Preface

ICCAL '89 is the second in a series of International Conferences on Computer Assisted Learning. The first one was organized by the Institute for Computer Assisted Learning (ICAL) of the University of Calgary, May '87. The success of this first ICCAL demonstrated the need for a regular international, high-caliber conference on post-secondary education which brings together an expanded list of issues concerning computer learning. The coherency of the ICCAL conference series is assured by an international steering committee, and a group of experts in the field acting as the advisory board.

ICCAL '89 is hosted by the Computer Learning Research (CLEAR) Center, the Erik Jonsson School of Engineering and Computer Science of The University of Texas at Dallas. This conference coincides with the university's twentieth anniversary celebration.

This volume consists of about forty papers selected by the program-committee from one hundred submissions. It also includes printed versions of a number of invited presentations by outstanding scholars in the field.

The program committee of ICCAL '89 consists of Bitzer (University of Illinois, USA), Bork (University of California, USA), Bonar (University of Pittsburgh, USA), Clark (University of Calgary, Canada), Davies (Open University, England), Friend (The University of Chicago, USA), Horowitz (University of Southern California, USA), Kovacs (Szamalk, Hungary), Makedon (The University of Texas at Dallas, USA), Maurer (Graz University of Technology, Austria), Norrie (University of Calgary, Canada), Oberem (Rhodes University, South Africa), Ottmann (University of Freiburg, Germany), Six (Open University, Germany), and Srisa-an (Open University, Thailand).

The chairman of the program committee would like to thank all members of the program committee for their meritorious work in evaluating submitted papers. Cordial thanks are also extended to those other additional scientists helping in the evaluation process; a certainly only partial list includes T. Bakos (Budapest), E. Berg (Hagen), J. Böhme (Hagen), J. Dobrinski (Freiburg), H.-D. Ebbinghaus (Freiburg), K. Fankhänel (Hagen), G. Holweg (Graz), F. Huber (Graz), A. Huszár (Budapest), K. Loose (Calgary), W. Niranatkomol (Bangkog), L. Reinsperger (Graz), H. Robinson (Milton Keynes), D. Rosin-Matthaei (Hagen), G. Sándor (Budapest), H. Sharp (Milton Keynes), W. Stern (Hagen), R. Stubenrauch (Graz).

As chairman of the program committee I am further much indebted to all of the contributors to the scientific program of the symposium, especially to the authors of papers and the invited speakers. But I would also like to gratefully acknowledge the support of the local arrangements committee, particularly those members helping to coordinate the program-committee's work and its meeting: S. Fickes, G. Oberem, and R. Riner.

Last but not least I would like to thank Springer-Verlag for excellent cooperation in the publication of this volume.

Graz, February 89   H. Maurer

Table of Contents

EDUCATIONAL KNOWLEDGE BASED SYSTEM DESIGN USING A DIAGNOSTIC APPROACH

Marie-Michèle Boulet, Ph.D.
L. Lavoie, P. Labbé, S. Slobodrian, L. Barbeau, graduate students
Department of Computer Science , Faculty of Science and Engineering
Université Laval, Québec, Canada G1K 7P4

Abstract.

In this paper we explain how we use formative evaluation tools to represent items of knowledge and the ties between these items. The expert system thinks using for that Prolog relations corresponding to many tables. The system has many knowledge bases related to formative evaluation and a global knowledge base which has more general knowledge about the psychology of learning which supervises the use of the other knowledge bases.

Introduction.

Research on the use of computers in education has enabled the identification of several pedagogical applications as mentioned by Brahan (1983) and Smith (1983). Among these uses, there are applications designed to aid the learning process, such as in games, simulations, drill and practices, as well as tutorial and problem solving applications (Brien and al., 1984). These uses of computers in curriculum development amount to, in fact, various modes of interaction between student and computer (Cohen, 1983). This student/computer interaction is as follows: 1. on-screen presentation of questions; 2. the entry of answers by the student; 3. analysis of these answers; and 4. adequate feedback according to their answers (Alessi and al., 1985; Gagné and al., 1981). One of the problems encountered by pedagogical software producers is difficulty in determining the appropriate level of sophistication for their computer programs' responses analyzer. In the case of a superior rule should the producer forsee all the possible wrong answers at every level of hierarchy of intellectual skill, including the consideration of prerequisites? Ideally the answer to this question should be "yes". However, in practice, considering the programing tools presently available, the answer can only be "no". That is where we believe that the utilization of knowledge bases can bring us closer to a solution and it is along these lines that we have directed our research.

The first part of this paper introduces the basic concepts of student/computer interaction and presents the partial uses made of these concepts. The second part is a partial description of the authoring languages and authoring systems presently existing. The third part discusses another omnipresent concept used in educational software: corrective teaching. Below, we will describe one of the tools of formative evaluation, the multiple facet scheme. This scheme will serve as the basis for the development of our knowledge-based system. Thereafter we will explain briefly the context of conceptual modeling of data. Finally, we describe the major characteristics of our prototype.

Question: the basic component of the interaction.

The first aspect that was considered was the determination of the questions, the basic component of the student/computer interaction; these questions serving to regularize the progress of each student. This concept of regularization implies the presence of an appropriate corrective teaching tool which suits a student in difficulty to get back on the right way. Regularization and corrective teaching are two expressions used in the concept of formative evaluation presented by Bloom and al. (1971). Formative evaluation of students is defined according to Scallon (1988b) as being a collection of tools used to measure or to observe progress, specifically designed to interact in a continuous way with the progress of each student engaged in a learning process. In fact, this entails comparing the students' knowledge at a given time, to what it should be. Barbier (1985) associates "present knowledge" to "what is evaluated" and the "should be knowledge" to "the standard of evaluation". This concept of the role of the evaluation is partially transposed in the principles used in the design of software curricula. Hazen (1985) states: "Frequent questions allow learners to check progress and focus on important points, and motivate learners to continue". Steinberg (1983) adds: "The question-and-response interaction can be fruitful or not, depending on how it is implemented. Opportunity for the learner to interact with the lesson is necessary, but this is hardly sufficient for learning. It is the quality of the questions and the demands they make on the students that are important". The local structures proposed by Godfrey and al. (1982) follows from this theory. It can be noted that this same concept of the role of the evaluation has been partially used in the development of the authoring languages and systems. We talk of partial uses of the formative evaluation concept because the questions are developed and used in a sequential order as is the feedback which is similarly executed in a sequential manner according to the wrong answers forseen by the software producer. However, the tools for formative evaluation are rather designed with an aim to classification of the errors by type through adopting a more global view as will be described in more detail later in this paper. For now, we will briefly describe the present structure of authoring languages and systems.

Structure of authoring languages and systems.

Authoring languages as well as authoring systems are tools design to assist programming aimed at facilitating the link between the questions, answers, comments and explanations which must be varied and adapted at each situation. Thus the authoring languages are programming languages in which the content of the lessons and all the commands or procedures are intermixed, while the authoring systems work interactively either by menu, by request and/or by macro-instructions.

Lets take, for example, software lessons produced with Super-Pilot. These involve several commands such as:

T:TYPE	To display text on screen
PR:PROBLEM	To change some aspects of the program execution
A:ACCEPT	To wait for the students' answer
M:MATCH	To assure that the answer given by the student corresponds to the appropriate answer

Let us now examine the pedagogical structure of the software lessons proposed by the authoring system "The Author". Three basic pedagogical formulas are avalaible: first, concept description, second, student questioning on his knowledge and third, situation simulation whereby the student is the main author. Four kind of questions may be used: multiple choice, incomplete sentences to be completed, multiple statement, and true or false. For each answer forseen by the authoring system the student can be directed within the same lesson content for revision, or into a different lesson in order to obtain additional explanation. For example, take a software lesson whereby a student is following a presentation of the theory of calculating compound interest and according to the expected answers the software guides the student to a situation simulation where he will have to apply this newly acquired theoretical knowledge (Régnier, 1984).

This brief description firstly highlights the omnipresent corrective teaching concept and then, the mechanism which triggers this concept. The decision to apply the corrective teaching concept is uniquely determined by the software following a wrong answer from the student and this for each of the questions.

In a non-computerized teaching environment the decision on whether or not to apply this kind of teaching method is made by the teacher. This decision is either based on tests given to the student which helps the teacher in determining general areas of difficulty of the student made at the students request. We observe once again that only part of the concept is used.

The corrective teaching concept.

The concept of corrective teaching is equivalent to a process, which uses a specific pedagogical diagnostic, suggesting to the student different ways in which to remedy his difficulties (Bonboir, 1970). Thus, in the light of authoring systems concept each incorrect answer given by a student will not automatically trigger corrective teaching mechanism; corrective teaching rather relies on the negative deviation between realization and expectations (Scallon, 1988b) and is based on diagnostic information supplied by formative evaluation (Provencher, 1985).

Having determined the necessity for a pedagogical diagnostic through the use of formative evaluation and corrective teaching, the next step was to examine the tools available for the conception. Subsequently, after modeling these tools we constructed a knowledge base system which respected the conditions necessary for each of the two above mentioned concepts. One of tools used in formative evaluation that we have used is domain referenced testing or, known as the more specifically, the multiple facet test (Scallon, 1988a).

The basis of the knowledge representation model.

The multiple facet test makes it possible to precisely evaluate the depth of understanding of an objective requiring intellectual skill (Scallon, 1988a). In view of the decision made there are two alternatives: either a student is redirected towards other goals which he can progress or the student is directed to apply corrective teaching in the area where the student experienced difficulties. This model, in conjunction with facets, allows the definition of a set of items or questions used to construct a specification matrix of two or more dimensions. By facet we mean any variation involving the formulation of the questions which are part of a performance test. The major investment is made during the elaboration of the test and in processing the results of the many questions making up this test; this processing is made to establish diagnostic profiles for each student. This kind of test has the following advantages: it applies to performance tests centered on a unique goal, and it allows the decomposition of the student's final score into profiles fitting the dimension of the test, that is, according to the variations or facets which are introduced during the formulation of the questions.

The construction of a facet test and of an analysis chart for the results may be done in three distinct steps. The first step consists of an indepth analysis of the subject to be taught, the second step is the formulation of the test and the third step is the construction of the tool used for correction. The following paragraphs describe each of these steps.

Steps description.

First step: subject analysis.

1. Identify the domain being evaluated.

Minor musical scales will be used as an example of a domain being evaluated during the following description of the steps.

2. Define the scope of the domain being evaluated.

During this step, we must answer the following question: "What are the difficulties a student could face if he has to write a minor scale". This question must be repeated until all of the dimensions of the domain has been identified.

Two major difficulties can be identified in the present domain (the minor scales): the student should be able to write a melodic minor scale and a harmonic minor scale (fig. 1).

HARMONIC	MELODIC

Figure 1. Identification of the first two dimensions of the domain.

The first sub-division allows a determination that a student has difficulty with harmonic and/or melodic scales if he does not achieve the suitable level of success. The information so far acquired seems insufficient to conclude with a specific diagnostic. Would there not be a way to obtain sufficient information enabling a more precise diagnostic and thus to construct a more adequate corrective action?

By asking more questions, it could be determined not only whether the student has difficulty with harmonic and melodic minor scales but also whether the problem lies with ascending or descending scales. This could be done by adding ascending and descending dimensions to the initial two dimensions (fig. 2).

HARMONIC		MELODIC	
ascending	descending	ascending	descending

Figure 2. Identification of subdivision of the domain.

A third sub-division of the domain evaluation of the initial question can be identified. We may determine whether the student has difficulty with minor scales possessing flats or possessing sharps. In fact it is common that some students will only have difficulties with scale possessing flats while others students will experience difficulty only with scales having sharps (fig. 3).

	HARMONIC		MELODIC	
	ascending	descending	ascending	descending
Sharp				
Flat				

Figure 3. Identification of another subdivision of the domain evaluation.

We could add other sub-division like the location of tone and semi-tone. Note that we will consider only three sub-divisions to illustrate our knowledge representation.

3. Identification of the domain facets.

After having established all the different dimensions of the domain of minor scales, we have to establish to which facets each of these dimensions can be related. Then when we will have analysed the students' results, it will be possible to determine with accuracy and fairness the precise domain of difficulties experienced by a student.

We now continue with the same example; the dimensions "harmonic" and "melodic" are grouped in a facet called "type"; the dimensions "ascending" and "descending" are grouped within a facet called "direction" and "sharp" and "flat" dimensions to a facet called "breaking". It can be seen that we have divides the breaking facets in smaller dimensions: "0 to 2 sharps or flats", "3 to 5 sharps or flats" and "6 to 7 sharps or flats" (Fig. 4).

Second step: writing the test.

1. Obtain evaluation items.

We have to establish the items which will allow to evaluate the learning of a student in regard with the various facets. For example, under the facets "breaking: 0 to 2 sharps", "type: harmonic" and "direction: ascending", it would be possible to ask to the student to write three minor scales (A, B and E).

2. Numbering each item.

A number, either attributed randomly or in an another way, has to be assigned to each of the question; for minor scales, there are sixty possible items. Figure 4 shows, using a circle illustrated many incorrect answers given by a student, a problem which an analysis table could precisely identify: that is a student that does not master the descending melodic minor scales. From that analysis, it is possible to give him effective corrective teaching.

			TYPE			
			Harmonic		Melodic	
			DIRECTION		DIRECTION	
			ascend.	descend.	ascend.	descend.
B R E A K I N G	S h a r p	0 to 2	5- A 9- E 60- B	14- A 30- E 36- B	31- A 37- E 42- B	16- A 55- E 44- B
		3 to 5	2- F# 25- C# 41- G#	7- F# 18- C# 49- G#	4- F# 27- C# 35- G#	12- F# 52- C# 57- G#
		6 to 7	17- D# 21- A#	29- D# 43- A#	10- D# 51- A#	32- D# 38- A#
	F l a t	1 to 2	6- D 53- G	22- D 58- G	56- D 59- G	13- D 28- G
		3 to 5	3- C 19- F 39- Bb	8- C 23- F 45- Bb	11- C 26- F 47- Bb	15- C 33- F 54- Bb
		6 to 7	20- Eb 40- Ab	24- Eb 46- Ab	1- Eb 50- Ab	34- Eb 48- Ab

Figure 4. Example of a problem which might be revealed by the use of an analysis table of results.

Third step: constructing the correction tool.

In this step, we have to produce an analysis table of the results. The seven following components have to be included in the table (Fig. 5):

1.   The facets which were identified when the test was developed, the questions to be presented to the student and the number associated to each of the question;

2.   the total number of questions used for each dimension;

3.   the minimum number of questions that must be answered correctly. Block and al. (1975), Bloom and al. (1981) set this minimum to be 80 or 90 percent of all of the items of a test;

4.   a place to be used to write the result of the student;

5.   a place to be used to write the result of the comparison between item 3 and 4;

6.   a place to be used to indicate if a student has mastered the evaluated subject or not;

7.   a place to be used to write what is (are) the cause(s) of the difficulty(ies).

Once these steps have been completed, this analysis table could be used by a teacher in order to obtain a better understanding of the specific area that a student did not master and the reason(s) behind the difficulty. It also allows the teacher to have a student to work a more specific part of a subject instead of simply telling him to work harder, such as is the case when the correction is an attribution of points to each question and that the overall result obtained by the student is weak. Since this tool is not used to make a classification scores are not used. It is rather a decision tool aimed to propose corrective teaching when necessary.

Thus, formative evaluation is a process allowing the collection of information on the progress or the difficulties of students and to diagnosis within limits the reason behind the difficulties.

DIMENSION TYPE	Questions	Minimum	Result	Mastered (X)
Harmonic Q- 2- 3- 5- 6- 7- 8- 9-14-17- 18- 19- 20- 21- 22- 23- etc.	30	24		
Melodic Q- 1- 4- 10- 11- 12- 13- 15- 16- 26- 27- etc.	30	24		

DIMENSION DIRECTION/TYPE	Questions	Minimum	Result	Mastered (X)
Ascending/Harmonic Q- 2- 3- 5- 6- 9- 17- 19- 20- 21- 25- 29- 39- 40- 41- 60.	15	12		
Ascending/Melodic Q- 1- 4- 10- 11- 26- 27- 31-37- etc.	15	12		
Descending/Harmonic Q- 7- 8- 14- 18- etc.	15	12		
Descending/Melodic Q- 12- 13- 15- 16- etc.	15	12		

DIMENSION TYPE/BREAKING	Questions	Minimum	Result	Mastered (X)
Harmonic/Sharp Q- 2- 5- 7- 9- 14- 17- 21- 25- 29-30- 36- 41- 43- etc.	16	13		
Melodic/Sharp Q- 4- 10- 12- 16- etc.	16	13		
Harmonic/Flat Q- 3- 6- 8- 19- etc.	14	11		
Melodic/Flat Q- 1- 11- 13- 15- etc.	14	11		

Figure 5. Example of a part of an analysis table.

Conceptual data modeling.

We have modeled using Merise methodology the process of formative evaluation which uses a multiple facet scheme. In short, an expert on the subject identifies the domain and analyzes it to determine the name of the dimensions, the elements and the facets. Each facet can be associated with a pool of questions or certain corrective teaching. All of that information can either be use to write different tests from which diagnosis could be made and a corrective teaching given or to provide additional information as requested by a student. This conceptual model (not depicted here) has been made used to develop a prototype on computerized formation system using knowledge base.

The principal prototype lines of development.

The domain of evaluation knowledge illustrated in a table is expressed in a knowledge base using Prolog relations. The relations can be seen like components of a tree structures in which each item identified in the table correspond to a node. For the case illustrated in figure 4, three trees are used (Fig. 6):

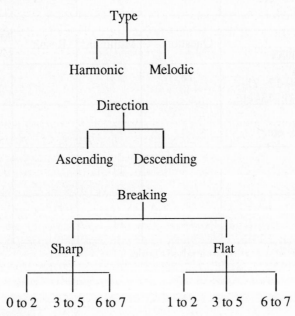

Figure 6. Tree structures.

The Prolog relations corresponding to these trees as per the syntax used in Turbo Prolog (Borland International), are as follows:

dimension	("A" "Type")
dimension	("B" "Direction")
dimension	("C" "Breaking")
element	("AA" "harmonic")
element	("AB" "melodic")
element	("BA" "ascending")
element	("BB" "descending")
element	("CA" "sharp")
element	("CB" "flat")
element	("CAA" "0 to 2")
element	("CAB" "3 to 5")
element	("CAC" "6 to 7")
element	("CBA" "1 to 2")
element	("CBB" "3 to 5")
element	("CBC" "6 to 7")

The codes (Ex.: "CAC" "6 to 7") are identifiant allowing a compact way to attach an element to a node of the tree. An interactive and convivial process is used in order to collect the knowledge to be used to build the relations: a pool of questions, of explanations and of corrective teaching. The teacher is required to point out the knowledge elements component of each question. The software then determines to which facet(s) a question or a explanation is to be related.

We have only presented the major concepts which are used in the conception of the system. As mention by Gagné (1977) categories using, superior rules have for prerequisite the rules, which rules have for prerequisites concepts, etc.; in addition, all these intellectual skills have for prerequisites verbal information which can be represented by a link of prerequisites. This hierarchy of the different capacities is part of the system. A formative evaluation is used with each of these capacities. For example, a student could fail all the questions on writing of minor scales. It is possible that his lack of success corresponds to a misunderstanding of the concept of scale, the concept of minor, the melodic or harmonic. The system can detect the student's weakness and decide to give him questions obtained from a table specifically oriented to his weakness. Thus the system has many knowledge bases related to formative evaluation and a global knowledge base which has more general knowledge about the psychology of learning which supervises the use of the other knowledge bases. Furthermore the student can take control of the lesson whenever he wants. For example, he could be writing a melodic minor descending scale and not remember the meaning of melodic; he could then ask the system to present him this concept. He can also ask the system for advice on his ability to reproduce the ascending minor harmonic scales, on the revisions that he should do, etc. In the same way the teacher could use the system to obtain information about the ability of each of his students or his whole class to achieve an objective.

Conclusion.

The important concept of our research is that we used formative evaluation tools not to build pools of items but rather to represent items of knowledge and the ties between these items. Instead of doing a list of key words describing potential mistakes from the learners, as per the traditional approach, our system "thinks" using for that many tables (diagnostic approach). It can explain the details of its reasoning in giving or suggesting corrective teaching. For each of the different parts of the domain, the author includes explanations, questions (principal component of the interaction as was seen) and corrective teaching. The use of the system for the conception of the knowledge base allows the author to be concerned only by his subject and not on the software to be used to produce a lesson. The conception of this system has been made possible by the implication of many persons being specialized in differents subjects: a learning psychologist, an educational technologist, a conceptual data modeling specialist and three specialists in artificial intelligence. The software prototype has been made possible with the help of a musician specialist. It is by studying the basis of pedagogical practice that all this was made possible.

We also have used the same knowledge representation for the design of an intervention module for an advisor system in conceptual data modeling because that in order to adequately advise a user within a specific domain, an advisor requires a knowledge of the domain, the capacity to determine the users knowledge level and a knowledge of the learning processes In the knowledge base of the advisor, the various question asked by or to the user are related to the matrix representing the appropriate scheme and change the value of the matrix. The scheme being related to a terminal objective, the value of a given call within the matrix representing the set of subjacent terminal objectives is also changed. This indicates that the user has needed advice. Before answering a user question or analysing a user's response to an advisor question, the advisor analyses each of the previously mentioned matrices in order to determine the frequency of the users query for the same material. The advisor may decide, based on its analysis, to answer the question directly or to suggest a revision of a set of concepts

Acknowledgements.

This research project was made possible by a grant obtained from Canadian Workplace Automation Research Center (CWARC) and from FCAR-EQ-3127 (Fonds des Chercheurs pour l'Aide à la Recherche).

References.

Alessi, S.M., Trollip, S.R. Computer-Based Instruction: Methods and Development. Prentice-Hall, Englewood Cliffs, N.J., 1985.

Barbier, J.M. L'évaluation en formation. Presses Universitaires de France, Paris, 1985.

Block, J.H. "Individualized Instruction: A Mastery Learning Perspective". Educational Leadership. Vol. 34, No 5, 1977, pp. 337-341.

Block, J.H., Anderson, L.W. Mastery Learning in Classroom Instruction. MacMillan, New York, 1975.

Bloom, B.S., Madaus, G.F., Hastings, J.T. Handbook on Formative and Summative Evaluation on Student Learning. McGraw-Hill Book Co., New York, 1971.

Bloom, B.S., Hastings, J.T., Madaus, G.F. Evaluation to Improve Learning. McGraw-Hill Book Co., New York, 1981.

Bonboir, A. La pédagogie corrective. Presses Universitaires de France, Paris, 1970.

Brahan, J.W. "CAL Technology - Decade Post, Decade Present". Comptes rendus du quatrième symposium canadien sur la technologie pédagogique. Winnipeg, octobre 1983, pp. 41-51.

Brien, R., Boulet, M.M. Le micro-ordinateur et l'enseignement: tomes 1 et 2. Université du Québec à Trois-Rivières, 1984.

Cohen, V.B. "Criteria for the Evaluation of Microcomputer Software". Educational Technology. January 1983, pp. 10-14.

Gagné, R.M. The Conditions of Learning. Third Edition. Holt, Rinehart and Winston, New York, 1977.

Gagné, R.M., Wager, W., Rojas, A. "Planning and Authoring Computer-Assisted Lessons". Educational Technology. September 1981, pp. 17-26.

Godfrey, D., Sterling, S. The Element of CAL: The How-to-Book on Computer-Aided Learning. A Softwords Book, Press Porcépic Ltd., Victoria, 1982.

Hazen, M. "Instructional Software Design Principles". Educational Technology. November 1985, pp. 18-23.

Provencher, G. "Les fonctions informatives et les principaux facteurs des feedback correctifs dans l'apprentissage scolaire". Revue des Sciences de l'Education. Vol. 11, No 1, 1985, pp. 67-81.

Régnier, L. "The Author". L'APOP. Vol. 2, No 2, février 1984, pp. 8-10.

Scallon, G. L'évaluation formative des apprentissages: l'instrumentation. Presses de l'Université Laval, 1988a.

Scallon, G. L'évaluation formative des apprentissages: la réflexion. Presses de l'Université Laval, 1988b.

Smith, P.R. "A Decade of Computer Assisted Learning". Comptes rendus du quatrième symposium canadien sur la technologie pédagogique. Winnipeg, octobre 1983, pp. 15-21.

Steinberg, E.R. "Reviewing the Instructional Effectiveness of Computer Courseware". Educational Technology. January 1983, pp. 17-19.

HyperLexicon, a Hypermedia-based Lexicon for Vocabulary Acquisition

Khanh P. Bui
U.S. Army Research Institute
and
George Mason University

Abstract

In this report Hypermedia, an emergent technology in search of applications, finds yet another home in Computer Assisted Language Learning, or CALL. Within CALL we focus on the subject of foreign vocabulary acquisition and promote the use of Hypermedia's hallmark, computer-based links among multi-media data, to support instructionally significant semantic links. The resulting instructional tool, which we term a HyperLexicon, appears as a natural extension of the classic vocabulary acquisition tools, the dictionary and thesaurus. This paper presents a conceptual design for the tool along with examples of coupled semantic / hypermedia links and illustrations of their use. We have implemented an interesting proof-of-concept demonstration system on a micro-computer which provides several HyperLexicon lessons incorporating many of the link-pairs discussed in this report.

Introduction

Hypertext (and its multi-media generalization, Hypermedia) have been around since Vannevar Bush wrote the historic 1945 article which essentially defined the concept (Bush 1945). The term itself was coined by another pioneer, Ted Nelson, back in 1965. It wasn't until recently however that the field experienced an explosion of interest in the subject's theoretical foundations and the search for new applications. In this report Hypermedia finds yet another home in Computer Assisted Language Learning, or CALL. Within CALL we focus on the subject of foreign vocabulary acquisition and promote the use of Hypermedia's hallmark, computer-based links among multi-media data, to support instructionally significant semantic links. The resulting instructional tool, which we term a HyperLexicon, appears as a natural extension of the classic vocabulary acquisition tools, the dictionary and thesaurus.

Much of the current interest in Hypermedia is due to the availability and affordibility of hardware and software suitable for Hypermedia applications. In particular the work reported on here was motivated in part by a feeling that these new tools represented an opportunity to develop some novel computer assisted language learning (CALL) techniques. Hypermedia is a significant extension beyond hardcopy and other "linear" media on which much of language instruction is based, therefore it follows that Hypermedia should have significant utility within the field. The availability of this new generation of Hypermedia tools on micro-computers, especially user-programmable software like HyperCard, addresses two issues of importance for any instructional computer-based tools, namely the cost of the tool and the ease with which instructors can produce courseware without requiring the services of programming professionals.

Another reason for the current popularity of Hypermedia techniques in (Intelligent) Computer Aided Instruction, or (I)CAI, has to do with the educational value of structured exploration. Although the goal of CAI and especially ICAI is to provide individual instruction, one is still left with an impression that basically all a student can do to control the learning experience is respond to the (I)CAI system's prompts. The system evaluates the student's reply and "decides" what to present next. Although a Hypermedia-based component of a (I)CAI system *can* conform to this instructional paradigm, we feel Hypermedia's inherently exploratory nature offers an attractive alternative, or complement, to more regimented (I)CAI approaches.

This report presents a conceptual design for a Hypermedia-based vocabulary acquisition system which we term a HyperLexicon. The design was guided by several requirements including the following. This system should be capable of teaching a wide range of vocabulary, from basic to sophisticated concepts, and from literal to idiomatic word usage. The mechanism by which the student learns should be "tunable" from an exploratory, student-driven learning environments, to ones whose options are constrained by a (human or automated) tutor to optimize knowledge transfer. Finally, the system should strive for universality in the sense that it makes minimal assumptions about a student's native language. We have implement a proof-of-concept demonstration system incorporating some of the features of the conceptual system. The demonstration is used to show the feasibility of the techniques proposed and to provide the basis for a preliminary assessment of their efficacy.

The sequel is organized into three sections. The first reviews existing aids to vocabulary acquisition and proposes our Hypermedia based HyperLexicon. In the second section we discuss the ways we envision the HyperLexicon would be used to teach vocabulary. The last section provides a high level description of the HyperLexicon system highlighting each of the functional components and data stores used. Throughout the report ideas are illustrated via with examples, many of which are drawn from the proof-of-concept demonstration.

1. Approach

Starting from the basic question of what it means to "learn the meaning of a word", and asking how this learning process could be improved, we are lead to a system which represents a generalization of the standard vocabulary acquisition tools, the dictionary and thesaurus.

1.1 Back to Basics

What *does* it mean to "learn the meaning of a word"?. In the simplest sense this can mean successfully recognizing positive examples which have been used to teach a target word. For example, a student taught the word "graze" via a picture or video of a horse grazing, recalls the correct word upon seeing a horse graze.

At a higher level "learning the meaning of a word" includes the correct identification of positive and negative examples to which the student has not been exposed. In this case we now require the student to generalize from the training example. The difficulty facing the student is knowing just how general the word under consideration is:

Is a *cow* eating grass "grazing"?

Is a horse eating *oats* from a trough "grazing"?

Is a *man* eating a *sandwich* "grazing"?

At yet a higher level "learning the meaning of a word" involves not only knowing when the word applies but when another semantically related word is more appropriate. For example a guard in front of Buckingham Palace is more correctly said to be "marching" than "walking".

Evidently "learning the meaning of a word" is only accomplished when a student uses the target word appropriately and understands the similarities and differences between the target word and words semantically "close" to it . Our approach to the vocabulary acquisition problem should therefore concentrate on ways to assist in this process.

1.2 Existing Aids to Vocabulary Acquisition

The standard tools used for vocabulary acquisition are the dictionary and thesaurus. A dictionary consists of a list of words, ordered by a scheme appropriate to the language, with accompanying textual and or graphic definitions. In the context of foreign language instruction the dictionary is usually employed in the form of a Target Language / Native Language glossary for each lesson. From our point of view such glossaries are limited in the information they provide regarding the generality or specificity of the target word and its relationships to related words, both of which we have seen are major components in learning the meaning of a word. Secondly, it requires a different glossary for each native language, primarily as a result of the medium which limits the use of universal forms of communication such as audio or (animated) graphics.

A thesaurus on the other hand provides, as a minimum, a list of synonyms for each index word, as in the online thesaurus "Word Finder®", or, as in the case of Roget's International Thesaurus, a categorized and cross-referenced list of related words together with examples of idiomatic usage. While a thesaurus clearly offers information lacking in a dictionary there are still shortcomings. First, as with the dictionary, hierarchical relationships between related concepts are not made explicit. For example under "eat" one finds "ingest" listed as a related word with no indication that ingest is a much more general concept. Secondly, a thesaurus allows one to "vary a concept" in some sense and provides illustrative examples, but it does not symmetrically allow the user to "vary the examples" and understand how the applicable concept varies in response. Removing this limitation will be seen to be a key feature in our approach.

In learning the meaning of the words, a language user must understand the semantic relations between concepts. A related question is , "how that knowledge is organized in human memory?" This psycholinguistic issue is addressed in (Miller 1988) and the implementation of his theory is an on-line lexical reference system called WordNet which attempts to mirror the organization of human lexical knowledge.

WordNet is an extensive computer-based lexicon which supports the conceptual relations of hyponymy, meronymy and antonymy. Lexical information (hyponymy and meronymy) are represented by semantic hierarchy and is extracted from a collection of dictionaries and thesauruses, liberally seasoned with linguistic intuition. This kind of information can be extracted from a machine-readable dictionary by automatic and semi-automatic procedures (Amsler 1980; Chodorow, Byrd & Heidorn 1985). One goal of the HyperLexicon system is to utilize such semantic hierarchies to organize lexical knowledge and to provide an environment through which student can access and acquire that knowledge.

1.3 Proposed tool: "HyperLexicon"

The vocabulary acquisition tool we propose is a natural extension, based on Hypermedia, of both the dictionary and thesaurus. The main idea underlying our tool is to use hypermedia links to support instructionally significant semantic links between the concepts to be taught. The following is a list of the semantic relationships we feel are fundamental and natural candidates for expression via hypermedia links in our system.

ISA: "ISA" is the hierarchical relation and is the means by which the student can explore the generality and specificity of the concepts to be learned. For example: "horse" ISA "animal", "shuffle" ISA "walk". In the HyperLexicon the student can branch from a selected word to related words on either side of the ISA relation via Hypermedia links.

Is-Part: "Is-Part" denotes "part-whole" relations so that a student can relate a selected concept to one of it's components or vice-versa. For example: "door" Is-Part "house", "head" Is-Part "man". From a selected word the student can branch to words on either side of the Is-Part relation via Hypermedia links.

Applies-To: "Applies-To" is a relation between the nodes of two ISA trees of concepts. For example the "fly" Applies -To "bird". The relation of Applies-To can be either "natural", as in the previous "bird / fly" example or idiomatic. As an example of the latter, "guzzle" Applies -To "car" in the context of gas consumption, but the abstraction "drink" of "guzzle" does not.

Analogy: An important relationship supported by the HyperLexicon is analogy. Thus words representing analogous concepts would be linked, for example "hand", "paw" and "hoof" represent analogous concepts for "man", "cat" and "horse".

Abstraction: The relation of "abstraction" is useful not only within a single concept hierarchy tree where it defines the ISA relation, but also between trees connected by the Applies-To relation. For example, given a word and a general concept a student could query the HyperLexicon for the least abstract form of the concept which is still general enough to apply to the word in question.

Definition: The student can explore audio / visual environments which define concepts lending themselves to textual, graphic or aural depiction. This straight forward Hypermedia extension of the a dictionary is a canonical example illustrating the capabilities of Hypermedia over conventional linear media.

Usage: Consider for example a student who must choose an expression for the concept "die". The concepts, "pass away" and "kick the bucket" would occur on the same level in the abstraction hierarchies and would provide no indication that it is appropriate to express condolences using the former expression but not the latter. There is a subtlety of usage involved in choosing the correct synonym of the concept "die" which we have not addressed previously. These subtleties can be explored through various "semantic attributes" including the following (some examples are taken from Zuckerman 1974).

Value Judgment: Synonyms may differ in expressing value judgments. The attribute values range from "negative" through "neutral" to "positive". (i.e "obstinate" is condemnatory, "determined" expresses no value judgment and to be "resolute" is considered a virtue)

Sophistication: Sometimes one synonym is more learned than other. The attribute values range through the following increasingly sophisticated categories: "crude", "colloquial", "informal", "formal" and "specialized". (i.e "domicile" is bordering on specialized, "residence" is more formal than the common "home").

Intensity: Some words express greater effect or degree than their synonyms. The attribute values range from "low" through "moderate" to "high". For example, contentment, happiness, joy and ecstasy.

Spectrum: Spectrum is the continuous version of the binary relation "opposite". The attribute values range from one extreme of the concept to the opposite extreme, thus the Spectrum is formed by concatenating the intensity scale of one extreme and (the mirror image of) the opposite For example, {(frigid, cold, cool), (tepid, warm, hot, blazing)} -> {frigid, cold, cool, tepid, warm, hot, blazing}.

2. Concepts of Use

In this section we discuss the ways in which we envision a user would interact with the HyperLexicon environment. We strove to minimize reliance on a student's native language skills. While we recognize that there are instances when cross-language instruction can be useful we wished to reduce the amount of duplication of HyperLexicon data, and so rely on more universal graphic and aural communication.

2.1 Learning Definitions

At its most simplistic level a hypermedia system can support student exploration of concept definitions via appropriate textual, graphical or aural representations. Although the graphical capabilities of the HyperLexicon are illustrated in the demonstration system through painstaking hand drawings, the technology exists to easily digitize existing hardcopy images, or video signals as well as store vast amounts of graphic or audio data on CD ROM. (Gildea 1988) has recently done work on vocabulary instruction using interactive videodisk. While a hypermedia dictionary is superior in concept to a linear dictionary, for learning definitions, more advanced types of learning become possible when the Hypermedia links are used to support the semantic links discussed in the previous section.

2.2 Learning by Analogy

Another useful aid to vocabulary acquisition involves the use of analogous concepts. For example: "'Foot 'is to man as _____ is to horse?" This type of learning could be aided in the HyperLexicon by presenting analogous concepts in a manner the student can grasp easily. Examples of this would include graphic presentation as in Figure 1, taken from the demo. In the example shown the user has selected the word "foot" and the analogous parts of the horse, cat and bird are indicated in a (structural) Is-Part decomposition as well as graphically. The user can interrogate either one of the two representations as each link in the tree has a corresponding mouse sensitive regions and graphics. Thus if the user selects "toe" from the tree or "mouses on" the toe in the graphic the claw and talon will be highlighted on the tree and a new graphic showing "toe", "claw" and "talon" will be displayed. The upward-pointing arrow in the lower right corner of the graphic takes the user "up" in the abstraction hierarchy.

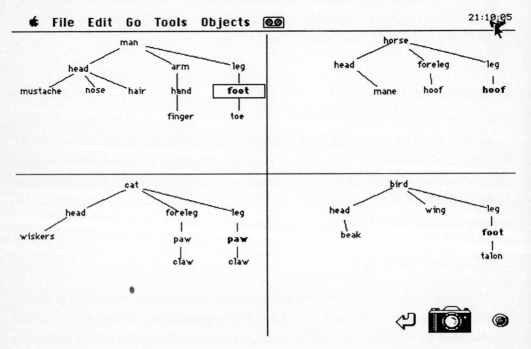

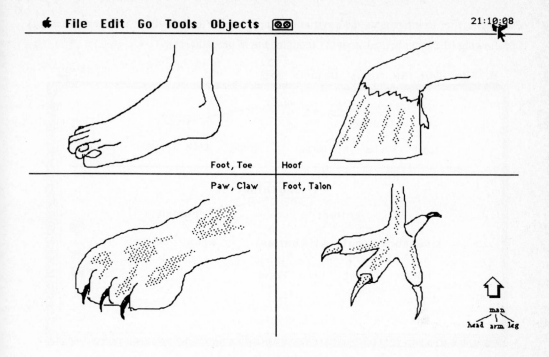

Figure 1.

We note that Is-Part hierarchies require a context for the decomposition. In the example above we have used a structural decomposition in which for example a man's arm is analogous to a horse's foreleg. This is not the only point of view to take in this and similar cases. For example, in Cruse's work, he indicates that a characteristic feature of parts is the possession of definite functions relative to their wholes (i.e. eye for seeing). If we had instead employed a functional decomposition the man's arm would have no counterpart for the horse and the horse's forelegs and hindlegs would instead correspond to the man's legs.

A different type of analogy which the HyperLexicon could support would be analogies between the native and target languages. Written words from the two languages could be depicted graphically in a manner which used geometric proximity to indicate semantic closeness.

2.3 Abstraction

The teaching aid which we originally envisioned when thinking about the HyperLexicon functioned like a generalized thesaurus, using the semantic relationships discussed earlier, in addition to the concept of semantic "nearness" used in a standard thesaurus. Two ISA-trees of concepts to be learned are presented graphically and the student can invoke Hypermedia links as described earlier to interrogate the environment and receive answers in visual dialogs such as the following (the hypothetical student's thoughts are in parentheses):

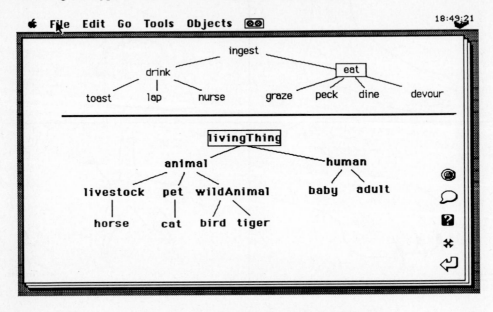

Student: What does "eat" apply to ? **HyperLexicon**: Man, Animal etc...

Student: (Hmm...I wonder if there is a more specific word for "eat" that applies to horse?)

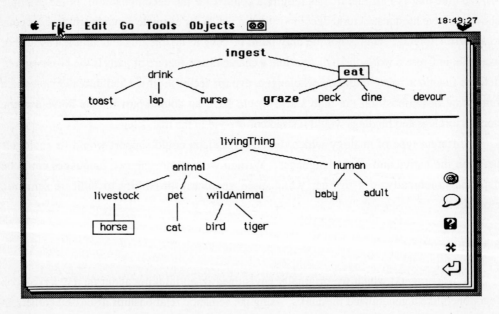

Student: What terms related to "eat" apply to "horse"? **HyperLexicon**: Ingest, eat, graze.

Student: ("Graze" is the most specific, I wonder how general it is?)

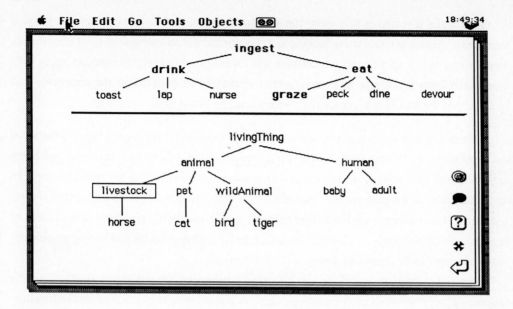

Student: Does "graze" apply to "livestock"? **HyperLexicon:** Yes.

Student: (Hmm…maybe graze is quite general, I wonder if it applies to human?)

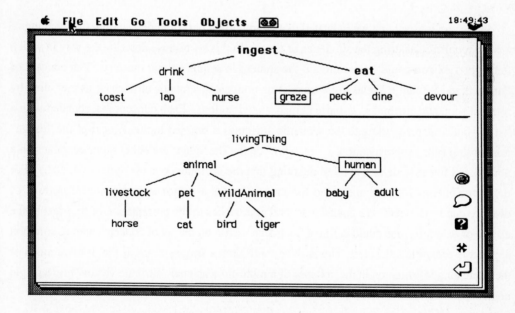

Student: Does "graze" apply to "human"? **HyperLexicon:** No.

Student: (O.K. now I think I see.)

One feature that makes this more flexible than a standard thesaurus is the fact that it is symmetric. A student can start by looking at a concept and see an example of what it applies to, then she can switch attention to the example and investigate what related concepts apply to *it*. Since both trees are hierarchical this helps the student to understand the generality and specificity of the concepts being learned, which was one of our main objectives.

In the demonstration system exploration of this environment is via student "interrogation" of the trees in the following three ways. First, by selecting a node in either tree and being presented with the nodes in the other tree which the initial node applies to, or which apply to the initial node, as the case may be. Secondly, by selecting a concept node and a referent node and seeing if that concept applies to that referent, and if not, being presented with the related concepts which *do* apply. And finally by selecting two referent nodes and seeing graphically which concepts apply to both of them.

Some interesting observations can be made concerning the graphical structure of the subtrees of hierarchy trees corresponding to images and preimages of the Applies-To function. These technical observations were used to develop efficient implementation schemes for the demonstration system. For more details see (Bui 1988).

2.4 Parametrized Semantic Views

In the previous section we indicated that an important part of understanding the meaning of a word requires mastering the subtleties of usage. In this section we describe the way in which the HyperLexicon could be used to aid the student in acquiring that mastery. The concept of Parametrized Semantic Views involves relating notions of semantic closeness, as measured by relevant semantic attributes, to basic human spatial notions. Each concept is associated with a list of values corresponding to the semantic attributes discussed in the context of the "usage" relationship (viz. "sophistication", "intensity" etc.). The values are either numeric values on a normalized linear scale or a symbol denoting that the attribute does not apply (e.g. NIL). For those attributes which do apply the list then becomes a vector and meaningful notions of distance can be defined. We consider several approaches to the presentation of this data to the user. For example, one could define a Euclidean metric on the set of concepts having common applicable semantic attributes. The problem with such a simple metric is that it loses much of the interesting information in the collapse of a multi-dimensional "attribute vector" into a single numerical value.

The presentation method we advocate is to display multi-parameter "semantic views" of the data as illustrated below. The user would select the desired concept (i.e. the word and the context) and one to three attributes of interest. The resulting display would show the semantic closeness of related concepts in the context of the attribute coordinate(s) selected. Figure 3. shows one- and two- and three- dimensional examples of the type of displays envisioned. We note that the three- dimensional views are similar to the "emotional solid" along dimensions of pleasantness / unpleasantness, attention / rejection, and intensity as illustrated in Miller (1985). For the three-parameter view the complexity may require a large, high resolution color display for effective use as an instruction aid. The semantic views we feel are most useful (and easiest to present on a small black and white screen) are those with one- or two-parameters.

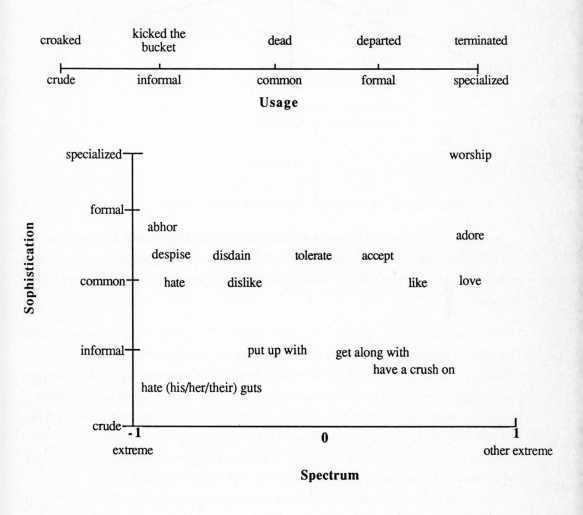

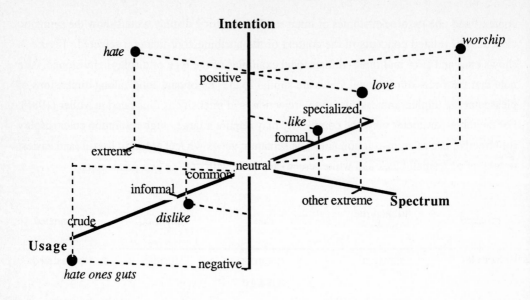

Figure 3.

2.5 Provide a Range of Student / Instructor Involvement

As mentioned before, the HyperLexicon is primarily a tool for learning by exploration. It is possible however, when designing HyperLexicon courseware, to create several "levels" of a lesson which could then be offered to students at their, or the (human or automated) tutor's, discretion.

For example, we have discussed how the concept of hierarchy is key in HyperLexicon. This offers a natural way in which the level of the lesson can be controlled. The hierarchies presented to the student could be pruned to suit a beginner by removing highly specific words or close synonyms which tend to be more advanced. For example, when learning types of motion the word "canter" for a horse, or "jog " for a man, would be suppressed. It is not, however, only the lower, more specific nodes of the ISA concept tree which are sophisticated. The upper nodes may be abstract to the point of being technical jargon or otherwise uncommon and uninteresting to the beginning student (take the word "biped" for example).

Instructors and courseware authors could use the Parametrized Semantic Views to help select appropriate teaching materials. A useful attribute for such users would be a concepts "level of sophistication". This would help the instructor to select, either by hand or automatically, words for a concept at a level appropriate level for the student audience.

2.6   Other Uses

The way the HyperLexicon concept could be integrated into a complete intelligent tutoring system is described in (Bui 1988). The HyperLexicon system could also be of use to teach or aid in exploration of a native language. A child could benefit from exposure to the inherent abstraction and analogy relationships, while an educated speaker could use the HyperLexicon in a manner similar to a standard thesaurus. We have not pursued these avenues since our focus is on foreign language instruction.

3.   HyperLexicon System Description

In this section we present a very high level functional description for the HyperLexicon system shown in Figure 4. We describe each of the functional components and data / knowledge sources from the online source "raw material" out of which the HyperLexicon data is made, to the user interface presenting the finished product. Once the HyperLexicon database exists, of course, the data and processing needed to create it are no longer necessary except for enhancement.

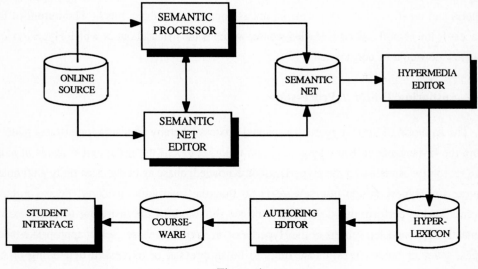

Figure 4.

3.1   Semantic Net Processor

The semantic net processor is envisioned as a principally automatic process to convert the raw online source into the semantic nets which form the basis of the HyperLexicon's

Hypermedia links. The input to the processor consists of online dictionaries and thesauruses and possibly other organized data such as Miller's WORDNET (Miller, 1988).

3.2 Semantic Net Editor

The purpose of Semantic Net Editor is to augment the semantic net with material not contained in the Online Source as well as to modify, when necessary, semantic links produced automatically by the Semantic Processor, to capture cases such as idiomatic word usage which are beyond automatic recognition. Related work in providing lexical support has been done by Ayuso (Ayuso et all 1988) in acquiring specialized knowledge for natural language interfaces and by Nirenburg (Nirenburg et all 1987) in acquiring lexical concepts for large scale applications such as machine translation.

3.3 Hypermedia Editor

The Hypermedia Editor is also a partly automated, but principally manual, process of building a Hypermedia knowledgebase to support the various semantic links in the Semantic Net. The automatic process could include translating the net links into the appropriate Hypermedia links while the manual process could include the selection of the appropriate media type(s) and creation of the Hypermedia nodes connected by those links. The output of this process is the HyperLexicon Knowledgebase, which is the material out of which HyperLexicon courseware would be constructed.

3.4 Authoring Editor / Processor

The Authoring Editor supports the manual process whereby an instructor extracts material from the HyperLexicon Knowledgebase and tailors it to suit the pedagogical needs at hand. The reason for envisioning the HyperLexicon Knowledgebase as being essentially a complete source for HyperLexicon courseware is so that the instructor need not be a computer professional to perform this task. The interface should allow the instructor to easily extract semantically connected subsets of the HyperLexicon Knowledgebase, select appropriate media types, sever or create links, cause links to be suppressed or expressed depending on the instructional level of the lesson etc. The output of the Authoring Editor is the HyperLexicon courseware which is run by the student.

3.5 Student Interface

The Student Interface is the man / machine interface which allows the student to interact with a HyperLexicon courseware lesson. This includes activating all supported HyperLexicon links for that lesson. The extent to which the student enjoys unconstrained browsing or moves within a (possibly dynamic) "envelope of options" is defined by the courseware author. The Student Interface requirements include the obvious ones of fast response and high quality graphics and audio.

Summary

Starting from a consideration of what it means to learn the meaning of a word and asking how this learning process could be improved, we were led to a Hypermedia-based system which generalizes the standard vocalulary acquisition tools, the dictionary and the thesaurus. We have presented a conceptual design for such a system, several important and natural classes of coupled semantic / hypermedia links and examples of their use. The demonstration system, which was implemented as a HyperCard stack, has shown that the HyperLexicon functionality we described can be implemented, indeed even on a micro-computer as small as a Macintosh Plus.

We did not have the time or resources to undertake a controlled assessment using a complete prototype system. Therefore questions concerning how the demonstration system would scale up using "fullsize" courseware, the practicality of actually generating the data required by the HyperLexicon and the pedagogical value of the HyperLexicon approach remain open for future investigation. What we have done is to propose a new CALL technique for teaching vocabulary, taken the first steps toward assessing its merit and found it worthy of further study.

Acknowledgements

The author wishes to thank Prof. Henry Hamburger and Dr. Joseph Psotka for their helpful discussions and continued encouragement. Appreciation is also extended to Dr. Robert Ruskin of the Consortium of Universities for financial support.

References

Amsler,R.(1980)   The Structure of the Merriam-Webster Pocket Dictionary.   Doctoral dissertation, DDJ81-09129, University Microfilms International, Ann Arbor, Michigan

Ayuso,D.M.,   Shaked ,V.,   Weischedel, R.M. (1987)   An Environment for Acquiring Semantic information. Proceedings of 25th ACL, pp32-40

Bui, Khanh. P. (1988) HyperLexicon, a Hypermedia-based Lexicon for Vocabulary Acquisition, MS Project, Computer Science Department, George Mason University, 1988.

Chodorow, M., Byrd R.J.and Heidorn G.E. (1985) Extracting Semantic Hierarchies from a Large Online Dictionary. Proceedings, 23rd Annual Meeting of the Association for Computational Linguistics, Chicago, Illinois, 8-12 July 1985. Association for Computational Linguistics, Bell Communications Research, pp. 299-304.

Cruse, D. A. (1986) Lexical Semantics. Cambridge University Press. (1986)

Miller, George. A. and Johnson-Laird Philip N. (1976) Language and Perception. The Belknap Press of Harvard University Press, Cambridge, Massachusetts (1976)

Gildea, Patricia M., George A. Miller, and Chery L. Wurtenberg (1988) Contextual Enrichment by Videodisc: A First Report. CSL Report # 12. January 1988.

Miller,G.A. , Fellbaum C., Kegl J., and Miller K.(1988) WORDNET: An Electronic Lexical Reference System Based on Theories of Lexical Memory, CSL Technical Report #11, Office of Naval Research, Arlington, VA . January 1988.

Nirenburg, S., Raskin V. (1987) The Subworld Concept Lexicon and the Lexicon Management System. Computational Linguistics, Volume 13, Numbers 3-4, pp. 276-289. (1987)

Zuckerman, Marvin S. (1974) Words, Words, Words. Glencoe Publishing Co., Inc., Encino, California.(1974)

SITUATED COGNITION AND
INTELLIGENT TUTORING SYSTEMS

William J. Clancey

Institute for Research on Learning
2550 Hanover Street
Palo Alto, CA 94304

Extended Abstract

The quest for intelligent machines is a problem of designing and constructing complex computer programs, whose style or reproducible framework we call an *architecture*. Architectures for intelligent machines fall into two categories-- psychological models of the human mind and engineering designs for expert systems. Most researchers have straddled this position between psychology (*cognitive science*) and engineering (*knowledge engineering*). We don't want to be held to scientific accuracy in describing human reasoning, yet we constantly draw on our understanding of how people reason and often hope that our work is advancing cognitive science.

What is the state of knowledge engineering today? On the one hand, the methods are unimaginably more sophisticated than ten years ago. Learning is finally becoming a central concern. Real-time processing, perception, and robotic control are finally being integrated with knowledge representation. Memory and problem-solving are no longer viewed separately, analogous to data structures and programs. Evaluative methods are slowly incorporating the mathematical analysis that befits an engineering discipline.

On the other hand, it is apparent that knowledge engineering has flourished and expanded its bounds so tremendously, that it totters on the edge of crisis. The crisis squeezes from two directions. To develop *a shared engineering approach*, we must reformulate our architectures so that commonalties and differences are more salient. But to do this we must establish *a scientific foundation*, as is required for any engineering discipline. We must understand why our programs work, when they will fail, and how to design them better.

Viewed from just a short way down the road, AI computer programs are like magnificent bridges, built by ambitious, imaginative engineers. Everyone uses different words to describe his structure and excitedly calls our attention to different concerns. But what have we learned about building intelligent programs? How are they different from computer programs of the 50's and 60's? More seriously, few people take seriously an increasingly pressing question: Why do the bridges hold up at all? Can we go on improving the design to get whatever performance we like, beyond human intelligence? Without a theory of representation, we are like bridge builders without knowledge of forces and material structure.

Thus, we have two foundational concerns: First, we need a descriptive analysis that characterizes our practice, a theory of commonalties that underlie the apparent differences of our programs. Second, we need a metatheoretical basis for justifying our practice, specifically, a philosophical reanalysis of the nature of representation.

The first part of this presentation views knowledge engineering as a methodology for modeling processes qualitatively (Clancey, in press), thus providing a coherent, readily understood, synthesis of current practice. I present several recommendations focusing on the role of formalization and methods for evaluation. This first part is intended to make clear that knowledge engineering has made a basic, lasting contribution to modeling methodology. My purpose in part two is not to undermine or dismiss this accomplishment, but rather to establish a new understanding of our methods so they can be more systematically applied and improved.

My study of the cracks in the bridges is presented as part two of this presentation. In part, this is an attempt to incorporate the work of my colleagues at the Institute for Research on Learning (IRL) into the knowledge engineering enterprise. But more fundamentally, Brooks' "situated" approach (Brooks, 1988) is behind my synthesis effort. Briefly put, Brooks does not build models of the world or explicit plans or schedules into his robot's memory. His work leads me to ask, "How does intelligent behavior come to be regular, if it isn't generated by interpreting grammars stored in memory?" With the help of diverse sources in linguistics (Stucky, 1987)(Tyler, 1978), anthropology (Rommetveit, 1987), and psychology (Bartlett, 1977), I describe an entirely different model of the mind, behaviorally consistent with all the regularities that knowledge engineering ascribes to experts, while integrating most of what we have ignored, including visual imagery, emotions, and physical skills. This alternative model explains how Brooks' non-representational approach and knowledge engineering can both be "right," and links both to connectionism.

But if our psychology is wrong, our engineering is seriously flawed, too. The implications are staggering. We can no longer talk about knowledge acquisition, explanation, learning, tutoring, consultation, or cognitive modeling without facing the basic epistemological matter of how our programs differ from human knowledge and reasoning. The very idea of *knowledge as structures* is reformulated, so all that we have taken to be static and "learned" is viewed as dynamic and constantly reconstructed. For the first time, our concern with reflection, introspection, and explanation is intricately tied to the very idea of representation, and if we believe the daring synthesis of Bartlett, consciousness itself.

When George Mandler used the "House of Cognitive Science" metaphor five years ago (Mandler, 1982), he suggested that AI might have the best room. The satisfaction of reconsidering the foundations of intelligence is knowing that the AI architecture work reported here did play and continues to play a pivotal part. For it is this community that established the strong "grammatical" regularities of knowledge representation, inference, and control. We showed that regularities carry across domains, and placed model-building--*understanding processes in the world*--as the central concern of intelligent action. We separated regularities of knowledge about the world from regularities of control. In effect, we have modeled the complex processes of diagnosis, interpretation, and design by the methods of linguistics: We describe knowledge structures by vocabulary typologies and transition networks, and show how to parse and generate problem-solving behavior by the production encoding and layered abstraction (e.g., "blackboard" and other hierarchical goal/context focusing mechanisms) previously developed for language research.

To transform knowledge engineering into a mature modeling discipline, we must view AI research for what it has accomplished--*a method for qualitative modeling of processes*--not in terms of its romantic quest for intelligent machines. To develop a suitable model of the human mind, cognitive scientists must be ready to collaborate with neural network researchers. Ultimately, they must generate by other means the problem-solving grammars that they explicitly and laboriously built into programs by hand. The difficulty of reconsidering the foundations of intelligence is that our psychology papers from the past decade are dumped back into our laps. For if my present understanding is right, most of the computer models constructed to date must be taken as the *specifications* for behavior we must now explain.

Our programs and how we talk about them are distorting our descriptions of how we think. For ten years, when I have explained NEOMYCIN's knowledge of diseases, I have visualized mechanisms such as TB organisms moving from the lungs to the meninges. But there is no place for pictures and presentational imagery in AI programs. Everything is discursive--words and more words--or worst, pictures supposingly reduced to words. So our experience must be ignored, even though we are constantly experiencing images and referring back to them when describing programs. The promissory note is coming due: The prevalent AI model has no place for dreaming, music, or art. And what of psychiatry, curiosity, or personal identity? We need a cognitive model that does justice to our everyday experience.

Closer to the concerns of present-day knowledge engineering, it is apparent that we must incorporate in our programs some representation of the *social context* in which they are designed to work. Indeed, one could argue that in designing a "glass box" representation, which facilitates multiple use of a knowledge base, such as for teaching, we must make visible not only the inner workings of the program, but render visible how it is intended to be embedded in some world. For example, in NEOMYCIN the crucial subject matter goes well beyond the disease processes and how to order requests for data. What we want to teach a student is the nature of the social setting in which these disease processes are encountered and in which this way of gathering data makes sense. Thus, medical knowledge is as much about the case population and hospital setting, as pathophysiological and therapeutic processes. This is a fundamental claim: The representations in a program like NEOMYCIN only make sense in the social context in which it is designed to be embedded.

How, then, should the new "intelligent tutoring system" be designed? We must shift from thinking of the computer as a delivery vehicle for prepackaged "knowledge." A better perspective is *the computer as a tool for facilitating collaborative work*. The SOPHIE-GAME program of the 1970's is probably the best example (Brown, et al., 1982). In this system, two teams of students compete against one another, using two machines in different rooms. One team inserts a flaw in an electronic circuit, the other team diagnoses the faulty circuit. The tutor flips back and forth, prodding the bug-inserting team to predict the results of diagnostic tests, just as it prods the diagnostic team to formulate hypotheses and good experiments in order to find the fault. Such a design emphasizes team-work as a way of learning together. Most striking is how each partner draws out his friend's knowledge and misconceptions in a way it would be difficult to design a program to do directly.

Here are some changes in perspective to inspire our future uses of computers in education:

1. Rather than teaching in a classroom, isolated from the context of materials and social organization where knowledge is used, we should find new opportunities for *apprenticeship learning*, on the job, in the workplace.

2. Rather than viewing teaching as a process of delivering a fixed, given curriculum of facts and procedures, we should engage the students in activities that *bring out the implications of personal experience*, primarily through telling, rationalizing, and critiquing stories. Rather than delivering someone else's conceptions, we should emphasize the capability to *form theories and design systems*.

3. Rather than viewing knowledge as static structures, we should think of it as a facility for *composing fugues*--thinking from multiple perspectives at once, integrating different trains of thought into a harmonious story with a rhythm and tone that fits the setting.

4. Our emphasis on discursive representations (reading and writing) should be balanced by promoting skills in *envisioning* (through drawing) and in *orchestrating complex designs* (through ensemble activity).

5. Rather than just designing a "glass box" computer model to be something that allows us to see through a complex mechanism to understand its inner workings, we should find ways to build in and reify the context in which that model makes sense, thus *reflecting back our social selves*.

If these new perspectives sound idealistic or overly romantic, it might very well be because of how our society has distorted our sense of what knowledge is, identifying it with stodgy, puritanistic principles to be learned and recited by rote--as if the mind is something mechanical, to be assembled and oiled and made predictable, like gears and pistons, and teaching is just a matter of following written manuals.

The time has come for some radical thinking. What we take for major religious schisms in AI are but quibbles among players crowded together on one end of a vast field of beliefs. What AI researchers question as irrelevant, intellects of the remaining academic world have established and built upon for a decade or more. Somewhere at the heart of AI's dilemma is the unquestioned belief that AI can go it alone, that intelligence is just a matter of mathematics and engineering, and that social scientists are wooly thinkers who just do things on paper. Yet anyone in the field with half an open eye must realize how much has been left out, how much of each person's day-to-day experience and passions are not captured by AI programs. In fact, it is this tendency to ignore our own personal experience and distort our own observations and goals that is most dangerous.

What's reputable in AI applied to education? What's left out of the paradigm? You must be creative. Keep asking questions about what is expected of you. Strive to know the boundaries and be sharp about what you are leaving out because your culture made it difficult to say.

> Surely we are all aware that more people know the name of Dante than have ever heard of Fibonacci. That Bach has given more joy to more people than Isaac Newton ever did. And that Cezanne and Monet will be remembered long after Brunel's bridges have crumbled and Riemann has been forgotten.... Figuring out how AI is to encompass more of human life and human needs than can be measured in economic terms constitutes the greatest challenge to the field. (Cohen,1988)

References

Agre, P.E. 1988. *Writing and representation.* Unpublished MIT Technical Report.

Bartlett, F.C. 1977. Remembering--A Study in Experimental and Social Psychology. Cambridge: Cambridge University Press.

Braitenberg, V. 1984. Vehicles--Experiments in Synthetic Psychology. Cambridge: The MIT Press.

Brooks, R.A. 1988. *How to build complete creatures rather than isolated cognitive simulators.* In K. vanLehn (editor), Architectures for Intelligence: The Twenty-Second Carnegie Symposium on Cognition. Hillsdale: Lawrence Erlbaum Associates. In preparation.

Brown, J.S., Burton, R.R., and deKleer, J. 1982. *Pedagogical, natural language, and knowledge engineering techniques in SOPHIE I, II, and III.* In D. Sleeman and J.S. Brown (editors), Intelligent Tutoring Systems, London: Academic press, pages 227-282.

Clancey, W.J. 1987. From Guidon to Neomycin and Heracles in twenty short lessons: ONR Final Report, 1979-1985. In A. van Lamsweerde (editor), Current Issues in Expert Systems. London: Academic Press, pages 79-123. Also, *The AI Magazine*, 7(3):40-60, Conference edition, 1986.

Clancey, W.J. (in press). Viewing knowledge bases as qualitative models. *IEEE Expert.* Also, KSL Technical Report 86-27, Stanford University.

Clancey, W.J. 1987. Review of Winograd and Flores's "Understanding Computers and Cognition." *Artificial Intelligence*, 31(2), 232-250.

Cohen, H. 1988. *How to draw 3 people*. Invited Talk. National Conference on Artificial Intelligence. Minneapolis.

Greeno, J.G. 1988. *Situations, mental models, and generative knowledge*. IRL Technical Report.

Mandler, G. 1984. *Cohabitation in the Cognitive Sciences*. In W. Kintsch, J.R. Miller, and P.G. Polson (editors), <u>Method and Tactics in Cognitive Science</u>, Hillsdale: Lawrence Erlbaum Associates, p. 305-315.

Rommetveit, R. 1987. Meaning, context, an control: Convergent trends and controversial issues in current social-scientific research on human cognition and communication. *Inquiry*, 30:77-79.

Roschelle, J. 1988. *Sufficiency and utility of physics problem solving processes*. Proceedings of ITS-88, Montreal, pages 123-138.

Stucky, S. 1987. *The situated processing of situated language*. Technical Report CSLI-87-80.

Tyler, S. 1978. <u>The Said and the Unsaid--Mind, Meaning, and Culture.</u> New York: Academic Press.

Visualizing A Channel Router: An Experimental Study

B.Codenotti   and   C.Montani

Istituto di Elaborazione dell'Informazione - CNR
Via S.Maria, 46, 56100-Pisa (Italy)

ABSTRACT

In this paper, visualization techniques are applied to the implementation and analysis of a known channel routing algorithm . The main features of the algorithm are visualized in order to make easier the user's approach to it.

1. Introduction.

Recently, several authors have studied the problem of visualizing algorithms with the goal of providing tools either to explore and better understand basic algorithms or to provide a framework for research in design and analysis of algorithms [2,3,4,5]. A variety of definitions for visualization have been suggested, depending on the application. The purpose of this paper is twofold, namely to extensively study the behaviour of a nearly optimal algorithm for **channel routing** [1], and to provide an animation tool capable of helping the user in the analysis of this complicated algorithm.

We deal here with the most efficient algorithm for channel routing in the **Manhattan model**, i.e. the approximation algorithm suggested by Baker, Bhatt, and Leighton [1], and we develope a visualization tool, which can be of great help in understanding as well as in optimizing this algorithm. In fact, the algorithm produces an asymptotically optimal channel width, but it does not perform as well as heuristics when applied to practical problems. We believe that simple local improvements would lead to a good performance, also in concrete applications. This will be discussed more deeply in section 3.

The animation of the algorithm is obtained by means of three stages: the development of the **algorithm** itself, the definition of **input** generators that provide consistent data, and the views presenting **pictures** of the algorithm during execution. This approach is in some sense intermediate between visual programming (e.g. replacement of the algorithm by graphic tools) and algorithm visualization (e.g. development of several tools (graphical or not) tailored to make easier the understanding of the algorithm. It turns out that we are oriented toward the definition of a tool that is application specific rather than domain specific.

We consider the problem of routing into a channel as given in [1]. For what concerns the popular terminology in channel routing, the reader is suggested to see [1]. Throughout the paper, the algorithm in [1] will be referred to as **BBL** algorithm.

2. The Channel Router (Programmer's Perspective).

We restrict ourselves to the version of BBL algorithm applicable to channels with 2-point nets. It is assumed that each net has exactly two terminals, one on the top track and one on the bottom track of the channel. The algorithm can be readily extended to treat the multipoint-nets case.

The algorithm is divided into four main stages.

BBL Algorithm [1]

Phase 1. Find the least integer k such that the channel can be partitioned into groups of k^2 consecutive columns, each group containing at least 3k grid points at which no terminal is placed (**empty** grid points) in both the top and the bottom tracks.

Phase 2. Divide each group of k^2 columns into k blocks of k columns each. Route wires from the first three points on the top (bottom) track of each block into columns that are empty on the top (bottom) track.

Phase 3. Route the correct number of wires between different blocks. If x nets have one terminal in the top track of block A and the other terminal in the bottom track of block B, then route x wires from the top track of block A to the bottom track of block B. Note that it is not necessary that the wires be routed into the correct columns, but only that the correct number are routed between blocks.

Phase 4. Route wires within each block. This can be accomplished without using extra columns, i.e. each net can be routed entirely within its block.

The extension of the algorithm to handle multi-point nets is straightforward. Details of this procedure can be found in [1].

3. The Visualization (User's Perspective).

In this section we first describe the general strategy which we think is appropriate to enhance the understanding of BBL algorithm, and then we state the results we have attained till now.

Our goal is to give a visualization of BBL algorithm. This router, although asymptotically almost optimal, is known to be complicated, so that a visualization tool seems to be very effective to capture the intrigued behaviour of the algorithm. Furthermore, in [1] many details of the algorithm (expecially for what concerns phases 2 and 4) are not explicitly developed, so that a number of practical choices are left to the readers.

The following arguments give an idea of the main strategies used and of the results achieved.

Each execution step leading to a wire-routing (e.g. a step of the algorithm corresponding to the selection of part of a path) is followed by **graphic** step, namely the segment corresponding to the wire routed is given in output on the screen. This choice, together with the possibility of deciding a **delay-rate** slowing down each execution step, allows the user to watch on-line to what the algorithm is currently doing. Moreover, some files containing feasible input data are provided, and the user can select one of them to perform experiments. The user can also create his own input data, and run the algorithm on them.

It is worth reporting on that the crucial step of the algorithm is **phase 3**, which provides the routing of wires which have to **change block** (see the previous section). In other words, this phase has to route (although not completely) wires which would be **long**. It is known that long wires are not desirable in practice, so that a heuristic improvement on this size has to interact with phase 3. It is possible to provide input data in order to put into evidence the behaviour of phase 3, by selecting data for which the other phases are trivial.

An analogous approach can be used in order to improve the behaviour of the other phases. For what concerns phase 4, different routing algorithms could be used, depending on the type of channel to be routed (as a function of its density, number of terminals, number of cycles,...). Therefore an **evaluation** of the **type** of channel to be routed could be performed interactively by the user, who could be allowed to choose different suitable routers to carry out each occurrency of this phase.

We have performed many experiments by applying the algorithm to many types of input data, obtained either at random or by selecting suitable **input parameters**, which allow to choose the type of channel.

More precisely, the user is allowed to choose channels with or without **cycles**, with given **density and/or flux**, with empty terminals inside.

Since the performance of channel routers heavily depends on these parameters, the choice of the **input parameters** allows to massively analyze BBL algorithm. We could observe that BBL algorithm naturally split itself into a **static** part (phase 3), which is the **core** of the algorithm, and a **dinamic** part (phases 2 and 4), which can be implemented by using different algorithms. These arguments make clear that interactive choices are recommended to improve the behaviour of BBL algorithm. For instance, phase 4 consists of a new channel routing problem whose features are known only after the completion of phase 3. It follows that only during execution one can choose an appropriate router to perform phase 4. Visualization helps the user in accomplishing this adaptive technique.

The main results we have obtained can be summarized as follows.

1. BBL algorithm can be highly improved (with respect to the upper bound to the number of tracks);
2. Channel routing algorithms can be better understood by means of visualization strategies;
3. BBL algorithm can be made versatile, by choosing adaptive strategies to carry out phases 2 and 4.

At the current stage of our project, some of the features of the visualization tool have been implemented. More precisely, we have visualized the core of the router, i.e. phase 3. In figs.1a-1d and 2a-2c, we are able to illustrate the main steps of phase 3, and the user can choose whether to watch a single block or the entire channel, as well as the whole routing within each block or only the routing of special types of nets (e.g. ending, falling, rising, continuing, and every combination of them). Figs. 3a-3d show the procedure of solution of a given CRP by BBL algorithm: the problem leads to a suitable partitioning (phase 1) of the channel (fig.3a); phase2 is then performed in order to distribute emty points (fig.3b); in fig.3c phase3 is shown; finally, the detailed routing within each block is illustrated (phase 4). The user can choose which phase he is interested to, and visualize only this one (or these ones).

The tool here described is being developed on an IBM AT computer, available at IEI-CNR, and C language has been used in the Microsoft 5.0 version.

4. Conclusions.

We have dealt with the most efficient algorithm for channel routing in the **Manhattan model**, and we have developed a visualization tool. On the base of the experimental results obtained, we have observed that the algorithm produces an asymptotically optimal channel width, but it does not perform as well as heuristics when applied to practical problems. We have seen that simple local improvements lead to a good performance, also in concrete applications.

This is only a first look to visualizing channel routers, but we believe that visualization will lead to better understanding and learning about channel routing problems.

This research will go on with the goal of providing a complete visualization tool for testing and/or implementing channel routing algorithms. The tool will be constructed by means of a set of algorithms, a set of input data, taken either as difficult examples or randomly chosen, and a set of visualization features.

REFERENCES

1.   B.S.Baker, S.N.Bhatt, and T.Leighton, An Approximation Algorithm for Manhattan Routing, Advances in Computing Research 2, 205-229 (1984).

2. M.H.Brown, Exploring Algorithms Using Balsa-II, Computer, 14-36 (1988).

3.   R.A.Duisberg, Visual Programming of Program Visualizations, Proc.Conf.Visual Languages (1987).

4. R.L.London and R.A.Duisberg, Animating Programs Using Smalltalk, Computer, 61-71 (1985).

Figure captions.

Fig.1a. A single block processed in phase 3 is illustrated. Numeric labels on the upper-left (lower-left) side of the block represent rising (falling) nets.

Fig.1.b. Rising- and falling-ending nets within a block are routed by means of a staircase pattern.

Fig.1.c. Rising- and falling-continuing nets are routed. Occupation of horizontal tracks is optimized by using the staircase previously generated to route ending nets.

Fig.1.d. A rising-starting net is routed to balance the number of starting-rising and starting-falling nets.

Fig.2.a. Vertical nets within a block are routed.

Fig.2.b. Remaining-starting nets are routed.

Fig.2.c. Starting-falling nets are routed via backtracking (see [1]).

Fig.3.a. A CRP is illustrated together with the corresponding partition of the channel (phase 1).

Fig.3.b. Phase 2: three empty columns are allocated for each block.

Fig.3c. Phase 3: interblock routing.

Fig.3d. Phase4: detailed routing within each block. (A simple routing strategy has been chosen, paying attention to the presence of conflict cycles inside the block, and routing trivially all the nets except than those involved in a cycle, for which an empty column has to be used).

47

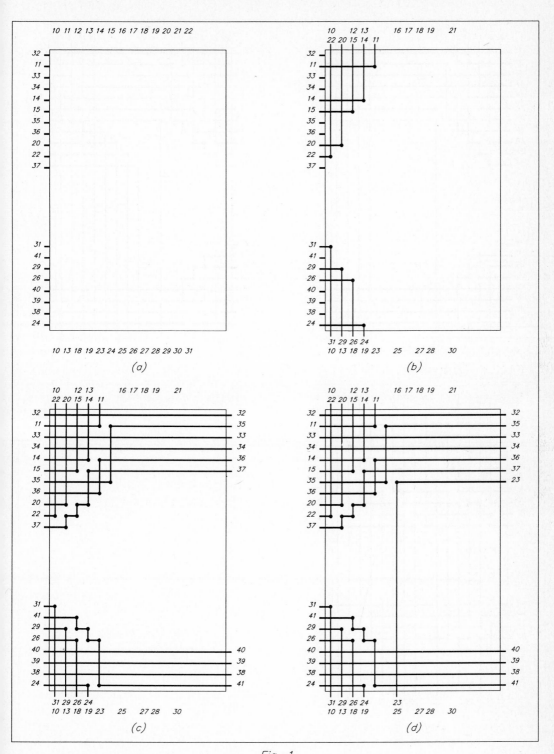

Fig. 1

48

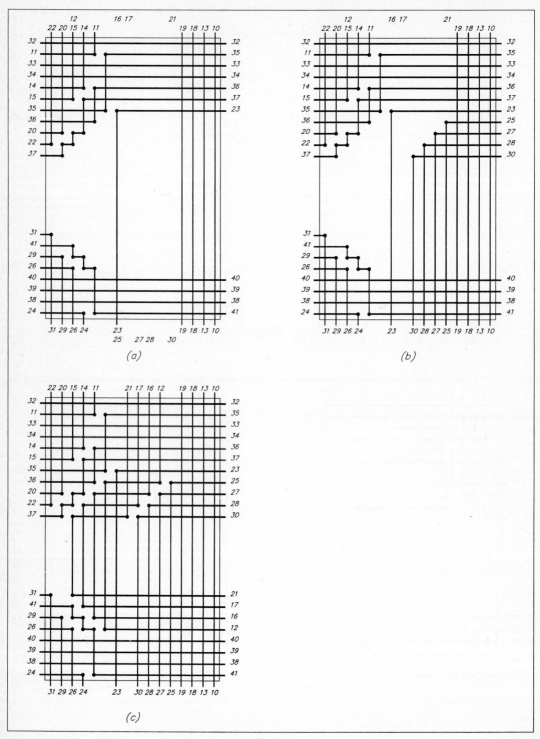

Fig. 2

11 12 13 14 15 16 17 18 19   20 21 22 23   24 25   26   27 28 29 30

25 30   28 29 18 27 23 16 20 24 11 13 15 14 12 21 17   19   26 22

Fig. 3a

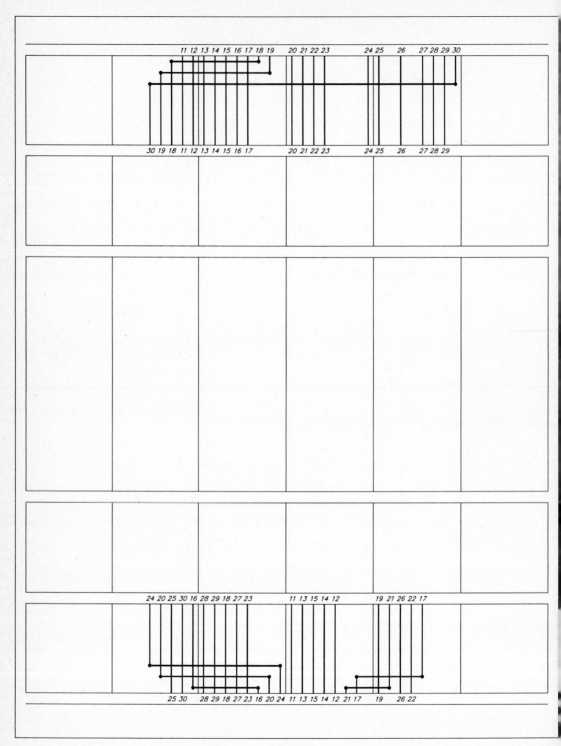

Fig. 3b

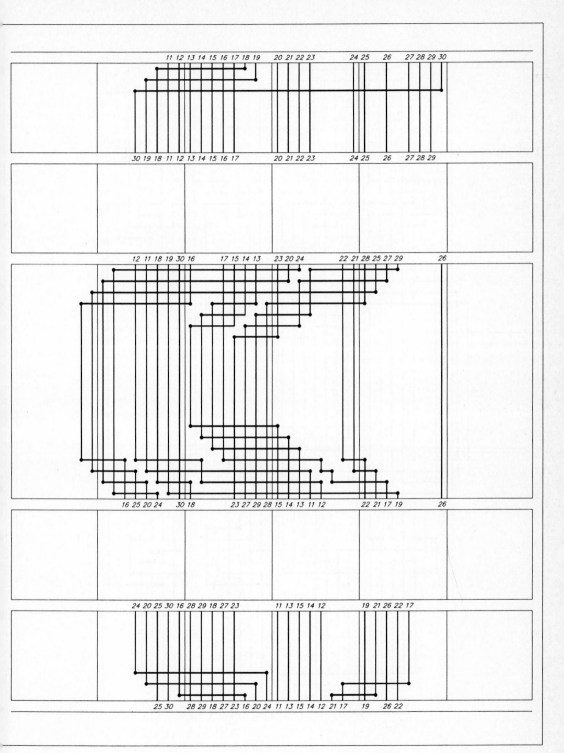

Fig. 3c

52

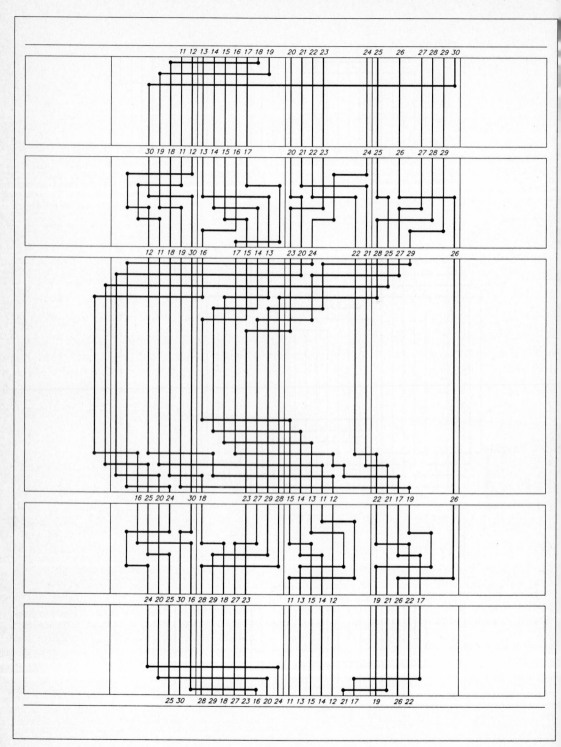

Fig. 3d

INTELLIGENT HYPERMEDIA IN EDUCATION

Amos Abayomi DAVID, Odile THIERY, Marion CREHANGE
Centre de Recherche en Informatique de Nancy (CRIN), Campus Scientifique, B.P. 239, 54506
Vandoeuvre-Les-Nancy, FRANCE.

ABSTRACT

Artificial Intelligence (AI) has found its way into Computer Aided Education (CAE), and several systems have been built to show its interesting advantages. We think that images (graphic or real) play an important role in learning. However, the use of images, outside their use as illustration, makes it necessary to have applications such as AI.

We shall develop the application of AI in an image based CAE and briefly present the system under construction to put in evidence our concept. We shall also elaborate a methodology for constructing such a system. Futhermore we shall briefly present the pedagogical and psychological activities in a learning process.

I.   INTRODUCTION

It is now many years that computer passed from the stage of a "studied machine" to that of "machine for study", which is known as CAE (Computer Aided Education). Initially simple "programmed teaching", where the student revises exercises applied to lessons received in the class, it evolves more and more towards a flexible machine. In fact, (Cf the analysis done in [8, 20, 19, 21, 5, 15, 25]) build a "good tutorial system" from the teacher's point of view as well as from that of the student is a complicated task. Very often, CAE softwares are rigid frames where even close responses are often rejected, thereby provoking a sort of weariness by the learner and a lack of interest. We think that the introduction of images in addition or even to replace text is a good factor for alertness and of interest especially in science of observation. Images in our context are used as a base for teaching and not just for illustration. At the same time, thinking of curiosity and the participation of the learner in the teaching process, we oriented our study towards a "discovery" type of system, where the learner's participation is important rather than towards a purely magistrate type. A flexible system capable of making deductions, accepting more or less well formed hypothesis is indispensable in this context: it must be intelligent in contents and in presentation with a friendly user interface. This is what we call an IICAE (Intelligent Image based Computer Aided Education) integrating images, text, sound and computer in a learning environment.

Even though there is an increasing need for IICAE system, few developments or research are done in this area. In training on the job, only big companies make use of equipement such as videodisc. Yet, for example, IBM evaluated to 30% the economy realized in training classes using videodisc. The introduction of Artificial Intelligence in CAE became, in the last years, a point of interest for research laboratories with interest centered on CAE in high schools, colleges or in universities (Cf [28, 24] in a special number of TSI dedicated to applications of computer science in training vol. 7 n°1-1988).

The objective of our work is to define a set of methods and software tools for building IICAE systems and to elaborate pedagogical scenarii by using the system. Our work started from the construction of a project called EXPRIM ("système **EXP**ert pour la **R**echerche d'**IM**age" : Expert system for image retrieval) [18, 10] whose objective was to develop an environment for image retrieval, the images being stored on a videodisc. The process adopted was to divide a retrieval into three stages:
- the the user's and then the system's request formulation stage (phase before observation);
    - the observation stage;
    - the user's choice analysis stage.
Image search consists of one or more retrieval steps. With this strategy, studied how this process could be used in CAE. We realized an "expert" tutorial prototype in ornithology whose direct application is planned for natural science classes at a high-school in Nancy, France. The knowledge in ornithology was built with the help of a natural science teacher in the school where we intend to use the system. After defining rapidly the four "supporting poles" for the elaboration of an IICAE system, we shall explain in section III the knowledge we modelized in the form of a semantic network applicable to various domains; in section IV we present the architecture of an IICAE system applicable in all types of training depending highly on the learner's model. We terminate with the presentation of the prototype that we have built using the C programming language and an inference engine called OPS5 on a PC-AT and a videodisc reader VP831. We conclude with the future developments of our work.

II.   THE FOUR SUPPORTING POLES

A review of the state of the art [12, 4, 17,19, 5, 8] brought us to distinguish between four parameters (or supporting poles) that condition teaching. They are respectively defined by the following questions illustrated in figure 1:

1)   what are the activities or processes within a teaching system ?
2)   what are the teaching objectives ?
3)   what are the predominant activities or processes for a given objective ?
4)   and last, given the answers to the precedent, what are the implementation methods considered as adequate?

Processes in Education	Pedagogical Objectives

Ex:
 	
Observation
             Motivation
Association of knowledge
 	
        Transfer of knowledge
Expression
          Control
      etc   *1*
	Ex:
	             Counting from 0 .. 9
	
	Gothic Architectural Structures
	
	              Recognition of birds
	
	     etc
	                              2

Pedagogical Strategies	Pedagogical Methods

Ex:
 	
Memorization
              Discovery
Examples
         Anology
       etc   *3*
	Ex:
	                    Simulation
	Page turning
	              EXPRIM process
	MCQ
	            etc
	                            4

Figure 1: THE FOUR SUPPORTING POLES TO EXPLORE

II.1   TEACHING PROCESSES

The activities or processes involved in teaching are to be considered from the learner's point of view as well as from the teacher's point of view. For a learner, the sub-processes involved are mainly observation, knowledge association and expression of the acquired knowledge. Though the teacher must of course take into account in his conception the transfer of knowledge and its control, he must also take into account the learner's motivation.

II.2   THE PEDAGOGICAL OBJECTIVE

The definition of the pedagogical objective is an important preliminary point. It must take into account the learner's level or at least that of a group of learners. The main objective must of course be decomposed so as to elaborate the desired IICAE scenario. For example if the main objective is the ability to count from 0 to 9, then the sub-objectives could be: a) the ability to recognize the 10 symbols and b) the ability to pronounce them.

II.3   PEDAGOGICAL STRATEGIES

These are rather classic learning strategies (of the learner), ranging from the most simple, like memorization, to the most complex, like "learning by reasoning", through one that is most interesting for us: "learning by discovery" (which could be simulation or recognition).

II.4   IMPLEMENTATION METHODS

These are also rather classic methods in CAE such as games, MCQ (multiple choice questions), simulation, etc ... with progression within the system more or less complicated. In our IICAE system, we intend to allow progression within the system as flexible as possible (while keeping to the defined objective and strategy). Furthermore, as implementation method nucleus, we have the three stage process of EXPRIM.

II.5   A METHOD FOR THE ELABORATION OF SCENARII

From the four precedent points, we have deduced an elaboratiion method of scenarii based on our IICAE system according to the following three stages:
1) define the general pedagogical objective taking into account the target population and then decompose it into sub-objectives;
2) define the teaching processes, which may be linked, and the pedagogical strategy;
3) define the implementation method that is better adapted to the desired scenarii.

This method is put into practice apparently with success in collaboration with a high-school in Nancy, France, within the framework of studies in natural sciences.

III.   BASIC KNOWLEDGE FOR CONSTRUCTING AN IICAE

With the above four supporting poles, we briefly present in the following section, the types of knowledge required for constructing an IICAE and their application.

III.1   HOW LEARNING CAN BE VIEWED

Learning can be viewed as consisting in the activity acquiring of ability or information. What is to be acquired (or more precisely what somebody wants to be part of himself) can be a mental activity or an habit. The starting point of all forms of learning consists in transforming concrete elements into their abtract form. The concrete objects are in general visible and when they are not, they can be transformed into their visible form. It is on this observation that we based our approach of the conception of an IICAE.

The concrete elements can be put into images. The learner can observe these and build an abstraction of what is observed. It is during the observation process that learning starts [4, 14, 17]. The result of the observation depends on the individual observer because observation is a process of image interpretation. The intellectual activity during observation consists in the association of knowledge already acquired. If the knowledge already acquired is considered as elementary concepts with associations, then one can interpret the intellectual activity as the association of elementary concepts or the creation of new concepts and associations.

In the following section, we elaborate the concepts that we have developed by giving an example of a pedagogical objective.

III.2 A PEDAGOGICAL OBJECTIVE

As an experimentation, we chose the objective as the ability to associate the morphological characteristics of birds and their types of nutrition. We have some knowledge on the types of nutrition and characteristics of birds. We established the links between the types of nutrition and the characteristics based on the knowledge we have on the general morphological caracteristics of the concerned birds. In figure 2, we give an example of our knowledge in form of semantic network [9, 32]. The network is a graph.

Figure 2:   Semantic Network (of the Knowledge Base)

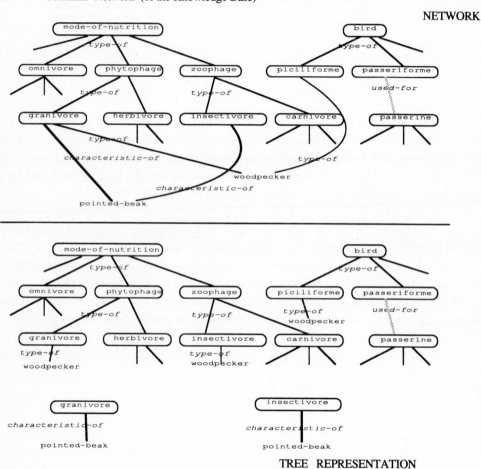

NETWORK

TREE REPRESENTATION

The nodes represent concepts or objects, that we can consider as elementary knowledge. The arcs represent the relationships between the elementary knowledge. For example, in the network, pointed-beak is at the same time a <u>characteristic of</u> **carnivore** and of **insectivore**, woodpecker is at the same time a <u>type of</u> **granivore** and also of **piciliforme** and passerine is <u>used for</u> "passeriforme".

Note that we have chosen a semantic network representation because our main interest is to know the relationships between the elementary knowledge. We built the network by classifying the types of nutrition and the birds according to their morphology. However, the implementation language used forced us to transform the network into a tree structure which is shown in the second part of figure 2.

We distinguish two types of elementary knowledge (concept or object), in our conception. There are visible objects such as trees, insects, grains, fruits, a long leg, and there are concepts that are not literally visible, or visible objects that are considered as concepts because of their use in a particular context, for example phytophage, beak (which is considered as a concept if it is not followed by a qualifier in the natural sciences' class).

III.3   THE USE OF THE NETWORK AND THE PEDAGOGICAL KNOWLEDGE

The pedagogical strategy that we try to implement is of the "discovery" type, where observation plays a very important role. The chosen implementation method is based on progression within the system in three phases. Note that in the "discovery" strategy, it is the learner who directs the system. The system tries to understand the needs of the learner so as to guide him eventually. The learner expresses his needs in the form of requests. For example, if he wants to see images which contain fish, and birds with long beak, he will type: "fish long-beak" (a free list of terms). The system will then try to understand this request. In order to realize this objective, we implement some heuristics that act on the request and at the same time on the learner's behavior. We give below some heuristics implemented in the system:

Heuristic 1: If a term in the learner's request is more general in sense than another one in the same request, then remove the most general term, considering the term that is more specific as a precision of the request. For example if the request is *"granivore   pointed-beak"*, the system will remove *"granivore"*, considering *pointed-beak"* as precision of the request (Cf figure 2). This heuristic attempts at reducing the number of possible responses.

Heuristic 2: If a term of the request is a general term regrouping others in the semantic network, then either establish a dialog so as to know more precisely the desired terms, or transform the general term into its more specific terms. This heuristic attemps at enlarging the possible solutions. For example, if the request is *"phytophage"*, the system will transform the request into *"granivore herbivore"*, or establish a dialogue with the learner so as to know which of the two terms to take as the request.

Heuristic 3 (Pedagogical): If a term is a concept (that is in the network, a non-terminal node) then establish a dialog with the learner so as to know the specific terms that has allowed him to infer this concept. For example, if the request is *"phytophage"*, either the learner really knows the significance of this term in natural sciences, or he came across it somewhere and he wants to know it better. In these cases, there should be a dialog between the system and the learner.

IV.   THE ARCHITECTURE OF AN IICAE

The following figure shows the architecture that we propose for an IICAE. It is composed of three modules:

- The **domain module** which should contain all knowledge related to the domain under study such as in the semantic network and the descriptive base for the used images;
- The **pedagogical technique module** which should define the heuristics, the objective and the method of progression within the system;
- In order to individualize and be capable of evaluating the performance of the learner as well as that of the system, the system should allow the creation of the **learner's module** (which contains his profile). The need

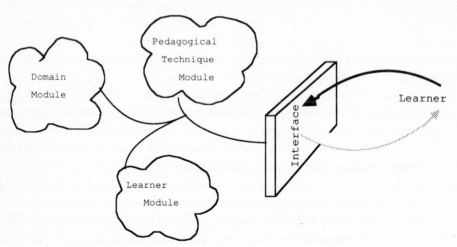

Figure 3.   ARCHITECTURE OF AN IICAE SYSTEM

for the exploitation of the learner's module is not a recent awareness. In traditional education for instance where a tutor is in front of 20 to 30 students in the same class, the need has long been proved for the necessity of individualization for a better academic performance. There are studies and synthesis done on the learner's module especially in [31, 11, 7, 17] on what the module should be, and what the module can be used for. In our project, we want to use the learner's model mainly for pedagogical need for example (among other things) for understanding the learner's need, help in changing pedagogical objective if the need be, and for evaluation facilities.

- The use of the system will then be facilitated by the use of an **intelligent interface**.

V.   THE PROTOTYPE

The prototype BIRDS is an intelligent hypermedia to be used in education, therefore the name IICAE. It integrates images on a videodisc and exploits the advantages of artificial intelligence. We are using the videodisc called BIRDS edited by BBC London. The pedagogical objective chosen in collaboration with a tutor in a high school is "the ability to recognize the external morphological characteristics of birds and link them with their modes of nutrition".

V.1   THE WORKING ENVIRONNEMENT

The working environment consists of: a videodisc reader, a television, a PC/AT and a mouse. In addition to the PC, we installed a supperposition board which allows image, text and graphics supperposition. Display of information can be in one of the following four modes:

- <u>Texte or graphic mode</u>: in this mode, only texts or graphics are displayed on the television;
- <u>Video mode</u>: in this mode, only images from the videodisc reader are displayed on the television;
- <u>Video + text/graphic mode</u>: in this mode, text/graphic is displayed over images from the videodisc reader. The PC and the videodisc reader can be synchronized to perform pedagogical objectives;
- <u>Transparent mode</u>: in this mode, images from the videodisc reader are seen through any colored region. Colored regions serve as tranparent screens. This technique is also useful as a pedagogical method.

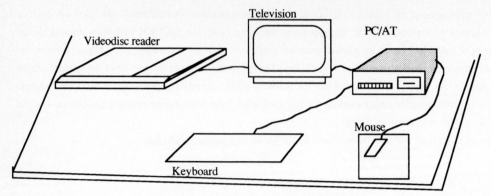

Figure 4: WORKING ENVIRONNEMENT

V.2   GLOBAL SCHEMA OF THE SYSTEM

The system can function in one of the four modes enumerated below. The main role of the controler is to initialize the environment before changing to a particular mode. The four modes are: videodisc reader command mode, illustration mode, interrogation mode and pedagogical scenarii mode.

Videodisc reader command mode:

This mode enables the learner to send any available command to the videodisc reader through the PC. Among the available commands are: chapter number search, frame number search, slow forward, slow backword, accelarate, select a commentary channel, etc.

Illustration mode:

Some lists of illustrations have been made using images on the videodisc. The learner can go through these illustrations. Illustrations examples are different flying styles; capture methods; displacement methods, etc.

Interrogation mode:

The system also allows interrogation with the EXPRIM process:
- presentation of a textual request;
- visualization of images found using the request, followed by image selection by the learner;
- analysis of the learner's choice of images for a new proposition.

<u>Pedagogical scenarii mode:</u>

Some pedagogical scenarii have been built using various pedagogical strategies. The learner can choose one of the scenarii or leave the choice to the system.

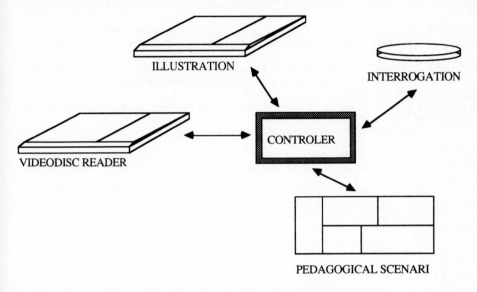

Figure 5: GLOBAL SCHEMA OF THE SYSTEM

VI.   CONCLUSION

In this paper, we tried to show which are our conceptual strategies for building an IICAE system with the four supporting poles [Cf figure 1]. We explained how we organized the knowledge and gave some heuristics for the reformulation of requests. Presently we are working more particularly on the definition of the learner's profile, the only guarantee for a really individualized IICAE. The problem is complex in its form ("how" to acquire) and in its content ("what" to acquire). It is one of research axes in collaboration with pedagogical experts.

VII.   REFERENCES

1. Congrès Francophone sur l'Enseignement Assisté par Ordinateur, Cap d'Agde 23-25 Mars 1987.
2. BARRIERE M., NAYMARK J., PAQUIER G., "Expérimentation du Vidéodisque: Parlez-moi Budget" [1].
3. BARRIL P., "Explication et Comptes Rendus d'Erreurs en Programmation Logique" [1].
4. BASSAN V.J., Eds(1976), "Comment Intéresser l'enfant à l'école". Paris, Presses Universitaires de France.
5. BESTOUGEFF H., FARGETTE J.P., Eds(1982), "Enseignement et ordinateur". Paris, Cedic/NAthan.
6. BOULET A. CHEVRIER J. "Typologie des Objectives et des Contenus des Programmes de Formation des Maîtres en APO au Quebec"[1].
7. CARR and GOLDSTEIN, "Overlays : A theory of modeling for computer aided instruction". MIT AI LAB, MEMO 406, Cambridge MA.
8. CERI, "Technologies de l'Information et Apprentissages de Base", Lecture, écriture, sciences et Mathématiques, OCDE.
9. COOMBS M.J., Eds(1983), "Developments in experts systems". Glasgow, Scotland, Academic Press.
10. CREHANGE M., et Al. ,"Les Structures de Données dans le Projet EXPRIM", Congrès Inforsid, Fontevraud, Mai 1986.
11. DEDE C., "A revue and synthesis of recent research in intelligent computer-assisted instruction". Int. J. Man-Machine Studies, 1986[24], pp. 329-353.
12. DUBE L., "L'Apprentissage << l'histoire de la science est aussi une science >>", Journal de la Formation Continue et de l'EAO, N°217.
13. DUBUC L., "EAO en Amérique du Nord", Revue Formation et Prospective, Septembre 1987.
14. DURAND J. Cl., MOITRIEUX G., Eds(1979), "Lire Les Images", CRDP Nancy.
15. FARGETTE J. P., LATGE G., "EAO et Formation professionnelle". Les Editions d'Organisation.
16. FONTAINE J. C., FENEUILLE D., Eds(1987), "Synthèse Vocale et Lecture"[1].
17. GARANDERIE A., "Les Profils Pédagogiques: Discerner les Aptitudes Scolaires", Le Centurion Collection Paidoguides.
18. HALIN G., et Al., "Semantics of User Interface for Image Retrieval : Possibility Theory and Learning Techinics applied on two prototypes", Congrès RIAO, Boston, Mar 1988.
19. HERMANT C., Eds(1985), "Enseigner apprendre avec l'ordinateur". Paris, Cedic/Nathan.
20. HENNART M., BERTHON J.F., BINSE M., Eds(1986), "Ecrire des logiciels pédagogiques". Paris, Cedic/Nathan.
21. LEFEVRE J.M., Eds(1984), "Guide pratique de l'enseignement assisté par ordinateur". Paris, Cedic/Nathan.
22. MOUNERAT C., LEFRANC R., PERIAULT J. Eds(1979), "L'Enfant et l'Image", CNDP Mémoires et Documents Scolaires.
23. NICAUD J. F. "APLUSIX: Un Système Expert en Factorisation pour un Logiciel d'EIAO"[1].
24. NICAUD J. F., VIVET M., "Les Tuteurs Intelligents: Realisations et Tendances de Recherche"[31].
25. PICARD M., BRAUN G. , Eds(1987), "Les Logiciels Educatifs". PUF, Collection que sais-je ?
26. QUAGLIA F., "L'Audiovidéographie Intéractive en Grande Section de Maternelle (MARION et NICOLAS)[1].
27. RACINE-LAZURE N., CHEVRIER J., "Une Expérience Réusie d'Implantation de l'Ordinateur à l'Ecole Primaire dans un contexte d'outil d'Apprentissage"[1].
28. REGOURD J. P., "GAMETE: Un Système Auteur pour l'EIAO"[31].
29. SELF J., "Student models: What are they ?", IFIP/TC3, FRASCATI, May 1987, North Holland (R. Lewis, P. Ercoli eds).
30. STUBBS M., PIDDOCK P., "L'Intelligence Artificielle dans l'Apprentissage et l'Enseignement", Revue Formation et Prospective, Décembre 1987.
31. Technique et Science Informatiques Vol 7 N° 1,Eds(1988), Numéro Spécial Consacré aux "Applications de l'Informatique", Dunod AFCET.
32. WINSTON P.H., Eds(1984), "Artificial intelligence". Massachusetts, Addison Wesley.
33. YANG J. S., "Individualisation de L'Enseignement: Perspectives ouvertes Par l'Intelligence Artificielle", Revue Formation et Prospective, Novembre 1987.

How Can Educational Software Survive Current Hardware[1]

J. Dobrinski,[2]
Th. Ottmann,
Institut für Informatik
Universität Freiburg
West Germany

Abstract:
We report about experiences gained when transferring an existing major database of educational software (courseware) to new computer systems. It is shown in particular that fairly different execution environments can help to make better use of the big effort invested into good courseware. We also derive some requirements for future authoring and execution systems. Our insights are exemplified by the COSTOC-library of computer science courses which contains already several hundreds of so called presentation type lessons and which is now available on a variety of computers like the IBM PC and the Macintosh II.

1.0   Introduction

Books are not bound to the printing technology; neither authors nor readers need to know what kind of technology the press may apply to produce a book. Furthermore, readers do not need any device (exept for glasses-may be) to utilize a book. Thus, good books often survive their authors. They become obsolete only when their <u>content</u> is outdated but not when their "production-" or "execution-" environment changes.

For their modern electronic counterparts (like stackware, hypermedia, courseware etc.) the situation is usually drastically different. All the nice additional features like animation, simulation, interactive and self-paced learning, etc, which go beyond the book, are available only if you have the right hardware and software. We believe that this is one of the main reasons why an expert in a certain field still prefers to write a textbook instead of a piece of educational software (courseware) about a topic in his field of expertise; and students still rely more on books than on computers. On the other hand, the advent of

[1] This work was partially supported by grants of the Stiftung Volkswagenwerk (I/62452) and the Computer Learning Research Center, University of Texas at Dallas, USA.
[2] Part of this work was done while this author visited the CLEAR-Center of the University of Texas at Dallas, USA.

modern personal computers and workstations and their widespread use at universities suggest to utilize them not only for number crunching, textprocessing, (simple) database applications etc. but also as a real educational tool. This is, of cource, not a new idea and was already around some 25 years or so but was not very successful. There has recently been a new wave of enthusiasm in CAI (Computer Aided Instruction). Strong evidence suggests a breakthrough for the use of computers as a tool in higher education at university level in the near future. The main problem in this context, however, is not the hardware but the software-supply problem: What is really missing is high quality software on as many computers as possible. In this paper we report about a successful attempt to make a large database of so-called presentation type CAI-lessons on computer science topics available on different computers.

Section 2 gives a short summary of the background of our project. Section 3 describes in some detail the execution environment developed for the Macintosh II. In Section 4 we derive some desirable features of future CAI-systems from our experiences. Our conclusions are summarized in Section 5.

2. A Sample of Hardware Independent Educational Software.

In 1985, a major project (COSTOC, Computer Supported Teaching of Computer Science) was initiated by the Institut for Information Processing (IIG) of the Technical University of Graz to create a database of hundreds of lessons on computer science topics. So far, some 30 well-known experts in computer science all over the world have become authors of educational software and currently there are about 400 computer science lessons available [MMO].

The main characteristics of this project are:

- Restriction to presentation-type CAI.

- All authors agreed upon the same authoring tool, AUTOOL ([GM], which   is a PLATO derivative.

- Fairly primitive hardware basis (according to the current standards).

The last point is a consequence of the intent to make the database of courses also accessible via slow, low-cost networks, such as the interactive videotext system.

One of the main features of AUTOOL and the COSTOC-database is , however, that COSTOC-lessons are _not_ bound the current hardware. The authoring system produces lessons in a kind of object oriented code. This code can be translated to so called GLSS-format (General Lesson Specification System [MS]). GLSS is a subset of Pascal objects combined with calls to a library that contains procedures for each command of the AUTOOL system. GLSS is in the public domain. Therefore with some effort it is possible to write transfer programs and procedure libraries which allow to execute lessons on a variety of different computers. More interestingly, one can embed the COSTOC-database into fairly different execution environments. The execution environment, however, may heavily depend on the respective computer.

To be more specific, let us first describe the AUTOOL system in some detail.

2.1 The AUTOOL System

AUTOOL is a PLATO based authoring and execution system that is running on MUPID computers. The MUPID is an interactive videotext computer with an inbuilt graphics package that includes procedures for drawing objects (like lines, polylines, splines, circles, arcs, rectangles and polygons). There are also filling algorithms available for painting objects like circles, arcs, rectangles and polygons available. For drawing graphical objects, 16 colors are available. The resolution of the graphic screeen is 240 X 320. For writing text, there is a special text mode with 25 lines and 40 characters per line implemented. Text can be displayed in 16 colors and have additional flashing effects.

The AUTOOL authoring system contains a menu driven graphics editor. The editor can handle all of the above mentioned graphic objects and functions.

Animation of objects or groups of objects along a defined path is also possible. Animation facilities include the definition of rotation angles, changes of the size of objects and control of the delay between the steps.

Furthermore, AUTOOL provides question/answer dialogues with multiple choice or free-text questions. The user´s answers to free-text questions are then compared with the structure of model answers that are designed and programmed-in by the author of the course.

AUTOOL combines the objects into frames (a frame has a size of 1K or less). A lesson contains normaly between 30 and 70 different frames. There are different types of frames like graphic, question/answer and index frames. The first frame of the lesson contains a listing of all the existing frames, their types and the structure of the lesson. Sometimes a lesson may use external groups of objects from a library.

Normally between 5 and 10 lessons form a course. In the execution system there is a 2-level-menu for selecting the courses and the lessons of the courses implemented. The courses can be stored on a fileserver and downloaded into the memory of the MUPID.

2.2 The Transfer Problem

In order to transfer a large database of lessons like the COSTOC-library to new and more powerful computer systems one has to find the balance between two conflicting goals: On the one hand the transfer process should not require the change or adaption of the CAI content; the authors of the educational software are usually neither willing nor able to become involved in such a transfer process. On the other hand, it is highly desirable to make full use of the specific, additional features of the new system (such as a window manager or a mouse controlled user interface). Therefore, a two-step procedure is obvious:

First, implement a one-to-one image of the execution environment of the source computer on the target system; this implies an exact translation of all graphics, texts, animation and navigation functions etc., i.e. emulate the source on the target machine.

Second, supply a number of additional features not available on the source machine as a front end to the database of lessons.

The first attempt in this direction was the implementation of GLSS on the IBM PC by the IIG of the Technical University of Graz. GLSS was implemented on a PC with EGA board by using Turbo-Pascal. The graphic algorithms for drawing and painting the objects are implemented in special include files. The interface for the special grafic board is an include file that provides procedures for drawing a pixel or a character in a specified color at a specified position on the screen.

It is possible to adapt the GLSS for other graphic boards only by changing this small interface. Therefore GLSS can be easily transported to other computer systems. However this type of implementation doesn´t support special features of the graphic boards or graphic interfaces. It may, therefore, not have the best possible performance time.

A later PC implementation offered annotation facilities. In this version the execution system is running in a specific area of the screen (execution window). Another area is reserved for annotations that can be made by the teacher or the students. The teacher can "customize" a course by making special explanations or references to the course. His or her notes cannot be altered by the students. Annotations can be made by the students, too. Student annotations may be personal comments or special explanations. Annotations can be supplied for every frame of the lesson.

3. MAC-COSTOC: An Execution Environment for COSTOC-Courses on the Macintosh II.

Our objective was to create a conversion program which makes COSTOC-lessons available on the Macintosh II utilizing the user-friendly facilities of this environment to the maximum possible degree.

As a first step GLSS was implemented on the Macintosh II. The Macintosh provides already a toolbox containing many powerful facilities for graphics and window-handling. Utilizing these tools has led to an implementation that is in many respects superior to the PC-implementation. The menu selection and the navigation through the lessons is implemented with mouse buttons. There is also a screen redraw implemented for using different other windows that are overlaying the execution window. In the current version, we have integrated 16 colors and color animation.

A major drawback is still the appearance of fonts. In order to obtain a one-to-one image of the text, the build-in fonts available in the font manager of the Macintosh could not be used. Therefore, the fixed-width fonts (including scaled fonts with double height and double widhts) had to be transferred from the source computer (MUPID) to the MAC, too. Because of the higher resolution of the screen, scaling the fonts was necessary, resulting in somewhat notched-looking fonts.

Our goal, of course, was not only to have the same picture graphics as on the machines currently running COSTOC (the dedicated MUPID station and the IBM PC with EGA board) but in a form of a fixed window on the screen of the MAC II. We were also interested in adding the typical inteface of Macintosh application software as a front end to COSTOC. So far the following additional features have been implemented:

A title bar has been created with pulldown menus to allow jumping, quitting, making annotations, calling and zooming a browsing graph. Desk accessories are supported and enable further individualization of lessons.

Navigation between frames is possible by pushing next-, back- and index buttons (with mouse click). In addition, a new feature, a browsing graph, is automatically extracted from the AUTOOL code by the converter program. The browsing graph can be displayed in two formats (standard and zoomed) in a separate window. The graph shows the relations between frames as designed by the author and also allows to navigate between frames by clicking over the nodes of the browsing graph.

Annotation facilities are provided both for teachers and students. The teacher can comment on the frames and customize the lessons. Students can also make notes which are stored in a separate file. The teacher´s notes can only be edited by the teacher. There is a special window for each of the notes available. If there is a note for a certain frame available, a button in the execution window is active. By clicking with the mouse at such a button, the note´s window is brought to front. For the student notes there is an editor with copy/cut/paste functions (mouse controlled) and automatic line break available. Text can be scrolled in the note´s windows. The annotations are stored in a "resource file".(This is a special file type of the Macintosh.) Because of the resource concept there is a dynamic management for all the frame-dependent annotations.

3.1 Extensions to the MAC-COSTOC Conversion

There are a number of obvious extensions which have not yet but will be implemented in the near future:

The AUTOOL to GLSS converter creates a Turbo Pascal program running on the MAC for each lesson. It is possible to start this program as any other application program from a uniform surface program like Hypercard. Hypercard is a modern hypertext system [C]. It allows to create a stack as a powerful and flexible menu structure to facilitate the access and management of the large number of COSTOC lessons. The GLSS Turbo Pascal program can be started from the stack; thus, Hypercard can easily be used as a front end for the GLSS system. It is even possible to implement additional links between frames and to provide operations like: "search and display all frames which deal with a special topic"; i.e. a limited access to the content of a lesson is possible without being forced to consult the authors of the lesson. Furthermore, our MAC-COSTOC implementation of GLSS on the Macintosh allows us to store all courses on a file server in a LAN. Thus, students may download and execute lessons on any Macintosh connected (via Apple-share) to the file server.

High quality educational software should not only consist of a tutorial part; good training and simulation parts are often even more important. Think of a course on programming in Pascal, LISP, UNIX etc. available in the COSTOC database. It should be easy to switch between the tutorial part explaining a certain feature and a "simulation part" where the student interacts with the real system. Of course, this is not possible on the MUPID; however it should be provided on the MAC and similar or more powerful machines. Using e.g. Hypercard as a front-end, the switching between a tutorial part and a simulation part can be implemented as an additional feature to existing courses. However, any "intelligent" interaction between these modes requires much more than just switching back and forth between different application programs running under the Hypercard surface.

4. Some Desirable Features of Future CAI-Systems.

The possibility to transfer existing high-quality courseware to new hardware and new execution environments is important but, of course, not the whole story. Authors should always have the best tools available which allow them to produce state-of-the-art educational software. Of course, upward-compatibility and hardware independence has to be guaranteed. That means, the software should be compatible with high-end workstations such as SUN, Apollo etc. Let us first briefly recall the basic features of current authoring systems and suggest a few desirable extensions.

4.1 Desirable Features from the System´s Point of View

The core of an authoring system must provide at least the following functions:

(a) <u>Text editor:</u>

A text editor must be available with different fonts and styles like underlined format or flashing format. This is necessary for emphasizing important text parts. It should also be possible to display text in different colors.

(b) <u>Graphics editor:</u>

A powerful graphics editor should support the definition of graphic objects like lines, splines, rectangles, circles, arcs, polygons etc; it should also support the filling of objects with a different pattern and different color.

(c) <u>Animation editor:</u>

One of the most attractive features of modern CAI-systems is the possibility of including animated graphics (like a "trick movie") into a lesson. It must be possible to define the path, the speed, rotation, scaling etc. of the animated objects.

(d) <u>Answer-judging:</u>

The main difference between a book and a piece of educational software is that the software allows interaction: The author of a computer lesson can include questions to be answered by the students. Multiple-choice and free-text questions should be supported. Answer-judging of free-text questions makes it necessary to edit and store the model answers.

(e) <u>Structure editor:</u>

The implementation of links between different pieces of information must be supported. These links determine the possible ways a student can "walk" through a lesson. Thus, the development of a new course should be done in a top down approach, where the structure of the course is designed first.

4.2 Desirable Features from the Author´s Point of View

In most cases the authors of educational software are not computer specialists. Hence, an appropriate user interface is extremely important. Such an interface can be mouse driven or (at least) menu-controlled. A special authoring language with many commands and a difficult syntax is <u>not</u> user friendly.

The corresponding execution environment must provide the student with <u>navigation</u> facilities such that he can find his own way through a lesson. A flexible <u>browsing tool</u> should also be available.

The <u>performance</u> of the execution system must be fast enough. Extremely slow graphics and animation are very boring for the student.

Some of the currently available CAI-systems, such as Course Of Action [CA] or Course Builder [CB] meet these standards. The current version of AUTOOL is not user friendly enough; on the other hand, it is the only system producing <u>public</u> code! CMU-Tutor [SS] uses a special language to define the course; thus, it is very powerful but extremely difficult to use.

Sometimes more general tools like Hypercard [HC] are used as authoring tools. As a hypertext systems, however, it provide powerful means to link pieces of information together but it does not have specific authoring system tools like animation editors and answer judging facilities. These functions must be programmed in. Therefore, we do not consider those systems like Hypercard as real authoring systems.

The advent of new computers (e.g. Macintosh II or powerful multimedia workstations) and the emergence of hypertext systems suggest a number of additional features for modern CAI-systems. In the following section we mention a few of them:

4.3 Features of Hypermedia-Based CAI-Systems:

(a) <u>Database /Hypertext oriented structure:</u>

Courses developed with existing authoring systems are usually completely independent of each other. It is not possible to link frames from different lessons together as in a database or a hypertext system. An authoring system should, however, allow and support this and thus open new ways through different lessons.

(b) Structured design of lessons:

The design of a good CAI-lesson is an art! In most cases authors are novices with (almost) no experience in courseware design. The authoring system should support the design process effectively. There are a number of possibilities to achieve this goal ranging from designing structured editors for the core features of authoring systems, defining course environments by professional courseware designers, to (rule-based) expert systems storing the knowledge of courseware experts.

(c) Reaction to unexpected answers:

Currently the author of a lesson has to anticipate all the possible (wrong) answers to questions in order to react reasonably. This is clearly rather impossible. Hence, a stepwise improvement of the answer judging process should be supported. In the first step unexpected answers should be directly reported to the tutor in the lab so that he can give some help to the students. In a second step, frequently unexpected answers should be reported to the author for expanding the model answers.

(d) Integration of (graphic) output of application software:

Think of CAI-lessons introducing into a software package (graphic editor, CAD system, text formatter etc.); both in the tutorial part and in the training and simulation part of such a lesson it is frequently necessary to refer to original intermediate or final output of the software package. Thus, like using the clipboard on the Macintosh , it should be easy to include those parts into a CAI-lesson. This goal may be, of course, in serious conflict with the hardware independence of the CAI-lesson!

(e) Integration of simulation parts:

We distinguish between the simulation of software packages and the simulation with mathematical models.

The simulation of software packages is more an interface to a real software package like an operating system, a database system or a word processing system. By a controlled use of the real package the student can get some practical experience with the software. The interface is necessary to exchange information between the tutorial part and the simulation part about special exercises or a feedback of the practical work of the student.

The simulation with mathematical models is often used in more theoretical areas like physics, chemistry, operations research or algorithms. The student can change the parameters of a model or the input data of an algorithm to get better insight into the model or the algorithm. This kind of simulation makes a CAI-lesson much more flexible then some fixed examples in a book.

(f) Individualization of lessons:

Annotation facilities are only a first step to customize lessons by the teacher and to handle an electronic notebook by the student. An authoring system should also support a rearrangement of lessons, tailoring sets of questions and exercises to different groups, etc.

Establishing and managing a large database of courseware, keeping track and coordinating the work of many authors, updating and correcting errors in hundreds of lessons etc. is a nontrivial task which requires effective computer support, too. These problems may not be much different from the problems occuring in other large software projects. However, no CAI-systems so far can handle these problems.

The main goal of future CAI-systems should be to achieve hardware independence of execution systems s.t. high quality educational software can run on as many computers as possible. For the authoring system the hardware independency is not as important. There are always relatively few authors; therefore they should have the best tools at their disposal in order to achieve the best results.

5. Conclusion

Educational software will survive current hardware,

- if it is of high quality (where, at least in a university environment, content counts more than style),

- if it is available on many different computers,

- if it can easily be transferred to new systems and embedded into different execution environments,

- if it can be customized to individual needs,

- if it is cheap.

We do not believe that a (worldwide) agreement upon standards of interchange formats for educational software is achievable. The experience gained in the COSTOC-project, however, suggests that it is possible to meet most of the above objectives if the interchange format of educational software is public. Developers of new authoring tools should always keep in mind that it might be more important to achieve hardware independence than to utilize specific "nice" features of specific computer sytems.

References

[C] Conklin, J: Hypertext: an Introduction and Survey, IEEE Computer, Sept. 87, pp. 17-41.

[CA] Course of Action Reference Manual, Authorware Inc, 1987.

[CB] Course Builder Manual, Tele Robotics International Inc, 1987.

[GM] J. Garatt, H. Maurer: Autool Version 2-Manual for COSTOC Authors, Report 244, IIG Graz, 1987.

[HC] Hypercard Reference Manual, Apple Computer Inc.

[MMO] F. Makedon, H. Maurer, Th. Ottmann: Presentation Type CAI in Computer Science at University level. Report 236, IIG Graz, 1987 and Journal for Micro Computer Applications (1987) 10, pp. 283-295.

[MS] H. Maurer, R. Stubenrauch: A General Lesson Specification System. Report 241, IIG Graz, 1987.

[SS] B A. Sherwood, J. N. Sherwood: The CMU-Tutor Language, Stipes, Champaign, Ill. 1986.

THE INFORMATION RESOURCE MODEL

Richard G. Epstein
Department of Statistics / Computer
and Information Systems
The George Washington University
Washington, DC 20052

Robert M. Aiken
Department of Computer and Information Sciences
Temple University
Philadelphia, PA 19122

Abstract

The goal of the information resource model is to develop a database technology specifically for education. The information resource model presents a formalism for the design and implementation of information resource systems. The heart of the model is a graphical query language, which achieves hypertext behavior while ameliorating some of the shortcomings of hypertext. This paper sketches the basic properties of the data model and the query language.

1. The information resource model

The information resource model is a data model for multi-media data base systems. A data model generally consists of two components:

1. a data model component, which specifies the nature

of data base objects.

2. a programming language component, which specifies

at least one formalism for performing computations with respect

to those objects.

For example, the relational data model of Codd (1970) is the de

facto standard for business data processing systems. The data

model component of the relational data model admits 'only one fundamental type of object: the table or relation. Codd presented two distinct formalisms for performing computations with respect to data base tables. These are relational algebra and relational calculus. These are discussed in the book by Date (1976).

The data model component of the information resource model is based upon the functional data model of Shipman (1981). The fundamental objects in both models are entity classes and functions. However, the programming language component of the information resource model takes the form of a graphical query language which is fundamentally new. This graphical query language is called the informatics calculus and it is intended as a user-oriented interface to multi-media data base systems. The information resource model is presented in detail in Epstein (1987a).

2. Information resource systems versus hypertext

The information resource model is a realization of the information resource paradigm for the use of computers in education (Epstein (1987b)). The basic philosophical premise behind the information resource paradigm is that when the computer is used in an educational setting, it must serve to amplify and not to stultify the intelligence of students. The information resource paradigm further states that we have yet to realize the full potential of data base technology for education. Furthermore, it defines an information resource system as a data base system which satisfies the seven criteria listed below. This definition states that an information resource system must:

1. be based upon a formal data model,

2. provide support for multi-media,

3. provide support for student exploration (browsing),

4. provide a powerful, user-oriented query language which can express complex relationships between data base objects,

5. provide support for quantitative analysis,

6. provide support for applications generation.

7. be based upon mathematical ideas which are themselves useful.

The information resource paradigm recognizes the significance of structure (by insisting upon the use of formal data models and query languages) as well as free activity (by insisting that the initiative must remain with the student).

Human factors researchers (for example, see Norman (1986)) have begun to recognize that overly intelligent systems are boring from the user's perspective. The information resource paradigm is presented as an alternative to the tutoring paradigm (intelligent or otherwise) which has been the dominant paradigm for the use of computers in education since the inception of this field. The information resource paradigm allows the student to maintain control and provides the student with a formal framework (based upon mathematics) for creative action upon the diverse kinds of information provided in an information resource system.

The seven criteria given above distinguish between information resource systems and hypertext systems as the latter are currently being defined. While hypertext is a multi-media access method which does provide support for browsing, hypertext systems are not based upon formal data models, nor do they provide powerful query languages which can capture complex relationships. Hypertext interfaces do not support quantitative analysis and applications generation from data. Finally, hypertext systems are not built around fundamental mathematical ideas such as sets, functions, etc. Nonetheless, hypertext clearly represents a technology with great promise for education.

Although there is no standard definition for Hypertext, Conklin (1987) has written an excellent introduction to the subject. He characterizes the essence of hypertext as a "data base method, providing a novel way of directly accessing data" (Conklin (1987), p. 33). In hypertext, the underlying data base is a network of nodes. Each node contains text (perhaps with annotations) and /or graphics and potentially access to other media. In hypertext, the link reigns supreme. The user explores the hypertext system by following these links, a process that is called "navigation". This process replaces the high level query languages associated with conventional data base systems.

The high level query languages associated with conventional data base systems have some important properties. They allow the user to perform quantitative tasks with respect to the information contained in the data base. They can be extended to allow for the generation of reports, line graphs and bar charts. One of the main thrusts of the research being reported here is that it is an error to abandon these powerful capabilities of conventional data base systems. On the other hand, in order for data base technology to realize its full potential for education, it must be extended in the direction of hypertext. What is needed is a melding of hypertext and conventional data base technology. That is what the information resource model represents.

In his survey of hypertext, Conklin identifies two fundamental shortcomings of existing hypertext systems. He calls these "cognitive overhead" and "disorientation". Cognitive overhead refers (in part) to the enormous mass of navigation links which can confront a hypertext user and difficulties associated with managing several tasks simultaneously. Disorientation refers to the tendency for users to lose themselves both spatially and temporally. Figure 1 shows the morass of navigation links that can confront a user of Intermedia, a state of the art hypertext system developed at Brown University.

In part, these problems are related to the fact that hypertext does not use a traditional data modelling approach to building its data bases. For example, the fundamental concept of "entity class" that occurs in one form or another in most data models (including the information resource model) immediately provides an ordering principle which can help the user manage complexity.

Figure 1. Screen from the Intermedia System developed at
Brown University. Source: Conklin (1987).
Reprinted with permission of the IEEE.

© 1987 IEEE

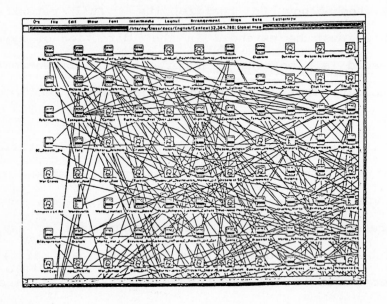

Hypertext is not designed to handle quantitative data
effectively. Yet, many learning situations naturally involve a
mixture of numerical facts, pictures and text. The information
resource model is designed to integrate these various data types
into one coherent framework. This can only be accomplished by the
use of a formal data model which allows numbers to be handled as
numbers and the other data types to be handled as appropriate for
those other data types.

Informatics calculus, the programming environment provided

by the information resource model, is designed to allow students
to handle quantitative data without losing the attractive
features of hypertext, which include the ability to store and
retrieve pictures and documents and to explore the data base by
following links. The informatics calculus is designed to realize
the best of both worlds.

3. The information resource data model

In this and subsequent sections we will present the basic
features of the information resource model. This section explains
the underlying data model, that is, the data base objects which
the model employs.

The information resource data model is an extended version
of the functional data model of Shipman (1981). The information
resource data model employs the terminology of the functional
data model in describing the contents of information resources in
terms of entity classes, scalar classes, functions and
subclasses. The notion of scalar class is extended to include
documents, pictures and audio output. The information resource
data model includes new objects not included in the functional
data model. These include class attributes, higher order
relationships and explicit intersection data. These additional
constructs were included to improve the expressiveness of the
data model.

A convenient method for documenting and displaying data base
structure is the schema diagram. In the following paragraphs, we

will introduce the basic constructs of the data model by means of a sequence of schema diagrams.

Figure 2 presents a schema diagram showing the entity class CITIES and its scalar attributes. The entity class is depicted using a box. Scalar attributes are depicted using arrows and scalar classes are depicted using ovals. An entity class represents a set of entities, in this case, a set of cities. The scalar attributes (including NAME, POPULATION, MAP and DOCUMENT) assign to each entity of the class CITIES a single value from the indicated scalar class. For example, the scalar attribute POPULATION assigns to each city a number whose meaning is the population of that city.

Figure 2. The entity class CITIES and its scalar attributes.

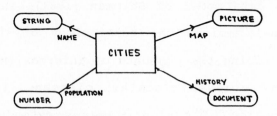

Relationships between entity classes are captured by means of entity-valued attributes, that is, functions which assign to an entity, either an entity or a set of entities from a second entity class. Figure 3 shows the entity-valued attributes which encode a one to many relationship between the entity classes CITIES and STATES. By "one to many" we mean that each city has just one state, but a state may have many cities. The single-valued entity attribute STATE in Figure 3 assigns a state to each city entity in the class CITIES. The multi-valued entity attribute CITIES assigns to each state the set of cities in that state. Note that single-valued attributes are denoted using single-headed arrows and multi-valued attributes are denoted using double-headed arrows. The line which connects the attributes CITIES and STATE in Figure 3 indicates that these attributes are inverse to one another, that is, they contain the same information.

Figure 3. A one to many relationship between the entity classes CITIES and STATES.

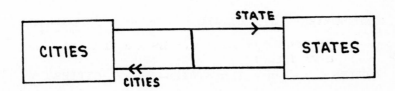

In Figure 3, the entity class CITIES is called the <u>domain set</u> and the entity class STATES is called the <u>range set</u> for the single-valued attribute STATE. In specifying whether an attribute is multi-valued or single-valued, we are giving the <u>arity</u> of that attribute. The name, domain set, range set and arity of an attribute can be conveniently displayed using "arrow notation". In the case of the attributes CITIES and STATE of Figure 3, the arrow notation is:

name		domain set	arity	range set
-------		-------	-------	-------
STATE	:	CITIES	----->	STATE
CITIES	:	STATES	---->>	CITIES

This notation is also used for scalar attributes. Hence,

> NAME : CITIES ----> STRING

indicates that the attribute NAME assigns a string to each entity
of the class CITIES.

Inverse multi-valued entity attributes encode many to many
relationships between entity classes. An example of this is shown
in Figure 4. The inverse attributes

> INDUSTRIES : CITIES --->> INDUSTRIES

and

> CITIES : INDUSTRIES --->> CITIES

encode the fact that a given city has a set of industries and a
given industry is associated with a set of cities.

Figure 4. A many to many relationship between the
entity classes CITIES and INDUSTRIES.

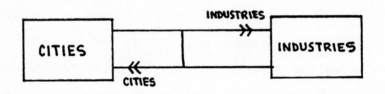

The examples given in this paper are based upon the simple
ideas given in Figures 2, 3, and 4. However, the information
resource model has many additional constructs. The interested

reader is referred to Epstein (1987a).

Figures 5 and 6 present a schema diagram for a social studies information resource. This schema will be the one assumed by all query language examples which are presented in subsequent sections. The social studies information resource is presented in two levels. Figure 5 shows the "top level" consisting of entity classes and their relationships. Figure 6 shows a second level, consisting of individual entity classes and their scalar attributes.

Figure 5. Top level schema diagram for the social
studies information resource, showing entity
classes and their scalar attributes.

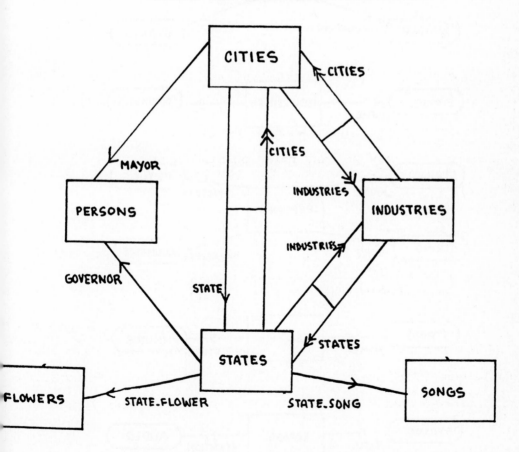

Figure 6. Lower level schema diagrams for the social
studies information resource, showing entity
classes and their scalar attributes.

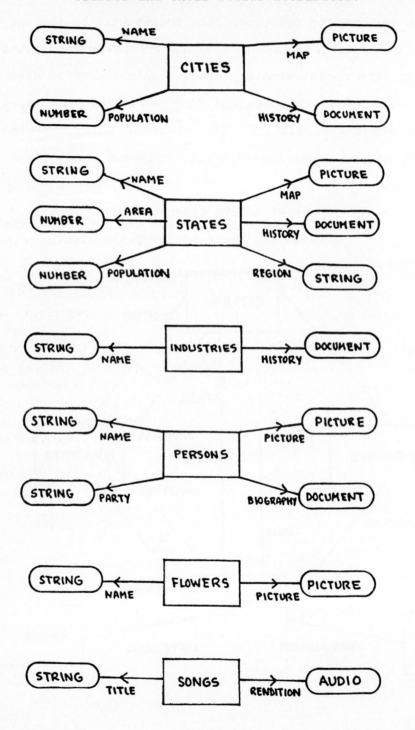

4. The informatics calculus

Informatics calculus is the programming language component of the information resource model. Informatics calculus is a graphical, functional query language. "Graphical" refers to the fact that queries, updates and other data base operations are expressed in the form of tableaus (mosaics) somewhat in the spirit of Query-by-Example (see Zloof (1977)). However, the graphical nature of the language is about the only similarity between the informatics calculus and Query-by-Example. "Functional" implies an indebtedness to Buneman's functional query language, FQL (1982). Buneman's idea of developing a query language using functions and functional combinators lies at the heart of the informatics calculus. However, the informatics calculus differs profoundly from FQL both in its intention and scope, the main differences being that the informatics calculus is intended as a user interface and also that it is designed to accommodate a multi-media data base.

Mosaics and programming by "tiling"

An informatics calculus expression takes the form of a "mosaic", as shown in Figure 8. A mosaic consists of a collection of rectangular boxes called "tiles". Each tile contains the name of an entity class or attribute or some other meaningful object or operation. These tiles must be arranged according to rules which define the syntax of the informatics calculus. The manner in which tiles are organized into a mosaic determines the manner in which functional combinators, such as composition and Cartesian product, are applied to the functions that the tiles represent.

Figure 8. A mosaic consisting of eight tiles.

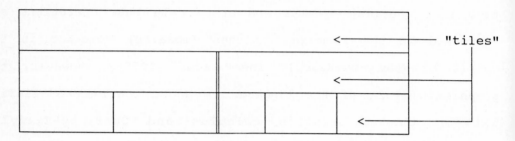

Users would formulate queries using a special editor which enables the construction of mosaics. This editor would support fundamental "tiling" operations such as extending a tile, building a new row of tiles, splitting a tile, and embedding a submosaic within a mosaic. Tiles would be "colored-in" with the names of entity classes, attributes, conditions and other objects which are meaningful with respect to the informatics calculus.

Composition and Cartesian product

In the informatics calculus, an entity class is formally defined as a function which can be composed with its attributes. In the informatics calculus, the composition of an entity class T with an attribute A is denoted by:

T
A

This can be read as "A applied to T" or "T composed with A". This

is an informatics calculus query which means retrieve the value
of attribute A for each entity in entity class T. For example,
the query

STATES
NAME

means, "Give the name of each state".

Suppose A and A' are attributes for the entity class T. The
Cartesian product of A and A' is depicted by horizontal
juxtaposition in the informatics calculus. Thus, the following
query means apply the Cartesian product of A and A' to the entity
class T:

T	
A	A'

For example, the following informatics calculus query applies the
Cartesian product of the attributes NAME and POPULATION to the
entity class STATES. The evaluation of this query would yield,
for each state, its name and population:

STATES	
NAME	POPULATION

Predicates

Predicates are defined as mappings from the power set of an
entity class to the power set of that same entity class.
Intuitively, a predicate selects a subset of the set of entities

to which it is applied by functional composition. Thus, the following query evaluates to the set of states whose populations are below 1,000,000:

STATES
POPULATION < 1,000,000

Applying the Cartesian product of NAME and POPULATION to the above query, we get a query which yields the names and populations of states whose population is below 1,000,000:

STATES	
POPULATION < 1,000,000	
NAME	POPULATION

This simple example gives some of the "flavor" of building a data base query as a mosaic.

The "join"

The "join" operation of the relational data model is related to the functional composition of an entity class by an entity-valued attribute in the functional data model. This sort of functional composition allows the user to combine related information from two or more entity classes into one query. Figure 9 shows an informatics calculus query which brings together information from the entity classes CITIES and INDUSTRIES. It asks for the names of cities with a population above 2,000,000 and for the names and histories of the industries within those cities.

Figure 9. An informatics calculus query which retrieves
information pertaining to large cities and
their industries.

line

	CITIES		
1			
2	POPULATION > 2,000,000		
3	NAME	INDUSTRIES	
4		NAME	HISTORY
	CHICAGO	BEEF GRAIN	document [ ] document [ ]
	LOS ANGELES	ENTERTAINMENT	document [ ]
	NEW YORK	FINANCE SHIPPING	document [ ] document [ ]
	PHILADELPHIA	PRETZELS BEER	document [ ] document [ ]

The tableau in Figure 9 includes the original query (shown
above the double line) and the result of evaluating that query
(shown below the double line). The query part of the tableau
provides meaningful labels for the query result. The line numbers
to the left of the tableau are included to facilitate the
discussion which follows.

Let us discuss the semantics of the query in figure 9 line
by line. Line 1 says, retrieve all the entities of the entity
class CITIES. Line 2 says, select those cities which satisfy the
condition POPULATION > 2,000,000. Thus, when we get to line 3, we
are working with a set of city entities, namely those that
satisfy the given condition on their populations. Line 3 says,

apply the Cartesian product of the attributes NAME and INDUSTRIES to each of the cities that we have. Thus, we get, for each city, a name and a set of industry entities. Line 4 says apply to each industry, the Cartesian product of the NAME and HISTORY attributes.

An important aspect of the informatics calculus is that certain types of scalar values and all entities are displayed as "menu elements". Scalar values that are displayed as menu elements include pictures, documents, and audio outputs. If the user wants to access the history of the pretzel industry when working with the tableau shown in Figure 9, the user would choose the relevant menu element in the result part of the tableau. The desired document would then "pop-up" at the screen in the form of a new panel. This is an example of how the informatics calculus supports hypertext behavior, a topic which we shall return to in the next section.

Derived attributes

A derived attribute for an entity class T is an attribute which is expressed in terms of the functional composition of intrinsic attributes. An intrinsic attribute is one of the attributes in the original information resource schema.

For example, since

CAPITAL   : STATES -------> CITY

and

POPULATION : CITY   -------> NUMBER

are intrinsic attributes of the social studies information resource given in Figures 5 and 6, the composition of POPULATION and CAPITAL, denoted in arrow notation by

POPULATION o CAPITAL : STATES -----> NUMBER

is a derived attribute for the entity class STATES. The derived attribute POPULATION o CAPITAL (read as "population OF capital") assigns a number to each state, namely, the population of the capital of that state.

The derived attribute POPULATION o CAPITAL can therefore be used in formulating predicates which can be applied to the entity class CITIES. For example, the tile

POPULATION o CAPITAL   <   200,000

denotes a predicate which can be applied to the entity class STATES or any subset of STATES. This predicate is true for all states that have a capital whose population is less than 200,000.

Predicates can involve the comparison of sets. For example, since

INDUSTRIES :   CITIES   ----->> INDUSTRIES

and

NAME   :   INDUSTRIES ------> STRING

are intrinsic attributes of the social studies information resource, the composition of NAME and INDUSTRIES, denoted by NAME o INDUSTRIES, is a derived attribute for the entity class CITIES. Since INDUSTRIES is multi-valued, the derived attribute

NAME o INDUSTRIES, computes, for each city, a set of strings, representing the names of the industries for that city. Consequently, the informatics calculus requires that in forming a predicate, NAME o CITIES must be compared to a set of strings.

These ideas are brought together in the query given in Figure 10. This query accesses the names, state flowers and state songs for states that have a state capital whose population is less than 200,000 and that have an insurance industry. Furthermore, the query asks for the names and pictures of the state flowers and the titles and renditions of the state songs.

Figure 10. A query mosaic involving derived attributes before its evaluation.

STATES				
POPULATION o CAPITAL < 200,000				
NAME o INDUSTRIES >= {"INSURANCE"}				
NAME	STATE_FLOWER		STATE_SONG	
	NAME	PICTURE	TITLE	RENDITION

5. Additional features of the informatics calculus

The informatics calculus is intended as a complete data base language, with facilities for data base updates, applications generation and data base relativism. In this section we introduce some of these additional properties of the informatics calculus.

A workspace of objects

The informatics calculus views the user as working in a

workspace which consists of program objects of various kinds. A program object represents a computation which is performed with respect to the data objects contained in the information resource.

Each object in a workspace has a name, a state and a type. The name and type of an object are displayed at the upper left corner of its mosaic. The objects of the previous sections were all of type QUERY. Objects are of type QUERY by default. Other object types include functions, constants and filters. The state of an object determines, among other things, its visual appearance at the computer screen.

Figure 11 shows two program objects, a QUERY called NEBigStates and a CONSTANT called AvePop. A constant represents a a single number, date or string. The query NEBigStates uses the constant AvePop and this ability of one object to refer to another object (inherent in the workspace organization of the interface) greatly enhances the expressive power of the informatics calculus. The constant AvePop denotes the average population of the states in the entity class STATES. It utilizes the functional #AVERAGE / x (read as "average OVER x") which computes the average value of the (numerical) attribute x for the set of entities to which the functional is applied. NEBigStates then gives the names, capitals and industries for states in the northeast whose population is above the national average. Figure 12 shows the result of evaluating the query NEBigStates, assuming the definition for the constant AvePop given in Figure 11. Each state entity in the result is shown as a panel and the panels are organized in a stack.

Figure 11. Two workspace objects, a constant AvePop and a query NEBigStates.

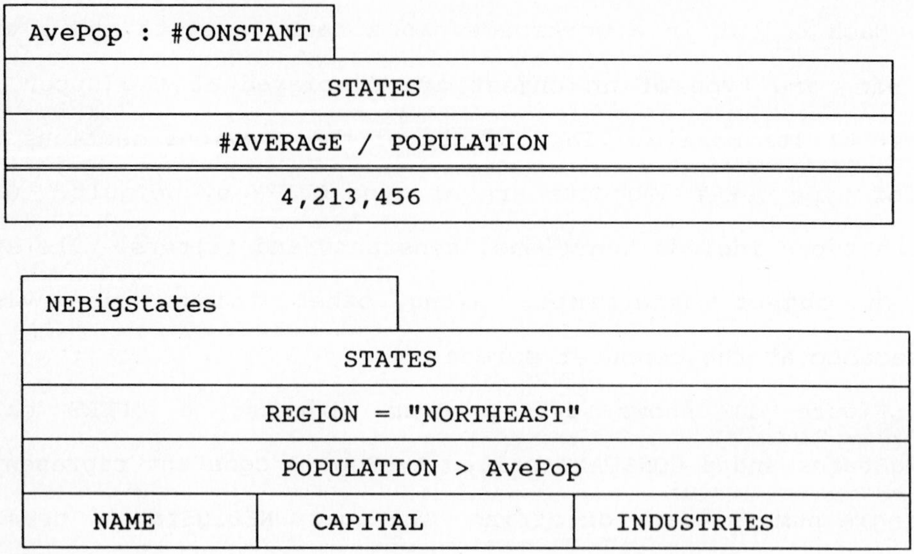

AvePop : #CONSTANT
STATES
#AVERAGE / POPULATION
4,213,456

NEBigStates		
STATES		
REGION = "NORTHEAST"		
POPULATION > AvePop		
NAME	CAPITAL	INDUSTRIES

Figure 12. The result of evaluating the query NEBigStates of Figure 11.

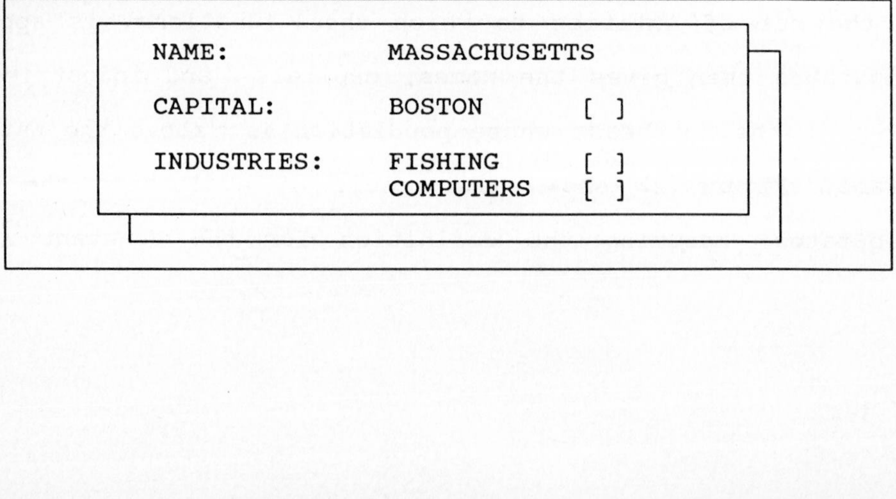

NEBigStates
STATES
REGION = "NORTHEAST"
POPULATION > AvePop

```
      NAME:          MASSACHUSETTS

      CAPITAL:       BOSTON        [ ]

      INDUSTRIES:    FISHING       [ ]
                     COMPUTERS     [ ]
```

Note that the information displayed for each state in the query, NEBigStates, of Figure 12 includes menu elements for entities (Boston of type CITIES and fishing and computers of type INDUSTRIES). If the user chooses one of these entity menu elements, all of the information for that entity would appear at the screen. That information would be displayed as a new panel with its own menu elements. Some of these will be entity menu elements. When a user chooses an entity menu element, the user is, in effect, navigating the information resource by travelling from one entity to another. This again illustrates how the informatics calculus achieves a melding of traditional data base and hypertext capabilities.

Data base updates

The informatics calculus includes sublanguages for performing data base updates. The update sublanguage includes four kinds of program objects:

1. insertion objects
2. edit objects
3. assignment objects
4. deletion objects.

These are important elements of the authoring interface which would allow information resource authors to enter and modify facts, documents, pictures and so forth with respect to an existing information resource schema.

Figure 13 shows an object of type ASSIGNMENT. Objects of

this type are used to update attribute values, possibly for a set of entities, all at once. The object UP_POP of Figure 13 updates the populations of all states in the northeast region by increasing those populations by 2%.

Figure 13. Changing the population of all states in the
Northeast all at once.

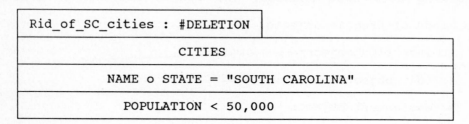

Objects of type DELETION cause the removal of entities from the information resource. Figure 14 shows a deletion object which will delete all cities in South Carolina with a population below 50,000 from the information resource.

Figure 14. Deleting a bunch of cities in South Carolina.

Rid_of_SC_cities : #DELETION
CITIES
NAME o STATE = "SOUTH CAROLINA"
POPULATION < 50,000

6. Summary and conclusions

The information resource model represents a melding of traditional data base and hypertext technologies. The model is a concrete realization of the information resource paradigm which asserts that we have yet to realize the full potential of data base technology in the classroom. Traditional data base systems are weak in their handling of pictures and text, yet these are essential in most educational settings. Hypertext is weak in its handling of quantitative data and in its inability to express complex relationships among data objects. The informatics calculus query language supports both hypertext capabilities as well as the ability of traditional query languages to handle numerical data and complex relationships.

References

Buneman, P., Frankel, R., & Nikhil, R. (1982) "An Implementation Technique for Database Query Languages", ACM Transactions on Database Systems, 7(2), pp. 164-186

Conklin, J. (1987) "Hypertext: An Introduction and Survey", IEEE COMPUTER, 20(9), pp. 17-41.

Date, C. (1987) An Introduction to Database Systems, third edition, Addison-Wesley, Reading, MA, 1976.

Epstein, R. G. (1987a) "Informatics Calculus: A Graphical, Functional Query Language for Information Resource Systems", doctoral dissertation, Department of Computer and Information Sciences, Temple University.

Epstein, R. G. (1987b) "A Formal Model for the Design and Implementation of Information Resource Systems", paper presented at the Third International Conference on AI and Education, Pittsburgh, PA, May 1987.

Norman, D. (1986) "Cognitive Engineering", in User Centered System Design, D. Norman and S. Draper (editors), Lawrence Erlbaum Associations, Hillsdale, New Jersey.

Shipman, D. (1981) "The Functional Data Model and the Data Language DAPLEX", ACM Transactions on Database Systems, 6(1), pp. 140-173.

Zloof, M. M. (1977) "Query-by-Example: A Data Base Language", IBM Systems Journal, 16(4).

A Workstation-Based Course Management and Instruction System

Gene L. Fisher
Lori S. Fisher

Division of Computer Science
University of California, Davis

1. Introduction

This paper describes the design of a workstation-based environment that provides facilities for the management of instructional materials at the post-secondary level. The facilities include:

- a graphical user interface, providing convenient access to instructional tools and data
- simplified access to multi-media facilities and resources available through external communications networks
- a means to customize system-supplied tools and to build interfaces to new tools
- integration with an object-oriented software development environment, providing uniform access to instructional applications written in standard applications languages

For the purposes of this paper, a "workstation" is defined simply as any machine capable of running the MIT X Windows system [Schiefler 86], which implies network access capabilities. X Windows is currently being adopted as a standard by a large number of hardware and software vendors, including DEC, Sun, IBM, and Apple. Significantly, the X Windows system is being targeted for a number of relatively inexpensive personal computers. Hence, a workstation need not be thought of as a expensive device out of reach of many instructional institutions. With the decreasing hardware costs, and the development of industry-wide standards such as X Windows, the workstation-based environment is now well within the reach of academic computing budgets.

The development of our system is based on experience we have gained using course management tools to teach computer science courses, in which computers are an integral part of instruction. It is natural for instructors in computer science to use the computer for activities such as grading, electronic messages to students, and distribution of course materials. We have found that in addition to saving instructor's time, computer-based facilities foster timely communication with the students. A primary motivation for the development of this system is to provide an environment that will foster the effective use of the computer as an instructional tool in disciplines other that computer science.

In addition to course management capabilities, we want to provide convenient access to instructional resources across mixed-media networks. We have gained experience in prototyping such networks, and believe that the widespread use of networks will be encouraged by providing access as an integral part of instructional and course management facilities.

2. The General Features of a "Control Panel" Interface

Several common forms of end-user interface are emerging in environments that support windows and graphics. One of the most common forms is what we refer to as a *control panel* interface in this paper. Basically, a control panel is a window on a bitmapped screen that includes a number of graphical controls, such as buttons, gauges, toggle switches, and the like.

In some other uses, the term control panel refers to a rather limited style of interface, used primarily to set system parameters or options. For example, the control panel in the Macintosh system [Apple 88] provides access to general system settings for the Macintosh operating system. On the Sun workstation, control panels are used most frequently in system configuration utilities, and similar tools [Sun 88].

In this paper, we will extend the use of a control panel to a more general-purpose interactive interface. This will be made possible by extending the forms of controls that can be used within a panel, and by defining a formal underlying model for the structure and behavior of a control panel. Hence, the control panel will be the primary top-level interface through which users access the environment. Control panels will provide access to data files, instructional tools, and other environment resources.

Figure 1 illustrates the structure of two typical control panels in our instructional environment. Shown are an instructor's view of the top-level course management panel, and a panel for compiling course tests. The annotations in the figure point out some of the different types

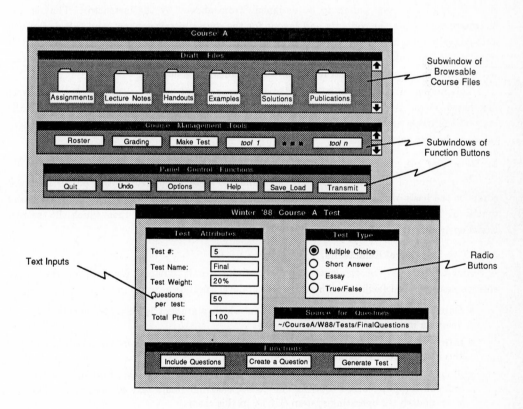

Figure 1: Two sample control panels.

of controls available in the panels. There are text input controls, in which the user types an appropriate value. There is a radio-button box, where the user selects one of a number of alternatives. The illustrated panels also contain a variety of function buttons, which when pressed activate a function or tool. Buttons can be depicted as labeled polygons or as iconic pictures. The general layout and operation of this form of interface should be familiar to users of graphical, window-based environments such as those available on the Macintosh and Sun, for example.

The control panel environment is designed to be an *extensible* basis. Instructors as well as students can conveniently enhance and modify the base set, and define entirely new control panels when desired. To allow instructors and system administrators to maintain some degree of managerial control, certain aspects of some panels will be unmodifiable. However, the general design philosophy is to allow, in fact to encourage, users to customize the interface to suit their specific needs and tastes.

A significant characteristic of the controls is that they are *hierarchically layered*. This layering allows a group of "child" control panels to inherit components of a common "parent" control panel. In the case of the course management system, a primary use of this inheritance is to allow student-level panels to be designed "from above" by the instructor. That is, the instructor will design the contents and layout for the course interface panel, and this design will automatically be inherited by the students' panels. By using an inheritance scheme instead of direct copies or links, students are able to further specialize their own panels if so desired, without interfering with the instructor's or other students' versions.

This notion of inheritance is a fundamental property of object-oriented design, and is in fact based on the facilities of the underlying software development environment on which the instructional tools are built. Section 5 below describes the underlying object-oriented representation in further detail.

3. Details of the "Scholars Workstation" Control Panels

This section of the paper describes the standard, system-supplied control panels that will comprise the basis of the instructional environment. Several salient features are illustrated and described. Technical details of the user interface management system upon which the instructional environment is built are found in [Fisher 88b and 89].

3.1. The Top-Level Selections

Figure 2 shows the top-level panel containing iconic buttons for each of the major environment-supplied facilities. There are six top-level selection categories:

- **Courses** -- the selection of all courses in which a student is currently enrolled, or which an instructor is currently teaching
- **Info** -- access to external information sources, such as the campus library, personal libraries, or external database services
- **Tools** -- general-purpose tools for conducting everyday business; these include the common computer-based tools for file access, electronic mail, text editing, and escape to an underlying operating system (UNIX in this case)
- **Accessories** -- electronic "desk accessories," such as a clock tool, calendar manager, etc.
- **Customize** -- selections to allow the electronic desktop to be customized to suit an individual user's needs and style
- **Help** -- general-purpose and special-purpose help for the user

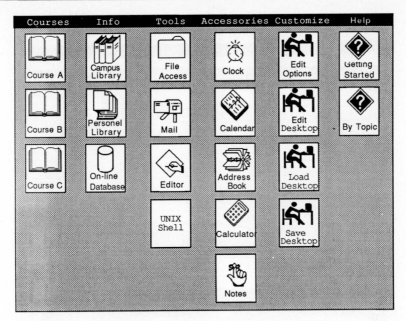

Figure 2: Top-Level Control Panel.

Each of these categories will be described in further detail in the following subsections.

3.2. The Course Control Panels

Data files and tools in the course control panels can be viewed from both instructor's students' perspectives. Figure 3 shows a sample student panel and a sample instructor's course preparation panel for a generic course "A." As seen in the figure, the student and instructor levels share some common course file elements and course specific tools, while having some additional independent files and functions.

The precise relationship between the different panel levels is shown in Figure 4. This figure depicts an inheritance hierarchy, based on the concept of inheritance in object-oriented programming languages (see for example [Horowitz 84] for a general definition of inheritance). Simply put, a control-panel at a lower-level in the hierarchy *inherits* all of the controls of the *super* control panel at the level above. For example, the most generic control panel at the top of the hierarchy contains the common set of course files (Assignments, Lecture Notes, etc.). From this topmost panel, all lower-level panels will inherit these file control icons.

The second tier in system administration level has two specializations of the topmost panel. These two specializations have analogous but different functions appropriate to student versus instructor usage. For example, the student specialization has a *Take Test* function whereas the instructor specialization has a *Make Test* function.

To maintain consistency between all student panels in a given course, the instructor modifies the super panel for that course. Working versions of course files will typically be

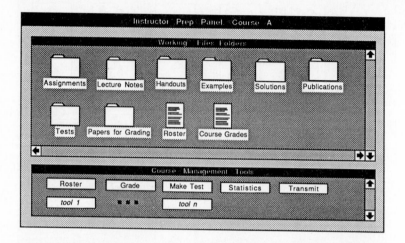

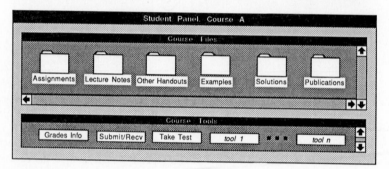

Figure 3: Sample Instructor and Student Control Panels.

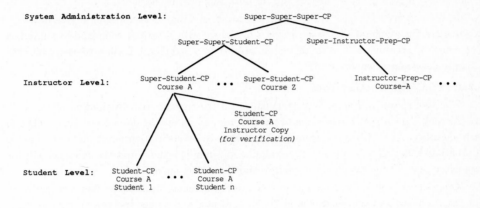

Figure 4: Control Panel Inheritance Hierarchy.

maintained in the instructor prep panel, and copied to the student super panel when ready to transmit to the students. The *Transmit* panel control function causes changes made in a super panel to become part of all subordinate panels. That is, the transmit function activates the inheritance mechanism. Transmit is an explicit function, as opposed to an automatic function, to allow an instructor to make and evaluate panel changes, and then transmit them when the changes are satisfactory.

3.2.1. Basic Course Data Files

The course data files are organized into the appropriate folders. This is a suggested organization that may modified at the system administration level if desired.

Any item of data depicted with a file icon represents a *plain text file*. That is, there is no hidden control information or other non-textual data contained in the file. All of the course management tools are designed to use input and produce output in the form of plain text. This allows any of the files to be viewed using any standard text editor, as opposed to only having access to the files via specialized tools. This notion of having all major system data files be readable as standard text is an "open architecture" approach, as in [Wasserman 87], for example.

3.2.2. Roster Management

The roster management function is designed to be coordinated with the campus registrar. The function on the control panel simply obtains the most recent roster information from the registrar, updating the instructor's roster file.

There are a number of alternatives for coordinating roster management between the course management system and the registrar. In some circumstances, there may be no direct electronic link from the registrar, in which case roster updates will have to be performed manually. There may be an intermediate form of electronic transmission, such as via tape.

3.2.3. Grading Tool

Figure 5 is an illustration of the grading control panel. The panel provides a standard set of functions for editing the grades file and for obtaining grading statistics.

In the current prototype, the grading tool has been designed as a graphical interface to an existing grading program that was designed originally with a textual command-line interface. The reuse of existing tools with textual interfaces is a significant feature of the underlying software development environment.

3.2.4. Test Construction Tool

The tool shown in Figure 6 is designed to aid the creation and distribution of tests. To use the tool, the instructor enters the test attributes and selects the desired test type. Then for each question, the "Create a Question" function is selected. Depending on test type, an appropriate subpanel will appear. For example, in a multiple choice test the subpanel will contain entry slots for the question, the choices, and the correct answer.

Once the questions are entered, the instructor will choose from one of two test generation options. A single test can be generated for all students, or a unique test can be randomly generated for each.

3.3. Information Access

Access to remote systems is provided in the environment. For example, at our site we provide access to the University of California Melvyl online library query system [UC 88]. At present, access is through the existing command-line interface to Melvyl, which appears in a separate window. We plan to construct a control panel interface to Melvyl. This will serve as a case study for constructing an interface to a wholly external system, for which we do not have

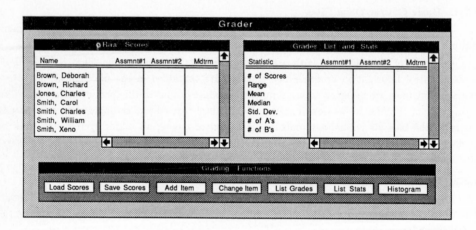

Figure 5: Grading Panel.

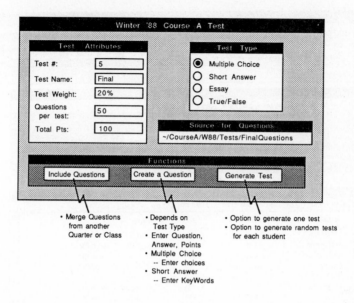

Figure 6: Test Construction Tool.

access to the source code.

Although not part of the current prototype, we have plans to extend the external information access facilities. A high priority item is interface to instructor databases stored on CD ROMs.

3.4. Environment Tools and Accessories

The system will provide consistent interface to the general tools and accessories. For example, there is control panel access to the underlying hierarchal file system, based on UNIX file access primitives. This is illustrated in Figure 7.

Other tools and accessories are based on currently available X tools. We have implemented several tools ourselves, and have enhanced existing tools to conform to the control panel interface style.

3.5. Basic Environment Customization

The top-level panel provides a number of facilities to tailor the environment to a particular user's style and needs. There are two basic forms of customization provided at the top level: option setting and desktop management. Also available to users who desire a more sophisticated level of customization are the panel construction facilities described in the next section of the paper.

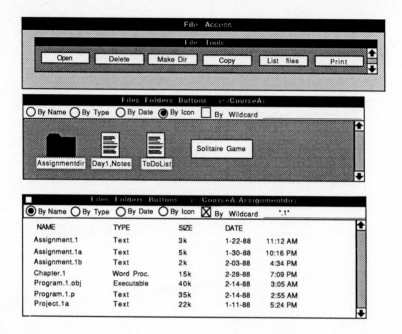

Figure 7: File Access Control Panel.

There is an environment-supplied options editor that allows the user to specify a host of general and specific options. General options include the standard set of X Window and operating system defaults, such as default fonts, window backgrounds, menu formats, etc. Specific options relate to course management and instructional tools. These options include default value inputs for each control panel as well as panel-specific formating and style options.

Desktop management in the environment is based on an X Windows facility to save the window configuration of a full workstation screen. Our environment allows configurations to be named, saved, and reloaded at any time.

4. The Control Panel Construction Facility

The basic workstation environment will provide a standard set of control panels containing the generally needed files and tools for managing course materials. By design, the control panels are intended to be easily customized by professors as well as by students. In order to customize a provided control panel, or to build an entirely new panel, the environment provides a graphical tool for this purpose.

4.1. Control Panel Canvas and Widget Menu

For the purposes of construction, a control panel is viewed as a basic window canvas onto which the individual controls are placed. In terms of the X window base, the individual controls are referred to as "widgets." As illustrated in Figure 8, the control panel builder provides a menu of widgets from which the user selects. To construct a panel, the user begins by choosing the base control panel widget (the lower rightmost item in the widget menu). This base panel becomes the background canvas on which the additional widgets are placed. The selection process is simply matter of pointing to one of the widgets in the menu, and dragging it to some location on the canvas. An existing panel may be modified in the same manner.

Once the basic widgets are placed on the control panel, different attributes of the widgets can be tuned to customize the widget's appearance and functionality. For example, the "pins" that define the maximum and minimum values of a gauge widget can be changed. Attributes of the control panel background can be changed, such as the background bitmap, and the currently visible layer(s).

To alter the attributes of any widget, one selects the *Options* alternative of the standard panel control functions. This will open the same style of options editor as is used to set top-level environment options.

4.2. Example of an Advanced Control Panel

The control panels thus far illustrated have contained only a few of the basic forms of available widgets. Files, buttons, menus, and text windows are the widgets that provide the majority of basic control functions in general-purpose panels, such as the top-level browsers and course management panels. Course-specific tools, including CAI applications, will make wider use of control panel widgets such as gauges, toggles, and plots. Examples of the use of control panels in an instructional setting have been presented in earlier papers [Fisher 87].

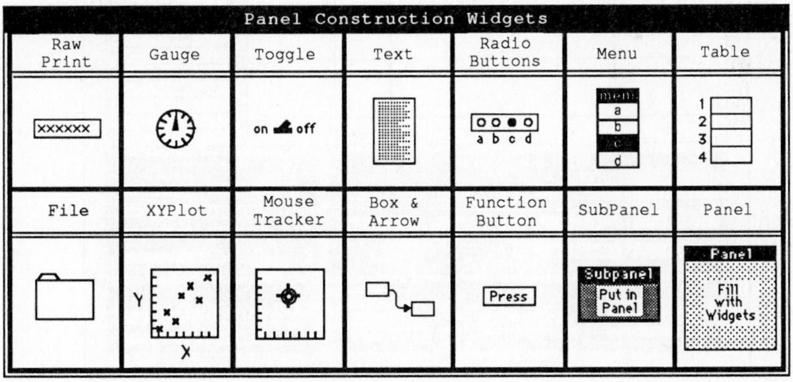

Figure 8: Widget Menu for Panel Construction.

To illustrate the use of some different widget types, Figure 9 shows an example control panel used in an engineering course, in the specific subject area of image processing. The overall function of the control panel is as a browser on a list of image files. The image file names appear in a check-box widget (a variant of radio buttons), with the currently viewed file checked. The top left portion of the control panel contains a "soft trackball" that allows the image cursor to be positioned to any X,Y coordinates. The two X,Y gauges in the upper right portion of the control panel indicate numerically the cursor position. This panel is used in conjunction with an image displayed on a high-resolution image processing device. The communication between the control panel display on the workstation and the remote image processing device is managed by the underlying software environment, as described in [Fisher 88a] and discussed briefly in section 6 below.

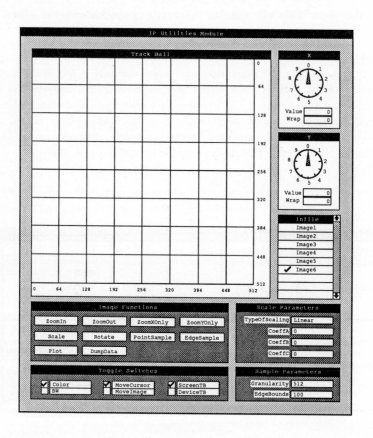

Figure 9: Example Control Panel for an Image Processing Class.

5. Integration with Object-Oriented Program Development Environment

As described above, the control panel interface is an entirely graphical language. Underlying the graphical interface, there is a formal representation for the control panel. Specifically, a control panel is the graphical view of a module in an object-oriented programming environment, and each of the panel widgets is the graphical view of a formal program datatype. It is not necessary for users and/or builders of control panels to understand the underlying representation. However, some understanding of it can be beneficial in order to understand the principles on which control panels are based, and how the control panels function. For the purposes of this paper, it is useful to introduce the underlying representation of the control panel to illustrate the foundations of the control panel principles, and to indicate that the principles are not ad hoc, but rather based on sound, and intuitively appealing concepts, from the domain of object-oriented program design. Finally, a consistent representational framework provides a uniform programmatic interface. That is, by defining control panels as formal program objects, they can be manipulated by programs as well as by human users.

The particular variant of object-oriented design used in our systems is an extension of the Modula-2 programming language. Modula-2 provides a basic form of object definition in terms of the *module* construct. It should be noted that the choice of Modula-2 as the base language is not critical. Other languages that support abstract object definitions could be used equally well (e.g., Ada, Smalltalk). In our case, Modula-2 was chosen as the base because it was well-supported in our environment [Fisher 88b], and because it provides a clean base on which to add extensions.

For purposes of interface design, two major extensions were made to the Modula-2 base. First, the two-part module definition scheme was extended to a three-part scheme. Specifically, standard Modula-2 subdivides the definition of an abstract object into two modular parts -- a *definition* part, containing the abstract specification, and an *implementation* part containing program-level details of the data representation and operational code. In the extended three-part scheme, a *display* part is added, to contain the specification of the graphical display of the abstract object specified in the definition part. Hence, just as the designer of an object's specification need not be aware of the concrete details of its implementation, the designer of an object's graphical interface also need not be aware of its implementation.

The second major extension to Modula-2 is the addition of a basic inheritance mechanism, using a *submodule* construct. Although the standard Modula-2 import/export constructs provide a means to effect inheritance, the explicit submodule feature allows inheritance to be specified in a more straightforward manner.

In addition to the two major extensions, a number of features were added to the environment in specific response to requirements generated while designing the instructional management system. For example, the explicit provision of the *Transmit* function was motivated by the need to provide the instructor explicit control over when the student panels inherit changes. Another added feature is display layering, which permits multiple display modules for a single definition, where each display represents a separate physical layer. The layers are distinguished by an integer index, representing the display depth of the layer.

The combination of inheritance and display layering features provide two dimensions of hierarchical organization. The inheritance hierarchy defines the layering that allows a parent control panel, owned by a course instructor, to have multiple child control panels which interhit all the structure of the instructor's panel. The student panels may be independently customized (i.e., specialized) by each student, without affecting the parent panel or any other students' panel. Displays may also be physically layered, to permit different groups of panel controls to be made visible or invisible selectively. This allows an instructor to design the controls of a panel in layers of successive detail, to be presented successively to the students.

6. Environment Interface to External Media and Systems

In addition to network access to systems such as the Melvyl library browser, we have developed some special-purpose mixed-media capabilities. In conjunction with the user interface component of the course management system, we have prototyped a multi-media network to allow physically separate instructional laboratories to be connected with a combination of workstation and video networks.

Figure 10 illustrates an example of such a mixed-media environment. The figure depicts how students in an instructional biology lab can have access to remote image processing facili-

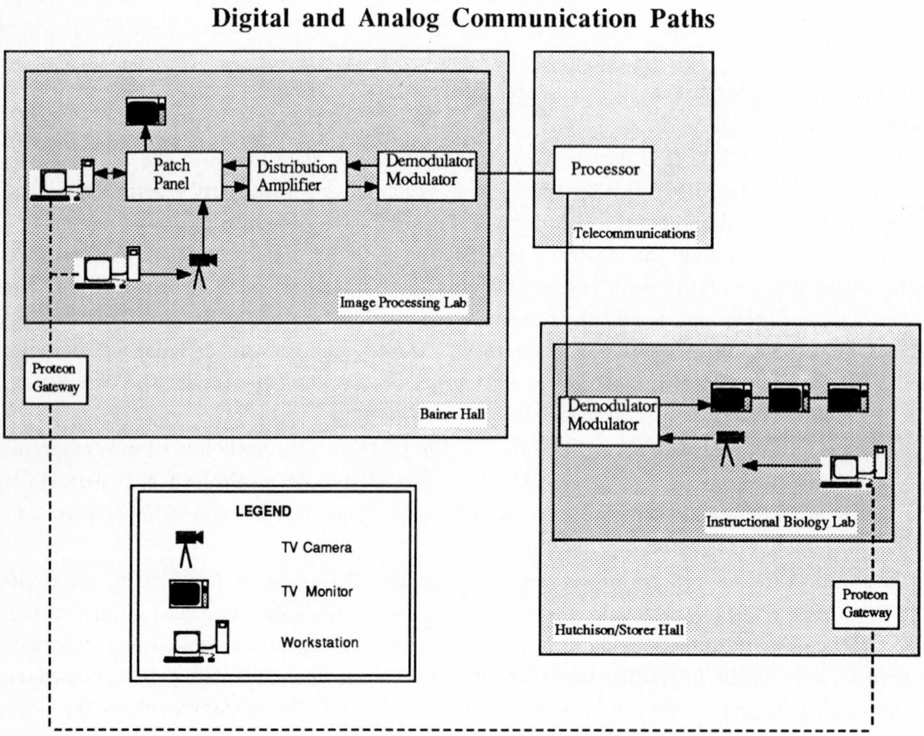

Digital and Analog Communication Paths

Figure 10: Example Mixed-Media Network.

ties in a lab located across campus. The biology lab is equipped with a workstation operated by an instructor, a television receiver, and several television monitors viewed by the class. At the remote image processing site, images on a high-powered image processor are transmitted via television video to the biology lab. The image processor itself is commanded using the control panel of Figure 9, which is displayed on the screen of the workstation in the biology lab.

The network was made possible through a combination of features that are part of the underlying software environment on which the instructional management system is built [Fisher 88a]. What this form of network demonstrates is how access can be provided to a remote instructional resource that is too costly to duplicate in all labs. Through the combination of a workstation network, and other communications media, instructional resources can be shared throughout the campus.

7. Current Status and Ongoing Work

Work on the underlying software development environment has been underway for several years, and a reasonably stable base has been produced [Fisher 87, 88a, 88b]. We are currently developing extensions to the user interface management component of the software environment [Fisher 1989]. These extensions will support in particular the object inheritance and graphical panel construction facilities described in this paper. We have a preliminary prototype of the new user interface features running under X11, and a fully functional prototype should be completed by December 1988.

In tandem with the development of the software environment, we have been prototyping the individual components of the course management system. Several individual tools have been prototyped, some integrated with the software environment and some standalone. We expect to complete development and integration of a base tool set, to produce a full-feature prototype of the course management and instruction system by December 1988.

References

[Apple 88]   Apple Computer Corp., "Macintosh System Software User's Guide," Version 6.0 (1988).

[Fisher 87]   Fisher, G. L., "Student-Oriented Features of an Interactive Programming Environment," Proceedings of the 18th SIGCSE Technical Symposium on Computer Science Education, pp. 532-537 (Feb. 1987).

[Fisher 88a]   Fisher, G. L., F. J. Leahy, and L. L. Lasslo, "Graphical Tools in a Workstation-Based Applications Environment," *Proceedings of the Second IEEE Conference on Computer Workstations*, March 1988.

[Fisher 88b]   G. L. Fisher, "An Overview of a Graphical, Multi-Language Applications Environment," *IEEE Transactions on Software Engineering*, to appear May 1988.

[Fisher 89]   G. L. Fisher, D. Bolden, "Direct Manipulation Interfaces as a By-Product of Modular Program Design," in preparation for submission to the CHI 89 Conference on Human Factors in Computing Systems (Apr 89).

[Horowitz 84]   Horowitz, E, *Fundamentals of Programming Languages,* Computer Science Press (1984).

[Scheifler 86]   Scheifler, R. W. and J. Gettys"The X Window System," *ACM Transactions on Graphics, 5, 2* (Apr. 1986), pp. 79-109.

[Sun 88]   Sun Microsystems, Inc., "SunView Programmer's Guide," version 4.0 (1988).

[Wasserman 87]   Wasserman, A. I. and P. A. Pircher, "A Graphical, Extensible Environment for Software Environment for Software Development, *Proceedings of the ACM Software Engineering Symposium on Practical Software Development Environments,* pp. 131-142 (Jan. 1987).

[UC 88]   University of California, "Melvyl Online Catalog Reference Manual," Tech. Report from Division of Library Automation (1988).

THE TELLER SIMULATOR:
AN AUTOMATIC PROBLEM SOLVER FOR EDUCATIONAL USE

Paola Forcheri and Maria Teresa Molfino
Istituto per la Matematica Applicata del C.N.R.
Via L.B. Alberti, 4 - 16132 Genova (Italy)

ABSTRACT

A knowledge based system, called the TELLER SIMULATOR, able to solve simple arithmetical problems, is herein presented. This system has been developed with an educational purpose, and is intended to be used with primary/secondary school children. The description of the system is aimed at analysing the kinds of knowledge and solution techniques which must be employed by an automatic problem solver, oriented to the arithmetic domain, in order to make it a tool apt to be used in order to improve the learning of arithmetic concepts.

1. INTRODUCTION

The development of cognitive science, as well as the idea of using artificial intelligence techniques, has allowed a gradual movement towards systems through which a teaching/learning process closer to the real one is possible [1,3,13]. This target is still a long way off. The teaching process is, in fact, particurarly difficult to automatize, mainly because of the number of factors concerned: the student, the teacher and the subject. The nature of the learning process, moreover, has not yet been fully discovered. Thus, teaching is particularly delicate and difficult to manage in itself, and its automatization, through the realization of knowledge based tutoring systems, has so far brought gross simplifications. Therefore, today's knowledge based tutoring systems are prototypes: the purpose is to analyse, through them, the nature of learning and, based on this analysis, to propose and to experiment automatic tools aimed at improving the teaching/learning of cognitive abilities.

In this field, knowledge based systems, able to explain their behaviour and the sequence of deductions which has been performed in order to find out the solution to a cognitive problem, are of particular interest, from two different points of view. On the one hand, they constitute the core of knowledge based computer coachs [5,11,12] able to supervise the problem solving activity carried out by the user. On the other hand, these systems can be viewed as learning environments, when specific knowledge and problem solving abilities used to automatically carry out the proposed task are carefully chosen: by observing the behaviour of the system, students are led to analyze the nature of their knowledge on a specific domain, thus learning to master the fundamental concepts this knowledge is based on; moreover, they are guided in finding out deductive chains of facts, thus discovering the role of knowledge in problem solving [14].

With these ideas in mind, a knowledge based system (called the TELLER SIMULATOR), able to solve simple arithmetical problems, has been developed. The aim of the authors was to carry out an operative analysis of the kinds of knowledge and solution techniques which must be employed by an automatic problem solver, oriented to the arithmetic domain, in order to make it a tool apt to be used to improve the learning of arithmetic concepts at primary/secondary school level (pupils from nine to twelve years old).

The system has been implemented in Prolog, and it has been developed on a VAX 750 under operating system VMS. A version of the system is running on Olivetti M24 under operating system MS DOS.

In the following, the overall organisation of the TELLER SIMULATOR will be described. The kinds of knowledge embodied in the system will be analysed, and the solution mechanisms which have been adopted will be discussed. A brief description of a coach system (the ENIGMA system) which has been developed around the TELLER SIMULATOR will constitute the final part of this paper.

2. THE TELLER SIMULATOR

The task of the TELLER SIMULATOR is to give arithmetical meaning to relations involving sums between two strings of alphabetic symbols, by interpreting every string as the sequence representing a natural number in the usual base 10 positional notation. That is, for every symbol a corresponding value in the set $\{0,1,2,3,4,5,6,7,8,9\}$ must be determined. Moreover, every symbol must correspond to only one value and different symbols represent different values.

For example, for the relation: CROSS+ROADS=DANGER the TELLER SIMULATOR finds: A=5, C=9, D=1, E=4, G=7, N=8, O=2, R=6, S=3.
For the relation XY+XY=YYY, the system comes to a stop and explains why no solution exists.
In both cases, the user is shown a detailed explanation of the solution process which has been carried out.

2.1 GENERAL ORGANIZATION

The teacher whose task is to make students learn problem solving abilities and specific concepts by examples, adapts his/her reasoning and the kind of knowledge employed to the pupil's minds. The same approach should guide the design of an automatic problem solver devoted to educational use. As a consequence, the TELLER SIMULATOR has been designed based on an experimental analysis of the behaviour of a sample of pupils. This experience pointed out that both domain oriented knowledge and general problem solving abilities are used to handle the set task; the pupil changes from one kind of reasoning to the other one during the solution process, depending on his expertise and on the particular problem which is faced. In particular, specific knowledge (facts and rules) is mainly used in the initial phase, in order to speed up the process of narrowing the sets of values which can be assumed by the symbols; attempts, guided by general heuristics and specific knowledge, are tried to assign specific values to symbols when the range of possibilities is judged small enough.
To simulate this behaviour, two different models of reasoning underlie the system: a declarative one, which corresponds to the "domain oriented" reasoning, and a procedural one which represents general problem solving abilities. Both models are constituted by knowledge on the problem and an inferential mechanism.

Figure 1 shows the overall organisation of the TELLER SIMULATOR.

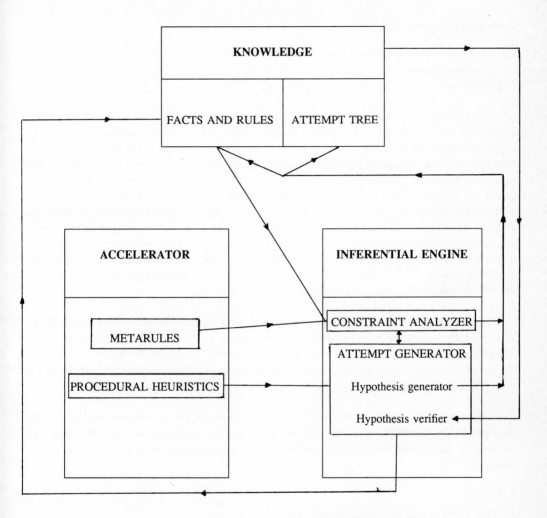

Figure 1. Overall organisation of the TELLER SIMULATOR

a) KNOWLEDGE REPRESENTATION

To solve the proposed task, the majority of pupils involved in the preliminary experiment placed the given relation in columns, explicitly taking into account the carriers, and analysed columns separately, when possible, by using arithmetic concepts and computation rules. Following this approach, the knowledge embedded in the domain oriented module is represented by a set of facts and rules. Facts correspond to the given relation, while by rules are represented arithmetic concepts and computation rules.

The reasoning, which is based on general problem solving procedures, uses knowledge about the effects of the different choices which can be made for the symbols. This knowledge is modelled by an ordered tree (the attempt tree).

b) INFERENTIAL MECHANISM

The inferential mechanism is made of two different parts:
- the inferential engine;
- the accelerator.

The inferential engine, which is designed to handle the two different models of knowledge, updates both representations. The constraint analyser, which takes as input facts and rules, performs a chain of deductions by applying rules to facts. If no rule can be applied, and the task has not yet been accomplished, the control is passed on to the attempt generator. The attempt generator, which handles the effects of different choices for symbols, builds, by using the hypothesis generator, a portion of the attempt tree and verifies, by using the hypothesis verifier, if this portion can be currently interpreted as part of the solution or if it must be rejected. The control is returned to the constraint analyser, which tries to apply the rules to the newly generated facts. The process is repeated, until a termination condition is reached. The termination condition is reached in two cases: when a solution is found; when an inconsistency is detected. If the inconsistency has been generated by an application of the attempt strategy, and another attempt can be tried, the hypothesis generator takes the control and the process continues. Otherwise, the solution process ends.

The actions performed by the inferential engine are supervised by the accelerator, which allows, among possible actions, the most promising one to be chosen.
Heuristic rules, called metarules, guide the constraint analyser in chosing the equation to process. Procedural heuristics operate on the hypothesis generator; these heuristics allow the attempt tree to expand by ordering symbols starting with the ones which allow for less possibilities.

The action of the engine is echoed back to the user, who can ask, at each step, the rule that has been applied, the situation to which it has been applied, and the newly generated situation. Moreover, the trace of the solution process can be shown, along with the transformations performed on the knowledge.

2.2 THE DOMAIN ORIENTED MODULE

This module uses knowledge on the type of problem in order to acquire new knowledge on the specific problem under examination.

a) MODEL OF THE PROBLEM

The specific problem is modelled by two sets of facts, which represent, respectively:
- the constraints on the values which can be assumed by the objects (symbols and carriers) involved in the problem;
- the decomposition of the relation under examination, that is the equations corresponding to the different columns of the bidimensional representation of the relation.

An example of the model for the relation XY+XZ=ZYZ, and its Prolog implementation are shown in Figure 2.

The rules, which represent knowledge on the type of problem, are subdivided into five different classes, according to their premisses and the effects they produce. These classes are as follows:

First step rules: allow reasoning on the symbols at the farthest left side of the initial relation, and they affect both the equations associated with the specific problem and the sets of admissible values connected to the objects.

Example: *IF a symbol is at the farthest left side of the string, and the length of the string is greater than 1*
THEN delete the 0 value from the set of admissible values

Computation rules: represent the constructive rules of arithmetic, that is, they allow equations to be simplified by substituting values for objects, or by performing computations among numerical values, when they appear in the equations.

Example: *IF the set of admissible values associated to an object (symbol or carrier) contains only one value*
THEN substitute every occurrence of the object in the equations with its value

Reduction rules: narrow the sets of admissible values which are associated to objects, by performing arithmetical reasoning on the current set of equations.

Example: *IF there is an equation $t(r(i))=0$*
THEN the set of admissible values for $r(i)$ must be reduced to $\{0\}$.

Deletion rules: they speed up the solution process by deleting facts which do not allow new knowledge to be acquired.

Example: *IF there is an identity*
THEN throw it away

Absurdity rules: they look for inconsistent situations, such as: the same digit is the only value associated with two different symbols; there exists at least one symbol to which no admissible value can be associated; the left and right sides of the same equation are composed of different numerical values; at least one equation has no solution.

Example: *IF there is an equation $S+S=n1$, where S is a symbol and n1 is an odd number*
THEN error

The given relation is:

> XY+
>
> XZ=
> ——————
> ZYZ

It is satisfied by choosing the following values for the symbols: X=5, Y=0, Z=1.

Six objects are involved in the problem: the symbols X, Y, Z and the carriers of the units, tens, hundreds columns, which are indicated, respectively, with r(1), r(2), r(3).

Sets of values which initially correspond to the symbols:

> X: {0,1,2,3,4,5,6,7,8,9}
> Y: {0,1,2,3,4,5,6,7,8,9}
> Z: {0,1,2,3,4,5,6,7,8,9}

Sets of values which initially correspond to the carriers:

> r(1): {0,1}
> r(2): {0,1}
> r(3): {0,1}

Equations corresponding to the column of the given relation:

> Y+Z=Z+t(r(1))
> X+X+r(1)=Y+t(r(2))
> r(2)=Z+t(r(3))

where t(r(i)) stands for 10*r(i), i=1,2,3

Prolog facts corresponding to the initial situation:

> admissible_value(x,[0,1,2,3,4,5,6,7,8,9]).
> admissible_value(y,[0,1,2,3,4,5,6,7,8,9]).
> admissible_value(z,[0,1,2,3,4,5,6,7,8,9]).
> admissible_value(r(1),[0,1]).
> admissible_value(r(2),[0,1]).
> admissible_value(r(3),[0,1]).
>
> equation(1,equal([y,z],[z, t(r(1))])).
> equation(2,equal([x,x,r(1)],[y,t(r(2))])).
> equation(3,equal([r(2)],[z,t(r(3))])).

Prolog facts corresponding to the final situation:

> admissible_value(x,[5]).
> admissible_value(y,[0]).
> admissible_value(z,[1]).
> admissible_value(r(1),[0]).
> admissible_value(r(2),[1]).
> admissible_value(r(3),[0]).

Figure 2. An example of representation

b) THE CONSTRAINT ANALYSER

The constraint analyser, which bases its action on rules, performs inferences from the current situation in order to narrow the sets of admissible values associated with the objects of the problem, and looks for inconsistency. To these aims, it applies the classes of rules, depending on the current situation, as follows: when acting on the initial knowledge, the first step rules are applied, generating a new state. To this state are applied, in order: computation, deletion, reduction, absurdity rules to the complete set of facts. When all facts have been examined, a new state is created and the process continues until a termination condition is found or no rule can be applied.
This choice allows the solution process to be simulated using the same two-step strategy which has been adopted by the children we observed: all the possible rules were applied to the same expression, and only when no other deductions could be performed, was a new expression examined and the reasoning restarted.

When no rule can be applied and a termination condition has not been reached, the attempt generator is activated.

c) THE METARULES

Two kinds of heuristics, expressed in the form of rules, speed up the constraint analyser: the first establishes an order among the classes of rules and among the rules of the same class; the second is aimed at ordering the equations to be considered.
As regards the classes of rules, the order is independent of the specific relation and does not change during the process. The ordering criteria depends on considerations on the effects produced by the different classes. As regards the rules of a same class, the ordering criteria which has been adopted consists in considering at first the rules which allow objects (symbols or carriers) whose corresponding sets of admissible values contain a low number of elements to be operated on.
As regards the equations, they are ordered based on the number of different objects they contain.

Moreover metarules, which implicitly use the simmetry property of the equality and the commutativity property of both the addition and the product, have been implemented. For example, the metarule corresponding to the commutativity property orders the expressions in such a way that in every side of every equation the objects (symbols and carriers) precede the numerical values.
The main advantage of using these kinds of metarules is that the above properties allow to considerably narrow the number of both computation and reduction rules but their direct application gives rise to a non-terminating process.

2.3 THE GENERAL PROBLEM SOLVER MODULE

This module is activated when no rule applies and there exists at least one object (that is a symbol or carrier) whose value is not yet determined.

a) THE MODEL OF THE PROBLEM

The basic idea is to hypothesize a correspondence between objects and values and to verify, by substituting values to symbols in the given relation, if the arithmetical equality is satisfied.
The solution process is seen as the search of a path in a tree. The root of the tree represents all

possible object-value correspondences. A node is expanded by choosing an object and assigning to it all admissible values. The leaves of the tree correspond to the "right" object-value correspondences, that is, they represent solutions to the problem. The nodes which can not be expanded and are not leaves correspond to inconsistent choices of values for the objects.

b) THE ATTEMPT GENERATOR

The attempt generator is made of two components: the hypothesis generator and the hypothesis verifier. The hypothesis generator explicits the "attempt tree" by proposing hypothesis of values (chosen among the admissible ones) for a chosen object. Thus, the expansion of a node corresponds to the choice of an object s* and the association to it of all admissible values. When a value v* is associated to the object s*, the set of values for s* is reduced to the set {v*}. Moreover, if s* is a symbol, v* is deleted from the sets of values connected to the other symbols when it is found. The hypothesis generator alternates a best-first technique with a blind one in order to explore the different possibilities.

The hypothesis verifier controls, based on the absurdity rules, the consistency of the attempt.

The attempt strategy works as follows:

1) the hypothesis generator picks up an object and chooses a value for it in the set of admissible values. If for every object all values have been tried the procedure exits with failure (that is, there are no solutions for the proposed relation) otherwise go to 2;

2) the value is substituted to the corresponding object in the current system of equation;

3) the control is passed to the hypothesis verifier: by using the absurdity rules a consistency check is performed;

4) depending on the result of this check the attempt is validated and the original situation is frozen. Otherwise backtrack to step 1);

5) when a consistent attempt is found the process stops successfully and the control is passed to the constraint analyser.

From now on, if some inconsistency is found, the last frozen situation is recalled and a backtrack is performed to the previously frozen situation.

c) PROCEDURAL HEURISTICS

A mechanism has been implemented, aimed at directing the action of the attempt generator. This heuristics consists in an ordering method. At every step, the objects are ordered depending on the number of elements of their associated sets of values, thus allowing for a best-first technique in the choice of the object to analyse.

The Appendix shows the output corresponding to the solution process of the relation XX+XX=ZZY ,carried out by the TELLER SIMULATOR.

3. EMBEDDING THE TELLER SIMULATOR IN A CONTROLLED ENVIRONMENT

As has been shown by wide experience, computer based learning environments, which lead students to learn powerful ideas and specific concepts as side effects of a stimulating and creative activity, can be particularly effective from an educational point of view [2,6,7,15]. Moreover, if these environments also include a student activity check system, then their educational efficiency can be increased, retrieving some traditional CAI ideas which are of particular importance in teaching [9].

Based on these ideas, a coach environment, called ENIGMA, has been developed [10], aimed at supervising the activity carried out by a pupil who plays a game centered on the kinds of problems which can be solved by the TELLER SIMULATOR.

The TELLER SIMULATOR constitutes the expert component of ENIGMA, which is organised in four modules:

1) Interface with the user;
2) Expert component;
3) Tutoring system;
4) Expert-Tutor interface.

1) The *interface with the user* is aimed at the following: to allow the user to choose the kind of assistance performed by the system during the execution of the game; to communicate the messages sent by the expert and by the tutor in a easy-to-understand form; to transform the user's request in the internal form.

The interface allows to use ENIGMA without superposing difficulties due to the system to ones depending on the handled problem. In particular, the following factors have been taken into account.

The user must clearly know the problem handled by the program and the meaning of the notations which are used: as a consequence, a brief explanation on the problem and on the notations is shown when the program starts.

The user must easily access the possibilities offered by the system; this has been obtained by using menus. With the initial menu, the user chooses the kind of use of the system; other menus, depending on the first choice, are subsequently shown. The option help is always present.

A simple language is used to ask questions to the user and to explain the action of ENIGMA. In particular, when a deduction is shown to the user, the rule which has been applied is described in a rather easy form.

The input is quite rigid but it does not require knowledge on the internal representation of facts and rules.

2) The *expert component* is a slight modification of the TELLER SIMULATOR. The main difference is that the possibility to handle problems previously memorized has been added, and to choose them based on their difficulty degree.

3) The *tutoring system* offers three kinds of assistance to the user: check, supervision, guide.

With the option "check", the user proposes a problem and its solution, and the system checks the correctness of his proposal. In case of error, or if explicitly requested, a chain of deductions to obtain both the solution and the result, are also shown. This option can be used by the teacher in order to chose the problems and to analyse their degree of difficulty.

With the option "supervision", the system shows the student, step by step, all the different possibilities, checks the correctness of his choices, points out errors and gives brief explanations.

By chosing "guide", the user is closely followed by the system during the solution process. In particular, the initial relation is built by the system, in order to allow students to focus their attention on the deductive activity. Moreover, if an attempt strategy is followed by the user, the system forces him to systematically choose values for the involved objects.

4) The *Expert-Tutor interface* manages the exchanges of messages between the Expert *(the expert*

component) and the Tutor *(the tutoring system),* and passes the control on to one or the other depending on the situation. The Tutor invokes the Expert in the following cases: to check the correctness of a deduction performed by the user; to perform deduction; to show a portion of the solution. When the action of the Expert is completed, a message is sent to the interface. The control is passed back to the Tutor, which chooses the action to perform based on the results of the Expert.

4. CONCLUSION

In this paper, we have described the overall organization of an automatic problem solver, called TELLER SIMULATOR, apt to improve the learning of arithmetic concepts at primary/secondary school level.
From a pedagogical point of view, the TELLER SIMULATOR, apart from being the expert component of an educational system, constitutes a learning environment in itself.

In fact, we think that knowledge based programs, which are able to explain their behaviour and the sequence of deductions which have been performed in order to find out the solution of the problem being considered, can be viewed as educational tools. In particular, students can be guided by the teacher to perform two different kinds of cognitive activities by observing the behaviour of an intelligent program which is based on rules carefully chosen to simulate human activities. On the one hand, students are led to analyze in depth the nature of their knowledge of a specific domain, thus learning to master the fundamental concepts this knowledge is based on. On the other hand, they are guided to find out deductive chains from facts, thus discovering the role of knowledge in problem solving. Moreover, students can compare not only the results obtained, but also the working methods which have been used to accomplish the proposed task. In this case, the analysis of the program performance can lead students to verify the need of choosing, among different solution methods, the most apt to the current situation. Thus, the program acts as a learning environment of powerful ideas.

These considerations derive from the work which has been carried out by the authors in the field of Computers in Education. The educational advantages which we noticed through experiments with students involving the use of computer based environments [4,8], aimed at improving the learning of mathematics concepts, prompted to analyse educational applications of knowledge based tools.

At present, we are working in two directions. From the one hand, we are setting an experiment with students of different ages, in order to evaluate the efficacy of tools, such as the TELLER SIMULATOR, for learning mathematical methods and concepts by examples (in particular, theorem proving techniques, natural numbers, ordering and quasi-ordering, set theory). On the other hand, we are studying the possibility of building, starting from the TELLER SIMULATOR, a more versatile tool, in order to take into account other learning approaches: "learning by discovery", through the independent choice of the strategy to be adopted and the rules to be applied in order to reach the solution, and finally, since the educational potential of a learning environment is very seldom utilized by children who are left to work autonomously, "learning by tutoring", through the action of a tutor who suggests, where necessary, a modification in the choice of behaviour.

ACKNOWLEDGMENTS

The authors are grateful to S. Antoy for helpful discussions and to A.M. Berta and E. Cheli for their help in implementing part of the system.

REFERENCES

[1] AAVV, Information Technologies and Basic Learning, Reading, Writing, Science and Mathematics, OCDE, Paris, 1987

[2] Anderson J.R., Boyle C.F., Yost G., The Geometry Tutor, Proc. of the 9th Int. Joint Conf. on Artificial Intelligence, Los Angeles, August 18-23, 1985, pp.1-7

[3] Barr A., Feigenbaum E.A. (eds.), The Handbook of Artificial Intelligence, Vol.2, cap.IX, William Kaufmann Inc., Los Altos (CA), 1982

[4] Bottino R.M., Forcheri F., Molfino M.T., Teaching Computer Science Through a Logic Programming Approach, Education and Computing (to appear)

[5] Burton R.R., Brown J.S., An investigation of computer coaching for informal learning activities, Int. J. of Man Machine Studies, Vol. 11, 1979, pp.5-24

[6] Cabrol D., Cachet C., Cornelius R., A Heuristic Problem Solver: George, Computer and Education, Vol.10, n.1, 1986, pp.81-87

[7] Forcheri P., Lemut E., Molfino M.T., The GRAF system: an interactive graphic system for teaching mathematics, Computer and Education, Vol.7, n.3, 1983, pp.177-182

[8] Forcheri P., Lemut F., Molfino M.T., Pedemonte O., Mathematical Teaching Experiences Using Computers, in Computer Assisted Learning, Lewis R. and Tagg E.D. (eds.), North-Holland, 1980, pp. 113-121

[9] Forcheri P., Molfino M.T., A historical approach to educational computer-based systems, Revue d'intelligence artificielle, Vol.1, n.3, 1987, pp.53-70

[10] Forcheri P., Molfino M.T.,ENIGMA: An Educational Knowledge Based System, 3rd Int. Conf. PEG '88, Copenhagen, July 6-8, 1988, pp.1-11

[11] Goldstein I., Carr B., The computer as Coach: an Athletic Paradigm for Intelligent Education, Proc. of ACM Annual Conf. '77, Seattle, October 1977, pp.227-233

[12] Goldstein I., The Genetic Epistemology of Rule Systems, Int. J. of Man-Machine Studies, Vol.11, 1979, pp.51-77

[13] Kearsley G. (ed.), Artificial Intelligence and Instruction. Applications and Methods, Addison-Wesley, Reading (MA), 1987

[14] Kowalsky R., Logic as a Computer Language for Children, in New Horizons in Educational Computing, Yazdani M. (ed.), Ellis Horwood Lim., 1984, pp. 121-144

[15] Lower R.W., Designing Computer-Based Microworlds, Byte, August 1982, pp. 138-160

APPENDIX

An example of use of the TELLER SIMULATOR:
solution of the relation XX+XX=ZZY by using rules and attempts.

In the rules the following notations are adopted:
S is a symbol;
r(j) is the carrier of column j;
n1, n2 are natural numbers.

```
relation:
xx+xx=zzy

initial system:
x+x=y+r(1)*10
x+x+r(1)=z+r(2)*10
r(2)=z

by rule rp1:
IF a symbol is at the farthest left side of the string
AND the length of the string is greater than 1
THEN delete 0 value from the set of values:
we have:
x: [1,2,3,4,5,6,7,8,9]
z: [1,2,3,4,5,6,7,8,9]

by rule rp2:
IF there is an equation r(j)=S
AND S is at the farthest left side in the string corresponding to the sum
THEN S: [1] AND r(j): [1]
we have:
z: [1]
r(2): [1]

by rule substitution:
IF the value of an object has been determined
THEN substitute it to the corresponding object in the equations
the current system is:
x+x=y+r(1)*10
x+x+r(1)=1+r(2)*10
r(2)=1

by rule substitution:
IF the value of an object has been determined
THEN substitute it to the corresponding object in the equations
the current system is:
x+x=y+r(1)*10
x+x+r(1)=1+1*10
1=1

by rule deletion:
IF there is an identity
THEN throw it away
applied to:
1=1
the current system is:
x+x=y+r(1)*10
x+x+r(1)=1+1*10
```

```
by rule multiply:
IF there is an expression n1*n2
THEN substitute it with the result of the product
applied to:
x+x+r(1)=1+1*10
we have:
x+x+r(1)=1+10

by rule addition:
IF there is an expression n1+n2
THEN substitute it with the result of the sum
applied to:
x+x+r(1)=1+10
we have:
x+x+r(1)=11

by rule even:
IF a symbol is the result of sum or differences involving only even numbers
THEN the symbol can assume only even values
applied to:
x+x=y+r(1)*10
we have:
y: [0,2,4,6,8]

NO ENOUGH RULES TO APPLY

the current system is:
x+x=y+r(1)*10
x+x+r(1)=11

TRY BY ATTEMPTS
symbols and carriers not yet determined:
r(1): [0,1]
y: [0,2,4,6,8]
x: [2,3,4,5,6,7,8,9]

attempt on r(1)
r(1): [0]

by rule substitution:
IF the value of an object has been determined
THEN substitute it to the corresponding object in the equations
the current system is:
x+x=y+0*10
x+x+0=11

by rule sum_neuter_element:
IF there is an expression S+0
THEN substitute it with S
applied to:
x+x+0=11
we have:
x+x=11

by rule mismatch_odd_even:
IF there is an equation S+S=n1 AND n1 is odd
THEN error
applied to:
x+x=11
we have:
error!!!
THE DOUBLE OF A NUMBER CAN NOT BE ODD
```

```
the current system is:
x+x=y+r(1)*10
x+x+r(1)=11

attempt on r(1)
r(1): [1]

by rule substitution:
IF the value of an object has been determined
THEN substitute it to the corresponding object in the equations
the current system is:
x+x=y+1*10
x+x+1=11

by rule add_same_value:
IF the non_zero numerical values n1 and n2 appear respectively in the
left-hand side and in the right-hand side of the same equation
AND n2 is greater then n1
THEN substitute n2 with the result of n2-n1
AND substitute n1 with 0
applied to:
x+x+1=11
we have:
x+x+0=10

by rule sum_neuter_element:
IF there is an expression S+0
THEN substitute it with S
applied to:
x+x+0=10
we have:
x+x=10

by rule half_evaluate:
IF there is an equation S+S=n1
THEN S=n1/2
applied to:
x+x=10
we have:
x=5

by rule substitution:
IF the value of an object has been determined
THEN substitute it to the corresponding object in the equations
the current system is:
5+5=y+1*10
5=5

by rule deletion:
IF there is an identity
THEN throw it away
applied to:
5=5
the current system is:
5+5=y+1*10

by rule addition:
IF there is an expression n1+n2
THEN substitute it with the result of the sum
applied to:
5+5=y+1*10
we have:
10=y+1*10
```

```
by rule multiply:
IF there is an expression n1*n2
THEN substitute it with the result of the product
applied to:
10=y+1*10
we have:
10=y+10

by simmetry property:
10=y+10
is equal to:
y+10=10

by rule zero_evaluate:
IF there is an equation S+n1=n1
THEN S=0
applied to:
y+10=10
we have:
y=0

A solution is:
y=0
x=5
z=1
r(1)=1
r(2)=1

Other solutions (yes/no)?
>
```

A CONCEPTUAL BASIS FOR THE ROLE OF THE MICRO-COMPUTER IN THE TEACHING/LEARNING OF COLLEGE MATHEMATICS

H.J. Greenberg (University of Denver) and R.M. Pengelly

ABSTRACT

Despite the appearance of more and more software packages for micro-computers designed to be used to improve the teaching/learning of introductory college mathematics courses including calculus, the acceptance and use of these packages as a regular part of the instructional paradigm is limited. The fact appears to be that we as yet do not know how to use them in mathematics education except as ad hoc add-ons to the course, simply because the relation between the subject matter and the software is unclear. The present paper is an attempt to provide the missing conceptual links between the topics, entities, operations, and problems treated in the texts, and the syntax and semantics of the software, to make the latter immediately understandable and therefore useable by student and teacher alike. In our view, there should be nothing extraneous to learn. To this end we adopt an object-oriented approach, the object-types being the mathematical objects themselves, and the actions being familiar mathematical operations on these objects. Next, we provide a modifiable tree-structure of menus of objects and actions as interface to the user to give flexibility. Lastly, we introduce "task descriptions" to guide, direct, record and communicate mathematical activities carried out by the student at the computer. We restrict ourselves here primarily to a discussion of object-types and actions, and the interface used, and illustrate with a prototype package for much of introductory calculus.

The Potential of the Micro-Computer

Current trends in the development of computer hardware and software mean that each year the computer becomes a yet more valuable and easily accessible tool that can be used to support the teaching/learning process in mathematics. Software packages are now created which run on inexpensive and reliable micro-computer systems, and which have the potential to support the teaching of whole areas of mathematics, and to enable "serious" users to tackle and solve mathematical problems arising in their work.

A good example of such a package is the PC-MATLAB System [1] which provides micro-computer users with relatively easy access to some of the most sophisticated software for matrix manipulation ever created. Then there are packages like MATH-CAD [2] which provide the user with easy access to a wide range of standard mathematical operations and the means to use them to solve a large variety of mathematical problems. Up to just a few years ago such software was available only to those working with large main-frame computers.

There are now also beginning to appear on micros, powerful symbolic mathematics packages such as DERIVE [3] and MATHEMATICA [4] which significantly expand the kind of mathematics that can be explored and developed with the aid of a computer.

The packages mentioned above are primarily created for practicing professionals. However, "easy to use interfaces" make them potentially useful in an educational environment. In addition, there is a rich variety of packages which have been created specifically to support the teaching of college mathematics.

Such trends will certainly continue and probably accelerate in the future, so that most observers agree that the micro-computer has an important role to play in the development of mathematics education. Some would go as far as to assert with John Kemeny [5] that "in this day and age it is [equally] ridiculous to teach mathematics, particularly certain branches of mathematics, without the availability of a computer terminal".

Clearly the technology now exists to change dramatically the teaching and learning of mathematics. The problem is to put this technology to good use in the mathematics classroom. Attempts to do this encounter serious problems, see for example B.W. Char and K.O. Geddes, [6]. We contend that progress in realizing the computer's potential as a tool to support the teaching of mathematics is slow and hesitant because the role and use of the micro-computer in the mathematics teaching/learning process, is so far not well understood.

The Computer and College Mathematics

The computer impacts college mathematics in two distinct ways. First, the computer has the potential to change the curriculum, both in content and emphasis. See for instance A. Ralston [7] who states that "the arguments in favor of change in the [college mathematics] curriculum are all motivated by the changes wrought in the fabric of science, technology and education by computers and computer science". Second, as indicated in the previous section, the computer has the potential to revolutionize the teaching of college mathematics.

Unfortunately, much work which has been done on the introduction of computers to support the teaching of college mathematics has inter-mingled these two aspects. The introduction of the computer has often been taken as a reason to change radically both <u>what</u> is taught and the <u>approaches</u> which are taken to teaching the material selected. For example, some authors have systematically developed an algorithmic approach to teaching large parts of the calculus, requiring the student to develop and use computer programs to solve calculus problems.

While we recognize that the existence of sophisticated software packages to support the teaching of mathematics inevitably changes to some extent what is taught and how it is taught, we believe that the introduction of the computer to support the teaching of college mathematics, and the need for the revision of the college mathematics curriculum brought about by the impact of computers and computer science, should be seen as two separate, albeit related issues, and tackled as two separate problems.

Current Approaches

We have chosen here to comment only on major current approaches to the use of micro-computers to support the teaching of calculus, because in that area a variety of alternatives have been tried, including computer-based supplements to texts, packages that attempt to integrate computer and text, algorithmic approaches, and computer-based instruction.

Briefly, our views on these various approaches are as follows:

Computer based supplements. If done well, this is a useful approach. It provides resources which the teacher/student can use. If the material is not based directly on specific parts of a particular book, then it can probably be used with practically any calculus book. The problem is that it is an "add on" to the course, and is seen as such.

Integrated packages. This is potentially a powerful approach but the most ambitious, difficult and costly. It also suffers from the fact that integration makes it relatively inflexible. The better the integration, the more you have to follow the author's approach, which may not correspond to how you would like to do things.

Algorithmic approaches. This can provide an interesting, challenging and stimulating course, but the focus is not directly on mathematics. The student and the teacher will have to spend much of their time learning to create programs (non-trivial ones if the course is to have any real mathematical content), and learning about numerical computation to a level at which they can understand the programs and the results which they produce, as well as understanding the mathematical concepts involved.

Our view is that the algorithmic approach is one with which most teachers cannot cope in an adequate manner, partly because they lack the background in computing and numerical techniques, and partly because what is being attempted is very complex, and it is not clear what the objectives are. Moreover, students will find the demands too heavy, particularly if the teacher tries to cover a large part of the normal calculus syllabus. While in the future such a course may be accepted as a part of the curriculum, at present it is simply not feasible to take this approach, as there is too much to cover that is not calculus.

Computer-based instruction. This approach suffers from the same disadvantages of cost and inflexibility as the integrated approach. There is the additional problem of deciding what part of the material to present via the computer, and what part to leave to the teacher and/or to a text-book. Often such approaches fail even to identify the teacher's role in the teaching/learning process.

Role of the Micro-Computer

In our view, the role of the micro-computer, by which we mean the hardware-software package operating as a system, is simply that of a tool -- a tool which helps the teacher to teach and the student to learn. However, it is a tool which beyond providing the means to do the mathematics, ought

* to be unobtrusive, i.e., provide a simple and natural interface for the student, based on a language and concepts which have already been mastered, or need to be mastered, in order to learn the mathematical content of the course;

* to be under the teacher's control, i.e., enable the teacher to decide what facilities are to be available to the student at any time, and how these facilities are to be provided;

* to provide a means by which the students and the teacher can record and share their mathematical activities.

The first requirement frees the student and the teacher to apply their intellectual effort to the task, rather than on the computer aspects of it. The second enables the teacher to use the tool to support the way in which he/she wants to teach the course, and to control what the students can do with the aid of the computer, and what they have to do for themselves. The third requirement is to facilitate the interaction between student and teacher.

In what follows we propose a conceptual basis for creating and using tools which conform to the above requirements.

The Conceptual Basis

The approach we have taken is based on the use of three key ideas:
Object types - which encapsulate the mathematical entities that we want to manipulate.
A tree-structured interface - which provides broad and flexible interaction between the student and the system.
Tasks and task descriptions - which provide a means of describing mathematical activities.

Objects

Object oriented programming [8], [9] was devised with the aim of making the programmer's job easier. The approach involves dividing the problem into objects and defining the actions that are "natural" for these objects. This enables the programmer to think about the job at a higher level of abstraction, and in terms of more chunks of information. Zimmer [10] has shown in a convincing way that using the concept of an object, without adopting the object-programming paradigm (he uses the normal algorithmic notation to express tasks), provides a valuable abstract basis for the process of program design. It is Zimmer's work that we take as the starting point of our development of an object-oriented approach. We have used his concept of an object-type as the means to provide a natural way of encapsulating the mathematical entities that we want to manipulate, defining these entities in terms of their properties - merely a somewhat different formalization of what mathematicians often do. The teacher can make use of the definition of object-types to help identify and clarify what is to be taught, and to design an approach to teaching it.

We envisage each object-type as being realizable in terms of an "object-type module" that enables us to sit at a computer and create and manipulate objects of that type. A collection of such object-type modules provides the basis for a software package used to support the teaching/learning process. The object-type definitions can be realized as object type modules in a variety of different ways depending upon the software available to create the realization, and the way the objects will be used. Moreover, the realizations of the object types may be incomplete, in that they contain just those properties that it is appropriate to manipulate with the aid of a computer.

For example, the teacher may choose at any time to limit the scope of the manipulations that can be performed on an object, in order to force the students to focus their attention on the objects in particular ways and carry out specific operations themselves. Our object-type modules are very similar to the objects defined in an object-oriented programming language. However, we have embedded them in a menu-driven user interface rather than in an object-oriented language, because we feel that at least initially the object-oriented style of programming is no easier to learn than the conventional procedural style of programming.

Our interface allows the user to perform either a single action on an object or to string together sequences of such actions, embodying what we call "task descriptions". If the objects have been appropriately defined, then task descriptions provide a realization of the exercises and examples normally found in textbooks and lectures, as well as a means of describing more significant and complicated mathematical activities.

Interface

The interface we have is based on a tree structure of menus. Each time a choice is made, the user is taken to the next level down in the menu tree. At each level in the tree HELP can be requested, and an explanation will be given of the options available at that point. The user also has at each level the option to go back up one level. [Technically, since "circuits" in this structure are desirable and available to avoid always having to retrace steps, the structure is a "graph" rather than a "tree", but we will continue to use the term "tree" to avoid confusion later with "graph" as used in calculus.]

The result of this choice of structure is a very flexible interface well suited to the learning process. By including only appropriate objects and actions, the carrying out of a task requires the user to be an active participant in the solution process. In contrast, interfaces which present a menu of programs to be invoked for the solution of any of a list of standard problems, require essentially no analysis of the task on the part of the student, since the course of solution is already predetermined by the program, and even the name of the program leaves no doubt as to which choice to make from the menu.

The levels in the menu tree generally present in the interface for a given course are as follows:

LEVEL 1: Course level -- list of TOPICS

The entries in this menu correspond to the topics covered in the course. Selecting one of the entries leads to a second level menu for the topic chosen.

LEVEL 2: Topic level -- list of OBJECTS

There is a separate topic level menu for each topic covered in the course. The entries in each of the topic menus correspond to the object-type modules used to cover this topic. Selecting one of the entries leads to a third-level menu for the object-type module chosen. If an object-type module is common to several topics then it can be accessed from each of the appropriate topic level menus.

LEVEL 3: Object level -- list of ACTIONS

There is a separate object level menu for each object-type module used to cover the topic. The entries in each of the object menus correspond to the actions defined upon the object concerned. Selecting one of these entries can lead to a further menu subdividing the action chosen into sub-actions, or can lead directly to a fourth level parameter table for the action chosen if it can be carried out directly. If an action is common to several object-type modules then it can be accessed from each of the appropriate object level menus.

LEVEL 4: Action level -- list of PARAMETERS (parameter table)

There is a separate action level parameter table for each action available to an object-type module. The entries in each of the parameter tables corresponds to the data required by the action. At this level what we have is essentially a data input table in that the user has to work down the table providing the parameter values requested. When the parameter table is satisfactorily completed, the action selected will be invoked. The user will be presented with any output generated by the action, given time to study it, and the opportunity to print it out and so on. The system will then return the user to the third-level menu.

While the above description of the menus is necessarily lengthy, in use the user moves quickly and naturally from object to action by single letter keystrokes as illustrated in the next section for a calculus interface.

An interface editor provided with the teacher's version of the package should allow the teacher to modify all levels of the HELP screens, menus and parameter tables to suit particular needs. The teacher should be able to add or drop object-types, actions, and parameters to simplify, refine, or combine them to move to higher or lower levels of analysis.

The interface editor might also provide a form of macro facility to allow the definition of new actions (on the existing object-types). For example, new actions could be defined in terms of a sequence of existing actions in which one or more of the parameters of an action are replaced by actions whose values are taken as the values for the parameters concerned. The facility should also allow the creation of "compound actions", for commonly occurring sequences of actions, which lead the user directly from action to action without the need to traverse the menu tree.

The interface described above focuses on the object aspect of the object/task approach because this is the simplest aspect of the interface and the one we have developed so far as a proto-type package. A more complete interface would provide at least a means to store and edit records of work done and allow the user to switch easily between such records and the execution of commands.

Even more advanced interfaces can be imagined that would provide facilities for such things as electronic note-taking, electronic mail and report preparation. Much experimentation will need to be done to arrive at an appropriate interface for doing mathematics so as not to burden the user with unnecessary complexities to be mastered. The model to be kept in mind here we believe is word-processing. While word-processors can and do provide very complicated and elegant options, it is not necessary for the "writer" to either learn or use them, and so only the task, i.e. writing, need occupy the user's attention. To pursue the comparison with word-processing a bit further, we believe that the tree-structured interface of object-types and actions we use is closer to a word-processor than is the interface commonly used in software packages for mathematics courses, consisting of a collection of programs to be run. For in the tree structure, the user is not made conscious of running programs. It is just this feature of current word-processing, the invisibility of programs, in addition to ease of use, to which we attribute its wide-spread acceptance and popularity.

CALCTOOL: A Prototype Calculus Interface

We have applied the object-oriented approach described above to produce prototype interfaces both for topics in a calculus course and for the Boolean logic portion of an introductory course in discrete mathematics. However, we describe below only the calculus interface.

For that part of a freshman calculus course ordinarily covered say up to the fundamental theorem, we find that the only object-types required are FUNCTIONS and GRAPHS. Thus, we have as our top-level menu

OBJECTS

F: FUNCTIONS
G: GRAPHS
H: HELP
X: EXIT TO SYSTEM

Selecting FUNCTIONS (by typing F), leads to the path indication FUNCTIONS\ being displayed at the top of the screen, and the second-level menu ACTIONS displayed alongside the OBJECT menu as below:

FUNCTIONS/

OBJECTS

F: FUNCTIONS
G: GRAPHS
H: HELP
X: EXIT TO SYSTEM

ACTIONS

C: CREATE
L: LIST
CP: COMPUTE
T: TRANSFORM
H: HELP
X: EXIT TO OBJECTS

Selecting CREATE leads to a parameter table requesting first the name of the function (any lower case letter such as f), and then the value of the function (any valid BASIC formula). Once functions have been created, say f and g , new functions may be created through operations on the function names alone. For instance we may take h to be f+g, f-g, fg, f/g, f(g) or g(f). We can create piecewise continuous functions using Boolean expressions, and functions with parameters.

Selecting LIST leads to a list of already created functions giving both names and values.

Selecting COMPUTE in the ACTIONS menu leads to a further menu, consisting of actions that require numerical computations to be carried out on previously created functions. This menu will include (only the first four are currently implemented):

SLOPES   -   displays a graph of the function and shows secants approaching a tangent at a selected point from both right and left.

LIMIT   -   displays a graph of the function and calculates values at a sequence of points approaching a selected point.

NEWTON -   displays a graph of the function and shows the successive tangents, and gives the first six approximations to the root following an initial value.

INTEGRAL -   graphs anti-derivatives of the function as well as finding approximations to selected areas on the graph of the function using numerical integration formulas.

TABLE   -   displays a value or table of values of the function.

COMPARE -   compares the values of two functions for equality at specified or random points.

INVERSE   -   displays the graph of the inverse function, i.e., the points $\{(f(x), x)\}$.

Selecting TRANSFORM in the ACTIONS menu leads to a further menu of actions yielding the symbolic representation of functions derivable from a given function f, including f', f'', $\int f\, dx$. (This is not currently implemented. However, the graphs of these functions are obtainable in the present version under the ACTION "CREATE" on the object-type GRAPHS, as described below.

Selecting GRAPHS from the OBJECTS menu leads to the second level menu of ACTIONS shown below along the path GRAPHS\:

GRAPHS\

OBJECTS

F: FUNCTIONS
G: GRAPHS
H: HELP
X: EXIT TO SYSTEM

ACTIONS

C: CREATE
L: LIST
P: PLOT
F: FORMAT
H: HELP
X: EXIT TO OBJECTS

Selecting CREATE leads to a parameter table requesting the name of the graph (required to be the capital letter corresponding to the lower-case name of the function), and the "window", i.e. x-interval and y-interval, to be displayed on the monitor. The graph is then displayed. (If no y-interval is specified, the y range is by default that determined by the domain of x.)

If the function f has already been created and the graph F, then typing F´ in the parameter table followed by the requested action P (for PLOT) will result in the graph of f´, the derivative of F, being displayed (along with the graph of f if it was saved) in the x,y window originally selected when F was defined. Similarly, typing F´´ and P will give the graph of f´´, and typing ´F and specifying a constant will give the graph of an antiderivative ∫ f dx.

Along the bottom of the screen displaying a graph, the FORMAT options are always listed as follows: C: CLEAR, S: SAVE, R: REDRAW, Z: ZOOM, A: ANNOTATE, P: PRINT, H: HELP. The results of choosing these are what you would expect. However, it is worth noting, first, that SAVE permits overlaying graphs, since the graph saved will be redrawn as well as succeeding ones on the same screen. Second, ANNOTATE permits the user to insert and edit text on the screen along with the graphs, such as labeling the axes, naming curves, giving the date and name of the user, etc. so that on printing (P), hard copy is obtained that can be handed in for an assignment.

We close this section with an example of a "task" that serves to point up the difference pedagogically between the use of a tree-structured, object-oriented package such as CALCTOOL, and the use of program-oriented packages of the type that currently are available. The task is simply to locate accurately the local maxima and minima of a polynomial over the whole real axis.

One popular package [11] (and a very good one) has on its menu the entry "Extrema" thereby identifying the proper choice to be made to carry out the task. Specifying the x-interval, the program displays a table of values of the function f , and the derivatives f´ and f´´ at a number of equally spaced points. Detecting a sign change in f´ over a subinterval, it gives that subinterval as the location of a zero of f´. This can be repeated on the subinterval if desired to locate the extremum more closely (and its nature from the sign of f´´), and the whole process can be repeated until the location is determined as closely as desired. If there are further sign changes in f´ along the axis, the program will repeat the process to find the next extremum. The role of the student in this process consists primarily of requesting or not requesting further subdivisions of the intervals.

A second popular package [12] (also a very good one) has on its menu the entry "Minimum/Maximum" again identifying the correct choice for performing the task. This program produces a graph of the function over the interval selected, and without further ado tells you the location and values of the relative and absolute extrema on that interval as well as the function values at the endpoints. This is excellent if you are only interested in the answer, but of limited pedagogical value if you wish to learn how to find extrema or apply what you have learned in class about extrema.

By contrast, to carry out the same task using CALCTOOL, the student would have to bring to bear what he/she knows about the behavior of polynomials at infinity, the difference between polynomials of even and odd degree, the number of extrema possible, and the fact that at a local extremum f´ is zero, and then evolve a strategy for accurately locating all such points, if they exist.

Moving forward and back in the tree structure, the student could view graphs of f and f´, find the approximate location of zeros of f´, invoke Newton's method for accurate determination (one possibility), and finally present the teacher with graphs of f and f´ in intervals where there are local extrema, as well as con-vincing evidence that all the extrema had been found.

The pedagogical significance, then, of the approach we have taken to the use of the micro-computer in a college mathematics course such as calculus, is that in the absence of fixed, pre-programmed "vertical" structures that lead at once to the solution of standard problems, the user must think about the task at hand and come up with a proposed method of solution, that can then be tried out on the computer by moving freely through a tree-structure of familiar mathematical objects and actions that hopefully will complete the task. And, as we all know, as much can be learned by failure, which can occur here, as by success.

The Teaching/Learning Environment

The addition of a micro-computer based component to the customary college mathematics course, if properly used, provides for a richer interaction between the teacher and the students. It also provides an opportunity to engage the student more actively in the learning process. However, the teacher must successfully integrate the computer with the other components -- lectures, text, homework, etc., making assignments and/or conducting labs in which the computer serves as an active learning aid and mathematical tool.

Two kinds of problems are then encountered. On the one hand, there are the problems of relating the subject material covered in the textbook and the lectures to the facilities provided by the software package that is being used. On the other hand, there are the problems of organizing and directing the student's work at the computer, individually and during the "lab-sessions".

We believe that both types of problems are more easily solved if the package is constructed as we suggest, around a set of familiar mathematical object-types and actions that correspond to the mathematical objects treated in the textbook and lectures. The relation between the abstract mathematical objects and the realization of these objects by means of the software package is apparent. In addition, because the user interface of the package is expressed in the same language and style as the textbook and lectures, students can approach and use the software package in a natural way, and the instructors are relieved of much of the burden of explaining how to interpret and use the facilities provided.

But even if the students' access to the facilities which the package provides, is enhanced in the way we have suggested above, it does not follow that the student will necessarily be capable of using the package to undertake significant mathematical activities. This requires more than just easy access to the facilities. What is needed, is a way for the student to organize and guide his/her work when tackling projects. We believe that the idea of a "task description" which we have begun to develop, can provide the right sort of basis for describing how to undertake mathematical activities with the aid of a software package, as well as provide the basis for interaction between the teacher and the students. A task description serves as a framework which can be used equally well either to guide and direct the student's work, or as a means of formally recording the student's work. By reading and working with some well prepared task descriptions, the student should come to understand both how to undertake various mathematical activities, and how to organize his/her own approach to a mathematical task. And finally, the task description provides a way to approach work in the micro-lab which can take the student well beyond simply learning how to use each of the facilities provided by the package to perform routine mathematical exercises.

The Course Creation Process

If the teacher has available a software package which will enable him/her to implement the object/task approach we advocate, just what is involved in creating the course beyond the usual preparation?

The first step is to inter-relate the mathematics covered in the textbook and the lectures, to the facilities provided by the software package. This means that the teacher should create (or review if they already exist) the object-type definitions for the subject material which is to be covered, and use these to review and revise the facilities provided by the object-type modules in the package to be used. At this stage, any documentation that the student will need to use the software package should be created if it is lacking.

Next, the teacher can review the sort of mathematical activities to be engaged in during the course, to decide what tasks can be supported by means of computer based activities. These include (1) examples and exercises -- for consolidation and practice, (2) exploration and discovery -- extending what has been learned, and (3) problem solving -- applying what has been learned.

In many courses, students spend most of their time just on (1) examples and exercises and even the problems (3) that are tackled are more like exercises, being typical of the sorts of questions that are found in homework and examinations. As indicated above, the object/task approach enables the teacher to extend the range of activities undertaken by the student, and allows them to be more open-ended. The teacher should work systematically through the course, identifying both simple and complex tasks which can be supported with the software available, and carefully consider just what actions each object-type module should provide at each stage in the course, so as to focus the student's attention on the appropriate ideas when attempting the tasks assigned. The teacher should take full advantage of the facilities available for controlling the actions open to the students. This not only makes it easier for the student to learn the package, but focuses the student's attention on the important basic ideas and skills.

When the tasks have been properly planned out, and the object-type modules defined, the teacher can attend to the preparation of the micro-lab sessions, deciding which tasks will be used for demonstrations, and which tasks the student will be asked to carry out during the lab sessions, and later for homework.

The work involved in carrying through the course creation process is not too demanding except for the planning of tasks. However, when a course has been taught once or twice, the teacher should have accumulated sufficient task descriptions and experience to be able to prepare the computer-based element just as easily and quickly as lectures. In a limited way this has been borne out by our experience with the calculus, which is now in its third year of a micro-lab component at the University of Denver. Except for revisions of demonstrations and homework assignments, the amount of extra time required has been minimal. However, a total reorganization of the course design based on the concepts we are presenting here has not been attempted yet, although we have begun to define the object-types, and have examples of tasks and task descriptions at various levels of difficulty.

A final word concerns actual classroom computer demonstrations given as part of the regular lectures, as distinct from lab sessions that students attend at other times. Last fall, one of the authors (Greenberg) made use of a cart set-up where, by a combination of a micro-computer, a special flat screen display, and an overhead projector, running programs can be projected on an ordinary wall screen. Unfortunately, CALCTOOL in a form required by our set-up was not available, so commercial packages of the type described earlier were used to illustrate topics in the text. In the author's opinion, good use can be made of this kind of set-up provided that the instructor is very well prepared and sufficiently experienced to be able to carry out a significant demonstration with an absolute minimum of wasted motion and time. By "significant" , is meant a demonstration of concepts and ideas that is a genuine step up from anything that can be done in the same time on a blackboard. One has to search to find those occasions in teaching calculus where the use of this technology in the classroom is justified.

Conclusions

What we have proposed appears to us as not merely a conceptual basis for a software package for a calculus or discrete mathematics course, or indeed for any particular mathematics course. Rather, what we have proposed here and illustrated for the calculus we see as a general approach to the software creation process that can be followed for any subject in search of a microcomputer component -- an approach based on a modifiable tree-structure of objects and actions appropriate to the subject matter of the course. The user's attention is focused on creating instances of objects and carrying out actions on them toward specific ends, similar to the way in which a word processor enables the user to write and edit. This approach provides a natural and easily understood interface between the subject matter as presented in textbook and lecture and the use of the microcomputer as a tool to carry out meaningful tasks.

REFERENCES

[1]   PC-MATLAB: The Math Works Inc., Portola Valley, CA 94025

[2]   MATH-CAD: Math Soft Inc., 1 Kendall Square, Cambridge, MA 02139

[3]   DERIVE, A Mathematical Assistant, Soft Warehouse Inc., Honolulu, Hawaii

[4]   MATHEMATICA: A System For Doing Mathematics By Computer, Steve Wolfram, Addison Wesley, 1988

[5]   J.G. Kemeny in The Future of College Mathematics, A. Ralston and G. Young, editors, Springer, 1983

[6]   B.W. Char and K.O. Geddes, Computer Algebra in the Undergraduate Mathematics Classroom, Communications of the ACM, 1986, p. 135

[7]   A. Ralston in The Future of College Mathematics, ibid.

[8]   Adele Goldberg, <u>Small Talk-80, The Language and Its Implementation</u>,
        Addison-Wesley, 1984

[9]   G.A. Pascoe, <u>The Elements of Object-Oriented Programming</u>, Byte, Vol. 11,
        August 1986, pp. 139-144

[10]   J.A. Zimmer, <u>Abstraction For Programmers</u>, McGraw-Hill, 1987

[11]   MicroCALC, 1987, Harley Flanders, MathCalcEduc, 1449 Covington Drive,
        Ann Arbor, MI 48103

[12]   CALCULUS: True BASIC Math Series, J. Kemeny and T. Kurtz, TBI, 39
        South Main St., Hanover, N.H. 03755

A REAL-TIME COACHING ENVIRONMENT FOR TRIANGLE CONGRUENCE PROOFS

Steven H. Greve
Department of Computer Science
University of Regina, Regina, SK, Canada S4S 0A2

Abstract — This paper describes a real-time system that coaches students in developing high school geometry proofs. The program consists of an expert that creates the proof solution and the coach that helps the student develop a proof. The expert is described elsewhere. The tutor consists of three parts: a student model module, the coach, and the interface. The student model keeps track of the student's progress through the geometry concepts and guides the coach if remediation is required. The coach manages the environment by responding to the student's questions and by posing problems and doing example solutions. The interface establishes communication between student and coach through the use of four windows. Two windows are used for text and two for graphics. The interface also handles the graphical dialogue, allowing the student to propose problems for the program to solve. The system is designed and implemented to provide students with a hands-on environment for real-time proof generation.

Introduction

The design of intelligent tutoring programs has advanced sufficiently in the last twenty years that it is possible to implement systems that are powerful enough to be effective and small enough to run on microcomputers commonly found in the public schools. This paper describes work on a coaching program for geometry that offers very fast response time while providing a discovery learning environment for students creating two-column proofs. The program is in two major sections, the expert system and the coach. This paper describes the coach portion of the project. The design of the expert is described elsewhere (Greve, 1988) and will not be covered in detail here.

The coaching module provides a student with a supportive, hands-on environment to learn the problem solving skills necessary to create congruence proofs in high school geometry. As an effective coach, the program ascertains the breadth of the student's knowledge and then provides facilities to remedy any deficiencies. To do this, the coach engages the student in "dialogue", analyzes the student's responses, and provides help when it is requested. In this paper, the student model, coach, and interface are discussed as designed and executed in the current system.

Student Model

The student model data structure is based on expert difference models (Carr and Goldstein, 1977; Burton and Brown, 1982) which compare the work the student is doing against the performance of an expert. The student is said to be weak in a skill or concept when deviating from the solution the expert proposes. This differential is recorded in the student model. The actual representation of the model is immaterial; importance is given to being able to recognize the difference. This activity is very dependent on the knowledge domain being modeled. Some domains (arithmetic, games) require the student to make moves that use combinations of many concepts in that domain. For example, in the arithmetic game WEST (Burton and Brown, 1982), the student's objective is to take the values on three spinners and create the most advantageous move for a given board position. This move is created by taking the three numbers and the normal arithmetic functions and determining an expression for a move. If the three numbers were 2, 4, and 3 the student might create the expression (2+4)*3 to move 18 spaces on the board. If the expert agrees that this is the optimal move, nothing is said. If the expert disagrees, the difference modeler will have to decide if the student has a faulty strategy for this board position or whether the student is weak on a particular type of arithmetic expression. In a board game, this modeling procedure is quite difficult. In the domain of geometry, the task is made easier by the fact that the space of possible next steps in a proof is small. All other moves would make no sense to the progress of the proof and can be quickly rejected.

The current geometry proof system uses a difference modeler that constructs the model based on the comparison of what the expert's solution says the next step in the proof should be and what the student offers as a next step. The model is a directed graph with 44 nodes that represent the rudimentary geometric knowledge required (points, lines, rays) and the concepts specific to triangle congruence proof generation (SSS, SAS, ASA). (See Fig. 1) In the figure, node number one represents a line segment, number five a triangle, and number 40 the side-side-side congruence postulate.

Each of the nodes on the graph records the student's correct and incorrect usage of that concept. Specifically, the modeler keeps a correct usage count, an incorrect usage count, and a should-have-used-but-didn't count. In addition, each node also maintains a complete history of these numbers, recording every change. By maintaining the various usage counts and histories, the coach can determine if the student is progressing from session to session and can estimate how much the student is forgetting over time. (See Fig. 2)

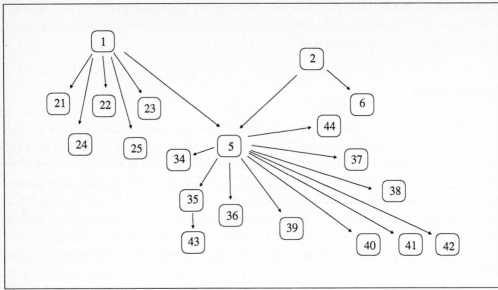

Fig. 1 - Partial Student Model Graph

Progress is monitored by the coaching module which uses the counts when deciding what type of remediation, if any, is necessary. The model also has pointers to show which concepts are considered to be prerequisite to other concepts. This allows the coach to delve deeper into the fundamental concepts of geometry to offer remediation if the student has reached an impasse at a higher level node. Finally, the model contains pointers to common misconceptions between nodes. For instance, a student might mistake the SAS postulate with the ASA postulate. In this case the misconception pointers on both nodes point to each other.

Node Number	42		
Student Model Name	ASA		
Explanation	If two angles and the included side of one triangle are equal to the . . .		
Correct-use	3		
Incorrect-use	2		
Should-have	1		
History	pointer		
Misconceptions	40	41	43
Prerequisites	4	5	

Fig. 2 - Graph Node Structure

There are two primary functions the modeler performs when analyzing the student's input. The modeler will first check the student's proposed step for conceptual agreement. If the student's step corresponds to the expert's step (ie they both propose SSS), the modeler will then check the step for syntax; is the student using the correct parts of the diagram and are they spelled correctly. This is important as a geometry proof is considered incorrect if certain references, triangles in particular, are not labeled correctly. The modeler increments the usage counts and passes control to the coaching module.

Coach

The coaching module has four primary purposes: to isolate and address apparent weaknesses, to generate examples that demonstrate concepts, to answer questions within the domain, and to solve problems that the student proposes. The system does not have a set of lessons or any type of agenda for the student, rather the student is encouraged to discover as much as possible about problem solving strategies for himself. As such this program is referred to as a coach rather than a tutor (Burton and Brown, 1982). As a coach, the program will sit quietly until the student makes a clear mistake in the proof or until he makes what the coach thinks is a sub-optimal move. At that point, the coach will attempt to isolate the weakness and remedy it.

When students deviate from the proof solution as supplied by the expert, it is for one of two reasons. Either the student has made an error in the solution or has used a different proof. The coach will first try to determine if there is in fact an alternate solution to the proof. The expert is called as a background task with the partial proof and tries to reach the goal using the student's step. If there is a solution path, this becomes the solution the coach uses. If it is not possible to reach the goal based on the partial proof supplied by the student, the expert signals the coach that this is an error.

When a deficiency is uncovered the tutor must decide on a course of action. First the coaching module checks the student model. If the correct usage counts in the student model indicate that the student should know the correct step, the example generator simply asks a leading question to jog the student's memory. There is a set of questions built into the student model, one question for each node, for this purpose. If the student model indicates that the student does not know this concept (no correct usage) or that it has been used incorrectly before (more incorrect counts than correct), the example generator creates a more in-depth example to explore with the student. Currently, the system can generate a completely new proof for the student based on the weak concept, it can quiz the student for short answers, and can do partial proofs having the student complete them. If none of this works, the coach supplies the student with the missing proof step.

The capacity of the coach to do demonstrations revolves around the example generator. When the tutor determines that the student is in need of help, the example generator then decides which type of help would be appropriate. For students that have little experience with the coach or with geometry, the generator will do a proof in the example window that demonstrates the weak concept. For example, if ASA was used as an intermediate step in the main proof and the student stopped at this point, the example generator would do a simple proof of ASA in the example window as a way to clarify this concept for the student. Examples of this type are produced from example templates. Each of the nodes in the student model that describes a concept specific to congruence proofs for triangles has one template. Each template describes a simple problem that can be proved in 3 or 4 steps. The expert solves the problem and supplies the proof. An advantage of this system is the generator's ability to vary the example each time it is presented. Currently the generator can do this in two ways. As the student uses the system the tutor maintains a count of the number of times each example has been used. If the student shows continual weakness on a concept, the tutor presents the same example again and again. To make each presentation different, the example generator adds a random amount of noise each time the same example is used. The first time, no noise is added. The second time noise will be added in the form of extraneous lines or triangles that have nothing to do with the proof. The generator can also rotate the example into unusual positions and vary the labeling of the vertices as further noise factors. As the student uses the system and becomes more adept at doing proofs, the generator will ask the student to supply important steps in the example proofs instead of simply displaying the answer. Through full and partial proofs developed for the student in the example window, the tutor focuses on and addresses the student's weaknesses.

Pedagogy of the Coach

One of the purposes in creating ICAI programs distinct from CAI is the simulation of the types of interactions commonly seen with human tutors. It is not enough to create examples and have the capability to solve arbitrary problems, the system must also teach the student problem solving strategies. How do you start a proof? What do you do when you are stuck? What is the goal? What are the sub-goals? The tutor must also address these concerns to be effective in the domain.

This coaching system approaches the issue of teaching by categorizing all proofs as either single goal or multiple goal proofs. Figure 3 is an example of a single goal proof.

In this case, the congruence between triangles is the goal of the proof. If congruence is the goal and the coach determines that this is a single goal proof, the problem solving strategy will be exhaustive search. Since the goal is to prove triangle congruence, the student has only three choices; SSS, SAS, and ASA. With single goal proofs the student has the option of "running" the expert and watching it try all the rules that could be used in a given situation. The domain is small enough that teaching this type of search is a reasonable problem solving strategy.

Multiple goal proofs use congruence as either an intermediate step in the proof or intermediate step and final goal. These proofs are commonly used after students learn the basics

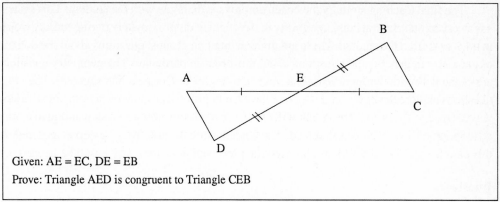

Given: AE = EC, DE = EB
Prove: Triangle AED is congruent to Triangle CEB

Fig. 3 - Single Goal Proof

of proof generation with single goal proofs. Multiple goal proofs try to extend the student's ability to use planning as a problem solving strategy as distinct from exhaustive search. Most of these proofs hinge on proving congruence between two triangles and then using parts of these triangles to prove the final goal. Rarely do proofs in high school geometry require more than two goals, for example, see figure 4 (from Anderson et al., 1985).

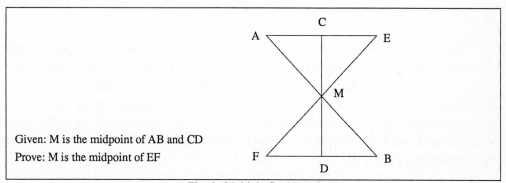

Given: M is the midpoint of AB and CD
Prove: M is the midpoint of EF

Fig. 4 - Multiple Goal Proof

In this proof the student must realize that there are the pivotal sub-goals of proving triangles AMC and BMD congruent and FDM and ECM congruent before ultimately proving M is the midpoint of EF. With this in mind, the program will coach the student NOT to use exhaustive search first but rather decide what congruences might be needed before the midpoint proof. The coach can differentiate between single and multiple goal proofs by searching the proof generated by the expert for any use of triangle congruence as an intermediate step. To make this idea of a pivot memorable for the student, the program will bring up a special window called "PIVOT" for the student's use in planning multiple goal proofs. The object of the PIVOT window is to have the student list the sub and final goals in the order they will be needed in the proof. If the student can not list them, the coach will provide assistance in identifying them.

The final teaching strategy the coach employs is dialogue with the student. This system has a very limited natural language ability that recognizes approximately two dozen key words in questions from the student. These are divided into two groups: questions about the domain of geometry in general and questions about this proof in particular. The geometry questions are of the definition variety. What is a scalene triangle? or Define a line segment. The other questions explore the how's and why's of the current proof. The student can ask "how" a step was derived in the proof. The coach will check the steps preceding that step and give a brief description of how each was deduced. The student can also ask "why" a step is required. In this case the coach looks forward through the proof and describes why it will be needed.

Interface

The interface to the tutor was designed to make use of graphics in support of proof generation (see Anderson et al.). To this end, the program was developed on a microcomputer where there is sufficient graphics support to have four windows open on the screen. The four windows the system uses are a dialogue window where the student types requests to the coach, a proof window where the main problem is displayed with the known facts and the proof goal, an example window where the coach guides the student through partial and complete proofs, and a small pivot window where the student can list the goal and sub-goals of the current problem.

The windowing environment for the system involves two graphics-based and two text-based windows. The two graphics windows are similar in nature allowing the student to draw components of problems and label them. Control choices in the program are accomplished through the use of pull-down menus controlled by the mouse and the mouse buttons or by typed commands, depending on the student's preference. For example, if the student wants to add the next step in a proof, she would pull down a menu of possible next steps and choose the appropriate one. All she would have to type would be the correct references to vertices currently on the diagram. The mouse is also used when the student wishes to propose a problem for the expert to solve. In this case, a menu comes up allowing the student to indicate points on the screen followed by the choice of either making line segments from the points or triangles. The program then requests placement of labels for vertices.

The two text windows are for dialogue between coach and student and for determination of goal and sub-goals. The coach is designed to be primarily graphic-based but there are occasions when the student may wish to type a request or when the tutor presents a text description or explanation. The program checks all input from windows against the diagram and known facts to make sure that the student is not proposing anything illogical. The use of two distinct presentation styles, graphics and text, has the advantage of more closely simulating the way a human tutor would vary the interaction with the student to make the best use of the tools within the environment.

Conclusions About the Coach

The goal of this research has been to design and develop an intelligent coaching system for high school geometry. The field of computer based tutors is still relatively new, where most tutors have been implemented on large machines and only a few completed and running on machines suitable for classroom use. This coaching system and interface are sufficiently well developed to both create a model of the student's understanding of the domain and to coach the student in solving problems with proof generation.

References

Anderson, John R., C. Franklin Boyle and Brian Reiser. (1985). Intelligent Tutoring Systems. *Science*, Vol. 228, pp. 456 - 462.

Burton, Richard R. and Brown, John Seely. (1982) An Investigation of Computer Coaching for Informal Learning Activities. In D. Sleeman & J.S. Brown (Eds.), *Intelligent Tutoring Systems,* pp. 79 - 98. New York: Academic Press.

Carr, Brian and Ira P. Goldstein. (1977) Overlays: A Theory of Modelling for Computer Assisted Instruction. *AI Memo No. 406.* MIT Artificial Intelligence Lab.

Greve, Steven H. (1988) Performance Considerations in the Design and Implementation of Intelligent Tutoring Systems. *Proceedings of the Third International Conference on Symbolic and Logic Computing.*

EXPLORATION IN COINLAND

Henry Hamburger & Akhtar Lodgher
Department of Computer Science, George Mason University
Fairfax, VA 22030

Coinland is a meaning-oriented approach to facilitating the learning
of arithmetic principles. Algorithms based on those principles, such as
those used to carry out operations like multi-digit subtraction, emerge
for the student through a process of guided exploration, rather than
inculcation. The visual representation is applicable to topics from
counting to elementary division. This paper treats only subtraction. An
alternative visual representation, Numberland, facilitates the important
transfer of concepts for use outside the computer environment.

Three Aspects of this Environment

Three essential characteristics of this computer-based environment
are its support for exploration, conservation, and translation. First,
Coinland permits exploration by a learner, thereby encouraging active
problem-solving in a domain where many children can succeed [Carpenter,
1985]. Second, it imposes meaningful constraints on the search space,
so that exploration does not degenerate into groping. In particular,
all available operations, such as moving coins from one location to
another, or putting a dime in the change-making machine to get ten
pennies, have the property that they conserve quantity. The third
important feature implemented in Coinland is explicit treatment of the
translation between alternative representations. The student can move
back and forth at will between Coinland and a Numberland that is iso-
morphic to it, carrying out an equivalent search. Facility with the
translation process carries the learner close to the ultimate transition, transfer of knowledge from the computer screen to the world of
pencil and paper. This step is important, since "strong semantic
understanding ... in no way guarantees ability to use [a corresponding
algorithm]" [Resnick, 1987]. We describe the Coinland environment for
subtraction and show how it can help a student circumvent documented
types of misperformance on such operations as borrowing across zero

[Brown and Burton, 1978]. Circumvention, if it can be achieved, is preferable to remediation.

Subtraction

The subtraction activity in Coinland comes into play only after the student gives evidence of having mastered many prerequisites embodied in earlier Coinland activities. To introduce and motivate the subtraction activity, we explain it to the student in terms of a real scenario, described below (expressed to the student in simpler language than that used below, and without the side comments). The explanation refers repeatedly to various parts of the Coinland screen, which appears here as Figure 1. The figure shows what a student would see at the start of the subtraction problem, 420 - 332. These two numbers, the minuend and subtrahend, remain in place on the screen throughout the problem. The student solves the problem by manipulating coins with the cursor ("+").

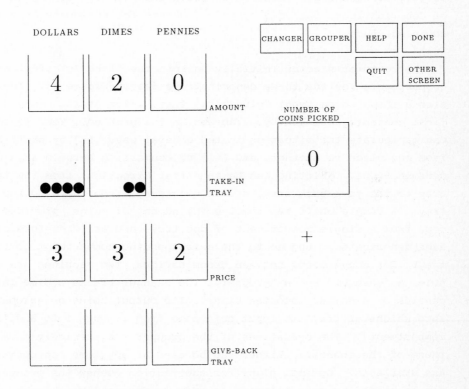

Figure 1: The Coinland Screen

You (the student) play the role of a cashier in a store. A customer
buys an item for some known price. The price appears on the screen in
numerical form, but the money tendered is in the form of monetary
objects (coins, bills) which appear on the screen as small filled-in
circles all the same size, with color-coded denominations (yellow for
pennies, etc.). You take in some money from the customer. It is your
job to give back the correct change, keeping for yourself a set of
coins specified by the price. You thereby solve a subtraction problem,
by finding the difference between the initially tendered amount and the
stated price.

Different sets of denominations may be used, for different parts of
the curriculum. In the examples here, we shall speak only of pennies,
dimes and dollars, which suffice to introduce base-10 subtraction with
borrowing across zero. The same technique, with pennies, nickels and
quarters, supports base-5 operations. (Intriguingly, base-5 not only
poses no new conceptual problems, but indeed promises to be particularly
easy, since the digit values are always small). By varying the number
of denominations, one readily gets problems for beginners or more
advanced students.

The customer's coins initially go into the "take-in" tray, with three
compartments for the three denominations (as in Figure 1). There is
also a three-compartment "give-back" tray, which starts empty and whose
final contents represent your answer to the problem. You (as cashier)
can manipulate the situation in two general ways: (i) by shifting coins
from one place to another, and (ii) by converting between adjacent
denominations. Shifting can be in either direction, from the take-in
tray to the give-back tray, or, if necessary, from there to the take-in
tray. A single shift can involve any number of coins, provided they all
come from a single compartment of one tray (and are therefore of the
same denomination) and go to the corresponding compartment of the other
tray. For conversions between denominations, two machines are available, a "changer" and a "grouper." The changer breaks a dime into ten
pennies or a dollar into ten dimes. Its output coins go automatically
into whichever tray its input coin came from (though into a different
compartment). The operations of the grouper are precisely inverse to
those of the changer. Either can be used at any time appropriate inputs
are available. Optimal plans for subtraction eschew the grouper, but it
may be needed by some learners to undo unnecessary breakings. Also, the
grouper is crucial earlier in the arithmetic curriculum for addition
problems and for the teaching of place value.

The screen has a variety of items. There are four rows, of which two
are the trays. The top row shows the minuend or "amount" originally
taken in, expressed in numerical form. Then comes the take-in tray,
initially representing the minuend in the form of coins. When the
student has solved the problem, the take-in tray will be equivalent to
the price, shown next, and the final row, originally empty, will show
the answer. To move coins, you first pick them up by moving the cursor
to the desired source compartment, either by mouse or arrow keys, and
either clicking or pressing the "enter" key, depending on the hardware
available. The region labeled "number of coins picked" is incremented
with each click and can itself be clicked as many times as desired to
undo picking up. To complete a shift, move the cursor to the destination and click. To convert a coin or coins to an adjacent denomination,
first pick them up, as above, and then click the changer or grouper.
If you have picked up, respectively, exactly one coin or ten, the
output of the changer or grouper will automatically go to the appropriate adjacent compartment of the source tray. "Done," "help," and
"quit" are self-explanatory. "Other screen" is for toggling back and
forth between Coinland and Numberland.

The Numberland screen is conceptually equivalent to that of Coinland
but differs externally in several ways. The sets of coins in the
various compartments are replaced by equivalent digits. The compartment
outlines are not shown, though the digits are arrayed in an orderly
fashion. The "amount" is removed to make room for the kind of trace of
a calculation that normally builds up with pencil and paper. After each
move, new digits can appear above the take-in tray and the corresponding
old ones get crossed off. If the problem is solved efficiently, the
original amount will still be on the screen, though crossed off, at the
end of a problem.

Exploration and Conservation

Some examples will indicate the pedagogical significance of exploration and conservation of quantity, specifically how conservation constrains the search space with a view to making it manageable and instructive. The conservation of quantity has as its simplest role the
gentle enforcement of one-digit subtraction facts. Take a one-digit
problem like 8 - 3 and suppose the learner begins by moving, say, 6
pennies to the give-back tray instead of 5. This person has, in effect,
tried to break 8 into 3 and 6, an attempted violation of the conserva-

tion of quantity, which the system does not support, in the sense that only 2 pennies (not 3) will be left in the take-in tray. Any learner who knows enough to check on the matter can see that the subgoal of having exactly 3 pennies in the take-in tray has not been achieved. The system provides the same type of subtle correction for subtraction facts like 13 - 4 = 9 whose need arises after borrowing. If a student signals "done" without having noticed some such discrepancy, the system points it out.

Consider now the more challenging example of 100 - 7, a problem that requires both subtraction from 0 and borrowing across zero. Both of these operations that are known to be rife with sources of bugs for those students who attempt mechanical execution of an algorithm that they have not yet mastered. In the Coinland version of this problem, the take-in tray has a dollar at the outset and the give-back tray, as always, begins empty. The cashier's goal requires the take-in tray to hold 7 pennies and nothing else. What can the learner do? Since the dollar is the only object available at the outset, there are only two possible moves: shift the dollar to the give-back tray or break it into dimes. Neither move directly addresses the need for pennies, and so the learner might reasonably select either. However the prospect of getting dimes may seem attractive to the learner who presumably knows that she can get pennies, her immediate need, once she gets ahold of a dime, that is, once she satisfies the precondition to the action that gets pennies from the changer. A student will have learned this way of getting pennies earlier in the curriculum from two-digit subtraction problems and from preliminary exercises with the changer.

Such problem-solving, with its use of a precondition to establish a subgoal may not occur immediately or at all to a child. Strategies for getting a student to consider such steps include coaching, instruction, and subtle alterations on the reward structure of the game. One such alteration involves the slotted or partially covered compartments discussed in the section, "Sequence and Translation." Even in this more directed environment, there is still the possibility of discovery. Moreover, what would be discovered if this scenario of problem-solving played out successfully is really the essence of some of the most difficult aspects of subtraction. We hold that such a discovery can plausibly take place in Coinland because the constraint of conservation keeps the search space small, and the situation correspondingly clear.

In comparison, a large search space is implicit in the repair theory of bugs [Brown and Van Lehn, 1982]. In that theory, bugs arise as repairs when an impasse is reached, so it would follow that the key to buglessness is preventing impasses from arising. But an impasse arises only if the learner has no relevant operator. In the algorithm-oriented approach, there are many operations and each is permissible only under conditions that are not always easy to determine. In Coinland there are very few operators and the tests for their legal applicability corres- pond closely to physical possibility, making impasses and hence the possibility of bugs relatively unlikely for graduates of this environ- ment.

We would make a final observation here with respect to enjoyability, games and game-like situations, as discussed by [Malone, 1982]. Note that Coinland has no conceptually wrong moves, just inefficient ones from the gaming viewpoint of taking as few moves as possible to reach a goal state. Consequently, there need be no inhibitions about trying things out.

Sequence and Translation

One unorthodox aspect of the curriculum implicit in Coinland subtrac- tion as presented so far is that no preferred sequence of operations is enforced. For example, in any problem without borrowing, the individual intra-column (digit-wise) subtractions can occur in any order, unlike algorithms commonly taught that prescribe a right-to-left sequence. This neutral stance, which is a natural consequence of the design, is compatible with Self's third slogan: "Empathise with the student's beliefs; don't label them as bugs" [Self, 1988].

Since order is not imposed, it becomes possible for a student to dis- cover a benefit of right-to-left order in some circumstances. If she prematurely shifts all the dimes to the answer, say, and then needs one to break into pennies, she will have to (at least partially) undo that shift. She may notice this, react appropriately, and ultimately reach the goal state, though not via a minimal length path. The system-resi- dent expert can readily detect that its own optimal solution is shorter and can inform the student that the "expert" finished the problem in fewer moves. Although we have not yet done so, it is straightforward to build a coach that interrupts only if a student has been persisting in this kind of inefficiency. Presumably the system would interrupt to do its coaching at the point of the move that commits the student to a suboptimal path (to the correct answer).

From this discussion of alternative paths, it may already be clear that there are many correct algorithms for subtraction. Various ones are taught around the world, so it is not possible for everybody to have the same one. That being the case, we may relax about letting children invent their own if they can. To stress the existence of variety, we express, in terms of Coinland moves, a little known but simple algorithm with the unusual virtue that it covers all cases, including borrowing across zero, with an unvarying sequence of steps: (i) go through the take-in tray from left to right, using the changer at every position; (ii) perform all intra-column differences (in arbitrary order); and (iii) go through the give-back tray, from right to left, gluing wherever possible. Coinland does not, however, support all possible algorithms. One that it does not support in any obvious direct way is one in which borrowing is accomplished by incrementing the subtrahend, because that method violates conservation of quantity, as noted by [Wenger, 1987].

We now turn to the matter of transferring the learning from the world of coins into the more abstract world of numerical subtraction. As noted earlier, transfer is not automatic but rather must for many children be explicitly learned. We also stated that our system provides a basis for such learning to take place by allowing the learner to toggle back and forth between two screens, Coinland and Numberland. Learning the translation would begin in the simpler realms of counting, regrouping, and addition, so its occurrence with subtraction constitutes a continuation.

Numberland is much like Coinland except that on its screen the several coins in a compartment are replaced by a number. This is true everywhere, so that there are no coins. For example, rather than seven pennies, one finds the numeral "7" in a penny compartment. Once the student has succeeded at the Coinland version, she is given it to solve in Numberland. She can then use her own valid knowledge of how to proceed in Coinland to instruct herself in Numberland, by solving the problem in both, more or less in parallel. In keeping with the role of Numberland as a transition to the world of pencil and paper, it shows some history of a calculation in the form of crossed off numbers.

Although free choice of legal moves can provide motivation and lead to discovery, it can also lead to an inefficient and possibly unen-

lightening search, as well as a lot of crossed off numbers in Numberland. We have argued that the small search space should help, and
ultimately we further tighten the search space by making it harder to
take coins out of the compartments of the give-back (answer) tray. Such
moves are not needed in (the coin analog of) the subtraction algorithm
that is taught in most U.S. schools. Even without such moves, there is
still some flexibility. Visually, the give-back compartments, which
appeared as cups without tops, now are drawn with partial tops: each top
is a line with a gap, to indicate the side view of a slot. We say it is
easy to drop coins in through the slot but hard to get them out once
they are in, and the game score reflects this. Notice that there is
constantly a visual clue to the physical basis for the scoring.

Future Directions

We are extending the curriculum both upward and downward from subtraction. In the downward direction, we have already implemented a
variety of games designed to foster learning of both the Coinland
interface itself and earlier topics in the curiculum, including the
notion of a place value system for expressing numerical quantity. In
the upward direction, we believe that we can succeed in teaching division by very small integers, independently of multiplication. We intend
to rely on an experience that many children have been exposed to,
dividing things up to share them. As the curriculum becomes more
thoroughly covered, it will be possible to make a more meaningful
selection of where within it a particular student ought to be. It will
then make sense for us to refine our currently primitive diagnostics and
tutoring decisions. We also plan to experiment with a technique we call
"heuristic guidance" for assisting a student within a problem without
relying excessively on diagnosis [Hamburger and Lodgher, ms].

We intend to to keep up a continual testing cycle with local elementary schools. Earlier we conducted a small pilot test and currently we
are awaiting the results and responses from a more extensive second
evaluation. We hope ultimately to provide new empirical results on the
transfer process. Finally, we will continue to seek the valuable advice
of Dr. Thomas Nuttall, an education specialist in Fairfax County who
recently concluded three years on the faculty of George Mason University. The system is written in C and is being developed on a PC/AT, but
can be delivered on a PC/XT.

References

Brown, J.S. and Burton, R.R., Diagnostic models for procedural bugs in basic mathematical skills, Cognitive Science **2** (1978) 155-192.

Brown, J.S. and Van Lehn, K., Repair theory: A generative theory of bugs in procedural skills, Cognitive Science **4** (1982) 379-426.

Carpenter, T.P., Learning to add and subtract: an exercise in problem solving, in: E.A. Silver (Ed.), Teaching and Learning Mathematical Problem-Solving: Multiple Research Perspectives (Erlbaum, Hillsdale, NJ, 1985).

Hamburger, H. and Lodgher, A., Constrained exploration and heuristic guidance, ms submitted to: J. Machine-Mediated Learning.

Malone, T.W., Heuristics for designing enjoyable user interfaces: lessons from computer games, in: Proceedings of the ACM Conference on Human Factors in Computer Systems (1982) 63-68.

Resnick, L.B. and Omanson, S., Learning to understand arithmetic, in: R. Glaser (Ed.), Advances in Instructional Psychology **3**, (Erlbaum, Hillsdale, NJ, 1987) 41-95.

Self, J.A., Bypassing the intractable problem of student modelling, in: Proceedings of the Conference on Intelligent Tutoring Systems, Montreal (1988) 18-24.

Wenger, E., Artificial Intelligence and Tutoring Systems (Morgan Kaufmann, Los Altos, CA, 1987).

HYPERMEDIA AND LEARNING: WHO GUIDES WHOM?

Nick Hammond
Department of Psychology,
University of York, UK

INTRODUCTION

The waves spreading from the surfacing of hypertext have left few areas of textual information processing unaffected. Certainly computer–aided learning has received more than mere ripples: many CAL centres now actively promote hypertext research alongside intelligent tutoring and instructional design.

Hypertext is of interest in education and training for a number of reasons, but particularly because it supports a mode of learning which contrasts both with traditional programmed instruction (Skinner, 1986) and with model–driven intelligent tutoring (Dede, 1986). This new approach is timely as the pendulum of fashion has swung away both from the behavioural underpinnings of programmed instruction and from the grander claims for AI techniques towards more pragmatic approaches based on exploratory and conjectural styles of learning (Stevens, 1986). At the same time, advances in storage, graphics and video technologies are making possible fast and cheap access to large multi–media information bases. In this paper I will explore the role that hypertext and hypermedia systems may play in CAL, and I will focus especially on issues concerning the nature of control.

HYPERTEXT AND HYPERMEDIA

The terms *hypertext* and *hypermedia* are subject to a great many interpretations. This is not surprising as the essence of hypertext lies in the support it provides for the user's task rather than in specific data structures, facilities or interfaces. It is easier, and perhaps more useful, to define what hypertext does than what it is: through direct interaction with information items it permits the rapid and efficient access to further relevant information. Hypertext systems may support the creation and modification of information networks as well as their exploration, and a number of authors point to the potential of hypertext for blurring the distinction between author, editor and reader (e.g., Megarry, 1988). The more general term *hypermedia* is used where materials are not limited to static text: video, computer graphics, animation, sound and indeed any technologically feasible form of presentation are all included. While the presentation medium will greatly influence the facilities and interface for both author and learner, many basic issues of hypertext and hypermedia use are shared, and it is these I shall discuss. In this paper I shall use the term hypermedia to refer to both textual and non−textual systems. For a general review of hypermedia systems and their use the reader is referred to Conklin (1987) and Halasz (1988).

Hypermedia systems fall broadly into those designed primarily for information presentation and exploratory browsing and those for information creation, organization and management, although these activities may overlap. I shall focus in the main on issues of information presentation. Presentation systems allow users to browse and explore large knowledge bases. Basic navigation relies on a pre−defined nexus of links between frames of information, and the user moves from one frame to another by pointing (usually with a mouse) to an item of interest on the screen. This may result in a new frame being shown or perhaps a *pop−up window* which overlays part of the screen with explanatory details. Since each frame may contain a number of branches, users can follow a great variety of paths through the material, and indeed in many systems can create new routes for others to follow. Multi−media systems support a wealth of verbal and non−verbal materials, allowing great sophistication in the design of the knowedge base.

Taking a task−centred view of hypermedia means that systems which do not explicitly support fixed network structures, such as *SuperBook* (Remde, Gomez & Landauer, 1987) or *StrathTutor* (Mayes, Kibby & Watson, 1988) should be included in the fold. Certainly these systems share with hypermedia the goals of rapid and effective information access, and however they are categorised it would be a mistake for CAL researchers to exclude them from consideration. SuperBook supports mainly textual knowledge bases and provides the user with a variety of viewing, access and search tools including (in its most recent implementation) sophisticated textual search based on statistical properties of the entire text (Deerwester *et al.*, in press; Dumais *et al.*, 1988). StrathTutor supports dynamic links between frames, computed on the basis of knowledge coding of the individual frames and the history of the user's session. In both cases, the author is freed from defining the network links explicitly, and interconnections are automatically re−computed when the knowledge base is altered.

In a similar vein, hypermedia concepts should be seen in the context of their common heritage with concepts of direct manipulation (Hutchins, Hollan & Norman, 1986; Shneiderman, 1984) where the goal is to engineer the interface to allow as close an engagement with task entities as possible. As output and input technologies develop, the influence of direct manipulation techniques on hypermedia in particular and on CAL in general will become more rather than less. Techniques for visual interactive modelling will lead to increasing use of visual simulations, microworlds and extended metaphors (Brooks, 1988; Smith, 1987), and advances in the sophistication of input methods will result in greater potential for direct task control and for procedural learning (Buxton,

1986). Hypermedia is but one stream within this wider tide of development and a stream with blurred boundaries; the point is that the wider context provides a fertile breeding ground for ideas on the application of hypermedia to CAL.

HYPERMEDIA FOR LEARNING

It is tempting to assume that a sophisticated system for browsing materials such as in an electronic encyclopaedia (Marchionini & Shneiderman, 1988; Weyer & Borning, 1985) or in a medical handbook (Frisse, 1988) will be suitable for learning. However, mere exposure to information does not guarantee learning and certainly does not ensure understanding. The temptation to assume that hypermedia is the panacea for CAL is reinforced by enthusiastic claims for the potential of its educational applications. Megarry (1988), for instance, states that the challenge that educational technologists face in harnessing the flexibility and capacity of hypertext and video technology is awesome. While this may indeed be the case, the problem of how to fit the harness is yet to be solved. Any instructional system must match its delivery to the changing informational needs, task goals and cognitive requirements of the learner, and the development of a cognitively based approach to handle the variety of learners, learning tasks and knowledge domains is no simple matter (Di Vesta & Rieber, 1987). The fact that hypermedia systems may promote quite a different style of learning from traditional forms of CAL (as claimed, for example, by Beeman*et al.*, 1987) only compounds the problem, as cognitively–based solutions may not transfer to the new style.

Problems with hypermedia

Before considering the rationale for using hypermedia systems in education, it is instructive to consider some of the documented problems in the use of hypermedia and hypertext systems to date. These problems do not of course occur in all cases, but they give some insight into issues which are likely to prove important in the use of hypermedia for CAL. Principal amongst the problems are the following.

First, users get lost (Jones, 1987). The knowledge base may be large and unfamiliar; the links provided will not be suitable for all individuals and for all tasks, and the user may be confused by the embarrassment of choice. Once in an unknown or unexpected part of the knowledge base, the user may have difficulty in reaching familiar territory; like a stranger in a foreign city without a map, he may miss the correct turning. Providing a*backtrack* facility is unlikely in itself to solve the problem.

Second, users may find it difficult to gain an overview of the material. They may fail to see how parts of the knowledge base are related and even miss large relevant sections entirely. In one study from our own laboratory (Hammond & Allinson, 1988a) we asked individuals to explore a small knowledge base for a fixed time using a variety of hypertext tools. All users had available the basic hypertext mechanism for traversing links from one frame of information to another, but some users also had access to additional facilities such as *maps* (providing an overview), an *index* of keywords or a number of *guided* tours through the material. Compared with users of systems with these additional facilities, users of the basic hypertext version thought they had seen the *most* material when in fact they had seen the *least*. Basic hypertext systems do not make it easy for users to know what's there or where they've been.

Third, even if users know specific information is present, they may have difficuly finding it. The knowledge base may not be structured in the way that they expect, or their lack of knowledge might mislead them. Jones (1987) has pointed out that the number of alternative choices often makes appropriate selection difficult. A related problem is that of uncertain commitment, where the user is unsure where a link will lead or what type or amount of information will be shown. Raskin (1987) gives an example of a user pointing to the leg of a butterfly on the screen: will the system take this to indicate the whole butterfly, the leg, the tarsus, legs in general or even the concept of symmetry? In other cases, the user might expect a short explanation, perhaps in a pop-up window, only to find that she has moved on to a new area in the knowledge base.

Fourth, users may ramble through the knowledge base in an unmotivated and inefficient fashion. This will be a crucial issue in instructional situations. When a person is uncertain of their immediate goals or of how to attain them, they will search their environment for clues. A system which gives a multiplicity of choice but the minimum of guidance may not be the ideal way for learners to ask themselves the right questions or to help them to formulate and attain their goals. This will be particularly so for non-experts (Gay, 1986).

Finally, coming to grips with the interface for controlling the various facilities may interfere with the primary task of exploring and learning about the materials. Raskin (1987) claims that the central lacuna of hypertext systems is the omission of any specification of the user interface (page 328), and even enthusiasts admit that the generic nature of hypermedia systems is both a blessing and a curse (Halasz, 1988). It is a curse because users are faced with a tool that may well be useful but is not well adapted to the specific task in hand. Getting the interface right is crucial in learning situations so as to prevent needless squandering of the student's resources on fighting the system.

These problems do not mean that hypermedia is inappropriate for exploratory browsing or even for learning, but rather that systems for specific activities should be supplemented by more directed access and guidance mechanisms and by appropriately tailored interfaces. Hypertext methods should be seen as one tool within the educational technologist's toolbox, to be used judiciously alongside others.

Instructional models for hypermedia

In view of these user problems, it seems that hypermedia concepts hold a hypnotic power over writers; the literature is enthusiastic and visionary but largely uncritical. Even the area of CAL has not been immune from missionary zeal, although at least some of the articles are tempered by the sobering effects of evaluation of educational efficacy. Perhaps the most extensive use of hypermedia for instructional delivery is that of the Intermedia project (Garrett, Smith & Myrowitz, 1986). The Intermedia group see hypermedia as a tool for promoting a *non-lineal* mode of thought by supporting the connectivity and integration of materials and the visualisation of concepts (Beeman *et al.*, 1987). Traditionally, educational systems (and the French and Japanese systems are singled out in particular) have focussed on a *linear* style where the "function of education is to exercise the brain through rote memorization and standard drill exercises with less attention to integration of that information" (page 68). Until recently, most CAL software supported this linear style of thinking through techniques such as programmed instruction and drill—and—practice. Although intelligent tutoring techniques may attempt to escape from this straightjacket by providing more directed remediation or conjectural forms of instruction, these have proved successful only in highly restricted and formal knowledge domains (Stevens, 1986). The requirement that the instructional dialogue should be driven by an explicit model of the student's state of knowledge places extreme constraints on the freedom that the learner can enjoy.

The contrast between intelligent tutoring methods and the potential for hypermedia is projected strongly by Megarry (1988): "the role of the computer should be organizing and representing knowledge to give the user easy access and control, rather than trying to create a model of the learner and seeking to prescribe her route through it" (page 172). According to Megarry, "a false trail has been laid by intelligent tutoring systems that try to create a model of the student (...) To treat the learner as a dumb patient and the computer system as an omniscient doctor is both perverse and arrogant" (pages 173—4). I have quoted from this paper because it captures succinctly the sentiments that many in CAL seem to feel about the mismatch between the quantity of the resources required for intelligent tutoring and the efficacy and scope of the final product. Whether or not the rejection of an explicit model—driven approach can be justified – and there are many reasons for questioning it as a general solution for CAL – it is still necessary to provide an alternative framework which can be used to link the design and use of instruction to the requirements of the teacher and the user. Attaining the goal of giving "the user easy access and control" is not just a matter of providing a hypermedia interface to the knowledge domain.

One spar of such a framework might be built from the observation that we know a good deal more about providing appropriate environments for learning than we do about the details of learning processes themselves. This is the case both at an applied level and at the level of cognitive theory. For instance in "teaching" a child to talk the parent merely needs to give appropriate stimulation at appropriate times; details of intermediate states of knowledge and the processes of acquisition can safely be left to the child and to the research psychologist.

In addition, cognitive theory furnishes us with a number of potentially useful distinctions in identifying conditions which will optimise learning. These include, for example, modes of learning (implicit, explicit), kinds of knowledge (declarative, procedural), forms of processing of materials (selecting, organizing, integrating), phases in learning (accretion, restructuring, tuning) and not least the consequences of learning activity for memorization and understanding (depth of processing, encoding specificity, schema integration). These issues will not be expanded upon here: see Bonner, 1988, Di Vesta & Rieber, 1987, and Hammond & Allinson, 1988b, for a more detailed discussion of their application to instructional design. The proposition is that such issues can take their place in a framework designed to support learning not by providing an explicit representation of the student's knowledge and the required activity to alter it but by suggesting how best to provide the right tools at the right time so that the student's learning processes – perhaps poorly understood – can flourish. The aims are theoretically more modest than those of model–driven intelligent tutoring: no attempt is made to develop a "complete" model of the student which can predict detailed learning behaviour, rather the aim is to ensure that the likely informational and cognitive requirements of the student can be helpfully met.

The distinction between implicit and explicit forms of learning is of particular interest when considering hypermedia techniques since the former may be achieved through appropriate "exposure" rather than by explicit instruction or strategically directed processing. It can be argued that much routine childhood learning and some adult learning occurs implicitly; psychologists are increasingly arguing for a distinction between explicit and implicit modes of learning (e.g. Hayes & Broadbent, 1988) and of memory performance (Graf & Schachter, 1985). For instance the latter authors demonstrated a dissociation between the two modes in amnesic patients. Models of learning based on connectionist principles (Pike, 1984) or on multiple–trace memories (Hintzman, 1986) have also given a spur to the idea that rules and structures can be abstracted from experiences without the need for them to be represented or taught explicitly. Indeed, adopting an explicit mode of learning for materials best suited to implicit learning can be counterproductive (Berry & Broadbent, 1988). It may be important, therefore, to identify when implicit rather than explicit learning is appropriate and what the optimal instructional approach for each type of learning might be.

LEARNING SUPPORT ENVIRONMENTS

We have attempted to tackle the two sets of issues raised above – the reported problems with hypermedia systems and the need for an alternative cognitive framework for the use of hypermedia techniques in CAL – by proposing the concept of a *learningsupport environment* or *LSE* (Hammond & Allinson, 1988c). This is a system which provides the learner with a set of tools to support exploration of, or instruction in, some field of knowledge. The tools will include both a set of learning activities and range of aids for accessing information and making best use of the available activities. The set of tools, the extent of learner control and characteristics of the interface can be tailored by the author or teacher to match the requirements of the student. They should not only allow the user to access the knowledge base without getting lost or bogged down in a morass of information but the nature of the tools should encourage optimal learning strategies.

Learner and system control

A presupposition which underlies the idea of an LSE is that handing some degree of control to the learner is appropriate. There are two types of control which are both educationally important and can be varied fairly easily in LSEs. These are control over the sequencing of the materials which the learner sees and control over the types and sequencing of learning activities (such as reading information, taking tests, solving problems or trying interactive demontrations). The optimal level of control is likely to depend on the nature of the learners, on their familiarity with the materials, on their learning goals and not least on the nature of the knowledge domain. Handing complete control to the beginner may be as ineffective as forcing the expert through a drill–and–practice tutorial. The question of appropriate level of instructional control has been the topic of a certain amount of research (Garhart & Hannafin, 1986; Gay, 1986; Gray, 1987; Hannafin & Colamaio, 1987; Hartley & Tait, 1987; Laurillard, 1987), and there seems to be a consensus that more knowledgeable learners can capitalise on self–directed learning. For instance Gay concludes that: "learners can be given more control if their prior understanding of a topic is relatively high; conversely, learners should be provided with more structure if their prior conceptual understanding of a topic is low." There is evidence, too, of strong individual differences in the optimal structuring of information (Laurillard, 1984). Finally, the nature of the learner's task will also be a strong determinant of the most appropriate level of control. A student who wishes to summarise a topic in preparation for an essay has different requirements from one who is studying the same material for the first time or from one who is revising for an examination.

Most research on learner control concerns the sequencing of materials: there is less work on control over learning activities, although, of course, there is a good deal on the activities themselves. For instance it is often a sound educational strategy to pose questions before presenting detailed information both to provide a structure in advance and to inform users of their current state of competence (Merrill, 1987). Issues concerning the appropriate provision, sequencing or control over different learning activities will not be discussed here: however if an LSE is to cater for a range of materials and users it should offer a number of mechanisms for sequencing both materials and learning activities, and it should allow flexible assignment of control to either system or learner.

The learner interface

Perhaps the most important requirement of all is to ensure that the interface to the LSE poses no barrier to the learner. It is useless to provide a dazzling array of facilities if the user never gets round to using them: there is ample evidence that users will stick with a "habitable subset" of facilities if the effort of learning new ones is significant, relying on familiar but circuitous routes to meet their objectives (Rosson, 1984). This means that the interfaces provided by generic hypermedia systems will usually be inappropriate for the average learner unfamiliar with abstract terminology such as nodes, links, browsers or filters. Nor is it just a matter of terminology: different classes of users will have their own idiosyncratic view of particular knowledge domains, and these may have to be catered for by altering the mix and organization of facilities available, the conceptual or metaphorical models in which they are embedded as well as the terminology itself. Ideally, the LSE should allow the interface to be tailored along the lines suggested by Trigg, Moran & Halasz (1987), the facilities being supported by more abstract and extended hypermedia software (eg, Campbell & Goodman, 1987).

AN EXAMPLE LSE: THE HITCH HIKER'S GUIDE

The Hitch-hiker's Guide is a general-purpose LSE for teaching non-formal fields of knowledge. We discuss its educational and psychological basis in Hammond & Allinson (1988b) and the system itself in described in more detail in Allinson & Hammond (in press) and Hammond & Allinson (1988c). It consists of an authouring component for generating materials and a presentation component which handles the interaction with the learner. During presentation all learner input is through a mouse, and the software records relevant user activity for subsequent evaluation. A typical display frame (with material on the history of York) is shown in Figure 1. The frame consists of a main display area, normally including mouse-selectable active areas (hypertext links to other frames) plus a number of boxes at the bottom of the screen. These boxes, also mouse-selectable, provide access and guidance facilities over and above hypertext links, namely maps, indexes and tours. These facilities are aimed in part at avoiding the characteristic "getting lost and confused" problems and in part at providing a range of control, customisable by the author of the knowledge base, over the sequencing of the materials.

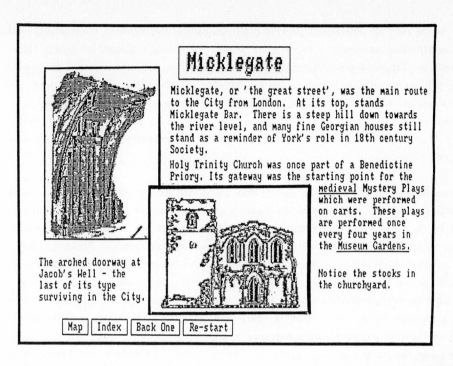

Figure 1. Example information screen, illustrating hypertext links (underlined here: colour-coded in the system) and bottom-line boxes.

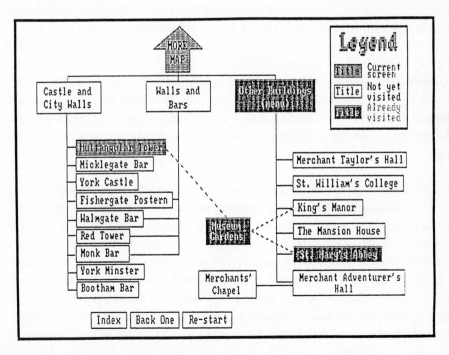

Figure 2. Example map screen, illustrating network structure and footprint information. Selection of any rectangle results in display of the associated frame.

Other boxes (not all illustrated) provide multiple—choice quizzes, help information, reading lists, backtracking and options to re—start or end the session. Embedded within the materials are further types of learning activities. For instance, materials for students taking a human cognition course includes a number of interactive experiments and demonstrations, where, for example, the learner can act as a subject in a classic experiment and then see a display of her results. This is an example of a "tailored" facility of relevance to teaching cognitive psychology but probably of little use in other domains.

Our aim for the interface was to ensure that users with no computer experience would be conducting real work after only a few minutes use, and that no paper documentation would be required. To achieve this, we embedded many of the facilities within a travel holiday metaphor. The rationale is duscussed further in Hammond & Allinson (1987). With selection of hypertext links, characterised as go—it—alone travel, the learner is free to move around the network by selecting items directly. Selection results in a frame containing further information on the item in question. Guided tours are initiated when the learner uses the mouse to select a coach icon (labelled with the topic of the tour). He or she is then guided round a sequence of frames on the topic until the tour ends, at which point the learner is returned to the starting point. To address one aspect of the problem of commitment, the student can call up a "destination board" which briefly describes the tour and the number of "stops" it includes. A further access mechanism is provided by the map facility: a typical map screen is shown in Figure 2, consisting of a graphical representation of the local part of the frame network. The facility is like a gazetteer, with one or more selectable arrows leading to further maps. Thus the learner can gain an overview of the available materials by navigating around the map screens. Direct selection can also be made — each rectangle is an active area — and colour is used to indicate footprint information (where I've been) and the screen from which the map was invoked (where I am). The final major access facility is an index which provides a list of keywords. Selecting a keyword results directly in the display of information about the topic.

The system has been evaluated by day—to—day use for undergraduate teaching, by targetted questionnaires and by specific experiments (using the materials of the type illustrated in Figures 1 and 2). Student reaction is positive: even after their first sessions (of average length 40 minutes) students rated the system easy to use, averaging a score of 11 on a scale running from 0 (very easy) to 100 (very difficult). Further details are given in Hammond & Allinson (1988c). The question of whether the access tools over and above hypermedia links do help learning, and if so to what extent they would be strategically deployed, has been addressed in a series of laboratory studies (Hammond & Allinson, 1988a; Hammond & Allinson, in preparation). These issues are central to the LSE concept as the intention is for the various facilities to shape and guide the behaviour of the learner along optimal lines. The results suggest that, even in the first twenty minutes of use, students can select access tools appropriate for their task: for example students conducting directed tasks (finding the answer to specific questions) used the index three times as frequently as students conducting exploratory tasks. Conversely, the latter students used tours three times as often as the former.

CONCLUSIONS AND FUTURE DIRECTIONS

Hypermedia systems have enormous potential in training and education. In this paper I have argued that a successful application of hypermedia to CAL requires the development of a sound understanding of the informational and cognitive needs of learners. Such an understanding must be based on a range of conceptual and analytical approaches, and some possibilities have been indicated above. Currently the design of successful delivery systems and instructional materials remains as much a craft as an engineering skill, although to an increasing extent a cognitive engineering stance is adopted. It is interesting, for example, that some recent analytical approaches to instructional design use hypertext as the means of representation (Russell, Moran & Jordan, 1988). A danger of too formal an approach to design is that the underlying model may flawed or incomplete: it is risky to put all your eggs in one basket if the basket is holed. A characteristic of the LSE approach is that empirical and principled approaches can be mixed, and formalism can be introduced in a gradual but well-motivated fashion. This contrasts with a strict model-driven approach to intelligent tutoring where the model is necessarily central to the course of instruction.

I have restricted discussion to situations where, in the main, information is presented to the learner; requiring the learner to generate materials is also a powerful technique in CAL (eg Hewett, 1988) and one to which hypermedia systems are well suited. Creation can run from private or public annotations of exisiting courseware to full-scale authoring of new materials. Particularly intriguing are possibilities for intermediate forms of creation, where, for example, a student might assemble exisiting fragments of knowledge into a coherent argument (a kind of knowledge jigsaw task, with tools to generate suitably labelled links), or conversely might fill in the factual details on a skeleton provided by the system. Hypertext techniques have already been used to support the representation of arguments in other domains such as system design (Conklin & Begeman, 1987; MacLean, Young & Moran, 1989) and in legal argumentation (Marshall, 1987) and ideas from these areas might well be applicable to CAL.

The future will also see the convergence of hypermedia with other direct manipulation techniques as improving input and output technologies expand the potential for simulations using sophisticated perceptual-motor skills in addition to cognitive ones. Already the talk is of hyperworlds rather than microworlds. Another development is likely to be the marrying of techniques from AI and intelligent tutoring with those of hypermedia. There are a number of systems which adapt their links on the basis of contextual variables (Campbell & Goodman, 1987) or of the prior history of interaction (Mayes, Kibby & Watson, 1988), and it is not hard to forsee these growing in intelligence. A somewhat different approach, that of intelligent agents, is also well—suited to hypermedia; one can envisage a system where an agent advises on the interaction between learner and knowledge base but without necessarily directing the course of the dialogue. However, before such a vision can be realised, much work is needed in understanding the cognitive foundation of hypermedia use.

REFERENCES

Allinson,L.J. & Hammond,N.V. (in press). A learning support environment: The hitch—hiker's guide. To appear in R.McAleese (ed.),*Hypertext: Theory into Practice*. Blackwell: Oxford.

Beeman,W.O., Anderson,K.T., Bader,G., Larkin,J., McClard,A.P., McQuillan,P. & Shields,M. (1987). Hypertext and pluralism: from lineal to non—lineal thinking. In *Hypertext '87*. North Carolina, pp 67—85.

Berry,D.C. & Broadbent,D.E. (1988). Interactive tasks and the implicit—explicit distinction. *British Journal of Psychology*, **79**, 251—272.

Bonner,J. (1988). Implications of cognitive theory for instructional design: revisited. *Educational Communication &Technology Journal*, **36**, 3—14.

Brooks,F.P. (1988). Grasping reality through illusion — interactive graphics serving science. In E.Soloway, D.Frye & S.B.Sheppard (eds),*CHI '88 Conference Proceedings: Human Factorsin Computing Systems*. ACM Press: New York (Washington, May), pp 1—11.

Buxton,W. (1986). There's more to interaction than meets the eye: some issues in manual input. In D.A.Norman & S.W.Draper (eds),*User Centered System Design: New Perspectives on Human—ComputerInteraction*. LEA: Hillsdale, 319—337.

Campbell,B. & Goodman,J.M. (1987). HAM: A general—purpose hypertext abstract machine. In*Hypertext '87*. North Carolina, 21—32.

Conklin,J. (1987). Hypertext: a survey and introduction.*IEEEComputer*, September, 17—41.

Conklin,J. & Begeman,M.L. (1987). gIBIS: A hypertext tool for team design deliberation. In*Hypertext '87*. North Carolina, 247—251.

Dede,C. (1986). A review and synthesis of recent research in intelligent computer—assisted instruction.*International Journalof Man—Machine Studies*, **24**, 329—353.

Deerwester,S., Dumais,S.T., Furnas,G.W., Landauer,T.K. & Harshman,R. (in press). Indexing by latent semantic analysis.*Journal of American Society for Information Science*.

Di Vesta,F.J. & Rieber,L.P. (1987). Characteristics of cognitive engineering: the next generation of instructional systems. *Educational Communication & Technology Journal*, **35**, 213–230.

Dumais,S.T., Furnas,G.W., Landauer,T.K., Deerwester,S. & Harshman,R. (1988). Using latent semantic analysis to improve access to textual information. In E.Soloway, D.Frye & S.B.Sheppard (eds), *CHI '88 Conference Proceedings: Human Factors in Computing Systems*. ACM Press: New York, (Washington, May), pp 281–285.

Frisse,M.E. (1988). Searching for information in a hypertext medical handbook. *Communications of the ACM*, **31**, 880–886.

Garhart C. & Hannafin M. (1986). The accuracy of cognitive monitoring during computer–based instruction. *Journal of Computer–Based Instruction*, **13**, 88–93.

Garrett,L.N., Smith,K.E. & Myrowitz,N. (1986). Intermedia: issues, strategies, and tactics in the design of a hypermedia document system. In *Proceedings of the Conference on Computer–Supported Cooperative Work*, (Austin, Texas, December), pp 163–174.

Gay,G. (1986). Interaction of learner control and prior understanding in computer–assisted video instruction. *Journal of Educational Psychology*, **78**, 225–227.

Graf,P. & Schachter,D.L. (1985). Implicit and explicit memory for new associations in normal and amnesic patients. *Journal, of Experimental Psychology: Learning, Memory, and Cognition*, **11**, 501–518.

Gray,S.H. (1987). The effect of sequence control on computer assisted learning. *Journal of Computer–based Instruction*, **14**, 54–56.

Halasz,F. (1988). Reflections on NoteCards: seven issues for the next generation of hypermedia systems. *Communications of the ACM*, **31**, 836–852.

Hammond,N.V. & Allinson,L.J. (1987). The travel metaphor as design principle and training aid for navigating around complex systems. In D.Diaper & R.Winder (eds), *People and Computers III*. Cambridge University Press: Cambridge, pp 75–90.

Hammond,N.V. & Allinson,L.J. (1988a). Taking the hype out of hypertext: Why it's inadequate for learning. In T.R.G.Green (ed), *Proceedings of Fourth European Conference on Cognitive Ergonomics*, (Cambridge, September).

Hammond,N.V. & Allinson,L.J. (1988b). Development and evaluation of a CAL system for non–formal domains: The Hitch–hiker's guide to cognition. *Computers and Education*, **12**, 215–220.

Hammond,N.V. & Allinson,L.J. (1988c). Travels around a learning support environment: Rambling, orienteering or touring? In E.Soloway, D.Frye & S.B.Sheppard (eds), *CHI '88 Conference Proceedings: Human Factors in Computing Systems*. ACM Press: New York, (Washington, May), pp 269–273.

Hammond,N.V. & Allinson,L.J. (in preparation). Extending hypertext for learning: An investigation of access and guidance tools.

Hannafin,M.J. & Colamaio,M.E. (1987). The effects of variations in lesson control and practice on learning from interactive video. *Educational Communication & Technology Journal*, **35**, 203–212.

Hartley,J.R. & Tait,K. (1987). Learner control and educational advice in computer based learning: The study—station concept. *Computers and Education,* **10**, 259—265.

Hayes,N.A. & Broadbent,D.E. (1988). Two modes of learning for interactive tasks. *Cognition,* **28**, 249—276.

Hewett,T.T. (1988). Some observations on applications of microcomputers in teaching. *Behavior Research Methods, Instruments, & Computers,* **20**, 191—192.

Hintzman,D.L. (1986). "Schema abstraction" in a multiple—trace memory model. *Psychological Review,* **93**, 411—428.

Hutchins,L., Hollan,J.D. & Norman,D.A. (1986). Direct manipulation interfaces. In D.A.Norman & S.W.Draper (eds), *User Centered System Design: New Perspectives on Human—Computer Interaction.* LEA: Hillsdale, 87—124.

Jones,W.P. (1987). How do we distinguish the hyper from the hype in non—linear text? In H.J.Bullinger & B.Shackel (eds), *Human—computer interaction — Interact '87.* North—Holland: Amsterdam, pp 1107—1113.

Laurillard,D.M. (1984). Interactive video and the control of learning. *Educational Technology,* **23**, 7—15.

Laurillard,D.M. (1987). Computers and the emancipation of students — giving control to the learner. *Instructional Science,* **16**, 3—18.

MacLean,A., Young,R.M. & Moran,T.P. (1989). Design rationale: Analysing and representing the product of user interface design. In *CHI '89 Conference Proceedings: Human Factors in Computing Systems.* ACM Press: New York, (Austin).

Marchionini,G. & Shneiderman,B. (1988). Finding facts vs browsing knowledge in hypertext systems. *IEEE Computer,* January, 70—80.

Marshall,C.C. (1987). Exploring representation problems using hypertext. In *Hypertext '87.* North Carolina, 253—268.

Mayes,J.T., Kibby,M.R. & Watson,H. (1988). StrathTutor: The development and evaluation of a learning—by—browsing system on the Macintosh. *Computers and Education,* **12**, 221—229.

Megarry,J. (1988). Hypertext and compact discs — the challenge of multi—media learning. *British Journal of Educational Technology,* **19**, 172—183.

Merrill,J. (1987). Levels of questioning and forms of feedback — instructional factors in courseware design. *Journal of Computer—Based Instruction,* **14**, 18—22.

Pike,R. (1984). Comparison of convolution and matrix distributed memory systems for associative recall and recognition. *Psychological Review,* **91**, 281—294.

Raskin,J. (1987). The hype in hypertext: a critique. In *Hypertext '87.* North Carolina, pp 325—329.

Remde,J.R., Gomez,L.M. & Landauer,T.K. (1987). SuperBook: An automatic tool for information exploration — hypertext? In *Hypertext '87*. North Carolina, pp 175—188.

Rosson,M.B. (1984). Effects of experience on learning, using, and evaluating a text editor. *Human Factors*, **26**, 463—475.

Russell,D.M., Moran,T.P. & Jordan,D.S. (1988). The instructional design environment. In J.Psotka, L.D.Massey & S.A.Mutter (eds), *Intelligent Tutoring Systems: Lessons Learned*. Lawrence Erlbaum: Hillsdale, NJ.

Shneiderman,B. (1984). The future of interactive systems and the emergence of direct manipulation. In Y.Vassilou (ed.), *Human Factors and Interactive Computer Systems*. Ablex: Norwood, NJ, 1—27.

Skinner,B.F. (1986). Programmed instruction revisited. *Phi Delta Kappan*, **68**, 103—110.

Smith,R.B. (1987). Experiences with the alternative reality kit: An example of the tension between literalism and magic. In J.M.Carroll & P.P.Tanner (eds), *CHI+GI 87 Proceedings*. ACM: Toronto, 5—9 April, 61—67.

Stevens A.L. (1986). The next generation of AI—based teaching systems. *Machine—mediated Learning*, **1**, 313—326.

Trigg,R.H., Moran,T.P. & Halasz,F.G. (1987). Adaptability and tailorability in NoteCards. In H.J.Bullinger & B.Shackel (eds), *Human—Computer Interaction — INTERACT '87*, pp 723—728.

Weyer,S.A. & Borning,A.H. (1985). A prototype electronic encyclopedia. *ACM Transactions on Office Information Systems*, **3**, 63—88.

TUTORING RULE AUTHORING SYSTEM (TRAS)

Mohammed M. Haque*
Allen A. Rovick+
Joel A. Michael+
Martha Evens#

*Department of Information Science
Northeastern Illinois University
Chicago, IL 60625
+Department of Physiology
Rush Medical College
Chicago, IL 60612
#Department of Computer Science
Illinois Institute of Technology
Chicago, IL 60616

ABSTRACT

An authoring program, TRAS (Tutoring Rule Authoring System) has been designed and written to allow teachers and other programming-naive individuals to create and assemble the rules for rule based programs. The program has two component parts: TRE (Tutoring Rule Editor) and TPT (Text to Prolog Translator). TRE enables the user to create rules by specifying the conditional and action clauses that are to be used and inserting them into rules. With TRE the user may also delete or add clauses to rules or delete or add whole rules. As predicates or arguments are specified within the program they are automatically numbered and segregated into "choice" files. Each choice file is associated with a specific subsegment of the program being built. When the author is creating new rules or editing existing ones, the relevant choice files are displayed on the screen for possible use by the author. When the rules of a program have been completed, they may be translated into Prolog using TPT, which automatically puts each rule into the appropriate format to run as a Prolog program. Both components of TRAS have been fully implemented except for minor elements. The program is in use as part of our smart tutor development efforts.

AUTHORING AIDS

The design and development of programs for computer-based education (CBE) has usually involved the co-operative efforts of several experts. Early on, when only conventional CBE was being written, a teaching program was likely to be produced by a teacher working with a programmer or by a teacher who had programming skills. However, once a fair number of people got interested in creating courseware, tools were developed that enabled the programming-naive teacher to work more independently. Some of these tools were specialized computer languages, so called authoring languages that had special functions which facilitated the programming of conventional CBE. These languages, like TUTOR of the PLATO system (Alpert & Bitzer, 1970) EnBASIC (Computer Teaching Corp, 1984), and PILOT (Yob, 1977) could be used to produce rather sophisticated teaching exercises. A teacher with a small amount of programming experience could learn to use these languages more easily than languages that lacked their special features.

A second group of tools that enabled teachers to be even more directly involved in creating their own CBE exercises are the authoring environments or systems (Hirsch, et al, 1978; Pogue, 1980; Pattison, 1985). These utility programs are generally menu driven and therefore do not require the teacher to learn to program. The programs prompt the teacher-author in a step-by-step manner to make appropriate entries which are automatically assembled into a working CBE program.

The principle advantage of these authoring aids is that they enable the teacher to be intimately involved in the creation of the instructional program.

The most recent phase of creating teaching programs involves the application of AI techniques to the production of complex, intelligent tutors. Many experts co-operate in the design and creation of these programs (e.g. knowledge engineers, cognitive psychologists, experts in student modeling and in natural language processing). As a consequence, the teacher has become less directly involved. Few teachers have the skill or the expertise to make direct contributions to the development effort.

Groups that are creating intelligent tutors use several techniques to reveal the tutoring rules and strategies employed by teachers, e.g. interviewing, observing or recording tutoring sessions. What is often not done, however, is to allow teachers to independently specify, modify and/or edit the strategies and rules as they think they use them. That was one of the primary purposes for the development of the Tutoring Rule Authoring System (TRAS) (Haque, 1988).

TUTORING RULE AUTHORING SYSTEM (TRAS)

The Tutoring Rule Authoring System (TRAS) has been developed as part of an ongoing project: the design and construction of the Pathophysiology Tutor, PPT, (Michael, et al, 1989) at Rush Medical College, Chicago. PPT is intended to instruct first year medical students in the solution of pathophysiology problems using the hypothetico-deductive method. PPT is a rule-based program in which the rules specify how the program proceeds and defines the interactions between the student and the Tutor.

While developing the PPT, we realized that the tactics that we had been using were rather awkward. Our approach had been to interpose a "software expert" between the "content/process expert" and the program during its construction. We felt that it would be more convenient and direct if we could eliminate the middle man during the initial phase(s) of rule construction. TRAS was developed as a tool which would enable the content experts, who have little or no programming expertise, to directly specify the rules that govern the functions of the tutor. Once TRAS was available, we realized that we also had a tool that provided us with an easy way to experiment with changes in the tutoring rules and strategies so that we could observe their effectiveness in guiding student learning.

Although TRAS was developed with the limited goal of serving the needs of the Pathophysiology Tutor project, it could be used as a general purpose authoring system to write the rules for any program that encodes its knowledge in the "IF conditions THEN actions" formalism.

TRAS consists of two programs, the Tutoring Rule Editor (TRE) and the Text to Prolog Translator (TPT). It works in the following manner.

CREATING A NEW RULE FILE WITH TRE

Each tutoring rule consists of two parts: one or more conditions (predicates) that must be satisfied in order for the rule to be executed and one or more consequences (predicates) that result when the rule is executed. When creating a new (tutoring) rule, TRE first prompts the user to specify a predicate. This is inserted into the rule that is under construction and is also numbered and stored in a predicate file. This predicate file becomes a menu that has been specified by the user and from which the user may make selections in constructing other rules. The user is then prompted to enter additional predicates for this rule which, if specified, are treated in the same way as the first entry.

When the user signals that there are no additional predicates to be entered into the rule being constructed, the program advances to the next step. The user is next requested to enter an action. This entry is numbered and stored in an file (another menu) and is assembled into the rule being built. Further prompts may elicit additional predicates which are treated like the first one.

Predicates and arguments are listed in their respective files as names. In order for them to function as intended they must eventually be programmed as subroutines.

When all of the desired predicates and arguments have been entered by the user, he signals that the rule is complete. The rule is then stored for later processing by the Text to Prolog Translator (TPT) and the user may proceed to create another rule or may edit an existing rule. Any entry in the predicate file or in the argument file may be used to construct any number of rules, not just the one for which it was originally created.

MODIFYING AN EXISTING RULE FILE

The Tutoring Rule Editor (TRE), as its name implies, may also be used to modify existing tutoring rules. These rules may be modified by adding, deleting or otherwise editing a predicate or predicates or an argument or arguments. Also, existing rules may be deleted, moved to a new position in a rule file or new rules may be created. In this process, new predicates or arguments may be added to the files or existing predicates or arguments may be deleted from these files.

In creating a new rule file or editing an existing one using TRE, the user merely names the predicates and the arguments or selects them by identification number. TRE itself assembles these entries into an English language IF...THEN format statement that satisfies the basic language requirements of Turbo Prolog. Thus the user, presumably a content expert and not a programming expert, need not be concerned about learning to program in Prolog.

As the rule writing process continues, the number of entries in the predicate file and in the argument file grows. This would make it increasingly more difficult to construct new or edit old rules as the number of predicates and/or arguments that would have to be scanned to select items for inclusion in rules would become more and more numerous. Therefore, TRE also allows the user to modify (add, delete or edit) the list of choices of predicates and arguments that are displayed during the rule editing or creating process at each point in the program. Since ITS programs tend to be modularized, one can thus assemble a number of predicate subfiles and argument subfiles (choice files) each of which specifically applies to one or more particular modules of the program. Since choice files are a subset of the whole, the number of elements that need to be scanned for the selection of predicates or arguments during the creation of new rules or the editing of old ones is greatly reduced.

TEXT TO PROLOG TRANSLATOR

The output component of the Tutoring Rule Authoring System is the Text to Prolog Translator (TPT). This program takes the tutoring rules that are assembled by TRE and converts them into syntactically correct Turbo

```
 TYPE NUMERIC ID OF YOUR CHOICE AND HIT RETURN:
 Window:1 File:\CBE\MOH\EXP                      Line:3      Col:1
 /* EX-new 1 */
     IF
 --->THEN
     END.



 Window:2              LIST OF AVAILABLE CHOICES




 Window:3 File:PROGRESS.RPT                      Line:1      Col:1

 --------------------------------------------------------------------
 ^A: ADD CLAUSE    ^F: ADD RULE    ^L: DELETE CLAUSE   ^W: DELETE RULE   ^P: HELP
 ^U: EXIT TRE      ^B: DISCARD CURRENT ACTIVITY        ^T: MODIFY CHOICELIST
```

FIGURE 1. THE BASIC TRE SCREEN

Top line = Prompt/Confirmation line
Window 1. Data Line contains file name, cursor location.
The window now contains the rule elements which are to be supplemented during the creation of the first rule in this file. The first line of the rule is the header. It will eventually contain the rule name and number. The next 2 lines are the conditions (IF) and actions (THEN) part of the rule. Predicates will be added after each part in building the rule. END is the rule terminator.
Window 2. Top line states the contents of thw window, in this case the list of available choices that can be inserted into the rule at the arrow (cursor) in window 2. Inserting a clause moves everything from the arrow downward. No predicates are yet listed in the window.
Window 3. The top line states the window contents. In this case the window will contain a progress report on the conditional clause that is going to be built. Nothing has been done so far so the window is empty.
Command lines. The bottom two lines list the available commands.

Prolog "IF...THEN" statements ready for compilation with other Prolog statements in a rule-based program.

Although TRAS allows the user to create and edit tutoring rules, it does not generate the programs that make them usable in an ITS (or any other rule based program). They need to be coded. This code does not have to be in Prolog. However, for each new entry (predicate or argument) a corresponding procedure must be designed and programmed. This requires the services of an expert programmer. Further, the rules, as specified by the teacher are not necessarily optimal for achieving the goals desired by this expert. Contributions from a computer scientist with experience in ITS building are also needed. Thus, the process of creating an ITS will continue to be a combined effort of individuals with different specialties. However, TRAS enables the teacher to become a more active member of the team.

USING TRE

Creating a new rule file

In order to create a new rule file, upon entering TRE the user selects the option create a new rule file. The basic TRE screen is presented in Figure 1.

When creating a new rule file there are no predicates or arguments in the "choice" files for the user to select. Hence, at each step in the rule creation process one or more choices must first be entered to provide predicates or arguments for insertion into the rules. Therefore, in the example being described here the user must first: 1. enter one (or more) predicates to be available for use in the IF (conditions) file (MODIFY CHOICE LIST, ^T; see figure 2a, window 2), then he may 2. select (by number) one of these for insertion into the rule as a condition predicate (ADD CLAUSE, ^A; figure 2b, window 1), 3. enter one (or more) predicates to be available for use in the THEN (actions) file (MODIFY CHOICE LIST, ^T; figure 2b, window 2), 4. select one of these for insertion as an action predicate (ADD CLAUSE, ^A). In the example shown the action predicate requires an argument. The incomplete clause is shown in figure 2b, window 3 until an argument has been selected. 5. Arguments for this predicate must first be inserted into its choice list (^T; figure 2c, window 2) before one may be selected for insertion into the rule. 6. Selection of an argument completes the rule (^A; shown in figure 2d). Of course more than one clause may be inserted into either or both the conditions part or the actions part of a rule.

Editing an existing rule file

In order to edit an existing rule file, upon entering TRE,

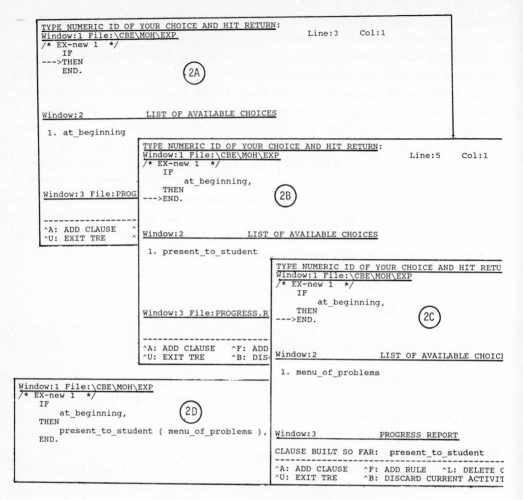

FIGURE 2. BUILDING A NEW RULE

A. User is building a new rule in window 1. Cursor shows where clause is to be added (line below IF). User has entered ^T (MODIFY CHOICE LIST) and inserted a choice into the list of predicates in window 2. He may now enter predicate in the rule by entering ^A (ADD CLAUSE) and typing clause number.

B. The conditional clause has been inserted into the rule (window 1). Action clause is being built. Author has entered a new action predicate in choice list (shown in window 2).

C. Action predicate has been selected for entry into the rule, but it requires an argument. The clause is held in window 3 while an argument is added to the choice list (window 2).

D. Selection of the argument completes the clause and the rule.

the user selects the file to be edited from a menu of existing files (figure 3). The basic TRE screen is presented along with the rules in the selected file. Note that each rule has a unique construction:

number of clauses, and predicates with and without arguments.

Suppose that the author wants to insert a new rule between present rules SF-2 and SF-3 (see figure 3a). The user positions the cursor at the end of SF-2 and selects the command ADD RULE (^F). TRE inserts a new rule skeleton at the designated location (see arrow, figure 3b).

```
Window:1 File:\CBE\MOH\SFRULES.RUL              Line:1      Col:1
/* SF-  1 */                          3A
    IF
        at_beginning,
    THEN
        present_to_student ( patient_description ),
        request_student_to ( identify_findings ),
    END.
/* SF-  2 */
    IF
        identified_finding ( garbage ),
    THEN
        comment ( SFGARB.TXT ),
        unhilite ( student_finding ),
        request_student_to ( identify_findings ),
    END.
/* SF-  3 */
    IF
        identified_finding (
    THEN
        comment ( SFMULT.TXT
-----------------------------
^A: ADD CLAUSE    ^F: ADD RULE
^U: EXIT TRE      ^B: DISCARD
```

```
Window:1 File:\CBE\MOH\SFRULES.RUL
        present_to_student ( patient_description ),
        request_student_to ( identify_findings )
    END.
/* SF-  2 */
    IF
        identified_finding ( garbage ),
    THEN
        comment ( SFGARB.TXT ),
        unhilite ( student_finding ),
        request_student_to ( identify_findings ),
    END.
/* SF-new  1 */
    IF                                        3B
    THEN
    END.
/* SF-  3 */
    IF
        identified_finding ( mult_cfroot ),
    THEN
        comment ( SFMULT.TXT ),
-----------------------------------------------------
^A: ADD CLAUSE    ^F: ADD RULE    ^L: DELETE CLAUSE
^U: EXIT TRE      ^B: DISCARD CURRENT ACTIVITY
```

FIGURE 3.   MODIFYING AN EXISTING RULE FILE
A.   The file to be modified is selected from a file list. The first 2 and part of the 3rd rule appear in window 1.
B.   The author positions the cursor at the end of rule 2 so that a new rule may be added at this point. Select ^F and the rule skeleton appears (see hexagon) between rules 2 and 3.

When the user moves the cursor to select an IF predicate and specifies ADD CLAUSE (^A), a list of available predicates appears in window 2 and the author is prompted to select one by number (figure 4a). If the author selects a predicate which requires an argument, the predicate is temporarily inserted in window 3 (see arrow in figure 4, CLAUSE BUILT SO FAR), a list of arguments appears in window 2 and the author is prompted (prompt line) to select one (figure 4b).

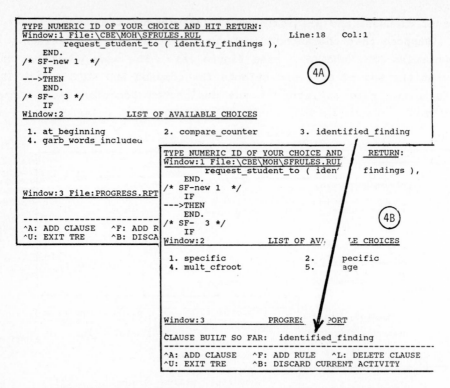

FIGURE 4. BUILDING A NEW RULE IN AN EXISTING FILE

A. The cursor is in place to add a clause below the IF and ^A (ADD CLAUSE) has been selected. All of the available conditions predicates have been loaded into window 2.

B. The user has selected predicate #3, which requires an argument. The list of arguments is loaded into window 2. The user may select one of these or add to the list. (See part 2 of figure 4 on next page.)

C. (See part 2 of figure 4 on next page.) The conditional clause has been entered into the rule (window 1). The cursor has been moved to build the action clause. A predicate has been selected from the list but it requires an argument. It is therefore stored temporarily in window 3. The list of arguments is shown in window 2.

D. These arguments are text files. When an argument is selected to append to the predicate, the file contents are displayed in window 3 so that the author can be sure that the correct text will appear when the rule fires. The author must confirm his choice (confirmation line) before the argument is appended to the predicate and added to the rule.

E. The completed rule (see box).

When the author has completed the IF part of the rule, the conditionspredicate with its argument is automatically inserted into the rule. Next, moving the cursor to THEN, he can proceed as he did above: select a predicate (actions, this time) from the choice list (see figure

4c, window 3). The selected predicate takes an argument which is a text file. The list of text files is shown in window 2. The contents of the selected file are displayed in window 3 (figure 4d) so that the author can see if this is the file that he wanted. Upon confirmation (prompt line figure 4d) the file is inserted into the clause. At any point items may be added to or deleted from the choice list. Figure 4e shows the completed new rule (see box).

FIGURE 4 (CONTINUED)

```
TYPE NUMERIC ID OF COMMENT FILE AND HIT RETURN:
Window:1 File:\CBE\MOH\SFRULES.RUL              Line:20    Col:1
/* SF-new 1  */
    IF
        identified_finding ( specific ),       (4C)
    THEN
--->END.
/* SF-  3 */
    IF
        identified_finding ( mult_cfroot ),
Window:2             LIST OF AVAILABLE CHOICES

  1. SFACK.TXT        2. SFEMPTY1.TXT    3. SFEMPTY2.TXT   4. SFEMPTY3.TXT
  5. SFGARB.TXT       6. SFINCOMP.TXT    7. SFMULTF.TXT    8. SFSTRIP.TXT


Window:3                 PROGRESS F

CLAUSE BUILT SO FAR:  comment
------------------------------
^A: ADD CLAUSE    ^F: ADD RULE
^U: EXIT TRE      ^B: DISCARD C
```

```
    IS THIS THE COMMENT FILE THAT YOU WANT?    (Y/N):
Window:1 File:\CBE\MOH\SFRULES.RUL                        L
/* SF-new 1  */
    IF
        identified_finding ( specific ),       (4D)
    THEN
--->END.
/* SF-  3 */
    IF
        identified_finding ( mult_cfroot ),
Window:2             LIST OF AVAILABLE CHOICES

  1. SFACK.TXT        2. SFEMPTY1.TXT    3. SFEMPTY2.T
  5. SFGARB.TXT       6. SFINCOMP.TXT    7. SFMULTF.TX

Window:3 File:\CBE\MOH\SFSTRIP.TXT                      I
You have included extraneous words in some of your f
displayed in red. Since they add nothing useful, the
you continue with the exercise. After you have revie
Window:4                  PROGRESS REPORT

CLAUSE BUILT SO FAR:  comment
```

```
Window:1 File:\CBE\MOH\SFRULES.RUL              Line:20    Col:1
/* SF-new 1  */
    IF
        identified_finding ( specific ),
    THEN                                       (4E)
        comment ( \CBE\MOH\SFSTRIP.TXT ),
    END.
/* SF-  3 */
    IF
        identified_finding ( mult_cfroot ),
    THEN
        comment ( SFMULT.TXT ),
        unhilite ( student_finding ),
        request_student_to ( identify_findings ),
    END.
/* SF-  4 */
    IF
        identified_finding ( partial_cfroot ),
    THEN
        comment ( SFINCOMP.TXT ),
        unhilite ( student_finding ),
------------------------------------------------------------------
^A: ADD CLAUSE    ^F: ADD RULE    ^L: DELETE CLAUSE   ^W: DELETE RULE   ^P: HELP
^U: EXIT TRE      ^B: DISCARD CURRENT ACTIVITY        ^T: MODIFY CHOICELIST
```

SUMMARY

TRAS is a program that enables programming-naive individuals to create and assemble the rules for rule based programs, using the module TRE. It translates these rules into Prolog using TPT. This facilitates the direct inclusion of teaching experts in creating rule based smart tutors.

REFERENCES

Alpert, D and Bitzer, DL (1970). "Advances in Computer-based Education"' Science 167, 1582-1590.

Haque, MM (1988). Tutoring Rule Authoring System for Intelligent Computer-Aided Instruction: Hypothetico-deductive Problem Solving in Physiology. Doctoral Dissertation, Illinois Institute of Technology, Chicago, IL, 60616.

Hirsch, JB, Hagamen, WD, Murphy, SS and Weber, JC (1978). "A tutorial System" in Deland, EC (Ed), Information Technology in Health Science Education, New York, Plenum Press, 297-318.

Michael, JA, Haque, MM, Rovick, AA, and Evens, M. The Pathophysiology Tutor:" A First Step Toward a Smart Tutor", Submitted to ICCAL, Dallas, TX, May 9-11, 1989.

Pattison, L (1985). "Software Writing Made Easy", Electronic Learning 4: 30-36.

Pogue, RE (1980). "The Authoring System: Interface between Author and Computer." J Research and Development in Education 14, 57-68.

Yob, G (1977). "PILOT", Creative Computing 3, 57-63.

"QUALITATIVE SIMULATION AND KNOWLEDGE
REPRESENTATION FOR INTELLIGENT TUTORING"

R. Hartog
Department of Computer Science, Wageningen Agricultural University
Dreyenplein 2, 6703 HB Wageningen, The Netherlands

ABSTRACT

This paper discusses the strong points as well as some consequences of
a newly emerging view on (computer assisted) learning (30). In this
view learning should be seen as acquiring mental models by students.
The models that are to be acquired should be the same models that drive
the simulations used in computer assisted learning. In order to facilitate the process of acquiring the target model intermediate models
should be implemented as well, in particular causal qualitative models.
These should be the first models to be acquired by the student. This
view forms a natural answer on criticisms with respect to the use of
computer simulation in education and at the same time enables a better
articulation of an existing paradigm for intelligent tutoring. The
important implication is that the student should acquire at least
certain qualitative causal models. A study of the literature on causality however shows that causality has been a much debated concept for
ages and that different forms of qualitative reasoning in artificial
intelligence are connected with different causality concepts. Thus the
"guess the model in the computer" view on computer assisted learning
leads to very fundamental philosophical questions, because in order to
implement a qualitative causal model we have to define very precisely
what we mean by causal reasoning. These same questions are encountered
in expert systems research where the QSIM approach (16, 17) was developed for representation of "deep models". Therefore this paper discusses those aspects of the QSIM approach that are relevant in the
context of intelligent tutoring and representation of deep models.

INTRODUCTION

This paper is about computer simulation in education, qualitative computer simulation, intelligent tutoring systems and causal reasoning. Learning should be seen as acquiring models by students. The model that is to be acquired by the student should be the same model that is the core of the system for computer assisted learning (30). This is the view that will be the backbone of this paper.

Not every model which is implemented as a computer program can easily be acquired by a student. The student must use his present knowledge in order to infer from interaction with the computer what the components of the model are and how these components interact. However there can be a large gap between the students' actual knowledge and the knowledge that is required to make the intended inferences. Metacommunication, enabling inspectability, introducing a number of intermediary models, or any combination of these can reduce the gap. This paper focusses on intermediary models, particularly on qualitative causal models.

The first chapter of this paper expresses dissatisfaction with the lack of clear learning objectives for the majority of applications of computer simulations in education. The "induce the model in the computer view" can resolve this dissatisfaction but disqualifies at the same time quantitative simulation for many educational applications. The second chapter shows that representation of domain knowledge is a central problem in intelligent tutoring and links this problem with qualitative simulation research. Chapter three shows that different concepts of causality will lead to different forms of knowledge representation. The concept of causality has been a much debated issue both in philosophy of science as well as in genetic epistemology. Research on qualitative causal models for intelligent tutoring cannot avoid this debate. The fourth chapter gives an impression of one (30) approach to qualitative causal modelling where generic component models are the primary places to store and use generic knowledge. The fifth chapter introduces a completely different approach to qualitative simulation and views QSIM (16, 17) as a knowledge representation tool partly pre-filled with generic knowledge of mathematical origin. This requires a substantial shift of attention: the focus is now on representation of knowledge about the qualitative behaviour of mathematical variables with respect to time and the chapter deals only implicitly with the way students should be able to inspect how such a model generates the qualitative behaviours. The summary highlights the important points of this paper in particular the fact that there is no generally accepted causality concept.

CHAPTER 1 QUANTITATIVE SIMULATION IN EDUCATION AND TRAINING

This chapter shows how thinking about the objectives of computer simulations in education naturally leads to research on qualitative simulation. I will present some types of computer simulations for education, in order to give the reader a feel for the relevant aspects.
All these simulations have in common that they are not meant to be used without instruction by a human instructor or without any other form of guidance such as a well-chosen series of exercises. Therefore the benefits of instruction with such computer simulations can certainly not be attributed to the computer simulation alone.

An instance of an important class of computer simulations is Steamer (9). Steamer simulates the propulsive machinery of a navy ship and is used to train operators. Conceptual similarity and inspectability are important features of Steamer. Thus the student can observe changes in behaviour of the system that would not be observable in reality. The goal of instruction with Steamer is essentially that the future operators learn a conceptual model that determines their reasoning about the functioning of the system. The philosophy behind Steamer forms a good basis for the creation of computer simulations as a tool to prepare students who are going to enter a laboratory course.

Another type of computer simulations (25) is popular in elementary science education where a number of concepts are closely connected with a visual representation. Interaction with computer simulations which visualize the behaviour of the objects (such as gas molecules) and show the student the effects of changing a value of a parameter should enable the student to discover the laws that are the core of the model which drives the animation. For some people this means that the student must build up a mental model of which the mathematical formulation is identical with the mathematical model on which the computer program was based, for others it means that the student acquires a different model, for instance a cause-effect model. Unfortunately there seems to be no empirical support for the hypothesis that the average student is able to build the intended mental model. The student still needs guidance in

the form of a textbook with series of exercises in some suggestive
order or guidance from a teacher.

A walk through the latest volumes of "Simulations and Games" shows
that the majority of publications on computer simulations are about
large mathematical models (say from 20 to 200 differential equations)
and that the computer is used to compute numerical solutions of these
models. While there exists a widespread belief that students can benefit from this type of computer simulations one can not deny that most
publications do not mention clearly defined learning objectives. Exceptions are simulations meant to be used in groups; here cooperation,
communication and group decision making are the learning objectives but
debriefing sessions guided by a teacher or other forms of guidance are
essential. In other words the actual learning effects are not attributed to the computer simulation itself. Also there is a growing interest in "wise decision making". Simulations place the students in
situations were they have to make decisions. The implicit suggestion is
that the output of a simulation run is sufficient feedback to the
student to develop a better decision making strategy. The last objective for using computer simulations of large mathematical models in
education is again acquiring models by students (32, 33). However this
objective is usually not very well articulated. Authors who describe
the purpose of interaction with a quantitative computer simulation
usually imply that the student should learn some form of reasoning
within the domain under consideration. This can be interpreted as
running mental models of systems in the domain. However I have not been
able to find an explicit description of the type of models that the
student should build. Apparently the student is not expected to build
the same mathematical model that is implemented on the computer when
this model consists of, say, 20 or even 200 differential equations. But
if the student is supposed to infer from a few runs of such a complicated model a much simpler model, it is unclear why this simpler model
is not offered to the student in a more direct way.
To recognise any regularity in the input output relations of a few
hundred runs of a large computer simulation model is virtually impossible, unless you hold most parameters and variables constant throughout
all experiments, in which case there is no reason to offer the full
complexity of the model at all. In other words: if the students are
supposed to learn model A and if computer simulation seems the best way
to reach this goal, what can be a reason to implement a much more
complicated or a completely different model B on the computer?
The conclusión should be that if there does not exist any good educa-

tional or pedagogical reason to make A and B different we should not make them different. This is the approach that is most clearly formulated in (30): ... "the central feature of the approach is that, at each stage of learning, the model driving the computer simulation should be the model that the student is to acquire."

CHAPTER 2 INTELLIGENT TUTORING

Until recently many of the following aspects were typical for intelligent tutoring systems (13, 22, 24, 29). Types of knowledge are separated into several modules. Domain knowledge, teaching knowledge, diagnostic knowledge and interaction knowledge are seen as separate types of knowledge. Some or all modules exhibit a structure which is also typical for expert systems. Therefore these modules are often called "experts" such as a domain expert, a teaching expert and so on. Hallmarks of expert systems are separation of program control and knowledge, use of heuristics, symbolic processing, and expert performance. The domain "expert" however seldom contains heuristics, is often not supposed to exhibit expert performance, and sometimes is just an quantitative simulation program. Except for the lack of expert performance the teaching, or tutor module and the diagnostic module usually have more in common with expert systems: they contain heuristics, knowledge is well separated from program control and symbolic processing is an important aspect. Lastly the computer tutor often uses a dynamic student model which enables adaptivity.

The domains of these systems are highly artificial. Popular domains for intelligent tutoring systems are: mechanics, electronics, mathematics computerlanguages, games, medical diagnosis. ("Real mechanics" and "real electronics" cannot be called artificial, but the domain expert module contains "textbook mechanics" and "textbook electronics".) Experience has shown that representation of domain knowledge proves to be very difficult for other types of domains such as meteorology (27), crop production systems (8), and certain technical knowledge (31). To some extent the problems with knowledge representation for intelligent tutoring in these domains can be traced back to different functional roles. The knowledge in an expert system has a specific functional role and is not without major changes fit for use in the domain expert of an intelligent tutoring system, even when for instance the original knowledge was 'diagnostical knowledge' and the learning objective is 'learning to make a diagnosis' (5).

Placing simulation central in intelligent computer assisted instruction, implicitly assigns a functional role to the domain expert in an intelligent tutoring system which is missing in many existing expert systems: domain experts in intellligent tutoring systems should be models that can predict how certain situations can develop. Furthermore in the literature on intelligent tutoring as well as in literature on expert systems we can distinguish a trend to attribute the lack of flexibility of knowledge represented in expert systems to the fact that expert systems usually do not contain "deep" knowledge (4, 26). This suggests that representing deep knowledge will make an expert system less dependant on a specific functional role. In particular the QSIM approach (16) is considered promising for representing deep knowledge in expert systems.

CHAPTER 3   CAUSAL REASONING

The "guess-my-model" view on CAL implies that there should exist at least one level where the reasoning steps of the student and the machine are equivalent. In fact this is the level where the student is supposed to employ some form of "causal reasoning". (Of course nobody wants the student to perform the same micro code operations that are executed by the machine.) Thus the question what type of mental models the students should acquire forces us to determine very carefully what causal reasoning is. One problem is, however, that the phrase "causal reasoning" stands for many different forms of reasoning (12, 18, 19). Therefore we should decide what type(s) of causal reasoning is/are acceptable from a scientific viewpoint. Throughout the history of philosophy of science the concept of causality always has been a much debated issue and it still is (3, 12, 28), but formal treatments of phenomena or formal explanations in science in the twentieth century usually avoid explicit reference to causes and effects.
Popper (20) defines a causal explanation as follows:
   "To give a causal explanation of an event means to deduce a statement
   which describes it, using as premises of the deduction one or more
   universal laws, together with certain singular statements, the
   initial conditions.......

> The initial conditions describe what is usually called the cause of
> the event in question......
> And the prediction describes what is usually called the effect.
> Both these terms I shall avoid."

Note that in this definition the cause (singular) is a set of conditions (plural), secondly that the effect also usually will refer to
more than one statement, and lastly that there is no reference to any
chronology.

Russell (21), however, goes further than just avoiding the terms cause
and effect: "the reason why physics has ceased to look for causes is
that, in fact, there are no such things." And Austin (1) even calls the
word causality "a source of confusion and superstition".

In fact causal reasoning is then reduced to a form of constraint satisfaction with as its most important instance the process of solving
mathematical equations. The rules that specify legal operations on
constraints normally allow for numerous paths through the problem
space. In particular constraint rewriting as well as forms of constraint propagation are legal types of constraint satisfaction. But a
particular path through problem space itself (in other words a sequence
of reasoning steps) has in Russell's and Austin's view no ontological
meaning.

The lack of asymmetry and especially the lack of temporal information
in mathematical formulations of many laws in physics causes serious
problems when students try to make connections with common sense models
of causal reasoning. For example the lack of information about temporal
causality in the mathematical formulation of Newton's third Law or
Ohm's Law is counter intuitive. Though students tend to think of action
being the cause of reaction, the equation

$$\vec{F}_{AB} = -\vec{F}_{BA}$$

does not contain such information. Every physics teacher can observe
this desire to attach asymmetric meanings - which are not supported by
mathematical logic - to mathematical equations.

While many researchers interested in qualitative reasoning are apparently dissatisfied with the shortcomings of the constraint logic
approach (11, 30) a renewed debate about causality has not made clear
yet that the lack of causal information in mathematical equations is

one of the weaknesses instead of one of the powers of mathematical formulations. Nonetheless it is now generally acknowledged that many people including many researchers have intuitive concepts about causality of which important aspects, in particular the temporal aspect, are not explicitly covered by a constraint logic view on causal reasoning. Protocols of thinking aloud experiments indeed show that children as well as novices and experts in certain domains refer explicitly to causes and effects. The question is, how we should handle this in a context of teaching and computer assisted learning.

One viewpoint is, that even if forms of cause-effect-reasoning are not scientific, tutors should not deny the fact that such forms of reasoning seem natural to students and that a teacher or computer tutor should strive to make effective use of pre-instructional forms of reasoning. This view is reflected in the following quotation (about Ohm's law) from a physics textbook (7):

> "A simple way to look at the law is to picture the potential as the 'motive power' (the British word for potential, 'tension, is suggestive), the current as the resulting effect. Doubling the potential across the circuit element causes a doubling of the amount of charge that flows through it in one second. This assignment of cause and effect, of course, is only an aid to visualization, and has no deep meaning."

Thus for Ford as well as for most teachers in science, two types of reasoning exist: first the formal method of constraint satisfaction, usually by means of constraint rewriting, second a form of thinking which I will call cause - effect - reasoning. In a way we can say that Ford teaches the students two different models. The second model is an intermediate model with references to causes and effects chosen for didactical reasons and is supposedly close to a form of reasoning that is already existent in the student (see also (6)).

De Kleer and Brown (11) go at least one step further as we can conclude from their definition of a causal account:

> "By a causal account,we mean a particular kind of explanation that is consistent with our intuitions for how devices function, i.e. causality. Device behaviour arises out of time-ordered cause effect interactions between neighbouring components of the device."

A causal account becomes a trace of how a disturbance is propagated through a constraint network that is a direkt mapping of the topology of a device. At the same time the choice of the constraint propagation algorithm is influenced by intuitions about what path of propagation is "natural". Iwasaki and Simon (10) have supported and formalized this

approach connecting it with the concept of causal ordering in sets of
equations (23). This can be regarded as an attempt to integrate two
forms of causal reasoning into a logic of scientific reasoning.
Though De Kleer and Brown do introduce a form of intuitive causality,
their way of modelling devices is still essentially a direct mapping
from descriptions of the target system (in the form of ordinary differential equations) to confluences (i.e. qualitative differential equations). We will see in the next chapter that White and Frederiksen
attribute a causal meaning directly to - for example - Ohm's Law. In
fact they do attach an asymmetric meaning to a mathematical equation.
Also the way information passes from one component to another, or the
way a change of the state of one component precipitates changes of
states in another component is regarded as precipitation of effects by
causes.

The preceding discussion shows that the choice for one specific constraint propagation algorithm (or an information passing algorithm) as
well as the choice to make this process visible to the student is based
on assumptions about the way humans generally reason. In this respect
the QSIM approach (chapter 5) is very much different. There exists no
connection between the constraint propagation algorithm that is built
into QSIM on the one hand and ideas about the way humans think on the
other hand. The constraint propagation algorithm could be changed at
any time or even replaced by a constraint rewriting algorithm for
reasons that have nothing to do with the way students reason. Although
the starting point for the development of QSIM was clearly not of
educational nature there are reasons to integrate the QSIM approach
with the view that White and Frederiksen have proposed for computer
assisted learning. The first is that QSIM models stay very close to the
formal concept of causal reasoning that has been dominant for long in
the twentieth century. The universal laws are - in the QSIM approach -
qualitative constraints on qualitative descriptions of variables, and
the initial conditions form part of the first qualitative state. Causal
reasoning consists of prediction and propagation through the constraint
network but is based on what operations can be proved to be legal and
not primarily on how people reason. Another reason is that we want
students to acquire mathematical models as well and that QSIM models
are by their nature good predecessors for these mathematical models.

CHAPTER 4 ZERO-ORDER QUALITATIVE MODELS OF ELECTRIC CIRCUITS

This chapter gives an impression of one of the types of causal qualitative models that are implemented in QUEST. QUEST (29) is viewed as a descendant of SOPHIE (2) and STEAMER (9, 29). However QUEST contains a progression of models that are to be acquired by the student. Also these models (which drive the circuit behaviour) are qualitative, not quantitative. The first models to be acquired by the student are zero-order models (i.e. models that reason only on the basis of presence or absence of resistance, voltage etc. QUEST also contains first order models reasoning on the basis of incremental changes in resistance, voltage etc.).

These zero-order qualitative models in QUEST have as basic elements instances of generic component models (like bulb, resistor, capacitor etc.). The structure of a circuit model that is build from these basic elements reflects directly the topological (physical) structure of the circuit that is modelled. Each instance of a generic component model can be in a certain state. For example a certain capacitor C-1 can be in a state CHARGED or in a state NOT-CHARGED. Each component model has a number of variables such as a variable to indicate if the component is conducting and one to indicate if the component is acting as a voltage source. The values of these two variables follow directly from the state. The model of a capacitor has a rule:

"if the capacitor is in the state CHARGED, then the capacitor is non-conductive and the capacitor is acting as a voltage source."

Also each generic component model has rules to determine the state of an instance of that model. For example the rule to determine if a bulb is in a state ON, would be something like:

"if there exists a voltage drop over the bulb then the bulb must be in the state ON."

To determine if there is a voltage drop across the bulb the bulb can call a procedure, which uses both the topological information of the circuit, and the states of the components of the circuit.
Such a procedure would look like the following rule:

"if there is a feed path from the negative terminal of a voltage source and there is a return path from the positive side of the voltage source and there is no short circuit then there is a voltage drop across the component"

A rule like the one that determines if there is a voltage drop across a component is necessary to establish which combination of states of the components of the circuit forms a valid state of the circuit as a whole.

A description of the state of a circuit is a set of descriptions of the
states of its components. A qualitative simulation starts with a description of a circuit state. A circuit state changes when the state of
one of the components changes. A change of the state of one of the
components can be precipitated by an increment of time (for instance
because a capacitor is discharging), when a state of one of the other
components changes, or by external intervention (like opening a
switch). A qualitative simulation ends with a (possibly temporary)
equilibrium.

The result of a qualitative simulation is a series of circuitstates and
intermediate circuitstates, including a causal account of all transitions
between circuitstates. During intermediate circuitstates time is frozen,
only changes propagate.

As an example this is a part of a causal account of a qualitative
simulation:

"....., suppose that someone closes switch #1. This change in the
internal conductivity of a component causes other components in the
circuit to reevaluate their states. The capacitor remains discharged
because switch #2 being open prevents it from having a good return
path. The light bulb has good feed and return paths, so its state
becomes on. Since in the course of reevaluation no component changed
its conductivity, the reevaluation process terminates..." ((30) p

19; originally the term "device" is used instead of "component").

Because one of the ways the model reasons is by reevaluating the state
of each component one by one and because more than one component can
change at the same time there can be a number of intermediate states
that form an essential part of the models' inference chain but can not
be observed in a real electrical circuit as separate states. During a
series of intermediate (not observable) states a change of state of one
component propagates through the circuit. Such propagation of changes
through the circuit and the fact that an ordinal instead of an interval
timescale form the inherent limitations of these zero order models.
These limitations can partly be resolved by introducing more sophisticated component models. In fact problems that bring limitations of a
model to the surface motivate students to learn a more sophisticated
model, i.e. to learn a next model of the model progression.

However one problem is much more fundamental. In the causality concept
which is built in QUEST cause is intrinsically coupled to time. When
more events happen at the same time it is impossible to attribute the
changes that follow to one of these events. It will be clear that this
problem cannot appear in a constraint logic approach.

In the limited context of this paper the following characteristics of
the models in QUEST are important:
- the direct mapping of the device topology and of the physical components of the device onto the model,
- the fact that generic knowledge resides primarily in generic component models,
- the fact that generic knowledge in QUEST is still domain specific,
- the clear choice for one interpretation of causality and causal
  reasoning based on information passing between components,
- the fact the design of QUEST has been fully based on didactical
  considerations.

The discussed zero order models contain only information about presence
or absence of components, voltagedifferences, currents and so on, and -
less explicit - directional information, but no information about the
direction of change of the quantities. While this is not important for
the main conclusions in this paper the reader should be aware that
QUEST also contains first order models that can handle qualitative
changes of quantities. These first order models are also essential in
the progression of qualitative causal models. But the causality concept
in these first order models is still the same as that in the zero order
models.

CHAPTER 5 THE QSIM APPROACH

In this chapter the approach to qualitative simulation that is described in (16, 17) takes a central place. In this QSIM approach a
direct mapping of the logical structure between variables onto the
model prevails over a direct mapping of the topological (physical)
structure. The QSIM approach is not developed with any didactic considerations in mind, the underlying notion of causality is better in
keeping with a notion of reasoning with mathematically formulated laws
and the models are based on proven theorems about variables that behave
as functions of time. Lastly the generic knowledge that is built into
QSIM is not domain specific and as such not comparable with the generic
knowledge in QUEST. In a way QSIM can be compared with an empty expert
system shell.

Modelling by describing a state as a finite set of state-variables has
been common practice in science for a long time, resulting usually in
mathematical models. In fact Kuipers' approach to qualitative simula-

tion stays very close to this traditional way of modelling.
The behaviour of a system is described as a sequence of states at time
points alternating with time intervals. While in mathematical models
the variable time usually is governed by the same axioms that are valid
for all real numbers Kuipers' QSIM algorithm is intrinsically based on
a treatment of time that is different from the way QSIM treats the
other variables. A qualitative state is a set of qualitative state
variables which consist of a qualitative value (qval) and a qualitative
direction-of-change (qdir). A mapping is defined between the qualitative state variable and the corresponding quantitative state variable
in such a way that critical values of a quantitative state variable are
mapped to so-called landmark values of the corresponding qualitative
state variable, and that all points in an interval between two critical
values of the quantitative state variable are mapped on one interval
description of the corresponding qualitative state variable. The mapping
preserves ordinal relationships. Zero, minus infinity (minf) and infinity (inf) are explicitly defined as landmark values. The qualitative
direction of change can be increasing (inc), steady (std), or decreasing (dec). The time axis consists of only those timepoints where one of
the state-variables reaches or leaves a landmark value (that is when
something interesting happens). For instance a ball thrown vertically
thrown upward could described as follows:

h(height)		v(velocity)		a(acceleration)	
qval	qdir	qval	qdir	qval	qdir
(0,inf)	inc	(v-start,0)	dec	-g	std

(0, v-start, -g are landmarkvalues for h, v, a respectively)

A complete state description like this will from now on be called a
state. On the next page we show the output of a qualitative simulation
run of QSIM for the same example of the ball.
QSIM generates the displayed qualitative behaviour without using any
numerical information. A quantitative computer simulation program would
need certain quantitative inputs in order to start a simulation run but
QSIM uses only non-numerical operations and just needs the information
that the ball is thrown upward. Note also that, in order to obtain a
description of the qualitative behaviour of the ball from the output of
a quantitative computer simulation, this output still has to be interpreted by the student. But the output of QSIM is in fact a direct
qualitative description (though not a verbal description yet).

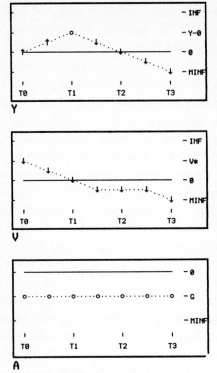

Y

V

A

Verbal transcription.
The ball starts at height zero, where it is going upwards with a positive but decreasing velocity. All the time the acceleration is negative and steady After some time - at time point Tl - the height reaches its maximum value. Note that this is <u>the discovery of a landmark which was not build into the model.</u>

At Tl the height is steady for one moment and the velocity is zero. The velocity is at this time point still decreasing. After having reached its maximum height the height is somewhere between maximum and zero and the velocity is now negative and still decreasing. After some time at a time point called T2 the height becomes zero but is still decreasing, the velocity is negative at this time point and also still decreasing. After this time point height and velocity stay negative and keep on decreasing.

DIAGRAM 5.1
Output generated by Kuipers' QSIM.

Qualitative simulation as described above produces a <u>tree of behaviours</u> given a certain state. In the example a starting state is given and the simulation produces a tree of only 1 behaviour i.e. at any time point or time interval only 1 state is possible according to the model. The model can be regarded as an operator that produces all states which can possibly be successors of a given state. In the example the number of possible successors (the branching factor) was 1 at every time point or time interval. This branching factor can only be 1 if the model contains enough knowledge. In fact it happens very often that the branching factor is larger than 1 leading to multiple behaviours. We will now see how different types of knowledge enable the qualitative simulation program to limit the number of behaviours that is produced.
The all pervading influence of a number of basic choices such as the asymmetry between time and any other variable and secondly the mapping of an infinite number of values in an interval between landmark values to one interval description and thirdly the mapping of an infinite number of values in a time interval to one interval description is

already taken for granted in the remainder of this chapter. Because we
are interested in representation of "deep" knowledge the distinction
between more generic knowledge and more domainspecific knowledge is the
most important. An instance of generic knowledge is, that for a variable only certain transitions from one qualitative value to another
qualitative value are possible. These transitions are given in a table
of P-transitions (from a time point to a time interval) and I-transitions
(from a time interval to a time point). The general knowledge about the
behaviour of reasonably behaving functions of time which is "hiding" in
the tables of P- and I-transitions reduces the upper limit of the
number of possible transitions from any qualitative value to only 4. As
a result the number of state transitions (i.e. the branching factor)
for the ball is limited to 64 by this non-domainspecific knowledge.
Other generic knowledge constrains further the number of possible
transitions. An example of a rule that expresses such knowledge is:
" IF   B is the time derivative of A   AND   A is increasing
    THEN   qval of B must be positive   "
This knowledge is valid for real numbers and for many more sets of
elements as well. Because quantities in many domains can be expressed
in real numbers rules like the rule above can be considered fairly
generic.
An example of more domain specific knowledge is:
"The velocity of a ball is the time derivative of the ball's height"
This example suggests that a special and interesting type of generic
knowledge is mathematically derivable knowledge about qualitative behaviour of variables.
When creating a certain model which generates all possible qualitative
behaviours given a qualitative state it makes sense to keep the generic
knowledge and the domain specific knowledge separated as strictly as
possible. In the first place this separation should enable us to reuse
the code with generic knowledge and secondly it forms the basis for a
qualitative modelling methodology. Exactly this is what has been done
in QSIM. Generic knowledge such as the knowledge expressed in some of
the rules above is built in QSIMconstraints. In the case of the ball
thrown upwards the number of possible next states is greatly reduced
because the user enters the domainspecific knowledge that the velocity
is the time derivative of the height and the acceleration is the time
derivative of the velocity. Qsim applies its generic knowledge about
time derivatives on the domainspecific knowledge that is entered in the
form of a constraint network and as a result the branching factor is
reduced from 64 to 1.

Just like QSIM expert system shells all contain some generic knowledge. For instance the fact that forward chaining is a valid inferencing mechanism forms in combination with an operational definition of
forward chaining together, generic knowledge. To put it differently:
the fact that one can build a separate inference engine means that
inference knowledge is generic. Major differences between QSIM and
empty expert system shells are that advancing time is rigidly build
into the QSIM algorithm and that QSIM contains generally applicable
mathematical knowledge but that QSIM does not contain general inferencing knowledge.
It would be ideal if an empty expert system shell could be prefilled
with the knowledge in QSIM in such a manner that QSIM models as well as
other domain specific knowledge could be added incrementally.
At this stage of qualitative simulation research however usually a
program for qualitative simulation is created in - for instance Lisp -
which contains the non domain specific knowledge and allows entering
only one type of domain specific knowledge in a very specific and
predefined way namely a constraint network. An example is shown below.

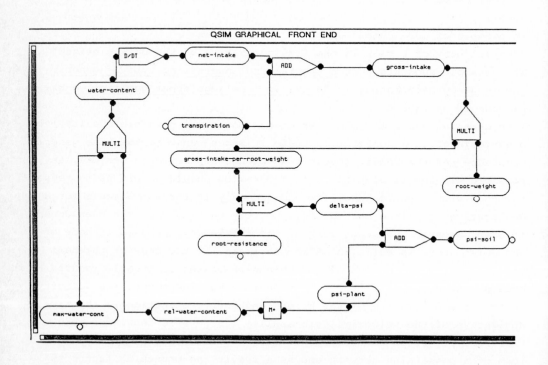

DIAGRAM 5.2

"water content"

A major problem is still the fact that QSIM often produces many
behaviours which cannot be derived from solutions of the corresponding
mathematical models (This is for instance the case for the model in
diagram 5.2). Much research is presently directed to solve this problem. The question is if there is still more generic mathematical knowledge that is not yet captured by QSIM, or if some of the knowledge in
QSIM is not optimally used or - lastly - if we must accept that qualitative mathematical knowledge is not enough for reducing the branching
factor to 1 at every node in the tree of behaviours. In the latter case
we want to be able to add incrementally other forms of knowledge, i.e.
we do not want to be limited to a constraint satisfaction network as
the sole form of knowledge representation. (remember though that this
is almost the same form of knowledge representation that is most widely
adopted by the scientific community during the last ages).
In QSIM an approach of separating generic knowledge like inference
knowledge and general mathematical knowledge from domain specific knowledge is easily recognizable. The generic knowledge in QUEST on the
other hand is still mostly domain specific, i.e. much less general than
the qualitative mathematical knowledge in QSIM. In QUEST the generic
knowledge is built in generic component models that work together with
knowledge of Kirchoffs' laws in such a way that it forces a type of
"topological" thinking on the user that is not applicable in many other
domains like meteorology, plant fysiology etc. This statement is not
only valid for the zero order models but also for the first order
models in QUEST. The fact that the topology of a QSIM model is not
necessarily based on the physical structure of the modelled system also
enables QSIM to handle more abstract models.
Finally the reader should be aware that, whenever there has been made a
comparison between QSIM and QUEST this comparison focusses on the
built-in concept of causality, the ways generic knowledge are captured,
the types of generic knowledge that are captured and the possibilities
of both approaches to enable representation of deep models. In particular QSIM was not developed in an educational context and QSIM is not
an intelligent tutoring environment like QUEST.

SUMMARY

An important thing to realize when we are talking about subjects like
intelligent tutoring, qualitative reasoning and qualitative simulation,

is, that we are talking about research and not about developing systems
that will soon be operational in many educational institutes. John Self
writes in the preface in (22):
"On the whole, it is <u>not</u> the prospect of improving educational efficiency - it is the prospect that ICAI will be an area where they (that
is the workers in the AI and Education field/RH) may refine their ideas
about important issues which interest them regardless of ICAI."
Only for a few domains ITS will soon be operational at a large scale.
To my knowledge there exists presently only one ITS that is used by a
substantial number of students and this is CHEM TUTOR which is operational at the University of Rhode Island.
For domains where qualitative reasoning about continuously varying
quantities takes an important place I foresee a future for a constraint
logic approach such as the QSIM approach. However we have no satisfactory solutions yet for the problem that the branching factors in too
many QSIM models are far too large.

The "induce the model in the computer" view on instruction (30) was
taken as the backbone of this paper because it expresses so clear what
has to be done in order to create an intelligent tutoring system: We
must implement exactly those models that we want to be acquired by the
student. This view guides the building of intelligent tutoring systems
and focusses attention on the central problem i.e. knowledge representation and reasoning. At the same time it disqualifies most types of
quantitative simulations for educational purposes.
If our goal is that students should learn to reason, then we need
generally accepted rules for correct reasoning. Such rules can be
formulated for constraint based logics. In the QSIM package for qualitative simulation of Benjamin Kuipers a number of these rules are
captured in an inference engine. For cause effect reasoning no set
exists of rules that are generally accepted and are sufficiently generic. But apparently many researchers in intelligent tutoring feel that
there must be generic knowledge about causes and effects which knowledge we must try to capture in an inference engine or - quite differently - in generic component models like in QUEST.

There is much confidence in the correctness of the knowledge in QSIM
and the connected constraint logic view on reasoning has in fact been
dominant in science for many decades in the twentieth century. At the
same time it is clear that the generic knowledge in QSIM is too often
not powerfull enough to reduce the branching factor in the resulting
tree of behaviours sufficiently. Also most of us are intuitively not

satisfied by the constraint logic view on causality on which QSIM is
based.
There is much less confidence in the scientific value of the knowledge about causes and effects that is captured in most other qualitative reasoning systems. On the other hand, causal explanations produced
by these systems are generally considered much more natural.

The most important thing is to realize that intelligent tutoring
research and knowledge representation research have stumbled upon a
fundamental question which has been a recurrent problem since ancient
history: Should we try to capture the many different intuitive aspects
of causality in some sort of inference engine (or logic), and if so
HOW, or should we banish these intuitive concepts? The trend seems to
be in favour of research in the direction of the former.
As said before, the fact that QSIM models are in better accordance with
the dominant view on scientific reasoning is in itself enough reason to
consider QSIM models in the context of qualitative reasoning in education. The scientific community would not have avoided all reference to
causes and effects for many decades if there were no good reasons. In
the first place we are not able to define cause effect reasoning in
such a way that all usual aspects of intuitive causality are covered.
Secondly cause effect reasoning is essentially asymmetric, while mathematical equations themselves as well as most operations on mathematical
equations or sets of equations are symmetric. In general we have not
yet succeeded in grasping causality in such a way that it conforms to
our intuition and at the same time is consistent with the existing and
scientifically accepted mathematical logic. (See (10) for an approach
that is at least applicable in certain classes of problems.)

Qualitative simulation research is in fact deep model research and
as such important in expert systems research as well as in intelligent
tutoring research. I do not expect that research in qualitative simulation will soon solve the knowledge representation problems for many
domains. But research in qualitative simulation wil surely offer us an
opportunity to refine our ideas about what forms of reasoning we should
teach our students as well as our ideas about what we should expect of
expert systems based on deep models. Maybe this research will even
provide us in the end with a generally accepted definition of causality.

REFERENCES

1. L. Austin, 1961. A Plea for Excuses. In Philosphical Papers Oxford 1961 on page 150.
2. J.S. Brown, R.R. Burton & J. De Kleer 1982 Pedagogical, natural language and knowledge engineering techniques in SOPHIE I, II and III. In Sleeman & Brown (eds.). Intelligent tutoring systems New York: Academic Press.
3. M. Bunge, 1959. Causality, the place of the causal principle in modern science Cambridge Mass.
4. B. Chandreshakaran, and S. Mittal, 1984. Deep versus compiled knowledge approaches to diagnostic problem-solving in M.J. Coombs (ed.) Developments in Expert Systems Academic Press.
5. W.J. Clancey, 1986. From Guidon to Neomycin and Heracles in twenty short lessons. Report 86-11 Stanford Knowledge Systems Laboratory.
6. A. DiSessa, 1983. Phenomenology and evolution of intuition. In D. Gentner, & A. Stevens, 1983. Mental Models. Hillsdale, New Jersey.
7. K.W. Ford, 1968. Basic physics, Waltham Mass.: Blaisdell Publ. Co.
8. R.J.M. Hartog, 1988. Representing knowledge of crop production for ICAI purposes. Int. Rep. Dept. of Comp. Sc. Agricultural University, Wageningen, The Netherlands.
9. J. Hollan, E. Hutchins, L. Weitzman, 1984. Steamer an interactive inspectable simulation based training system. The AI Magazine Summer 1984.
10. Y. Iwasaki & H.A. Simon, 1986. Causality in device behaviour Artificial Intelligence 29 pp. 3-32.
11. J. De Kleer & J.S. Brown, 1985. A Qualitative physics based on confluences. In D.G. Bobrow (ed.) Qualitative reasoning in physical systems Cambridge Mass. 1985.
12. D. Lerner (ed.), 1965. Cause and effect The Free Press New York.
13. G. Kearsley (ed.), 1988. Artificial intelligence and instruction, applications and methods. Reading Mass.
14. T.S. Kuhn, 1962. The structure of scientific revolutions. sec. ed. Chicago 1962.
15. T.S. Kuhn, 1959. The essential tension: tradition and innovation in scientific research. In: T.S. Kuhn, The essential tension selected studies in scientific tradition and change. Chicago 1977, pp. 225-239.
16. B. Kuipers, 1986. Qualitative simulation. Artificial Intelligence 29 (1986) 289-338.
17. B. Kuipers, 1987. Qualitative simulation as causal explanation. IEEE Transactions on Systems, Man, And Cybernetics, Vol. SMC-17, no. 3 May/June 1987.
18. J. Piaget, 1927. La causalite physique chez l'enfant Parijs 1927.
19. J. Piaget, 1977. (with the collaboration of R. Garcia) Understanding Causality. Norton & Comp. New York 1977.
20. K. Popper, The logic of scientific discovery London, 1959 (quotations from second edition 1967).
21. B. Russell, 1953. On the notion of cause. In Mysticism and Logic on page 171 Pelican Books 1953.
22. J. Self, 1988. Artificial intelligence and human learning. London.
23 H.A. Simon, 1953. Causal ordering and identifiability in D. Lerner, (ed.) 1965 Cause and Effect The Free Press New York.
24. D. Sleeman & J.S. Brown (eds.), 1982. Intelligent tutoring systems. Academic Press London.
25. R.B. Smith, 1986. The Alternate Reality Kit; An animated environment for creating interactive simulations. Proc. of the 1986 IEEE Computer Society Workshop on Visual Languages Dallas Texas pp. 99-106.

26. L. Steels & W. van der Velde, 1986. Learning in second generation expert systems. In J.S. Kowalik, (ed.) Knowledge Based Problem Solving, pp. 270 295 Prentice Hall 1986.
27. A. Stevens, A. Collins, S. Goldin, 1982. Misconceptions in students' understanding. In Sleeman & Brown (eds.). Intelligent Tutoring Systems. London. pp. 13-24.
28. W.A. Wallace, 1972. Causality and scientific explanation Vol I and II University of Michigan.
29. E. Wenger, 1987. Artificial intelligence and tutoring systems. Morgan Kaufman publ. Los Altos.
30. B.Y. White & J.R. Frederiksen, 1987. Causal model progressions as a foundation for intelligent learning environments. BBN report nr 6686 To appear in Artificial Intelligence.
31. B.P. Woolf, 1988. Representing complex knowledge in an intelligent machine tutor. In: J. Self, (ed.) Artificial Intelligence and Human learning. London.
32. W. Zernik, 1987. Economic theory and management games. Simulation & Games 18 360-384.
33. W. Zernik, 1988. Economic theory and management games II. Simulation & Games 19 59-81.

A Proposal for an Authoring System Avoiding Common Errors in Tutorial Lessons

Friedrich Huber

Institutes for Information Processing Graz
(Grundlagen der Informationsverarbeitung und Computergestützte neue Medien)
Graz University of Technology and the Austrian Computer Society, Schießstattgasse 4a,
A-8010 Graz (e-mail: fhuber@tugiig.uucp)

Abstract

Courseware development systems enable non-programmers to write lessons on almost any subject. Based on a large courseware project, we classify common errors usually made by novice authors. We also propose a solution where most of the errors are recognized by the courseware development system at definition time.

1   Introduction

This paper deals with aspects of quality control of courseware. The results presented are based on lessons created for the HyperCOSTOC project [Maurer86a] (the project was called COSTOC in the beginning, so many of the references just mention "COSTOC" in their titles.) The aim of the HyperCOSTOC project which has about 350 lessons already available, is to create tutorial lessons about computer science. As has been discussed in several places, (e.g. in [Maurer85]) successful computer assisted instruction is based on several premises like:

- Powerful student terminal: CAI can only be successful if high-resolution, bit-mapped color workstations are available at a moderate price. In many cases it is also extremely useful to have workstations that can be networked. With the advent of relatively cheap high-powered workstations like Apollo or Sun the situation for CAI has improved dramatically in the last years.

- Data base of lessons: It has been proved that CAI is a pedagogical success in many cases. To make it an economical success, courseware must be available as a mass product: it must be simpler to obtain good courseware than to create it (no one would write a new book to have a supplementary text for a class, but rather one just looks for the appropriate book). The time needed for creating courseware must not be underestimated. Even when using interactive courseware development tools one still needs about 30 to 100 hours to create a lesson which takes about one single hour to work through. This effort only pays off when lessons are not created for a single class but rather for many classes (or universities) as in the case of HyperCOSTOC.

- Quality: As with all products the success depends largely on the quality of the product. Courseware often is of inferior quality, as findings have shown ([Ridgeway87]). Within HyperCOSTOC, all lessons are written by experts in their field (mostly university professors), and so the lesson content is of good quality.

In this paper we consider the last aspect, quality. We are talking in this context about quality of presentation, not content. The computer medium like any other medium – blackboard, transparencies, video etc. – demands that specific rules are obeyed. Unfortunately even experienced teachers are in most cases novices as far as creation of courseware is concerned. Additionally, existing courseware development systems lack sufficient support of the author [Merrill85].

Therefore we investigate how the quality of lessons can be controlled not after but during lesson-creation. Many of the rules for good courseware can easily be checked – nevertheless they are neglected by authors again and again, making quality control of lessons a tedious task. Furthermore, re-editing of the courseware is necessary. (For a overview and evaluation of different approaches to classify courseware see [Marshall84].)

The importance of a sensible support for the author is undisputed. One of the most promising ideas is to use methods from artificial intelligence, but almost all effort in this area is applied to the student's side of CAI. As many examples of prototypes have shown (e.g. [Bonar87], [Harris86], and [Hartog87]), one of the weaknesses is that solutions are completely tailored to a specific subject area. As soon as one wants to move to a new area, a new model has to be developed. Only a few papers deal with applications of artificial intelligence for authors, e.g. [Bonar87], [Dear87], [Merrill87], and [Roberts87].

The rest of the paper is structured as follows: in Chapter 2 results and experiences of the HyperCOSTOC project are summarized, Chapter 3 deals with some possible solutions for automated quality control of lessons, and a summary and references conclude the paper.

2 What does a "good" lesson look like ?

In this chapter we first describe the features of the courseware development system[1] that formed the basis of all courseware which we have analyzed. We then summarize what lessons were expected to look like. Of course the features that make up a "good" lesson are highly subjective, but some of the rules can even be found in other courseware projects. The last subchapter lists the most common rules that were neglected.

2.1 Features of the courseware development system

The courseware development system used within HyperCOSTOC is called Hyper-TRAIN and is based on a similar system developed by our Institute [Garratt87]. It allows programming-free creation of tutorial material like text, graphics (lines, arcs, circles, rectangles, polygons, sectors, ...), question/answer dialogs and animation. Text and graphics can be displayed in up to 16 colors in different resolutions. It is an WYSIWYG-type editor with mouse interface and pop-up menus.

---

[1]Since the term "editor" has ambiguous meaning in the context of this paper, we use "courseware development system" for the SW-tool that is used for creating courseware, and "editorial staff" for a group of people who are the publishers of that courseware

The courseware development system heavily relies on the mouse: except for text and model answers, the author just clicks on icons or buttons inside menus.

In the terminology of AUTOOL2 the basic entities of the courseware development system are called *objects*. A set of objects forms a *frame*. A frame is in most cases just the information contained on a single screen; using key pauses and (partial) erasure, a frame can contain more information than can be written on a single screen. The frames of a *lesson* are linked to each other by the author and are presented to the student in the same order. This linkage may be static or dynamic, e.g. depending on the evaluation of answers. The student may jump directly to the beginning of any frame, but normally students work through lessons in the recommended order, especially when working through a lesson for the first time.

The recommended structure of a HyperCOSTOC lesson is shown in Figure 1. Lessons start with a welcome frame. After an optional short introduction, the student is shown a table of contents from where the different chapters (about 5 to 8) can be reached. A chapter itself consists of about 7 frames and may be followed by questions related to the material in the chapter. The authors have to supply at the end of each chapter and each question block choices on where to continue; all end-of-chapter menus within a *course*, which normally comprises 10 lessons, have to be organized in the same way.

A branch like at the end of a chapter or the main table of contents is made up of two components: a list of all possible choices and an index object. The list is plain text, the index object is defined by the number of choices and references to corresponding frames. During execution the student has to enter or click on a valid number. Figure 2 shows a typical branch situation.

2.2 Necessity of rules

As a novice, one easily makes mistakes even when creating transparencies, such as writing to much text on a single sheet, or writing in small letters that are unreadable. It is obvious that when using the computer for creating courseware one can make even more mistakes. The computer as medium has strong advantages

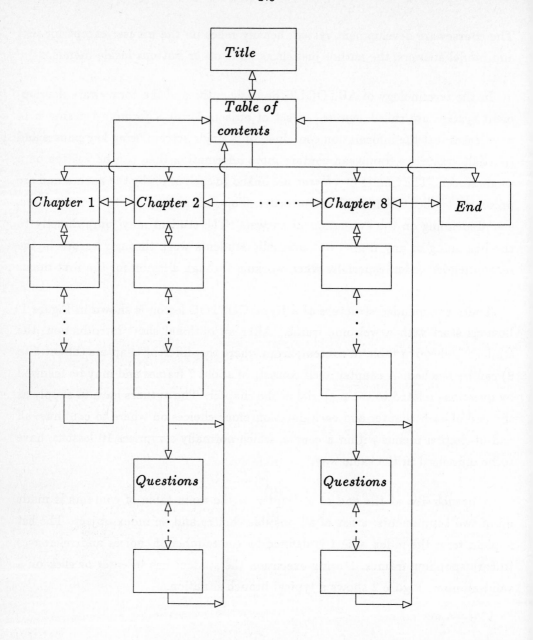

Figure 1: Structure of a HyperCOSTOC lesson

over books or lectures (like animated color graphic, self paced progress etc.), but
on the other hand, it also has many pitfalls.

---

1 ... *Continue with next chapter*

2 ... *Questions to this chapter*

3 ... *Repeat chapter*

4 ... *Go to table of contents*

PLEASE ENTER A NUMBER BETWEEN 1 AND 4

Figure 2: A typical branch menu

The courseware development system used for HyperCOSTOC lessons does not put any constraints on authors, i.e., they can design lessons completely the way they want to. Nevertheless experience has quickly proven that authors should obey certain rules for lesson creation. They have been summarized in a manual that was made available to each author [Kaiser86]. A small part of the rules is mentioned below.

The rules result from the analysis of the most common errors after many lessons have been created. Most authors create courseware for the first time. Based on the feedback of the students who use their lessons, almost all authors end up with a similar set of criteria of what constitutes a good lesson. The rules are also intended to reduce the time spent in the initial learning phase.

The rules are of particular importance in HyperCOSTOC. If hundreds of lessons are created from different authors and used at different universities [COSTOC], then a certain amount of coherence is of utmost importance. As soon as students have worked through some lessons, they should know the typical form of the rest of the lessons, thus improving the acceptance of the system. Therefore, the structure of lessons, menus and other things like appropriate use of colors are described by the rules mentioned.

A major point of interest in HyperCOSTOC is, of course, the creation of high-quality courseware. To this end all lessons are carefully checked by editorial staff, a list of errors is sent back to the author and only revised lessons are published. Since all authors are expected to write professional impeccable lessons, this quality control does not put emphasis on the content of lessons but rather on stylistic aspects. This control creates much work: the editorial staff has to work through all lessons of an author (normally 10 lessons) and afterwards all errors found have to be corrected.

If it were possible to reduce the amount of work spent on control and correction, the productivity of lesson creation could be improved. As reality has shown, only 5% of about 300 lessons conformed to the rules ([Huber87a], [Huber87b]), although all authors were given the rules in a manual. Therefore it would be optimal if neglectance of rules could be recognized immediately by the courseware development system. This would be analoguous to the paradigma that is also recommended for e.g. software development, where one goal is to find design errors in early stages of the development cycle. Another positive side effect would be that authors probably learn rules quicker if they are given immediate feedback right after violating a rule.

2.3   A classification of errors

In this sub-chapter we classify the most common errors made in lessons. This classification is of course only true for HyperCOSTOC lessons and cannot be applied to other courseware, even if determining quantitative measures for courseware quality has been dealt with in some work ([Al-Jaberi84], [Marshall84]). The classification is based on the units an author deals with: lessons, frames and objects.

- Errors on lesson level

  (1) Wrong branches.
      The most annoying effect is that frames can not be reached or exited using normal browsing operations during execution. This error is very common with novice authors who try to force students to answer a question correctly and give them no chance of leaving the frame.

  (2) Wrong lesson structure.
      Some lessons are either not divided into chapters, or chapters have

subchapters. Lessons with this error demand too much attention to just find one's way through them.

(3) Inconsistent naming of chapters in table of contents, menus and chapter headings.

The first frame of a new chapter should repeat the name of the chapter in the header line to give an indication of the place in the lesson. If names differ, one often assumes to have taken a wrong branch, and goes back for a retry, only to discover that just names don't match.

(4) Inconsistent layout of specific frames.

The first and the last frame of a lesson have to conform to certain rules. Authors are also asked to create consistent end-of-chapter frames with uniform menus. Otherwise students are forced to read all entries very carefully where a standard choice could be possible (e.g. "1" for just continuing execution in the standard way through the lesson).

(5) Lesson too big.

The size of lessons is restricted for two reasons: lessons are also distributed over slow networks, like the Austrian videotex system with rather small memory available for execution([Maurer86b]). Furthermore it should be possible to work through a complete lesson in one session.

(6) Too many or too few chapters.

This can be an indication of a bad classification of the subject area and may inhibit finding specific topics within a lesson.

(7) Inconsistent layout of chapters.

Authors are asked to stick to the same background color within chapters and to use a header line (at least for the first frame of each chapter) indicating the name of the chapter. In this way a change of background color also indicates a slightly different topic.

- Errors on frame level

(8) Wrong sequence of objects.

In some cases authors forget to insert pauses before parts of the frame are erased, and consequently students cannot study the material. In other cases text and graphic are not synchronized properly.

(9) Too many or too few colors, bad color combinations.

Authors can choose between 16 foreground colors and 8 background colors. Especially with text, color can be extremely helpful in highlighting certain keywords or establishing a logical connection between the word and a specific concept. On the other hand, too many colors are distracting. Some combinations of foreground and background colors are hard to read and irritate the eye.

(10) "Book-style" frame.

Many authors do not see the power of dynamic screen changes and create lessons that looked more or less like an electronic book.

(11) Too much text on a frame.

Too much text on a frame may turn the computer into an electronic page turner. Language in lessons should be short and concise.

(12) Wrong background colors.

Frames containing questions should have a red background.

(13) Badly arranged frame.

The layout of the frame should be clear, e.g. different areas for text and graphic.

(14) Wrong size of a frame.

The size of a frame should not be too big since frames are the smallest units within a lesson that can be reached directly.

- Errors on object level

(15) Errors in text.

Normally text makes up at least half of the information kept in a frame (see e.g. [Sherwood86]). In many cases, several persons assist the author in editing lessons, i.e. they "implement" a script written by the author. As a result of this, typing of certain words varies slightly from lesson to lesson ("heap-sort", "heapsort", ...). Typing errors are also common.

(16) Timed pauses instead of key pauses.

Many authors use timed pauses where key pauses would have been better.

(17) Errors in graphics.

Very often the graphics are logically incorrect or do not conform to the explanation given in text; when drawing a tree, authors e.g. forget some connections between nodes in the tree, or elements of the tree are labeled differently in the graphic representation and in the explanation found in the text.

(18) Unnecessary definition points of graphic objects.

Some graphic objects (like polygons or polylines) look quite the same if additional definition points are defined near each other. Since they only cost memory space and make re-editing more complicated they should be eliminated.

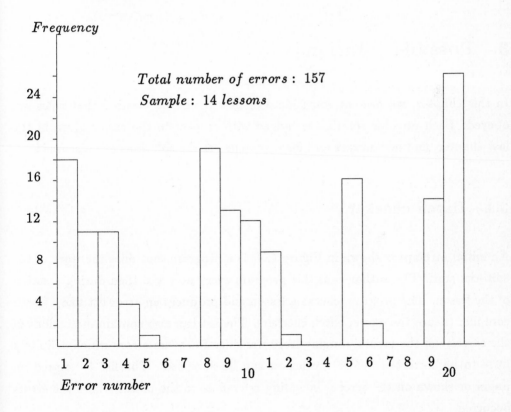

Figure 3: Frequency of errors in lessons. Error numbers correspond to the numbers in the text, except for 19: wrong wording, and 20: other errors.

The above error list is not exhaustive, but contains the most common errors which cover about 75 percent of all errors in a lesson. If all of these errors could have been avoided, the work needed for revision could have been reduced to about 25 percent. Figure 3 shows the number of errors for 14 lessons that were arbitrarily picked from the HyperCOSTOC database. To obtain these numbers, letters listing errors as sent from the editorial staff to the authors were used. Some of the errors that are mentioned above did not occur in the picked lessons. This is partially due to the fact that they can not be recognized by just working through the lesson (e.g. error 18). Other errors cannot be found in Figure 3 because authors first had to deliver two lessons which were used to set a certain standard and only then started to work on the remaining lessons. Information exchanged was only available for the second "round", consequently some errors were no longer made. Another class of errors was style of text and imprecise or even wrong wording.

3 Possible solutions

In this chapter, we present some ideas of how it can be assured that rules are obeyed. Each possible solution is judged with respect to the errors given in the last chapter, and advantages and disadvantages of the solutions are discussed.

3.1 Batch checker

An initial attempt is shown in Figure 4. It is a program that does the work of the editorial staff. The author runs this program every now and then during creation of the lesson. The program checks a lesson and produces an error list like a batch compiler (hence the name, batch checker). The list can also contain indications of the severity of the errors, ranging from warnings to severe errors which definitely have to be corrected before the lesson can be accepted. The list is printed on paper or shown on the screen, including references to the places where the errors occurred.

Even a rather simple program could detect almost all errors from the above list of errors, except for errors 3 (inconsistent naming of chapters in table of contents, menus and chapter headings), 4 (inconsistent layout of specific frames), 15 (errors in text) and 17 (errors in graphics).

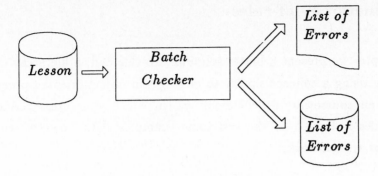

Figure 4: Structure of a batch checker

The advantage of a batch checker is its easy implementation. Disadvantages are that not all errors are detected and that errors are found only after they have been made. Authors will still produce errors; an ideal solution would be to keep them from making errors. Another disadvantage is that the batch checker has to be changed if the rules for "good" lessons change, like e.g. a new structure of lessons, different sizes of frames and so forth.

3.2   On-line checker

A solution that is not as easy to implement as the last one might be to incorporate the checker into the courseware development system. Some routines would check a lesson as soon as the author starts to modify it, and a list of errors would be created. As soon as a new object has been defined, the courseware development system would see how this definition affects the current status of the lesson. If the status of the lesson worsens, the author will be warned. Upon exiting the courseware development system, the author will be shown the current list of errors.

This on-line checker can find the same errors as the batch solution. The advantages and disadvantages of both solutions are the same with the exception that an author is given an immediate hint on errors. There is no delay as in the first case, and authors probably will learn faster.

3.3 A hierarchy of rules

In this chapter we present a better solution. To this end, a hierarchy of rules is introduced. Using a concept similar to messages in object-oriented programming languages, an courseware development system which guarantees verification of different rules is built. At the end some examples show how this courseware development system works.

3.3.1 The hierarchy of the courseware development system

One goal of an ideal courseware development system would be to avoid the disadvantages of the first two solutions. The courseware development system should detect errors as soon as they are made, and it should be possible to change the set of rules for different authors.

This adaption of rules is an extension of the mechanism for customizing an courseware development system, as explained in more detail in [Huber88]. We do not repeat here the basic facts of this work but refer the reader to the paper mentioned.

A lesson consists of different building blocks which are called classes: objects form the lowest class, followed by frames and lessons. As has been discussed in Chapter 2, errors can be associated with these three classes in a natural way. All rules that have to be checked can be defined for one of these classes depending on what classes they apply to.

The hierarchy formed by objects, frames and lessons is not complete yet: a class called "block" lying between frames and lessons is introduced. A block contains all frames which belong logically together like frames of a chapter, frames of a series of questions etc. All frames of a block form a linear list which can only be accessed in sequential manner. At the end of a block there is usually an index frame. The definition of the block includes a description of the structure of this index frame. This structure can e.g. prescribe that the first choice of the index has to lead to the next block, the second one to the beginning of the current block and the third one to the main table of contents.

Since the structure of a lesson is of great importance, we will focus on this aspect. The most common lesson structure has already been dealt with, and two others are explained now. The first one consists of three blocks: a pre-test, a tutorial part and a post-test. At the end of the pre-test students can decide whether they really want to go through the lesson or do some other work first. At the end of the tutorial block they can again decide upon repeating the lesson, leaving it or taking the final exam. The second lesson structure consists of several sequential blocks. Each block explains an important concept. If the students need more explanations, they can work through an additional block. After the additional block, they continue in the main stream of blocks. Both structures are shown in Figure 5.

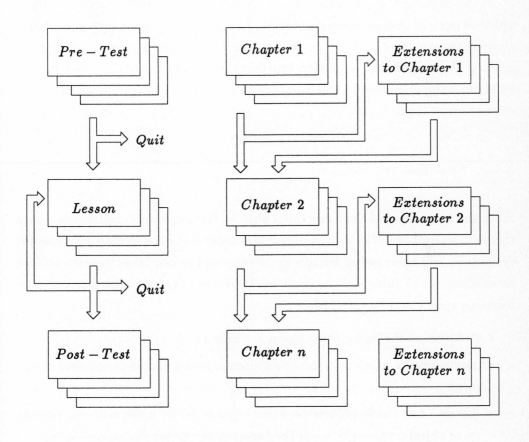

Figure 5: Two other lesson structures

During customization of the courseware development system, these structures are defined as choices for the layout of a lesson. When working with the courseware development system, authors have to specify what block they want to edit. If the block is empty, the author can immediately start to define a frame; otherwise, the author has to indicate where the new frame should be inserted into the sequence of frames. If the frame is inserted at the beginning of a block, all references of other blocks to the beginning of this block are corrected. If the frame is inserted in the middle of the block, only the references of the predecessor and the successor are adjusted. If the frame is appended at the end, references from the former end frame are copied to the new frame. This ensures that the structure of a lesson is always correct, even if only part of a lesson has been defined.

When defining the end frame of a block, the author is also forced to define a index object and the corresponding menu. The author can have a look at a sample showing the structure of the index object. The position and aesthetic design of the menu is the author's responsibility, but branches are set under all circumstances as in the sample menu. In this way, coherent menus are ensured throughout a certain lesson type.

3.3.2 Specification of rules

Since the four stages of the hierarchy – objects, frames, blocks, and lessons – are the units an author works with, it also makes sense if the courseware development system can edit these units. By specifying rules on the four levels one can achieve an effective set of rules with minimal work. For the topmost class "lesson", the following rules could be specified:

- structure of the lesson (how blocks are linked)
- maximum size of lesson (storage requirements and maximum number of frames)
- the set of available objects (in some cases it might make sense to exclude some objects, especially when they are not be used in the subject area)

In a similar way one specifies rules for lower levels: for "block" one might specify the maximum number of frames per block or the background color of all frames within a block. The "frame" class will contain rules about the size of a frame, maximum number of different colors and so on. To reduce the work, a mechanism similar to inheritance in object oriented languages is assumed: a rule on a higher level applies to all lower levels unless it is overriden by a specific rule. As an example, think of the set of objects available. This is normally specified on the lesson level, but may be overriden on the block level to exclude questions in a tutorial block or to enforce questions in a question/answer block.

Rules are set up during customization and stored under the name of a lesson type; when working with the courseware development system later, authors have to choose the type of lesson they want to edit; all corresponding rules are activated.

Rules are also used for initializing new variables of a certain class. This can be used to set the background of a frame to a prescribed color or to automatically define fixed texts like the header line.

3.3.3 Sending of messages

Rules are checked during the definition and editing of lessons. First of all, the rules on the specific level the author is working on are checked. Thus, if an object is defined, all rules on the object level are checked (e.g.: Does the object have unnecessary definition points? Is a word spelled incorrectly?). In the same manner, rules on other levels are checked (deletion of a frame, moving a block, etc.).

Additionally, a message may be sent to the next higher level in the hierarchy. This message is handled as in object-oriented programming languages: first the receiver checks whether the message is understood on the receiving level. If not, it is passed on to the next level, until the message is finally discarded at the top level. If a message is understood on a certain level, a corresponding action is carried out; a new message may be passed to the next higher level.

If a message triggers an error condition on a certain level, authors are only given a warning which they must acknowledge. It is almost impossibel to really prevent the author from making an error. Just think of the interactive definition of a complex graphic object: the courseware development system would have to check for unnecessary definition points, definition points lying outside the recommended graphic window, the total size of the frame and the total size of the lesson as each definition point is defined by using a rubberband function. This would clearly deteriorate the performance of the courseware development system. Another problem is how the system should react when an error is encountered and the author still wants to move the cursor to the next definition point. Therefore rules are checked after an object has been defined or modified. For each operation in the courseware development system, specific messages have to be defined during customization. For objects there will be messages for definition, modification and deletion, and some rules on the object level. On higher levels in the hierarchy, there will probably be fewer messages but more rules that have to be checked.

3.3.4 Examples

In this section some examples are given to show how messages and rules work together. Let us assume the author begins with the definition of a new frame. After s/he has defining some objects the author may e.g. want to define a red circle. The definition of the circle creates two messages: the first one passes the color information, the second one the storage requirements to higher levels. The first message is received on the frame level, since there is a rule established on this level that checks the maximum number of different colors per frame. If this number is exceeded, a warning appears in a separate window ("The maximum number of different colors has been exceeded!"); the author has to click on a field in the alert box before s/he can continue to work. The message is not passed further. The second message is also checked on the frame level and leads to a warning if the size of the frame has become too large. This message, however, is passed to the next higher level. On the block level, there is no corresponding rule, and the message is handed to the top level. On the lesson level, another warning may be triggered when the total allowable size of the lesson has been reached.

The next example shows how the definition of the background color in a frame is handled. On the frame level, the definition of a specific color may reduce the set of colors available for graphic objects to avoid color combinations that are difficult to distinguish. After defining a half intensity blue background, it is not possible to define a full intensity blue line. The message is passed on to the block level. There the courseware development system checks whether the defined color is the same as of all other frames in the block, assuming that frames within a block should have the same background color. If the author has inadvertently switched to a new color, another warning will be given. At this level the message is discarded.

Rules can also be used to achieve a certain style of the layout of frames, e.g. that graphic is only drawn in a window on the left part of the frame, whereas text is written in another window on the right half. To this end, a rule on the frame level is defined which checks whether all definition points of graphic objects are within the specified window. Another rule does the same for text. As soon as an author defines an object outside the recommended area, a warning is given that this object may only be defined there when it is really necessary, e.g. for a highlighting text with a box or as labelling of some graphic information. This shows another advantage of just giving warnings and not really keeping the author from making a mistake: not even a very intelligent courseware development system will be able to decide whether a box around the text is allowed or not.

Messages can also be used for mutual exclusion of objects within a frame. Many current courseware development systems forbid that indexes and questions are defined in the same frame. The standard message that is produced when an index object is defined will trigger a rule on the frame level that removes questions from the set of available objects. Together with the corresponding rule for questions, it will not be possible any more to define both objects within one frame. Note in passing that this solution is more flexible than the static standard solution where this would have to be defined during the programming of the courseware development system.

Messages and rules are not only useful for operations on the object level. All lesson structures that have been mentioned restrict questions to certain blocks. If during customization questions are removed from the set of available objects on block level, one can be sure that no questions can be defined in tutorial blocks. To ensure that a frame in a question block really contains at least one frame, a message is produced when the frame is stored. This message is received at the block level. If no question has been defined in the frame, a warning is given that there should be at least one question in the frame.

Even at the block level messages can be useful, e.g. when a new block is defined.

This message is dealt with at the lesson level: a corresponding rules checks whether there are too many or too few blocks in the lesson.

4 Summary

We have proposed a system that can avoid most of the errors novice authors make when they create their first tutorial lessons. The system uses mechanisms of object-oriented programming and is customizable, i.e., new rules can easily be introduced. A system like this should further reduce the work necessary for creating courseware.

Acknowledgement

Support of part of this research by the Austrian Federal Ministry of Science and Research (Grant Zl. 604.508/2-26/86) and the Fonds zur Förderung der wissenschaftlichen Forschung (Grant P6042P) is gratefully acknowledged.

References

[Al-Jaberi84] Al-Jaberi M. R.: *Developing and Validating Criteria for the Production of Computer-Based Courseware*, Thesis, Ohio State University, 1984.

[Avner84] Avner A., Smith S., Tenczar P.: *CBI Authoring Tools: Effects on Productivity and Quality*, Journal of Computer-Based Instruction, Vol. 11, No. 3, Summer 1984, p. 85-89.

[Bonar87] Bonar J., Cunningham R., Schultz J.: *An Object-Oriented Architecture for Intelligent Tutoring Systems*, Technical Report No. LSP-3, University of Pittsburgh, 1987.

[COSTOC] COSTOC Newsletter No. 1, IIG, Graz University of Technology, 1988.

[Dear87] Dear B. L.: *AI and the Authoring Process*, IEEE Expert, Vol. 2, No. 2, Summer 1987, p. 17-24.

[Fairweather84] Fairweather P.G., O'Neal A.F.: *The Impact of Advanced Authoring Systems on CAI Productivity*, Journal of Computer-Based Instruction, Vol. 11, No. 3, Summer 1984, p. 90-94.

[Garratt87] Garratt J., Huber F.: *AUTOOL Version 2 Reference Manual*, Report 237, IIG, Graz University of Technology, 1987.

[Harris86] Harris S. D., Owens J. M.: *Some Critical Factors that Limit the Effectiveness of Machine Intelligence Technology in Military Systems Applications*, Journal of Computer-Based Instruction, Vol. 13, No. 2, Spring 1986, p. 30-34.

[Hartog87] Hartog Robert J.M.: *Better More Efficient or Different Education in the Future?*, Report of the Wageningen Agricultural University (Holland), 1987.

[Huber87a] Huber F., Maurer H.: *On Editors for Presentation Type CAI*, Applied Informatics, Vol. 29, No. 11, 1987, p. 449-457.

[Huber87b] Huber F., Maurer H.: *Extended Ideas on Editors for Presentation Type CAI*, Report 240, IIG, Graz University of Technology, 1987.

[Huber88] Huber F.: *On Customizing a PT-CAI Editor*, to appear in Journal of Microcomputer Applications.

[Kaiser86] Kaiser D., Maurer H.: *How to develop a COSTOC Course*, Report 229, IIG, Graz University of Technology, 1986.

[Marshall84] Marshall K. W.: *A Comprehensive Evaluation Model Developed by a Panel of Experts for Use in Evaluating Educational Courseware/Software*, Doctoral Thesis, Pepperdine University, L. A., 1984.

[Maurer85] Maurer H.: *Authoring Systems for Computer Assisted Instruction*, Proc. of the ACM National Conference 1985, Denver, p. 551-561.

[Maurer86a] Maurer H., F. Makedon: *COSTOC: Computer Supported Teaching of Computer Science*, Proc. IFIP Conference on Teleteaching '86, Budapest, F. Lovis (Ed.), North Holland Pub. Co., Amsterdam, 1986, p. 107-119.

[Maurer86b] Maurer Hermann: *Nationwide Teaching Through a Network of Microcomputers*, Proc. of IFIP World Congress 1986, Dublin, North-Holland Pub. Co., Amsterdam, p. 429-432.

[Merrill84] Merrill Paul F., Wood Larry E.: *Computer Guided Instructional Design*, Journal of Computer-Based Instruction, Vol. 11, No. 2, Spring 1984, p. 60-63.

[Merrill85] Merrill M. D.: *Where is the Authoring in Authoring Systems?* Journal of Computer-Based Instruction, Vol. 12, No. 4, Autumn 1985, p. 90-96.

[Merrill87] Merrill M. D.: *An Expert System for Instructional Design*, IEEE Expert, Vol. 2, No. 2, Summer 1987, p. 25-37.

[Ridgeway87] Ridgeway Jim: *Development and Evaluation of CAL Materials*, Trends in Computer Assisted Education, R. Lewis, E. D. Taff (Eds.), Blackwell Scientific Publications, Oxford, 1987, p. 203-212.

[Roberts87] Roberts Franklin C.: *Developing a Library of Knowledge-Based Instructional Models for Authoring Systems*, Proceedings of the 2nd International Conference on Children in the Information Age, Sofia, Preprint 2, 1987, p. 186-201.

[Sherwood86] Sherwood B.: *CMU Tutor and Language Design: Talk and Discussion*, ICEC - Carnegie Workshop Guide, 1986.

Incidental Learning During Information Retrieval : A Hypertext Experiment

Tricia Jones *
Department of Computer Science, University of Maryland
College Park, MD, USA 20742

Abstract

A study was conducted in a hypertext environment in order to examine the effects of the type of fact–retrieval search (browsing vs. index-using) on incidental learning. It was hypothesized that browsing would lead to more incidental learning; from a cognitive viewpoint, it would appear that browsers would have more opportunity to make connections between the various articles, which would result in a more complete understanding of the material. No significant results were found at the level of overall performance; however, by examining individual questions and the log files of various subjects, insight was gained into the search process. These trends were discussed in terms of implications on the use of hypertext for education. Many suggestions for designers of hypertext databases were given, along with suggestions for further research.

1   INTRODUCTION

There is a growing awareness that current educational software often is not based on strong educational or cognitive theories, and does not reflect the cutting edge of software development. To create better educational software, some educators and software developers are beginning to use hypertext environments (see Yankelovich, Meyrowitz, and van Dam (1985), pp. 22-28, for an overview of the systems in development and in use at Brown University). While these and other hypertext applications are blossoming, research regarding their efficacy has not kept up the pace. In addition, research examining how users search in such an environment has been minimal. The current study explored the use of two navigational aids, embedded menus and indexes, within Hyperties, a hypertext system for personal computers. In particular, the interaction between the navigational aid and incidental learning was examined. Conclusions will be drawn regarding the appropriateness of the hypertext environment for educational software, and implications will be made for designers of general purpose hypertext systems.

---

* This material is based upon work supported under a National Science Foundation Graduate Fellowship.

1.1 Hypertext

Hypertext can be compared to 'electronic books', yet it is inherently much more than just an electronic analogy to our familiar concept of a book. One essential characteristic of hypertext is the connectivity of information. One author describes it as "linking together discrete blocks to form webs of information, following different paths through the information webs, and attaching annotations to any block of information" (Yankelovich, Meyrowitz, and van Dam, 1985, p. 19). An extension of hypertext is hypermedia, which can include graphics, sound, videodiscs, or animation...all interconnected.

Why should a teacher choose a software system built upon a hypertext framework? As Marchionini and Shneiderman (1988) point out, due to the relative newness of hypertext, "we have sparse evidence for it's effectiveness, let alone proven principles to guide design" (p. 71). Why should the use of hypertext be promoted for learning?

One of the major assets of such a system is the ability to make explicit links between concepts. Such explicit links may lead to an increase in knowledge, as the users gain an understanding of the information's underlying structure. This notion of connectivity is one of the main selling points of hypertext, since it corresponds to cognitive models proposed by research psychologists. Hypertext systems, with their emphasis on related ideas and webs of information, should lead to a better understanding of concepts and how they are related. Such knowledge is beneficial to one who seeks to understand a particular domain. Ausubel has given us the notion of "anchoring ideas to an ideational structure." Cognitive psychologists promote the notion of spreading activation. If knowledge is represented cognitively as an associative network or hierarchy of information, then systems which are organized along similar lines would seem to be desirable. Browsing, with its decreased cognitive load, might allow more short-term and episodic memory resources to be freed for the processing of incidental facts. By emphasizing the existing interrelationships among ideas, it would be easier to tie together related webs of information.

One of the aims of the present research is to determine if browsing strategies have an effect on a user's overall grasp of the knowledge structure in a database. If incidental learning can be enhanced through the use of hypertext, and through the use of navigational aids such as embedded menus, there should be many fields in which to apply this technology. Educational software is one arena. Kreitzberg and Shneiderman (1988) give direction to this idea by suggesting types of instruction for which Hyperties will be appropriate, including dynamic glossaries, familiarization, and diagnostic problem-solving. Perhaps students could read a lesson in the hypertext environment, followed by a comprehension test, or a vocabulary test, or some other appropriate measure. When an incorrect response is given, the system could return the student to a point in the text where he or she could reexamine the relevant information and hopefully gain a broader perspective on the item in question. If education is, as George Landow puts it, the act of seeing connections and following links (Yankelovich, et.al, p. 16), and if hypertext systems encourage the understanding of the interconnections between concepts, then these systems might have a substantial role in the development of educational software. If they are beneficial in "observing existing connections and making new connections" (Yankelovich, et.al, p. 16) between various disciplines, then they can contribute to an interdisciplinary understanding of the world.

1.2 Information Seeking in Text

Methods of seeking information range from highly structured, analytical searching to random forms of browsing. Search is a well-defined discipline in computer science; however, searching for information within text—a topic falling within the realm of information science—is not nearly as formalized; therefore, much remains to be learned. For example, it is an open question how previous knowledge of the task domain influences search strategies. Similarly, the effect of the user interface is relatively unknown. The present study examines two specific search methods, index-using and browsing, within the hypertext environment.

Indexes or tables of contents are familiar metaphors from the realm of 'hard-copy books'. Most literate people feel quite comfortable with the concept. Browsing, on the other hand, does not seem to be as well-defined or concrete. Browsing can be defined as "an exploratory, information-seeking strategy that depends on serendipity. It is especially appropriate for ill-defined problems and for exploring new task domains." (Marchionini and Shneiderman, 1988, p. 71). Marchionini defines browsing as "a highly interactive process with multiple decision points which depend on feedback to help determine what to do next." He goes on to explain various browsing techniques, ranging from random and informal to systematic and formal. He gives three broad reasons why people resort to browsing (Marchionini, 1988a, p.3):

> First, they browse because they cannot or have not defined their search objective... Second, people browse because it takes less cognitive load to browse than it does to plan and conduct an analytical, optimized search... Third, people browse because the information system supports and encourages browsing.

The browsing examined in this study falls into the third category. Many environments support and encourage this form of search, such as the stacks in a library. Hypertext systems in general, and the use of embedded menus in Hyperties in particular, also tend to support and encourage browsing.

An electronic-text system with powerful full-text search capabilities is Grolier's Electronic Encyclopedia on CD-ROM. Experiments conducted with the system, involving elementary school students and high school students, suggest that novices benefit from having hypertext features which allow browsing. Elementary school students, with less proficiency in the search techniques and insufficient mental models of the system, tended to use the low cognitive load browsing strategies. High school students using an analytical approach were no more effective in finding information than those using a scan and select (browsing) strategy (see Marchionini (1988b) and Marchionini and Shneiderman (1988)).

A pilot study involving a simple fact-retrieval task was conducted using the Hyperties system, with the primary aim of identifying research questions and methods (Wang, Liebscher, and Marchionini, 1987). Two experiments were performed; one examined display formats (print and electronic), the other examined two search strategies (index-using and browsing). Subjects in the print condition were more efficient; however, no significant difference was found in mean number of questions correctly answered. In the second experiment, subjects in the Index group tended to view fewer articles and screens during the search, but no significant difference was found in terms of success. The index users rated the system higher in terms of ease, speed, and lower in level of frustration.

The above experiment involved a highly specialized student group, consisting of graduate level Library Science students, all with considerable experience in reading printed text, as well as in using indexes and similar searching aids. As discussed by Feibel (1984), established habits of users play a large role in learning situations. This notion seemed to be reflected in the subjective satisfaction scores. Furthermore, many of the Browse group were found to have migrated to use of the index. Rather than adapting to the new situation they were learning, the subjects turned to a more common method—the index. This study attempted to identify significant differences between library science graduate students and undergraduates from the psychology pool in terms of performance, both in browsing or use of an index. Furthermore, search strategies of the two populations were compared.

1.3 Incidental Learning

Incidental learning takes place when acquisition of knowledge occurs despite a lack of intention. A large body of literature exists concerning incidental learning. Primary producers of the research are educators and psychologists. Studies can also be found in paradigms as diverse as medicine (incidental learning of child-oncology interns in two different hospitals), and political science (knowledge of New York political campaigns gained by residents of New Jersey contrasted by geographical region and media population).

The traditional psychological literature is full of experiments involving lists of words—not full-text situations. Classic studies examined word recognition and the determination of frequencies of words. Many studied the effects due to age differences (generally attributed to the development of selective attention). Many, including Craik and Tulving, lean towards an 'elaboration of encoding' theory, and examine the effects of depth of processing and episodic memory (see Lindberg and Wickens, 1979). Dixon studies the effect of personality factors such as motivation and locus of control on incidental learning conditions (see Dixon and Cameron, 1976). Another study investigated "pupillary dilation as a possible index of task difficulty for various orienting tasks during incidental learning" (Krinsky and Nelson, 1981).

Educational psychologists seem to have a less diverse range of research experiments, but more diverse results. Their research tends to focus on the impact of behavioral objectives and pre-organizers on the amount of intentional and incidental learning. Some researchers state that behavioral objectives increase intentional learning and decrease incidental; some claim both are increased. To help sort this out, Klauer (1984) attempted a meta-analysis of 23 reports generated during the decade of 1970 to 1980. He analyzed variables such as text length, test difficulty, and type, level, and number of objectives. His main finding was that

> "giving behavioral objectives, learning directions, or questions before an instructional text is read leads to some improvement in the learning of goal relevant material; however, these preinstructional acts impede the learning of goal irrelevant material (i.e. incidental learning)" (Klauer, 1984, p.323).

Barker and Hapkiewicz (1979) also attempted to account for various types and levels of behavioral objectives. The two types they focused on were *knowledge level* (e.g. the learner will accurately define X) and *evaluation level* (e.g. the learner will effectively compare and contrast the theories of Y and Z). These obviously require different levels of understanding from the student. Whereas Klauer simply concluded that general (i.e. knowledge level) objectives "produce negative effects on incidental learning", Barker and Hapkiewicz studied the interaction of the level of the objective and the level of knowledge subsequently measured. They found that the learning objectives did not depress incidental learning at lower levels; however, such learning was depressed when the questions required a higher level of understanding than the objective demanded. In other words, subjects given an evaluation level objective ("compare Y and Z") probably could define X, but subjects given a knowledge level objective ("define X") could not effectively evaluate the theory of Y in the context of Z. They concluded that students given evaluation level objectives must obtain a better understanding of the basic information in order to reach their objective. This is not in contradiction with the theory that behavioral objectives steer one's attention away from goal-irrelevant details, since the lower-level details *are* relevant to a higher goal.

The task in our experiment was primarily a fact–retrieval task. Wang, Liebscher, and Marchionini have developed a taxonomy to classify questions used in fact–retrieval. This same taxonomy was utilized in the selection of questions for the current experiment. The taxonomy will be explained fully in the next section; but in light of the previous discussion on learning objectives it deserves mention here that the level of fact–retrieval question posed may have an effect on the knowledge acquired. Questions which are more complex and less focused may lead to more incidental learning, as more information must be processed in order to obtain the correct answer. It is conjectured that such questions might be better explored through browsing than by use of an index (Wang, Liebscher, and Marchionini, 1987, pp. 6, 14).

One recent study involving incidental learning from a full-text environment (as opposed to word lists) investigated the effects of text features on vocabulary acquisition (Herman, Anderson, Pearson, and Nagy, 1987). The unique focus of this experiment has direct implications for the users of hypertext systems in creating databases.

Educators have hypothesized that meanings of words can be acquired through normal reading of text, with no emphasis on vocabulary learning. This is known as the *incidental acquisition hypothesis.* Herman points out that there is little clear empirical evidence for this hypothesis, and offers a possible explanation as to why this might be. She contends that the acquisition occurs in small increments, with portions of a word's meaning being learned from context rather than a full grasp of the complete definition being obtained. Previous research may have failed by requiring students to generate a complete, adult-level understanding of the word.

With this in mind, the authors devised a measure sensitive to various levels of word knowledge. They produced one study which provided convincing evidence for the incidental acquisition hypothesis. A follow-up study gave further support. However, discrepancies in the results led to further reflection. It was determined that anomalies could possibly be a result of the quality of the text. This insight led to a study in which the authors attempted to systematically control three different text features through successive rewriting of a text. These features are macrostructure, microstructure, and the completeness of the explanation of concepts and the relations between them. It was found that the degree of incidental learning was significantly influenced by the version of the text that was read. Macrostructure revisions—more complete titles, topic sentences—did not produce significant results, nor did the combination of macrostructure with microstructure revisions (making temporal and logical relations explicit). However, students reading the elaborated version, containing the above improvements as well as an elaboration of key concepts and presentation of concrete examples, gained more word knowledge, regardless of ability or any other factor.

Hypertext is an approach which involves a more definite and elaborate presentation of concepts and their interrelationships than can be found in straightforward presentations of the same material. Designers of hypertext databases should be aware that concepts which are elaborated in this manner will be more memorable. Short text is not necessarily better; rather, it is critical that a text "convey important information precisely, with interconnections fully explained at a level of specificity appropriate for readers who do not know much about the subject matter" (Herman et al., 1987, p. 281). The functionality of hypertext makes this quite easy; in Hyperties, for example, selection of a highlighted term through the embedded menus can lead to a more elaborate explanation of a concept or an example of an obtuse phenomenon. Readers who are already familiar with the concept need not follow such paths, but those who are unsure of their meaning can explore until they are satisfied.

2 EXPERIMENT

2.1 Introduction and Hypothesis

The experiment used a 2 x 2 design with navigational aid (index vs. browse) and subject type (CLIS students vs. psych pool) as between-subjects factors. The dependent measures were success in finding the answer to a question and score on an incidental learning task. The hypotheses were:

1. Navigational aid will have no effect on search success.

2. Library Science students in the index group (having more familiarity with the use of searching aids such as indexes) will perform better than index-using subjects from the psychology pool on search tasks.

3. Browsing will have a positive effect on incidental learning; that is, the browse treatment group will have a significantly better score on an incidental learning measure.

2.2 Subjects

A total of 40 subjects were used. Eighteen subjects were graduate students in the College of Library and Information Sciences (CLIS); eighteen subjects were volunteers from the undergraduate psychology subject pool. Four subjects were obtained by personal contact, and were treated as part of the psychology pool group.

2.3 Materials

System: A version of the Hyperties 2.3 browser was used on IBM PCs having two disk drives. This version of Hyperties captured selections made by users, and noted the time (in seconds) between choices.

Database: The Hyperties database was compiled by downloading articles related to environmental pollution from Grolier's Electronic Encyclopedia. A search was done for articles containing the word 'pollution'. The encyclopedia presented a list of article titles, along with a frequency count for the word 'pollution'. Articles with a high frequency count were downloaded to a floppy disk, as were articles with a low frequency but which seemed to be directly related to other articles. For example, **Recycling** only had a frequency count of one, but was relevant to **Land Pollution** and **Pollution Control**.

In order to structure the text files into a database, the **Environmental Pollution** article was selected as the introduction. This article, like many others, was quite lengthy. To produce shorter articles and take advantage of hypertext capabilities, the outline provided by the Electronic Encyclopedia was used to divide the article logically. The main sections were **water, thermal, land, pesticide and herbicide, radiation, noise**, and **air pollution**. The first few paragraphs were rewritten and retained as the introductory article. References were made to the various forms of pollution and to pollution control. The main sections of the original entry were divided among the three experimenters, who rewrote and restructured them according to the outlines. Bibliographies from the original entries were maintained at the ends of articles. If a file was split up into subarticles, the bibliography was maintained in the article at the head of the network.

Internal links to other articles were determined with the following procedure. First, a concordance was constructed for each file, giving the frequency count for each word in the article. Words with a high frequency were examined for clues to other, related articles. This method was not complete in itself, since phrases were broken into their constituent words (e.g. there would be no consistent measure for the frequency of the phrase 'pollution control'). Furthermore, higher frequencies which could be attributed to the use of synonyms and derivations would be obscured. To circumvent these problems, articles were read over with attention paid to key points. Important details that led to other articles were noted. Further assistance was generated by the "(See XYZ)" citations present in the text of the encyclopedia entries. The experimenters met and drew a map of articles and links. Where any obvious connections were being neglected, refinements were suggested and implemented.

Titles for articles were generated by maintaining section headings present in the encyclopedia, or by expanding them into more complete ideas. Definitions were produced with the aid of key points in the article.

Questions The experimenters each generated a set of questions for the set of articles they had constructed. Questions were then classified according to the taxonomy developed by Wang, Liebscher, and Marchionini. Five criteria are used to classify questions:

complexity : the number of concepts (facets) represented in the question.

specificity : the variability of a correct or appropriate answer. A three point scale was used in the studies; the higher the score, the more open-ended the answer could be.

focus : the determinability of the primary facet. A three point scale was used; the higher the score, the harder it is to choose a main entry point.

path : the length, in terms of articles selected, of the optimal route to find the information needed to answer the question.

	Complexity	Specificity	Focus	Path	Accessibility
Practice 1	2	1	1	1	1
Practice 2	3	1	2	2	3
Question 1	2	1	1	2	2
Question 2	2	2	2	2	1
Question 3	4	1	3	2	3
Question 4	3	1	3	2	2
Question 5	4	1	2	4	2

Table 1: Taxonomy Rankings for Target Questions

	Complexity	Specificity	Focus	Path	Accessibility
Question 1	2	2	1	2	2
Question 2	3	1	2	4	2
Question 3	1	1	1	2	1
Question 4	3	3	1	2	2
Question 5	2	2	2	2	3
Question 6	3	1	2	2	1
Question 7	2	1	1	2	2
Question 8	3	1	3	3	3
Question 9	3	1	2	2	2
Question 10	3	1	2	2	2

Table 2: Taxonomy Rankings for Incidental Questions

accessibility : the difficulty of finding the right path to an answer. A three point scale was used; the higher the score, the more difficult it is to find the path.

According to Wang, et al.,

> "complexity and specificity are generic [system-independent] and objective; focus is generic but subjective; path is objective but system–based; accessibility describes the interaction of the user's knowledge base, the search task, and the system". (1987, p. 6)

All questions generated were ranked independently by the experimenters. Agreement on the ratings was checked before selecting a question. Target questions were chosen by examining the rankings and attempting to mix levels of difficulty. The first five incidental learning questions were a result of the choice of target questions; the sentence preceding a target was used to construct an incidental learning question. The last five posttest questions were picked randomly from available questions. The questions selected can be seen in Appendix A; the taxonomy rankings for the questions are in Tables 1 and 2.

2.4   Procedure

Subjects were trained in the use of the system by watching a demonstration of a search for the answer to the question 'Why is there a continued need for treatment in the reclamation of chemically polluted land?'. The Index treatment groups were only shown how to use the index. The highlighted terms in the index were explained as "clues to other index entries." They were *not* told that these items were selectable. Similarly, the Browse groups were not shown the index. After the demonstration, subjects were given ten minutes to look up two practice questions in order to familiarize themselves with the use of the system. Clarification was given to anyone needing it, but no clues regarding search strategies were given. Some of the CLIS subjects in the Browse group were noted to be using the index; the group was then specifically told *not* to use the index. All groups were explicitly told that there was no need to hurry when looking up answers. Subjects were primarily run in groups, although a few were run individually due to scheduling conflicts.

After completion of the two practice questions, subjects were given five questions, one at a time, for five minutes each. Subjects were instructed to push the **F1** key after answering a question. This generated a timestamp uniquely indicating 'task completion' in the log file on the computer and returned the user to the outermost level on the system. If a subject finished before time was up, they were instructed to wait until told to begin the next question. Upon completion of all the searches, a short questionnaire was handed out, which contained the ten incidental learning questions (see Appendix B) and a short set of questions regarding background and experience.

2.5 Grading

From the log files, search times were calculated for each question. An alternative measure to search times can be thought of as 'success'. This was determined by the correctness of the answer recorded by the subject. For reasons discussed below, this may even be a better measure for the current experiment. If the answer was the same as our intended answer, it was given a score of 1; otherwise, it received a 0. The questions had been worded virtually identically to the sentence containing the desired answer; therefore, incorrect answers were a result of following an incorrect path.

The incidental questions were scored by two different measures. The first can be called 'complete learning', in which only the precise answer was awarded a score of 1. Anything else resulted in a score of 0.

An incremental knowledge measure, inspired by Herman, et al., involved partial credit. This was somewhat subjective and involved assigning fractions of a point to answers which reflected a portion of the correct answer, or which contained related information from the target article. An example of this phenomenon occurred many times in question 5: the answer 'agriculture' was awarded 1 point, 'erosion' received .75 points. Erosion was mentioned as the result of strip mining and agriculture in the target article. If a subject wrote an **R** beside a question, indicating they remembered seeing the fact but did not remember the answer, a score of .1 was awarded.

3 Results

Data on the search questions were analyzed according to performance on each individual question as well as collectively across all five question.

CLIS students had marginally faster total times than the subjects from the psychology pool, but this result was not significant ($F = .505$, $p = .5$, $df = 1, 36$). Neither could

	Navigational Aid		
	Index	Browse	totals
CLIS	2.6	2.8	2.7
	(1.2)	(1.3)	(1.2)
Psych pool	2.1	2.6	2.4
	(1.4)	(1.4)	(1.4)
	2.3	2.7	2.5
totals	(1.3)	(1.3)	(1.3)

Table 3: Success Measure for Questions 1–5
Mean Number Correct per Subject

any significant effect be attributed to navigational aid. Although some significant results were seen when examining individual questions, search times were determined to be an inaccurate measure for two reasons. Inadvertently, not all treatment groups were given the same amount of time per question. For example, all CLIS subjects had been given six minutes for question 1; CLIS index-users had been given 6.5 minutes for question 5; some of the Psych browsers had been given six minutes for question 4. Furthermore, there is the question of correctness. More than a dozen subjects wrote down an incorrect answer for question 1. A smaller number (6) responded with an incorrect answer on question 2. The logs for these subjects would indicate a shorter time on the question, yet they had not actually completed the task. If we were to attempt to normalize the search times as a percentage of total time given to the group, it would tend to reduce the variability of the time measure, but it would not nullify the fact that some people had a longer amount of time to look up an answer. In addition, it doesn't correct the second problem mentioned above, that of incorrect answers. It is for these reasons that 'success' should be considered a more accurate measure of the searches done, and used in subsequent analysis.

Basic statistics for the success measure are shown in Tables 3 and 4. Under this measure, CLIS index subjects outperformed their psych pool counterparts, and CLIS browsers outperformed psych pool browsers. Furthermore, psych pool browsers outperformed their companions in the index group. As with the time measure, no significant effect was found overall for either of the independent variables or their interaction. However, if we examine the percentage of subjects with a correct answer on each individual question, the following pattern is observed:

Q2 :	Navigational Aid	$F = 6.42$	$p = .02$	$df = 1, 36$
Q3 :	Navigational Aid	$F = 8.37$	$p = .006$	$df = 1, 36$
Q5 :	Navigational Aid	$F = 6.46$	$p = .02$	$df = 1, 36$

For question 2, browsing was superior by a factor of seven to four. Browsers were also more successful in finding·the answer to question 3. On the other hand, the index was clearly a better access method for question 5. As a matter of fact, every one of the CLIS subjects in the index treatment group found the answer to question 5. All of the CLIS browsing subjects found the answer to question 3, but the effect of subject type for this question was not significant.

A table of overall means for the incidental learning questions can be found in Table 5, showing the number of correct answers within each treatment. On the 'true' incidental

Question 1

	Index	Browse	totals
CLIS	0.0	.22	.11
	(0.0)	(.44)	(.32)
Psych pool	.36	.18	.27
	(.50)	(.40)	(.46)
totals	.20	.20	.20
	(.41)	(.41)	(.40)

Question 2

	Index	Browse	totals
CLIS	.56	.89	.72
	(.53)	(.33)	(.46)
Psych pool	.54	.91	.72
	(.52)	(.30)	(.46)
totals	.55	.90	.72
	(.51)	(.31)	(.45)

Question 3

	Index	Browse	totals
CLIS	.56	1.0	.78
	(.53)	(0.0)	(.43)
Psych pool	.36	.73	.54
	(.50)	(.47)	(.51)
totals	.45	.85	.72
	(.51)	(.37)	(.48)

Question 4

	Index	Browse	totals
CLIS	.44	.22	.33
	(.53)	(.44)	(.48)
Psych pool	.18	.36	.27
	(.40)	(.50)	(.46)
totals	.30	.30	.30
	(.47)	(.47)	(.46)

Question 5

	Index	Browse	totals
CLIS	1.0	.44	.72
	(0.0)	(.53)	(.46)
Psych pool	.64	.45	.54
	(.50)	(.52)	(.51)
totals	.80	.45	.62
	(.41)	(.51)	(.49)

Table 4: Mean Success Measure for Individual Target Questions
Proportion of Subjects with Correct Answer

	Incidental Learning Questions 1–10			Incremental Incidental Learning Questions 1–10			Questions 1–5		
	Index	Browse	totals	Index	Browse	totals	Index	Browse	totals
CLIS	1.56	0.90	1.22	2.71	1.68	2.19	2.38	1.54	1.96
	(0.88)	(1.27)	(1.11)	(1.16)	(1.17)	(1.25)	(0.87)	(1.19)	(1.10)
Psych pool	1.27	0.82	1.04	2.44	2.09	2.26	2.20	2.06	2.13
	(0.47)	(0.87)	(0.72)	(0.61)	(0.73)	(0.68)	(0.71)	(0.69)	(0.69)
totals	1.40	0.85	1.12	2.56	1.90	2.23	2.28	1.83	2.06
	(0.68)	(1.04)	(0.91)	(0.88)	(0.95)	(0.96)	(0.78)	(0.96)	(0.89)

Table 5: Incidental Learning
Mean Number Correct per Subject

learning questions (1–5, where subjects were virtually guaranteed to see the answer if they correctly answered the target question), no significant effects were found. When all ten questions are taken into account, navigational aid is a significant factor (F = 5.45, p = .025, df = 1, 36). Examining Table 5, we see that the index group outperformed the browsers on the incidental learning task. This was contrary to expectations.

4 Discussion

While it is perhaps discouraging that there were no significant results at the overall level, insight into the design process can be gleaned by examining the effects that did occur at the level of individual questions.

Success was not found to be a significant measure for overall performance. However, examining individual questions shows a number of effects. This indicates that different techniques are appropriate for the various information seeking tasks. Hayes and Williges (1986) present a three-way division of search tasks, calling them explicit, clued, and non-clued. An explicit task is one in which the target is "essentially revealed" by the question. In terms of the taxonomy discussed above, this would correspond to a question with an accessibility of 1. Clued tasks are those in which a clue to the file is provided, corresponding to an accessibility of 2. An example of such a question in the present experiment is question 1. A non-clued question is one which provides no information regarding the path to the answer. An example of such a question is number 8 on the post-test; in terms of the taxonomy, the accessibility ranking would be large.

4.1 Analysis—Question 1

From Table 1, we can see that question 1 has a focus rating of 1 and an accessibility of 2. This would seem to imply that most subjects should find the answer. However, if we examine the success scores (see Table 4), we determine that only eight subjects found the correct answer! In particular, note that none of the CLIS index group found it. There were numerous problems associated with this problem that should be mentioned here. The web of articles for pollution control was created by splitting the file along the guidelines of the encyclopedia entry. This included major subtopics of air treatment systems, water treatment systems, problems of pollution control, and the EPA, with the **air treatment systems** article containing the answer. The introductory paragraph to this pollution control web was a section about *general approaches* to pollution control. Two of the four methods discussed within that article did directly mention air pollution. Therefore, many of the subjects were misled into writing down an answer from a sentence stating "this method of pollution control is most effective...", when in fact that method was not even specifically related to *air* pollution control.

Many subjects began this search with the *air pollution* articles and then got lost in the information web. This was partially due to the fact that a link had been misplaced, causing the phrase 'abatements of air pollution' to reference the **global air pollution** article, instead of the intended **air treatment systems** article. Unfortunately this was not detected during the testing performed by the experimenters, or in pilot tests.

Another common problem was that index users never connected the phrase 'air treatment systems' with the concept of air pollution control. This title was provided by

Grolier's; apparently it did not fit into the context that the users were building for pollution control. None of the CLIS index group found the right answer; 4 out of 11 subjects from the psych pool index group did. Examining the log files for these four, we find that only one of them made **air treatment systems** his first choice. Two of the subjects made a browsing selection. It was obvious, from watching the index-users perform their tasks, that the index entry was not a clear enough clue. Furthermore, the fact that only two people were able to use the index to find the answer is a strong indicator that something was awry. It appears that this question, for the index-users at least, corresponds to a 'non-clued' question. A few comments regarding the structure of the index and its entries were made by the subjects. It was suggested that entries be better organized along the lines of "Air Pollution, Global", "Air Pollution, Local" (the existing situation being "Global Air Pollution", "Local Air Pollution", ...).

Four browsers found the correct answer, with five more citing the misguided answer. Question 1, as stated, gives a pair of clues: one being **air pollution**, the other being **pollution control**. By examining the log files, it appears that many browsers in a clued situation tend to take the first path presented which fits a clue. Due to the faulty structure of the database, the first clue in this case led to an unfruitful search. This shed some insight into the behavior of users without a clearly defined search goal. More study is needed to determine exactly how choices are made.

4.2   Analysis—Question 2

Now let us examine the questions for which a statistical significance was discovered. Question 2 had a significant main effect for navigational aid. The focus for this question was 2; accessibility was 1. Browsers outperformed those in the index group. The search path for browsers was clearly outlined within Hyperties: choose **land pollution** from the introduction, then select **soil misuse**, whose definition contained a clear reference to strip mining. On the other hand, many index users selected articles with clear references to mining, such as **agricultural and mining waste disposal**, rather than **soil misuse**. Again, the title for this article was carried over from the Electronic Encyclopedia. Within the index, it had no context to give it the intended meaning; in other words, there was no overt 'clue'. As a result, index-users had more difficulty in finding the correct answer. The accessibility rating of 1 (implying a clued situation) which we gave to the question seems to apply only to the browsing path.

4.3   Analysis—Question 3

Interestingly, the third question had been given accessibility and focus ratings of 3, yet it was also easier for browsers. All of the CLIS browsers found the correct answer; two-thirds of them were finished in under three minutes. Some of the browsers went straight from **air pollution** to **local air pollution**. It may be that the word 'London' triggered an association with cities and 'local'-ness, it may be that some had previously read the article and remembered seeing the answer. Index users seemed to frequently choose **L** as the entry point into the index; it would be insightful to know how many of them were looking for an entry on *London*. The quickest search was only 51 seconds; it was conducted by a CLIS index-user. Her first choice from the index was **local air pollution**. Examining the log file indicates that the article had not previously been read; in fact, neither had the main **air pollution** article. It would be interesting to know what intention or knowledge was behind this search.

It seems that questions 2 and 3 are clear indicators of the use of context in linking clues during browsing. In cases where the index titles were out of context, little information was given to the index-users to help them on their path.

4.4   Analysis—Question 5

Question 5 also showed a significant main effect for navigational aid. The accessibility of this question was ranked at 2. For this question, however, the index group was the winner, with a mean success rate of .8 as compared to .45 for the browsers. All the CLIS index subjects found the correct answer, as did 64% of the psych pool index-users. Of those who found the correct answer with the aid of the index, 67% of the CLIS and 57% of the psych pool subjects made **recycling** their first choice from the index.

For this question, contextual clues were not as clear for the browsers; consequently, their performance suffered. The correct path for question 5 was **land pollution** to **solid wastes** to **recycling**. It seems logical to have a direct link from **pollution control** to **recycling**, and perhaps even to have a direct link from **land pollution** as well. However, neither of these existed in the original structure of the encyclopedia, so neither was brought into the Hyperties database. Again, the browsers were presented with two clues at the introduction level. Those who followed the wrong clue (associating recycling with pollution control, rather than litter with land pollution) tended not to find the answer. In fact, nearly 80% of the browsers who found the right answer took the correct path from their initial step. Interestingly, this corresponds to the first of a pair of clues, which supports the notion that users are persistent in following their first path.

4.5   General Analysis

It appears, given the results cited above, that the interaction of context and clues does have an impact on the paths people take through a database. More study is needed, however, to determine exactly what this interaction is.

Using the complete learning measure of incidental learning, where only fully correct answers are given a score of 1, we find that index users scored nearly twice as well as the browsers (see Table 5). Likewise, if we consider the incremental learning measure, we still find index-users outperforming the browsers. However, the margin drops to only 37%.

It seems intuitive that the presence of context in selections through the use of embedded menus should lead to a better overall understanding of the knowledge contained in the database. This hypothesis, however, is not substantiated by the data. It could be an artifact of the test; that is, the type of questions asked may not be the most appropriate measure of incidental knowledge. Another explanation is that the search for particular facts tended to suppress other learning. This is supported by research involving behavioral objectives discussed above. Since the questions tend to reflect 'knowledge-level' behavioral objectives, it is reasonable that only a small degree of incidental learning occurred. Questions at an 'evaluation level' might have triggered more incidental learning. However, it does not explain the difference between index-users and browsers. This could be a result of previous knowledge, reading skills, or various other factors not controlled in this experiment.

There is another explanation as to why the intuitive notions were not supported (assuming, of course, that our intuition is correct), and that is that the results were an artifact of the task. Subjects were focused on looking up isolated bits of information. It may be that the context effects are not significant for incidental learning in such a situation. If, on the other hand, this database had been a unit on environmental pollution used in a classroom-type situation, in which students were responsible for *all* the information contained within it, rather than scattered bits and pieces, the desired effect might have been found. In other words, it may be the case that context clues in Hyperties only have a significant impact when a complete body of information must be understood.

5   Conclusions

5.1   Impact for practitioners

Many of the problems with this experiment offer clear advice to designers of hypertext systems, particularly those using Hyperties. The designers of the database under discussion had not actually written the material contained within it. Many of the problems encountered in the experiment can be attributed to the fact that articles were imported from another source. Furthermore, they had not been written in such a manner as to convey the underlying network of associations. In such a situation, it is imperative that the whole body of articles and their interrelationships be understood, and then rewritten and restructured to convey the intended connections. In our case, using an approach where individual articles were treated outside the context of the gestalt information content of the database resulted in missing links. References that logically should have been made were overlooked due to our focus on the structure of the entries from the encyclopedia. The perceived impact of hypertext results from the ability to convey the structure of information; it became clear that oftentimes extra effort must be expended in order to make this structure clear.

Another issue for designers is the index. The index in the database we used was not consistent in its naming of articles. Two areas where consistency was practiced are the water pollution web and the reclamation web. Titles for articles splintered out of the Grolier's **reclamation** entry all began with the word 'Reclamation'. This was mainly due to a lack of creativity, as well as an attempt to use unique names, but it resulted in a clearer representation of the contents of the articles. Such a method was not used uniformly by the three designers, or even by this writer. From research with menu structures, we know that consistency is an important design issue; this must be carried over as a design principle of indexes within Hyperties and other hypertext systems with an index. The index can serve as an aid to understanding, so it is important to work on the index (and other such aids) in order to take full advantage of their capabilities.

Hyperties provides users with definitions of selectable items so that they can determine whether or not to follow a particular path. If these definitions are well-written in order to convey the meaning and structure of the article, accessibility is increased. Within hypertext systems, it is important that links between concepts are clearly defined and represented to the user; otherwise, the result may be 'hyperchaos'.

Education has been discussed as an application area for hypertext systems. This experiment sought to provide evidence that Hyperties and its embedded menus leads to an increase in incidental learning, thus lending support to the use of hypertext in educational settings. Unfortunately, such support cannot be garnered from the current research. However, this result alone does not necessarily imply that hypertext is not a good tool for educational software. Clearly, results are specific to the database used and the task required. We sought to examine the navigational aid; perhaps an even more important issue than the effect of such aids that arose from this work is that the database must form a strong, cohesive, logical entity. This was not the case with the environmental pollution database; perhaps it was this factor that suppressed the incidental learning.

It was noticed that browsers had different strategies for highlighted terms; for example, some scanned the highlighted terms for meaningful connections. Others would read an entire article before traversing any paths. Still others would follow the highlighting in order—sort of a depth first search strategy. It is not clear if these methods were a result of the task, that is, attempting to answer specific questions, or a reflection of individual backgrounds and training. However, from close analysis of search patterns, their results, and subsequent incidental learning, we should be able to understand what methods are most effective, if indeed a difference exists. More experimentation is needed in this realm. Once an 'optimal' method for a particular task domain is determined, however, users should be trained in its use. For example, if it is better to follow a path in its context rather than reading an entire article and then following paths in order, students should be taught how to apply this method.

5.2 Suggestions for future researchers

Many experiments can be generated from the framework of this research. Domains outside of pollution could be examined for incidental learning effects. Perhaps some subjects are better treated in this manner; perhaps the material needs to be either familiar or entirely new for there to be a significant incidental learning effect. Since behavioral objectives have shown to decrease incidental learning, it might be worthwhile to study subjects who are given access to a database but have no specific framework to follow. These subjects could be divided into two groups by navigational aid. Maybe then the results would be those we hypothesized for the current work. Another experiment would be to compare users with no specific task to those given a set of facts to look up.

It might be the case that users need some sort of 'road map' to keep track of their place in the database, as well as to visualize the underlying structure. It may be that this sort of guide is what is needed to make hypertext fully compatible within a traditional educational setting. It would be worthwhile to examine incidental learning and search paths in such situations. One could compare subjects given such a map to those who have no orienting framework to guide them.

To explore the issue of index consistency, two versions of a database could be constructed, differing only in their index. Subjects would be given a set of questions which rely on information present in index entries to guide the search. It is hypothesized that the index which is both consistent while reflecting the underlying structure would be a better aid.

Another possible study is to use a Hyperties database in the manner alluded to above;

that is, to create a unit of instruction that subjects must read and understand in order to complete their task. Incidental learning could then be measured, comparing subjects which used embedded menus to those who had only the index, or perhaps who had read a 'linear' text which had not been broken up into constituent articles.

Much more research is needed to study search habits of individuals, both in guided and undefined settings. One possible approach is to require users to conduct 'think-aloud' searches, in order to see what thought patterns they are using, and how these can be facilitated by search aids. In order to truly understand the interaction of previous knowledge with information, we need some measure of a person's understanding of the structure of information. A network diagram seems like a good first pass, but a more robust measure should be designed.

5.3   Theoretical implications

It appears that people presented with an interface which encourages browsing tend to use low cognitive load search methods. This finds support in log files which show that the first item selected is often the first presented. When a path is explicitly defined, it will usually be followed. If it is clued, but the clues are vague, it is easy to get misled. In the absence of clues, an individual will tend to examine all possible paths.

It is fairly clear from the discussion of individual questions that context clues play a large role in defining the search task in a full-text environment. Goals and plans are derived from a person's understanding of the underlying relationships. This understanding directs the way an individual conducts a search. No definite model of a user's performance in full-text information retrieval has been formulated.

6   Acknowledgements

This paper was originally prepared as a student project for CMSC 828 at the University of Maryland, under the direction of Ben Shneiderman. Many thanks go to Gary Marchionini for valuable input in both practical and theoretical issues; to Peter Liebscher and Xianhua Wang for their involvement in the development and implementation of the experiment; and to my husband Matthew for believing in it even when I didn't. Hyperties is available from Cognetics Corporation, 55 Princeton-Hightstown Road, Princeton Junction, NJ 08550, USA. The Grolier's Electronic Encyclopedia was used with the written consent of the publishers.

REFERENCES

1. Barker, D. and Hapkiewicz, W.G. 1979. The effects of behavioral objectives on relevant and incidental learning at two levels of Bloom's taxonomy. *Journal of Educational Research* , 72(6):334–339.

2. Dixon, P.N. and Cameron, A.E. 1976. Personality and motivational factors on an intentional-incidental learning task. *Psychological Reports* , 39:1315–1320.

3. Feibel, W. 1984. Natural phrasing in the delivery of text on computer screens : discussion of results and research approaches. *Proceedings of the NECC* . Della T. Bonnette (Ed.), 160–167.

4. Gagne, R.M. 1986. Instructional technology : the research field. *Journal of Instructional Development* , 8(3):7–14.

5. Hayes, B.C. and Williges, R.C. 1986. Defining search strategies in information retrieval. *Proceedings of the 1986 IEEE International Conference on Systems, Man, and Cybernetics* , 1108–1112.

6. Herman, P.A., Anderson, R.C., Pearson, P.D. and Nagy, W.E. 1987. Incidental acquisition of word meaning from expositions with varied text features. *Reading Research Quarterly* , 22(3):263–284.

7. Kreitzberg, C. and Shneiderman, B. 1988. Restructuring knowledge for an electronic encyclopedia, *Proceedings of the Tenth International Ergonomic Association* .

8. Krinsky, R. and Nelson, T.O. 1981. Task difficulty and pupillary dilation during incidental learning. *Journal of Experimental Psychology: Human Learning and Memory* , 7(4):293–298.

9. Lindberg, M. A. and Wickens, D.D. 1979. Are incidental learning tasks measuring elaboration of coding, or just overloading retrieval cues? *Bulletin of the Psychonomic Society* , 13(1):47–49.

10. Marchionini, Gary. 1988a. An invitation to browse : designing full-text systems for novice users. *Canadian Journal of Information Science* , in press.

11. Marchionini, Gary. 1988b. Making the transition from print to electronic encyclopedias : assimilation and accommodation of mental models, *International Journal of Man-Machine Studies,* in press

12. Marchionini, Gary and Shneiderman, Ben. 1988. Finding facts vs. browsing knowledge in hypertext systems. *IEEE Computer,* 21(1):70–80.

13. Wang, Xianhua, Liebscher, Peter and Marchionini, Gary. 1987. Physical format and search strategy in hypertext: effects on information seeking, *University of Maryland Human Computer Interaction Lab Technical Report* (CAR-TR-353, CS-TR-2006).

14. Yankelovich, Nicole, Meyrowitz, Norman, and van Dam, Andries. 1985. Reading and writing the electronic book. *IEEE Computer,* October 1985: 15–30.

Appendix A—Search Questions

Practice Question 1. Give 3 examples of high-level sources of noise pollution.
Practice Question 2. At what rate is the concentration of carbon dioxide in the atmosphere increasing?

1. Which of the four methods of air pollution control is most efficient?
2. Why does strip mining cause land pollution?
3. How many deaths were attributed to the severe fog of 1952 in London?
4. What nutrients may accelerate the natural aging process of lakes?
5. According to a 1975 report, how much did litter decrease in Oregon due to their recycling law?

Appendix B—Incidental Learning Questions

Knowledge Questions This questionnaire relates to information in the database. You may or may not have seen the answers to these questions, depending on your search path. Please answer according to the best of your knowledge. If you remember seeing the fact during your search, but do not remember the answer, write an '**R**' beside the number of the question.

1. Which of the four methods of air pollution control is most commonly used?
2. When did Oregon's litter law (the first of its kind in the United States) go into effect?
3. What is smog?
4. What is the effect of a high concentration of suspended solids in rivers and navigational channels?
5. What is the other major cause of land pollution besides strip mining?
6. What are the two safest types of storage sites currently used for radioactive nuclear wastes?
7. When was the EPA established?
8. How many people were killed in the Aberfan disaster of 1966?
9. Who maintains the International Registry of Potentially Toxic Substances?
10. About what percentage of all water consumption, excluding agricultural uses, is for cooling or energy dissipation?

CIRCSIM-TUTOR:
AN INTELLIGENT TUTORING SYSTEM FOR CIRCULATORY PHYSIOLOGY

Nakhoon Kim, Martha Evens
Computer Science Department, Illinois Institute of Technology
Chicago, IL 60616

Joel A. Michael, Allen A. Rovick
Department of Physiology, Rush Medical College
Chicago, IL 60612

Abstract

The aim of this research is to develop an intelligent tutoring system (ITS) which teaches students the causal relationships between the components of the circulatory physiology system and the complex behavior of the negative feedback system that stabilizes blood pressure. This system will accept natural language input from students and generate limited natural language explanations. It contains rules that identify the student's errors and build a "bug-based" student model. It uses tutoring rules to plan each response based on its model of the student and the dialog history so that it can tailor the dialog to fit the student's learning needs. The tutoring rule interpreter manages the dialog and determines strategy and tactics to achieve its educational goals.

Since we assume that our students have already been taught the relevant domain knowledge, our system is designed to help the students integrate their piece-by-piece knowledge and correct their misconceptions by working through set of predefined problems, which were selected to deal with physiological phenomena of particular importance or difficulty.

1. Introduction

We are developing an intelligent tutoring system, CIRCSIM-TUTOR, which assists students in mastering the causal relationships between the components of the circulatory system and the complex behavior of the negative feedback system that stabilizes blood pressure.

A qualitative change in one component in our causal model, for example, "a decrease in blood volume," directly causes many components to change. Later, in the reflex stage (with neural feedback to stabilize the blood pressure) another set of qualitative changes occurs. Finally a steady state is achieved as a balance between the qualitative changes directly caused by the initial perturbation and the further changes induced by negative feedback. Our major goal is to teach these complex mechanisms to the students and to assist them to correct their misconceptions.

Unlike other computer tutors, CIRCSIM-TUTOR has a set of predefined problems, designed by expert teachers to uncover most of the common student misconceptions in this domain. Since the students may make multiple errors in predictions for each procedure, it has a collection of domain-dependent planning rules to determine what to teach next. It will then replan these instructional goals dynamically as the student model changes. The system organization is an extension of the discourse management network system designed by Woolf for her MENO-TUTOR (1984) to incorporate a multi-level planning module. All tutoring rules are explicitly stated in a structured form of English, then translated into Prolog form by a rule interpreter called by the planner. This makes it easy for the system to explain its plans and goals to the student and also makes it easy for the expert to change the tutoring rules. The tutor incorporates a simple natural language understander and text generator that makes it possible for the system to understand student questions, to ask questions itself, and to sometimes understand the answers.

2. Circulatory Physiology Problems

The subject area of the system that we are implementing is cardiovascular (CV) physiology. CIRCSIM-TUTOR deals with the complex behavior of the cardiovascular system, which incorporates a negative feedback system to stabilize blood pressure. This feature is particularly difficult for the novice to understand.

The CV system consists of many mutually interacting components, and the student must understand the input-output relationships for each individual component of the system. A qualitative change in one component of the system can cause many other components to change. A perturbation in the system will have a direct and immediate effect on some components. Other components are only affected by neural reflexes called into play by the negative feedback mechanism to stabilize blood pressure. The complex behavior of the negative feedback system cannot be captured by simply understanding the causal relationships between individual components. Hence, the students must learn to integrate the piecemeal facts about the relationships between the components into mental models of the operation of the overall system.

For effective learning, the students must be able to use this knowledge reliably, that is, without errors or ambiguities, and flexibly, so that they can apply it consistently in diverse and unfamiliar situations (Ohlsson, 1987; Reif, 1985). This means that the students must know how to use their knowledge to make correct predictions when a perturbation is introduced. The blood pressure system, like any negative feedback system, is very complex. Ordinarily, students have only limited opportunities to integrate and use the knowledge they learn from lectures and textbooks. CIRCSIM-TUTOR is designed to give them a chance to integrate and apply this knowledge in a number of different situations that require explicit qualitative answers.

3. Background and motivation

Rovick and Brenner (1983) developed a simulation experiment, HEARTSIM, on the PLATO system, with which students can explore the mechanisms of the cardiovascular system that are responsible for the regulation of blood pressure. HEARTSIM requires the student to make qualitative predictions about the responses of the system. Later Rovick and Michael developed a personal computer based instruction system, CIRCSIM (1986), in which additional attention is given to assisting the student to develop an algorithm to solve problems involving blood pressure. If there is any error in the student's predictions, CIRCSIM identifies the errors and then presents explanations to help the student correct misconceptions.

Work with CIRCSIM has shown that it is an effective instructional system capable of making the students recognize their misconceptions and correct them as they proceed through its eight problems. However, it lacks the ability to model the student's knowledge and thus cannot react flexibly to different student needs (Michael, 1986). It can only compare the prestored correct answers with the student's answers and output canned text. Michael and Rovick have become increasingly frustrated with the inability of CIRCSIM to communicate with students in natural language; they feel that they cannot really explore the student's understanding without language facilities. Also an important part of understanding this kind of complex process, they find, is learning to discuss it in the correct technical language. This paper presents a first step at moving from a CBI system, CIRCSIM, to an ITS, CIRCSIM-TUTOR, with some natural language capability.

4. Implementation

4.1. Scenario.

The curriculum for CIRCSIM-TUTOR is a set of predefined experimental procedures. Each one begins with the description of a possible perturbation of the cardiovascular system, such as a sudden loss of blood. Then the student is asked to predict how the parameters that control blood pressure will be affected. Each problem procedure stresses different topics that the students must understand. The tutor evaluates the student's predictions, looks for patterns of errors, makes hypotheses about the underlying misconceptions that might lead to those errors, and plans a tutoring discourse to remedy those misconceptions. CIRCSIM-TUTOR terminates when the student has gone through all the procedures successfully or when the student indicates a wish to stop working with the program. Provision is made for students to restart the program partway through at a later time.

A typical tutoring session proceeds as follows. After a brief introduction to the program, the tutor presents the first procedure from the curriculum, beginning with a description of the perturbation. Then the tutor asks the student to predict the qualitative changes in seven components in the CV system, by marking the appropriate square in the Predictions Table displayed on the screen (see Figure 1), using a "+" sign to represent an increase, a "−" to represent a decrease, and a "0" to indicate that the variable will not change. The first column is used to predict the Direct Response of each variable to the perturbation; the second is used to predict the changes produced by the Reflex Response after the negative feedback system has been activated; and the third to predict the Steady State.

Parameters	DR	RR	SS
Cardiac Contractility			
Right Atrial Pressure			
Stroke Volume			
Heart Rate			
Cardiac Output			
Arterial Resistance			
Mean Arterial Pressure			

Figure 1. Predictions Table

For example, the tutor may ask the student to predict the changes that occur when the arterial resistance is decreased to 50% of normal. The student may predict all the changes in the seven variables correctly, or may show multiple errors in the table. Based on the student's errors, the tutor updates the student model and then builds a lesson plan using the lesson planning rules. These rules set up tutorial goals starting with the most serious misconception first. The tutor may ask a Socratic question to achieve the first tutorial goal and evaluate the student's answer. Looking up the dialog history record and the student model, it responds to that answer. It may provide an informative explanation or merely give a hint. It may replan tutorial goals to include a sub-goal or ask a question to better understand the student's misconceptions (Stevens et al., 1882). When it asks a question, it can solve the problem in order to evaluate the student's answer. If the tutor judges that the student does not understand the experimental procedure or does not know more important and basic concepts, then it must replan the lesson.

The dialog is organized (from the tutor's side at least) by the discourse rules which determine tutorial strategy and tactics. Of course, the student may interrupt the tutor-initiated dialog to ask some question of the tutor. The natural language understander first analyzes the sentence and passes its semantic form to the tutor. The tutoring rules then look at the student model and the dialog history and decide on the best instructional action in response to that question. Both the system's goal and the student's response are recorded in the dialog history record at every step. If one tutorial goal is achieved, the tutor selects the next goal and executes the same tutorial cycle. However, if the student seems to achieve a goal which has not been selected from the goal list, the tutor replans the lesson goals. When all the goals are satisfied, the tutor chooses the next problem from the curriculum list.

4.2 Representation of Domain Knowledge

The system uses domain knowledge for several purposes: (1) to solve the problems that it asks the student to solve; (2) to provide explanations to the student, (3) to understand questions and answers generated by the student, and (4) to aid the tutor in planning the tutoring discourse (Clancey, 1983). Hence, the knowledge base must be a glass box rather than a black box and must be organized to serve in natural language understanding and text generation as well as problem solving.

The domain knowledge of CIRCSIM-TUTOR is represented in two different forms, frames for declarative knowledge and rules for procedural knowledge. Figure 2 shows an abstract representation of the components of the cardiovascular system compiled by our experts (Michael and Rovick), called a Concept Map. The frame knowledge base is built as a two level hierarchy, the lower level contains the concept map and the higher level contains the entities to which the components in the concept map belong such as the nervous system and the heart. Our first step was to convert this graphic representation into frames. Figure 3 shows a sample frame and Figure 4 shows some causal rules.

4.3 Student Model

Ordinary classroom teaching and tutoring have similar goals – helping students learn domain knowledge and learn how to apply that knowledge in problem-solving situations. However, the former puts more emphasis on organizing and delivering the domain knowledge effectively while the latter focuses on providing adaptive instruction, finding out what the student knows and does not know, and helping fill in the gaps and correct the misconceptions (Wilkinson, 1984).

An intelligent tutor must have a student model that represents an estimate of the student's current understanding of the domain knowledge in question. By using the student model, the tutor can give adaptive explanations and hints and generate questions dynamically rather than presenting predefined questions during instruction. Also the tutor can consult the student model when it determines the next topic (Van Lehn, 1988). It is evident that the more the tutor knows about the student, the more adaptive instruction the tutor can provide. However, it is very difficult to access the mental states that the student traverses in the problem solving process since only the keyboard inputs are available. But, the tutor can track student's approximated reasoning processes by asking enough questions as LISP TUTOR does (Reiser et al., 1985).

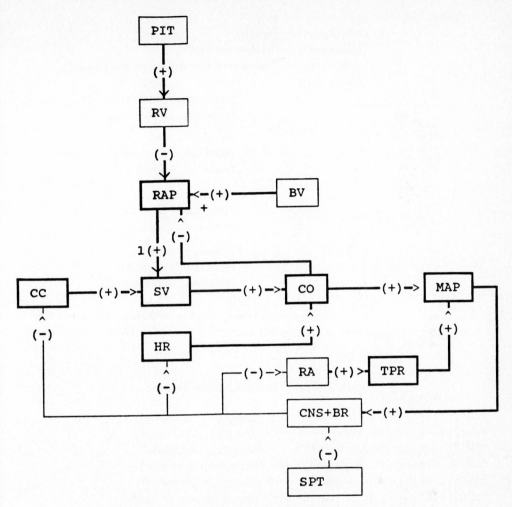

Figure 2. A Concept Map of Domain Knowledge

The goal of our research on student modeling is to obtain more information about the student's cognitive state from the keyboard input in order to provide more individualized instruction. We are also experimenting with different tutoring rules that determine how and when the controller uses and updates the student model and what should be represented in that model.

```
frame   ([      (name,          sv),
                (member,        [heart]),
                (fullname,      "stroke volume"),
                (definition,    "volume of blood ejected each beat"),
                (affected_by,   [   [   (name,      rap),
                                        (medium,    physical),
                                        (relation,  positive)],

                                    [   (name,      cc),
                                        (medium,    physical),
                                        (relation,  positive)],

                                    [   (name,      hr),
                                        (medium,    physical),
                                        (relation,  negative)]]),

                (affects,       [   [   (name,      co),
                                        (medium,    physical),
                                        (relation,  positive) ]]),
                (value,         [   (min,           65),
                                    (max,           80) ]),
                (unit,          ml)
        ]).
```

Figure 3. The Frame for Stroke Volume

rule(1) :– change(pit, increased) ==> change(rv, increased).
rule(2) :– change(pit, decreased) ==> change(rv, decreased).
rule(3) :– change(rv, increased) ==> change(rap, decreased).
rule(4) :– change(rv, decreased) ==> change(rap, increased).
rule(5) :– change(rap, increased) ==> change(sv, increased).
rule(6) :– change(rap, decreased) ==> change(sv, decreased).

Figure 4. Causal Rules

4.3.1. *Data for the Student Modeler.* The student's keyboard entries in the Predictions Table indicating qualitative changes of seven variables are our major data about the student's level of understanding. As shown in Figure 1, the the student is asked to answer what qualitative changes would happen to seven CV variables in three separate stages. Thus the student's intermediate causal knowledge at each step is available to the tutor. Not only the student's answers about the causal changes of variables at each step but also the order in which the answers are entered in the Predictions Table are important sources of knowledge to the student modeler. Unfortunately, the sequence of entries does not always correspond to the sequence of thought; some of the very best students work the whole procedure out in their heads and fill in the predictions table systematically from top to bottom.

4.3.2. *Representation of Student Model.* We assume that the student has already been taught the subject matter. But even students who know individual relationships may not have integrated knowledge about the domain. To diagnose the student's misconceptions, CIRCSIM-TUTOR uses a set of carefully selected predefined procedures. The model of a particular student is based on the student's entries in the predictions table and answers to questions. The student modeler in the initial version of CIRCSIM-TUTOR uses the student's errors to fire the student-modeling rules. These errors may involve actual prediction values or relationships between predictions of variables that affect each other. The rules also use the order in which entries are made in the Predictions Table to try to trace the course of the student's reasoning process. The student model consists of a set of terms in Prolog which have two different functors, namely, donot_know and wrong_order. The general forms are:

    (1) donot_know(Type, Variable, Count, Corrected).

        For example, donot_know(causality, sv, 1, yes).

    (2) wrong_order(Variable, Count, Corrected).

        For example, wrong_order(ra,1,no).

The student's errors are classified into three different types called "causality," "equation," and "concept." A count is associated with each error; if the student repeats an error, the count for that error will be incremented by 1.

4.3.3. *Student Modeler.* The student modeler uses the modeling rules to build a student model, based on the student's answers, the right answers, and a list of expected misconceptions. Two examples of the modeling rules follow:

```
rule(1) :-
      student_ans(hr, increased),
      student_ans(sv, increased),
      student_ans(co, nochange),
      then, store(donot_know(equation,co,1,no)).

rule(2) :-
      student_ans(co, X),
      correct_ans(co, Y),
      X ≠ Y,
      then store(donot_know(causality,co,1,no)).
```

After the error is remediated, the slot value of "corrected" is changed to "yes."

4.4 Discourse Control

This module consists of a collection of tutoring rules that control the overall tutoring discourse and determine what instructional action to perform next. Our main design goal was to achieve context-dependent tutoring. Thus it is essential for the tutor to maintain a coherent dialog while tailoring the discourse to fit the student's dynamically changing needs.

Since the control mechanisms of traditional CAI systems are tightly coupled with the domain knowledge, it prevents them from handling new domains. One new approach to avoiding this problem is the discourse management network that explicitly describes the tutorial states with a fixed control mechanism to handle transitions between states as in an augmented transition network (Woolf, 1984). As Murray points out (1988), the major flaw in this organization is the difficulty in supporting lesson planning and mixed-initiative interaction. We have tried to combine a discourse managment network with a planner modeled on Russell's (1988) IDE system.

In our system, it is very important to determination the order of remediation goals in cases when the student shows evidence of multiple misconceptions. Hence, we have domain-dependent rules to determine the sequence of teaching goals based on the student's misconceptions, called lesson planning rules. We have another set of more generic rules to control tutoring discourses and to handle situations where the student takes the initiative.

Once the remediation discourse is complete, then the system comes back to the main discourse rules and continues. If the student asks a question, the discourse rules for student's initiative are applied. Similarly, when the student's intiative is completed, the main cycle resumes. The framework for managing tutoring discourse (main tutoring process and remediation process only) appear in Figure 5 and some examples of explicit rules appear in Figure 6. These rules are executed by a rule interpreter.

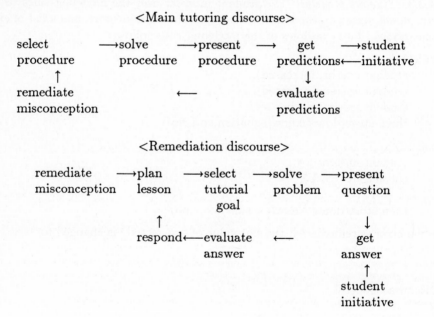

<Main tutoring discourse>

```
select        →solve      →present   →    get        →student
procedure      procedure   procedure      predictions←—initiative
  ↑                                            ↓
remediate                    ←             evaluate
misconception                              predictions
```

<Remediation discourse>

```
remediate    →plan     →select   →solve   →present
misconception lesson    tutorial  problem  question
                         goal
              ↑                               ↓
         respond←—evaluate    ←              get
                  answer                      answer
                                               ↑
                                             student
                                             initiative
```

Figure 5 Organization of the Main Discourse

Rules for tutoring strategy of main discourse:

Rule 1: if current_state = SELECT_PROCEDURE then
execute tactic(SELECT_PROCEDURE),
current_s_state = SOLVE_PROCEDURE.

Rule 2: if current_state = SOLVE_PROCEDURE then
execute tactic(SOLVE_PROCEDURE),
current_s_state = PRESENT_PROCEDURE.

Rule 3: if current_state = PRESENT_PROCEDURE then
execute tactic(PRESENT_PROCEDURE),
current_s_state = GET_INPUT.

Rules for tutoring tactics:

Rule 1: if tactic(PRESENT_PROCEDURE) then
execute text_generator(PRESENT_PROCEDURE).

Rule 2: if tactic(RESPONSE) then
call student_model(Count)
if Count = 1 then
execute text_generator(WEAK_NEGATIVE_ACKNOWLEDGE).

Figure 6 Rules for Tutoring Discourse

4.5 Lesson Plan

Typical ITSs need three levels of instructional planning: curriculum planning, lesson planning, and discourse planning (Murray, 1988). CIRCSIM-TUTOR's curriculum is preplanned and stored as a set of experimental procedures, which deal with different instructional objectives. However, it needs to build a lesson plan based on the student's answers and it must be able to dynamically replan the lesson as the student model is updated. New tutorial goals may be added and some of the lesson plans may be omitted. The lesson planner fires all the lesson planning rules which satisfy the current tutoring environments. At the moment it is crucial that the rules are fired in the order of the most important tutorial goals. Hence, the order of rules in the rule base must be determined by our experts since it is completely a domain dependent matter. Here are some examples of lesson planning rules.

rule 1: if the procedure variable is X
and X affects Y directly
student predicts the causal change in Y incorrectly
then teach(object(direct_effect),variable(Y)).

rule 2: if student does not know hr is under neural control
and does not know cc is under neural control
then teach(object(neural_control),variable(hr,cc)).

    rule 3: if student predicts the causal change in rap incorrectly
        then teach(object(causality),variable(rap)).

5. Natural Language Communication

Since we believe that two-way natural language communication is indispensible to any ITS, we are also designing a robust and efficient natural language system for our limited domain knowledge.

Clearly, the current state of the art in computer science is unable to provide the world knowledge that humans use in generating a dialog. Hence, designing a natural language understanding system that allows the user to type whatever they want to say does not make sense (Tennant, 1986). However, a robust understanding system can be designed that is powerful enough to carry on tutoring goals in a limited domain with agreement between the users and the system about the sublanguage that the system can support (Grishman and Kittredge, 1987). All natural language systems in use today are based on the assumption that the system knows in advance what the users are likely to say. These systems need to make clear to their users the limitations of the linguistic and conceptual coverage of the system, otherwise the users may be frustrated by the deficiencies in the system.

Several natural language interfaces to databases have been very successful. Among the best are Tennant's NLMenu system, NaturalLink, and Symantec's Q& A; we explored ways to adapt this kind of strategy to a frame-based knowledge base and were not successful. We also looked very carefully at the semantic grammar underlying Brown's (1982) SOPHIE, but we were afraid that the semantic grammar notation might confuse our users. We have therefore implemented a simple parser for Lexical Functional Grammar (Kaplan and Bresnan, 1982), using the Definite Clause Grammar system (Pereira and Warren, 1980) built into our Arity Prolog system. The controller receives the outputs of the parser (semantic forms) and passes them to the problem solver. Currently, we are using simple semantic forms to make the entire system work properly.

The text generation module has a collection of predicates and rules to generate sentences. It generates questions, answers, and explanations, but this first version generates only a sentence at a time. The controller passes the predicate to the text generator along with the information to be displayed. Each predicate has a corresponding rule to translate the passed information into the sentences. However, the initial version of CIRCSIM-TUTOR will not try to produce sophisicated text output.

The following are some examples which we have implemented of student questions and system answers.

(1) Q: By what components is SV affected?
         Internal form is: RETRIEVE(sv, affected_by)

     A: Stroke Volume is affected by Right Atrial Pressure
         and Cardiac Contractility.

(2) Q: What would happen to MAP if RA is increased?
         Internal form is: SOLVE(change(ra,increased), change(map,X))

     A: MAP is increased.

(3) Q: Why is SV decreased if PIT is increased?
         Internal form is: REASON(change(PIT,increased),
             change(SV, decreased))

     A: If PIT is increased then RV is increased.
         If RV is increased then RAP is decreased.
         If RAP is decreased then SV is decreased.

(4) Q: Is MAP increased if CO is increased?
         Internal form is: PROVE(change(co, increased),
             change(map,increased))

     A: Yes.

Summary

This research represents a first step at moving from a useful but not really intelligent CAI program, CIRCSIM, to an ITS, CIRCSIM-TUTOR. Its educational objective is to tutor the complex causal relationships of the cardiovascular negative feedback system. It has two sets of tutoring rules, discourse rules and lesson planning rules, which are interpreted by the system planner. Using these rules the tutor can plan and replan in response to the changes in the student model and organize the discourse to serve the goals of the tutor and respond to the students's errors and questions dynamically. All these rules are explicitly stated so that they can easily be changed by the expert and so that tutoring actions can be explained to the student. The tutor also has some simple natural language capabilities, which we are working to expand.

References

Brown, J. S., Burton, R. R., and de Kleer, J. (1982). Pedagogical, natural language, and knowledge engineering techniques in SOPHIE I, II, and III. In D.H. Sleeman and J.S. Brown, (Eds.), *Intelligent Tutoring Systems*, Academic Press, New York, 227-282.

Clancey, W. (1983). The epistemology of a rule-based expert system: A framework for explanation. *Artificial Intelligence*, 20, 215-251.

Grishman, R. and Kittredge, R. (1986). *Analyzing Language in Restricted Domains.* Hillside, NJ: Erlbaum.

Kaplan, R. M. and Bresnan, J. (1982). Lexical Functional Grammar: a formal system for grammatical representation. In J. Bresnan, (Ed.). *The Mental Representation of Grammatical Relations.* Cambridge, MA: MIT Press, 173-281.

Michael, J. A. (1986). Making CBE programs "smart": one goal of artificial intelligence research. *Computers in Life Science Education*, 3, 19-22.

Murray (1988). *Control for Intelligent Tutoring Systems: A Comparison of Blackboard Architecture and Discourse Management Networks.* Santa Clara, CA: FMC, Report R-6267.

Ohlsson, S. (1987). Some principles of intelligent tutoring. In R. W. Lawler and M. Yazdani (Eds.). *Artificial Intelligence and Education*, Vol. 1. Norwood, NJ: Ablex, 203-237.

Pereira, F. and Warren, D.H.D. (1980). Definite clause grammars for language analysis - a survey of the formalism and a comparison with augmented transition networks. *Artificial Intelligence*, 13, 231-289.

Reif, F. (1985). Acquiring an effective understanding of physical concepts. In Leo West and A. Leon Pines, (Eds.), *Cognitive Structure and Conceptual Change.* Orlando, FL: Academic Press, 133-151.

Reiser, B.J., Anderson, J.R., and Farrell, R.G. (1985). Dynamic standard modeling in an intelligent tutor for Lisp programming. *Proceedings of IJCAI*, 8-14.

Rovick, A. A. and Brenner, L. (1983). HEARTSIM: A cardiovascular simulation with didactic feedback. *Physiologist*, 26, 236-239.

Rovick, A. A. and Michael, J. A. (1986). CIRCSIM: An IBM PC computer teaching exercise on blood pressure regulation. Paper presented at the XXX IUPS Congress, Vancouver, Canada.

Russell, D. M. (1988). The instructional design environment: The interpreter. In J. Psotka, L.D. Massey, and S.A. Mutter, (Eds.), *Intelligent Tutoring Systems: Lessons Learned.* Hillsdale, NJ: Erlbaum, 323-349.

Stevens, A., Collins, A., and Goldin, S. (1982). Misconceptions in student's understanding. In D.H. Sleeman and J.S. Brown, (Eds.), *Intelligent Tutoring Systems.* New York: Academic Press, 13-24.

Tennant, H. R. (1986). The commercial application of natural language interfaces. *Proceedings of COLING 86*, 167.

Van Lehn, K. (1988). Student modeling. In M.C. Polson, and J.J. Richardson, (Eds.) *Foundations of Intelligent Tutoring Systems.* Hillsdale, NJ: Erlbaum, 55-78.

Wilkinson, J. (1984). Varieties of teaching. In M.M. Gullette (Ed.), *The Art and Craft of Teaching.* Cambridge, MA: Harvard University Press, 1-9.

Woolf, B. P. (1984). *Context Dependent Planning in a Machine Tutor.* Doctoral dissertation, Department of Computer and Information Science, University of Massachusetts, Amherst, MA.

An Intermediate Representation for
Mathematical Problem Solving

J. F. Koegel
Dept. of Computer Science
University of Lowell
Lowell, Massachusetts

N. Lakshmipathy and J. Schlesinger
Dept. of Mathematics and Computer Science
University of Denver
Denver, Colorado

Abstract: An intermediate representation for an intelligent tutoring system for elementary combinatorics is presented. The representation appears to satisfy both the requirements for a relevant environment for students' problem solving and for adequate diagnosis of student actions for the domain of interest. We present these ideas in the context of a tutor currently under development.

1. Introduction

The student module component is a major bottleneck in the development of effective Intelligent Tutoring Systems (ITS). It has been suggested [Self 88] that getting enough meaningful feedback from students can do a great deal towards alleviating this problem by enabling simpler, cheaper techniques like model-tracing. Most recent systems, in fact, have incorporated this idea by providing graphics interfaces that encourage feedback from students. Such screen notebooks seem to fall into two ends of a spectrum. At one end are systems (e.g., the Geometry tutor [Ande 85]) that demand meaningful responses from the student at each step so that they can facilitate model-tracing and other similar diagnostic methods. At the other end are learning environments which allow the student much more flexibility to explore. A drawback in such systems is that one has to resort to rather distributed diagnostic techniques like issue-based diagnosis [Burt 82] and critics [Fisc 88]. With these methods a cohesive, deep-level understanding of the students' problems is hard to formulate from their responses.

The Bridge tutor [Bona 88] presents an elegant solution that provides an exploratory environment which allows for simple, cohesive diagnosis. In addition, the proposed intermediate representation provides a convenient mental model by which students can grasp the concepts of the domain. This feature assumes greater importance for domains like mathematics since it provides a convenient means of reification of abstract concepts.

In this paper we describe an intermediate representation language that provides similar advantages. Our scheme is incorporated in a tutor being built at the University of Denver to teach students elementary counting principles. Although it is currently customized to our domain, we believe it should be easily extendible to other problem-solving domains, especially mathematical ones.

2. The Tutor

The tutor is designed to teach simple principles of counting. This includes the rules of addition, multiplication, inclusion-exclusion, permutations, combinations, and strategies of how to solve problems requiring arbitrary composition of these rules. The target population is college students at the junior to graduate level who may not have an adequate background in mathematics. The system is open-ended in the sense that all problems posed by students (which is one of the tutoring modes) cannot be solved by the system as it may not have enough expertise.

The principles of the domain are generally taught by solving word problems involving combinatorics. Word problems posed in English typically require two stages of problem solving. The first stage is to understand the problem in an unambiguous way, including unstated specifications. The second stage requires applying the principles of combinatorics to solve the problem. Consider the following problem:

Example 1. There are three cities A, B, and C, linked by roads. There is a direct road from A to C.
  Between A and B there are 4 roads and two direct roads from B to C. How many different
  paths are there to city C from city A?

The first stage includes the realization that to go from A to C, one can either take a direct path or go through city B. Also, going through B involves taking an A-to-B road followed by a B-to-C road. Our tutor assumes that the student can do this part; it tutors him only on how to use counting principles to accomplish the second stage.

The tutor consists of four modules--the tutorial module, the student module, the domain or expert module, and the interface module. The tutorial module implements the teaching strategy. It decides on how a concept is to be taught and, usually, illustrates the concept through an introduction and examples before posing exercises to the student. While the student has the option to enter problems for the system to solve, the usual scenario is for the tutorial module to select an appropriate problem from its problem library and turn over control to the student module.

The student module decides on the level of the student based on the current student model and, with the help of the interface module, poses a problem in English to the student. The natural language component of the interface module is responsible for translating the internal predicate calculus-like notation into English and vice-versa. Section 4.2 contains more information on this component. The feedback from the student, at each step, is reported by the interface to the student module. The domain module and the diagnosis routine (in the student module) are used to decide if the student is making errors; feedback to the student, if necessary, is also provided by the student module. At the end of a problem-solving event the student module updates its current student model and reports back a summary to the tutorial module; the latter then considers its next action.

The next section describes the intermediate representation. Section 4 provides details of the interface module. Section 5 describes the consequences of having such an intermediate representation on the design of other modules. Finally, Section 6 summarizes the paper and indicates directions for future work.

3. The Intermediate Representation

3.1 Introduction

The intermediate representation is based on the idea that the problem solving process can be modeled as a tree. It provides a tree-based environment for the user. The notion of using trees is certainly nothing new. It has been used in diverse applications from medical diagnosis [Buch 84] to teaching geometry [Ande 85]. Teachers of combinatorics, as evinced by our resident experts, seem to work with them internally, even if they do not use them explicitly to explain problems. While many systems use trees as the working memory structure, very few systems use them as the basis for an exploration environment. We feel that the tree structure and its operators are ideally suited for our domain and the target student population.

Viewed in the context of our tutor, each node of the tree represents a problem. Connected nodes represent related problems. Children of a given node represent subproblems; in particular, they describe a subset of the given set whose cardinality is sought. Similarly, parent nodes (there could be more than one as there can be more than one line of reasoning) represent more general problems (supersets of the given set). Siblings represent the complementary problem (other subsets of the superset). Alternative lines of reasoning represent other trees anchored at a common node. Note that this feature mandates use of an AND/OR graph. However, it is easier to regard them as an AND tree with the property that some nodes can have attached alternate subtrees. For other domains, the semantics may be different.

3.2 The problem solving process

The problem solving process is best illustrated through an example. Assume that the student is presented with the problem of Example 1. Now the answer may not be immediately apparent. So, assume that he uses the addition rule to decompose the problem into the following two subproblems:

Subproblem 1: How many direct paths are there from city A to city C?

Subproblem 2: How many indirect paths are there from city A to city C?

If N(1) is the answer to the first subproblem and N(2) the answer to the second one then the answer to the original problem is N(1) + N(2). Figure 1 illustrates this situation.

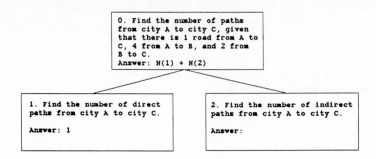

Figure 1. A partial exploration tree for Example 1

The student may now realize that the answer to the first subproblem is 1, as it is supplied in the problem statement. The second subproblem may in turn need another decomposition, this time using the multiplication rule, to yield:

Subproblem 3: How many paths are there from city A to city B?

Subproblem 4: How many paths are there from city B to city C?

If the answers to these are known as N(3) and N(4) respectively, then the answer to Subproblem 2 is N(3) * N(4). At this stage, if he realizes that the answers to the remaining subproblems are available in the problem statement, all he now has to do is to calculate 1 + (4 * 2) to yield 9. The fully explored tree is shown in Figure 2.

3.3 A basis for an exploration environment

The exercise of the previous section can be done on a screen "workbook" if we provide proper facilities. We describe the facilities needed for such an exploration environment. Operators like "CREAT CHILD" and "CREATE PARENT" can be used to extend a tree to any shape. In particular, the "CREATE CHILD" operator will create a new node that is a child of the current node and will ask the student to fill in the associated subproblem (in English).

At any given node, the student can open a new line of reasoning with the "CREATE ALTERNATE" operator. This can be used in situations where the first line of reasoning does not directly lead to a solution. It may also be possible that a student may want to deliberate over some problems in isolation before deciding how they will be related to the original problem. The operator "CREATE NODE" enables such a bottom-up mode of exploration. The forests can later be "CONNECT"-ed together, once the relationships become apparent.

Another activity typically performed in a notebook is recording numbers and formulae, and performing calculations. Facilities for enabling some of these activities are provided. Each node has an answer field in addition to the text of the problem statement. The student can enter the answer to the problem in this field, if he knows it. Otherwise, if he knows the answer in terms of the answers of some other problems, he can specify it using variables. These variables are indexed to refer to their corresponding node as follows.

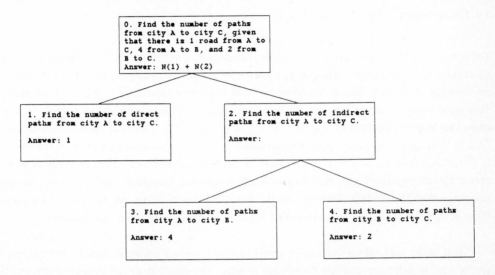

Figure 2. An exploration tree for Example 1

When a node is created, it is automatically labeled with a unique number generated by the system. The variable N, subscripted by a node number, refers to the answer of the problem associated with that node. Thus in the exercise of the previous section the answer to the original problem can be related to that of the subproblems as $N(1) + N(2)$. An alternate notation, which is a relative mode notation and so more local in nature, can also be used. In this notation $A(d1)$ refers to the first child, $A(u)$ to the parent, and $A(s1)$ to the leftmost sibling. To refer to nodes in an alternate window, doubly subscripted variables like $A(2)(d1)$ can be used. In this case, visualize the alternate windows as corresponding to different sheets of a notebook. the first subscript then refers to the page number. Absence of this number indicates working on the current page (sheet).

The selection of given variable notation is totally at the discretion of the student. The two notations can be freely intermixed.

A calculation facility is also provided. Once the answer to a given node is entered by the student, the system can automatically evaluate it and propagate it to all other nodes that specify that node through a variable. Thus, in the exercise of the previous section, if the student had written down the formulae, the answers could have been computed for him. Apart from its utility to the student, this facility avoids one source of noise during diagnosis--arithmetic mistakes. This facility can be disabled by the system and/or the student.

These operators constitute the main elements of the exploration environment. There are some other high level operators available; these are listed in Section 4.1.

3.4 Interpretation of the Exploration Tree

The domain module uses a tree as its working memory data structure. The knowledge is encoded as rules and each rule corresponds to a particular way of extending the tree. For example, in the exercise of Section 3.2, the addition rule will create the equivalent of Figure 1 internally. This close correspondence between the interface representation and the internal representation helps the diagnosis process to a great extent. The action of the student at each step is reported back to the student module, which then can match it with the expertise rules to see if the student is proceeding without errors. If the student is showing all steps and they correspond to the granularity of the expert rules then diagnosis can be enabled through model-tracing (we use terminology from [VanL 88]). There is also the the possibility of immediate feedback. This possibility is very similar to that of Anderson's Lisp and Geometry tutors [Reis 85, Ande 85].

Just as the exploration tree can be used to gauge a student's domain-specific knowledge, it can be used to judge his strategic knowledge as well. The ability to decompose problems can be detected by seeing if he creates children for a given node. Similarly, creation of parents and siblings is evidence of working on the complementary problem. Problem reformulation manifests itself as creation of a single child. Knowing a formula and its applicability corresponds to direct filling of the answer slot. This last inference may not be always true as a student may have gone through the necessary steps internally. A request to the student to show some intermediate steps may resolve this hypothesis.

The above determination of strategies can be used in many ways:

1. Identification of *a priori* strategic knowledge in new students

2. Absence or even sparse use of some strategy may suggest tutorial remediation

3. The preponderance of a particular strategy may suggest the preferred way of introducing new concepts

4. Explanations and hints can be given at a more abstract level--the strategic level

Further interpretations are possible by analyzing the way trees are extended. Interpretations along this line have not yet been fully investigated.

4. The Interface

The intermediate representation is used by many components of the system. The tutorial module, for example, uses it to illustrate concepts through examples and guided exercises. An expert user of the system--a consultant mode--can use it to explore solutions to more complex problems. The greatest use is made by the student module when it poses exercises to the student and seeks to interpret the responses in terms of the current student model. We concentrate on explaining the features of the interface from this viewpoint, as it will explain most of the facilities. We begin with an overview of the screen as seen by the student. Section 4.2 describes the natural language understanding component. Finally, Section 4.3 goes through a hypothetical session with the student that will illustrate a typical use of the interface.

4.1 Overview of the Screen

Figure 3 illustrates the screen available to the student when the student module presents a problem. The screen is divided into three regions: the workbook area where the exploration tree is displayed, a dialog window where communication can take place in English, and the operators panel where buttons are available for manipulating the tree. We first concentrate the operators.

There are three kinds of operators: the basic operators, the mode operators, and special operators. The first type is used to manipulate the exploration tree. For example, if the mouse is moved to the "CREATE CHILD" button, the system creates a new child to the current node in the workbook area, associates a new number with it, and asks the student for a problem statement. This is entered by the student in the dialog window. The new node becomes the current node. The focus can be changed by moving the mouse to another node of the tree. The operators "CREATE CHILD", "CREATE PARENT", "CREATE NODE", "CONNECT", and "CREATE ALTERNATE" have all been explained in Section 3.3. "CREATE ALTERNATE" opens a new line of reasoning, anchored at the current node. Operators like "CREATE CHILD" work on this new tree as well. The mouse is used to return to another sheet of the node that has alternates.

"SHOW FUNCTIONS" can be used to display functions available to form formulae in the answer slot of a node. "EXPLAIN" details the use of the operators. "UNDO" can be used to withdraw the just-previously performed operation.

If enabled by the student module, a button to control the auto-propagation of results will appear. This allows the user to take direct control of the calculation of answers at each node.

The number and kind of special operators available is also determined by the student module, based on the current model of the student. The operator "QUIT" can be used to exit from the system, if the student is not interested in pursuing the problem. "TAKE OVER" is a directive to the system to go ahead and finish solving the problem. "HINT" is a request for the next best move. "REMIND ME" is a less specific form of hint--the system will list out a possible set of moves which it thinks the student knows. Note all the options may not be feasible at that situation. Functions such as "USE MULTIPLICATION RULE" and "FIND COMPLEMENT" are intended for experts who use the system as an aid in exploring solutions to more complex problems.

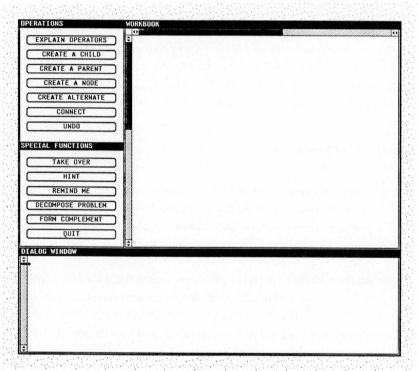

Figure 3. A sample screen

The workbook area is not directly manipulatable, except for picking the current node. Answers, formulae and problem statements are entered in the dialog window. These are used by the system to update the workbook area.

Finally, we intend that the syntax of the interface will be controlled by the user to a large extent. This gives the user the flexibility to choose whether interaction will be driven by the mouse, function keys, text entry in the dialogue window, or some combination of these.

4.2 The Natural Language Component

All natural language communication between the user and the system takes place via the dialog window. The user initiates this communication each time a new node is created; the system initiates it whenever it must communicate with the user: when posing new problems, during tutorial feedback, when the user requests a clarification or reformulation of a problem, etc. If the user's communication is not readily translatable, queries and/or reformulations are requested until a proper parse is possible.

The natural language component (NLC) is being developed in parallel with the tutoring system. While its primary purpose is to be embedded in the interface module, the NLC has been designed to be independent from the specific domain of the ITS. Both the dictionary and the syntax/semantic rules are input to the language processor in order to expedite changes in the domain.

Figure 4 shows the major functions of the NLC. The operation of the NLC is bidirectional--English input must be translated for ITS use into a predicate calculus notation and the ITS must be able to communicate in English with the user.

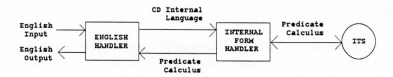

Figure 4. The natural language component

The English Handler (EH) utilizes a dictionary and a set of syntax/semantic rules to translate the English input to a conceptual dependency representation [Scha 72]. This operation relies heavily on the fact that the domain is very well defined and, in terms of language, very restricted. When English is to be output to the user, the EH uses pre-defined "frames" to match the conceptual dependency relations that are sent to it. The operation of the EH follows conventional techniques in natural language processing within a restricted domain. Details of this process are beyond the scope of the paper.

The Internal Form Handler (IFH) translates from the intermediate form of the conceptual dependency representation to the ITS' "language" form, predicate calculus, as well as from predicate calculus to the conceptual dependency representation. This step is fairly mechanical since both input and output languages are very well defined.

4.3 A Hypothetical Session

Let us assume that the tutorial model decides to present the following problem:

Example 2. How many two digit numbers are there where the first digit is greater than the second digit?

This example can not be solved by the present domain module, except possibly by enumeration. Enumeration, in our representation, involves defining a tree where each leaf represents only one possibility, i.e., the answer to each leaf is one.

The student module, which controls the interaction, enters the problem as a node in the workbook area and waits for the student to respond. Note that this involves using the NLC to translate the English form of the problem as stored in the problem library to the internal form.

An average student might first use the multiplication rule to decompose the problem into the subproblems of choosing the first digit and then the second digit. At that time, he probably would have realized that there is no easy way of expressing the dependencies between the two subproblems. He then might abandon this line of enquiry and decide to look at upper bounds by generalizing the problem. We will assume this thought pattern and see how he would progress using the interface functions.

To create a more general problem a parent node has to be created. Let us assume that he uses the "CREATE PARENT" operator. The interface would then lead him to state the general problem. Let us say he responds by typing "Find the number of two digit numbers." The NLC will translate this to the internal predicate calculus form.

At this stage, the multiplication rule might occur to him, as a way of obtaining the cardinality of this problem. He must, however, first create an alternate window for this line of enquiry. The "CREATE ALTERNATE" operator will have to be used for this purpose. We will assume that he uses this first, then states the answer to the problem as A(d1) * A(d2), and uses the "CREATE CHILD" operator twice to state the subproblems of finding the number of ways of choosing the first and second digits. Figure 5 depicts the workbook area of the screen just after he types in 10 as answer to each of the two subproblems. Note how the use of relative variables and the alternate windows allows the student to focus completely on the current subline of enquiry without getting enmeshed with the entire exploration tree.

After he has typed in the answers to the two subproblems the system will automatically calculate the answer as 100, assuming the auto-propagate mode is available and is set. To return to his original window, he can point the mouse at the alternate view of Node 5.

The student then may decide to generate the complement to the original problem, once again using the "CREATE CHILD" operator on the original parent node and entering:

"Find the number of two digit numbers where the first digit is less than or equal to the second digit".

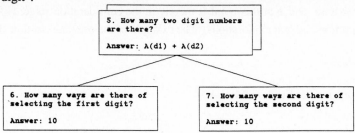

Figure 5. A partial exploration tree for Example 2

There are other ways he could proceed. For example, he may choose to obtain two complements--first digit strictly less than the second digit and first digit equal to the second digit. We will assume that he will use the addition rule to break the complement into these, after entering the answer to the original problem as $A(u) - A(s1)$. In the auto-propagate mode this will be translated as $100 - X(s1)$ by the system. We show the screen at this juncture as Figure 6.

Let us now assume that he enters the answer for Node 10 as 10. Now the student may realize that, by symmetry, Node 9 has the same answer as the original problem. This is the step where the system has no corresponding domain rule. However, if the student types in $N(0)$ as the answer for Node 9 and the auto-propagate mode is on, the system will calculate the final answer to the original problem as 45. The system will assume that the answer may be right, as the student used valid rules for all other steps. In fact, it will store this tree for later ratification as a possible rule to acquire into its knowledge base.

After updating the student model, the student module will return control to the tutorial module.

5. Implications for the Other Modules

We discuss in this section how the use of the intermediate representation has positive impact on the design of the other modules.

5.1 Implications for the Domain Module

As mentioned in Section 3, the domain module uses a tree, very similar to the exploration tree, as its working memory data structure. It contains domain specific rules for possible ways of extending the tree and strategy rules for deciding among the alternatives. One immediate consequence of this correspondence is that the tree-based language provides yet another convenient means for explanation.

Another feature, which at this point is merely in the consideration stage, is for the domain module to learn from student explorations. The example of the previous section shows how this might occur.

5.2 Implications for the Student Module

While the student module provides most of the support to the environment, it in turn reaps many benefits. First of all, the detailed feedback available enables easier diagnostic techniques like model-tracing. If the student does not show all his intermediate steps, the student module can request explanation of the intermediate steps on the exploration tree. Thus it is possible to match the granularity of the student's responses and the expert's rules to implement model-tracing.

Another problem encountered, especially when tutoring mature students, is how to find out what general problem solving heuristics they bring from their past experiences and exactly how they use these heuristics in the problem solving process. The tree representation enables one to express general problem strategies as different tree exploration classes. Thus, they be might be captured as knowledge chunks in the domain module and the system could diagnose these just as they would domain-specific knowledge. In most systems it is very difficult to relate past experiences to domain-specific rules.

Finally, storage of the exploration trees could allow other forms of diagnosis such as episodic modeling proposed by Weber [Webe 88]. While we are not implementing such a diagnostic method, we merely wish to point out that the representation mechanism allows the freedom to use many choices of diagnostic methods.

5.3 Implications for the Tutorial Module

One immediate consequence of this scheme is the feasibility of a learning environment that at the same time allows cohesive monitoring possibilities. The intermediate representation also permits a very convenient medium for demonstrating examples and guided exercises.

Inspection of trees created by student sessions can lead to observations of a particular student's learning pattern. For example, patterns such as top-down or bottom-up problem solving could be observed. As mentioned previously, proclivities towards particular strategies could also be determined. This kind of information can be used to influence the teaching focus, not only in terms of what to teach but also how to introduce new concepts.

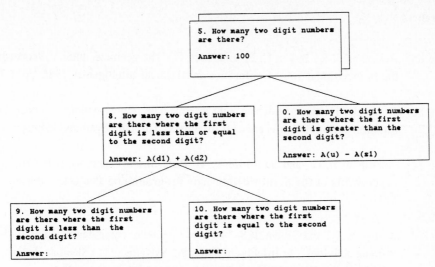

Figure 6. A more developed exploration tree for Example 2

6. Summary

In summary, we propose a tree-based intermediate representation for a tutor to teach the principles of counting. This representation provides a flexible and intuitive basis for a learning environment while facilitating use of diagnostic techniques like model-tracing. In addition, it has several positive implications for the other components of the tutoring system. We strongly feel that this representation can be transported to other mathematical domains. In such domains, providing a natural exploration environment is crucial in order to permit reification of abstract concepts.

A version of the domain module and a very rudimentary version of the interface described has been implemented on a Xerox 1186 using LOOPS. We are in the process of implementing a more complete version of the interface, as described in this report. The next step is to create a user interface shell that provides this exploration environment and test it in other domains.

Acknowledgement

We would like to acknowledge our colleagues Herb Greenberg, Paul Pedersen and Jim Hagler for their countless hours of patience in serving as our domain experts. We also wish to acknowledge the effort of several graduate students, in particular, Dan Dorenfeld, Tadashi Sakamoto, James York, Bobbi Young and Yunlong Zhao.

References

[Ande 85]   Anderson, J. R., Boyle, C. F., and Yost, G. "The geometry tutor". **Proceedings of the International Joint Conference on Artificial Intelligence**, 1985, pp. 1-7.

[Bona 88]   Bonar, J. "Intelligent tutoring with intermediate representations". **Proceedings of the International Conference on Intelligent Tutoring Systems**, 1988, pp. 25-32.

[Buch 84]   Buchanan, B. G., and Shortliffe, E. H. **Rule-Based expert systems: the MYCIN experiments of the Stanford Heuristic Programming Project**. Addison-Wesley, 1984.

[Burt 82]   Burton, R. R., and Brown, J. S. "An investigation of computer coaching for informal learning activities". In **Intelligent Tutoring Systems** (eds.) Sleeman, D. and Brown, J. S. Academic Press, 1982, pp. 79-98.

[Fisc 88]   Fischer, G., and Morch, A. "CRACK: A critiquing approach to kitchen design". **Proceedings of the International Conference on Intelligent Tutoring Systems**, 1988, pp.176-185.

[Lang 84]   Langley, P., and Ohlsson, S. "Automated cognitive modeling". **Proceedings of the National Conference on Artificial Intelligence**, 1984, pp. 193-197.

[Mill 88]   Miller, J. R. "The role of human-computer interaction in intelligent tutoring systems". In **Foundations of Intelligent Tutoring Systems** (eds.) Polson, M. C., and Richardson, J. J. Lawrence Erlbaum Associates, 1988.

[Reis 85]   Reiser, B. J., Anderson, J. R., and Farrell, R. G. "Dynamic student modeling in an intelligent tutor for LISP programming". **Proceedings of the International Joint Conference on Artificial Intelligence**, 1985, pp. 8-14.

[Scha 72]   Schank, R. C. "Conceptual dependency: A theory of natural language understanding". **Cognitive Psychology 3**, pp. 552-631.

[Self 88]   Self, J. A. "Bypassing the intractable problem of student modeling". **Proceedings of the International Conference on Intelligent Tutoring Systems**, 1988, pp. 18-24.

[Webe 88]   Weber, G. "Cognitive diagnosis and episodic modeling in an intelligent LISP-tutor". **Proceedings of the International Conference on Intelligent Tutoring Systems**, 1988, pp. 207-214.

[VanL 88]   VanLehn, K. "Student Modeling". In **Foundations of Intelligent Tutoring Systems**
(eds.) Polson, M. C., and Richardson, J. J. Lawrence Erlbaum Associates, 1988.

CircuitWorld
An Intelligent Simulation System For Digital Logic

Barry L. Kurtz
Cathy Cavendish

Computer Science Department
Box 30001
New Mexico State University
Las Cruces, NM 88003

Captain Byron Thatcher

United States Military Academy
West Point, NY 10996

ABSTRACT

CircuitWorld is an Intelligent Simulation System for digital logic developed at New Mexico State University. The digital logic expert and human-computer interface are completed. With the addition of a student model and pedagogical model, currently in the planning stages, the system will become a robust intelligent tutoring system. This paper describes the human-computer interface program written in C using X-11 windowing software and discusses the implementation of the expert in Prolog. Although there were considerable difficulties in using Prolog for circuits with feedback, these problems have been overcome and Prolog will offer many advantages for features being planned, such as the automatic translation of a device state table into Prolog code.

1. Introduction

CircuitWorld is an Intelligent Simulation System for digital logic. It allows users to build arbitrarily complex circuits out of discrete components and then to test these circuits based on specified inputs. The final system will have four main components: the digital logic expert, the human computer interface, the student model, and the pedagogical model. The digital logic expert and the human computer interface have been completed. The student model and pedagogical model are currently under development; they will form a layer between the digital logic expert and the human computer interface. The system is currently running on Sun 3 computers, using Prolog, C, and the X-ll windowing software.

2. Background and Project Goals

The CircuitWorld methodology is influenced by the Micro-World methodology developed by Seymour Papert in his Logo Project at MIT. The basic paradigm is to give the student an interactive, problem-rich environment designed to enhance the student's interests in learning the subject domain. This notion stems from Papert's acquaintance with Piaget's work in learning methods which states that, "Learning is done naturally, and spontaneously by interaction with the environment" [Papert 1980]. The Micro-World is a constructed reality whose structure matches that of a given cognitive mechanism so as to provide an environment where this mechanism can operate effectively and where a student may discover the workings of this mechanism.

The Steamer Project brings the ideal of self-discovery one step closer to a conventional ITS. [Hollan, 1984] Steamer emphasized the use of Qualitative Process Theory. This theory states that the student should learn the underlying principles of a domain and should not get bogged down in the details of the actual working components. The Steamer project also contains a limited tutoring system in the form of the Feedback Mini-Lab. In the Mini-Lab the student is able to build devices out of generic components and test them while a tutor critiques the device and points out any obvious defects. CircuitWorld uses Steamer as the model for its interactive simulation based on self-discovery. Unlike Steamer, in the completed ITS system, an opportunistic tutor will be integrated directly into the simulation and self-guided discovery portions of the program.

Quest, like Steamer, uses the Qualitative Process Theory and the idea of an interactive simulation in the domain of electrical system troubleshooting. [White, 1985] The pedagogical help given to the student is extensive, but this is at the expense of flexibility: the student is not allowed to modify the given circuit in any way. This is where CircuitWorld differs from Quest. CircuitWorld allows the student self-guided discovery yet, the complete ITS system will use a "shadow" tutor to provide pedagogical input.

The West program introduces the concept of a "shadow" tutor. [Burton, 1979] In West, the object was to win a game against the computer by constructing mathematical formulas to move around a game board. When the student model indicated that the student was lacking in a certain mathematical skill, a tutor would interrupt the game and give the student some helpful advice on how to play better. This intermittent tutor is the prototype tutor of CircuitWorld.

The other project that influenced the design of CircuitWorld was the ACTP Lisp Tutor. [Anderson, 1986] This project implements a very restrictive interaction with the students. Each keystroke is traced and any deviation from a top-down, left-to-right answer to their Lisp programming problems is immediately caught by the system and an error message is given to the student. While CircuitWorld does not trace every keystroke by the student, it traces every interface with the expert system and this will allow the tutor to find opportunities to interject pedagogical guidance and motivational messages.

The completed CircuitWorld system will combine two distinct teaching methodologies: the conventional Intelligent Tutoring System method and the Micro-World method. This will be done by creating a Micro-World environment for the student that is enhanced with an opportunistic, intelligent tutor that provides student model diagnosis and conventional ITS didactics. There are two distinct portions of CircuitWorld corresponding to the two methodologies: the Micro-World for circuit exploration, as described in this paper, and the "shadow" tutor, under development, for teaching circuit analysis and design.

3. CircuitWorld - The User Perspective and the Interface to the Expert

The student can enter circuit diagrams in graphical form and have the expert analyze the circuit for a specific set of inputs. At least two windows are used, one to display the circuit diagram and one for interaction with the student. The circuit components are selected from a menu and then placed on the screen. A mouse is used to draw wires to connect components. Keyboard input is used to assign component names and wire names. When a student decides to evaluate a circuit, the expert performs the analysis and output values appear on the circuit diagram. This human-computer interface is written in C and uses the X-11 graphics routines [Cavendish 1988].

Consider the presettable three bit binary counter shown in Figure 1. After the circuit is entered, the interface program generates the appropriate Prolog clauses and sends them to the expert. The clauses associated with the binary counter in Figure 1 are shown in Listing 1.

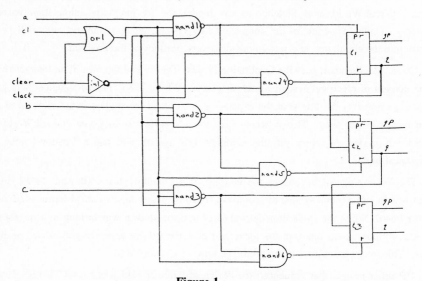

Figure 1
Presettable Three Bit Binary Counter

Each component definition includes a name for the component, which is used on the circuit diagram, a list of input signals, a list of output signals, and the generic component type. After the Prolog expert instantiates the circuit, control is returned to the C interface program so that the user can specify the simulation conditions. For example, suppose that the user wants to clear the binary counter and preset it to 101 before it is allowed to count. The interface program sends the following clause to the expert.

```
:- new_component(or1,[cl,clear],[out],or),
   new_component(in1,[clear],[out],inverter),
   new_component(nand1,[a,in1_out,or1_out],[out],nand),
   new_component(nand2,[b,in1_out,or1_out],[out],nand),
   new_component(nand3,[c,in1_out,or1_out],[out],nand),
   new_component(nand4,[or1_out,nand1_out],[out],nand),
   new_component(nand5,[or1_out,nand2_out],[out],nand),
   new_component(nand6,[or1_out,nand3_out],[out],nand),
   new_component(t1,[cp,nand4_out,nand1_out],[q,qp],t_ff),
   new_component(t2,[t1_q,nand5_out,nand2_out],[q,qp],t_ff),
   new_component(t3,[t2_q,nand6_out,nand3_out],[q,qp],t_ff).
```

Listing 1
Binary Counter Definition
at C to Prolog Interface

```
new_input([clear,1,0,clear,0,1,cl,1,1,a,1,1,c,1,1,cl,0,2]).
```
This is a sequence of triplets of the form

..., signal name, signal level, time, ...

So at time 0, clear is set to 1 and then reset to 0 at time 1. The cl line (clear and load) is set to a 1 at time 1 and back to 0 at time 2. Inputs a and c are set to a 1 at time 1; since b is not listed, it is set to a 0 by default. This sequence of inputs presets the counter to 101. The clock is built into the simulation and need not be specified as an input signal.

After running the simulation, the expert sends back to the interface a list of triplets in the form (wire name, new value, time) that gives a complete history of circuit behavior during the simulation. All of this data is available to the interface program. The user can set the clock to a starting value and click the mouse to step the clock through the desired time period. At every clock tick each wire is labeled after its name with a /0 or /1, as appropriate.

Since the student model and pedagogical model under development will be layered between the interface program and the expert, the current communication between the user interface written in C and the expert written in Prolog is extremely simple: the programs use shared files to pass information to one another. When the complete ITS becomes functional, Unix sockets will be used for interprogram communication.

4. Implementation of the CircuitWorld Expert

The current program contains AND, OR, NOR, NAND, and inverter gates, as well as *rs*-flip flops, *jk*-flip flops, *jk*- master-slave flip flops, *d*-flip flops and *t*-flip flops as generic components. The addition of generic flip flops was done to illustrate a limited encapsulation facility and to increase the evaluation speed for large circuits. Listing 2 shows the generic AND gate from the logic base.

```
                                        \*  AND gate  *\
logic([Node],and,In,[0],Time,Clock) :-   \* zero is output *\
    zero_present(In).                     \* any zero input results in a zero output *\
logic([Node],and,In,[1],Time,Clock) :-   \* one is output *\
    not zero_present(In),                 \* provided there is no zero input *\
    not member([A,feedback],In),          \* and there is no feedback *\
    not member(uncertain,In).             \* and none of the inputs are uncertain *\
logic([Node],and,In,[Out],Time,Clock) :- \* last value output is used temporarily *\
    not zero_present(In),                 \* because so far there is no zero input *\
    (member([A,feedback],In);             \* and there is either some feedback *\
      member(uncertain,In)),              \* or one of the inputs is uncertain *\
    last_val(Node,Out,Time2),             \* in this case, return the last value *\
    asserta(lastval).                     \* and set a global flag that a last value was used *\
```

Listing 2
Sample Logic Base for AND Gate

In this system, flip flops remember values by asserting a last value clause into the program data base stamped by component name and evaluation time. When the evaluation determines that the current output of a component is a remembered value, it gets the required information from the last value clause.

Prolog was chosen as the language for implementing the expert since there is a direct correlation between the abstract knowledge of the state table and the actual representation in Prolog. This direct correlation should make it possible for a user to input a state table for any device and generate the appropriate Prolog code to add this component to the generic database. In order to implement this feature a state table parser and code generator will have to be built and integrated into the current system. Figure 2 illustrates this approach for a *jk*-master-slave flip flop.

Following the component name, jk_ff, is an input list (J, clock, K, reset, preset) and an output list (Q, not Q). The first clause states that if the reset line goes low while the preset is high, then the Q is forced low and the not Q is high. The second clause is for preset and also follows directly from the

J	K	Reset	Preset	Clock	Q(t+1)	Comments
_	_	0	1	0	0	Reset
_	_	1	0	0	1	Preset
0	0	1	1	0	Q(t)	No change
0	1	1	1	0	0	Clear
1	0	1	1	0	1	Set
1	1	1	1	0	Q'(t)	Complemented
_	_	1	1	1	Q(t)	No Change Clocked

Figure 2a: State Table for jk-flip flop

* Reset *\	logic([Node,Node1],jk_ff,[_,_,_,0,1],[0,1],Time, Clock).
* Preset *\	logic([Node,Node1],jk_ff,[_,_,_,1,0],[1,0],Time, Clock).
* No Change *\	logic([Node,Node1],jk_ff,[0,0,0,1,_],[Out,Out1],Time, Clock):-
	last_val(Node,Out,Time2),
	switch(Out,Out1),
	asserta(lastval).
* Clear *\	logic([Node,Node1],jk_ff,[0,0,1,1,_],[0,1],Time, Clock).
* Set *\	logic([Node,Node1],jk_ff,[1,0,0,1,_],[1,0],Time, Clock).
* Complement *\	logic([Node,Node1],jk_ff,[1,0,1,1,_],[Out,Out1],Time, Clock):-
	last_val(Node,Out1,Time2),
	switch(Out1,Out),
	lastval(Clock,1,Time3),
	interval(Val),
	Time3 is Time - Val,
	asserta((last_val(Clock,1,Time):-!)).
* No Change *\	logic([Node,Node1],jk_ff,[_,1,_,1,_],[Out,Out1],Time, Clock):-
* Clocked *\	last_val(Node,Out,Time2),
	switch(Out,Out1),
	asserta(lastval).
* No Change *\	logic([Node,Node1],jk_ff,[1,0,1,1,_],[Out,Out1],Time, Clock):-
* Clocked *\	last_val(Node,Out,Time2),
	switch(Out,Out1).
* Error *\	logic([Node,Node1],jk_ff,[_,_,_,_,_],[uncertain,uncertain],Time,Clock):-
* Handling*\	asserta(lastval).

Figure 2b: Code Corresponding to State Table

truth table. The third line of the truth table (no change due to J,K both being low), corresponds to the next logic clause. Notice that the last Q value is fetched in Out, switch sets Out1 to the opposite value, and the global last value flag is set. The clear and set (lines 4 and 5 of the table) are very similar to reset and preset, however, the outputs are caused by the J and K inputs rather than the reset or preset lines. If both the J and K are high, the flip flop toggles. The complement logic has been set up so that there can be multiple pulsing within a time interval. The next two logic clauses correspond to the last line of the truth table, No Change Clocked. The first of these is the rising edge of the clock and the second is for the falling edge of the clock. In evaluating circuits with feedback, one or more inputs might have the value uncertain. The last logic clause handles this by simplying stating that at this time the outputs of the flip flop are also uncertain.

The evaluation of feedback was the most challenging task in implementing the expert system. It required the addition of clauses that checked for feedback and clauses that continued evaluation of the circuit when feedback was found. The general scheme for evaluating a circuit with feedback is to try to evaluate the circuit in the normal manner. If an output cannot be determined due to feedback, then that output is "short circuited" and other components of the circuit are evaluated in the hope that some stable components will be found that will lead to stable inputs into the component(s) that could not be evaluated.

CircuitWorld evaluates a circuit as a function of time. The user specifies inputs with a time stamp on them so that circuits can be evaluated relative to a system clock. Listing 3 gives the evaluation clauses which simulate the system clock. The output clause (arity 2) is a request for the output of a named component at a particular time. Once the current time is determined, the catch_time clause steps through the simulation from the previous time to the current time. Finally, the circuit is evaluated. The eval clause using the logic clauses discussed previously. A history of each component output is saved, in the form of last value clauses, and can be used to analyze the circuit dynamically as the inputs change. This added component allows for future development of output waveform analysis for the circuits.

Since CircuitWorld is still under development, it has not been tested with "real" students. Field testing will begin once the student model and pedagogical model are completed.

5. Ongoing Development of CircuitWorld

The current version of CircuitWorld consists mainly of the Micro-World expert and the human-computer interface program. The shadow tutor along with its didactic and diagnostic strategies are currently under development. Other additions will be the encapsulation facility, enhanced graphical interface, and the addition of a waveform output analysis facility.

The shadow tutor will include the didactic and diagnostic components and will be driven by the student's interaction with the system in an opportunistic manner. The shadow tutor itself will be implemented in Prolog by adding an intelligent interpreter as a layer between the C program's

```
output([]).
output([Head,Time|Rest]) :- output(Head,Time),
                    output(Rest).
output(Name,Time1):- Time is Time1 * 2,
        current_time(Ctm),
        Time >= Ctm,nl,
        catch_time(Ctm,Time),
        eval([Name],Output,Time).


catch_time(Time,Time):- retract(current_time(A)),
             asserta(current_time(Time)),!.
catch_time(Ctm,Time):- NewTime is Ctm + 1,
        PTime is NewTime  2,
        bagof((Name,Val),
        input(Name,Val,NewTime),Bag),
        remove_input(NewTime),
        interval(Fudge),
        NewTime1 is NewTime + Fudge,
        assert_bag(Bag,NewTime1),
        eval_all(NewTime),
        catch_time(NewTime,Time),!.
catch_time(Ctm,Time):- NewTime is Ctm + 1,
        eval_all(NewTime),
        catch_time(NewTime,Time),
        !.
```

Listing 3

Output Evaluation Clauses with System Clock

graphical interface and the current expert system. The shawdow tutor will detect simple errors, such as outputs from two devices wired together, and will provide more sophisticated guidance when the student has been challenged to design a particular circuit, such as a four bit decoder.

The encapsulation facility will allow the inclusion of any circuit into the system as a generic component. This can be used by teachers and students to add components to the system. No knowledge of programming or the underlying knowledge representation will be needed to use this facility. The user will enter the state table of the component and it will be entered into the generic component database. The state table can also be generated by the system for any component built and be entered into the generic component base in this manner. A state table parser will parse the table into a usable form and a code generator will write the Prolog code needed to add the component into the generic component database. It has already been shown, by the inclusion of the flip flops, that it is feasible to generate this Prolog code from the state table information.

The graphical human-computer interface will be enhanced to include alternative forms of circuit display, such as state tables and will include the use of pop-up menus to minimize keyboard interaction. The X-11 graphics system has the capability to include these features into the system.

The addition of waveform analysis of circuits will require an interface to the expert system's history data base to pass the needed waveform information that has already been generated by the expert system. A graphics facility will be needed to display and manipulate these data.

6. Conclusions

CircuitWorld shows that an expert for circuit design and analysis can be implemented in a reasonable manner using Prolog and that an interactive simulation environment can be developed using C. The main problem encountered during the development of the CircuitWorld expert occurred when the program tried to evaluate circuits with feedback. An evaluation scheme was developed that recognized circular definitions and, even more difficult, evaluated circuits after feedback had been detected. The "short circuit" approach of evaluating circuits with feedback produced correct results, but the logic is complicated and not very efficient. This was perhaps the greatest drawback in using Prolog for this expert system.

The merging of logic based programming in Prolog with imperative programming in C was a basic goal of this project. A simple prototype expert system (without feedback) was developed quickly using Prolog, then this was expanded as the complexity of the expert increased. The C language, chosen for the user interface, has also proven to be a good choice. The C language's interface with the X-11 graphical system makes it a powerful and flexible language in which to construct a user interface. The resultant graphical displays are very useful and have great potential for further enhancement. The user interface, written in C, must make numerous C-system calls to the expert system whenever evaluation or analysis is required. Data sharing is accomplished via two permanent files, however, once the system is fully developed Unix sockets will be used.

The development of this portion of the CircuitWorld program has been relatively successful. The major problems in the expert system area and user interface have been worked out and provide a firm basis for further enhancement and development.

References

Anderson, John R., and Edward Skwarecki. "The Automated Tutoring of Introductory Computer Programming." *Communications of the ACM* Volume 29 (September 1986), pp. 842-849.

Burton, Richard R., and John Seely Brown. "An Investigation of Computer Coaching for Informal Learning Activities." *International Journal Man-Machine Studies* Volume 11 (1979), 5-24.

Cavendish, Cathy. "CircuitWorld's Graphical User Interface." Unpublished Project Report, New Mexico State University (1988).

Hollan, James D., Edwin L. Hutchins, and Louis M. Weitzman. "STEAMER: An Interactive, Inspectable, Simulation-Based Training System." *The AI Magazine* (Summer 1984).

Papert, Seymour. **Mindstorm: Children, Computers and Powerful Ideals**, Basic Books, Inc. (1980).

Wenger, Etienne. **Artificial Intelligence and Tutoring Systems**, Morgan Kaufmann Publishers, Inc. (1987).

White, Barbara Y., and John R. Frederiksen, "QUEST: Qualitative Understanding of Electrical System Troubleshooting." *SIGART Newsletter* Number 93 (July 1985), 34-37.

A CAL ENVIRONMENT FOR HYPERCARD

Brigitte de LA PASSARDIERE

Université Pierre et Marie Curie (PARIS VI), Laboratoire MASI
4 place Jussieu, 75252 Paris cedex 05
FRANCE

Abstract :

In this communication, we present a special Computer Assisted Learning environment for the HyperCard development tool. We create a dedicated version of a benchmark courseware, which has already been previously developped under other authoring systems in order to compare HyperCard facilities for CAL. On the strength of this first experience, we have designed a programming environment adapted to the particular nature of CAL problems, in order to develop educational stackwares. This environment tries to provide CAL functions which are missing such as response analysis or automatic student recording. Two further advantages are both the simplification of the HyperTalk learning process and the improvement of productivity by reducing the development time.

This paper reports on a special **C**omputer **A**ssisted **L**earning (CAL) environment for HyperCard. The basic features of HyperCard and HyperTalk will first presented. Then, we will describe an environment designed to facilitate the development of instructional software based on the use of HyperCard.

1. INTRODUCTION

HyperCard is a development tool for Macintosh material [1]. It benefits from the very convivial environment of this type of computer (e.g., mouse and graphic interface) which seems to make it both a "user's friendly" software and an appropriate medium for CAL. Most importantly, it enables the student to avoid the material difficulties that often disturb the learning process.

HyperCard is based on concepts taken from Smalltalk, such as the notion of objects and programmation through messages. So, it works as a database connected to an object-oriented language. Objects have static and dynamic properties. In terms of CAL, static properties define how the object is seen by the student, while dynamic properties describe how the software reacts to the student's responses or requests such as "help", "dictionnary", "calculator" or "break".

There are several types of objects in HyperCard : `stack`, `card`, `background`, `field` and `button`. A courseware would be best described as a `stack`. If the courseware consists of several lessons, then it can be broken into more than one stack (a stack for each lesson, for example). A learning situation will be described by one or more `Cards`. If the situation is complex, it can be done either by a succession of cards which are visually related (e.g., animation or help) or by the overlay of informations on the starting card (e.g., emphasis, comment, complementary information or instructions). Finally, `fields` contain editable text, while `buttons` are action objects that can recognize and deal with mouse events.

Given the powerful features of HyperCard as a general purpose development tool, it was evaluated for its suitability in CAL and compared to other authoring languages and systems. The different functions usually required for CAL were tested on a courseware specifically designed for this study [2]. It was found that HyperCard's graphic and browsing tools were particularly useful but that programming was necessary if exercices were to be included in the courseware [3]. For example, HyperCard misses special facilities for CAL, such as grading, student recording or response analysis, and this means that all these functions have to be programmed by the author. Although the programming language of HyperCard (**HyperTalk**) is very powerful, its learning can take a long time especially if the author want to create a sophisticated courseware in interactive rather than artistic terms.

Taking into account these difficulties, we have designed a programming environment, compatible with CAL, that improves the development of educational stackware with HyperCard.

2. A CAL ENVIRONMENT

The environment includes CAL facilities with an emphasis on functions that deal with response analysis. Basically, such an environment is a stack including HyperTalk programs. Therefore, we will first review some of the major features of this language.

2.1. HyperTalk features

Every HyperCard object has a script. A script is a collection of handlers including HyperTalk statements. There are two types of handlers : the message handler (beginning with on) and the function handler (beginning with function). When a message or a function is received by the object whose script contains the handler, it executes it. For example, when you release the mouse button while the browse tool is inside a button's rectangle, HyperCard sends the message mouseUp to the button. HyperCard then looks in the button script for a handler matching the mouseUp message. If found, it executes the statements included in the handler. Otherwise, the message is transmitted further on, according to the existing objects hierachy (Figure 1). On the other hand, the function handlers are user-defined functions. Functions as messages use the same object hierarchy.

```
Buttons or fields
       Card
   Background
      Stack
   Home Stack
    HyperCard
```

Figure 1 : object hierachy

2.2. Facilities

HyperTalk being an object-oriented language, the programming is scattered among the objects. One consequence of this characteristics is that object hierachy must be respected in order to select the appropriate position of a function. Thus, CAL functions will now be reviewed according to HyperCard objects.

2.2.1. *stack script*

The stack script only handles system messages that are related with the stack itself (`openStack`, `closeStack`) and with unexpected card deleting (`doMenu deleteCard`). The `openCard` handler covers various initializations. Some are concerned with predefined feedback messages to the student (e.g., congratulations, encouragements, errors and warnings) which can be randomly selected after. Others can fix courseware parameters or define the student's level (mostly, level 2-typing). In this environment, there are many global variables which caracterize, for example, the learning session (number, duration), the student (name, grade) or the courseware (title, lesson number). These are mainly initialised at this step. This handler also determines whether the student is starting this courseware for the first time or not.

```
on closeStack
  global sPrénom, sNote, sNuCarte       -- global variables
  global sDébut, sDurée

  --                   -- compute time spent in the session
  get the seconds - sDébut
  put it into temps
  put it div 3600 into heures
  get it - (3600 * heures)
  put it div 60 into minutes
  get it - (60 * minutes)
  put heures & ":" & minutes &":" & it into total

  --                        -- save session parameters
  lock screen
  go to card "Résume session"
  put sPrénom into card field "Prénom"
  put sNote into card field "Note provisoire"
  put sNuCarte into card field "Dernière carte vue"
  add temps to sDurée
  put sDurée into card field "Durée"
  put total into card field "Temps session"
  unlock screen
end closeStack
```

Figure 2 : extract from closeStack handler

Indeed, it is possible for the student to stop learning at any time, in which case the session parameters are initialized accordingly. The `closeCard` handler (Figure 2) computes the time spent in the session and saves the session parameters such as the student name, the number of the last card seen, the grade or the duration. All this information is stored in a card specially designed for this use (named "Résume session"). In HyperTalk, there is no way to discreminate variables concerning the full courseware from those which are used inside one card (to transmit parameters from a handler to another one). To single out full courseware variables, we name them with a prefix "s", meaning superior level or system level.

2.2.2. *background*

In this environnement, there is only one background shared by all cards of the courseware (Figure 3). The header includes the lesson's name, the courseware's title and a card's reference. The footer contains only icones symbolizing the facilities given to the student. Some are classic buttons such HOME, ARROWS (next, previous) while others are more adapted to CAL functions. The HELP button provides the instructions for the stackware and specially an explanation of all the icones used. This is the *global help*. The GLOSSARY button allows the student to access the definition of words by

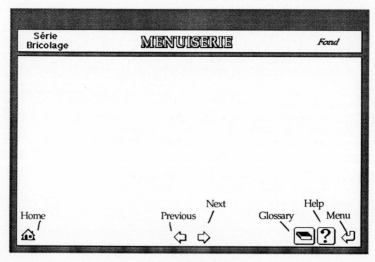

Figure 3 : background

three ways : directly by the word, by a hierachy of themes or by alphabetical order. The MENU button allows to return to the last menu seen.

2.2.3. *background script*

The background script includes various functions and utilities for CAL. Some handlers show or hide buttons of the background, whilst others display texts with visual effect or sound for warnings. The most important part of the background script however concerns response analysis and student recording.

(i) - response analysis

There are functions for the pretreatment of the student's response (UpperCase, VerifyNum, VerifyAlpha) and others for pattern matching (Présent, Absent). Others functions are used to recognize synonyms which are included in a list and to accept answer for which the model includes jokers (Figure 5, next page).

```
function Tolérance texte,min,max
   --           -- check if the text value is between min & max
   if not VerifyNum (texte)
   then  return false                        -- not a number
   else
      if texte <= max and texte > min
      then return true
      else return false                      -- not between
   end if
end Tolérance

function Précision texte,rép,ordre
   --           -- check if the text value has a given precision
   if not VerifyNum (texte)
   then return false                         -- not a number
   else
      put rép + rép * ordre into max
      put max
      put rép - rép * ordre into min
      put min
      if texte <= max and texte > min
      then return true
      else return false
   end if
end Précision
```

Figure 4 : numerical functions for response analysis

An example of pattern matching analysis is presented in section 2.2.5. In case of numerical responses, there are others functions that recognize if a number falls whithin a given interval or with a given precision (Figure 4).

```
function Synonyme liste,texte
   --          -- check if an item of the list is in the text
   put the number of items in liste into lg
   repeat with i = 1 to lg
     if item i of liste is in texte
     then
        return true                          -- there is one
        exit Synonyme
     end if
   end repeat
   return false
end Synonyme

function Joker élément,texte
   --        -- check if the element with joker is in the text
   global sJoker
   put offset(sJoker,élément) into i         -- joker position
   put the length of élément into lg
   put empty into prem
   repeat with j = 1 to i-1
     put prem & char j of élément into prem
   end repeat
   put empty into deus
   repeat with j = i+1 to lg
     put deus & char j of élément into deus
   end repeat
   if prem is empty
   then
     if deus is empty
     then return false                -- prem & deus empty
     else return Présent (deus,texte)    -- only prem empty
   else
     if deus is empty
     then return Présent (prem,texte)     -- only deus empty
     else                          -- prem & deus non empty
       if SuiviDe(prem,deus,texte)
       then return true
       else return false
     end if
   end if
end Joker
```

Figure 5 : text functions for response analysis

(ii) - <u>student recordings</u>

A student recording can be set up in many different ways according to its further use. Options include creating a file, creating another stack, or using a scrolling field. If a file is created, its elements should be isolated using the tab key or carriage return, so applications such as Multiplan and Cricketgraph can be subsequently used for editing statistics or graphics. Creating an additional stack can be annoying since it involves interferences and time consumming procedures such as opening and closing stacks in order to switch from one to another. We have found that the best solution is to use a scrolling field. In such a case, a card, unknown by the student, will be dedicated. It will be composed of a single scrolling field holding a line or a paragraph in which the student's activity will be stored. We propose that two types of student recording should be managed. In the first, only the number of the card seen and the time alloted to it will be stored ; in the second, previous informations will be saved along with the student's answer and the pattern matching in the response analysis. This option calls for the compulsory use of fonts such as `courrier` or `monaco` whose letter spacing is fixed. Moreover, all the information within line should fit in a fixed format so that columns are adequately reproduced.

(iii) - grading

To perform this function, one needs to create a dedicated global variable that will be initialized upon opening the stack and a function handler will increment the variable according to given parameters.

2.2.4. *card script*

The card script has been restricted to two handlers (`openCard`, `closeCard`). The first handler takes care of the initialisations specific to the card. Both of these handlers hold some important statements that are needed to facilitate the applications of the CAL functions involved. Some statements are used to influence the visual effect of shifting from one card to another (`lock screen`, `unlock screen`). Others instructions call automatically utilities such as scoring and student recording. A last set of instructions is needed to retrieve a card with its current status after a call for help or use of the dictionnary, since these procedures involve the temporary use of a different card. In order to return to the starting card, we have at first to save it (`push card`) then to restore it (`pop` card). Unfortunately, this last command triggers automatically an `openCard` message which resets the card to its very original status and erases the student's answers. To avoid such situation, a boolean variable is tested in the `openCard` handler (Figure 6).

```
on openCard
  global sAide
  --    -- initialisation only if aid has not been requested
  if sAide is true
  then put false into sAide
  else                                    -- card initialisation
  -- any statements
  end if
  --                                      -- clean card change
  unlock screen
end openCard
```

Figure 6 : openCard handler

2.2.5. *exercises*

Since almost everything can be created with HyperCard, one should not limit its imaginative use to only to a few exercises. In order to make developments, easier, we have included in the stackware some cards to be used as sample exercises. At any rate, one has to remember that the author HAS TO write some scripts or at least to modify button scripts. For example, a special button is often needed in order to trigger the response analyis at the end of an exercise. A new message of HyperCard 1.2, `returnInField`, will also permit the detection of the end of the exercies if text typing is required. The related script will describe the list of the synonyms, the answer patterns and also how the responses analysis has to be done. To illustrate this, we use cards from the benchmark courseware on carpentry. Figure 7 shows how buttons are used for mutiple choice question, while Figure 8 shows how all the answers are stored in order to display a result array. Figure 9 shows a response analysis that checks if any thing is missing. In case of open questions, we use the different functions already present in the background script in order to recognize the answer. It is also possible to handle questions whose answer is among a set of words, and possibly involving minor misspellings (Figure 10).

In this exercise, there are two tools not belonging to the set. The student has to click these two objects then the "OK" button.

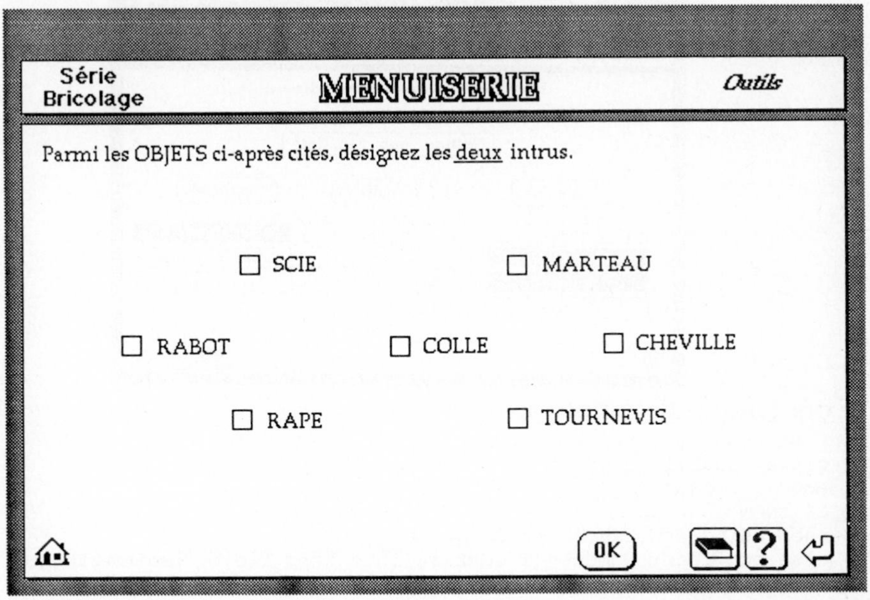

Extract from the "OK" button

```
on mouseUp
   global sBravo,sCourage,sErreur          -- global messages
   global SNote

   --                                       -- initialisation
   put "Seuls sont intrus les deux éléments qui ne sont pas"¬
   & "des outils" into laRéponse
   put 0 into bon                          -- good answer number

   if not hilite of button "Scie" then add 1 to bon
   if not hilite of button "Marteau" then add 1 to bon
   if not hilite of button "Rabot" then add 1 to bon
   if hilite of button "Colle" then add 1 to bon
   if hilite of button "Cheville" then add 1 to bon
   if not hilite of button "Rape" then add 1 to bon
   if not hilite of button "Tournevis" then add 1 to bon
   if bon = 7                              -- everything good
   then
      Répond line (random of 3) of sBravo
      add 4 to sNote
   else
      Répond laRéponse
      add 2 to sNote
   end if
   afficheFlêche
end mouseUp
```

Figure 7 : multiple choice question

In this exercise, each tool passing in the rectangle window has to be returned to his owner. The student has to click on a profession button. After the last tool, the result is given as an array and the wrong answer are highlighted by reverse effect.

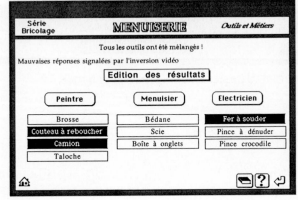

Extract from the script card

```
on montreUn
  global cOutils,cNuméro
  add 1 to cNuméro
  if cNuméro > 10
  then editeRésultat
  else put item cNuméro of cOutils into card field "NomOutil"
end montreUn

on editeRésultat
  global cBon
  put "Mauvaises réponses signalées par l'inversion vidéo"¬
  into card field "Enoncé"
  put "Edition des résultats" into card field "NomOutil"
  lock screen
  repeat with i = 1 to 10
    put "Récap" & i into leChamp
    show card field leChamp                    -- the tool
    if item i of cBon is false
    then                                  -- reverse effect
      put "Couvre" & i into leBouton
      set hilite of button leBouton to true
    end if
  end repeat
  afficheFlêche
  unlock screen
end editeRésultat
```

Extract from the "PEINTRE" (painter) button

```
on mouseUp
  global cNuméro,cBon
  --                                      -- initialisation
  put "3,4,6,10" into aLui                -- good answers

  if cNuméro is in aLui
  then put true & "," after cBon
  else put false & "," after cBon
  montreUn
end mouseUp
```

Figure 8 : result array

In this exercise, each tool has to be associated with its use. The student has to click on a tool button and a use tool, then on the "PAIRE" button and at the end on the "OK" button.

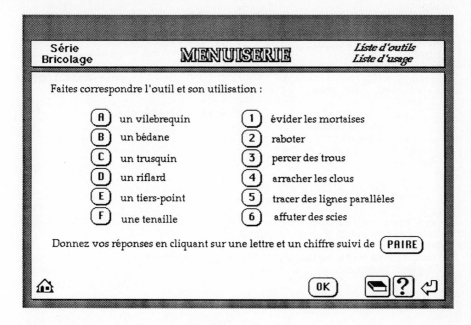

Extract from the button card "OK"

```
on mouseUp
   global sBravo,sNote,sMenu
   global cRéponse,cNb

   if cNb is not 6
   then                                        -- incomplete answer
     answer "Il manque des paires"
     exit mouseUp
   end if
   put "A 3, B 1, C 5, D 2, E 6, F 4" into modèle
   put 0 into bonrep
   put empty into mauvrep

   repeat with j = 1 to cNb                     -- missing numbers
     if j is not in cRéponse
     then
       put cRéponse & "," & j
       answer "Il manque le numéro : " & j
       exit mouseUp
     end if
   end repeat

   repeat with j = 1 to cNb                     -- response analysis
     if item j of cRéponse is in modèle
     then add 1 to bonrep
     else put item j of cRéponse && ";" after mauvrep
   end repeat
   afficheFlêche
end mouseUp
```

Extract from the "PAIRE" button

```
on mouseUp
   global cLettre,cChiffre,cRéponse,cNb
   if (cLettre is empty) or (cChiffre is empty)
   then                                              -- not a pair
      answer "Cliquez sur UN outil et UNE définition"
      exit mouseUp
   end if
   if cNb is not 0
   then
      repeat with j = 1 to cNb                       -- pair updating
         if word 1 of item j of cRéponse is cLettre
         then
            put cChiffre into word 2 of item j of cRéponse
            Répond "Réponses : " & cRéponse
            exit mouseUp
         end if
      end repeat
   end if
   add 1 to cNb                                      -- new pair
   if cNb = 1
   then
      put cLettre && cChiffre into cRéponse
      Répond "Réponse : " & cRéponse
   else
      put "," && cLettre && cChiffre after cRéponse
      Répond "Réponses : " & cRéponse
   end if
end mouseUp
```

Figure 9 : pair list

In this exercise, the student has to explain the use of a tool. He can do it with his own words. In the handler below, the response analysis checks if the answer has at least a word in a predefined set of words, if another word is present and thus, if there is not a third word. The answer can have mispelling, but the joker is not used as the pattern is given only by the root of words.

Extract from the "OK" button

```
on Trusquin
   global cLocFenêtre
   put card field "Réponse" into réponse
   --                                              -- checking words
   put Synonyme ("tir,fai,dessin,trac",réponse) into m1
   put Présent ("parral",réponse) into m2
   put Absent ("courb",réponse) into m3
   if m1 and m2 and m3 then
      Répond "Félicitations"
      exit Trusquin
   end if
   if m1 or m2 then
      Répond "Précisez votre réponse, elle est incompléte"
      click at cLocFenêtre
   else
      Répond "le TRUSQUIN sert à tracer des lignes paralléles"
   end if
end Trusquin
```

Example of a good answer

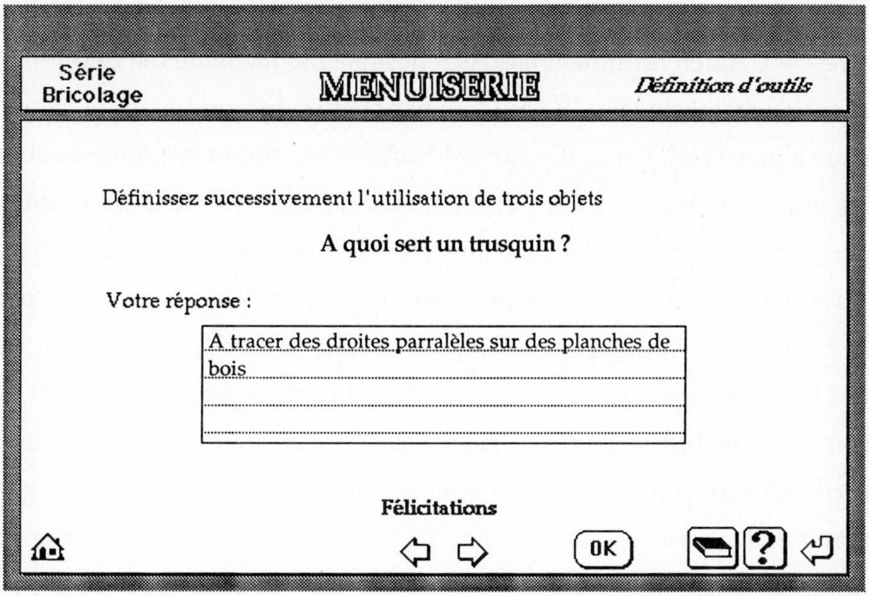

| Série Bricolage | MENUISERIE | Définition d'outils |

Définissez successivement l'utilisation de trois objets

A quoi sert un trusquin ?

Votre réponse :

A tracer des droites parralèles sur des planches de bois

Félicitations

Example of an answer with misspelling and a word missing

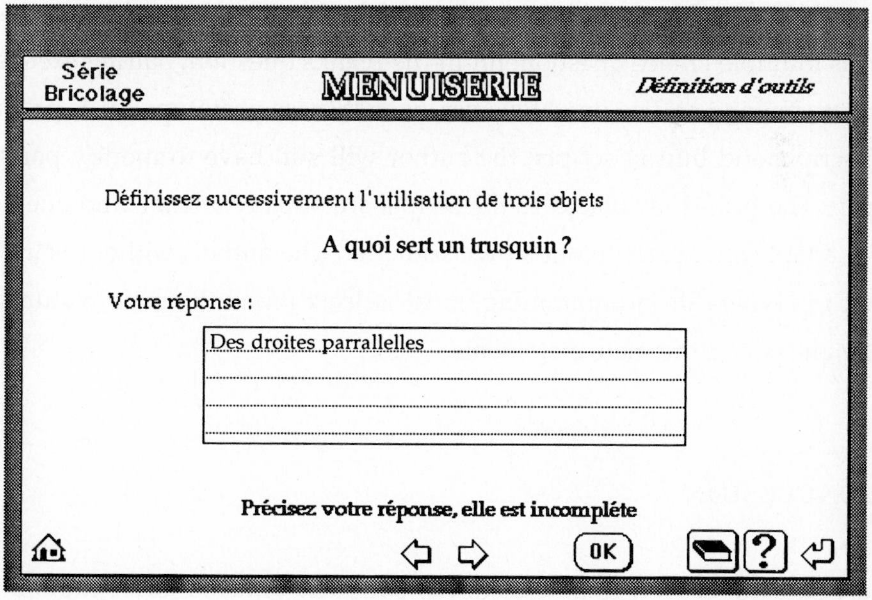

| Série Bricolage | MENUISERIE | Définition d'outils |

Définissez successivement l'utilisation de trois objets

A quoi sert un trusquin ?

Votre réponse :

Des droites parrallelles

Précisez votre réponse, elle est incomplète

Figure 10 : open question

2.3. How to create your own stackware

The present CAL environment has been designed to facilitate the development of educationnal stackware. It could be handled in different ways. One use is to create a new stack using the current background option set. One can create a stack with one's own graphics, ergonomy and even style, with the additional benefits steming from all the functions already present in the stack script and the background script. Therefore, important functions such as response analysis, grading, student recording are readily available in order to write card or button scripts. A second use is when an author wants to create a stack without writing full scripts. In such cases, one is limited to the style and exercices already provided by the environment but benefits from the global help and the glossary. The author just has to save a copy of the CAL environment stack, delete unnecessary cards, copy and paste prototype cards and then update each card according to his own needs. For each different prototype cards, there is a help card that explains exactly which changes has to be made and where they are to be done. The prototype cards consist of the differents forms of typical exercises as in other specialized authoring systems, such as multiple choice question, fill-in-the-blanks question, pairing exercises, elements ranking and so on. However, even if these prototype cards provide card scripts and button scripts, the author will still have to modify parts of scripts. The task is facilitated as the scripts are already written and one only has to adapt some parts to one's own scenario. The author, without being an expert in HyperTalk programming, must at least know the main features of the language and the main statements.

3. CONCLUSION

Although it can be easy to quickly develop a stack aimed at basic exploration of knowledge (effort being mainly devoted to graphics effects), writing a courseware that involves response analysis is a more demanding task.

HyperTalk is a powerful language, with many features, functions and commands, and its learning takes time. With the environment described above, we wished to provide a set of functions usually required in the authoring systems and not to impose a style of stackware or limit the pedagogical creativity.

Finally, to validate this environment, we have created an educational stackware based on a courseware defined in the European project DEGEL (Didacticiels en Génie Logiciel - European coursewares of software engineering). The aim of this courseware, specified without reference to any specific realisation tool, is to present the rules of the Man-Machine interface. The environment has enabled the stackware development in a short time, although it shows the limits of a such environment and the difficulties if a good experience in HyperTalk programmation is not available.

REFERENCES

[1] **BRANDEIS** P., **KERTESZ** J., "Le livre d'HyperCard", Editions P.S.I, 1988
GOODMAN D., "The complete HyperCard handbook", Bantam Computer Bks, 1988
KAEHLER C., "HyperCard, power techniques and scripts", Addison Wesley, 1988
RINALDI F., "HyperCard : la programmation en HyperTalk", Cedic Nathan, 1988
SHAFER D., "HyperTalk programming", Haydan Boos, 1988
VAUGHAM T., "Using HyperCard from Home to HyperTalk" Que Corp., 1988

[2] de **LA PASSARDIERE** B., "Quels outils informatiques pour réaliser des didacticiels : une étude sur HyperCard", Université Paris VI, Rapport MASI, n° 250, 1988

[3] de **LA PASSARDIERE** B., "HyperCard et les fonctionnalités de l'EAO", Sixth Canadian Symposium on Instructional Technology, Halifax, 1989

THE ROLE OF SCHEMATA
IN CONCEPT ACQUISITION AND DIAGNOSIS

Jean-François Le Ny
Institut des Sciences Cognitives et de la Communication
Centre d'Etudes de Psychologie Cognitive,
Universite de Paris-Sud, Centre d'Orsay, Bat. 335,
91405 Orsay, France

Summary

A module of automatic cognitive diagnosis has been constructed in
the framework of a tutorial system for transmission of knowledge
through language. It takes responses of students trying to
characterize newly acquired concepts and evaluates them. The module
contains a syntactico-semantic analyzer, a summarizer-schematizer, and
an evaluator. It uses a conceptual base of knowledge organized in a
hierarchy of schemata. This paper presents an important class of such
schemata, concerning scientific phenomena, more specifically those in
the field of animal behavior. They contain information on the entities
or relations involved in the concept, their successive states, and
times. They are represented in an attribute-value format. They are
implemented by insertion of their components in the semantic part of
the dictionary associated with the analyser. When processing a
particular student response the system constructs from these schemata
both a representation in working memory of the target concept and an
instantiated representation of the response. Comparison of these two
representations yields a diagnosis of the corresponding individual
concept.

Development of intelligent tutoring systems is often based on use of reasoning about situations or micro-worlds designed to enable students to acquire knowledge, in particular concepts (Bonar and Cunningham, 1988; Caillot, 1985; Carbonell,1970; Chi, Feltovitch and Glaser, 1981; Reiser, Anderson and Farrell, 1985; Sleeman and Brown, 1982; Wenger, 1987; Woolf, 1988). However there is also a distinct advantage in having intelligent tutorials deal with concepts directly acquired through natural language. Acquisition of highly abstract concepts -- for example in mathematics, logic or computer science -- may also require manipulation and reasoning in specific formal languages, but less abstract concepts in various empirical sciences often require as much semantic accuracy as formalized concepts, even though their use does not necessarily imply as high a degree of symbolic reasoning and computation (Anderson, 1983; van Dijk and Kintsch, 1983; Le Ny, 1986; Le Ny, Carite and Poitrenaud, 1986).

The field of knowledge I will use to illustrate this type of concept is animal behavior and conditioning. I will give a description of one concept in this field later.

A general cognitive model of concepts must encompass descriptions of their structure, their formation in individuals through perception, their acquisition in instruction through language and other media, as well as their historical elaboration in science through reasoning and experimentation. Thus, to be universal and valid such a cognitive model must apply both to rational concepts, i.e. concepts considered to be adequate in a given scientific field -- such as described, in particular, by knowledge representation -- and natural concepts, i.e. concepts actually existing in the mind of people, in particular students -- such as described by cognitive psychology. Thus, cognitive science research and modeling must combine these two approaches and its models must include a higher order description, i.e. an adequate meta-concept of conceptual representations (Le Ny, 1989): I will use the concept of "schema" as such a meta-concept.

Approaches to conceptual diagnosis

To infer the individual content of a natural concept in the mind of a particular student can be considered as a crucial requirement in long-term instruction. However this may not in any case be within the grasp of the teacher. Thus it is both theoretically and practically useful to construct an intelligent system, or sub-system, that can produce such a diagnosis automatically.

I will restrict myself here to a method where students provide a verbal characterization of a concept. This consists of a response to a simple question such as : "What is a C ?", where "C" is the name of a concept.

Let us take the concept of "spontaneous recovery" in the field of animal conditioning as an example. Thus if we ask a student a question such as: "What is spontaneous recovery ?", we actually are instructing him or her to put the content of his or her concept as such in memory into words. Cognitive conceptual diagnosis will here consist of inferring in an inductive way the content of the natural concept from its verbal characterization by the student. This diagnosis must of course take into consideration the psychological processes involved in solving this cognitive problem.

Now, the problem that arises if we place ourselves in the context of cognitive science is the following: given responses in natural language obtained in such educational situations, is it possible to devise an intelligent, automatic knowledge-based system performing conceptual evaluation of these responses ? Such a system should of course be both theoretically well grounded and technically efficient. I have constructed an automatic module of our CINACC tutorial system (Le Ny, Carite and Poitrenaud, 1986) that is one possible solution to this problem.

The conceptual diagnosis module

In short this module comprises three main layers. They are : 1. the analyzer-interpreter, 2. the summarizer-schematizer, and 3. the evaluator

The first, lowest layer, the analyzer-interpreter, consists of an automat of the Augmented Transition Network type (Winograd, 1983; Woods, 1972) which performs a syntactico-semantic analysis of students' responses and provides a first representation in machine as its output.

This representation contains detailed information on both the syntactic and semantic aspects of the response. The function of the second layer will be to summarize this information according to pre-determined requirements.

This second layer, the summarizer-schematizer, works by using schemata of texts and concepts. These schemata represent intensional knowledge as frames expressed in a predicative language. They are assumed to correspond to organized bundles of semantic features in the teacher's or student's minds.

The third and highest layer of the automat has an evaluation function. Its task consists of automatically matching two representations created in machine, one after interpretation and schematization of the student's response and another constructed according to a description of the target concept stored in the knowledge base of the system.

An overview of the schemata

In short, I use a hierarchy of schemata, the highest being the hyper-schema for an event. Immediately below is the super-schema for scientific phenomenon.

The event hyper-schema depicts the change taking place between two states of a given entity. These states are associated with two successive points in time. A formal description is:

Event
           State 1:   Px, t1   or   Pxy, t1
           State 2:   Not Px, t2   or   Not Pxy, t2

where P is a predicate, either unary or binary, x (or x and
y) the concerned entity, t1 and t2 two moments in time. The
different states are opposed, in this case, by negation
applied to one state.

       The lower scientific phenomenon super-schema in addition
includes mention and description of the condition, or cause,
of the change described above. In principle, universal
quantification should be added for all standard scientific
phenomena. Thus:

Scientific phenomenon
           State 1:   Px, t1   or   Pxy, t1
           State 2:   Not Px, t2   or   Not Pxy, t2
           Condition of change: j

Below these two high level schemata, other specific
schemata or sub-schemata for various scientific phenomena
can be described on the lower levels of the hierarchy. They
are obtained by restrictions on the components in their
super-schema. This kind of description is of course close to
object oriented description and programming.
       Let us see an application concerning a particular field.
In conditioning, for example, all phenomena have "animal" as
the entity a possibly subject to change, i.e. restricting x.
The successive states of this entity must be described in a
complex way with a relevant predicate B, which is a
restriction of P. These states in this case encompass the
likelihood that a given animal will produce a conditioned
reaction when presented with an appropriate conditioned
stimulus at a given time. A formalization of this is
presented below.

Scientific phenomenon in conditioning
           State 1:   Ba, s, r, t1, e
           State 2:   Not Ba, s, r, t2, e
           Condition of change: k

where a is a variable denoting an animal, s a stimulus, r a response, e an environmental condition, B the likelihood of producing the relevant behavior, interpretable as the predicate "produce", and k a suitable condition of learning change. That is "animal", "stimulus", "behavior", and others are terms in a language specifically defined for this sub-field, with an appropriate semantics.

In this sort of schema, concepts from the field of conditioning, and many others, can be described easily: for example "learning", "conditioning", "forgetting", "habituation", "extinction", "relearning", and, lastly, "spontaneous recovery".

In any description of a scientific phenomenon the change condition is of major importance and must be indicated in a separate way. As has been already pointed out, the super-schema contains a specific slot, where this information will have to be inserted in the instantiated representation.

This change condition is, in Pavlovian conditioning, the role of the unconditioned or reinforcing stimulus, which is the key to most modifications of the behavior taking place in the conditioning process. For extinction to take place the change condition is absence of reinforcement and for spontaneous recovery it is simple rest. It turns out that the main, albeit small, difficulty in acquisition of the latter concept by students comes from the change condition and lies in the difference between this and the neightbouring phenomenon of re-conditioning after extinction. Knowledge or ignorance of the right change conditions is a crucial point in the mastery of the two corresponding concepts.

Thus, such schemata are used extensively in my system. The task of the summarizer-schematizer in the second layer of the automat consists of exploring the first representation obtained as a result of the syntactico-semantic analysis in order to detect all or part of the components that can instantiate the relevant conceptual schema and construct an instantiated representation of the student's response.

In the same framework the task of the evaluator is then to match this instantiated representation to the target representation. This is constructed by the system after the "correct" description of the concept stored in memory according to the knowledge of an expert in the field.

Thus, according to my general cognitive model the final goal of this evaluative task clearly is: to compare the linguistic expression and, by inductive inference, the intentional content of the corresponding natural concept existing in the mind of the student at this given time, with the content of the rational scientific concept forming the instructional cognitive target.

Implementation of schemata

I would now like to say a little more about the schemata and their implementation.

The conceptual information on the target concepts is stored in the dictionary under the corresponding word, or words, more precisely in the semantic part of the total information devoted to each word in the dictionary. This conceptual information, which is formally undistinguishable from the other semantic information (or from grammatical information), will be thereafter called the "conceptual base".

Of course these same conceptual words can be used in the normal way in a sentence. Their entry first contains a marker indicating that they are potentially words-to-be-characterized. The automat has an especial graph which detects when the word is in the role of word-to-be-characterized and when it is not.

The conceptual information is stored in an attribute/value format. For any target word the first attribute given in the dictionary is the type of schema it belongs to. It may be for example the schema of scientific phenomenon I presented above. This value is stored for all concepts falling under this schema and hence all the remaining conceptual information is stored in the same conceptual structure.

Each sub-schema in the conceptual base is organised in the form of a tree, the root of which is the name of the type of schema being just above this concept. Each attribute is then stored as a pathname, which represents a complete branch in the tree, and traces back to the root of this. Each pathname is followed by the value for this attribute.

For example, one attribute concerning the concept of "extinction", stored in the schema of "scientific phenomenon in conditioning" is: "1ag1" (for state1_agent1, or argument a in the schema) and its value is "animal". Another attribute is: "2pat1" (for state2_patient1, or r) and its value is "comportment".

It may be observed that this particular concept, as several others in the schema of "scientific phenomenon in conditioning" has two case role attributes, or branches, of similar types, called "agent1" and "agent2", for arguments a and s.

The corresponding core proposition from the schema is:
produce (x, behavior)
which partially restricts Pxy. Of course many synonyms or approximate equivalents of "produce" are actually used in students's texts and are, as a rule, impossible to distinguish on an accurate semantical basis.

Consequently, a problem arises as concerns the first argument in the proposition above: it may as well be said that an animal "produces" a behavior or that a stimulus, or a situation, "produces" a behavior.

There is no such problem concerning the second argument: in this proposition: "behavior", or any equivalent, is considered by default as referring to conditioned behavior. That is presence of the word "conditioned", or any synonym of it, in the student's text is optional: it makes no difficulty to decide that a characterization correctly matches the conceptual description even if this mention is not given in an explicit form.

The problem concerning the first general argument is apparently due to the status of causality in this domain. We can briefly examine the cognitive content of this schema.

First, if we only consider the facts, it is clear that a double causality must be taken into consideration for the concepts in the whole field of behavior, which makes an important difference with many concepts concerning physical scientific phenomena. In classical conditioning (and in general for all reflexes or responses to stimuli, that is for any behavior that was formerly called "respondent" in the analysis of Skinner, 1938), both the organism and the external stimulus can be correctly considered as partial determinants, or causes, of the behavior.

This shows that three possibilities must be kept open for the linguistic agent in students' responses: mention of one agent, the other, or both. In practice, this problem is solved by inserting two slots for agents in the conceptual base, and then allowing the evaluator to accept, either one "agent1", or one "agent2", or both, in the students' responses.

It may be pointed out that only the organism is as a rule considered as a determinant of the behavior in non-classical, instrumental, conditioning ("operant" in the language of Skinner). However, some authors consider as necessary to take into account the situational factor also in this form of behavior.

If we wanted to go deeper into this aspect of the concept, we should further say that any characterization of a concept in this field is necessarily given by the student on the basis of his or her individual general, presumably implicit, representation of causality in the physical and animate world. The way the response is expressed is presumably a result of this.

However, this is a very general problem as concerns our students, and we have no serious reason to consider this general representation of causality as directly relevant to the particular concepts under study (for example "extinction"). This only shows how we could go deeper into a conceptual representation if necessary.

Let us now return to the format of the conceptual base. From the point of view of knowledge representation each attribute in a given target schema has the status of a slot and each value of a correct instantiation in this slot.

But from a psychological point of view, each attribute, considered at its terminal level, is considered to be a particular sort of semantic, cognitive feature, and each value another sort. The psychological theory underlying this model is presented in detail elsewhere (Le Ny, 1989). Thus, the information stored in the dictionary of our system is considered as an external description of the mental, internal, information stored in a structured form in the experts' or students' memory.

Use of the conceptual base

How is this information extracted from the dictionary and practically used by the system ?

At the beginning of the processing, a graph detects the name of the word-to-be-characterized, as previously said, and searches for all the information associated with it in the dictionary. This same graph then constructs a representation of the target concept by using the information stored in the conceptual base. This is, when constructed, stored in one particular register. Thus, this representation is now in the working memory of the system and consists of the complete relevant schema and the values correctly instantiating it .

Later, the list of the attributes in this conceptual schema is also used by the second layer of the system during the phase of interpretation, as was said above, to summarize and schematize the result-of-the-analysis constructed by the first layer.

Thus, this list of attributes is used twice: first to construct the target representation, and in this case the correct instantiations in the slots are extracted from the dictionary at the same time as the attributes. And secondly to construct the predicative summary of the response, and in this case the actual instantiations are extracted from the response itself, more precisely from the result-of-the-analysis obtained from this response.

Thus, when this double construction has been completed the working memory of the system contains two instantiated representations, placed in two different registers: one corresponding to the target concept and the other to the student's response. They are written in a standardized language of representation.

This language has a closed lexicon, which is composed of words that refer to all main objects or entities in the domain under study. These standardized words are inserted in the general dictionary as components in the semantic part associated with all entries: every word that does not belong to the closed lexicon points to a word from this lexicon that is either a synonym or a superodinate of it at a pre-determined basic level.

So, all content words in the text are substituted during interpretation by a suitable word from the closed lexicon so that the final representation only contains standardized words. For instance all animal species ("dog", "rat", "cat", etc,) are substituted by "animal", all words as "reaction", "response", "reflex", etc, are substituted by "comportment". That many words point to "produce" has been mentioned above.

Given these two representations in working memory written in the same language and the same format, it is very easy to match them and detect similarities or differences between their instantiation for each attribute. This is the basis of the evaluation task performed by the third layer of the system.

Results of the evaluation

The third layer yields several types of information as output. First, if all the sub-matches were successful, the output contains the judgment: "wholly correct", which may be printed out for the teacher. In this case the student's concept is inductively inferred to be correct, unless there is different information from other evaluations.

If some difference appears as a result of evaluation it is interpreted as a partial or micro-error. In this case the particular instantiations and whole clauses that are correct are separately indicated.

In addition, the evaluator has the task to detect the nature of errors. That is: either the corresponding information is missing in the student's response, and this lack is pointed out in the evaluation result, or a different instantiation has been found instead of the correct one. In this latter case the evaluator interprets this as an error and picks up its content in the form of the main incorrect word or concept.

Table 1

```
****************************************************************
```
extinction is the fact that a dog previously gave a
conditioned response to a stimulus in consequence of a
period of conditioning and later this animal no longer
produces this reaction after a rest.

characterization_of_the_concept_of:

    : extinction

evaluation:

    state 1:   correct
    state 2:   correct
    condition_of_change: error: rest

instanciated_schema:

    state 1:
                 afneg: af
                 predic: produce
                 agent1:   animal
                 agent2:   stimulus
                 patient: comportment
    state 2:
                 afneg: neg
                 predic: produce
                 agent1:   animal
                 patient: comportment
    condition_of_change: rest

****
```
Translated reproduction of a print-out. Top: partially
incorrect student's text. Bottom: its summary in the form of
an instanciated schema. Middle: result of the final
evaluation.



     In the working version of the module presented in this
paper the existence and nature of the partial errors have
been printed out as a message sent to the teacher or human
supervisor (Table 1).
     In addition, the most frequent errors concerning the
concepts under study are being collected from empirical
observation. Consequently, typical schemata for
```

misconceptions can be constructed in the same form as for correct concepts. Then, the evaluation process can assign particular responses to such types and make diagnosis more accurate.

In the operational version of the module when used as a part of the CINACC system (Le Ny, Carite and Poitrenaud, 1986) such messages are not mainly transmitted to the human supervisor but to the system itself. These messages are then used as inputs for production rules contained in CINACC, and corrective texts are presented to the student.

REFERENCES

Anderson, R. (1983) - The Architecture of Cognition, Cambridge, Mass., Harvard University Press.

Bonar, J.G. and Cunningham, R. (1988) - Intelligent Tutoring with Intermediate Representations, Proc. Intelligent Tutoring Systems, Montreal.

Caillot, M. (1985) - Problem representations and problem-solving procedures in electricity, in R. Duit, W. Jung and C. Von Rhoneck. Aspects of Understanding Electricity, Kiel, IPN-Arbeitsberichte, 139-151.

Carbonell, J. R. (1970) - AI in CAI: An Artificial Intelligence Approach to Computer-Assisted Instruction, IEEE Trans. Man-Machine Systems, 11, 4, 190-202.

Chi, M.T.H., Feltovitch, P.J. and Glaser, R.G. (1981) - Categorization and representation of physics problems by experts and novices, Cognitive Science, 5, 121-152.

van Dijk, T. and Kintsch, W. (1983) - Strategies of Discourse Comprehension, New-York, Academic Press.

Le Ny, J.F. (1986) - Discourse comprehension and memory for concepts. In: F. Klix and H. Hagendorf (eds). Human memory and cognitive capabilities. Amsterdam, Elsevier.

Le Ny, J.F. (1987) - A quels risques peut-on inferer des representations ? In: M. Siguan (ed). Comportement, cognition, conscience. Paris, Presses Universitaires de France.

Le Ny, J.F. (1989)- Science cognitive et comprehension du langage, Paris, Presses Universitaires de France, in press.

Le Ny J.F., Carite, L. and Poitrenaud, S. (1986) - Construction of individualized texts for the transmission of knowledge through discourse. In: I. Kurcz, G.W. Shugar and

J.H. Danks (eds). Knowledge and Language, Amsterdam, Elsevier.

Maida, A.S. and Shapiro, S.C. (1982) - Intensional concepts in propositional semantic networks, Cognitive Science, 6, 291-330.

Reiser, B.J., Anderson, J.R. and Farrell, R. G. (1985) - Dynamic Student Modelling in an Intelligent Tutor for LISP Programming, Los Angeles, Proc. IJCAI-85, 8-14.

Skinner, B. F. (1938) - The Behavior of Organisms. An experimental Analysis, New York, Appleton Century Crofts.

Sleeman, D. and Brown, J.S. (eds) (1982) - Intelligent Tutoring Systems, Cambridge, Mass., Academic Press.

Wenger, E. (1987) - Artificial Intelligence and Tutoring Systems, Los Altos, Morgan Kaufman.

Winograd, T. (1983) - Language as a cognitive process, Reading, Addison Wesley.

Woods, W.A. (1972) - An Experimental Parsing System for Transition Network Grammars. In R. Rustin (ed.) Natural Language Processing, New-York, Algorithmic Press, 113-154.

Woolf, B. (1988) - Intelligent Tutoring Systems: A Survey, Survey Lectures from the American Association of Artificial Intelligence, Los Altos, Morgan Kaufman.

COURSEWARE DEVELOPMENT BY TOPDOWN CONCEPTUAL ANALYSIS

Albert Le Xuan
Alphamega Knowledge Craft, 4987 Walkley Ave, Montreal, Que H4V 2M3, Canada

And

Rajjan Shinghal
Concordia University, Computer Science Department, 1455 De Maisonneuve West
Montreal, Que H3G 1M8, Canada

Key Words: Topdown Conceptual Analysis, Conceptual Structure, Subordinate
Concepts, Coordinate Concepts, Supra-ordinate Concepts, Generalization,
Discrimination & Chains.

ABSTRACT

This paper describes the methods and techniques used to design and develop the
courseware called INTRODUCTORY NEW MATHEMATICS FOR PARENTS & CHILDREN, using authoring systems like SCENARIO which has been used by teachers in Quebec and the US
to produce courseware with little help from programmers.

The methods and techniques that have been used are called Topdown Conceptual Analysis (TCA) which takes most of the guesswork out of the design of knowledge-based
systems. Given a list of specifications of objectives and a description of the
target population , different groups of people who are trained in TCA, and working
independently, should be able to generate - without involuntary omissions or repetitions - equivalent knowledge bases to build a system.

1. INTRODUCTION

In this paper we present the notion of TCA and how it can be used to produce the
knowledge base for the development of the courseware. We explain some of the prerequisites and basic theories behind TCA. We discuss what is meant by learning
and teaching a concept, and how a complex concept can be taught in terms of simpler or contributory concepts. We emphasize the importance of examples and non-
examples in learning and teaching a concept, and then we discuss how we used TCA
to develop the courseware called INTRODUCTORY NEW MATHEMATICS FOR PARENTS AND
CHILDREN.

2. THE PROBLEM OF DEVELOPING HIGH-QUALITY INSTRUCTIONAL MATERIALS

2.1 A Great Composition: MIT Professor Jerrold Zacharias suggested in a 1956
memorandum which led to the creation of the Physical Science Study Commission
(PSSC) that, "Education is like hi-fi. To have a good hi-fi, you need a good per-
former on a good day, a good recording, a good pressing of it, a good pick-up and
amplifier; you need a room with good acoustical qualities and a person with the intent to listen. But most important of all is the composition itself; without a
great composition, everything else is pointless." Silberman (1970)

2.2 Cooperation Between Knowledge Engineers & Domain Experts: The planning of a
good learning system development project ideally provides for close cooperation between knowledge engineers (KE) and domain experts (DE). The DE usually holds a
higher position than the level for which the system is to be built. He (for brev-
ity's sake, we shall use masculine pronouns for both genders) should know the domain of his field thoroughly as well as the problems encountered at various levels

within the specialization. The KE applies learning theories to the practical task of learning and teaching. Ideally he should have also acquired the methods and techniques of TCA.

2.3 Allocation of Responsibilities: Although a course can be developed by one KE working with one DE, or by a person acting as both, it is better to have one KE working with several DEs, programmers, artists and editors, to ensure quality and reduce the costs.

2.4 Set of Steps: While designing a learning system, the KE and the DE go through a set of such steps as:

1. Determining the needs
2. Identifying the problem
3. Specifying the target population of learners
4. Specifying pre-requisite entering behavior
5. Specifying terminal behavior
6. Generating the knowledge base (NB)
7. Converting KB into story-boards
8. Testing and revising until the materials meet specifications
9. Entering the materials into the computer
10. Testing and revising the courseware,etc.

Some textbooks explain quite clearly how to perform all the steps except Step Six: "Generating the knowledge base". The success of a learning system depends on the quality of the knowledge base. It is the raw material with which we build a learning system, and it is the Topdown Conceptual Analysis that generates that raw material.

3. SOME THEORIES BEHIND TCA

3.1 Introduction: The term Topdown Conceptual Analysis may be new but the idea of TCA is not. Every good teacher or educator has been using it in some form or other without realizing that it is called TCA.

3.2 Some Examples: In his Discourse on the Method (1637), René Descartes was certainly using a topdown technique when he wrote about dividing each problem into as many parts as feasible and requisite for the solution of a problem. Unfortunately Descartes never showed us exactly how to go about such division.

According to Richard Skemp (1971), "Concepts of higher order than those which a person already has cannot be communicated to him by a definition, but only by arranging for him to encounter a suitable collection of examples. And since in mathematics these examples are almost invariably other concepts, it must first be ensured that these are already formed in the mind of the learner." In other words, lower-order concepts must be present before the next stage of abstraction is possible. In building up the structure of successive abstractions, if a particular level is imperfectly understood, everything from there on is in peril. This dependency is greater in mathematics and related domains than in any other domain. One can understand and learn the geography of Asia even if one has missed that of Europe; one can understand and learn the history of the nineteenth century even if one has missed that of the eighteenth. To understand algebra without having really understood arithmetic is an impossibility. To learn calculus without having a working knowledge of algebra, trigonometry, and analytic geometry is not possible.

Robert Gagné (1985) maintains that readiness to learn is essentially a function of pre-requisite learning. "Ensure that he has acquired the pre-requisite capabilities and he will be able to learn. When he is capable of tasks d & e (Figure 1), he is ready to learn b; when he is capable of tasks f & g, he is ready to learn c; and when he is capable of tasks b & c, he is ready to learn a", which is the most abstract concept or task in the hierarchy.

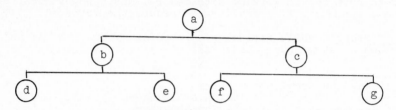

Figure 1: Tree diagram representing a hierarchy

Ausubel (1960), who is in agreement with Gagné on this issue, has stated the point eloquently thus: "If I had to reduce all of educational psychology to one principle, I would say this: "The most important single factor influencing learning is what the learner already knows. Ascertain this and teach him accordingly."

4.   TOPDOWN CONCEPTUAL ANALYSIS

In practice, what Skemp, Gagné and Ausubel say amounts to this: before one can understand and learn a new concept, one has to discover and learn its subordinate concepts and related rules, and so on, until one reaches those one already knows. Unfortunately, Skemp, Gagné and Ausubel have not shown us how to discover the subordinate concepts of a concept - at least in a concrete, simple and systematic way.

Le Xuan & Chassain (1975, 1985) have developed a method and technique which allows us to generate - without involuntary omissions or repetitions - all the necessary subordinate concepts and rules of any concept, rule, principle or text. It is called Topdown Conceptual Analysis (CTA). Doing a TCA is like decomposing a composite number into its prime factors. If one has to factor the number 24, for instance, one will always obtain the prime factors 3, 2, 2, 2, no matter how one decomposes the number 24, as shown in Figures 2, 3, and 4.

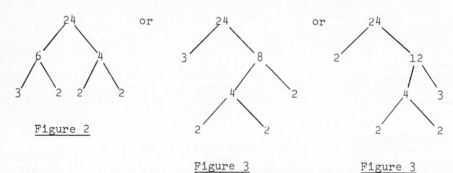

Figure 2   Figure 3   Figure 3

5.   SOME PRE-REQUISITES TO TCA

5.1 Relations: Relations are links that connect objects. Relations are usually represented by verbs, verbal phrases, arrows or any sym-

bol. The following underlined verbs and verbal phrases are examples
of relations:

5.1.1 Peter <u>loves</u> Jane. Notation: loves(Peter,Jane) arrow diagrams:
Peter————→Jane. This relation connects two objects: It is a binary,
dyadic or two-ary relation.

5.1.2 Peter <u>gives</u> a book <u>to</u> Jane. Notation: gives-to(Peter,book,Jane)
This relation connects three objects: It is a ternary, triadic or 3-ary
relation.

5.2 <u>Concepts</u>: Concepts are classes or categories of

1. objects (table, computer, chair, man,etc)

2. qualities (good, bad, large, narrow,etc)

3. quantities (one, two, much, many,etc)

4. events (work, play, run,etc)

5. relations (above, below, west of, east of,etc)

5.3 <u>Conceptual Structures</u>: Conceptual structures are structures in
which lower-order concepts are pre-requisites to higher-order concepts.
A conceptual structure can be visualized by the following tree diagram
(Figure 5).

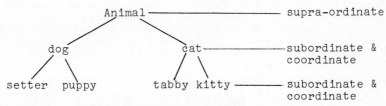

Figure 5: Tree diagram representing a structure

5.4 <u>Chain</u>: Chain is a technical term for what is sometimes called <u>pro-</u>
<u>cedure</u>, <u>sequence of action</u>, or <u>reasoning sequence</u>. A more precise defi-
nition of chain is "a sequence of stimuli and responses where each response produces the stimulus for the next responses, and so forth." Some
common examples of chain are: (1) uttering a sentence; (2) performing
an experiment,etc.

5.5 <u>Generalization</u>: Generalization is a technical term for what is commonly called "lumping things together," "seeing similarities," or "dis-
regarding differences." This leaves open the question of whether or not
a generalization is appropriate or inappropriate, desirable or undesirable. A more precise definition of generalization is "making the same
kind of responses to different stimuli (objects)." The following are
some examples of generalization.

5.5.1 Saying "good morning" to all kinds of people, regardless of what
time of the day it is so long as it is before noon.

5.5.2 Saying "dog" in the presence of setters, puppies, pointers, regardless of whether the animals are brown or black.

5.5.3 Proceeding when the traffic light is green, regardless of whether the light is suspended or on a post, regardless of whether you are in a car or on foot, and regardless of whether it is morning, noon or night.

5.6 <u>Discrimination</u>: Discrimination is a technical term for what is commonly called "making distinction,""classifying," or "categorizing." A more precise definition would be "a tendency to make one kind of response in the presence of one kind of stimulus situation, and another kind of response in the presence of other kinds of stimulus situations. Note again, that this leaves open the question of whether or not the discrimination is the desired or the appropriate one. Discriminations may be either correct or incorrect, desirable or undesirable. The following are common examples of discrimination.

5.6.1 Saying "good morning" before 12 and "good afternoon" after 12.

5.6.2 Proceeding when the light is green & stop when the light is red.

5.7 <u>When Can We Say That an Individual Has Learned a Concept?</u> In other words, what must he do to show that he has learned a concept.

1. He must be able to generalize within a class of objects, qualities, quantities, events and relations; and

2. discriminate between that class and other classes.

5.7.1 <u>Example</u>: When an individual makes the same response "triangle" to each member of class T (Figure 6), and the same response "rectangle" to each member of class R, he is generalizing within a class of triangles and a class of rectangles; he is also discriminating between a class of triangles and a class of rectangles. The psychologist would say that the individual has learned the concept of triangle and the concept of rectangle.

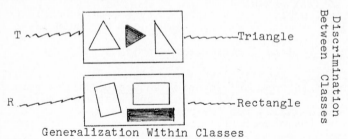

Generalization Within Classes

<u>Figure 6</u>: Generalization & Discrimination Between Classes

5.7.2 <u>Non-example</u>: When an individual is capable of recognizing a dog, but is unable to distinguish a dog from a fox, he has not learned the concept of "dog".

5.8 <u>How To Teach a Concept</u>: When one analyzes the behavior of the learner to see what he does when he learns a concept one sees that the learner generalizes within a class and discriminates between that class and other classes. Now what does the teacher do when he teaches a concept? He creates situations which will allow the learner to generalize and to discriminate among things; that is, he provides the learner with enough examples and non-examples. Suppose one has to teach the concept of primitive term to an adult learner, here is one way one can proceed:

A. Tell him why he should learn the concept of "primitive term". This is the <u>introduction</u>:

"To define a term (word) we must use other terms, but we cannot go on defining terms for ever. We must at some stage reach terms which cannot be defined by other terms without turning in circles. Such terms are called <u>primitive terms</u>."

B. Show the learner at least two examples of the term "primitive term", as one cannot generalize from one example:

"Terms such as 'point', 'line', 'plane',etc cannot be defined without using less familiar terms. Point, line & plane are said to be <u>primitive terms</u>." Note that some concepts need more than two examples before the learner can learn to generalize within classes.

C. Next, show the learner as many non-examples as necessary so that he can discriminate between "primitive terms" and "non-primitive terms":

"Terms such as 'addition' and 'subtraction' can be defined by more familiar terms, but sometimes we do not need to define them because most people (or at least the people for whom the material is designed) alread know how to use these two terms. In this case, 'addition' and 'subtraction' are called <u>undefined terms</u>."

D. If necessary, show the learner another non-example:

"The term 'mortar' can be defined as 'a mixture of cement, sand, and water used for holding together bricks and stones. 'Mortar' is a <u>derived term</u>. It is derived from the terms 'mixture','cement' and'water'.

E. Perhaps it is now time to give the learner a test to see if he can recognize a primitive term among different types of terms:

"Which of the following are primitive terms: table, on, the, an? Answer: on, the, an are primitive terms, because they cannot be defined without using less familiar terms."

F. Next, give the learner another test to see if he can give an example of 'primitive term' other than point, line & plane:

"Give another example of 'primitive term'." "Answers: or, at, in, out,etc."

G. Next come the definitions, because by this time the learner should be able to define 'primitive term', 'undefined term' and 'derived term'.

"Define 'primitive term', 'undefined term' and 'derived term'. Answers: (1) A <u>primitive term</u> is a term that cannot be defined without using less familiar terms; (2) An <u>undefined term</u> is a term that can be defined by more familiar terms but which we do not want or need to define; and (3) A <u>derived term</u> is a term that has been defined by other terms. Note: More examples and non-examples might be needed for some learners. All depends on the level of pre-requisite knowledge of the learners and the complexity of subject matter to be taught.

5.9 Positive & Negative Examples: We see that (1) to teach a concept we must teach the learner to generalize within a class and to discriminate between that class and other classes; (2) to teach the learner to generalize and to discriminate, one must present him with enough positive examples (or simply examples) and negative examples (or non-examples) of the concept to be taught.

5.9.1 Examples of Pos. & Neg. Exs. (1) A foxhound belongs to a class of objects called DOG. A fox hound is said to be a positive example of of the concept dog; (2) A fox which looks somewhat like a dog but is not a dog: a fox is said to be a negative example (or non-example) of the concept dog; (3) Chair is an excellent negative example of stool, because both have the same attributes except one: a chair has a back whereas a stool does not.

5.9.2 Definitions: (1) A positive example (or simply example) of a class or concept is the member of that concept or class; (2) a negative example (or non-example) of a class or concept is the member of a class which is similar to but different from the class or concept under investigation.

5.9.3 Different Forms of Examples: A example may be an experiment, object, diagram, table, photograph, description, explanation,etc.

6. USING TCA TO GENERATE THE KNOWLEDGE BASE

6.1 Introduction: The knowledge base is the raw material with which we build learning systems. It is made up of two component parts: the declarative knowledge structure which contains concepts, rules, facts, opinions or principles; and the procedural knowledge structure which contains procedures to perform such tasks as experiments to illustrate science concepts which call for experiments, or such tasks as starting a car, or changing a tire.

The following is the TCA the authors have developed to generate the knowledge base for the development of the first lesson: SET. It is the first component part of the INTRODUCTORY NEW MATHEMATICS FOR PARENTS & CHILDREN. The knowledge bases for the rest of the course were generated in the same manner. This TCA was developed from the term SET, but a TCA may also be developed from any stimulus: a symbol, phrase, diagram, photograph, sentence or a test with or without answers.

6.2 Procedure   *TCA : Set*
              Part A : Input-output Inventory

Input	Output
1.0 Set ⟶	*2.0 Introduction: This is a step-by-step study course in the INTRODUCTORY NEW MATHEMATICS FOR PARENTS & CHILDREN. The concepts presented are: set, one-to-one matching, expanded notation, inverse operations and arithmetic properties. In this lesson we shall see what is meant by the term SET.*
	3.0 Examples of Sets:
	3.1 This is a collection of stamps: The mathematician would say "a set of stamps."

1.0 Set

3.2 *This is a group of people: We can also say "a __set__ of people".*

3.3 *This is herd of elephants: We can also say "a __set__ of elephants".*

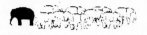

4.0 *Definition: A __set__ is a collection, group, herd or family of objects or things. The things that make up a set are called __members__ or __elements__ of that set.*

5.0 *Related Rule: A collection, group or herd must be well-defined to be a set; that is, given an object, we must be able to tell immediately whether or not that object is a member or an element of that collection or group.*

6.0 *Examples of Well-defined Collections*

6.1 *Consider the collection of letters: a, b, c, d, & e. Given an object f, for instance, one can tell immediately that f is not a member of that collection of letters.*

6.2 *Consider the collection of numerals: 1, 2, 3, 4, 5 & 6. Is the object 3, for instance, an element of the collection? We can tell immediately that 3 is an element of the collection. The collection of letters and the collection of numerals are well-defined collections.*

7.0 *Examples of Not-well-defined Collections*

7.1 *The collection of "beautiful" paintings cannot become a set, because given a painting, it is not possible to tell whether or not the painting is beautiful: not everybody agrees on what is beautiful and what is not.*

7.2 *The group of "intelligent" boys is not well-defined, because not everybody agrees on which boy is intelligent and which boy is not.*

8.0 *Exercises*

(a) *Is the "collection of carpets" well-defined?*

(b) *Is the "collection of beautiful rugs" well-defined?*

(c) *Is a "group of well-dressed men" well-defined?*

(d) *Is a "group of psychologists" well-defined?*

(e) *Define "set" and "element of a set".*

(f) *When can we say that a collection of things is well-defined?*

(g) *What is the mathematical term for collection or herd?*

9.0 *Answers*

(a) *The "collection of carpets" is well-defined.*

1.0	Set ⟶	9.0	(b) The "collection of beautiful rugs" is not well-defined because not everybody agrees on the meaning of the term 'beautiful'.
			(c) A "group of well-dressed men" is not well-defined, because not everybody agrees on the meaning of the word 'well-dressed'.
			(d) A "group of psychologists" is well-defined in the western world.
			(e) A set is a collection or group of objects; and the objects that make up a set are called members or elements of that set.
			(f) We can say that a collection is well-defined when given an object we can tell immediately whether or not the object is an element of that set.
			(g) The mathematical term for collection or herd is set.
2.0	Introduc- ⟶ tion: This is ...	NTBA	Short for Not To Be Analyzed, by which we mean that, by convention, we shall not break down the content of this item, as each of the new concepts announced here will be treated later in the analysis proper.
3.0	Examples		
3.1	This ... ⟶	PR	Short for Pre-Requisite, by which we mean that this item contains no new terms which call for further analysis (breakdown).
3.2	This ... ⟶	PR	
3.3	This ... ⟶	PR	
4.0	Definition ⟶	PR	
5.0	Related Rule ⟶	PR	
6.0	Examples		
6.1	Consider ⟶	PR	
6.2	Consider ⟶	PR	
7.0	Examples		
7.1	The ⟶	PR	
7.2	The ⟶	PR	
8.0	Exercises ⟶	PR	
9.0	Answers ⟶	PR	

TCA : Set
Part B : Representation of TCA

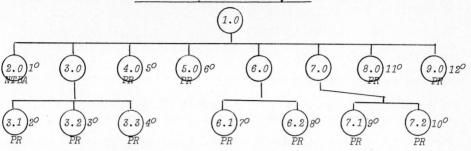

Note: The usefulness of this tree diagram would be more apparent if the domain is more complex. In the present case, we could visualize the hierarchy of the concept by mere inspection. 1° = 1st, 2° = 2nd, etc.

TCA : Set
Part C : Sequential Index

1°	(2.0 - 1.0)	Introduction
2°	(3.1 - 3.0)	1st example of set
3°	(3.2 - 3.0)	2nd example of set
4°	(3.3 - 3.0)	3rd example of set
5°	(4.0 - 1.0)	Definition
6°	(5.0 - 1.0)	Related Rule
7°	(6.1 - 6.0)	1st example of well-defined collections
8°	(6.2 - 6.0)	2nd example of well-defined collections
9°	(7.1 - 7.0)	1st example of not well-defined collections
10°	(7.2 - 7.0)	2nd example of not well-defined collections
11°	(8.0 - 1.0)	Exercises
12°	(9.0 - 1.0)	Answers to Exercises

TCA : Set
Part D : Converting the Sequential Index Into
Story-Boards

Once the sequential index has been completed, it was converted into story-boards for the production of the program. The rest of the course was produced in the same manner.

6.3 How Was Part A Generated: To generate Part A of the analysis we proceeded as follows:

1. We divided each page into two parts, forming two columns: one for inputs and the other for outputs;

2. We recorded the material to be analyzed (the term SET) in the input column and numered it 1.0;

3. Input 1.0 produced eight outputs: 2.0, 3.0. 4.0, 5.0, 6.0, 7.0, 8.0, & 9.0;

4. Next, we drew a horizontal line under the 1st input & its eight outputs;

5. Then, we brought down output 2.0 (introduction) in the input column to turn it into an input, and recorded it under the line we had just drawn;

6. Input 2.0 produced NTBA, short for <u>N</u>ot <u>T</u>o <u>B</u>e <u>A</u>nalyzed. This means that, by convention, we shall not analyze (breakdown) this item as it contains concepts which are analyzed elsewhere;

7. We drew another horizontal line;

8. We brought down output 3.0 in the input column to turn it into an input and wrote it under the line we had just drawn;

9. Input 3.0 produced PR, short for <u>P</u>re-<u>R</u>equisite, by which we mean that we will not pursue our analysis any further, assuming that all the concepts in this item are known to the target population.

10. We drew another horizontal line.

11. We brought down output 4.0 in the input column and treated it in the same manner until all the outputs were turned into inputs and produced PRs.

<u>6.4 How Was Part B Generated</u>: To reorganize the input-output inventory into a hierarchy or structure we proceeded as follows:

1. As one can see, input 1.0 produced eight outputs. We drew a tree diagram like this:

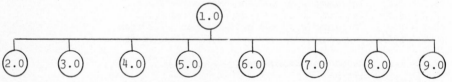

2. As input 2.0 produced NTBA, we added NTBA to the partial tree diagram which now looks like this:

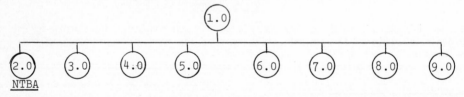

3. We proceeded in the same manner until we exhausted all the inputs and outputs of the inventory and obtained the final tree;

4. The symbols 1°, 2°, 3°, etc. represent the order of the component parts of the hierarchy. The ordering begins with the branches, from left to right, and from bottom upwards;

5. As one can see, the TCA begins at the top and moves downwards. But the concepts and rules or examples, represented by the nodes, are ordered from the bottom upwards. This means that the analysis proceeds from the higher-order concepts to the lower-order concepts, and the presentation of concepts, rules or examples, proceeds from the lower-order concepts to the higher-order concepts.

6. Note: When the domain is complex the tree diagram may occupy quite a large space. In that case it is necessary to break the tree diagram into as many branches as necessary. Some tree diagrams can give a sense of awe, but without the help of tree diagrams we will have to resort to intuition and guesswork which are usually more time-consuming.

6.5 How Was Part C Generated: To generate Part C we proceeded as follows:

1. We picked out the first item (1°) on the tree diagram, then looked at the input-output inventory, and copied the content of 1° on a separate sheet of paper. This is the first element of the structure.

2. Next, we picked out the second item (2°) and copied its content. We proceeded in the same manner until the last item was disposed of. The end-result is the knowledge base with which we build the course.

3. Note: Usually the conceptual structure or knowledge base is made up of the following elements:

.1 Introduction
.2 Definition
.3 Positive examples(or experiments)
.4 Negative examples
.5 Notation (if necessary)
.6 Diagram or table or procedure
.7 Related rules
.8 Exercises with answers
.9 References & bibliography

6.6 How Was Part D Generated: As the reader can imagine, Section 1, Step 1 represents the title of the program:

INTRODUCTORY NEW MATHEMATICS

FOR PARENTS AND CHILDREN

By

Albert Le Xuan & Rajjan Shinghal
With the Collaboration of a Group of
Parents & Children

Section 1, Step 2 represents the introduction:

This is a step-by-step study course in the INTRODUCTORY NEW MATHEMATICS FOR PARENTS & CHILDREN. The concepts presented are: Set, one-to-one matching, expanded notation, inverse operations and some arithmetic properties. In this lesson we shall see what is meant by the term SET.

Section 1, Step 3 represents the first example of SET, and so one, until the learner can generalize within a class and discriminate between that class and other classes.

7. USING SCENARIO TO PRODUCE THE PROGRAM

7.1 What Can Scenario Be Used For: According to its authors, SCENAR-
IO can be used for Writing, Drawing, Explaining, Learning, Teaching,
Organizing, Telling, Having Fun, Composing Music, Buying & Selling,
Being Heard, Being Seen, Questioning, Gathering Statistics, Simulat-
ing Conversation Events, Laboratory Experiments or Mathematical Mod-
els, Creating Interactive Software, Formative Documents, Images and
Text Banks, Dictionaries, Animation, Video and Educational Games, or
all of the above.

7.2 Scenario's Weakest Point: Scenario's weakest point is documentation. It is the number of errors that its manuals contain. What
makes it more serious is that it is impossible to correct these errors with the three documents available because one cannot find the
numbers of the items to be corrected, with the consequence that we
have been obliged to grope around for quite a while before we can
even enter the system, and even then we have not been able to find
all the commands necessary for our work. It has not been easy to add
graphics to the text so we have had to re-write the story-boards to
"fit" Scenario.

8. STATUS OF INTRODUCTORY NEW MATHEMATICS FOR PARENTS & CHILDREN

We were half way through with the production of the program using
SCENARIO when we discovered that we would succeed better with HYPER-
CARD which we will try out in May 1989. In the meantime we are using
the methods and techniques of TCA to build a knowledge base for the
development of the course entitled PATTERN RECOGNITION for beginning
students of Artificial Intelligence.

9. HOW USERS USE TCA IN A CAL ENVIRONMENT

We believe that the methods and techniques of TCA are one of the most
powerful tools for CAL systems designers. The following are some of
the uses of TCA:

1. Generating knowledge bases for the development of CAL system;

2. Generating materials for the construction of tests: performance
    tests, pre-tests, post-tests, etc:

3. Measuring the level of difficulty of a term, sentence or text;

4. Teaching oneself new subject matters quickly and surely to be
    able to interact intelligently with domain experts.

What is really important about TCA is the idea that a concept, rule,
task or any stimulus can be broken down into meaningful pieces, and
that these pieces can be broken down into yet finer pieces, and so on,
until one finally reaches a stage at which the detailed writing of
line after line of a program is appropriate. 'Topdown Analysis' is
an important phase in knowledge engineering (KEg), and it implies a
from the abstract whole ('top') to the particular sub-components
('bottom'). An automobile engineer who starts his work by drawing
blue-prints of a proposed car is using the topdown approach, whereas
an engineer who starts by consulting a tyre catalogue is using the
bottom-up approach. In the same manner, a knowledge engineer who
starts his work by writing frames or lines is not using the topdown
approach. Education is accomplished through a combination of bottom-

up and top-down approaches. Teaching is bottom-up - from the lower-order concepts to the higher-order concepts, and preparation for the teaching is top-down - from the higher-order concepts to the lower-order concepts.

10. REFERENCES & BIBLIOGRAPHY

1. Ausubel, D.P. (1960). The Use of Advance Organizers in the Learning of Meaningful Verbal Material. Journal of Educational Psychology, 1960, 51, pp. 267-72.

2. Descartes, René (1637). Discourse on the Methods. London: Nelson's University Paperbacks.

3. Gagné, Robert (1985). Conditions of Learning. New York: Holt, Rinehart & Winston.

4. Le Xuan & Chassain (1975). Analyse Comportementale. Paris: Nathan.

5. _____ (1985). Topdown Conceptual Analysis. Montreal: Pedagogical & Technological Innovations.

6. Martin, James & Oxman, Steven (1988). Building Expert Systems. Englewood Cliffs, N.J.: Prentice Hall.

7. Schoen, Sy & Sykes, Wendell (1987). Putting Artificial Intelligence to Work. New York: John Wiley & Sons.

8. Skemp, R.R. (1971). The Psychology of Learning Mathematics. London: Penguin Books.

9. Walters, R. & Nielson, Norman R. (1988). Crafting Knowledge-Based Systems. New York: John Wiley & Sons.

11. TABLE OF CONTENTS

FINDING THE APPROPRIATE INSTRUCTIONAL TEXT FROM QUESTION PERFORMANCE EVALUATION : A PROTOTYPE INTERFACE

Kenneth D. Loose

Department of Computer Science, The University of Calgary
Calgary, Alberta, Canada T2N 1N4

Abstract

The purpose of this paper is to describe the development of prototype software which would interface with instructional text so that the appropriate text could be presented on the basis of responses to multiple choice questions. Ease of implementation from a user point of view and potential generalizability to formal text or CAI materials were considered during the development. The text is analyzed to determine key words which are placed in three lists -- concept, quantifier, and sequence/level. The software analyzes the text to determine the line location of the words and create a tree structure of the word locations. Questions are analyzed to find the key words which appear in the three key word lists and the text appropriate to the question is located by attempting to find the best match for word combinations which occur in the text and the question. The software can locate text appropriate to a specific question for highly structured, relatively short text. Deficiencies in software performance are identified to provide the basis for further enhancements.

Introduction

This paper summarizes work completed thus far in building a prototype piece of software appropriate for inclusion in a tutoring system. Ever increasing quantities of information are stored in computer

files, many containing prose varying from formal presentations to
information which forms a part of presentation CAI. In order for
this information to be optimally useful for instructional purposes,
some effective but reasonably simple technique for finding the
appropriate portion of the text is required. Hypertext systems now
exist which make possible the linking of multiple files of various
types and enable the user to carry out complex searches [Conklin,
1987]. However, complex software is often avoided by many individuals and relatively extensive or complex instructional software does
not live up to expectations because of this avoidance [Kurland and
Kurland, 1987]. The prototype is designed to be relatively simple
and easy to implement. The user answers a series of questions to
determine current mastery of the subject and the appropriate position
in the text is determined and presented to the user. Alternately, a
series of questions can be used to find those areas where there are
deficiencies and the appropriate text identified and presented. The
prototype interface developed and investigated essentially functions
as a rather simple tutor which attempts to determine the current
mastery level of the student through a set of questions and then
branch to the appropriate text.

The approach used in the prototype is to analyze the instructional
material to produce three different lists which contain concepts,
quantifiers, and sequence/level indicators. Questions posed for the
student are analyzed on the basis of the words in the three lists,
appropriate search combinations are produced and the textual information accessed on the basis of these words. The expectation is that
the initial work in producing the three indicator lists might be
somewhat time consuming but having constructed the list pertinent to
some specific subject matter and level, any set of questions and text
could then be used. The construction of the three word lists and
questions which are pertinent to the information presented in the
instructional text are separate from the software which uses this
information to locate appropriate text position. The intent is that
the interface will be general enough so that class notes and
appropriate questions could be used, or, with small modification, the
questions often contained in presentation CAI modules could be used,
given the production of the appropriate keyword lists. The prototype
uses the subject matter from a first course in computer programming
in Pascal and the text files contain reasonably extensive notes
designed for the course.

The remainder of the paper discusses the production of the external data which provides the basis for the development of the interface, followed by a description and function of the interface. Finally a summary of the findings of the project will be presented.

Development of the External Data Files

Background

Two basic features guide the production of both the lists which are required and, ideally, the questions which will be used to locate appropriate text position. These are a limited model of the learning process and some basic assumption about the components of effective instruction.

Many theories exist which attempt to explain how individuals learn. Estes [Estes,1984] defines learning as all systematic processes of acquiring information or knowledge. The same article reviews some of the theories of learning, but there are features common to all. Learning requires that information or knowledge be acquired and assimilated into the larger base of information through additions and modifications, processes most commonly associated with Piaget and Inhelder [Piaget,1969]. Learning new information requires integration of new information with existing information to build an ever larger base. Isolated facts do not function as part of the background diversity of the individual until these facts are also related to those which already exist. Sternberg's [Sternberg,1984] work provides an interesting and practically useful model which helps in the analysis of features of instructional text and which serves as a guide for the prototype.

A critical component of this model is the basic tenet that knowledge acquisition is a bottom-up process. The computing analogy is that knowledge is incorporated in the same way as new keys are inserted into a B-tree. Thus when there is sufficient knowledge at the lowest level to enable some generalization, another level is created. The inference here is that the sequence in which the knowledge is added at the lowest level is not entirely critical but moving to the next

level requires some critical amount of information. Good sequence
may, however, enable the generalization to occur more readily. In
practice, good teachers often iterate the concept before beginning at
the bottom to provide the framework which will allow the learner to
grasp the concept. From the point of view of the model, such a procedure may be an aid because it provides a focus for incorporating
the appropriate bits of information to make the generalization.

Effective instruction should be enabled when the new information
builds upon the knowledge which currently exists and is presented
with some sequence which allows the learner to incorporate separate
entities readily. In some disciplines, the subject itself provides
substantial cues with respect to sequence and it becomes easier to
determine those aggregate pieces of information which are required to
build understanding at a more general level. Behavioral objectives
are a way of specifying the components and the desired relationship
among components which are to be acquired. The availability of such
objective specifications for instruction is one tool in determining
the simple knowledge specifications used in the prototype. While the
behavioristic approach to learning suggested by behavioral objectives
is not as popular as it once was, the hierarchy in Bloom's [Bloom,
1956] taxonomy can still provide a useful tool for the analysis of
instructional text.

Creating the Key Word Files

Three different lists are used by the software to try to determine a
position within the text. Analysis of the instructional text and the
behavioral objectives provides most of the first list termed the concept list. These are words which convey the essence or principles of
the subject matter, for example, words like 'structure' and 'block'.
Most often concepts are subjects or objects of sentences, but some
may also be the verb (usually the more difficult ones). Words in
this list can be elaborated or quantified by the words in the second
list termed the quantifier list. Quantifiers may indicate how concepts can be decomposed into some component parts or specific structural features of the concept. They may also help determine a
specific instance of some key piece of information or may also help

the learner discriminate between two different pieces of seemingly similar information. The process of discrimination is involved in deciding how the new information integrates with the old [Estes, 1984]. The quantifiers provide some information as a cue for discrimination. In some cases these may also be in the concept list such as 'block' which could be combined with 'program block' and also be a part of 'block structure'. The third list contains words which can indicate sequence, level, or a progression. Examples of these words are 'first', 'finally', 'simple', 'complex'. Once again, some of the words may appear in another list. 'Begin' has special meaning in Pascal when used as a reserved word, and would appear on a concept list. It may also appear as a sequence indicator.

Structure of the Software

Virtually all of the code is written in Pascal. The exception is a small portion written in C which allows random access to specific lines in the original text file. Development was done on a Sun 4 running UNIX which allows the insertion of executable code segments during compilation of the Pascal code. One minor modification is made to the original text file. A special indicator appears before and after any Pascal code. While the code is used to illustrate the concepts and is an integral part of the explanation, the code itself is not used to do sequence analysis incorporated into the prototype. This feature may be useful in other types of text where an example is used to explain some concepts but would not usually become part of the test which is searched for key words.

The software currently exists in two distinct parts. All of the processes which produce the data structures required for the analysis, and which are completed before any analysis of questions, form the first part. The second portion deals with the analysis of user response to questions covered in the textual material and the attempts to match user response to the appropriate text. A more detailed description follows.

Creation of the Data Structures

The original instructional text is scanned one line at a time. Only alphabetic characters are considered valid and all punctuation, numeric characters, and control characters are eliminated. As well all characters are converted to lower case to make string comparisons simpler. As the scan proceeds, each word and the line on which it occurs is written to a temporary file. These words along with their locations are then used to create a binary search tree. Each node in the tree has a field for the word (fixed length array set with a global constant), a frequency field, a boolean which indicates whether the word is being used in the structure (initially set to 'true)', and a head pointer to a linked list which contains the line number, a field to indicate if the word is on one of the three lists (concept, quantifier, sequence), and finally a left and right pointer.

Having determined a unique list of words in the original text, the next portion compacts the list since a large majority of these will not be used in any analysis. Two global constants, CUTFREQ and MAX-FREQ, are declared. If the frequency of occurrence of the word exceeds MAXFREQ, that word is no longer considered. If the frequency of occurrence is between CUTFREQ and MAXFREQ, the implementor is asked if the word should be retained. This eliminates many of the words which add coherence to the text but are not specific quantifiers or concept words while attempting to retain those words which indicate concept, sequence, or level and occur quite often.

A second compaction process also occurs in which the locations of words which contain the same root are combined into one list. This process at present is not elegant, or even particularly efficient. Two strings are compared to determine whether the second string contains the same characters as the first and then uses a set of simple rules to determine whether they should be combined. The rules distinguish plurals and a limited set of suffixes. For example if one string is the word 'character' and the second 'characters', the two are combined. Rules for coping with root words which end in 'e' and are another example (such as use using, and useful). This process may at some point be done with a more intelligent algorithm.

The compaction process results in a modification of the tree structure. Some words are discarded (boolean set to false). When two words are combined into the root word, the locations of the occurrence of the second word are merged with the location list for the root resulting in one list in line sequential order. All words merged in this way have access to the total list of variations of the same word. Because the algorithm is crude, an option exists which allows the implementor to go through the list of words again and combine those words which were not included in the scope of the algorithm but which should reasonably be combined. At this point, the flag in the tree node indicates those words which are still included and those which are being ignored. If the prototype proves effective and reasonably generalizable, additional code will be inserted to rebuild the tree with only active words.

A final set of processes are required to complete the building of appropriate data structures. The three lists produced from the analysis of the instructional text must be marked in the tree structure. In order to keep the algorithm simple, an initial check must be made to ensure that the form used for the word in any of the three lists is that which occurs first in the search of the tree. For example, if 'execution' is considered a key concept word, and 'execute' also occurs in the text, then the second form is used to identify the keyword in the data structure. As well, all words linked to the same list are also marked so that any occurrence has access to all locations of all forms of the word.

Matching Performance with Text

A series of multiple choice questions were designed on the basis of the material in the instructional text. All questions have four choices. For simplicity, neither the question stem or the answer options contain negations. These were avoided because the algorithm for determining where text matches the questions is still very crude and no analysis of sentence structure is done making it difficult to determine which part of the sentence is negated. For the purposes of initial test of the capability to locate appropriate text, all questions were analyzed and the text chosen by the software. Questions are presented interactively to the user and each answer analyzed.

The analysis procedure first requires that the question stem and the correct answer be evaluated to determine the words which appear in one or more of the three lists. This is done by checking each of the words against those in the tree structure produced previously. Since the tree nodes indicate which of the three lists contains the word, a pointer reference to the node can be kept in the appropriate list of pointers for easy access to the locations of the word and its various forms in the text. A given word may be in more than one list although this is not usually the case. The choice of some of the reserved words in Pascal means that 'begin' and 'end' may be key conceptual features but might also indicate some sequence or level.

The attempt to locate the appropriate text is really an attempt to find the best match of quantifiers, concept, and sequence. Thus the location of concept words is examined in relation to the location of quantifier words and the best combinations chosen. Best in this case is the closest match of line location of concept and quantifier, with the best being the occurrence of both on the same line. If sequence keywords also exist, then the closest combination of sequence, concept and quantifier is used. Note that the search compares line locations of various combinations of chosen words rather than search the strings for the appropriate combinations. This allows some flexibility as well since the quantifiers may occur before or after the concept which they modify and need not be adjacent.

The incorrect answers can be analyzed using the same process. However, some of the search can be shortened using the assumption that the misconception occurs at some position prior to the text which is appropriate for the correct answer. In other words, the failure to answer correctly is interpreted as an inadequate grasp of all of the features which comprise the correct or complete understanding of the concept.

When the algorithm has made a choice of the portion of text which should be appropriate, the text is accessed and presented to the user. Currently twenty lines are given and the user may request the next twenty or the previous twenty. At the users option, the system can be asked for another choice of text.

Performance of the Prototype

Performance of the prototype has been variable, however, many of the features which affect performance have been identified and these will be the focus of the discussion.

As would be expected, the performance is better with small quantities of text as opposed to large ones since there are fewer key words. As the size of the text increases, the number of unique words begins to level off. Thus the chance of finding a good textual match for the question is relatively easier for short pieces of text since the recurrence of the key words is less. A more important feature is the three lists. Initially, the lists were found to contain too many concept words. Analysis indicated that many of the words in the concept list were actually components of the concept and more rightfully belonged in the quantifier list. The quantifier list initially also contained words which really added no discriminatory value but were often chosen because they were modifiers of a concept word but were relatively situation specific rather than more global quantifiers. Finally, the sequence level list proved to be rather short in most cases, not because they could not be readily identified. It seems that much instructional text does not provide cues on the difficulty or simplicity or the steps in the sequence for developing the framework for the concept.

Because of these difficulties, the user option for choosing another possible text location was inserted. This proved effective and only rarely was it impossible for the software to locate appropriate text. Problems sometimes existed when the concept was the verb of most sentences rather than a subject or object. The indication seems to be that some parsing ability might improve the performance. One other situation presents itself quite often. Repetition is a common feature in instructional text. Without the capability of finding other possible text locations, repetition of concepts (with the same quantifiers) is hard to deal with unless there is some previous information about the position in the text which indicates the quantity of the text already mastered.

Conclusions

The initial intent was to investigate the effectiveness of a software package to choose appropriate text on the basis of answers to multiple choice questions. It was also to be relatively simple to use and generalizable to various forms of instructional text. The prototype functions well enough to encourage further refinement. Generalizability has not been established to this point since the text used for evaluation has been highly structured and topic specific. However, many of the shortcomings have been identified. From an implementor's point of view, much of the effort required to use the system is already expended in developing or analyzing the instructional text to be used. Enhancements to the prototype which try to overcome deficiences will then indicate whether this can be a useful software tool. Should this be the case, the final test of usefulness will be to determine if a set of files for concept, quantifier, and sequence can be used for different textual information about the same concepts without having to again generate another set of keyword lists and to determine the generality of the approach.

References

Bloom, B.S. 1956. *Taxonomy of Educational Objectives: The Classification of Educational Goals.* (Handbook 1, Cognitive Domain). NY: David MacKay.

Conklin, Jeff. 1987, Hypertext: An Introduction and Survey. *Computer,* 20(9):17 – 41.

Estes, William K. 1984. Learning, Memory, and Intelligence. In *Handbook of Human Intelligence.* ed. Sternberg, Robert J. Cambridge: Cambridge University Press. pp. 170 – 224.

Kurland, D. Midian and Kurland, Laura C. 1987. Computer Applications in Education: A Historical Overview. *Annual Review of Computer Science,* 2:317 -358.

Piaget, J., Inhelder, B. 1969. *The Psychology of the Child.* NY: Basic Books.

Sternberg, Robert J. 1984. *Beyond IQ: A Triarchic Theory of Human Intelligence.* Cambridge: Cambridge University Press.

Quadratic Grapher: An Intelligent Tutoring System for graphing quadratic equations

Marilyn Loser
Barry Kurtz

Computer Science Department, 3CU
Box 30001
New Mexico State University
Las Cruces, NM 88003
505-646-3723

Section I: Introduction

Few Intelligent Tutoring Systems (ITSs) have left research laboratories to augment instruction in the high school or college classroom. This research project produced an operating ITS, *Quadratic Grapher*, which runs quickly on a microcomputer. This ITS effectively teaches students to graph quadratic functions of a single variable. *Quadratic Grapher* is a practical teaching tool designed for high school classrooms and remedial mathematics laboratories at the college level.

We need good mathematical tutoring systems to supplement instruction and help ameliorate problems arising from a shortage of qualified high school mathematics teachers, to assist students in meeting increased mathematics requirements of more college majors, and to aid students in overcoming difficulties and anxieties associated with learning mathematics. Few students of elementary algebra graph quadratic equations, but once they make the transition from equation to graph, they quickly develop an understanding of properties of quadratics from the visual representation. In mathematics, "a picture is worth a thousand words" [Stevenson 1948]. Classroom overcrowding and time constraints limit the teacher's opportunity to plot graph after graph to illustrate important properties of functions. With its precision, accuracy, and speed, the computer can provide this service.

Quadratic Grapher produces a graphing environment where students can explore the graphs of quadratics. Students move graphs around the plane and infer, through the transformations of the equation, the relationship between functions and their graphs. The system evaluates a student's ability to graph quadratics and to understand quadratic concepts. *Quadratic Grapher* also illustrates quadratic graphing and has an interactive tutorial.

Quadratic Grapher uses AI methodologies in several ways:

1) a set of production rules generates quadratic functions of varying difficulty,

2) fuzzy set operations update the dynamic student-model database,

3) in the computer-driven mode, the current student state and recent history of consulted functions and questions dictate student activity selection,

4) pedagogical approaches involve three paradigms: microworld, diagnostic tutor, and coach,

5) it has a parser that allows simple natural language input, and

6) the database design allows an instructor to alter or to make additions to the system using an expert shell currently under development.

The remainder of this paper is divided into five sections. Section II contains a review of the current literature, Section III describes the nature of the project, Section IV explains the implementation, Section V presents testing methods and results, and Section VI includes possible future work and conclusions.

Section II: Review of the Literature

The realms of ITSs and CAI (Computer Aided Instruction) are not distinctly divided; they span a spectrum with pure ITSs at one end and CAI at the other, and with extant systems falling in between. Wenger [1987] feels that ITSs are distinguished from CAI since ITS encode knowledge instead of decisions resulting from knowledge. ITSs generally employ AI techniques and are dynamic, process-oriented structures. They are based on the idea that the most natural way to learn is in the context of doing [Anderson 1986]. ITS developers are motivated by the hope that a program can understand a student's misconceptions, then behave as a master teacher and provide appropriate instruction [Knezek 1988].

ITSs generally require powerful, expensive computers, so reside only in research laboratories. In 1985 only two ITSs were commercially available, *Proust* and *Lisp Tutor* [Yazdani 1986]. Hence, most schools use CAI systems. Unfortunately, CAI packages that are not user friendly or robust have sullied the reputation of CAI. Complaints range from the page-turning nature of courseware to the often limited or meaningless interaction [Bonner 1987].

Wenger [1987] describes four components basic to an ITS: domain knowledge, the student model, pedagogical knowledge, and the user interface. Current ITSs address one or more of these issues; they rarely attempt to deal with all four in depth.

Domain Knowledge

The domain knowledge, generally called the expert, is the representation of knowledge to be communicated and is frequently the best developed module of an ITS. Experts take many forms. *Steamer* [Hollan 1984], *Quest* [White 1985], and *SOPHIE* [Burton 1979] are sophisticated simulations. *Scholar* makes extensive use of semantic networks, and *Guidon* uses the *MYCIN* expert system [Wenger 1987]. *Buggy* employs a procedural network for subtraction skills [Brown 1978]. The *Lisp Tutor* [Anderson 1986] and *Quadratic Tutor* [O'Shea 1979] rely on sets of production rules.

Student Model

The ITS student model encodes the student's current state of knowledge. This model may be compared with that of an expert to determine proficiency or mastery or to diagnose student errors. An ITS analyzes student behavior and decides how that behavior alters the student model.

To classify student behavior, many ITSs, such as *Buggy*, store and search a large database of likely errors or misconceptions. *Quadratic Tutor* uses a state vector to store estimates of a student's knowledge. *Proust* extends the *Buggy* concept into the realm of debugging student programs and tries to understand the intentions of the programmer [Kearsley 1987]. *West* uses differential modeling to analyze student behavior.

Pedagogy

System control ranges from complete control by the student, in guided-discovery and coached programs such as *Motions* [Thompson 1987], *Steamer*, and *West*, through the give and take of mixed-initiative dialogues (where control may switch from student to computer and back) to monitoring systems in which the computer never relinquishes control, as in *LISP Tutor*. *Quest* [White 1985] employs a variety of pedagogical strategies.

User Interface

To the user, the human-computer interface is as important as the other three components. The more sophisticated the system's understanding of natural language inputs, the higher the likelihood the computer can communicate with the student. *Scholar's* interface is limited to simple sentences and it understands only correct responses; *Guidon* understands simple sentences and a list of commands. *Meteorology* parses user input questions by keyword matching. *SOPHIE* (SOPHisticated Instructional Environment) [Burton 1979] uses a semantic grammar parsing mechanism.

Users appreciate fast computer response time; the performance, however, of many ITSs is unsatisfactory. The response of *Quadratic Tutor* could be as much as two minutes [O'Shea 1979]. A single *Buggy* subtraction lesson took about 100 hours of a Lisp machine's time [VanLehn 1983].

Use of Microcomputers

Few extant ITSs have been ported to microcomputers--experts in the field of AI dismiss the current generation of personal computers, and suggest that the next, more powerful, generation will be more applicable to AI programming. Kearsley [1987] says, "... to me this is unrealistic and out of touch with the reality of the nation's classrooms. If ICAI is to have any practical impact on the world of education in the next five years, it will involve programs that run on those current machines." Among ITSs that do run on microcomputers are *MicroProust* and *MicroSearch*, and *Motions Micorworld*.

Section III: System Overview

Quadratic Grapher helps students graph quadratic functions of one variable. The program provides two environments: learning and evaluation. The learning environment includes reference materials (*Reference*), tutoring and coaching (*Tutorial*), and exploration (*Play*). The introduction is a reference section that explains the concepts involved in graphing quadratics. The interactive *Tutorial* provides the basics of graphing and coaches the student to improve his/her ability to graph quadratics. The *Play* section prompts a student to enter the coefficients of a quadratic in standard form, graphs the function, allows the student to alter function characteristics, then graphs the resulting quadratic. The evaluation environment, *Knowledge Evaluation* , can be driven by the student or the computer. It assesses and stores a student's knowledge of graphical concepts and his/her ability to correctly graph quadratics. A student's past history determines the level of function difficulty and the concepts on which the student is queried. The program displays its current assessment of student performance upon request.

Quadratic Grapher assumes that the student wants to learn how to graph quadratics and wants to know the computer's evaluation of his/her ability. However, even motivated students may find pure discovery to be too threatening, too difficult, or too time-consuming, so the program gives the student the freedom to choose other activities from a global menu.

Master teachers use a variety of methods to teach and assess students; no single approach suffices. *Quadratic Grapher* also uses a variety of instructional approaches. *Play's* microworld approach encourages students to freely explore graphing quadratics. Konrad Lorenz [1973] states that most of human cognition is based on pattern matching. *Play* exploits this attribute by letting students see pattern changes that occur when they change coefficients or translate the graph vertex and two other points. The program prompts the student for a quadratic to transform. After each transformation, it graphs the original function and the transformed function. While non-threatening, this free environment does not provide the guidance many students need; *Tutorial* provides this guidance. To make the *Tutorial* as flexible as possible, a coach monitors student application of various graphing concepts and encourages the student to use methods that s/he has overlooked or avoided.

Assessment also needs to be flexible and responsive. Since *Quadratic Grapher* maintains a record of a student's current knowledge, it can avoid asking questions about concepts the student understands. If a student response is partially correct, the computer acknowledges those portions that are correct and gives hints or suggestions for improving performance on incorrect portions.

The program displays four windows that provide a rich but uncluttered visual interface (see Figure I). The dialogue window at the bottom of the screen allows human-computer interaction; the graph window, on the right side of the screen, displays quadratic graphs. Two information windows, at the top left, display the original and the current function in both standard and vertex forms along with the coordinates of the vertex and two opposing points for the two functions.

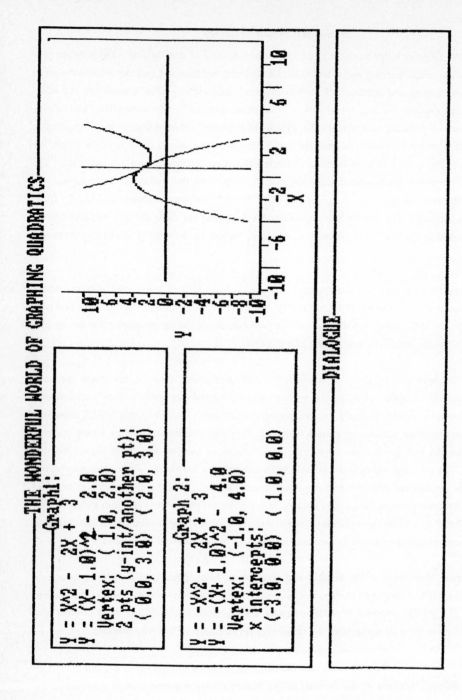

Figure 1: Sample screen during *Quadratic Grapher's Play* section

Quadratic Grapher understands natural language responses that use a limited vocabulary. It recognizes a variety of answers to questions which have more than one correct answer, and it replies to many incorrect responses. The program evaluates multiple concepts involved in many questions and answers.

Table 1 contains a sample of questions and recognized responses from the *Knowledge Evaluation* section. A correct response to a question triggers the computer to display a message and to update the student database. Incorrect responses result in hints or suggestions if the computer understands the response.

Concept questions		
Question	Correct	Incorrect
What do you know about the graph of a function if coefficient a is positive?	The graph opens up. The vertex is a minimum.	It opens down. The vertex is maximum.
Given a graph in standard form with b = 0, what do you know about the graph of the function?	The vertex is on the y-axis. The y-intercept is the vertex.	The vertex is on the x-axis.

Table 1: Sample of questions and recognized responses
from the *Knowledge Evaluation* of *Quadratic Grapher*

The *Knowledge Evaluation* section also checks the student's ability to calculate the coordinates for the vertex and two other points for a given equation. On correct responses, the computer flashes the entered function points in the graph window and updates the database. After required points are entered, the computer plots the complete graph.

The program deals with incorrect key point responses in a variety of ways.

1) If the student enters coordinates for a point that is in the function, but is not the requested point, then the computer prints an appropriate message (if the point is another key point, the computer explains the error) and reprompts.

2) If part of the response is correct, then the computer reprompts for the incorrect portion. For example, if the student enters correct x-coordinates for two opposing points, but incorrectly enters the y-coordinates, the computer tells the user that the x-coordinates are correct and only reprompts for the y-coordinate.

3) If the student has exceeded the maximum number of tries, then the program displays the correct coordinates.

When the student chooses "Student evaluation", the program then displays its estimate of the student's level of understanding (see table 2).

```
┌─────────────────────────────────────────────────────┐
│                 Student Evaluation                   │
│  Graphing:                                           │
│    Elements needed to graph function: ok             │
│    Vertex: needs more work                           │
│    X-intercepts: not enough information              │
│    Two opposing points: needs more work              │
│    Overall function graphing: not enough information │
│  Concepts:                                           │
│    Coefficient a: ok                                 │
│    Coefficient b: ok                                 │
│    Coefficient c: not enough information             │
│    Axis-of-symmetry: not enough information          │
│    Vertex: knows very well                           │
│    X-intercepts: not enough information              │
│    Y-intercept: ok                                   │
└─────────────────────────────────────────────────────┘
```

Table 2: Example of displayed Student Evaluation

The program saves a student database at the end of each session, so the student can start the next session where s/he left off.

Section IV: Implementation

Quadratic Grapher is a compiled Turbo Prolog system with an external database. It runs on an AT&T PC6300 computer with an AT&T graphic's board (640 x 400) or on IBM compatibles with CGA cards and monochrome or color monitors.

Domain

The program generates four difficulty levels of quadratic equations using production rules. The examples in Table 3 illustrate the nature of the production rules.

An external dynamic database stores question information used in the *Knowledge Evaluation* section. The database design allows an instructor to extend or change any of the question database information using an expert shell currently under development.

Student Model

The program develops two student models, one in the *Knowledge Evaluation* section and the other in the *Tutorial* section. A 12-element fuzzy set stores the *Knowledge Evaluation* student model. These elements are the concepts and abilities listed in the student evaluation table (Table 2). Fuzzy sets have a degree of membership assigned to each element; this degree, a real number in the range 0.0 to 1.0 measures the plausibility of an element being in a set (with 1.0 representing full set

Levels of function difficulty $f(x)=ax^2+bx+c$		
Level	Coefficient Characteristics	Examples
1	$b=c=0$ $b=0$ $a=b,\ c=0$	$f(x)=2x^2$ $y=x^2+3$ $f(x)=2x^2+2x$
2	difference of squares $b=ka\ \&\ c=0$ simple perfect squares $a=1\ \&$ easily factorable	$y=x^2-4$ $y=2x^2+4x$ $f(x)=x^2+2x+1$ $f(x)=x^2+5x+6$
3	failry easily factorable simple non-integer roots	$f(x)=2x^2+5x+8$ $y=2x^2-x$
4	random	$y=-6x^2+3x+5$

Table 3: Examples of quadratic functions
generated by *Quadratic Grapher*

memebership). Fuzzy set theory allows for reasoning with uncertainty, so models human reasoning better than traditional set theory.

The database also stores the number of times the computer consults each fuzzy set element. The combination of a fuzzy element's degree of membership and number of consultations is used to assess student knowledge. Simply printing the percentage of correct responses or the number of correct responses compared to the number of incorrect responses does not supply enough information and may be misleading. Correctly answering one question or 100 questions would produce a rating of 100% correct. Saying a student answered five out of 10 correctly provides no information on improvement. Which five were correct--the first five? the last five? every other one?

This program initializes degree of membership for each element to zero. The first time a student demonstrates ability or understanding of a particular concept in the *Knowledge Evaluation* section, that set element degree is changed to 0.2. Preliminary testing showed that this initial degree produced, after several student interactions, set membership degrees that corresponded to master teacher assessments.

Thereafter, student responses cause the program to update set elements using the fuzzy set operations dilation (returns the square root) and concentration (returns the square) [Schmucker, 1981]. A subset of concepts is associated with each student assessment. The "less" an element is there (the lower its degree of membership), the more it is altered; this gives a weighting to student responses. These operations model the way master teachers evaluate student performance. For example, once a student has demonstrated a high level of understanding, a teacher is more likely to attribute an incorrect response to a simple mistake, rather than to a lack of understanding, and reduce his/her estimation of student understanding less than if the student had only demonstrated a low level of concept understanding. Similarily, if the estimation of student understanding is very high, further demonstration of understanding increases the estimation level only slightly. However, for a student with a low level estimate, an additional demonstration of understanding increases the estimate to a greater degree.

Humans tend to communicate fuzzy information through natural language rather than through numbers; hence, the program uses the evaluations: not enough information, needs more work, ok, and knows very well [see Table 4].

Evaluation	Degree of set membership	Number of consultations
not enough information	-	< 3
needs more work	< 0.67	≥ 3
ok	≥ 0.67 & < 0.95	≥ 3
knows very well	≥ 0.95	≥ 3

Table 4: Natural language evaluation of fuzzy set membership
and number of consultations of fuzzy set element

The *Tutorial* section student model collects two types of information in a dynamic database. It keeps tract of the number of times a student uses each key point graphing technique and it stores information on the student's approach to graph a particular function. The database exists only during a particular session of *Quadratic Grapher*.

Pedagogical

The *Knowledge Evaluation* section is either computer or student driven to the extent that a student can choose functions and concepts on which to be evaluated or can have the computer make those choices.

If the student elects to graph a function selected by the computer, the program generates one of the appropriate level. It chooses functions of Level 1 [see Table 3] if fuzzy set membership for graphing vertex, x-intercepts, and two opposing points are all < 0.4. Level 2 graphs are appropriate if elements have degrees ≥ 0.4 but at least one has degree < 0.7. The range for Level 3 functions is 0.7 to 0.95. If membership degree for all three concepts is ≥ 0.95, the program selects a random function. The computer keeps a history of the last five functions and will not repeat them.

Students may select their own integer coefficients (absolute value <= 10) with the limitation that the entered function cannot be in the recent history. Students enter coordinates for the vertex and two opposing points. If the student points are incorrect, the computer tests for a variety of errors. It checks to see if the entered point is on the graph, and if so, if it is another key point. If the student inputs coordinates for two opposing points, the computer checks to see if either or both points are in the function. It checks whether the x-coordinates are for opposing points, or the y-coordinate is wrong. The program displays appropriate error messages and reprompts the user for needed information. The user has a maximum of three tries after which the computer displays the correct values for point coordinates.

The database of questions and responses keyed to a student model assesses student understanding. In the computer-driven mode, the program sorts the database in ascending order of concept fuzzy set membership, and selects a question based on lowest set membership and recent history. It will not repeat a recent question and it will not select a question with the same main concept as the previous question. If the student selects the question category, recent questions are not repeated.

The program parses a student response to a query by key words, then matches these key words with lists in the database. If the user's list matches an acceptable database list, the subset of fuzzy concepts associated with the answer is updated. A match with an unacceptable database list produces a hint or suggestion and reprompts the user. A student has a maximum of three tries.

The *Tutorial* presents students with functions and guides them through the graphing procedure. The *Tutorial* student database and a set of production rules (see Table 5 for examples) are used to guide the presentation. Anytime the computer expects a student response, the student may type "help" to receive hints or instruction. The program monitors student progress in two ways. First, the program uses differential modeling. Using production rules like those in Table 5, it selects the most direct approach to graphing a function and compares it to the student's approach. If the approaches are different, the computer explains it's selection to the student. Secondly, to encourage students to employ a variety of graphing techniques, the program--after the first few examples--selects functions that can be graphed using techniques the student has never or only seldomly used.

Interface

The key-word parser selects up to four key words from each student natural language input--a noun, verb, modifier and negative. It makes four passes at the sentence, searching first for a noun, then in subsequent passes for a verb, modifier and negative. The database stores understood words along with their associated part of speech. On each pass, the parser, moving from left to right, repeatedly strips off a word and checks for the first word and part of speech match in the dictionary.

Production rules for selecting graphing technique		
Vertex:	**IF**	$b=c=0$
	THEN	Vertex = (0,0).
	IF	$c=0 \ \& \ b \neq 0$
	THEN	Vertex = $(c,0)$.
	IF	$b \neq 0 \ \& \ c \neq 0$ & two opposing points have been found
	THEN	apply midpoint formula.
Two points:	**IF**	$b=c=0$
	THEN	find two opposing points (no x-intercepts or y-intercept & point)
	IF	$c=0 \ \& \ b \neq 0$
	THEN	find x-intercept by factoring
	IF	*discriminant* <0 and vertex has been calulated
	THEN	find two opposing points

Table 5: Examples of production rules used
for coaching in *Tutorial* section

Section V: Testing

Preliminary evaluation of the *Play* and *Knowledge Evaluation* sections was informal and involved five high school and college mathematics instructors. After a brief introduction, instructors experimented with the program and kept a log of comments and reactions. Responses resulted in adding correct and incorrect responses to the question/answer database and alternating the notation of presented function examples between $f(x) =$ and $y =$. Student testing is scheduled for mathematics students at two college campuses and one high school.

Section VI: Future Work and Conclusions

As Kearsley [1987] pointed out, if ITSs are to have any practical impact in education in the near future, it will be through programs that run on microcomputers. *Quadratic Grapher* demonstrates that producing an ITS on a microcomputer is viable today. Turbo Prolog is a good language choice since it runs on microcomputers, supports a rich user interface through its windows, has adequate execution speed, and provides for easy data updating and the development of expert shells through its dynamic database facilities.

During preliminary testing, the response to the use of fuzzy set theory in the student model was positive. Instructors felt weighing student responses and communicating in natural language made the program seem reasonable and friendly. Instructors requested a greater variety of responses, however.

A weakness of the program is the rudimentary language interface. Fortunately, the realm of quadratic graphing has many domain specific words and can be discussed in straightforward, fairly simple terms. Robust parsers are a study in themselves and as they require large amounts of memory and are often relatively slow, they were not suitable for this project.

Two improvements are under development. First, the expert shell will allow additions and changes to the database of questions and response giving instructors the opportunity to tailor the program.

The second desired improvement is the ability of the program to more fully explain its method in graphing a particular quadratic. Currently, it gives an English explanation as to why a particular method was chosen, but doesn't show any mathematical calculations. One of the major limitations of a microcomputer (at least those one can expect to find in a classroom) is the small memory size. Unfortunately, *Quadratic Grapher* can not grow much in size and many of the desired improvements require additional memory.

High school teachers have requested programs similar to *Quadratic Grapher* for graphing lines and trigonometric functions. It would be interesting to see how much of the framework of this project could be used for either of the suggested projects.

References

John R. Anderson and Edward Skwarecki, "The automated tutoring of introductory computer programming," **Communications of the ACM,** 29: 9, 1986

Jodi Bonner, "Computer courseware: frame-based or intelligent?," **Educational Technology,** pp. 30-33, 1987

John S. Brown, Richard R. Burton and Frank Zdybel, "A model-driven question-answering system for mixed-initiative computer-assisted construction," **IEEE Transactions on Systems, Man and Cybernetics,** SMC-3, no. 3, 1973

Richard R. Burton and John Seely Brown, "An investigation of computer coaching for informal learning activities," **Int. J. Man-Machine Studies,** pp. 5-24, 1979

James D. Hollan, Edwin L. Hutchins and Louis M. Weitzman, "STEAMER: An Interactive, Inspectable, Simulation-Based Training System," **The AI Magazine,** Summer 1984

Greg Kearsley (Ed.), **Artificial Intelligence and Instruction. Applications and Methods,** Addison-Wesley Pub. Co., Reading, Mass., 1987

Gerald A. Knezek, "Intelligent tutoring systems and ICAI," **The Computing Teacher,** 15:6, pp. 11-13, 1988

Konrad Lorenz, **Behind the Mirror,** Harcourt Brace Jovanich, New York, 1978

T. O'Shea, "A self-improving quadratic tutor," **Int Jrnl Man-Machine Studies,** vol. 11, pp. 97-124, 1979

Kurt J. Schmucker, **Fuzzy Sets, Natural Language Computations and Risk Analysis,** Computer Science Press, Rockville, 1984

Burton Stevenson, **The Home Book of Proverbs, Maxims, and Familiar Phrases,** pg. 2611, Macmillan Company, New York, 1948

Patrick W. Thompson, "Mathematical microworlds and intelligent computer-assisted instruction," **Artificial Intelligence and Instruction,** Addison-Wesley Pub., Reading, Mass., 1987

K. VanLelhn, "Human procedural skill acquisition: theory, model and psychological validation," **Proceedings of the National Conference on Artificial Intelligence,** pp. 420-423, Washington, D.C., 1983

Etienne Wenger, **Artificial Intelligence and Tutoring Systems: Computational and Cognitive Approaches to the Communication of Knowledge,** Morgan Kaufmann Pub., Inc., Los Altos, CA, 1987

Barbara Y. White and John R. Frederiksen, "QUEST: Qualitative understanding of electrical system troubleshooting," **GART Newsletter,** July 1985

M. Yazdani (Ed.), **New Horizons in Educational Computing,** Wiley, 1984, New York

ANALYSIS OF HEURISTIC REASONING FOR THE VISUALIZATION OF CAD HEURISTICS

Fillia Makedon

The Computer Learning Research Center
and Computer Science Program
University of Texas at Dallas
Richardson, Texas, 75083-0688

Malgorzata Marek-Sadowska

Electronics Research Laboratory
University of California,
Berkeley, CA 94720

ABSTRACT

In this paper we develop a conceptual model for CAD algorithm visualization. We analyze the knowledge requirements necessary and formalize a visualization model called FOVISTA. FOVISTA has four essential "functional views" which emphasize the visualization of the computational behaviour of CAD heuristics, rather than the final result. The aim is to provide a learning and research tool for the design of heuristics. As an example, we consider a VLSI (Very Large Scale Integration) heuristic, that of detailed (switchbox) routing.

1. INTRODUCTION

The use of visualization for teaching, learning and research has gained a great deal of interest recently [Fr, My]. Although limited by advanced workstation requirements, the claimed advantages of visualization in algorithm design are to help "see the unseen" [Fr] of data structure behaviour, provide new techniques for exploring the potentials of a heuristic (or combination of heuristics), and provide new tools for comprehending data interaction and complexity. Since the field is new and relatively undefined, specialists of various domains have been approaching it in an application-specific manner.

This paper describes a domain-specific yet application-independent model for the class of intractable computational problems encountered in chip design.We introduce the FOVISTA visualization model as a way for (a) theoretically understanding and learning already known algorithms and (b) making the invention or design of new, more powerful heuristics intuitively easier for the novice and more efficient for the expert designer. We hope that this approach will also help in the development of a theory for heuristics. In another paper in these proceedings [MO], we present ALGO, an object-oriented programming environment for designing and learning algorithms.

1.1. VISUALIZATION OF CAD HEURISTICS

Analyzing heuristic behavior from a computer scientist's point of view, one places emphasis on improving the space and time performance of an algorithm. Thus, a good visualization system must provide support for questions of the form, how/when/why a heuristic works, what is the effect of parallelism on the time requirements, how to design for testability and fault tolerance, etc.

Recent advances in VLSI (Very Large Scale Integration) technology make it possible to put large numbers of components on a chip. Hence, the problem of efficiently designing a chip automatically is a very important one in Computer Aided design (CAD). Unfortunately, almost all VLSI algorithms are inherently intractable or NP-Complete (i.e., the time/space requirements of an exact solution grow exponentially with the size of the input). Hence, the development of algorithms which are based on human intuition and which work fast in practice, i.e., HEURISTICS, are the only alternative. Heuristics is an area where visualization, properly applied, can play a great role. For example, visualization can provide new techniques for the analysis of tradeoffs between competing cost parameters, assessment of available space, of architecture capabilities, for monitoring the effect of local parameters on system design, etc.

By an algorithm visualization system we mean the intelligent application and interplay of software tools at "key places" of the algorithm for a conceptual, comprehension of the method, rather than a visual illustration of the result. FOVISTA is a conceptual visualization model for VLSI heuristics.

The user is able to define how the system is to be used, e.g., for understanding theory versus real time behavior, to learn about algorithms, or how to design new ones, for drill and practice or to design a simulation, etc.

We consider the CAD process from the designer's point of view, how he/she structures and uses knowledge. Switchbox routing is a classic VLSI Layout problem which appears in a variety of forms at various levels of the VLSI physical design process. We consider the development of a heuristic for this problem which one of the two authors has developed [M].

1.2. BACKGROUND: VISUALIZATION EFFORTS IN GENERAL

Visualization research as it applies to learning is still in a fuzzy state. Several issues are still not clear, such as what techniques are needed for guiding simulations interactively, for monitoring the parameter space graphically in real time [F], how this should be done for the visualization of a graph algorithm versus the visualization of a computer memory architecture, etc. Other open questions concern the degradation of the algorithm's performance due to the annotation overhead and how to incorporate a variety of already developed instructional techniques [BS,MMR,SHA], such as diagnostic modeling and student monitoring capabilities. Detection of when a student does not perform well, and what skill he is lacking, may be possible by comparing the student's answer with that of the expert's [GR, SHA].

A variety of visualization definitions have been given for different applications [Fr,Gr,My]. A basic distinction has been made, however, between visual programming [J] and program visualization. Visual programming means that the graphics itself replace the program. In program visualization, on the other hand, a mixed set of tools is applied to enhance the intuitive understanding with textual, graphical and other strategies [Gr,My]. Our approach falls more within the second category.

We mention below some of the approaches to program visualization, very few of them complete systems:

a. algorithm animation software environments, such as ALADDIN [HHRa], Brown's BALSA system [B, BS] and London and Duisberg's Smalltalk [D, LD];
b. interactive programming environments which are used as teaching coaches of the form described in [Te] and [F]; programming by example, as in [H]; teaching by graphic aids [BCJK, ME], tools for programming learning [G];
c. languages of the form described in [R] and in [J] and operating systems which allow for analyzing complex explanations [SHA].
d. visual educational strategies in general, such as advanced computer aided instruction (CAI) systems, as in [MMH, MMO, MMR], modular approaches to program visualization, as in [St];
e. end-user programming facilities for using graphics [MV, My];
f. hypermedia (information linking) facilities, as in [CTHP, MV, MS, YHMD];

Most visualizations have been application specific, or towards the development of general software-support environments, such as in [B] and [LD], which emphasize the graphics and the tools over the concept, a hard trade-off.

For certain domains, such as computer science, this is not adequate. Certain principles need to be developed which (a) visualize the method of an algorithm, rather than the result, (e.g., the principles, limitations and strengths of a heuristic should be explained), (b) visualize algorithm execution with expert guidance, (c) monitor data structure changes during execution and (d) allow user-defined creation of domain-specific views of the algorithm.

A central feature in algorithm visualization is how the user can increase his/her understanding of the algorithm via the interplay between graphical interfaces and his cognition, how the algorithm designer "programs" these interactions in a modular way, and how the system controls the access of the various models. In [CPF], window-based computer dialogues are studied and seven functional uses for windows are identified, based on operating system theory. The basic idea of multiple windows is that it leads to a multiplicity of contexts. Thus, a window is a particular view of some data object in the computer and can be multiplexed with other windows [CPF].

Among various algorithm animation systems, the most known one is BALSA ([B],[BS]), a powerful software environment which provides tools for the easy development of algorithm animation programs. BALSA constitutes only a part of what we view as algorithm visualization because it does not have certain essential CAL (computer assisted learning) facilities for tutoring, or for computational insight into what is going on. Little conceptual guidance is provided [Gi] by the expert and limited intelligent access to a library of related algorithm visualizations or background information. BALSA provides facilities for annotating the algorithm, i.e., identifying essential operations which cannot be inferred automatically. While several algorithms are running, the user can synchronize them, can suspend them to change the combinations of views on the screen, and can change the annotations. There is also a scripting facility which records the user's actions and can replay them. There are menus offered for this purpose, called algs, views and inputs, all with parameter options for active windows.

ALADDIN has also been designed to animate graph algorithms for the purpose of teaching algorithms. It provides facilities for user-controlled creations of multiple views of an algorithm, creation of the objects to be animated, printout, and dialogue facilities which help in programming. In [MSKW], an intelligent aid for circuit redesign is described that is a knowledge-based system and is called REDESIGN. REDESIGN takes into account knowledge of circuit structure, function, purpose and interrelationships. Such a system is closer to our view [MO] of algorithm visualization because it analyzes circuit operation and reasons about its purpose.

2. PRELIMINARIES

2.1. DEFINITION OF AN ALGORITHM VISUALIZATION SYSTEM

In order to visualize how an algorithm works, we need the following two components: (a) the reasoning behind the algorithm displayed (with interruptions, graphics and links to other aids), and (b) an appropriate interface with the user for defining parameters to experiment with, for accessing demonstrations of related algorithms, relevant definitions, and for searching the relevant knowledge space. There are many implementation questions that arise here and which are not considered in this paper: How should these two components of knowledge interact for an efficient, modular, easy to maintain and to update system? How should they be synchronized? How should we guide exploration in the knowledge space of algorithm design? How should this occur for the user who is a novice versus an expert designer? How should we provide access to computer science concepts stored in a an electronic library [St], and how should we link them with hypertext facilities?

From the literature, we can conclude that, for a multiple-viewing of the inner workings of an algorithm, a visualization system must be composed of the following three sets of tools:

(1) A set of tools for the DISSECTION of the algorithm (or heuristic) into visualizable components A1, A2, ..., An, which we call "algorithmic snapshots".

These snapshots depict the behavior of the algorithm and are taken at "computationally critical" events, E1, E2, ..., Em. That is, snapshots may occur at an exchange of values, a comparison, the end of an iteration, the return from a recursive call, the escalation of time/space complexity to a higher order of magnitude. A set of designer-defined "computationally significant" ANNOTATIONS, N1, N2,..., Nm are mapped onto the snapshots A1, A2,..., An at different events Ei. Annotations (see [MMR]) serve the purpose of routing the user through a set of paths which make sense for the algorithm, rather than allowing the user to arbitrarily experiment in a vast information system. (Algorithm animation is then defined in terms of computationally significant events).

(2) A set of INTERACTIVE PROCESSES which are domain-dependent in that they are possible for a range of heuristics within a certain domain. Thus, for a given event Ei, expressed by snapshot Ai, the user can direct his/her next action based on a set of available operations. For example, he/she may wish to access a variety of tools which are part of the visualization knowledge base, and external to the heuristic (simulation, tutors, a CAI lesson on VLSI, etc.)

For this, he may use hypermedia type of links and a graphics-based, high level programming language). Depending on the domain of problems, the FOVISTA visualization system defines these processes taking into account the applications possible, in a similar manner as described in [MMH].

(3) An advanced and highly graphical USER INTERFACE which "embeds" the facilities described in (1) and (2) in a "Visualization Learning Support Environment", similar to what it described in [SKW]. The aim of FOVISTA is to formalize the user-interface so that it does not vary greatly from heuristic to heuristic, but allows a set of domain-specific facilities which take into account the requirements of the problem, conventual complexity measures, etc. The interface should be interactive, with a knowledge base, and with a hypermedia mechanism of linking and accessing information [HA].

2.2. INTRINSIC FEATURES OF VLSI LAYOUT HEURISTICS

There have been several papers on understanding algorithm design, for the purpose of automating it and developing an artificial intelligence program, see, for example [K] and [SK]. Our approach to visualization differs in that we place emphasis on intelligent aids to heuristic design, rather than on the development of an automated AI system which solves the problems for us. A set of salient features which we believe are inherent to designing heuristics in VLSI is listed below:

1. Almost all VLSI design problems are NP-hard and heuristic approaches are taken. (Since an algorithm is considered to be a heuristic if it has a fast and practical solution without any guarantee that it works all the time, for all instances of the problem, a visualization system must provide for "what if I tried this" facilities.)

2. Because of the inherent computational complexity of VLSI problems, most heuristics are artificially broken into phases although a design decision of one phase has immediate effect and is dependent on the design decision of the next phase. (Since the goodness of one phase can only be judged by its effect and performance on the next, a visualization system must provide for input generator modules which can be executed in a reasonable amount of time).

3. For any given problem, there is (usually) an array of possibly conflicting optimization costs, (such as, minimizing total wire length, minimizing space, number of vias, and possibly other costs). The priority given to a certain problem's cost functions may vary from implementation to implementation and model to model and a good visualization system should allow for this.

2.3 HEURISTIC DESIGN : DOMAIN VS PROBLEM KNOWLEDGE

In designing a heuristic solution, there is "apriori" knowledge [K] which a designer must have before starting to solve a VLSI problem which is "domain-specific" :

(a) UNDERSTANDING THE PROBLEM: computational understanding of the general problem (switchbox routing), i.e., the assumed generic model, what the problem tries to solve;

(b) CLASSIFICATION OF PROBLEM: understanding of where the problem belongs in the whole physical design process (i.e., what implications it has for the design phase following),

(c) EFFICIENCY KNOWLEDGE: knowledge of the problem's worse case space/time complexity whether an exact solution has been proven to be NP-hard (i.e., efficiency knowledge [K]);

(d) IMPLEMENTATION KNOWLEDGE: knowledge of the problem's real-time performance, what strategy other heuristics have followed and what has been their best performance;

(e) MODEL ASSUMPTION KNOWLEDGE: what are the goals (cost criteria to optimize) and in what priority;

During the design of a new heuristic, a good visualization system must provide the designer with intelligent aids for developing "problem-specific" knowledge, i.e., new rules, definitions, etc. Problem-specific knowledge is "evolving knowledge" in that it is developed from the interaction of the given problem requirements, accepted "domain-specific" knowledge and the creativity of the designer. The result of this interaction is a solution to the problem.

For a CAD algorithm visualization system, the following observations can be made about what problem-specific knowledge consists of:

(a) HEURISTIC SPECS: knowledge of new rules (assumptions) and model constraints introduced by the heuristic;

(b) HEURISTIC BEHAVIOUR: knowledge of the conflicting situations which may arise and which force making a choice or a DESIGN DECISION, (such as choosing to connect x and y versus u and v); we note here that a decision is taken based on the algorithm's central optimization strategy, i.e., domain knowledge; several to many special cases that appear and to which the central strategy of the heuristic must apply; these special cases propagate algorithmic "assertions", of the form described in [K, SK]. Each of these cases are treated using problem-specific and domain-specific knowledge.

(c) SKETCHPAD FACILITIES: facilities of learning from examples or modules for generating instances of the problem with user-defined parameters. Here is where a certain heuristic guess (or decision of a pattern) taken can be evaluated, monitored, and the feasibility of the solution verified for an instance of the problem.

(d) UNDERSTANDING THE RELATIONSHIP BETWEEN UNIQUE SOLUTIONS AND HEURISTIC STRATEGIES: An optimal solution to an NP-hard problem tries to detect all unique patterns (or design decisions). To do this, all solutions need to be examined simultaneously, something which is computationally too expensive or not feasible. Thus, a good heuristic strategy should try to incrementally solve the problem by finding patterns (as efficiently as possible) which do not violate undetected unique patterns. Otherwise, there may not be a solution possible after a certain configuration of patterns have been chosen.

The above observations will become clear as we consider our specific example of switchbox routing in the next section.

3. SWITCHBOX ROUTING EXAMPLE: A HEURISTIC PARADIGM

Typically, the systems for VLSI layout consist of two phases: placement and routing, an artificial division of the layout process since the two are really one problem. Switchbox routing [M] is a typical VLSI layout problem which involves two-dimensional routing in two distinct layers. It appears after the global routing phase of VLSI design, i.e., after placement of modules and after the global assignment of nets to channels.

DEFINITION OF THE PROBLEM: In switchbox routing, we are initially given a rectilinear routing region ("switchbox"), (with or without obstacles present and with or without initial routes present) which encloses horizontal and vertical grid lines which model the design rules. The terminals of the nets to be connected are placed on the boundary of the routing region. The problem is to interconnect all terminals with the same number assigned so that no more than one net is routed over any given row-column path in the routing region.

If we have not connected all the nets and we run out of row-column paths to achieve this, we say that the routing is "not realizable" and try another routing possibility. One basic assumption (rule) of this model is that two different nets can intersect only in a cross-type way (see Figure 1 for explanation).

GOAL TO BE ACHIEVED: The goal is to find a routing which (1) connects all the nets, (2) fits into the given grid, and (3) satisfies the intersection requirements. Like most routing problems, this problem is NP-hard, i.e., it takes an exponential time in terms of its input size (number of nets) to find an optimal solution because it has to try all possibilities for an optimal solution.

Thus, the algorithm which we will outline is a heuristic in that it may fail to find routes for some connections even when a complete routing exists.

3.1. UNIQUE SOLUTIONS AND HEURISTIC STRATEGIES

Before we proceed, the relationship between unique solutions and heuristic strategies needs to be elaborated. In fact, the relationship is true for many NP-hard problems. Let $\{S_i\}_i = 1,2,\cdots,k$ be a set of all different solutions to our routing problem P. Two solutions S_i and S_j are different if $S_i - (S_i \cap S_j) \neq 0$, $S_j - (S_j \cap S_i) \neq 0$. Now let us consider $\overset{k}{\underset{i=1}{\cap}} S_i$. If $\overset{k}{\underset{i=1}{\cap}} S_i \neq 0$, we say that the routing problem P has "unique" routes. In particular, we may have k=1, which means that P has a unique solution. From the definition of unique routes, it follows that if a portion of a net has a unique route which has not been identified, then solution to P can not be found.

However, there is a problem in finding unique routes. It is as follows: Suppose that in order to solve P, we have to complete m nets. For each net we consider all possible routes. If all routes for net N_i have to contain some common grid line segments, then those grid segments constitute unique routes. Such unique routes are easy to detect.

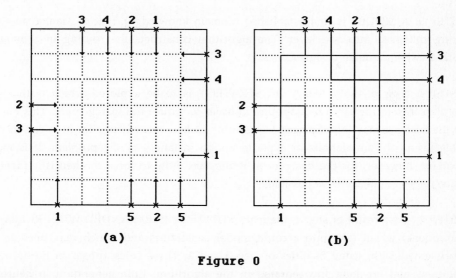

Figure 0

The situation is quite different when each unfinished net can take at least 2 different routes but unique routes still do exist (i.e., not all routes have to contain certain segments). Consider the switchbox routing example in the Figure 0(a and b). Figure 0(a), shows the unique routes when each net is considered independently from the other unfinished nets. In Figure 0(b) this is a unique solution. We could find all unique routes if we could examine all routes of all nets simultaneously. We do not know how to do it.

In the switchbox routing algorithm, when no unique patterns are detected, it does not mean that there are none. The heuristic strategy tries to suggest such routes which do not violate those undetected unique routes. In fact, to be on the safe side, each route should be completed incrementally. After adding each segment based on heuristic reasoning, we should check if it causes detection of occurrence of unique routes and the feasibility of the solution should be monitored. This is computationally too expensive in a practical router but could be monitored in a LEARNING SYSTEM. Our heuristic's main strategy to external boundary strategy usually results in easy to detect unique routes. However, routing in the middle of the grid makes it hard to force unique routes.

In a visualization system, the emphasis should be on the relationship guess --> consequence. In fact, if we store these relationships, they could be used for a rule-based rerouting system.

3.2. A STEP BY STEP ANALYSIS

Let's now follow through the steps involved in producing a heuristic for our problem so that we may be able to better understand the requirements of a good visualization system for CAD heuristics.

STEP 0: A MODEL is first established (domain knowledge), that of Manhattan-style routing collapsed into one layer. The algorithm constructs the routing in a manner similar to what a human designer does:

STEP 1: Now a MAIN IDEA OR STRATEGY is to be explored which is that the algorithm tries to identify unique routes in order to reduce the search space. This means that the designer may initially need to visualize (a) how other heuristics have solved this problem, and (b) simulations of experiments on instances of the problem. It is more important, however, for the designer to understand how to force the heuristic identify unique routes as efficiently as possible.

STEP 2 : As a result of step 1, the main STRATEGY IS EXPANDED WITH RULES (or assumptions) which take into account model constraints and which may need to be experimented with, using facilities of step 3 and 4. These rules appear in the form of definitions and are later incorporated in the algorithm. Rule generation in heuristic problem solving [K], is a divide and conquer approach which breaks the problem into smaller ones (special cases) with certain "idiosyncrasies". The main strategy still exists but it is particularly important to visualize how the different cases adapt to it so that the ability to recognize anticipated or unanticipated results in the evolution of the heuristic [K] is provided to the learner.

STEP 3: GENERATION OF DEFINITIONS which fall into two categories now occurs, (a) domain-specific, i.e., have to do with the model structure and (b) problem-specific, i.e., intrinsic to the algorithm (such as the data structures/operations of the algorithm).

Examples: The first five of the following definitions are domain-specific while the rest are problem-generated: a) a certain wire intersection pattern is excluded, that of knocked-knee routing (see Figure 2 for explanation); b) definitions of a "routing region", a "terminal", a "net", a "route", a "connection", an "endpoint", a "corner", a "hanging connection", a "current routing region". Efficiency knowledge is used only when the definitions are being incorporated into the algorithm. Definitions are incorporated into the algorithm as operations which become associated with the algorithm's data structures. These form what we call "dynamic definitions".

Examples of "dynamic definitions": (a) "lines of expansion", as they are defined for corners, terminals and hanging connections; (b) what to do when the expansion lines are "directed"; (c) what to do when two expansion lines "converge', when they "semiconverge"; (d) what to do when two expansion lines "diverge".

STEP 4: RESOLVING CONFLICTS: when no unique wire patterns are detected, the heuristic tries to route one or more connections which have high probability of not obstructing the further routing. The decision of which connection to route and what pattern to choose is based on "heuristic reasoning" which is described in greater detail in step 5. Each time a route or set of routes is added to the existing routing, it may cause some other wires to take unique routes at this juncture. Thus, the strategy of forcing routes which are unique propagates down. After adding a route based on heuristic reasoning, the algorithm identifies and routes those wires which have to take a unique pattern hereafter.

STEP 5: The routing ALGORITHM IS FORMULATED below:

(1) FIRST ROUTE CONNECTIONS WHICH HAVE A UNIQUE SHAPE AND ARE CLASSIFIED AS "NON-CONFLICT" (heuristic reasoning is applied here).

(2) Then COMPLETE THE ENTIRE ROUTING BY CAREFULLY CONSTRUCTING IT FROM THE BOUNDARY INWARDS, (i.e., use the boundary to force unique routings, pull out all wires whose routes become unique so they will not be blocked adjacent to the boundary).

(3) USE one of the following 5 RULES in order to decide what connection to select and how to route it in the current step. (The interested reader should study the paper in [M]

in order to fully understand the implications of our analysis):

RULE 1. HOW TO FILL THE CORNERS OF THE ROUTING REGION (Figure 4)

RULE 2. STRAIGHT-THROUGH CONNECTIONS (Figure 5): this rule considers how to connect those terminals of the same net appearing in the same column or row with their lines of expansion being convergent. Since several situations may arise for each case, an interactive visual aid of these situations is valuable for juxtaposing, keeping track and refining the heuristic.

RULE 3. NON-CONFLICT CONNECTIONS: This rule characterizes as "non-conflict" two convergent (crossing) routes.

RULE 4. EXPANSION FROM CORNERS: This rule considers how to interconnect partial routes, the case when a net A is partially routed and the wire patterns create corners. The designer trys to complete the routing of a net A as soon as possible by deciding to interconnect if two partial routes of a net A have a straight line expansion from a corner that joins them (see Figure 8).

RULE 5: REMAINING CONNECTIONS ALONG THE BOUNDARY: now all those nets which remain unconnected from rules 1-4 are connected so that the route is pushed to the boundary (uniqueness) as much as possible (Figure 9 shows an example routed by a program which implements the algorithm).

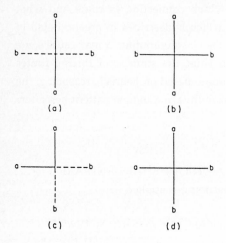

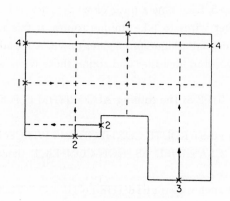

Fig. 1. Wire intersection styles:
(a) Cross-type intersection with layering shown
(b) Cross-type intersection in collapsed routing
(c) Knocked-knee intersection with layering shown
(d) Knocked-knee intersection in collapsed routing

Fig. 2. Examples of lines and directions of expansion for: a terminal of net 1, a corner of route of net 2, hanging connection of route of net 3, and a corner of route of net 4. Solid lines show routes, broken lines are lines of expansion.

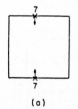 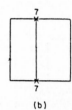 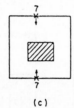 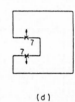 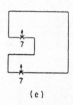

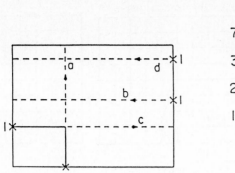

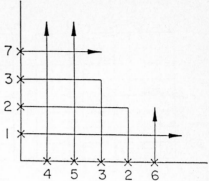

Fig. 3. Convergent and divergent pairs of lines:
    i) a and b are convergent,
    ii) b and c are semi-convergent,
    iii) b and d are divergent

Fig. 4. An example of unique routing pattern near the boundary corner.

Fig. 5. Possible situations for pins of the same net placed in a common column.
    (a) Convergent directions of expansion, no obstacle on the straight line connection the pins.
    (b) Connection routed for the case (a).
    (c) Convergent directions of expansion, obstacle present, no straight-through routing possible.
    (d), (e) Divergent directions of expansion.

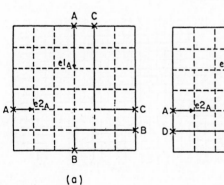 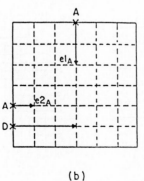 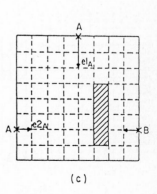

Fig. 6. Connection for net A is a non-conflict one in all the (a), (b) and (c) situations.

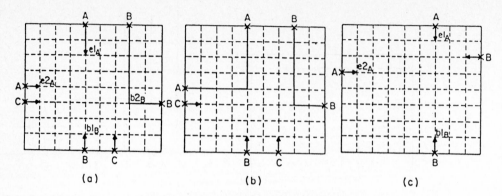

Fig. 7. Non-conflict and conflict connections.
(a) Only the connection for net A is non-conflict here
(b) and can be routed, nets B and C have a mutual conflict.
(c) Nets A and B have a mutual conflict.

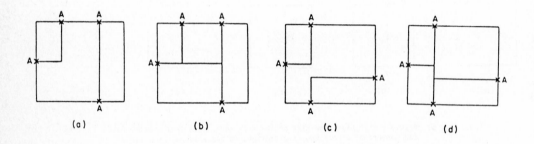

Fig. 8. Expansion from corners.
(a), (c) The situation before the expansion
(b), (d) The situation after expansion

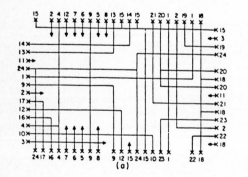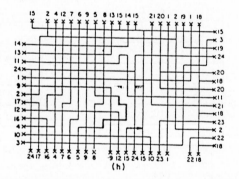

Fig. 9. Example routed by the computer program
(a) The situation after Step 7.
(h) Situations after routing consecutive nets selected in Step 9, routed in Step 10 and unique routes caused by these routes.

3.3. FOUR FUNCTIONAL VIEWS FOR CAD ALGORITHM VISUALIZATION

For effective algorithm visualization, user-controlled windows should be functionally related to the intricacies of the heuristic. We have identified four functional views or vistas the user needs to have during algorithm exploration:

(1). A "vista" for generating carefully chosen examples that illustrate the properties of the problem, not just arbitrary examples. This vista should give the user an understanding of which input representation is most appropriate for a given algorithm, how does it reflect on the algorithm. A LIBRARY OF BENCHMARKS and/or difficult examples for a particular VLSI algorithm should be generated based on key cost parameters, ability to look/compare at results of other solutions to the problem.

(2). To visualize the goodness of a heuristic, one needs a "computational vista" which can visualize the following: DATA STRUCTURE BEHAVIOUR, its evolution during execution; feedback on the interaction of input data with the data structures, (e.g., how many times the algorithm interacts with data structures representing input data); monitoring time versus space requirements, the use of memory for intermediate or temporary data, the upper bound estimates of space and time used, how much time is used for operations versus data structures.

Such a vista for algorithm comprehension, should depict the expert's explanation of strengths, weaknesses, computationally significant events of the algorithm. There should be facilities for recognizing what are the important cost parameters to watch in the heuristic's behavior, not just rules about the heuristic, but also suggestions of remedies at critical places.

(3). A vista for "HANDS-ON EXPERIMENTATION" on a wisely chosen instance of the algorithm which is synchronized with the other three vistas. This will allow the user to try out different ideas, see the result of a certain design choice or pattern he picked, test it for feasibility, look at unique patterns, gain an insight or suggestions for making better choices, try different heuristics on a given example. An "analysis - coach" can be built-in to this as well as a user-dialogue facility which allows the user to provide and receive information on issues (from the other 3 vistas), from the knowledge base, to exert parameter control, to be tested and monitored for cognition.

(4). A vista for sparking creativity to the design process: This is a set of tools which can AID THE HEURISTIC REASONING process by accessing related algorithms, thus gaining insight and being able by analogy to find better solutions; tools for checking available layout space, quantifying it (with a highlight facility), would be very useful in deciding how to reduce a problem into smaller cases of the problems and either apply variations of the same heuristic to the cases or COMBINE DIFFERENT HEURISTICS at different stages (phases) of the heuristic.

4. FOVISTA: DESIRABLE FEATURES IN VLSI ALGORITHM VISUALIZATION

This section presents the four components of the FOVISTA concept in the figures 11 (a-e) : Figure 11(a) shows the general architecture of FOVISTA: Component (1) creates an instance of the problem for, say, a specific class of VLSI problems, such as Channel Routing. This component will generate a list of relevant cost measures for channel routing (see Figure 11 (b)), such as n = number of terminals, d = density, etc. Component (2) is described in Figure 11(c). This component describes the algorithm chosen in component (1), gives analysis of performance and statistics and helps the user decide which algorithm to use. The user can (i) update the actual performance of each algorithm by running it on benchmarks, (ii) read the description of the algorithm expressed in high level language, and (iii) visualize data structures to be used by the algorithm.

Component (3) is a sketchpad facility for the designer (Figure 11(d)) and Component (4) gives the ability to combine various heuristics to solve cases of a given problem. Specific features of Component (4) for routing problems could be:
- "colors" to evaluate the goodness of a layout;
- mean case performance versus worst case performance;
- strategies to combine algorithms;
- strategies to visualize features (e.g., behavior with respect to given parameters).

Figure 11(e) gives a scenario of the interaction of the four components. Figure 12 explains how visualization is achieved with the FOVISTA model from the user's point of view and from the programmer's point of view. The user can choose to be given either a "tutorial" description of the problem or an effective input data (randomly generated over the set of feasible input or selected among difficult examples). In the former case, the user can choose to be given an example of problem instances, in the latter, a visualization of data structures.

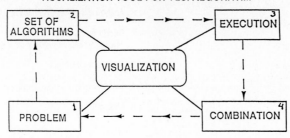

FOVISTA:
VISUALIZATION TOOL FOR VLSI ALGORITHM

TOOL BASED ON FOUR MAIN COMPONENTS

Figure 11 (a): Architecture of the FOVISTA Model

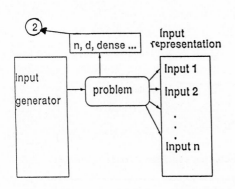

PROBLEM COMPONENT :

1.1 creates problem instance (input generator)

1.2 gives problem description to user

1.3 problem instance, analyzed w.r.t. given "measures" (i,e., density, flux, ... for CR)

1.4 visualizes data structures which represent the input

1.5 links to components 2 , library of algorithms

Figure 11 (b): Description of Component (1), the PROBLEM generator component

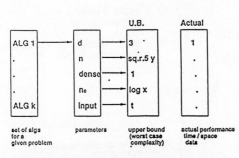

2.1 Description of the algorithms

2.2 Analysis of performance (w.r.t. given parameters)

2.3 Statistics of actual performances

2.4 Link to 1 . (choose another algorithm)

2.5 Link to 3 (perform execution)

2.6 User Chooses What to See (parameters)

COLLECTS A LIBRARY OF BENCHMARKS OR DIFFICULT EXAMPLES FOR A PARTICULAR VLSI PROBLEM (e.g., CHANNEL ROUTING) AND TESTS THE VISUALIZATION OF THEM TO SEE HOW EFFICIENT IT IS.

Figure 11 (c): Description of Component (2)
SET OF ALGORITHMS Component

③ EXECUTION COMPONENT

3.1 "Plain" execution of algorithm

3.2 Link to 2

3.3 Link to 4

④ COMBINATION COMPONENT

4.1 Analyze execution dynamically

4.2 Decide (w.r.t. to given parameters) whether to improve locally on a given result

4.3 Provide a new input

4.4 Link to 3

4.5 Link to 1

Figure 11(d): Description of FOVISTA Components 3 & 4

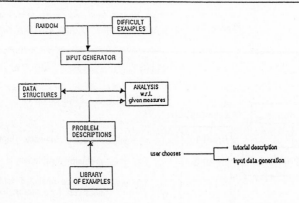

Figure 11(e): A scenario of interaction of the four FOVISTA components

VISUALIZATION   WINDOWS

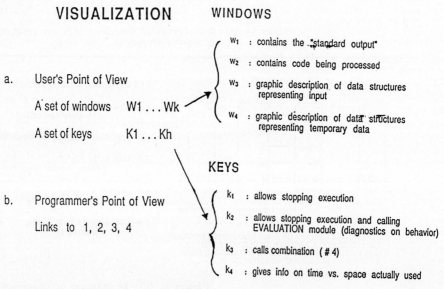

a. User's Point of View

A set of windows W1 ... Wk

A set of keys K1 ... Kh

W_1 : contains the "standard output"

W_2 : contains code being processed

W_3 : graphic description of data structures representing input

W_4 : graphic description of data structures representing temporary data

KEYS

b. Programmer's Point of View

Links to 1, 2, 3, 4

k_1 : allows stopping execution

k_2 : allows stopping execution and calling EVALUATION module (diagnostics on behavior)

k_3 : calls combination (# 4)

k_4 : gives info on time vs. space actually used

Figure 12: Visualization with FOVISTA (programmer's and user's point of view)

REFERENCES

[BK]   Bentley, J. L., and Kernighan, B. W., "A System for Algorithm Animation: Tutorial and User Manual.
        Tech. Rep. 132, Computer Science, AT&T Bell Laboratories, Murray Hill, N. J., Jan. 1987.
[B]   Brown, M. C., "Exploring Algorithms Using Balsa-II", in IEEE Computer, May 1988, pp. 14- 36.
[BS]   Brown, M., and R. Sedgewick, "Techniques for Algorithm Animation", IEEE Software, Vol. 2, No. 1,
        Jan. 1985, pp. 28-39.
[BCJK] Brown, G. P., R. T. Carling, C. F. Herot, D. A. Kramlich, and P. Souza, "Program Visualization:
        Graphical Support for Software development", IEEE Computer, Aug. 85., pp. 27-37.
[CPF]   Card, S.K., Pavel, M. and Farrell, J. E., (1985), "Window-Based Computer Dialogues", Human-
        Computer Interaction, Interact '84, Austin, Texas, North Holland Proceedings, pp. 239-243.
[CTHP] Christodoulakis, S. M. Theodoridou, F. Ho, M. Papa and A. Pathria, "Multimedia Document
        Presentation, Information Extraction, and Document Formation in MINOS: A Model and a System, in
        ACM Trans. on Office Information Systems, Vol. 4, No. 4, Oct. 1986, PP. 345-383.
[D]   Duisberg, R. A., "Visual Programming of Program Visualizations", Proc. Conference on Visual
        languages 1987, Linkoping, Sweden, Aug. 1987.
[F]   Fisher, G., "Student-Oriented features of an Interactive Programming Environment", in ACM (1987),
        pp. 532-537.
[Fr]   Frenkel, K. A., "The Art and Science of Visualizing Data", in Communications of the ACM, Feb. 1988,
        Vol. 31, Number 2, pp. 111-121.
[G]   Giannotti, E. I., "Algorithm Animator: A Tool for programming Learning", in ACM, pp. 308-314.
[GR]   Goldstein, I. and Rapert, S. (1977), "Artificial Intelligence, language and the Study of Knowledge",
        Cognitive Science 1, (1), 1-21.
[Gr]   Grafton, R., "Guest Editor's Introduction: Visual Programming", IEEE Computer, Vol. 18, No. 8, August
        1985.
[H]   Halbert, D. C., "Programming by Example", Ph. D. Thesis, CS Division, Dept. of EECS, UCB, 1984.
[HA]   Hammond, N. and Allinson, L., "Travels Around a Learning Support Environment: Rambling,
        Orienteering or Touring?", in ACM proc. of CHI'88, (1988), pp. 269-273.
[HHR]   Helttula, E., Hyrskykari, A., and Raiha, K., "The Magical ALADDIN Tour", in HICSS-22.
[J]   Jacob, R., "A State Transition Diagram Language for Visual programming", in IEEE Computer Aug. 85,
        pp. 51-60.
[K]   Kant, E., "Understanding and Automating Algorithm Design", in IEEE Trans. Software Eng., vol SE-11,
        No. 11, Nov. 85.
[LD]   London, R. L., and R. A. Duisberg, "Animating programs Using Smalltalk", in IEEE Computer, vol 18,
        No. 8, Aug. 1985, pp. 61-71.
[MMH]   Maurer, H., F. Makedon and F. Huber, "HyperCOSTOC" a ComprehensiveComputer-Based Teaching
        Support System", in J. for Microcomputer Applications, to appear.
[MMO]   Makedon, F., H. Maurer, and T. Ottmann., "Presentation Type CAI in Computer Science Education at
        University Level", J. of Microcomputer Applications 10 (1987), 283-295.
[MMR]   Makedon, F., H. Maurer and L. Reinsperger, "Active Annotation in HyperCOSTOC", IIG Technical
        Report, No. 256 (1988), Inst. of Informatics, Graz U. of Technology, Schiesstattgasse 4a, A-8010 Graz,
        Austria.
[MO]   Makedon, F and M. Ouksel, "The Anatomy of an Object-Oriented Visualization System for Learning
        Algorithm Design", Technical Report, CLEAR Center, The U. of Texas at Dallas, Richardson, Tx,
        75083-0688.
[M]   Marek-Sadowska, M., "Two Dimensional Router for Double Layer Layout", in 22nd Design Automation
        Conf. (1985), pp 117-123.
[MS]   Marchionini, G., and B. Sheiderman, "Finding Facts vs. Browsing Knowledge in Hypertext Systems",
        in IEEE Computer, Jan. 1988, pp. 70-80.
[ME]   Maxim, B. R., and B. S. Elenbogen, "Teaching Programming Algorithms Aided by Computer Graphics",
        in 1987 ACM, pp. 297-301.
[MV]   Meyrowitz, N. and A. Van Dam, "Interactive Editing Systems: Part II", in Computing Surveys, Vol. 14,
        No. 3, Sept. 1982, pp. 353-415.
[MSKW] Mitchell, T., Steinberg, L, Kedar-Cabelli, S., Kelly, V., Shulman, J, and Weinrich, T., "An Intelligent
        Aid for Circuit Redesign", in Proc. of the National Conference on Artificial Intelligence, Washington,
        D.C., Aug. 1983, pp. 273-278.
[My]   Myers, B.A., "Visual Programming, Programming by Example, and Program Visualization, A
        Taxonomy", in CHI'86 Proceedings, pp. 59-66.
[SHA]   Sleeman, D. H., Hendley, R, and Ace, J., "A System which analyzes Complex Explanations", in Intern.
        J. of Man-machine Studies, 11, pp. 125-144.
[SKW]   Smith, D. R., G. B. Kotik and S. J. Westfold, "Research on Knowledge-Based Software Environments at
        Kestrel Institute", IEEE Trans. on Software Engineering. vol SE-11, No. 11, Nov. 85, pp. 1278-1295.

[S]   Soukoup, J., "Circuit Layout", in Proc. of IEEE, vol. 69, pp. 1281-1304, 1981.

[SK]   Steier, D. M., and E. Kant, "The Roles of Execution and Analysis in Algorithm Design", IEEE Trans. Software Eng., Vol. SE-11, No. 11, Nov. 1985, pp. 1375- 1386.

[S]   Stone, D. C., "A Modular Approach to Program Visualization in Computer Science Instruction", in 1987 ACM Proc. of Human-Computer Interaction, pp. 516-522.

[Te]   Teitelman, W., "A Display Oriented Programmer's Assistant", in Int. J. Man-machine Studies (1979) 11, 157-187, Acad. Press Inc., pp. 157-187.

[YHMD] Yankelovich, N., Haan, B., Meyrowitz, N., Drucker, S., "Intermedia: The Concept and the Construction of a Seamless Information Environment", in IEEE Computer, Jan. 1988, pp. 81-96.

A Teachware Concept for Education in CAD

Luiz Ary Messina
Institute for Graphic-Interactive Systems
Department of Informatics
Technische Hochschule Darmstadt
D-6100 Darmstadt
Federal Republic of Germany

The main task is aimed at supporting the teacher and the student with hardware and software tools for a CAD training environment.

Teachware is the term designating the new technologies developed in the last decades (e.g. overhead projector, large screen projector, video, film, hardware and software) and the techniques applied for teaching purposes.

The reference model for the general concept is shown in fig.1. In the center there is the subject to be taught. Around it there is the knowledge supporting the subject, which comes from different sources (e.g. books, procedures, peoples' experience). This knowledge is shared among teachers and students; and this knowledge must be evaluated. The description of the school organization serves as a filter to the choice of a technological infrastructure. In order to support and establish a teachware environment for CAD the following guidelines are considered and are being implemented based on Autocad, IBM PS 2 systems and a pedagogical network.

1. Journaling guidelines

A journal file is broadly speaking a file containing the users' actions. In a CAD environment these actions are the solution paths for design/drawing tasks.

Journaling designates the storage and the use of an input sequence. In the relation teacher/student the teacher stores the solution of a task and the student may at all times use this solution to conduct the task.

How can then a journal file today help the teacher's tasks?

1) The teacher stores a stepwise solution of a drawing task in the journal file.
2) Stored solutions may serve as examples for classroom work, explanations and homework.
3) The stepwise characteristic of the solution facilitates the comprehension.
4) The student's solution may be visually compared with the teacher's solution.
5) The teacher may show right away the student's mistakes. This may occur graphically, by superposing both solutions, or through the analysis of both journal

files.
6) A task-oriented menu may be obtained from the journal file.

What additional functions should the journal file support in regards to the teacher facilities:
1) The teacher should be able to correct and complement the solution without having to do the whole task again.
2) The teacher should be able to specify steps and alternative paths for a solution.

How can a student benefit from the journal file?
1) Already stored exercises may be provided in floppies.
2) The solution commands are also stepwise shown.
3) Simple tasks do contain complete solutions, so that correpondence course may be supported.
4) As long as alternative solutions may exist, these may be shown to the student.
5) A comfortable recovering tool, in case of inoportune deletion.

What additional facilities should be provided to the students?
1) Explanation facilities
2) Solved tasks should provide an associative feedback, so the students themselves go fetch the solution.

Therefore, the following functions are being implemented to support the journaling : on, off, undo, change, explain, or, step.

2. Analysis and comparison of solutions

Two different approaches are distinguished here. "Passiv" designates the visual comparison of two solutions. The journal file from the teacher has the structure shown in fig.2, which describes the history of the design/draft process for the task. The solution of the student presents in this case a deviation from the muster.
"Active" designates an associative feedback.As it was stated at the journaling guidelines, the teacher has the tools to create the solution so as to minimize the complexity of the active approach, which is aimed at prototyping and simple tasks. It must be pointed out that geometric as well as system functional knowledge may be practiced. Solving a task, the student may ask for help. The system answers, giving back an association, which should bring the student to conduct the search for the solution.
Three cases may be distinguished:
1) The student waits too long to give an input: The system may help the student finding the next step. This does not mean the next step will be given, but hints (associative

feedbacks) could help in deriving a next correct action.

An example in the field of architecture is: to draw the walls of a room on a base plan. Two commands may be used "line" and "polyline". Both are correct, but "polyline" may contain a thickness argument, which draws directly the wall, without having to draw four lines to complete one wall. So, a possible associative word is "line thickness".An associative word for the whole task in fig.2 is "symetry".

2) In case a false step is made by the student or a step is forgotten, the program helps the student to find the correct step or to introduce the forgotten one.

3) In case a better solution exists, this should be shown and explained to the student.

The comparison is dedicated to tasks with a fixed solution. There exists also tasks, where the student should be actually motivated to create its own solution. In this case, the measures for analysis may only be constrained on the application matter.

3. Task-oriented menus

CAD systems are not adequate for teaching purposes. The functions are organized for an experienced designer/drafter. The main purpose is to give the user the whole functionality and completeness needed at a certain design level. This does not correspond to the demands of a beginner, whose objective is to learn each function of the system in connection with the next probable ones to solve a simple application appropriate task.

The domain of possible functions should therefore be reduced in order to facilitate and speed up the learning process. The big amount of functions do complicate rather than impress the user.

Following this concept, the CAD systems must be restructured for teaching purposes. Autocad is one of the few systems which support this facility. Menus may easily be restructured and adapted to local demands.

Broadly speaking, this learning process starts with very simple menus of points, lines and goes gradually through arcs, circles, tangent to e.g. dimension and symbol generation.

Since the tasks have already been formulated for the CAD course and the journaling functions have been used to create the journal files corresponding to the tasks to be exercised by the students, these files contain in fact the CAD functions (commands) necessary per task. Another program, also written in Auto-Lisp as the one for the creation of the journaling functions, is being implemented to generate automatically the task-oriented menus. So that, when the journal file is done, the correspondent menu for the task is also ready.

4. The support of CA-Libraries

Libraries are a "common place" for students and researchers. One of the most important aspects of a research/training is to come to a number of issues, relevant to the concept being studied/considered at that time. This is properly "the search for information", given a central idea. This work is tiresome and discouraging. Therefore, the use of CA-Libraries is a major factor to support and guide the development.

Drawing departments have still the necessity of organizing drawings in numbering systems, so that they can be easier found. Such systems contain none or little knowledge of the drawing content. In fact, only the direct personnel knows how to access a specific drawing. This difficults enormously the personnel training.

A classification of drawing parts and field of application is conceptually not difficult to realize. It depends on the available personnel and adequate qualification. An example of such a classification for the field of architecture and house construction could be the division of necessary subfields of architecture, classes of object per subfield and objects per class. This is to say e.g.: graphical objects such as oven, dish-washer, refrigerator ... belong to the class kitchen, which may belong to the subfields house, restaurant etc. Restaurant its turn could belong to, say shopping center, airport and so on.

What one could aim at, considering the state of the art, is the realization of such a classification, for showing to the students the possibility of organizing a symbol or part library.

5. The classroom subject

The classroom subject here is CAD. A course on CAD may have very different approaches, which depends basically and heavily on the teacher's background. This dependence presents an important advantage if the students' and the teacher's main field of interest coincide. Otherwise, it brings very little information. CAD classes are held today mainly for draftspeople and students from departments like mechanical, civil, electronic, electrical engineering, architecture and mathematics. As one can see, the approach given to each field must be different, although a basic course could be general.

The description of the subject of a CAD introductory course, which could be held independently from the field, is:

1) CAD-Hardware
   CPU
   Mass storage

    Terminals
    Keyboard
    Graphic tablet
    Mouse
    Plotter
    Printer, etc.
2) CAD-Software
    Geometric kernel
    DBMS
    Dialogue interfaces
    Libraries
    Notations 2D, 2 1/2 D, 3D
    CAD/CAM concepts
    Market Analysis
3) CAD fundamentals
    Mathematical fundamentals
    Geometry generation
    Attributes
    Geometric modification
    Control/help functions
    Drawing generation
    Areas of application
4) Introduction to Autocad
5) Practical demonstrations
6) Hands-on exercises

6. Presentation facilities

The most used presentation material today is still foils, followed by slides. The introduction of video, large screen projector and terminal based presentation has begonnen and will turn out to be an usual presentation media.

According to the classroom subject above, items 1, 2 and 3 are provided to the students in a sequence of concepts simulated visually. This facility is provided at the moment by using the program Show Partner. The students take home a floppy with the simulated concepts and may also take a demo version of Autocad.

Three questions are very important and should be analysed:

1) What sort of media should be used for a specific subject?
2) How can this subject be made attractive for learning purposes?
3) How can these media improve the learning process?

From a systems' organization point of view two factors influence directly the acceptance (from both teachers and students) of such teaching media: the allowed interactivity and the context dependent information. There is also no doubt that the systems used to develop teaching material are still imature although some interesting combinations may already be executed as here is the case. The advantage in the CAD case is the fact that for such a matter already systems exist.

Qualified teaching personell is seldom. Books are then the support material for "holding the course sequence" and for "establishing a general understanding" of the course subject. In a similar way, electronic media is introduced, adding new features to the teach/learn process. Some advantages are:

1) Enhancement of the visual process, giving emphasis to the visual memory
2) Direct use of existing hardware/software, training the student on these new work tools
3) Improvement of interaction and self learning facilities
4) Search through keywords
5) Stored material: text, images, graphics
6) Structures: logic, set theory, class, list, inheritance
7) Interactive explanation
8) Save place and is cheaper!!

7. Classroom types

Regarding a classroom environment, three alternatives classify the teaching purpose:
a) Self learning
b) Guided classroom work
c) Knowledge transfer

"Self learning" is education and/or training aimed at single individuals. The student himself determines the times and speed of learning. This learning process could happen at home and/or at school.

The planned next level of "guided classroom work" is the mapping of self learning onto a small group or team. A teacher is in charge of, and all participants have access to computing equipment. To allow for efficient teaching, all the training systems are networked with the teachers machine. Basically two ways of information exchange are provided:
a) The students can request additional help from the teacher.
b) The teacher can monitor and improve the students progress.

This two-way electronic communication between teacher and students supports work in small groups. In addition, the training can be complemented e.g. with video presentation and slide projections.

"Knowledge transfer" is done by a lecturer to a potentially large auditorium. Individual feedback with students is no longer possible. The information/knowledge to be transfered is distributed via the video signal network to

all participants in the training. This way of teaching is
suitable for teaching fundamentals and structures.

8. Network

Specially the guided classroom work demands a network. The
available configuration for teaching CAD for draftspeople
and students of architecture, civil and mechanic engineering
is shown in fig.3. It shows some possibilities of such a
network for training purposes. Additionally it offers also
access to a printer/plotter, and file transfer, which are
important features for the organization of the classroom
works. The new possibility of interaction given to the
relation teacher/student must be practiced and studied in
order to be used efficiently.

9. Summary

The evolution of a CAD class teachware-based is therefore: 1) Transfer of concepts through electronic media
followed by explanations from the teacher, 2) Individual
work on the concepts, 3) Exercise the concepts through the
task-oriented menus based on the journal file, 4) Repeat
steps 1,2 and 3 for the necessary concepts.
The use of a journaling function for solving tasks and
supporting the design/draft work through dedicated menus
provides new facilities for training teachers and students.
Some advantages and guidelines have been pointed out in
order to assist the relation teacher/student and to improve
the learn process. The design/draft history and its analysis
gives also support to the development of new features in a
CAD system.
A learning process supported by electronic media, by
simulation of concepts, structures, processes and by
interactive work, approaches the qualified demands of the
market.
Courses have already been held under this model and their
success provides a means for continuing the research and the
implementation work.

10. References

COMETT Vertragsunterlagen 87/2/B1-D/00695, 25.01.88, ZGDV

Verlängerungsantrag zum COMETT-Vorhaben 87/2/695, 31.03.88,
ZGDV

Havemann D., Funk J., Erstellung eines Journalfiles
innerhalb von Autocad, Dokumentation März 1989

Biefang K., Optimierung von CAD-Schulung durch dedizierte

Benutzermenüs und Journaling-Unterstützung, Diplomarbeit Juni 1989

11. Aknowledgment

Most of the concepts developed in this paper are due to the intensive discussions originated at the COMETT (Community Action Programme for Education and Training for Technology, from the Commission of the European Communities) meetings at the ZGDV (Zentrum für Graphische Datenverarbeitung) in Darmstadt. Thanks to all the colleagues which participate in the meetings and support the next developments. In particular: Annelore Buhmann, Georg Köberle and Marion Günther.

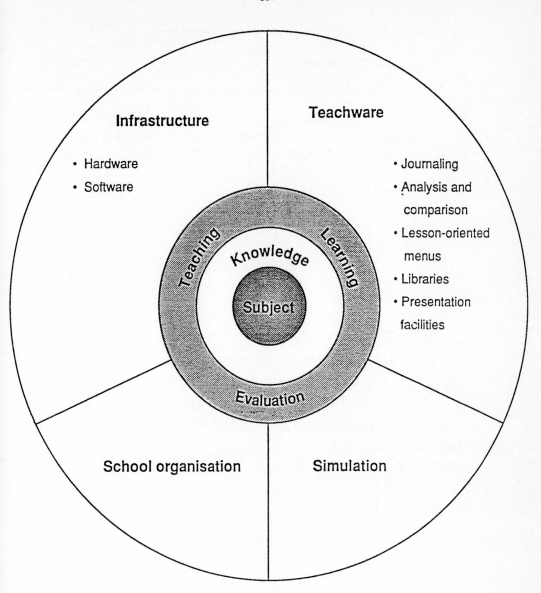

Fig.1 : Approach model for a teachware concept

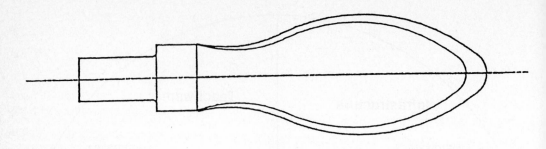

linetype dashdot
line 2,3 11.5,3
linetype solid
pline 3,3 3,2.5 4.5,2.5 4.5,2.2 5.3,2.2
arc direction 6.2,2.5 7,2.2 10,2.5 10.7,3
line tools osnap endpoint 4.5,2.5 4.5,3
line 5.3,2.2 5.3,3
mirror 3,2.5 4.5,2.7 5.3,2.6 2,3 11.5,3

Fig.2 : Teacher's design task history (outermost) and

student's solution (innermost)

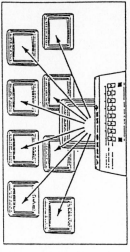

All users work independent.

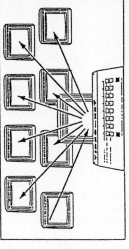

Teacher observes the student.

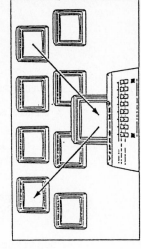

A student receives the screen of the teacher.

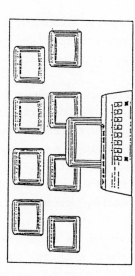

All students receive the screen of the teacher.

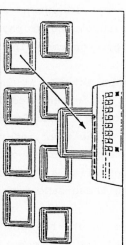

Teacher shows the screen of a student to all students.

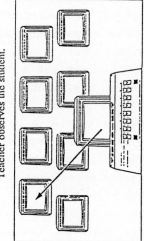

Teacher shows the screen of one student to another student.

Fig.3 : The pedagogical network

THE PATHOPHYSIOLOGY TUTOR:

A FIRST STEP TOWARDS A SMART TUTOR

Joel A. Michael[*]
Mohammed M. Haque[+]
Allen A. Rovick[*]
Martha Evens[#]

[*]Department of Physiology
Rush Medical College
Chicago, IL 60612

[+]Department of Information Science
Northeastern Illinois University
Chicago, IL 60625

[#]Department of Computer Science
Illinois Institute of Technology
Chicago, IL 60616

ABSTRACT

The Pathophysiology Tutor (PPT) is intended to assist students to integrate their knowledge of cardiovascular physiology and to learn to apply it to solve pathophysiology problems using a hypothetico-deductive reasoning process.

While PPT is not yet a "smart tutor", it incorporates a number of features of such programs. It is implemented in Turbo-PROLOG using a rule-based formalism. Tutoring rules are distinct from the cardiovascular knowledge base. The user interface employs menus and simple keystroke entries and output text is obtained from stored text files. The tutoring rules incorporate a primitive student model based on eight years experience using these same pathophysiology problems in small group tutorials.

The lack of natural language inputs has not proven to be a serious limitation, although the inability of generate text outputs does significantly limit the extent to which individualized tutoring can be provided. Nevertheless, the PPT is a valuable first step towards the development of a "smart tutor".

INTRODUCTION

The Pathophysiology Tutor (PPT) has been developed as a part of an on-going collaboration between the Department of Computer Science at

IIT and the Department of Physiology at Rush. The long-term goal of this effort is the creation of an intelligent, natural language based, computer tutoring system or ITS [8, 9]. Such a system would be used to assist students in integrating facts and concepts into useful, large-scale mental models and in developing problem solving skills, two of the most difficult steps in mastering physiology.

An intelligent tutor, whether a human teacher or a computer, requires: (1) domain expertise - knowledge which allows the tutor to solve problems or answer questions in the field and to explain those answers; (2) tutoring expertise - knowledge about how to correct student errors and guide student learning in the domain (including the ability to model the student's knowledge and skills, and the ability to use a variety of strategies and tactics to explore and improve student knowledge and skills); and (3) the ability to generate a context specific dialogue that will most effectively assist the particular student being tutored.

The Pathophysiology Tutor is not yet a "smart tutor" - it has no natural language capability, can not model the student, and has only limited domain problem solving ability. Nevertheless, it is a sophisticated teaching resource in its present form. This has been achieved by applying some of the ideas and concepts that have arisen out of ITS research, without using "expensive" AI software or hardware tools. Furthermore, PPT is a system with which we can experimentally attack new questions about computer tutoring, questions whose answers will assist further development efforts towards truly intelligent systems.

We will describe the Pathophysiology Tutor, focusing on those features which we think have general applicability to the writing of educationally useful teaching programs.

DESIGN CRITERIA FOR A "SEMI-SMART" COMPUTER TUTOR

In designing the Pathophysiology Tutor we were guided by several fundamental design decisions and resource limitations.

(1) We wanted to utilize a rule-based formalism that clearly separates tutoring rules from domain knowledge.

(2) The tutoring rules are based on personal experience (JAM and AAR) tutoring students solving the same pathophysiology problems in small group tutorials at Rush Medical College.

(3) In the absence of robust language understanding capabilities, we were limited to using an interface between student and system that would accept simple inputs from menus, multiple-choice items, and other simple key-stroke entries.

(4) Lacking the ability to generate text on-line, we were limited to

using stored text as outputs to the student.

(5) We wanted to explicitly teach a particular problem solving method, an algorithm to be used by the students in solving a wide range of problems in physiology.

(6) Nevertheless, we wanted to give the student the maximum opportunity to determine the direction of his or her interaction with the program.

After describing the nature of the problems to be solved and the actual implementation of PPT, we will discuss the extent to which we succeeded in incorporating these goals into our program. We will also consider whether these goals and approaches to implementation have general applicability to other programs.

PATHOPHYSIOLOGY PROBLEMS AND THE HYPOTHETICO-DEDUCTIVE METHOD

A pathophysiology problem of the kind we intend the PPT to deal with begins with the presentation of a brief description of a patient as she or he might present in a doctor's office. Following is an example of such a patient description [5]:

> Mr. A.B., a 56 year old patient, was admitted to PSL
> Hospital complaining that he recently began to tire
> upon exertion (a round of golf) and that he had
> occasional heart palpitations. He did not appear to
> be in acute distress. Physical examination revealed a
> moderate systolic murmur.

After being presented with the patient description, the student is asked to (1) select the significant findings (SF step) or symptoms in the patient description, (2) generate a hypothesis (HG step) about the possible cause of the patient's problem, (3) justify (JU step) the selected hypothesis by identifying one of the selected findings that would specifically follow from it, and (4) validate (VA step) the hypothesis by means of data such as laboratory results that could be obtained from the patient. In this way, the student reaches a solution that defines the pathology causing the entire constellation of findings present in the patient description. Finally, (5) the student is asked to explain (EX step) the sequence of cause-and-effect relationships that give rise to each finding, beginning with his/her proposed causative pathology.

The educational objectives of this exercise are to assist the student in organizing his or her "facts" about the cardiovascular system into usable mental models or schemas, and in developing problem solving skills [4]. This approach to solving problems is an example of the hypothetico-deductive method [1]; and it is applicable to physiology in general and to a wide array of problems from many different domains. We are <u>not</u> trying to teach medical diagnosis.

THE PATHOPHYSIOLOGY TUTOR (PPT)

PPT is written in Turbo PROLOG to run on an IBM XT (640 K RAM) with EGA graphics; this will make possible more widespread use of PPT than would be the case if PPT ran only on a more expensive AI workstation. A "semi-smart" editor for assembling and editing tutoring rules was developed in the course of this project and has been increasingly used in the development of PPT [2, 3].

PPT presently incorporates three different cardiovascular pathophysiology problems. The student first proceeds through a brief introduction that provides instructions about the operation of the program, and then selects a problem from the Index.

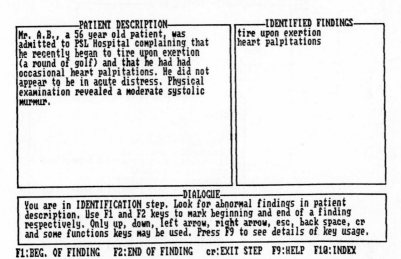

Figure 1: Screen print from the Select Findings step

The student is taken through the five step problem solving process just described. At each step, student input is either from menus ("enter desired letter or number" or "move the cursor to your choice and press return") or via operations carried out with simple key strokes ("use the F1 key to signal the beginning of your finding, use the cursor keys to move to the end, and signal with F2 key"). All output text is written to the screen from stored text files. The problems themselves, and all information needed to specify a solution, are also stored as files.

The interaction between the student and PPT is determined by the tutoring rules. However, PPT is a mixed initiative system, and at several junctures the student may elect which of the available steps to turn to next, thus individualizing the progress made towards a solution of the problem. Evaluation of student inputs is carried out by accessing the stored solution and a limited cardiovascular knowledge base that has been provided (used in the EXplain step).

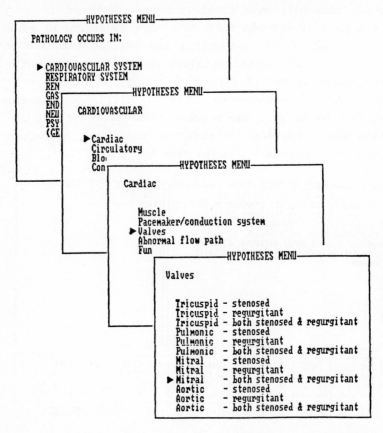

Figure 2: The nested menus used in the Hypothesis Generation step

We can illustrate how the PPT functions by going through a problem one step at a time with screen prints from each of the steps.

The student selects a problem from the Index, and is directed to the first step, identifying the significant patient findings in the patient description (Figure 1). Two universal features of the user interface can be seen here; the last line of the screen always contains a list of the active function keys and their action, and immediately above this there is a window in which instructions and comments from the program are displayed (the "dialogue" window). The procedure for identifying findings is described in the "dialogue" window of Figure 1; the identified findings are high-lighted in the "patient description" window (illustrated here by underlining) and transferred to the "selected findings" window. When the student confirms that this step is completed, PPT carries out some editing of the selected findings to put them in standard form and then proceeds to the next step.

The student is now asked to select an hypothesis from a nested menu (Figure 2). The current version of PPT forces the student to pursue cardiovascular hypotheses, although latter versions will allow selection of other, erroneous pathways and will lead the student to reject them in the next step. The hypothesis selected is displayed in the "selected hypothesis" window (Figure 3); PPT forces the selection process to be carried through to a terminal point along any pathway selected. The "selected findings" window continues to be displayed to remind the student of the data being used to select an hypothesis.

In the next step the student must justify the selected hypothesis by identifying one of the selected findings as specifically arising from the hypothesized pathophysiology. The solution file contains the links between findings and hypotheses that will be accepted. If the student is in error about the finding he uses to justify his hypothesis (Figure 4) he then has two choices available. He may continue in the JU step and select another finding to justify his hypothesis, or he may return to the preceding step (HG) and select a new hypothesis (these choices are visible in the middle window).

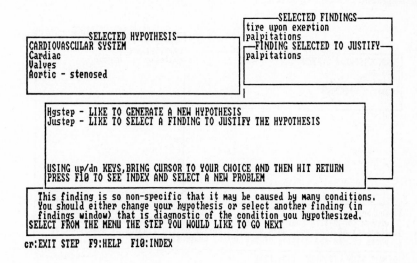

Figure 3: Screen print from the Hypothesis Generation step

A justified hypothesis may or may not be a correct hypothesis. Validation of the hypothesis is, therefore, the next step (the rules for which are still not complete). This requires the student to request additional data, generally obtained from laboratory studies of the patient, evaluate whether it is normal, and then determine whether this data validates the hypothesis. To carry out this process the student will be presented with nested menu from which he can request that information be retrieved from a data base containing a complete description of the patient's lab work-up. Decisions about the appropriateness of the data requested, the correctness of evaluations of the normality of that data, and whether the data is thought to validate the hypothesis must all be made by PPT using the tutoring rules and the stored solution.

The final step in the problem solving process (also under development) requires that the student begin with the hypothesized pathology and explain _all_ of the patient's findings (whether or not they were identified by the student), including the laboratory data that is available for validating the hypothesis. In the domain of cardiovascular physiology, such an explanation can consist of a representation of the cause-and-effect relationships that link the hypothetical pathophysiology to the findings. The student will begin with the hypothesis placed on the screen and a menu available from which to chose the finding and intermediate steps to be explained. The cursor keys will then be used to move the selected items on the screen. Other keys will permit the student

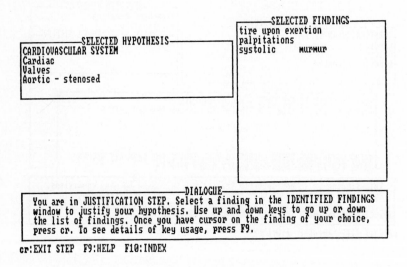

Figure 4: Screen print from the Justify step

to indicate the relationship (A causes B to increase or decrease) between the items being manipulated. The student's ability to generate a graphic representation of the cause-and-effect relationships involved, a kind of "concept map," is the final test of the student's ability to integrate the individual concepts into a useful mental model or schema of the functions of the system.

DISCUSSION

We feel that we have been moderately successful in realizing the design goals that were described above.

PPT is written in a rule-based manner that separates the tutoring rules from the data and text that are also used by the program. This provision, and the availability of an editor [2,3] has made it possible for non-PROLOG programmers, the teaching experts (JAM and AAR), to interact with the PPT program in an effective way, changing tutoring rules as needed to repair bugs or altering the way in which PPT interacts with the student in order to test hypotheses about teaching.

Our user interface is a mixed success. On the one hand, the use of menus etc. provides us with a mode of input that has proven more useful and robust than we had anticipated. It constrains the student only minimally, since the content and complexity of the domain (cardiovascular physiology) is so great that menus provide very little prompting of student responses. At the same time, these simple to implement inputs are rich in information about the student knowledge and allow us to model the cognitive state of the student [6].

However, the use of stored text files for all of our output continues to be a serious limitation. It is very difficult to produce a context-dependent interaction [10] with such pre-determined text. This is a particular problem in a domain that is as complex and language dependent as cardiovascular physiology. We think we have also succeeded in combining the explicit teaching of a particular problem solving approach with the maximum student flexibility in directing the tutorial interaction. As students have experience with PPT we anticipate being able to write tutoring rules that allow a still greater number of options to the students without having to abandon our intention to teach a particular process in an explicit manner.

Finally, what can be said about the general applicability of the approach to computer-based education that is illustrated by PPT? It is clear that there are important advantages to a programming style that separates tutoring rules from data etc. While PROLOG is ideally suited for this mode of programming, it would be possible to utilize other programming languages in a similar way, languages likely to be more familiar to educators writing teaching programs. It is also clear that a simple input interface can provide considerable information with which to assess the state of the students' thinking. While single choice answers (A, B, C, D or E) are limiting, the use of nested menus, student high-lighting of text, on-line graphical assembly of concept maps, or the use of a predictions table [Rovick and Michael, 1986; Michael et al, 1988] allow complex decision-making by even a "semi-smart" tutor. Finally, there is evidence that allowing the student the perception of directing the sequence of interactions with the program has a positive effect. That this can be accomplished while nevertheless completing a teacher-centered agenda requires careful program design (tutoring rules), but not necessarily the application of sophisticated AI tools.

As the collaborative effort between Rush and IIT continues, we are increasingly focussing our efforts on developing the language capabilities required by a smart tutor, developing both the capability to understand student input (as ill-formed, ungrammatical, and incorrect as it may be) and to generate content-dependent text. We have also begun to examine the problem of student modeling.

REFERENCES

Elstein, A.S., Shulman, L.S., and Sprafka, S.A. (1978). Medical problem solving: an analysis of clinical reasoning. Harvard University Press, Cambridge, MA.

Haque, M. M. (1988). Tutoring rule authoring system for intelligent computer-aided instruction: hypothetico-deductive problem solving in physiology. PhD dissertation, Department of Computer Science, Illinois Institute of Technology, Chicago, Illinois.

Haque, M. M., Rovick, A. A., Michael, J. A. and Evens, M. (1989). Tutoring rule authoring system (TRAS). Submitted to ICCAL, Dallas, TX, May 9-11.

Michael, J.A. and Rovick, A.A. (1983a). CV pathophysiology problems in small group tutorials. Physiologist, 26(4), 225-227.

Michael, J.A. and Rovick, A.A. (1983b). Cardiovascular physiology syllabus. Rush Medical College, Chicago, Illinois.

Michael, J. A., Rovick, A. A., Evens, M., Kim, N., and Haque, M. M. (1988). From CAI to ICAI: two examples along the way. Proceeding of the 30th International Congress of the Association for the Development of Computer-Based Instructional Systems, Philadelphia, PA, November 7-10. pp. 268-273.

Rovick, A. A. and Michael, J. A. (1986). CIRCSIM: an IBM PC computer teaching exercise on blood pressure regulation. XXX Congress of the International Union of Physiological Sciences, Vancouver, Canada.

Sleeman, D. and Brown, J. S. (editors). (1982). Intelligent tutoring systems. Academic Press, London.

Wenger, E. (1987). Artificial intelligence and tutoring systems. Morgan Kaufmann Publishers Inc., Los Altos, CA.

Woolf, B. (1984). <u>Context dependent planning in a machine tutor</u>. Ph.D. Dissertation, Dept. of Computer and Information Science, University of Massachusetts, Amherst, MA.

REQUIREMENTS AND CONCEPTS FOR NETWORKED MULTIMEDIA COURSEWARE ENGINEERING

M. Mühlhäuser *

University of Karlsruhe, Institute for Telematics

Zirkel 2, D-7500 Karlsruhe, W. Germany

Abstract

The Digital Equipment Corporation CEC Karlsruhe and the University of Karlsruhe - along with other associated institutes - are cooperating in the field of computer-assisted learning (CAL). The joint project, codenamed NESTOR (NEtworked Stations for TutORing), is intended to create a suite of integrated software aids giving high-level intelligent support for the planning, development, and execution of courseware in an environment of networked multimedia workstation/server topologies. The NESTOR kernel technical team is currently growing to ten people permanent staff plus a large number of students and temporary aids.

We introduce the notion of (networked multimedia) *courseware engineering* in order to indicate that we intend to support continuous support throughout the 'lifecycle' of courseware, a high level of integration of tools and a common methodological framework.

In the remainder of this paper, we present fundamental NESTOR requirements (chapter 1), feasability considerations (chapter 2) and the coarse NESTOR architecture (chapter 3).

1 NESTOR Required Properties

A look at recent CAL-related projects ([ATHTP,FRI88,KSK88,SHI86,STA86]) and at comparisons and evaluations ([ADF86,OSG87,OTT86,PIC87]) shows that 'classical' Personal Computers are largely insufficient as a CAL means. Intolerable response times, low resolution graphics with too little information content, expensive 'learning-to-learn' phases, and restrictive user guidance are among the drawbacks inherent in this technology.

The 'workstation' generation which is well under way should be able to overcome these limitations. Among the requirements for an appropriate on-desk CAL-qualified computer for the NESTOR project are (cf. [LSC87]:

- high resolution graphics with virtually no noticeable drawing delay for 2-D images and multifont documents,
- windowing and direct manipulation interface,
- multitasking, virtual memory operating system,

---

*presenting joint work of K. Coyle, B. Neidecker, F. Spanachi, P. Tallett, and I. Varsek of the Digital CEC Karlsruhe, W. Germany, and M. Duerr, T. Rüdebusch, and the author of the University of Karlsruhe

- 'several M' in processing speed (MIPS) and main memory (Mbyte),
- fast local disk and high-bandwidth highly integrated network access.

1.1 Multimedia Based

Digitized and synthesized audio [ADS86], electronic documents with multifont text and graphics, still pictures [RAS87] and computer animations, and especially full motion video [PAR88] do not present just 'nice to have' media in a CAL environment. As CAL should be able to address non-computerscientists and as it should allow fast perception of complicated subjects, the amelioration of cognitive processes through the use of the most efficient media becomes a central requirement.

Our studies, however, showed that many multimedia courses and authoring systems used today [STA86, ICC87, AMH88, APP87, COA87] are very limited in the way computerbased and media-based course parts are integrated. Only recently - e.g., in the ATHENA multimedia workstation experiments [ATHPR,LAM88] - we found attractive integration of media: frame-sequences are selected according to the user's decisions in the course, and text is well synchronized with the information displayed via video. However, even better combinations of computer-generated I/O and video information has to be achieved: input 'hot spots', highlighting and other overlayed graphics should be coupled with 'real-image' video, and the integral handling and synchronization of multimedia information fragments should be supported by dedicated sophisticated services. The lack of the latter at present is one of the main reasons for the tremendous and unacceptable effort necessary to author a multimedia course. Multimedia data management is as well not clearly separated from the applications and intermixed with other data management functions.

In order to provide sufficient multimedia authoring support we need to find new ways of combining multimedia storage / management / editing [WLK87,LWH87,MEI88] and hypertext / hypermedia features [AMH88,NEL88,YAN88,AAH88,CAC88,CON87,LIN87] with courseware engineering.

1.2 Distributed

Distribution plays a central role in virtually every field of modern CAL technique. One may identify three different categories of distribution support:

- ACCESS: As in the forseeable future we don't expect to have sufficient on-desk power and peripheral capabilities for each and every need, *server access* will continue to be a major driving force for distribution: among the required services to be accessed are

  - compute power, e.g. for manipulating complex graphics,

  - special peripherals, e.g. for high-quality media production, and

  - storage capacity, especially for the 'storage crunching' multimedia information.

In addition, remote *information access* has to be supported not only in the form of radial access to dedicated storage servers (see above), but also in terms of a irregular mutual information access in a meshed topology, where information is produced at many different places and stored where it is produced.

- DISSEMINATION: networks of author's and student's workstations - either in a LAN type topology like on campuses, or using WANs as in distance learning situations [HMS87,JSO87] - should no longer follow the 'down-line load' or 'broadcast' metaphor. Efficient 'backlinks' for the students to pose - and communicate among one another - questions, remarks and additions are required. Tutors should be able to interact closely with a student on an on-demand basis, still using the computer as a vehicle. Coupled with the requirement of multimedia capabilities, this represents very hard demands for the communication facilities (cf. chapter 2).

- COLLABORATION: the collaboration metaphor is highly important primarily from a social standpoint, but in its consequence also in an economical sense: the isolation imposed by modern education will become even more drastical if we do not require courseware to become much more group oriented [JOJ87]: elements of collaborative work [GIB88] such as brainstorming, subgrouping, and parallel work, should be reflected in the capabilities offered by a courseware engineering toolset like NESTOR.

1.3 Didactic

Common authoring systems and languages offer many constructs and features suited for building courseware: notions and setups for information frames, dialogue forms, evaluation aids and so on. However, they typically do not endorse didactical aspects. Many systems rely on the experience and education of the instructional designer for applying instructional strategies, methods, and rules [BPB87,GAG87]; the didactical quality of courseware relies totally on the author's capabilities; we believe that for a widely used system, computer-assistance for didactial, cognitive and instructional concepts is a major prerequisite. As there is no common terminology in this field, the more detailed prerequisites below can be considered as our glossary for the terms used, too.

- Appearance: Activities such as screen design, storyboard editing, or planning of media use relate to what we call 'appearance' [HEI84]. During these activities, part of the functionality of the system should be devoted to cognitive aspects, concerning e.g. the use of colour, scaling and ordering of graphics layouts, appropriate media mix, and so on.

- Goals, Strategies: Overall didactical goals and instructional strategies should be used to plan the sceletal structure of a course. Instructional strategies can be related to terms as different as 'model-building' [CTJ88], 'play' [HOR88], or 'tutorial'. Examples for goals are 'high retention rate' or 'management level understanding of topic', but also reasoning about the information space the course covers, and the contents to be taught. NESTOR will provide a more classified and systematic approach to this field.

- Instructional Methods: experts follow quite a large number of rules and methods both when authoring a single piece of courseware and in the process of composing such pieces: rules like reasonable percentages of redundancy, mix of pure presentation and interactive teaching, different methods for teaching principles, and many many others. Computer-assisting the use of methods and partly automating the endorsement of rules is another goal for NESTOR.

Goals and strategy selection have to be coped with in early phases of courseware engineering. The enforcement of a strategy and the application of rules and methods pertain mostly to the development phase. NESTOR intends to support a switch to another strategy even at or after development by decoupling the content taught from the didactical concepts applied.

1.4   Adaptive

We use the term 'adaptive' to avoid the overloaded notion of 'intelligent'. What we require NESTOR to be in this sense, however, will require the use and extension of concepts commonly referred to as 'user modelling' and 'intelligent / knowledge based tutoring' [SEL84, MAL88, BCS86, CLA87]. As we saw in requirement 'didactic' already, many a required feature is related to expert knowledge, coming mostly from educators, instructional designers and cognitive psychologists. As NESTOR is to be designed in a way to allow continuous knowledge acquisition and adjustment even past its implementation, expert system technology has to be partly used in order to provide the necessary flexibility.

Around course execution, i.e. learning, we require the system to 'learn about the learner'. This knowledge acquisition comprises information about

- **background knowledge**: Reasoning about the learner's background knowledge is possible by analyzing the way s/he uses a course and by tracking and analyzing the relevant information acquired along a series of courses a student took in the past; this information can be used to adapt the course execution accordingly and to contrast it to the predicted background knowledge as assessed in the course planning phase.

- **user preferences**: This relates especially to the way s/he 'likes' the information to be presented (related to 'appearance', see above).

- **learning history**: The history knowledge is used together with the background knowledge information, e.g., in order to decide whether or not a term has to be explained (especially important in combination with the requirement 'modular', see below).

- **problem context**: This relates, e.g., to the depth in which the student is interested in a subject matter. In the case of on-demand learning, ways have to be seeked for teaching in the context of the problem a user is confronted with in his current 'real world situation'; in the special case of teaching computer applications, the application may even be enabled to interact with the courseware, discribing the student's 'real world situation', switching over to the courseware, and getting back the 'solution' which a course unit worked out together with the student.

1.5   Comprehensive

Comprehensiveness in this sense means that the author and student should find their 'toolbox' to contain all the support they may need in the process of authoring a subject or learning about it. It also means that these tools have to be well integrated across all layers (see requirement 'uniform' below). Care is to be taken in the way different courseware lifecycle phases (e.g., planning, development, learning) are separated. Support for these phases should be designed such that a learning environment can be configured with a flexible level of integration of them, e.g.,

- with no to little 'coauthoring' (cf. 1.4) allowed to be fed back into the original course, or
- with a seamless integration of authoring and learning aspects in an environment targetted towards a 'group coordinated knowledge acquisition' metaphor.

1.6   Portable

Portablity is required in two ways in the NESTOR project:

- **Base-independend**: NESTOR tools, as well as the courses developed with it, should be easily portable to another hardware/software/peripherals base, they should even survive a generation change in underlying technology as drastical as the one we currently encounter in the change from the PC generation to the workstation generation. The level of achievability and some architectural concepts to achieve this goal will be discussed in sections three and four.

- **Distributable**: Easy distribution of courses from the authoring site to the learning site should be possible even if authoring stations and learnstations are different in hardware and capabilities. This requires a well-defined and well-documented way of 'describing' a course to be distributed. Based on such an interface, different vendors may even set up very different learning environments on their machine base, while the course may still stay the same. This requirement is by far not trivial in the context of other NESTOR requirements like 'distributed' and 'adaptive'.

1.7   Modular

Modularity in our sense is meant to support three important aspects of authoring/learning environments, namely **individualized learning**, **composite authoring**, and **coauthoring**.

Individualized learning means that a learner can determine the time, sequence, speed, and depth of learning, as well as important aspects of the dialogue between her/him and the CAL system. On-demand learning, where the student learns along the line of the problems s/he encounters in her/his (professional) live, is a special facette of individualized learning.

Composite authoring is something well known from classical (book and lecture) authoring. Authors tend to scan existing material, select (and maybe slightly modify) convenient parts like definitions, graphs and photographs, they may even paste complete paragraphs and sections, and intermix them with self-authored parts. Both in rapidly changing high-technology fields and in more traditional disciplines with 'classical canonical lectures', lectures could not be written in an acceptable timeframe without this possibility of composition (*and*, of course, an appropriate framework about rights and royalties).

Coauthoring finally denotes a seamless integration of and continuous iteration between learning and teaching; e.g., if a group tries to acquire expertese about a subject together, everybody may be both a teacher and a learner. Different degrees of coauthoring may be desirable at different times.

CAL up to now has largely failed to support individualized learning, composite authoring, and coauthoring. While computers as such are well prepared to provide these features, it seems to be necessary to design them from the very beginning into a courseware engineering environment, starting with a sophisticated framework for modularity.

1.8 Iterative

Iterativity alludes to a 'rapid prototyping' like property of the authoring system. As for some of the design and authoring tasks, WYSIWYG is not feasable or desired, care has to be taken to allow quick and easy execution (simulation, animation) of incompletely authored courses.

1.9 Uniform

Uniformity has to be realized in all three 'classical' layers of engineering environments: the human interaction layer, the functional layer, and the storage access layer. 'Common look' human interfaces are commonly required for highly interactive systems these days. Such interfaces can be supported or enforced with, e.g.,

- Library modules for provision of conformant course routemaps, glossaries, etc. and their presentation.
- Equally looking, named, and/or formatted screen artifacts (commands, options, menues, icons, forms, lists, output graphs etc.) for equal functions; system-support can be provided by guidelines or again libraries.

In the functional layer, uniformity relates to the 'behaviour' of different tools. Equally 'looking' operation-invokations should also operate equally. This feature is sometimes referred to as 'WYSINS' (what you see is no surprise).

An economical way to enhance functional uniformity is by providing generic basic (atomic) operations, out of which tools can be more or less 'composed': identical basic operations in different tools are by nature behaving identically.

In the data layer, finally, uniformity means that tools use common data. While this sounds trivial, it becomes less trivial to support in a growing and open environment. Data descriptions decoupled from the data, data integrity and support for modifiable data definitions can only be provided if recent technical advances like in data base technology are used for data storage ([ORE88], more References cf. 1.8). The meshed information structure encountered specifically in CAL environments poses another requirement to data management. This requirement is currently best met by hypermedia tools. It is the combination of such requirements (to be coupled with that of multimedia support and distribution support) which raise the need for very advanced information management technology.

2 Technological Restrictions

Considering NESTOR promarily as a software project, we have to accept limitations introduced by hardware technology. Some of these can be expected to be resolved in the forseeable future, others appear to be more persistent. Uncertainties about the technological development can not totally be avoided in a large, multiyear advanced project which relies on a variety of hardware features. Fullmotion video – used in the way pointed out in section two – is obviously the most challenging component of our project to technology; this chapter will therefore focus on this aspect. Main technological influences and restrictions for NESTOR in this respect can be grouped into communication, storage, and video recording/presentation.

2.1 Communication Technology

The NESTOR requirements 'multimedia-based' and 'distributed' (with subrequirement 'collaboration') together impose the most critical requirements with repect to communication technology.

As both by nature analog (e.g., video) and by nature digital information have to be transmitted, and as separate channels for these obviously hinder integration and efficient linkage in the long run, all information should to be transmitted by the same means, and hence analog information, like motion video, should to be digitized. Collaborative learning, on the other hand, discourages broadcast technologies. Finally, continuous education tends to require long distance connections.

These considerations sum up to the requirement of two-way individualized digitized WAN connectivity, capable of transmitting realtime fullmotion digitized video. While at present the available technology cannot meet this combination of requirements, there are a number of intermediate solutions which are or will soon be economical and feasable:

- The best solution to be expected for the medium range future is as follows [LAR88, DIX87, SIE86]: image compression technology is likely to reduce the necessary bandwith for realtime digital video transmission much below that of the the upcoming fibre optical networks (FDDI for metropolitan area networks and, especially in Europe, broadband ISDN for WANs, both around 100 Mbits/sec); the required speed of an individual video transfer can be pushed even below Ethernet capacity, but with extensive compute efforts for compression.

  FDDI has reached a first stage of commercial availability, and B-ISDN is tested in pilot installations. Acceptable compression technology is still in laboratory stage, but on the other hand entered the standardization process. This means that in not too long a time, multiplexing (a small to moderate number of) 'individualized video sessions' over such a network will become feasable. For large numbers of concurrent sessions, even another generation of networks will have to come into being.

- In broadband LAN topologies, video may still be transmitted in analog form in a transition phase, sending digitized information over the same communication medium. Multiplexing 'individualized learning sessions' will be possible only in a very restricted form.

- Non-realtime video transmission (via highspeed broadcast or lower-speed individualized links) is another choice, if videos can be stored on local random-access storage. Courses can than be transmitted in batch mode, using lower-speed individualized channels for student's feedbacks. This implies, of course, the existence of appropriate local storage (see below) and is a much less interactive approach. NESTOR will therefore not focus on this alternative.

2.2   Storage

Modular (individualized) learning requires courses to be stored for random access. This requirement is most limiting for motion video once again. While all kinds of digital storage continue to become faster, cheaper and bigger, random access motion video seems to remain the domain of optical disks in the near future. Especially as analog recording has to bridge the time until digitized video storage becomes mature, optical disks – suited for both analog and digital video storage – present the only viable choice.

On the other hand, composite iterative authoring and integrated multimedia are best supported with *erasable* video storage:

- cut & paste operations and highly iterative video editing/authoring are likely to produce large amounts of waste information.
- better integration of video information with other media (hot spotting and the like, see paragraph 1.2) will require video information to be 'enriched', a process which also tends to produce waste video information.

The above sums up to the requirement of erasable optical disks for digital video recording, which are not readily available. Once again, intermediate solutions have to be sought. It seems that video authoring can best be done on VCR recorders in the meantime, offering erasability. The final course can then be written to WORM or read-only (CD-ROM or video) disks. Main disadvantages are the impact of VCR use on the authoring process, limited CD-ROM capacity, and the high compression effort mentioned.

2.3   Recording and Presentation

Standard CD-ROM players cannot be used to play non-compressed motion video as their bandwith is too low. Standards for multimedia CD-ROMs and for compression are, however, emerging on the market. A more persistent problem lies in the fact that both CD-ROM and video disk technology suffer from the high cost and turnaround time for disk production, restricting their use to high-quality and/or large volume course production.

Recently, write-once (WORM, [ONC88]) disks for recording analog video became economical. As there are no master disks required, the volume of individual courses is irrelevant. With this technology, turnaround time and volume requirements are no more an issue; however, presentation device (player) costs and non-erasability still restrict feasability. Economical WORM recording

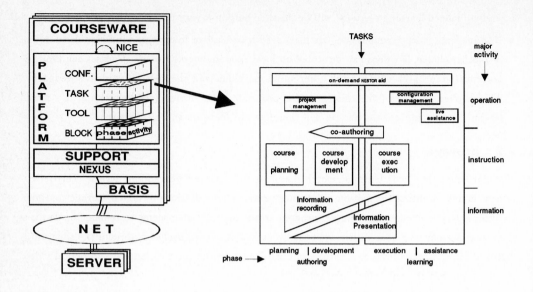

Figure 1: Coarse NESTOR architecture

along with affordable per-learnstation players, coupled with tape recorders for authoring, are regarded as a feasable mid-range solution for NESTOR.

3 NESTOR Architecture

Note that for the ease of reading and in order to better remember the many terms used (most of which represent special meanings of common vocabulary), we introduced a specific way of writing: NESTOR itself and terms used in its overall architecture are written with SMALL CAPS, phases and activities of the engineering process are *emphasized*, and functional bodies (like the individual NESTOR tasks and tools) are written sans serif.

3.1 Overall Architecture

The overall NESTOR architecture is shown on the left of figure 1, the right side showing the TASK-level view as exported to the user (cf. 3.2). It is to be retained that NESTOR has only recently and partly entered the implementation phase, so the architecture presents mainly a conceptual view. The main components of the overall architecture will be introduced below.

Applications under development (COURSEWARE): This term comprises COURSEWARE both as it is created and as it is used in the NESTOR environment. In the course of development, COURSEWARE exists in different representations like 'specification or 'executable code'. Remember that COURSEWARE may also be in the form of a distributed program, with different elements to be executed by different students on different workstations.

NESTOR intermediate courseware exchange format (NICE): NICE is the format in which executable courses are described and distributed to the learner's workstations. NICE will consist of three main parts:

- A formal, human and machine readable *language* for the description of courses. Different abstraction levels can be expressed in the one language, from the overall conceptual framework such as the instructional strategies pursued, down to in-depth issues such as the concrete structure of the user interaction. Both interpreters and compilers for NICE can be imagined, (pre)compilers being the likely choice for the early NESTOR project phases.

- An object-oriented interface to the multi-media objects referenced by a course (called *clip-objects*)

- An interface and interaction model for interacting with different functional modules which form selfcontained TOOLS in the development/learning process (for description see below), such as simulation or sf student evaluation.

Platform for individualized authoring/learning environments (PLATFORM): This is the very heart of NESTOR, all relevant functions visible to the user being realized in PLATFORM. Sections 3.2 and 3.3 will describe some of its functional aspects. Here we only present the logical architecture PLATFORM adheres to. PLATFORM can be viewed in four different levels of abstraction (layers, say), where the components of each layer are basically a composition of several components of the underlying one, plus the necessary 'glue', i.e. support for the composition itself. Higher layers are more complex, more comprehensible for the user, more individualized in terms of a user's personal workstation, and less 'pure' in their adherence to the two-dimensional PLATFORM classification scheme (see below).

In increasing order, the layers are as follows:

- BLOCK: BLOCKs are selfcontained small programming modules of all kinds. Making lowlevel functions (e.g., file/object access and manipulation primitives, self-contained common compute algorithms, windowing primitives) public to all TOOLs, we hope to reduce production time and to increase the level of 'common feel'.

- TOOL: TOOLs are composed of both common and TOOL specific BLOCKs, limited in their functionality for example to the manipulation of one or few classes of objects in a specific lifecylce phase. Section 3.3 will describe the TOOL layer in more detail.

- TASK: TASKs are composed of TOOLs, together with mutual dependency rules and constraints. A TASK presents a much more substantial and long-range functional entity than a single TOOL. An example is the whole development of the instructional part of a course. TASKs can also be seen as toolsets or workbenches, concentrating on a major activity of the authoring/learning process. The TASK layer, as shown in figure 1 on the right side, will be described in section 3.2.

- CONFIGURATION: A CONFIGURATION determines mainly the TASKs a user is allowed to carry out on his/her specific workstation and the phase in the courseware engineering lifecycle in which s/he is allowed to use it. Sometimes the right to use specific TOOLs within a TASK must be specifically decided upon, too. For example, according to the CONFIGURATION, the user is or is not allowed to do, e.g., *development* (a phase, see above), **information recording** (a TASK, see below), or certain aspects of **annotation/ammendment** to a course (a TOOL). As workstations are typically reserved to a single user or a group of users, our notion of CONFIGURATION has a direct relation to the common idea of a workstation's configuration.

Two-dimensional PLATFORM classification scheme: BLOCKs, and TOOLs, to a lesser degree also TASKs and CONFIGURATIONs, are classified according to two orthogonal aspects:

- Phase aspect: the principle phases we distinguish in a courseware engineering environment are the *authoring* phases called *planning* and *development*, and the *learning* phases called *execution* and *assistance*.

  By *assistance*, we denote all kinds of human controlled activity in the learning environment except for the learning process itself, e.g., operating the learning environment, or giving 'live assistance'. The latter term means that a human tutor helps the student in executing a course, using computer based means. Note that we distinguish the human tutor from the author as they need not necessarily be the identical person.

  As to the *planning* phase, note that in media-based courseware production technique as used today, this phase is computer assisted to a small degree only, e.g., with storyboard editors and some non domain specific software (project planning etc.).

- Activity aspect: we use the term 'activity' to describe a specific aspect of the courseware development process supported by NESTOR. These activities will be described in section 3.3. The activities are grouped into three socalled major activities: *operation*, *instruction*, and *information*.

NESTOR support system (SUPPORT): PLATFORM is built on top of the NESTOR SUPPORT system. The latter can be viewed as a sophisticated kernel providing operating system like support for the rest of the environment. It exports three main functional modules to PLATFORM:

- **Execution**: The object oriented execution service provides (optionally location transparent) runtime support for the objects in PLATFORM. It also contains the necessary functional parts and human computer interaction for 'bootstrapping' the PLATFORM functionality. The functional and human computer interaction parts can be seen as extensions to NEXUS-O and NEXUS-W (see below).

- **HyperSync**: this service offers to the user a sophisticated multimedia access, following the hypermedia paradigm. Special emphasis is put on providing a general purpose, media-independent interface for the description of media synchronization aspects. It is by this layer that, e.g., different clip-objects represented in different media can be integrated into a selfcontained 'composed media' clip-object to be easily handled by the PLATFORM TOOLs.

- **Cooperation**: Built on top of the hidden distribution service, the cooperation service offers the basic functionality necessary to implement PLATFORM features which by nature cope with the network of workstations NESTOR is intended to run on. Most relevant examples of such features are the **collaboration support**, **distance learning support**, and **live assistance** TOOLs (cf. 1.3, 3.3).

Three functional modules are hidden from the user in SUPPORT:

- **Information Management**: here we use an object-relation base extended by multi-media handling features and by special features needed by HyperSync.

- **Multimedia Management**: since in the forseeable future we will not have access to a robust object-relation base which can integrally store all types of media, there will be types of media only described and referenced in information management, but stored externally. The necessary storage/access features are provided by **multimedia management**.

- **Distribution**: The distribution service provides basic communication and remote invocation features. It is used by the cooperation service as an underlying basic service and by all other services for implementing these as distributed services (usually following the client/server model, accessing the NESTOR SERVERs (see below).

NESTOR access to underlying services (NEXUS): NEXUS is an interfacing layer designed to provide portability of SERVICE and PLATFORM and transparency of system specific characteristics of the underlying hardware, operating system and imported software components (to the desired degree).

Four major components of NEXUS can be distinguished:

- NEXUS-W (windowing): NEXUS-W defines the interface to the underlying windowing system and graphical diplay component.

- NEXUS-O (operating system): NEXUS-O gives access to local operating system services and allows remote execution.

- NEXUS-S (storage): The elementary storage access primitives offered in NEXUS-S provide independence from storage mechanism pecularities of different systems used.

- NEXUS-M (multimedia): NEXUS-M reveals the specific aspects of different media and their manipulation (generation, recording and/or presentation, storage). Only the differences necessary to be seen at higher layers are exported via its interface, however.

Figure 2 shows the interdependencies of the functional modules within SUPPORT and of NEXUS.

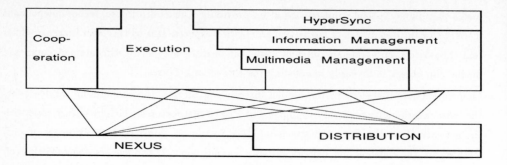

Figure 2: SUPPORT and NEXUS: functional dependencies

Local basic hard/software (BASIS): this stands for the hardware and software which is 'imported' into, i.e., used as a base for, NESTOR. While the NEXUS layer allows, in principle, to import a varying range of equipment, early phases of NESTOR will only allow a very restricted number of components as BASIS in order to reduce the adaption effort in NEXUS. Primary choice for the early NESTOR basis are: workstations like DECStation^{TM}, the operating system service specifications according to the POSIX^{TM} standard, the windowing system X-Windows^{TM} [SCG87], and a number of multimedia peripherals, some of which are contained in the ATHENA multimedia workstation [ATHTP].

NESTOR extended transport (NET): While TCP/IP and DECnet Phase IV will have to be used as an interim solution for 'classical' data communication purposes, a fast migration towards the OSI standards is planned here. More open is the area of highspeed multimedia communication (cf. chapter 2), a decision not yet being made at present.

NESTOR dedicated servers (SERVER): Dedicated servers include specialized high-performance multimedia workstations, compute- and database-serving machines and, in a larger timeframe, specialized number crunchers for dedicated purposes such as graphics manipulation.

3.2 PLATFORM Task View

As can be seen in figure 1 (right side), major courseware engineering TASKs lie within major activity *instruction* and are divided according to the first three lifecycle phases; they are called course planning, course development, and course execution. Section 3.3 will give more insight into their structure. The arrow-shaped TASK coauthoring indicates that there is explicit support for this feature (cf. 1.8) even at TASK level.

The TASK view also shows that a clear distinction is made between on one hand the didactical, instructional, and cognitive aspects of the courseware lifecylce (all treated in the major activity *instruction*) and on the other hand the pure information handling (major activity 'information').

Recording, selection, and integration of the contents taught as well as their presentation are reflected in two major TASKs. The triangles indicate that the TASK of information recording is to a high degree that of the author, while information presentation occurs to a larger extent at the learner's side. The use of different and multiple media is to be reflected at the TOOL level view of these two TASKs (cf. section 3.3), as well as the use of hypermedia TOOLs for coping with the integration of and navigation through multimedia information.

Four TASKs can be distinguished in major activity *operation*. As courseware authoring usually represents a substantial, long-duration project, often undertaken by more than one person, project management support is desirable. And as the typical environment envisioned at the learning side is a network of workstations, considerable configuration management efforts are necessary to support the operation of a learning environment. We also consider the possibility of computer assisted interaction between a student and a human tutor as another essential (although optional) TASK, called live assistance in NESTOR. Finally we think that being a flexible courseware engineering environment, capable of coping with on-demand learning, NESTOR should be its own best customer, i.e. we want to provide lifecycle spanning on-demand learning about NESTOR itself, comprised in the TASK on-demand NESTOR aid.

The following section will show in a bit more detail how the TASKs break into TOOLs.

3.3 PLATFORM Tool View

A first glance at figure 3, the TOOL layer of PLATFORM, gives an idea of the extent of a comprehensive computer aided courseware engineering environment. The three major activities have been further devided into eight activities. The ten TASKs described in section 3.2 are realized via 35 different TOOLs or TOOL types (an example for a TOOL type is the media object editor which has to exist for every class of media supported; for the sake of simplicity, we will mostly use the term TOOL in the remainder to comprise both).

Although the NESTOR team with its restricted size will not be able to write 35 TOOLs plus the NESTOR SUPPORT system in four years, we intend to realize at least the major part of the functionality as described in this paper and to provide the architectural and conceptual framework for the parts that will have to be left out.

In the remainder, we give an overview about the key characterisics of the TOOLs, using the eight activities as a guideline.

• Activity *guidance* is responsible for tutoring the user (author, learner, operator, human tutor etc.) about NESTOR itself. This activity matches one to one with a TASK described in 3.2, namely on-demand NESTOR aid. It is realized via four TOOLs. TOOL information management aid spans the whole courseware lifecycle, as all NESTOR users have to cope with navigating through and recording or presentation of multimedia information. TOOL courseware authoring aid provides on-demand learning support throughout the phases *planning* and *development*. The learner is assisted by course execution aid, and human tutors as well as learners are guided in the use of the live assistance TOOL (see below) by live assistance aid.

- The second activity within major activity *operation*, called *management*, supports the planning and supervision of other activities and the management of a NESTOR environment. TOOL project planning is one of the first used in a courseware authoring project. To a larger degree, this TOOL is a derivate of general-purpose project planning software; the domain specific parts are fed by other TOOLs of the *planning* phase to determine timeframes and coarse project structures as related to the pecularities imposed by goal/strategy selection and as related to the content structure. Project planning in turn feeds TOOL project control, supervising the whole project authoring process.

  The configuration support to be given in the *execution* phase of a course is determined in TOOL configuration support establishment. This relates to, e.g., live assistance, distance learning, or collaboration support in their effect on management and operation of the NESTOR execution environment.

  In the *execution* phase, TOOL access/capability control provides the kernel functionality to other TOOLs for supervising the learner's access to, or manipulation of, course data and information. Environment control / course administration renders the key features for operating a NESTOR environment. Distance learning support helps in the operation of an execution environment which is located remote to the human tutors and / or authors, especially in terms of dedicated communication facilities between the remote sites envolved. The actual computer support for a (local or remote) human tutor is realized in TOOL live assistance, partly belonging to the activity described next.

- *Instructional control* is the principal of four activities within major activity *instruction*. Herein, the goals of a course and the instructional strategy/ies (cf. 1.4) are determined in the *planning* phase (activity goal/strategy planning). Then, the instructional strategies and instructional methods are implemented in the course using TOOL strategy/method development; the computer assistance for enforcing strategies and for implementing methods at course development is given in this TOOL. Two specific aspects, only relevant to some of the strategies, are realized in seperate TOOLs, called collaboration development and simulation development. The former prepares a course for collaboration of the learners, the latter lets an author easily create simulations for use in courseware (microworlds, 'tachistoscopes'). In the *execution* phase, the enforcement of strategies and methods is coupled with the kernel runtime support system for course execution in TOOL runtime control/dispatch. Analogous to the *development* phase, TOOLs for collaboration control and simulation control exist.

- Activity *human interfacing* is represented by three TOOLs: in appearance planning, rules and layouts for the interaction are predefined (among others, the process of storyboarding finds its NESTOR equivalent in this TOOL). At *development* time, these rules and definitions are implemented using human computer interaction establishment, a TOOL which in turn uses a library of interaction artifacs created on the basis of NEXUS-W. During *execution*, student dialogue provides the functionality according to the establishment TOOL. Note that of course most other TOOLs interact directly with their user (author, learner etc.), and that the respective human interfaces are not regarded as TOOLs to be identified here.

- Activity *user modelling* realizes the NESTOR functionality according to section 1.5. A respective software design TOOL named **student profile assessment** is entered first. The TOOL's name reflects the subject of the interaction with the instructional designer; however, its functionality is also devoted to the preparation of the *development* phase, for which specifications and preselections are generated. TOOL **student model development** actually enforces user modelling within the course development. The development of the student evaluation part of a course is realized by a separate TOOL, **evaluation development**. Once again, the *development* TOOLs find their analogy in phase *execution*, the respective TOOLs are called **student modelling** and **student evaluation**.

- The fourth activity within *instruction* is called *feedback*. While we expect the NESTOR courseware lifecycle to be very iterative, we identify three points in the cycle where iterations are particularly supported by TOOLs. In the *authoring phase*, we support **prototyping/verification** to give an early feedback on a development which is under way. For prototyping reasons, we provide a subset of the execution TOOLs, comprised in a single TOOLsframe and complemented by support for the execution of partly developed courses. Verification is made explicit by the TOOLs generating attributes of the course parts under development which can be matched to specifications generated by TOOLs in the *planning* phase.

TOOL **course evaluation** offers three levels of feedback by the students to the authors (not all levels offered for every strategy): in the 'hidden' level, invisible monitoring modules observe the way in which a student is using a course. False assumptions made during user modelling, badly presented contents and other problems can be found according to this analysis. At the 'half open' level, questionnaires are presented to the student about the course, with the intend not to evaluate the student but the course. This level is called 'half open' because only an analysis of the questionnaires leads to statements about the course. At the third, 'open' level, the student gets direct insight into the instructional strategies and methods and into the content structure via special, human and machine readable specifications as supported by NESTOR (webs, see below). He can either annotate or directly change these specifications according to his views. The evaluation TOOL supports an author-driven feedback into the course.

The **coauthoring** TOOL matches one to one to the TASK with the same name as described in 3.2. For example, it allows the feedback of a course evaluation into the course not to be determined by a human but via (semi-)automated rules, merging the authoring and the learning process.

- *Navigation* is one of two actions within major action *information*. It comprises everything in this major action that has to do with the relations between several pieces of information. The TOOLs in this action follow the hypermedia / hypertext paradigm and have large functional parts in common. In early stages of *planning*, TOOL **info-space assessment** allows to specify the whole set of information that is related to the course planned. **Content assessment** determines the information (including meta-information, principles etc.) to be taught in the course, relates the contents to the info-space and defines information-inherent dependencies (like single terms explained by some information, information based on other information and so on). Dependencies which have to do with the instructional design are not regarded here; they are entered using TOOL **hypermedia editing**, the principal navigation TOOL for authors and learners (pertaining to TASK **information recording** as well as to **information presentation**). Any class of relations between and dependency among pieces of information is expressed via a subset of the set of hypermedia links, called a 'web' in NESTOR. TOOL **annotation/ammendment** is realized as a separate TOOL (partly pertaining to the *media management* activity, see below) because special control is necessary in the way a student's changes to a course are stored and fed back to other students or into the initial course.

- *Media management* is the activity which deals with the plain information taught and is largely influenced by the multi media aspect of NESTOR. **Template handling** is shown as a separate planning level TOOL; it is used to prerecord incomplete information and partial course contents (cf. TOOL **content assessment**). TOOL **media object editing**, as mentioned above, represents a TOOL class, standing for quite a number of media recording/presentation TOOLs for different media. The sophisticated support for creating and synchronizing 'composed media', the basis of which is provided by HyperSync (cf. SUPPORT in 3.1), is rendered to the user in this TOOL, too.

4 Conclusion

Requirements, feasability considerations, and architectural and conceptual issues have been discussed for a next-generation networked multimedia courseware engineering environment. The concepts presented obviously represent an agressive goal for the four-year NESTOR project which is only in an early phase today. Nevertheless we regarded the analysis and concepts found to date interesting enough to be presented to a larger audience, as similar activities are planned or going on in quite a number of educational institutions around the globe, requiring mutual fructification in order to sucessfully lead from today's common 'course hacking' to widely accepted courseware engineering methodology and standards.

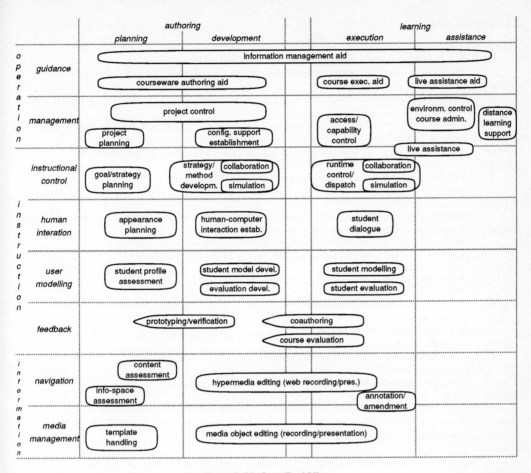

Figure 3: Platform Tool View

418

References

[AAH88]   Aambo, K.H., Hovig, I.
           The Term Hypermedia & a Thought-Experiment Hypatia
           Proc. Res. Networks & Distributed Applications, Wien April 1988, pp. 259-270, North-Holland
[ADF86]   Adams, D.M., Fuchs, M.:
           Educational Computing – Issues, Trends and a Practical Guide, *Charles C. Thomas, Springfield 1986*
[ADS86]   Ades, S., Swinehart, D.:
           Voice Annotation and Editing in a Workstation Environment, *Proc. AVOIS Voice Application 1986*
[AMH88]   Ambron, S., Hooper, K.: Interactive Multimedia, *Microsoft Press, Redmond, WA 1988*
[APP87]   Appleton, B.: Course Builder Manual, *TeleRobotics International, Inc., Knoxville TN, 1987*
[ATHPR]   Stewart, J.A. (Ed.)
           PROJECT ATHENA: Faculty/Student Projects (periodisch erneuert)
           Massachusetts Institute of Technology, Cambridge, MA
[ATHTP]   Saltzer, J., et al.:
           ATHENA Technical Plan (periodisch erneuert), *Massachusetts Institute of Technology, Cambridge, MA*
[BPB87]   Berger, D.E., Pezdek, K., Banks, W.P. (Eds):
           Applications of Cognitive Psychology: Problem Solving, Education, and Computing
           Lawrence Erlbaum Associates, London 1987
[BSC86]   Bonar, J., Cunningham, R., Schultz, J.:
           An Object-Oriented Architecture for Intelligent Tutoring Systems
           Proc. ACM OOPSLA '86, pp. 269 - 276
[CAC88]   Special Issue on Hypertext *Communications of the ACM, Vol. 31, NO. 7, 7/1988*
[CLA87]   Clansey, W.J.:
           Knowledge-Based Tutoring: The GUIDON Program, *MIT Press, Cambridge, MA 1987*
[CTJ88]   Coyle, K., Thompson, A.D., Jarchow, E.M.:
           Computers in Education: A Call for Exemplary Software
           Journal of Research on Computing in Education, Spring 88, pp. 245 - 257
[COA87]   Course of Action Product Description, *Authorware, Inc., Minneapolis MN, 1987*
[CON87]   Conklin, J. :
           Hypertext: An Introduction and Survey, *IEEE Computer, Vol. 20, No. 9, 9/1987, pp. 17 - 41*
[DIX87]   Dixon, D.F.: DVI Video/Graphics, *Computer Graphics World, July 1987, pp. 125 - 128*
[FRI88]   Friedlander, L, : The Shakespeare Project, *in [AMH88]*
[GAG87]   Gagné, R.M.:
           Instructional Technology: Foundations, *Lawrence Erlbaum Associates, Hillsdale, NJ 1987*
[GIB88]   Gibbs, S.J.:
           LIZA: An Extendable Groupware Toolkit
           MCC Tech. Report No. STP-042-88, MCC Austin, TX, 1/1988
[HEI84]   Heines, J.M.:
           Screen Design Strategies for Computer-Assisted Instruction, *Digital Press, Bedford, MA 1984*
[HMS87]   Hodgson, V.E., Mann, S.J., Shell, R. (Eds.):
           Beyond Distance Teaching – Towards Open Learning
           Society for Research into Higher Education & Open University Press, England 1987
[HOR88]   Horowitz, E.:
           An Integrated System for Creating Educational Software
           Perspectives in Computing, Vol. 8, No. 1, Spring 1988, pp. 35 - 42
[ICC87]   The University of Calgary:
           Proc. Intl. Conf. Computer Assisted Learning in Post-Secondary Education, Calgary, CDN, 5/1987
[JOJ87]   Johnson, D.W., Johnson, R.T.:
           Learning Together and Alone - Cooperative, Competitive & Individualistic Learning
           Prentice-Hall, Englewood Cliffs, NJ 1987
[JSO98]   Jones, A., Scanlon, E., O'Shea, T.:
           The Computer Revolution in Education: New Technologies for Distance Teaching
           The Harvester Press, Sussex 1987
[KSK88]   Krause, B., Schreiner, A. (Eds. Vol. I) – Krüger, G., Müller, G. (Eds. Vol. II)
           HECTOR - Heterogeneous Computers Together, Volume I/II, Springer Verlag 1988
[LAM88]   Lampe, D.R.:
           ATHENA MUSE: Hypermedia in Action, *The MIT Report, Vol XVI, No. 1, 2/1988, pp. 4f*

[LAR88]   Lambert, S., Ropiequet, S. (Eds.): CD-ROM - The New Papyrus, *Microsoft Press, Redmond, WA 1988*

[LIN87]   Linton, M.A., et al.
The Design and Implementation of InterViews, *Proc. USENIX C++ Workshop, Santa Fe, NM, 11/1987*

[LSC87]   Lerman, S.R., Saltzer, J.H., Champine, G.A.:
Requirements for Meeting the Needs of Next Generation Educational Computing
MIT ATHENA Report, Cambridge, MA, 1987

[LWH87]   Lum, V.Y., Wu, C.T., Hsiao, D.K.:
Integrating Advanced Techniques into Multimedia DBMS
Report No. NPS52-87-050, Naval Postgraduate School, Monterey, CA, 11/1987

[MAL88]   Mandl, H., Lesgold, A.:
Learning Issues for Intelligent Tutoring Systems, *Springer, New York 1988*

[MEI86]   Menasce, D.A., Ierusalimschy, R.:
An Object-Oriented Approach to Interactive Access to Multimedia Databases on CD-ROM
Proc. RIAO 88, Cambridge, MA, 3/1988, pp. 237 - 246

[NEL88]   Nelson, T.H.: Managing Immense Storage, *BYTE, 1/1988, pp. 225-238*

[ONC88]   Ooi, B.C., Narasimhalu, A.D., Chang, I.F.:
Integration of Write Once Optical Disc with Multimedia DBMS
Proc. RIAO 88, Cambridge, MA, 3/1988, pp. 213 - 226

[ORE88]   Orenstein, J.A.:
Can We Meaningfully Integrate Drawings, Text, Images, and Voice with Structured Data?
Proc. IEEE 4th Intl. Conf. on Data Engineering, Los Angeles, CA, 2/1988

[OSG87]   Osgood, D.:
The Difference in Higher Education, *in: Gurney, M.C.: Educational Computing, BYTE, 2/1987*

[OTT86]   Ottmann, T:
Can Teaching by Computers Replace Teaching By Professors?
FB 173/1986, Inst. angewandte Informatik u. formale Beschreibungsverfahren, Univ. Karlsruhe

[PAR88]   Parkes, A.P.:
CLORIS: A Prototype Video-Based Intelligent Computer-Assisted Instruction System
Proc. RIAO 88, Cambridge, MA, 3/1988, pp. 24 - 50

[PIC87]   Dedicated Issue on Academic Software / Courseware
Perspectives in Computing, Vol. 7, No. 2, Fall 1987

[SCG87]   Scheiffler, R.W., Gettys, J.:
The X Window System, *ACM Trans. on Graphics, Vol. 5, No. 2, 4/1986, pp. 79-109*

[RAS87]   Rashin, R., Stone, M.D.:
Picture Databases: Coming into Focus, *PC Magazine, Vol. 6, No. 14, 8/1987, pp. 341 - 376*

[SEL88]   Self, J. (Ed.):
Artificial Intelligence and Human Learning – Intelligent Computer-Aided Instruction
Chapman and Hall Ltd., London 1988

[SHI86]   Shields, M.:
Computing at Brown – an Ongoing Study, *Perspectives in Computing, Vol. 6, Nr. 2, Herbst 1986*

[SIE86]   Siegel, M.R.:
The CVD Format in the Development of the Video Book and the Impact of the Video Book on Electronic
Publishing, *Proc. Compcon Spring 1986, S.F., CA, 3/1986, pp. 220 - 227*

[STA86]   Creating Courseware: Faculty Author Development Project
Stanford University, ACIS/IRIS, Stanford, CA, 10/1986

[WLK87]   Woelk, D., Luther, W., Kim, W.:
Multimedia Applications and Database Requirements
Proc. IEEE Office Automation Symp., Gaithersburg, MD, 4/1987, pp. 180 - 189

[YAN88]   Yankelovich, N., et al.:
INTERMEDIA: The Concept and the Construction of a Seamless Information Environment
IEEE Computer, Januar 1988

KNOWLEDGE BASED INTELLIGENT TUTORING SYSTEM

Liu Ning and Krzysztof J. Cios

The University of Toledo
Toledo, Ohio 43606

ABSTRACT

Declarative programming languages are more difficult to learn especially after being first exposed to procedural languages. The tutoring system was developed to help in learning of how to write Prolog programs, majority of which are recursive. The system requires initial definition of basic concepts about the problem to be solved in a form of facts and then form examples, supplied by a student, generates Prolog program. The method used for learning from examples is an incremental, inductive learning algorithm based on an zero-one integer programming model.

INTRODUCTION

A system was designed to assist students in the process of learning a declarative, logic programming language Prolog. To achieve that goal there are two possible approaches. One is to develop an expert system which requires a huge knowledge base [Polson and Richardson, 1988; Clancy,1982], and the other is to develop an incremental inductive learning system which is able to learn from examples [Michalski, 1986] in a way which is similar to that of a student. The latter approach was taken here. The learning system generates the program solution for the problem being studied and at the same time it requires substantial student involvement in defining the background/initial knowledge about the problem's domain. Only correct definition of this initial knowledge base and appropriately chosen examples will result in the correct program.

The only input required from the student is the name of the concept to be studied and a few examples supporting the concept. Then the tutoring system generates individual rule covering a given example and upon getting another example generalizes the rules incrementally using induction.

The tutoring system requires a priori definition of knowledge about the problem being studied rather than specifying production rules used in expert systems. This simple requirement results in a compact knowledge base. The generalization algorithm makes the system more flexible than one using production rules, moreover, expert systems may have problems in dealing with extreme cases due to the incompleteness of the rules.

At the beginning of the process of learning, the tutoring system requires the same background knowledge as specified for (and thus possessed by) a student about the problem to be solved. The student becomes a teacher for the system but in fact he is both, the learner and the teacher. The student learns from the output of the system and from correcting her own mistakes. The student only needs to provide positive or negative examples to the system. She also has the freedom to emphasize some distinguishing characteristics of the given example since an example used to train the system is merely the name of a concept. The system works in the following way. First, it lets the student to define a domain upon which the learning is to be performed. Second, after reading an example, the system searches its knowledge base (domain) and generates the interpretation based on a priori knowledge about the problem. Third, the system combines the generated hypothesis, if available, with newly derived interpretation of another example to generate a new hypothesis about the problem. The above mentioned processes are repeated for each new example. When the student finally decides that she has provided enough examples, the last interpretation constitutes the correct program-solution for the problem, at least to the extent that the resulting program correctly covers all given examples. At the end of the process of learning the system transforms the program into a corresponding recursive form if desired and possible.

METHODS

The tutoring system is designed in three levels. The first level is the construction of a knowledge base which serves as the platform for the process of learning [Miller, 1982]. The knowledge base is divided into several domains, each domain covering different problem area. An interpretation of a given example constitutes the second level of the system. The developed system learns from positive and negative examples. If the student is able to provide some additional information, even incomplete, or emphasize some predicates in machine-found interpretation (conjunction of predicates) then the learning is performed in more efficient way. The more information the student provides the easier the correct Prolog program is generated by the system. With each part of a Prolog program a corresponding network can be associated. In the later analysis of the generalization algorithm a program-equivalent network [Bratko, 1986] will be discussed. The basic idea of generalization is to find the common part of two networks which is achieved by solving a corresponding 0-1 integer programming model. Recursive form is also obtained by using the same model.

Knowledge Base Description

Knowledge base used in a tutoring system consists of different domains. A domain covers a certain area of a problem being solved/learned. For example, family relations, such as father, mother, grandfather, aunt etc. can be classified into one domain. If we use term "concept" as the basic unit representing a small "piece" of knowledge, then we have, for instance:

parent(X,Y).

male(X1).

female(X2).

three concepts representing that a person X is a parent of Y, person X1 is a male and person X2 is a female. Let us introduce the following definitions:

Definition 1: The concepts used to explain or define other concepts are called basic concepts.

Example: grandfather(X,Y) :- parent(X,Z),

parent(Z,Y),male(X).

where parent(.,.) and male(.) are basic concepts.

Definition 2:   All the concepts that could be defined, or explained, by basic concepts comprise knowledge domain. These basic concepts are called concept coordinates.

There are no restrictions on how to choose a concept coordinate, but we recommend the most commonly used, simple concepts to be chosen as the coordinates. For instance we might use concepts of:

```
father(X,Y).
mother(X,Y).
```

as the concept coordinates for a family relation domain, but they result in an unconsise two-rule description of a grandfather:

```
grandfather(X,Y):-father(X,Z),mother(Z,Y).
grandfather(X,Y):-father(X,Z),father(Z,Y).
```

Proper definition of concept coordinates is related to linguistics and information theory [Uszkoreit, 1988; Lehman, 1988]. Often a non-concept coordinate of a domain serves as a concept coordinate of another domain and different domains may have common coordinates. The relations between different domains in a knowledge base may be complex. When a new example is read a decision has to be made to which domain it belongs. For the sake of simplicity of the implementation we let the new example to belong to the current active domain, that is the one defined by the student. At the beginning a student is asked to chooses or creates a domain.

A student can define concept coordinates by:

a) Specifying other domains which may be the subdomains of the new domain.

b) Adding new concept coordinates directly.

c) If the facts in a domain are incomplete the system asks
   for more facts. If a new fact represents a new coordinate
   this new coordinate is added to the domain automatically.

d) Deleting coordinates which are redundant.

Interpretation of Examples

An example is only the name of a concept (predicate) to be
studied. The system generates an interpretation of each example. This
interpretation is given in terms of the coordinate names of the domain
to which the example belongs. When an example is given, the search of
the coordinates/facts is performed. An individual rule gives
interpretation of one example only and is formed by the example
becoming a head of the rule and the newly formed interpretation of
this example the body of the rule. The interpretation constitutes the
body of a rule, or the subgoal list. We shall use the two terms
interchangeably in the following discussion. The procedure of forming
a subgoal list is discussed in detail in [Cios and Ning, 1988].

A weight is associated with each coordinate fact to allow a teacher
to emphasize its importance. The weights representing the truth
likelihood of a fact range from -10 (most unlikely) to +10 (most
likely). The facts with large absolute values of weight indicate the
characteristic descriptions of an individual rule.

When a subgoal list is found, an initial weight is assigned to each
fact. If the example is negative, every fact in a subgoal list is
assigned a -1, which means that all the facts are equally negatively

important.   If the example is positive, all of the facts are assigned a +1.

The system then asks a student if there are any facts to be emphasized.   If this is the case the weights for these emphasized facts are changed according to the student's assignment.   In a negative example, the facts that have not been emphasized no longer keep their initial negative weights and are changed to 0.   In addition to the change of the weights in a subgoal list the student can also add/delete facts to/from the subgoal list.   This, of course, accelerates the process of learning but needs more input from the student.   The above can be seen as the strength of this tutoring system since if student knows more she would direct the system to quick solution - the correct program. For the very beginners they need only to specify an initial knowledge base and just keep giving examples till the correct program is found. The correctness of the program must be eventually checked by the student for some general case, which is usually provided with a problem specification.

In some instances, due to the absence of some facts in a domain the search for the subgoal list may not succeed.   In such a case the system terminates a search and asks the student for more facts.   The implemented system is capable of :
a) Asking questions when the search fails.
b) Providing information to the student about what kind of facts may help in a search.

The new facts are automaticly checked by the system whether the newly specified concept coordinates are to be stored in a knowledge base. This updates the knowledge base and helps in learning other concepts later.

Generalization Algorithm

A generalized rule covers all examples used for learning a new program, which means that its body is contained in every individual rule [Stepp and Michalski, 1986]. The generalization algorithm finds common part of all individual rules and creates the body of a general rule. To find a common part the subgoal list of the first individual rule becomes the body of the general rule. Then, when the next example is available its subgoal list is compared with the body of the general rule to find the common part. This common part becomes the new general rule. To find a common subgoal list a suitable correspondence of predicates and variables between the two lists must be found. Let us consider two lists represented by two graphs. The variables of a predicate are the nodes and the relation specified by the predicate is an edge from one variable to the other variable.

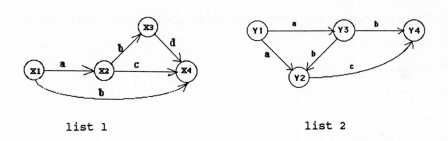

list 1   list 2

These two graphs correspond to two lists of predicates:

list 1: a(X1,X2), b(X1,X4), b(X2,X3), c(X3,X4), d(X3,X4).

list 2: a(Y1,Y2), a(Y1,Y3), b(Y3,Y2), c(Y3,Y4), d(X3,X4).

Each network may have some matching nodes with other networks when the generalization algorithm is applied. In our example node X1 matches node Y1, node X4 matches node Y4. The generalization algorithm will match the rest of branches and nodes. The matching conditions are concisely represented in the following table:

Zij	X1	X2	X3	X4
Y1	1	0	0	0
Y2	0	1	1	0
Y3	0	1	1	0
Y4	0	0	0	1

table 1

Where a "1" in matrix represents that there is a possible match of nodes between the corresponding row and the corresponding column. For example, the element $Z23$ from the above matrix has value 1 which represents a possible match between X3 and Y2.

Because a variable in a subgoal list can match at most one variable in another subgoal list, the sum of columns and rows should be smaller or equal to one. In order to find common sublist of list 1 and list 2 the following integer programming problem [Schrijver, 1986] is solved:

$$\max (S_1 + S_2 + S_3 + S_4 + S_5)$$

$$Z_{22} + Z_{23} \leq 1$$
$$Z_{32} + Z_{33} \leq 1$$

$$Z_{22} + Z_{32} \leq 1$$
$$Z_{23} + Z_{33} \leq 1$$

$$Z_{11} + Z_{23} \geq 2 * S_1$$
$$Z_{11} + Z_{22} \geq 2 * S_2$$
$$Z_{32} + Z_{23} \geq 2 * S_3$$
$$Z_{32} + Z_{44} \geq 2 * S_4$$
$$Z_{23} + Z_{44} \geq 2 * S_5$$

Where $Z_{ij}, S_k = 0, 1$

The optimal value of objective function is 5 and the optimal solution results in matchings:

X1=Y1, X2=Y3, X3=Y2, X4=Y4.

The common sublist of the above two subgoal lists is :

a(X1,X2),b(X2,X3),c(X2,X4),d(X3,X4).

Its correctness can be easily checked by drawing the equivalent network:

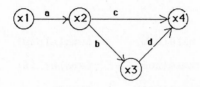

Forming Recursive Rules

If the rule is complex it may be changed into a recursive form [Bratko, 1986]. A recursive definition usually requires two rules: a basic rule and a general rule. The general rule is formed by substituting the common part in the body of the non-basic rule by the head of the basic rule. The details of the procedure are given in [Cios and Ning, 1988]. First, several rules in the knowledge base with the same head as the general rule are found and then their common part is found by calling the generalization algorithm. Next, if the common part covers completely one of the rules, the common part in the general rule is substituted with the head of the basic rule.

EXAMPLES OF TUTORIAL SESSIONS

Two examples of tutorial sessions how to write simple Prolog programs will be shown.   As a domain a family relations will be used. Let us suppose that a student wants to write a recursive program defining the concept of a PREDECESSOR. At first, the student is asked to define concept coordinates. Let us suppose that she has defined

      parent(X,Y).   male(X).   female(X).

Then she has to specify some initial knowledge about some family relations, for instance:

      parent(pam,bob).   male(bob).   female(pam).

      parent(tom,liz).   male(tom).   female(liz).

      parent(tom,bob).   male(joe).   female(pat).

      parent(bob,ann).   male(jim).   female(ann).

      parent(pat,jim).   male(sam).   parent(bob,pat).

      parent(liz,joe).   parent(liz,sam).

The following paragraph shows the actual dialog between the tutoring system and a student. After the prompt,   'Please input an example which supports a concept to be learned', a student gives an example:

|: PREDECESSOR(PAM,BOB).

Is there any predicate you want to emphasize ? |: no.

The individual rule is :

    predecessor(A,B):-[parent(A,B),1],[female(A),1],[parent(C,B),1],

                [parent(B,D),1],[parent(B,E),1],[male(B),1].

Do you have more examples to teach the system ? |: yes.

Please input an example which supports a concept to be learned.

```
|: PREDECESSOR(BOB,ANN).
```

Is there any predicate you want to emphasize ? |: no.

The individual rule is :

```
   predecessor(A,B):-[parent(A,B),1],[parent(C,A),1],[male(A),1],
                     [parent(D,A),1],[parent(A,E),1],[female(B),1].
```

Do you have more examples to teach the system ? |: no.

The new concept learned in this learning cycle is:

```
   predecessor(A,B):- parent(A,B).
```

The above is the Prolog-program output. The weights are used only
by the algorithm in the process of learning.

Do you want the system to learn another concept ? |: yes.

Please input an example which supports a concept to be learned.

```
   |: PREDECESSOR(PAM,ANN).
```

Is there any predicate you want to emphasize ? |: no.

The individual rule is :

```
   predecessor(A,B):-[parent(A,C),1],[female(A),1],[parent(D,C),1],
                     [parent(C,B),1],[parent(C,E),1],[male(C),1],
                     [female(B),1].
```

Do you have more examples to teach the system ? |: yes.

Please input an example which supports a concept to be learned.

```
   |: PREDECESSOR(BOB,JIM).
```

Is there any predicate you want to emphasize ? |: no.

The individual rule is :

```
   predecessor(A,B):-[parent(C,A),1],[parent(D,A),1],[parent(A,E),1],
                     [male(A),1],[parent(A,F),1],[male(A),1],
                     [parent(F,B),1],[female(F),1].
```

Do you have more examples to teach the system ? |: no.

The new concept learned in this learning cycle is:

    predecessor(A,B):- parent(A,C),parent(C,B).

Do you like this system to learn another concept ? |: no.

Do you want to form a recursive rule ? |: yes.

The recursive rule is :

    predecessor(A,B):- parent(A,C),predecessor(C,B).

The above recursive Prolog program constitutes correct solution of
PREDECESSOR.

The next example shows how to write a program defining the concept
of BROTHER. In this example negative examples and even wrong examples
will be used.

From the example:

    |: BROTHER(BOB,LIZ).

the system generates:

    brother(A,B):-[parent(C,A),1],[parent(D,A),1],[parent(A,E),1],
                  [parent(A,F),1],[male(A),1],[parent(D,B),1],
                  [male(D),1],[female(B),1],[parent(B,G),1],
                  [parent(B,H),1].

From another, this time a negative example:

    |: NOT(BROTHER(ANN,PAT)).

Is there any predicate you want to emphasize ? |: yes.

Please input the predicate(s) and the weight(s):

    |: not(female(ANN)), 1.

the system generates:

      brother(A,B):-[parent(C,A),0],[female(A),-1],[parent(D,C),0],
                    [parent(E,C),0],[parent(C,B),0],[parent(B,F),0],
                    [female(B),0].

From next wrong example:

  |: BROTHER(ANN,PAT)).

the system generates:

      brother(A,B):-[parent(C,A),1],[female(A),1],[parent(D,C),1],

              [parent(E,C),1],[parent(C,B),1],[parent(B,F),1],

              [female(B),1].

After the generalization, the rule takes form:

      brother(A,B):- parent(C,A),parent(C,B),male(C),female(B).

As one can see, this result is not correct due to the fact that the student gave an incorrect example. In the next learning cycle this incorrect program is corrected.

Upon giving another example:

  |: BROTHER(BOB,LIZ).

and associating a weight with a predicate male:

  |: male(BOB),1.

the system generates:

      brother(A,B):-[parent(C,A),1],[parent(D,A),1],[parent(A,E),1],

              [parent(A,F),1],[male(A),2],[parent(D,B),1],

              [male(D),1],[female(B),1],[parent(B,G),1],

              [parent(B,H),1].

and after generalization:

      brother(A,B):-parent(C,A),parent(C,B),male(C),

              male(A),female(B).

From the next example:

  |: BROTHER(SAM,JOE).

the generated individual rule is:

brother(A,B):-[parent(C,A),1],[parent(D,C),1],[parent(C,B),1],
[male(A),1],[female(C),1],[male(B),1].

and after generalization, the final correct program is obtained:

brother(A,B):-parent(C,A),parent(C,B),male(A).

CONCLUSIONS

Intelligent tutoring systems are supposed to use "intelligence" to help in learning how to solve problems. Unlike tutoring systems which use expert system approach to simulate a teacher with a sophisticated knowledge base, the implemented tutoring system performs its function in the same environment and learns along with a student. It is obvious that to simulate a student's background knowledge is easier than to simulate the background knowledge of a teacher. Different definitions of a knowledge base results in different comprehension abilities of the system, resembling student's understanding of a problem. By learning along with a student the system uses the student's inputs and produces the machine-written program for her. Similarly to a student who is flexible at learning different kinds of concepts, the system is designed to perform learning without requiring a priori definition of large knowledge bases.

Two basic problems were faced in developing this tutoring system: 1) How a student should communicate with the system and 2) What should be extracted by the system from a set of student's instructions. First, like many others [Utgoff, 1987; Spackman, 1988] the system is taught by giving examples. There is no uniform way in which the

.examples are supplied. In general there are two basic ways. One is to provide an example by giving the name of a concept without any detailed explanation.   This requires the system to perform the search of its knowledge base and "understand" the example by giving an interpretation in the form of a rule.   Second, a student gives an example with some additional explanation at the same time. Now there is no need for the system to "understand" the example.   The described tutoring system has the ability to interpret given examples. However, the system makes it possible for the student to emphasize some facts and change weights of the machine-found interpretation.

To find a general description from a set of individual rules a method which is independent of the knowledge to be learned is needed. Heuristic rule-based generation methods are extensively used [Mitchell, 1982; Minton, Carbonell, Etzioni, Knoblock and Kuokka, 1987], but they are knowledge dependent. Such learning systems either have to include sophisticated heuristic rules or they lose their learning abilities.   The described zero-one integer generalization model is knowledge independent and can be used for general purpose learning.

The weights generated by an interpretation procedure are used by generalization algorithm.   By letting the value of weights in the system to be in the range between -10 to +10 the scope of the learning abilities is broadened. In addition to learning from both negative and positive examples, the system takes into account also their weight which expresses uncertainty or fuzziness associated with some facts.   Another advantage of the method is that it generalizes the individual rules using zero-one integer programming model. When at least two such rules are generated the program changes them into a recursive form whenever possible.

The system also allows learning expert systems methodology. In particular it enables knowledge acquisition in a form which is often used to represent knowledge, namely in the form of rules. Since descriptions of initial facts are already stored in a knowledge base and descriptions of new concepts are added to the same knowledge base the system is very suitable not only for tutoring how to write programs but also for constructing knowledge bases from examples.

REFERENCES

Bratko, I. (1986) : " Prolog Programming for Artificial Intelligence", Addison-Wesley.

Cios, K.J. and Ning, L.(1988):"Learning New Concepts in Closed-World Domains", The Proc. of Third Annual Rocky Mountain Conf. on AI,Denver Colorado.

Clancey, W. J. (1982): "Tutoring Rules for Guiding a Case Method Dialogue", Intelligent Tutoring Systems, Academic Press.

Lehman, H. (1988): " The LEX-Project - Computers and Results", Natural Language at the Computer", Springer-Verlag.

Michalski, R. S. (1986):" Understanding the Nature of Learning: Issues and Research Directions", MACHINE LEARNING --- An Artificial Intelligence Approach, Vol II , Morgan Kaufmann.

Miller, M. L. (1982): " A Structured Planning and Debugging Environment for Elementary Programming", Intelligent Tutoring Systems, Academic Press.

Minton, S., Carbonell, J., Etzioni, O., Knoblock, C. A., and Kuokka, D. R. (1987) : " Aquiring Effective Search Control Rules:Explanation_Based Learning in the PRODIGY System", Proc. of the Fourth Inter. Workingshop on AI, Irvine, CL.

Mitchell, T.,(1982): " Generalization as Search ", Artificial
    Intelligence,   Vol 18, pp.203-226, North-Holland.
Polson, M. C. and   Richardson, J. J. (1988): " Foundations of
    Intelligent Tutoring Systems", Lawrence Erlbaum Associates
    Publishers.
Schrijver, A. (1986) :   " Theory of   Linear   and   Integer
    Programming",   John Wiley and Sons.
Spackman, K. A. (1988):" Learning Categorical Decision Criteria
    in Biomedical Domains", Proc. of the Fifth Inter. Conf.
    on Machine Learning, Ann Arbor, MI.
Stepp, R. E. and Michalski, R. S. (1986): "Conceptual Clustering:
    Inventing   Goal--Oriented   Classification of   Structure
    Objects ", MACHINE   LEARNING --- An Atrifical Intelli-
    gence Approach,Vol II,Morgan Kaufmann.
Utgoff, P. E. and Saxena, S. (1987) : " Learning a Preference
    Predicate", Proc. of the Fourth Intertnational workshop on
    AI, Irvine, CL.
Uszkoreit, H. (1988): " From Feature Bundles to Abstract Data
    Types: New Directions in the Representation and Processing
    Linguistic Knowledge ", Natural Language at the Computer,
    Springer-Verlag.

THE ANATOMY OF AN OBJECT ORIENTED VISUALIZATION SYSTEM FOR ALGORITHM DESIGN

Mohamed Ouksel and Fillia Makedon
The Computer Learning Research (CLEAR) Center
The University of Texas at Dallas
Richardson, Texas 75083-0688

ABSTRACT

The components of an object-oriented visualization system for algorithm design and algorithm learning are described. This system, called ALGO, provides an environment in which both instruction and the design of algorithm can be conducted. It combines intelligent tutoring techniques, hypermedia linking tools to a computer-aided instruction library, facilities for assessing understanding of complex concepts via goal-directed dialogue aids, simulation packages and algorithm animation, and algorithm design through analogies and constraint satisfaction.

1. INTRODUCTION

The aim of this paper is to describe the architecture of a system conceived primarily to provide an environment for both the instruction and the design of algorithms. This system, entitled ALGO, is based on the idea that learning and design may be thought of as "discovery" [19,20] and "exploration" process. If so, the difference between these two functions lies more in the amount of control they exercise over these processes than in the methodology pursued to attain these goals, which, in one case is the understanding of an algorithm, on the other the discovery of a new one. Below we elaborate on this approach.

1.1 THE LEARNING ENVIRONMENT

The ultimate goal in the learning environment is to understand the intricacies and the implications of an algorithm that already exists. As we see it, the objective of instructing statement of the problem specifications to the solution embodied in the algorithm and ending with the program implementing the algorithm. The rate and the manner in which the algorithm is dissected can be controlled, depending on the learner's progress.

At each stage, a goal-directed dialogue may be conducted, using aids or techniques such as in [9, 10, 11, 42] and language interfaces [29, 31] to assess the student's understanding of problem specifications and the appropriateness of model, control abstractions, data structures utilized, etc ... A decision must be made as to what complementary knowledge the learner must grasp in order to get a clear insight into the choices made by the designer. This additional knowledge will constitute the context and circumscribe the search space in which the learner can explore and reason. It can include fundamental concepts to be reviewed as well as material which might elicit associations to other problem solving techniques. This context is necessarily dynamic since it must reflect the results of analyzing and explaining the dialogue with the learner. The learner is provided with a set of hypertext mechanisms to access and navigate around large semantically decomposed knowledge bases that form the "Learning Support Environment"[17]. The context will be utilized to delineate the scope of this environment within the knowledge base and thus provide a way of avoiding disorientation in a forest of information as can be the case with unbridled use in hypertext systems [42, 24]. Instruction structure can also be achieved through problem decomposition at each level of abstraction, identification of various subgoals, and finally supervision of the integration of partial solutions.

In ALGO, graphical visualization is but one facet of the system. It plays a role in allowing, at some stages in the design, a film-like description of the data interactions during the running of the partial solutions proposed by the learner, using techniques such as the ones described in [5, 6, 21]. From the behavior, the learner will be able to extract clues as to how his initial guesses can be amended. However, this type of visualization cannot be relied upon entirely to understand the anatomy of the algorithm or the justification for the choices made in the design. Our aim is to achieve a conceptual comprehension of an algorithm and thus, visualization is viewed as an all encompassing set of tools that include textual, graphical and other strategies such as the ones discussed above and in [14, 36, 40].

The combination of the top-down methodology [1] and contextual constraints is geared to provide a certain amount of instructional control, which was found to be particularly important in the case of a novice [15, 17, 35]. The system integrates ideas found in classroom instruction in that it focuses on the specifications of the problem at hand and decomposes the learning process into refinement stages, hypermedia environments and tools [42, 31] to allow exploration of related knowledge, animation [5, 6] and simulation packages to visualize graphically [7, 13] and experiment with proposed solutions. At the same time, the learner is an active participant in that he is allowed to explore, albeit in a controlled environment, and discover the constraints on the solution space and the appropriateness of specific constructs, strategies, or heuristics.

1.2. THE DESIGN ENVIRONMENT

The task in the design environment is one of charting a path from the statement of the problem to an algorithm that does not yet exist. As we contemplate this objective, it is apparent that a methodology is necessary to provide structure to this process. In our case, design will share with the learning approach discussed previously the step-by-step refinement technique proposed in [1]. This framework is the only systemized portion in the design process. Unlike instruction, the ability to control the "exploration" and "discovery" processes is considerably more restricted, and other structural aspects are more dependent on the designers expertise.

ALGO is designed to be an interactive system that makes it easy for an algorithm developer to try out a variety of ideas. For example, at the level of problem formulation and specification, when a designer determines the mathematical model for a given problem, the solution may already exist and its performance be recorded under different implementations. Alternatively, suggestions or clues as to the implementation required may be extracted from the other problems that use the same mathematical model. This entails a sophisticated knowledge representation for the object "algorithm" in the database, that captures the salient features of a dissected algorithm and facilitates reasoning by analogy. In particular, it must be capable of representing the specifications of the problem, the strategy adopted and its properties, the abstract data types utilized and their implementation under different data structures. Additionally, this class "algorithm" may be partitioned into a set of non-disjoint subclasses based on the strategies, and/or problem areas, and/or time and space complexity. All these aspects will be used to build a base of assertions about the algorithm to be devised. In turn, theses assertions will constrain the search space, reduce ambiguities, eliminate contradictions, and finally allow inferences and analogies to be made [3]. Presumably, some of these inferences will lead to discovery.

The base of assertions about the solution space can also be augmented from observation. In this respect, the system must provide ways for experimenting with different implementations of abstract data types and various heuristics, and examining the evolution of different implementations for purposes of comparison. The behavior of the proposed solutions can also be observed through the graphical visualization of the algorithm, or through the plotting of monitored statistical parameters.

In this paper, we present the architecture of a visualization system which is based on an object-oriented programming approach [4, 31, 27, 32, 34]. This system combines intelligent tutors, hypermedia linking tools, and integration of algorithm visualization with other existing aids (e.g. CAI lessons) in the visualization library [22, 23, 25], facilities for assessing the level of understanding via goal-directed dialogue, simulation packages and algorithm animation, and algorithm design through analogies and constraint satisfaction. In section 2, we summarize the desirable features of such a system. In section 3, aspects of the representation of algorithms are discussed, and in section 4, the components of the ALGO system are described.

2. DESIRABLE FEATURES IN AN ALGORITHM VISUALIZATION SYSTEM

We have designed ALGO to embody the following conceptual features necessary for algorithm design [18]:

a) Understanding the problem: facilities for comprehending the problem which the algorithm is to solve, and the computational costs to optimize. The user is presented the notions in a visual and interactive form which include:

(i) formal specification of the problem and
(ii) examples, complications, instances and cases.

b) Understanding relevance, applicability and explaining need for an efficient solution. This is achieved by:

(i) relating or accessing real-world problems, possibly in the form of simulation packages, industrial CAD tools.
(ii) links to background via a theoretical framework (e.g. drilling over logarithms, a reduction which proves a similar problem to be NP-complete);
(iii) tutoring facilities which coach a solution (can direct student to intelligent tutor, CAI frame, etc.)
(iv) conversion and relationship to other problems areas.

c) Evaluation facilities (analysis coaching) which explain how good the algorithm is from two points of view:

(i) a theoretical framework which has links to how similar algorithms work and their visualizations, animations, or simply descriptions,
(ii) a practical framework with analysis facilities for real-world cost savings resulting: real-world instances for interactive assessment with user in terms of productivity, man-hours, time, space, etc.

3. REPRESENTATION OF ALGORITHMS

A sophisticated representation is required to accomplish the objectives of ALGO. It must capture all the features of the algorithm which provide an insight into the model, structure, and behavior of the algorithm and be flexible to allow various types of search techniques pattern matching and reasoning. We decompose this representation into two types:

a. LOGICAL REPRESENTATION : This gives a formal abstraction (creation of the abstract data types) of the problem. The purpose is to (i) motivate the physical representation (e.g., creation of data structures), in the form described in the first chapter of [1]; (ii) justify the physical representation and (iii) explain how and why certain formal tools were used (e.g., graph versus Petri Nets, versus first order logic, versus prepositionalcalculus) and capture the intricacies of the problem. Hypertext facilities will be helpful in this case since they can provide further explanations of concepts if needed.

b. PHYSICAL REPRESENTATION: The purpose of this representation is to serve as

(1) an exploration medium for making analogies, and mapping one problem to another by tools which :
-give ideas about strategies (e.g., divide and conquer, or greedy versus dynamic programming approach); with this facility we determine a strategy that is a functional object and which gives you operations that can be applied to an instance of the problem;
-help understand how this problem's data structures were designed
-identify by analogy other, similar problems and help make associations

This type of representation is not easy to achieve. Several research issues have been raised which cannot be answered in this paper, such as: How is analogy done? How is it done efficiently? How should the problem be presented? What kind of search mechanism through the visualization database is necessary? How should the mapping take place between the specifications of one formal model to another?

(2) an aid in choosing the strategy for the solution: since the formal abstraction of the problem has been decided on at the logical representation phase, this phase helps explain/choose the data structures, how they interact with the input, etc.

4. AN OBJECT-ORIENTED APPROACH

An important question in designing visualization systems is to determine what are its components and how they interact. For our algorithm visualization, we shall adopt the

Object-Oriented Programming (OOP) paradigm in which systems are constructed form self-constrained objects that interact via messages [38, 34, 26, 27]. It is thought that this approach aids design, implementation, and maintenance of complex systems by supporting modularity. This, in turn, aids code reuse and the extensibility of system through inheritance.

An object oriented architecture uses objects as the unit of access and manipulation. A user is allows to define, create, and relate objects and object interactions. The advantages of the object oriented approach in handling multimedia type of information (as would be true with an algorithm visualization system) are: information hiding, abstraction, typing of objects into classes, and independence among active objects.

Furthermore, for an automated storage and retrieval system in algorithm visualization, especially in CAD/CAM problems, two very important problems will be how to find desired information and how to vow it effectively. Very powerful presentation and browsing facilities are needed for this and OOP is geared to handle these problems.

Before embarking in the description of the main modules of our system, temporarily baptized ALGO, a clarification of the objectives is warranted:

4.1 OBJECTIVES OF ALGO

The system will consist of two main (and not necessarily distinct) parts: a TUTOR SUBSYTEM (for pedagogical tools) and a DESIGNER SUBSYSTEM (for adaptive design algorithms):

(1) The ALGO-TUTOR SUBSYSTEM: PEDAGOGICAL TOOLS, GOAL DIRECTED DIALOGUE AND EVENT-DRIVEN EVALUATION

The ALGO will provide the capabilities to tech students the mechanics of algorithm design and assess their understanding of specific algorithms and concepts therein.

The idea is to provide a human tutor through sophisticated interfaces and a variety of pedagogical tools to help in preparing tutoring sessions.

GOAL DIRECTED DIALOGUE: The most appropriate pedagogical tool can be chosen on the basis of several factors such as: user's/student's level of expertise, the objective of the training, and the teaching/learning philosophy adopted. The system will also allow the monitoring of a continuous goal directed dialogue between the tutor and the student.

EVENT DRIVEN EVALUATION: A subsequent evaluation of the history of events that occurred during the dialogue will provide a way to identify where the weaknesses lie and, in turn, aid in planning the explanations required. The dialogue will be conducted at different levels of abstractions to localize the detection of concepts not understood.

ANIMATION AND OTHER HELP FACILITIES: Additionally, the system will offer the capability for the student to directly plan and then monitor the features requiring careful examination at both the Abstract Data Type and the implementation levels. A variety of help facilities, such as animation, will also be provided.

(2) THE DESIGNER SUBSYSTEM: ADAPTIVE DESIGN, RECOGNITION DISCOVERY, MULTIPLE SOURCES OF KNOWLEDGE, INTERACTIVE DESIGN, ANALOGICAL REASONING, DESIGN METHODOLOGY FACILITIES

The DESIGNER subsystem will provide tools for the designer in order to explore the various sketches of partial solutions elaborated during the step-wise refinement [1] of the algorithm.

ADAPTIVE DESIGN: The new knowledge acquired in this manner, i.e., difficulties and/or opportunities (as described in [18], will be expressed in the form of assertions [K, SK], about the solution and will then be injected into the searching techniques used in the form of constraint propagation. The idea is to progressively limit search in subsequent stages of this adaptive process.

RECOGNITION DISCOVERY AND SEARCH IN MULTIPLE SOURCES OF KNOWLEDGE: The system will also provide capabilities to recognize patterns in the way operators are applied to a) satisfy subgoals, b) to discover similarities to known strategies by examining interactions between states in the search space and the propagation of constraints, c) to avoid meaningless guesses , notice difficulties and d) other similar facilities which promote the element of chance and creativity necessary in the design of algorithms. This part will require enriching the set of assertions from multiple sources of knowledge such as the application domain (i.e., having instances of problems to execute partial algorithm descriptions on concrete data in order to help visualize the algorithm).

INTERACTIVE DESIGN: Unlike Kant's approach [18], we do not wish a complete automation of the algorithm design process. Rather, we aim at the opposite: that the designer be as much an active participant in formulating the kernel ideas of the partial solutions and in deciding the kind of objects (mathematical or otherwise) to be manipulated during the exploration of the search space. ALGO will help him/her do this, not replace him/her.

We can observe here that, since ALGO will be based on the OOP paradigm, new modules (embodying concepts not clearly understood at present) can be integrated later without affecting the existing ones in a modular, independent fashion.

ANALOGICAL REASONING : In section 3 (Representation of Algorithms), we identified analogy as an essential task for algorithm design. ALGO will include a component dedicated to analogical reasoning. This module will use the formal specifications of a problem to search the data base. More specifically, it will search the object algorithm or a class of algorithms and its subclasses, the class strategy and its properties. The purpose of this search is to identify other algorithms (or properties of algorithms) whose problem specifications are relevant to the current one. This process can provide clues as to the possible strategies for handing this problem.

DESIGN METHODOLOGY FACILITIES: When designing algorithms, there is a certain methodology which is acceptable and which includes the sequence and formulation of general principles, integration with problem-specific principles, and model constraints to systemize the process. In our system, we shall impose the following one, extracted verbatim from chapter 1 of [1]:
(a) Understanding the problem
(b) Problem formulation and specs
(c) design and solution
(d) Implementation
(e) Testing and documentation
(f) Evaluation
This methodology does not greatly differ from the observations made by Kant in [18, 39].

4.2 ALGO ARCHITECTURE

As illustrated in Figure 1, the ALGO architecture is based on modules that represent the various structural and behavioral objects we have identified in previous sections. The architecture reflects the abstract description requirements of an algorithm design process and an algorithm tutoring system.

Unlike most current Intelligent Tutoring Systems (ITS), such as the WEST tutor [8, 4], this object oriented methodology will allow the addition of new knowledge (automatic design of algorithms or new approaches to pedagogical tasks) without resulting in an overhaul of the whole implementation. It is thus a very pragmatic approach.

In what follows, we will describe only some of the modules involved, to give the reader a flavor of our system. A more complete description will be given in the final version of the paper.

4.2.1 The PROBLEM SOLVING MONITOR MODULE (Figure 1) :

Problem solving is viewed here as a search in a problem space [28]. As such, it is characterized by an INITIAL STATE and a GOAL STATE description. A transformation from one state to another is called an OPERATOR and the set of states describes the set of partial solutions. The objective is to find a sequence of operators which lead to a goal state.

In our system, the algorithm designer is asked to explicitly state all the transformations they consider to be appropriate to the task and the type of objects to be manipulated. For example, in a geometrical problem, an object might be a set of points in the 2-dimensional space and an operator might be a segment drawing function. In addition, the designer might suggest a strategy.

The PROBLEM SOLVING MONITOR MODULE will then provide means to systematically explore the complete search space. This part will be based on the findings of [12, 35]. The difference now is that the ideas will be implemented for designing algorithms, rather than tutoring. Another difference is that the ideas will be used in conjunction with several other modules which will feed it a vast (and increasing) array of knowledge.

SEARCH SPACE ISSUE: The major disadvantage with this approach is the potential size of the search. It is therefore necessary to add some knowledge for controlling the expansion of the search and limiting inferences and constraint propagation.

In our system, this additional knowledge will be extracted from the ASSERTION MODULE (figure 1) which serves as the repository of all the information we have learned so far about the solution space. This information will be organized in the form of constraints and will have either been imposed by the designer i.e., his knowledge about the problem, algorithm design principles, etc...) or from the domain space or from knowledge acquired in the previous explorations and evaluations of partial solutions. The system in [2] provides a good example of how domain space, in this case geometry, has been used to limit search.

For every exploration of the search, the problem solving monitor will provide an AND/OR TREE OF GOALS AND RULES (where the "OR" nodes would be the goals and the "AND" nodes the rules [30]) that were pursued during the monitoring of the corresponding instance of the problem. The tree will constitute a trace of the alternatives (in the case of ORs) and the decomposition of the problem (AND nodes).

This tree will be fed to the EVALUATION MODULE (Figure 1) for later evaluation. To maintain the insularity of modules, the transmitted object will be the corresponding Abstract Data Type (ADT), rather than its implementation.

4.2.2 THE ALGORITHM DESIGNER MODULE

As mentioned previously, our designer is an active participant in the design of an algorithm. The function of the ALGORITHM DESIGNER MODULE, will be to allow the designer to intervene in several aspects of the design. As Figure 1 shows, this module will communicate with several components of the algorithm design subsystem, including:

(1) The ASSERTION module, where the designer will be able to insert and propagate his knowledge about the problem at hand, about algorithm design principles which may limit search, his expectations and conclusions about efficiency, about the set of constraints, relationships and properties in the solution space.

(2) The PROBLEM SOLVING MONITOR module, where the designer will be able to perform initialization of the search to determine subgoals, and to influence the search strategy (i.e., by defining the criteria on which the evaluation of the"goodness" of states will be based).

(3) The EVALUATION MODULE, where the designer will be able to suggest the types of structural and behavioral objects to look for in the analysis of events and indicate whether the foreseen difficulties and opportunities are worth pursuing.

(4) The ANALOGICAL ANALYZER AND CONVERTER, where the designer will be able to limit search by suggesting which problem areas are more likely to be similar to the current one and what kind of analogies we are looking for. Additionally, the designer will be able to help in converting the specifications of a problem from one formal system to another so that the search for analogies becomes easier.

(5) The SOLUTION SKETCH MODULE, where the designer will be able to examine the integration of the content in the ASSERTION MODULE and the results in the ANALOGICAL ANALYZER modules and help in verifying the plausibility of the resulting steps.

4.2.3. THE DISCOVERY MODULE

The DISCOVERY MODULE will provide rules to analyze sequences of events that occurred during the problem solving exploration and notice patterns in the application of operators, the use of strategies, factors that reduce the search. In this aspect, search as well as heuristics play an important role, as established by Doug Lenat [19, 20]. In our system, the conditions to be monitored will be simple so as to allow a feasible solution.

4.2.4 THE GOAL-DIRECTED DIALOGUER MODULE

The goal-directed DIALOGUER (see figure 1) will provide the user/learner with an instance of the problem. (front end of this will determine level of expertise). The learner/user will then be asked to figure out the solution in a step-by-step goal-directed approach. In addition, the student can be quizzed at each level of abstraction to assess his level of understanding. This will enable the system through an analysis of dialogue "events" to figure out whether the student understands the overall approach of the algorithm and the details embodied in the data structures and operations. This part is inspired from the GUIDON System [10] which tutors a student to understand the knowledge in the MYCIN expert System [33]. This module will also show similarities to the Problem Solving Monitor presented previously in that the student will be allowed to explore the search space. However, in this case the search will be completely controlled since the algorithm will be known in advance, and therefore the subgoals will be precisely stated.

4.2.5 EXPLAINER Module

This module is directly tied to the GOAL-DIRECTED DIALOGUER and DIAGNOSER modules. The idea is first to design a model of interaction in the cas of discourse in specific problem areas such as VLSI design so that we determine in our tutorial session where questions are warranted and where explanations are necessary. This may serve as the tuggers towards the explanations of other concepts.

4.2.6. ALGORITHM MONITOR Module

This module is designed in such a way as to be accessible to the novice student and not to hinder the expert algorithm designer. Various features make the monitoring flexible so that the students use their judgement to control the depth and detail of the discussion. the module will have the capabilities to monitor: change of parameters, effect of Abstract Data Types, state after control abstractions, effect of heuristics at specific points. It will also be able to plot the implementation of the Abstract Data Type, save events for later analysis, and offer additional help facilities, similar to techniques in [11]. Finally, it will be able to indicate a list of descriptions of all data relevant to a particular goal and exhibit a subgoal tree for a goal. To achieve this objective, the monitoring of the algorithms will be viewed as a multilayered state-space problem [30] so that each level captures the monitoring at different levels of abstractions, expressing hence the step-wise refinement followed during the design of the algorithm. Clearly, it is important that an algorithm monitor be able to recognize and generate arguments at several levels of abstraction.

4.2.7 ALGORITHM Module

This module provides a structured and behavioral description of the ALGORITHM object. This object forms a lattice where there is one maximal object which describes the common components of all algorithms. for each element of the top class to which ADT is used, what are the control abstractions, specifications of the problem addressed, what heuristics was used, etc.... One can envision a set of non-disjoint subclasses: one based on the strategies, one on problem areas, one on complexity.

5. CONCLUSION

In this paper we give the anatomy of an object-oriented visualization system which captures the essential features of algorithm design and algorithm instruction in a system called ALGO. This system is based on the principle that both learning and design are "discovery" and "exploration" processes. We discussed visualization of algorithms as we see it, then gave some of the knowledge needed to perform certain tasks in algorithm design and finally we described the main modules of ALGO and explained how they integrate. The development of a system such as ALGO requires sophisticated software tools. These should integrate several Artificial Intelligence problem solving paradigms, including frames, inheritance, production rules, access-oriented programming techniques, object-oriented programming, multiple-worlds, and truth maintenance with facilities for querying, altering, and displaying the resulting structures.

REFERENCES

[1]   Aho, A. V., Hopcroft, J. E. and Ullman, J. , ""From Problems to Programs", in Chapter 1, Data Structures and Algorithms, pp. 1-10, Addison Wesley Pub. Co., 1982.

[2]   Anderson, J. R., "Tuning of Search of the Problem Space for Geometry Proofs", in Proc. of IJCAI-81, pp. 165-170, 1981.

[3]   Barstow, D. R., "The Roles of Knowledge and Deduction in Algorithm Design", pp. 201-222 in Automatic Program Construction Techniques, ed. Alan E. Biermann, G. Guiho and Y.Kodratoff, Macmillan Publishing Co., New Yor (1984).

[4]   Bonar, J. Cunningham, R. and Schultz, J., "An Object Oriented Architecture for Intelligent Tutoring System", OOPSLA 1986 Proceedings, pp. 269-277, Sept. 1986.

[5]   Brown, M. C., "Exploring Algorithms Using Balsa-II", in IEEE Computer, May 1988, pp. 14- 36.

[6]   Brown, M., and R. Sedgewick, "Techniques for Algorithm Animation", IEEE Software, Vol. 2, No. 1, Jan. 1985.

[7]   Brown, G. P., R. T. Carling, C. F. Herot, D. A. Kramlich, and P. Souza, "Program Visualization: Graphical Support for Software development", IEEE Computer, Aug. 85., pp. 27-37.

[8]   Burton, R.R. and Brown, J.S., 1982, "An Investigation of Computer Coaching for Informal Learning Activity", Append in Intelligent Tutoring Systems, ed. by Sleeman, D.W. Brown, J.S. Academic Press.

[9] Card, S.K., Pavel, M. and Farrell, J. E., (1985), "Window-Based Computer Dialogues", Human-Computer Interaction, Interact '84, Austin, Texas, North Holland Proceedings, pp. 239-243.

[10] Clancey, W.J., "Tutoring Rules for Guiding a Case Method Dialogue", Intern. J. of Man-Machine Studies, 11, 25-49.

[11] Fisher, G., "Student-Oriented features of an Interactive Programming Environment", in ACM (1987), ----pp. 532-537.

[12] France, S.A. and Sleeman, D. H., TSEARCH: A Data-Driven System to Help Students Solve Non-Deterministic Algorithms", Technical report, Dept. of Computer Studies, Univ. of LEEDS, England.

[13] Frenkel, K. A., "The Art and Science of Visualizing Data", in Communications of the ACM, Feb. 1988, Vol. 31, Number 2, pp. 111-121.

[14] Grafton, R., "Guest Editor's Introduction: Visual Programming", IEEE Computer, Vol. 15, No. 8, August 1985.

[15] Gray, S.H., "The Effect of Sequence Control on Computer Assisted Learning", in Journal of Computer Based Instruction, 14 (1987), 54-56.

[16] Halbert, D. C., "Programming by Example", Ph. D. Thesis, CS Division, Dept. of EECS, UCB, 1984.

[17] Hammond, N. and Allinson, L., "Travels Around a Learning Support Environment: Rambling, Orienteering or Touring?", in ACM proc. of CHI'88, (1988), pp. 269-273.

[18] Kant, E., "Understanding and Automating Algorithm Design", in IEEE Trans. Software Eng., vol SE-11, No. 11, Nov. 85.

[19] Lenat, D.B., "The Ubiquity of Discovery", Artificial Intelligence", vol. 9, No.3, 1977.

[20] _____, "The Nature of Heuristics", Artificial Intelligence vol. 19, No.2, 1982.

[21] London, R. L., and R. A. Duisberg, "Animating programs Using Smalltalk", in IEEE Computer, vol 18, No. 8, Aug. 1985, pp. 61-71.

[22] Makedon, F., H. Maurer, and T. Ottmann., "Presentation Type CAI in Computer Science Education at University Level", J. of Microcomputer Applications 10 (1987), 283-295.

[23] Makedon, F., H. Maurer and L. Reinsperger, "Active Annotation in HyperCOSTOC", IIG Technical Report, No. 256 (1988), Inst. of Informatics, Graz U. of Technology, Schiesstattgasse 4a, A-8010 Graz, Austria.

[24] Marchionini, G., and B. Sheiderman, "Finding Facts vs. Browsing Knowledge in Hypertext Systems", in IEEE Computer, Jan. 1988, pp. 70-80.

[25] Maurer, H., F. Makedon and F. Huber, "HyperCOSTOC" a Comprehensive Computer-Based Teaching Support System", in J. for Microcomputer Applications, to appear.

[26] Meyrowitz, N., Ed., 1986, "Intermedia" The Architecture and Construction of Object Oriented Hypermedia System", In OOPSLA Conf. Proc., (Portland, Oregon, Sept 1986), ACM SIGPLAN 21, 11 (Nov), 186-201.

[27] _____, 1987, OOPSLA Conf. Proc. (Orlando, Fla., Oct.), and in ACM SIGPLAN 22, 12 (Dec).

[28] Newell, A. and Simon, H, "Human Problem Solving", Englewood Cliffs, N. J., Prentice Hall, 1972.

[29] Nievergelt, J. and J. Weydert, (1980), "Sites, Modes and Trails: Telling the User of an Interactive System Where He is, What He Can Do, and How to Get Places" in Methodology of Interaction, North Holland pp. 327-332.

[30] Nilsson, N. J., "Principles of Artificial Intelligence", Tioga Publishing Co., 1980.

[31] Rich, E., "Natural Language Interfaces", IEEE Computer, Sept. 1984, pp. 39-47.

[32] Rich, E., "Introduction to Artificial Intelligence", McGraw Hill 1983.

[33] Shortliffe, E.H., "Computer-Based Medical Consultations: MYCIN", New York:Elsevier.

[34] Shriver and Wegner, P., eds, 1987, "Research Directions in Object Oriented programming", MIT Press, Cambridge, Mass.

[35] Sleeman, D.H., "A Problem Solving Monitor for a Deductive Reasoning Task", Intern. j. of Man-machine Studies, 7 (2), 183-211, 1975.

[36] Sleeman, D. H., Hendley, R, and Ace, J., "A System which analyzes Complex Explanations", in Intern. J. of Man-machine Studies, 11, pp. 123-144.

[37] Stefik, M. J., et al., "Integrating Access-Oriented Programming into a Multiparadigm environment" IEEE Software, Vol3, No. 1, pp 10-18, January 1986.

[38] Stefik and Bobrow, 1986, "Object-Oriented Programming: Themes and Variations", AI Mag. 6, 4, 40-62.

[39] Steier, D. M., and E. Kant, "The Roles of Execution and Analysis in Algorithm Design", IEEE Trans. Software Eng., Vol. SE-11, No. 11, Nov. 1985, pp. 1375- 1386.

[40] Stone, D. C., "A Modular Approach to Program Visualization in Computer Science Instruction", in 1987 ACM Proc. of Human-Computer Interaction, pp. 516-522.

[41] Teitelman, W., "A Display Oriented Programmer's Assistant", in Int. J. Man-machine Studies (1979) 11, 157-187, Acad. Press Inc., pp. 157-187.

[42] Yankelovich, N., Haan, B., Meyrowitz, N., Drucker, S., "Intermedia: The Concept and the Construction of a Seamless Information Environment", in IEEE Computer, Jan. 1988, pp. 81-96.

The ALGO Architecture

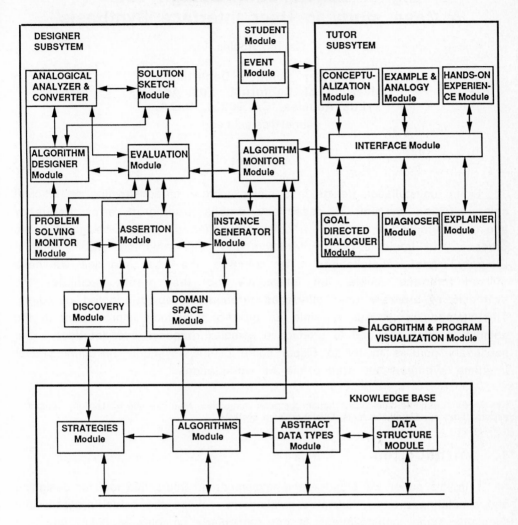

Figure 1: An Object-Oriented Architecture for Algorithm Design Visualization

Signal Constellation Design Tool:
A Case study in User Interface Synthesis

Gabriel Robins

Computer Science Department
University of California, Los Angeles
Los Angeles, CA 90024, U.S.A.
gabriel@cs.ucla.edu

Abstract

Signal constellation design is a major subtask of constructing an efficient communication system; it essentially entails trading-off error frequency against information throughput, a chief occupation of modem designers. We propose and implement an interactive tool for designing and simulating arbitrary signal constellations. To construct the user interface we have utilized Interface Builder, an interactive tool that greatly facilitates the synthesis of arbitrary user interfaces through an object-oriented paradigm. This methodology makes possible an order-of-magnitude improvement in the amount of effort required to produce a complex graphical user interface. Our secondary goal is to try to dispel some of the mystique surrounding user interface synthesis on state-of-the-art workstations.

Keywords: User interface tools, Human computer instruction, Man-machine interaction, Computer-assisted learning, Simulation tools, Object-oriented systems.

1. Introduction

In this paper we propose and implement an interactive tool for designing and simulating arbitrary signal constellations. While the actual program that simulates signal constellations is not particularly complex in itself, the user interface to this code is by contrast quite elaborate. To design and construct this user interface we have used Interface Builder, an interactive tool that greatly facilitates the synthesis of user interfaces through an object-oriented paradigm. Using the Interface Builder package and the Signal Constellation Design Tool as the target prototype, we demonstrate how an order-of-magnitude improvement can be achieved in the amount of effort required to produce a complex user interface.

A secondary goal of this paper is to try to dispel some of the mystique surrounding user interface synthesis on state-of-the-art workstations. Many otherwise informed researchers have very little experience in user-interface design, and consequently view user interface design as some sort of a black art, best left to specialized hackers to dabble in. By user interface we mean a collection of functionality (running on a graphics-capable workstation) that interacts with the user in a friendly manner via menus, scroll bars, control buttons, icons, mouse clicks, key strokes, etc.

Our intention is to show that, quite to the contrary of these myths, given the proper tools and methodology, the synthesis of complex user interfaces could become rather trivial. As a case in point, the user interface described in this document was implemented on a MacIntosh, and required only several days of coding, including the overhead in learning how to use the Interface Builder. As a by-product of our inquiry, we have synthesized an interactive tool for computer-assisted learning in the area of signal-constellation design.

2. Signal Constellation Design

In designing an efficient communication scheme for band-limited channels, invariably of chief concern are the effects of noise, distortion, and other kind of interference on the system [Forney, Gallager, Lang, Longstaff, and Qureshi]. To combat such interference, and while still aiming to achieve high throughput, one must carefully design an appropriate signal constellation [Carlyle] [Schwartz] [Sklar].

The task of signal constellation design essentially entails trading off error frequency against information throughput and is the chief concern of modem designers. Our goal is to implement a signal constellation design and simulation tool; our tool is to graphically display and simulate a signal constellation in two dimensions, allowing the user to visually observe the progressing simulation under interactive modifications of the noise and distortion parameters of the system.

2.1. The Desired Functionality

In this section we describe in greater detail the functionality that we would like our Signal Constellation Design Tool to exhibit. Later we explain how this functionality was actually achieved in the implementation.

First, we would like to allow the user to select any of a number of "canned" standard signal constellations. For example, the user may elect to simulate an N-in-a-circle signal constellation and observe its performance under various levels of noise and distortion. Next the user may wish to select a certain probability distribution that would control the generation of random signal points; for example, the user may wish to select a Gaussian distribution with a specified variance.

Now the signal constellation is to be displayed on the screen and the simulation may proceed. During the simulation, the user may interactively modify a number of system parameters, such as the phase jitter and the additive white Gaussian noise level. This would be accomplished by dragging "scroll-bars" identified with the corresponding parameters, or by directly typing in the desired numerical values.

Using a random number generator, random signals are generated, according to the probability distribution function specified by the user, and are then plotted against the signal constellation diagram. After a few moments, a cumulative scatter-plot of the received signals will form, giving the user an indication of how the chosen signal constellation is performing under the given distortion parameters. A cumulative total of the number of errors encountered so far is to be displayed, as is the empirically derived error-probability (the number of errors encountered divided by the number of signals transmitted.)

The various commands should be accessible via clicking appropriate buttons, or alternatively via menus or keystrokes. In addition, the user should be provided with some on-line information describing the concepts of signal constellation design, as well as the operation of the simulation tool. Such a facility has proven to be quite useful in many successful software systems.

2.2. The Main Panel

To make the appearance of the user interface more concrete, Figure 1 gives an illustration of how the main panel may appear. Towards the left we observe the main drawing area, where the signal constellation appears; in this case the signal constellation itself consists of 20 signal points evenly distributed on 4 concentric circles. The interference parameter are located near to top right corner, as are the scroll bars and click boxes used to modify them. The mouse-sensitive "buttons" are used to invoke commands. Towards the lower right there is a printing area where the run-time statistics of the simulation appear.

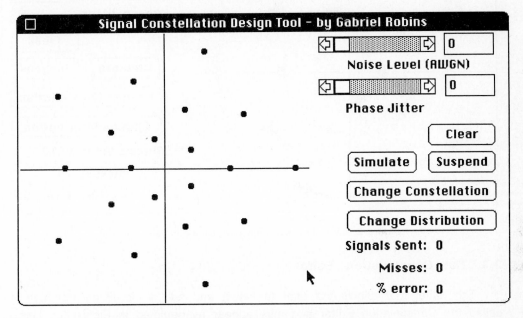

Figure 1: the main panel of the Signal Constellation Design Tool

The user may invoke several operations simply by clicking the corresponding buttons. In addition, all of these commands are also available from the pull-down menus, as well as through keystrokes (i.e. single character keyboard inputs). We would also like to have at the top of the display a pull-down menu bar, representing other various commands that the user may invoke; the menu bar is not visible in this diagram.

After a simulation has been underway for some time, the main panel might appear as in Figure 2. The clouds around the signal points represent the randomly generated signals that fell around the actual signal constellation points. In this particular simulation, given the specified noise parameters, we are observing an error rate of over one percent, an undesirable situation.

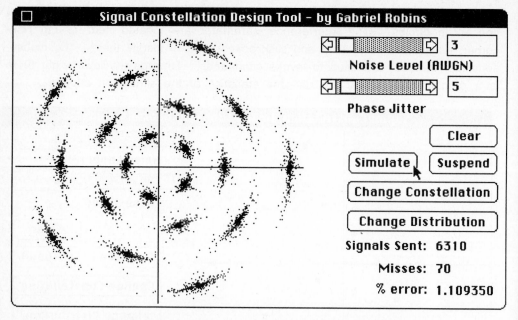

Figure 2: the main panel a few minutes into the simulation

2.3. The Constellation Editor

The panel that allows the user to select and edit a signal constellation is called the Constellation Editor and may appear as depicted in Figure 3. Using the clickable items at the top left corner of the panel, the user may select one of several "canned" signal constellations, parametrized by the variables M and N; these parameters are also user-specified: to change them, the user simply clicks in the corresponding box and types in the new value. An optional editing grid is available, and may be either rectangular or polar; the purpose of this grid is to make the manual placement of individual constellation points more precise. The resolution of the grid is user-controllable: in the case of a rectangular grid, the number of horizontal and vertical lines may be specified, and in the case of a polar grid, the number of circles and rays may be specified.

The user may add or delete constellation points, redraw the display, or obtain on-line help, simply by clicking the corresponding buttons. In addition, all of these commands should also be available from the pull-down menus, as well as through keystrokes (i.e., single character keyboard inputs). Note that one of the points of the constellation is highlighted; this happens when the mouse is clicked anywhere in the drawing area, whereupon the closest point to the click coordinates becomes highlighted. A "delete" command would subsequently remove the highlighted point, while an "add" command would wait for a new mouse click, whereupon a new point would be added to the constellation at the coordinates corresponding to the location of that click.

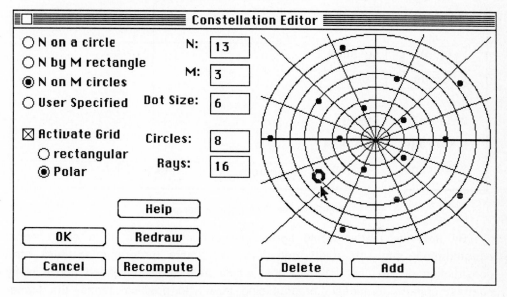

Figure 3: the Constellation Editor panel

On-line help should be available from any panel. The "OK" command saves the current signal constellation and uses it in all future simulations, while the "Cancel" command reverts back to the previous signal constellation, ignoring the effects of the current editing session.

2.4. The Distribution Editor

The panel that allows the user to define and edit a signal constellation is called the Distribution Editor and may appear as in Figure 4. The user may select from either a uniform distribution on a given interval, or a Gaussian distribution with a given variance. The "Plot" command starts generating and plotting random points according to the distribution specified, while "suspend" stops this generation process. The "graph" command draws a graph of the probability density function in the X/Y plane. The average X and Y coordinates for the points generated so far are displayed to the lower left area of the panel.

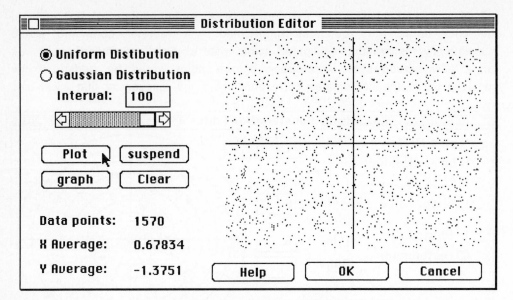

Figure 4: the Distribution Editor panel

By now the reader would agree that although simulating a given signal constellation may by itself constitute a simple programming task, the construction of the user interface that would behave as described above is by contrast quite a formidable programming task. In practical terms, the former could be easily accomplished in a couple of hours, while the later may take many weeks to implement. Using the Interface Builder tool and an object-oriented programming methodology, all of these tasks were implemented on a MacIntosh in only several days of coding (including the overhead time that was spent reading the manuals and learning how to use the software).

3. Using the Interface Builder Tool

The process of constructing the user interface using the Interface Builder mostly entails interactively specifying the various menus, dialogue-boxes, scroll-bars, and menu-buttons, as well as where they should appear on the screen, and what should happen when each is clicked, selected, or dragged. The latter is accomplished by providing the relevant program code associated with each object. The Interface Builder performs all of the user-specified functions at the appropriate times by usurping the workstation's "main event loop" and substituting the user-specified functionality in place of the defaults.

The result is an attractive user interface which is easy to build and modify. The Interface Builder tool was pioneered by ExperTelligence Inc. several years ago, and only recently has met with competition when Apple Inc. produced the HyperCard program [Goodman]. Although both the Interface Builder and HyperCard have a large body of functionality in common, each can accomplish things the other can not, and both have their drawbacks. For example, HyperCard is not well-integrated into a standard professional programming environment, and can only display one stack card on the screen at a time. On the other hand, the Interface Builder Tool (as implemented for the MacIntosh) is currently restricted to work strictly within ExperCommon LISP.

The importance of such tools has only recently been fully appreciated, although it has been known for quite some time that most of the effort associated with constructing computer software is invariably spent in programming the user interface; moreover, in many cases the user interface directly determines the utility of a piece of software [Kaczmarek] [Robins].

3.1. The Methodology of Interface Builder

Interface Builder uses an object-oriented paradigm to create a user interface. Objects are general entities such as windows, bitmaps, icons, records, scroll bars, buttons, text strings, regions, points, lines, files, and mouse clicks, among others. Objects communicate by sending *messages* to one another, and each object has a set of messages that it knows how to respond to; for example, a "redraw" message sent to an icon will cause the icon to redraw itself on the display. In addition to various useful default messages (or *methods*, in LISP parlance), a user may specify additional hand-crafted methods to be associated with an object. Messages may contain zero or more arguments and are essentially equivalent to function calls.

An Interface Builder *editor* is a panel consisting of a collection of objects, each with an associated set of methods. In addition to methods, an object may also have some local variables that may store arbitrary values, including other objects. When an object is defined, it is specified to be a child of some other object, and thus automatically inherits all the methods that apply to its parent; in addition, new methods may be added to the child, specializing it from its parent. An object may have multiple parents, in which case it inherits all of their parents' methods. The astute reader will note that this schema necessitates a conflict-resolution or priority scheme when methods clash through inheritance, but these details are not particularly relevant in this discussion.

As a concrete example, let us consider the Distribution Editor described earlier, whose panel inside Interface Builder appears as shown in Figure 5.

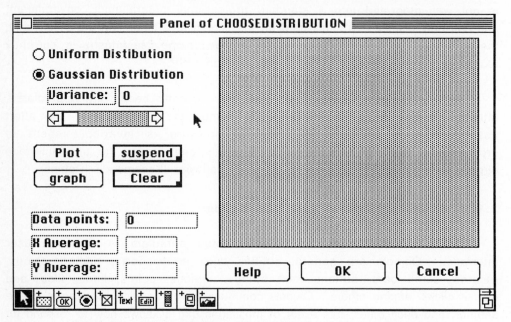

Figure 5: an Interface Builder editor defining the distribution-editor panel

Each visible item is an object to which we may send various messages, and with which there is an associated functionality that is invoked whenever (during execution) it is clicked, dragged, resized, etc. The icons at the lower left side are Interface Builder commands and are used to create the various types of objects that they represent pictorially. Once such an object is created, it may be further modified, resized, and redefined.

For example, the "click" method of the main drawing area may be specified by double-clicking on the main drawing area and filling in the required fields in the resulting dialogue panel, as shown in Figure 6. In this example, the function

REDRAW-MAIN-CANVAS is a piece of code that will clear out and redraw that print area.

Scroll bars of arbitrary sizes may be similarly created and placed in arbitrary window locations by specifying an appropriate "click" method, as well as minimum and maximum values for the scroll interval; an example of this is given in Figure 7.

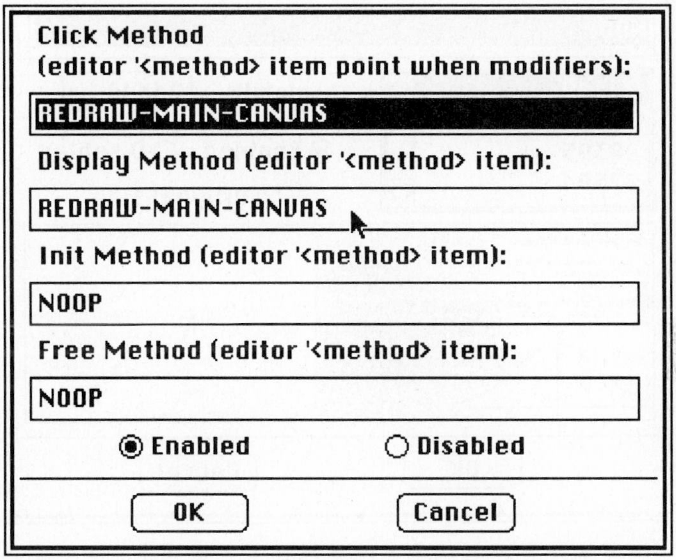

Figure 6: defining a click-method for a "drawing-area" object

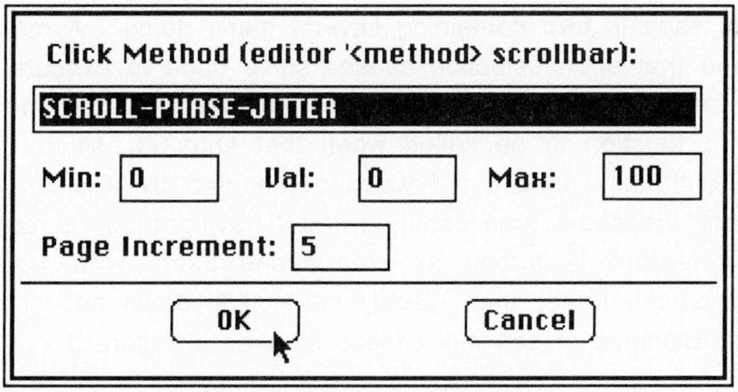

Figure 7: defining a scroll bar

Arbitrary icons and bitmaps may also be included as part of the editor panel being constructed. This is done by a dialogue as shown in Figure 8, in which a previously created bitmap is designated as part of the display in one of the Distribution Editor help screens.

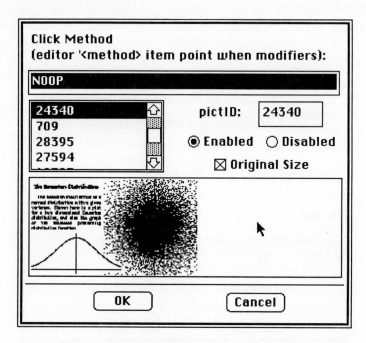

Figure 8: inserting a bitmap into an editor window

An editor panel has associated with it a pull-down menu bar containing several menus, each in turn containing several menu items. A menu item is an entry in a menu that upon selection causes some code to execute. Menus are constructed interactively in Interface Builder: for each named menu entry the user specifies a function to be called when that entry is selected. In addition the user may optionally specify a keystroke (denoted by a slash and a letter) that will execute the same functionality *without* having to go through the menu system. This feature is aimed at experienced users who would prefer to memorize a keystroke rather than waste time pulling down and clicking a menu item. A sample dialogue of defining a menu is given in Figure 9.

Proceeding in this manner, panels for the rest of the Signal Constellation Design Tool were constructed.

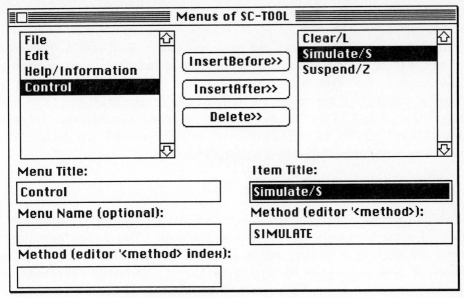

Figure 9: defining a menu in Interface Builder

4. Correctness and Functional Orthogonality

Since the underlying paradigm of Interface Builder is object-oriented in nature, a certain functional orthogonality exists in the finished software in the following sense: messages sent to an object do not directly affect any other object, and moreover objects can only communicate by passing messages to one another. Hence the execution flow of control is highly constrained and therefore the formation of side-effects, although possible, is nevertheless tightly controlled.

If a set of objects has been debugged and is found to operate correctly, adding new objects is not likely to affect the correctness of any of the old objects. Moreover, the functionality of any of the objects may be invoked at any point in time via an appropriate message from any other object. Although at first glance this would seem to give rise to a certain "non-determinism" in execution, in practice, the programmer will remain quite informed about what code should/would execute under various circumstances, and experience has shown that if the programmer has adhered to the standard object-oriented programming conventions, the "right thing" usually happens even in the presence of pathological boundary-conditions.

The programmer's code does not have to concern itself with a "main-event-loop" nor with dispatching certain event-dependent functions, because Interface Builder usurps the system's "main-event-loop" already and does all the necessary dispatching based on the programmer's specifications. This takes much of the complexity out of the application code, a complexity that would otherwise have had to be duplicated from scratch in each application. Thus considerable programmer effort is saved by this scheme.

5. The On-Line Help Screens

As part of our user interface design, we have provided a mechanism for presenting some interactive on-line help to the user. This on-line help may be invoked via clicking a button, pulling a menu, or pressing a key. The help consists of sets of one of more screens full of information, directions, and diagrams. The user may jump between these screens, or quit and return to the original mode from which help was called. In order to illustrate this discussion, and also to further clarify some of the concepts relevant to signal constellation design, we give in Figures 11-13 a few of the help screens included in the user interface.

6. The Software/Hardware Used

The Signal Constellation Design Tool is implemented in ExperCommon LISP [Bollay, McConnell, Reali, and Ritz]. The user interface was constructed with ExperInterface Builder, an interactive package that allows a user to quickly and easily design a graphical user interface from scratch in an object-oriented paradigm [Hullot]. The hardware configuration used was the MacIntosh Plus with 2 megabytes of memory and a 20-megabyte hard disk.

The annotated Common LISP sources for the Signal Constellation Design Tool are available upon request. Although this tool was developed on the MacIntosh, it should be readily portable to any system which supports Common LISP and reasonable window and graphics conventions. To obtain the sources, either in hardcopy and on a MacIntosh diskette, please contact the author at P.O. Box 8369, Van Nuys, CA 91409-8369.

Additive white Gaussian noise (AWGN)

The term *noise* refers to <u>unwanted</u> electrical signals that are superimposed on the transmitted signal and tend to obscure it; it limits the receivers ability to make correct symbol decisions, and thereby limits the rate of information transmission.

Usually we model noise as being of the <u>additive white Gaussian</u> type; that is, as a random process whose value n(t) at time t is statistically characterized by the Gaussian density function p(n):

$$p(n) = \frac{1}{\sigma\sqrt{2\pi}} \exp\left(-\frac{1}{2}\left(\frac{n}{\sigma}\right)^2 \right)$$

where σ^2 is the variance and the mean is zero.

[▲ Next]   [Quit]

Figure 11: explanation of additive white Gaussian noise

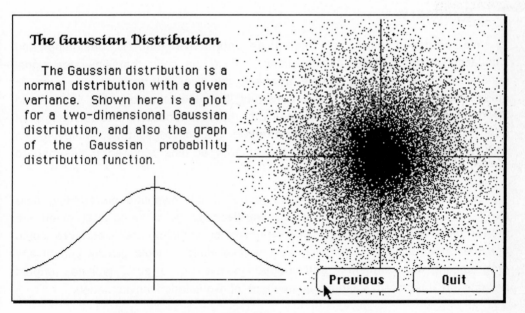

The Gaussian Distribution

The Gaussian distribution is a normal distribution with a given variance. Shown here is a plot for a two-dimensional Gaussian distribution, and also the graph of the Gaussian probability distribution function.

[Previous]   [Quit]

Figure 12: plot of a 2-dimensional Gaussian distribution

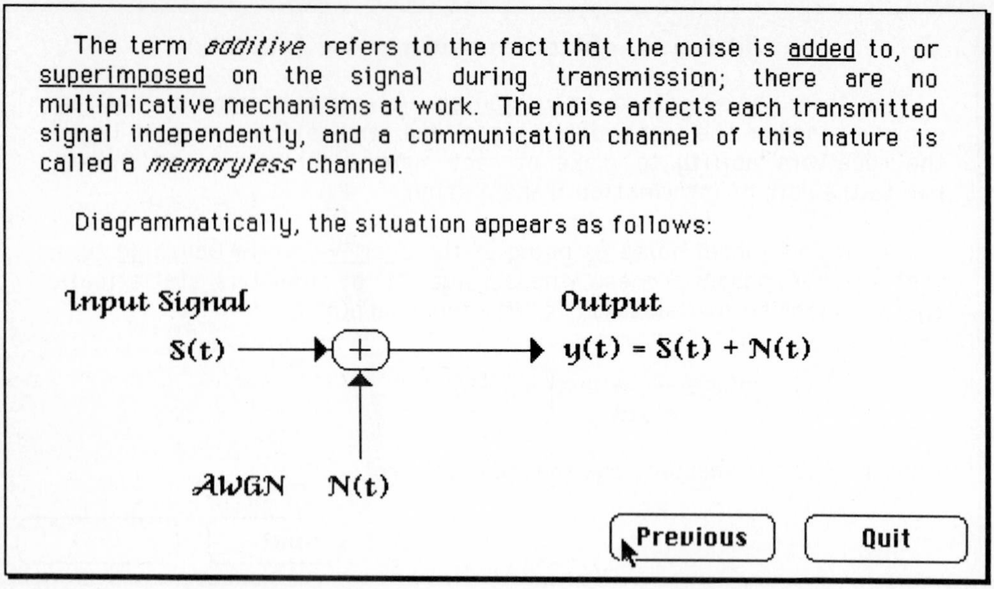

The term *additive* refers to the fact that the noise is <u>added</u> to, or <u>superimposed</u> on the signal during transmission; there are no multiplicative mechanisms at work. The noise affects each transmitted signal independently, and a communication channel of this nature is called a *memoryless* channel.

Diagrammatically, the situation appears as follows:

Input Signal   Output

S(t) ──────▶(+)──────────▶ y(t) = S(t) + N(t)

AWGN   N(t)

Previous   Quit

Figure 13: explanation of superposition of noise and signal

7. Summary

We proposed and implemented an interactive tool for designing and simulating arbitrary signal constellations. While the code that simulates signal constellations is relatively simple in itself, the user interface to this code is quite complex. To design and construct the user interface we have used Interface Builder, an interactive tool that greatly facilitates the synthesis of user interfaces through an object-oriented methodology, thus achieving an order-of-magnitude improvement in the amount of time required if this had to be accomplished starting from scratch.

Hopefully we have also dispelled some of the mystique surrounding user interface synthesis on state-of-the-art workstations by showing that given the proper tools and methodology, the synthesis of complex user interfaces could become rather trivial. Tools such as Interface Builder would greatly benefit any programming environments, and indeed in the future such facilities should become an integrated standard component of workstation environments.

8.   Acknowledgements

I thank Professor Jack Carlyle for igniting my interest in this subject, and for his thoughtful advice on numerous occasions. I also thank ExperTelligence Inc. for providing the software which made possible the implementation of the Signal Constellation Design Tool.

9.   Bibliography

Bollay, D., McConnell, J., Reali, R., Ritz, D., ExperCommon LISP Documentation: Volume I, II, and III, The ExperTelligence Press, Santa Barbara, California, 1987.

Carlyle, J., Analog Transmission/Reception for Digital Communication, CS214 Class Notes, Computer Science Department, University of California, Los Angeles, Winter, 1988,

Forney, D., Gallager, R., Lang, G., Longstaff, F., Qureshi, S., Efficient Modulation for Band-Limited Channels, IEEE Journal on Selected Areas in Communication, Vol. SAC-2, No. 5, September, 1985.

Goodman, D., The Complete HyperCard Handbook, Bantham Books, New York, 1987.

Hullot, J., ExperInterface Builder Documentation, The ExperTelligence Press, Santa Barbara, California, 1987.

Kaczmarek, T., Mark, W., & Wilczynski, D., The CUE Project, Proceedings of SoftFair, July, 1983.

Robins, G. The ISI Grapher: A Portable Tool for Displaying Graphs Pictorially, Invited Talk in Symboliikka '87, Helsinki, Finland, August, 17-18, 1987. Reprinted in Multicomputer Vision, Levialdi, S., Chapter 12, Academic Press, London, 1988.

Schwartz, M., Information Transmission, Modulation, and Noise, McGraw-Hill, Third Edition, pp. 212-235, 1980.

Sklar, B., Digital Communications: Fundamentals and Applications, Prentice Hall, New Jersey, pp. 412-424, 1988.

DESIGN AND IMPLEMENTATION OF INTERACTIVE PROGRAMS FOR EDUCATION IN ENGINEERING AND NATURAL SCIENCES

Walter Schaufelberger
Project Center IDA, Swiss Federal Institute of Technology
ETH Zentrum, CH-8092 Zurich, Switzerland

Abstract: The availability of reliable and cheap software is crucial for a successful use of computers in teaching. An environment that has been implemented for the generation of software for teaching purposes at ETH Zurich is described in the paper. It is based on Modula-2 and allows the realization of highly interactive programs running on Macintosh and IBM compatibles.

Keywords: Computer aided instruction, DialogMachine, interactive software, layers of software, Modula-2 programming, simulation and animation in teaching, software design, tools for learning and teaching.

Introduction

ETH Zurich is an engineering school with some 10,000 students. A major project for an integrated use of personal computers and workstations in all areas of teaching is under way since 1986 with the aim of installing and operating 2000 small computers for teaching by 1991. About 1000 computers are already installed and in regular use now (about 400 Macintosh, about 400 IBM compatibles, and about 200 workstations (SUN, VAX etc.)). A Project Center (IDA : Informatik dient allen) was formed in 1986 as a consulting unit for staff members, and several pilot projects for advanced uses of computers in teaching were initiated in 1985. This paper is mainly based on the work of the consulting unit and on experience gained in a pilot project on simulation and modelling in natural and engineering sciences.

Interactive software for animation and simulation

Software is important when computers are used in education. The following are typical applications that we have implemented for teaching, especially for computer science, natural and engineering sciences.

- ModelWorks, a complete simulation environment
- Differential equation solvers
- World2, a training program implementing Forrester's world model
- Desktop calculators for drawing graphs of functions
- A set of training programs for control engineering students, containing:
  - tuning of two term controllers
  - antiwindup problems in two term controllers
  - state variable feedback and observer design
  - decision table analysis
  - petri net simulation and analysis
  - rule based controller design (small expert system shells)
- A set of training programs for computer science basics, containing:
  - sorting algorithms
  - random number generation
  - iteration and recursion
  - real arithmetic
- A set of programs for natural science students (population dynamics) :
  - stability, explaining Lotka-Volterra equations
  - Euler integration techniques
  - Drosophila
  - Automaton
  - Identification

Our own designs are based on Modula-2 and on the very efficient one pass compiler developed by the group of N. Wirth (1988). Beside these we use some public domain programs (especially Matlab and Xlisp), programs implemented by other groups within ETH, and software for which we obtained site-licences.

A Hypercard stack describing some 30 programs developed at ETH for teaching is available from the project center IDA.

The software we produce and describe in this paper is mainly used to replace paper and pencil exercises during the exercise periods. The course material is presented in the traditional way during lectures where the theory is explained and where a general attitude towards the problem area and the methods available is developed. Based on this knowledge, students then spend one to two hours on computers to apply the theory to a practical problem. These problems may be formulated much more realistically since we use computers. Many more attempts to solve a given problem can be made, and more complex cases can be looked at. These exercises are not used to replace laboratory work, which also plays an important role in our educational system (Mansour and Schaufelberger, 1989).

Layers of software

The availability of good and reasonably priced software will be crucial for the future of computer assisted instruction. As an example, the following summarizes our views on software in the area of signals, systems and control. From our teaching in these areas four distinct layers of software can be distinguished:

Layer 1: Specific training programs
These are programs used in a specific situation during the education. They serve no other purpose than to aid the student in mastering a certain subject as i.e. tuning of a controller or comparison of sorting algorithms.

Layer 2: Mini tools
Mini tools can be used in different situations and in several courses. They allow handling simple tasks such as drawing the graph of a function, inverting matrices of restricted order, solving differential equations with limited order etc.

Layer 3: Tools
Tools may be used for professional work, without necessarily providing a fully developed environment as the professional tools. Typical examples are matrix calculation or simulation environments.

Layer 4: Professional tools
These are the fully developed systems usually marketed by software houses. Typical examples are ProMatlab, CTRLC, ACSL, Mathematica.

It is hoped that agreement may be reached that software up to layer 3 must be made available for all students in the corresponding disciplines (i.e. engineering) at minimal cost in a way that this software may be used freely on machines belonging to institutions or to the students. At the Project Center IDA we strongly work towards this goal and we do have a corresponding environment available for all students of ETH at no cost. Software at layer 4 is also used in many educational programs (CAD, VLSI design), but the number of stations on which this software must be available is limited.

We will illustrate and clarify the meaning of these layers by providing some examples from system and control education. A training program for two term controllers as shown in fig.1 is a typical example of a program at layer 1. A step response such as the one represented in fig. 2 shows the use of a program at layer 2, the same for the van der Pol differential equation that is entered into the system in fig. 3 and produces results shown in fig. 4 . A step response of a state variable feedback controller obtained from ModelWorks (fig. 5 and listing 1) demonstrates the use of programs at layer 3, where Matlab of C. Moler (1981) that is still one of our favorites is also positioned (fig. 6). Programs at layer 4 are also used in education but due to licensing conditions and to complexity use is usually restricted to students projects.

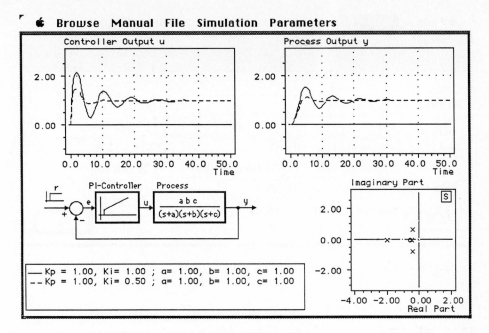

Fig. 1: Screen of a training program for two-term controllers:
Students may change controller and process parameters and run simulations. The manual part contains a manual and the exercises.

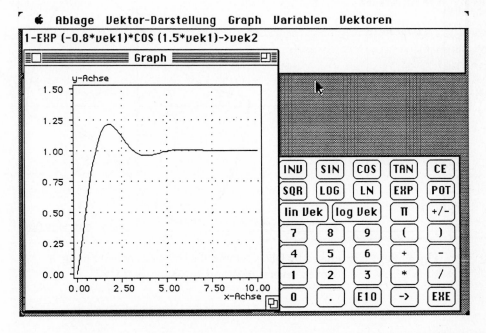

Fig. 2: A calculator for drawing graphs of functions composed from the graphic keyboard.

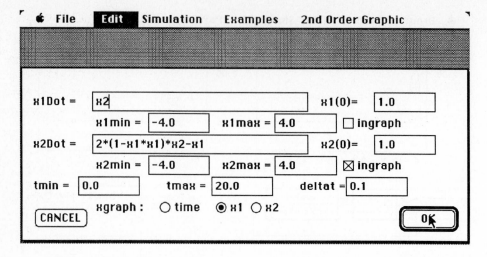

Fig. 3: Mask for entering second order differential equations into DESolver.

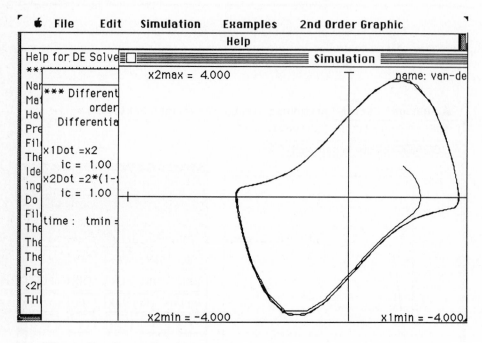

Fig. 4: Results produced by DESolver and the equations entered in fig. 3
shown in several overlapping windows

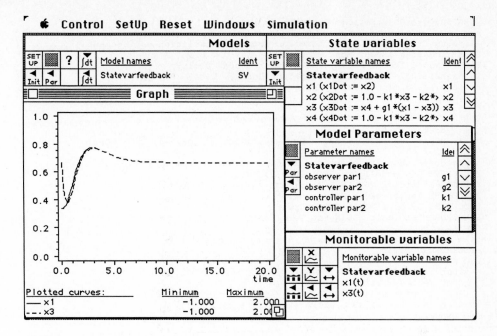

Fig. 5: Simulation of a state variable feedback control system with observer.

```
         < M A T L A B >
  Macintosh Version 2 of 20/10/87

HELP ▶ is available

<>
HELP
 TYPE HELP FOLLOWED BY
 INTRO   (TO GET STARTED)
 NEWS    (RECENT REVISIONS)
 ABS   ANS   ATAN  BASE  CHAR  CHOL  CHOP  CLEA  COND  CONJ  COS
 DET   DIAG  DIAR  DISP  EDIT  EIG   ELSE  END   EPS   EXEC  EXIT
 EXP   EYE   FILE  FLOP  FLPS  FOR   FUN   HESS  HILB  IF    IMAG
 INV   KRON  LINE  LOAD  LOG   LONG  LU    MACR  MAGI  NORM  ONES
 ORTH  PINV  PLOT  POLY  PRIN  PROD  QR    RAND  RANK  RCON  RAT
 REAL  RETU  RREF  ROOT  ROUN  SAVE  SCHU  SHOR  SEMI  SIN   SIZE
 SQRT  STOP  SUM   SVD   TRIL  TRIU  USER  WHAT  WHIL  WHO   WHY
 < > ( ) = . , ; \ / ' + - * :

<>
```

Fig. 6: Working environment of Matlab

```
MODULE StateVarObserver; (*WS 29/Mar/88*)

(* Imports from the DialogMachine and from the simulation environment *)
  FROM SimMaster IMPORT RunSimMaster;
  FROM SimBase IMPORT DeclM, IntegrationMethod, DeclSV,
    StashFiling, Tabulation, Graphing, DeclMV, DeclP, RTCType,
    Model, SetSimTime, SetMonInterval, SetIntegrationStep;

(* variable declarations *)
  VAR
    m: Model;
    x1, x1Dot, x2, x2Dot, x3, x3Dot, x4, x4Dot,g1 ,g2, k1, k2 : REAL;

(* procedures that are only used in more advanced models *)
  PROCEDURE DoNoModelInfo; BEGIN END DoNoModelInfo;
  PROCEDURE Initial; BEGIN END Initial;
  PROCEDURE Input; BEGIN END Input;
  PROCEDURE Output; BEGIN END Output;
  PROCEDURE Terminal; BEGIN END Terminal;

(* the differential equations *)
  PROCEDURE Dynamic;
  BEGIN
      x1Dot := x2;
      x2Dot := 1.0 - k1*x3 - k2*x4;
      x3Dot := x4 + g1*(x1 - x3);
      x4Dot := 1.0 - k1*x3 - k2*x4 + g2*(x1 - x3);
  END Dynamic;

(* definiton of objects *)
  PROCEDURE Variables;
  BEGIN
      (* state variables with names,initial value,range etc *)
      DeclSV(x1, x1Dot,0.0, -1.0, +2.0,
        "x1 (x1Dot := x2)", "x1", "");
      DeclSV(x2, x2Dot,0.0, -1.0, +2.0,
        "x2 (x2Dot := 1.0 - k1*x3 - k2*x4)", "x2", "");
      DeclSV(x3, x3Dot,1.0, -1.0, +2.0,
        "x3 (x3Dot := x4 + g1*(x1 - x3))", "x3", "");
      DeclSV(x4, x4Dot,0.0, -1.0, +2.0,
        "x4 (x4Dot := 1.0 - k1*x3 - k2*x4 + g2*(x1 - x3))", "x4", "");

      (* measurable variables for output *)
      DeclMV(x1,-1.0,2.0,"x1(t) ","x1","",notOnFile,notInTable,isY);
      DeclMV(x3,-1.0,2.0,"x3(t) ","x3","",notOnFile,notInTable,isY);

      (* parameters for observer and controller *)
      DeclP(g1,4.0,-10.0,10.0,rtc,"observer par1","g1","");
      DeclP(g2,4.0,-10.0,10.0,rtc,"observer par2","g2","");
      DeclP(k1,1.0,-10.0,10.0,rtc,"controller par1","k1","");
      DeclP(k2,2.0,-10.0,10.0,rtc,"controller par2","k2","");
  END Variables;

(* definition of the complete model *)
  PROCEDURE ModelDeclaration;
  BEGIN
      DeclM(m, RungeKutta4, Initial, Input, Output, Dynamic, Terminal,
            Variables, "Statevarfeedback", "SV", DoNoModelInfo);
      SetSimTime(0.0,20.0); SetMonInterval(0.2); SetIntegrationStep(0.05);
  END ModelDeclaration;

BEGIN
  (* start of the interactive simulation environment with the model *)
  RunSimMaster(ModelDeclaration);
END StateVarObserver.
```

Listing 1: Definition of the differential equations for state variable feedback control

Design of interactive software

The above mentioned programs must be very easy to understand and to handle if we want our students to accept the computer as a new interactive medium for learning. It should be a pleasure to use the programs and little time should be lost in learning how to use and operate them.

On the other side, programs that serve only a very limited purpose in the education and that for example are used only for one hour must be developed with a limited effort that is justified by the results obtained.

From this we need something like a rapid prototyping environment that yields high quality software, and we must support staff members that are not computer scientists with concepts and the corresponding tools.

We advocate the use of a user's model of the system approach as outlined in Norman and Draper (1986) as the basic design idea for man machine interfaces.

Typical models that we we have repeatedly applied are:
- the textbook model (the teaching program behaves like a textbook)
- the laboratory model (the screen looks like a laboratory bench)
- the calculator model (imitating the behaviour of a desk top calculator)

These models can easily be explained to the students. From our experience we lose about ten minutes for general informations when the first program is introduced.

If a model is used in the design, tools may be prepared that allow easy implementation and considerably shorten the development time. To this effect a frame program generator has been implemented to generate the module structure directly from the description of the menus and commands in the textbook model (Vancso, Fischlin, 1988).

The environment described so far is used to produce programs that are used in a specific way during the course. The integration of these isolated programs into an environment is done via Hypercard leading to what might be called electronic textbooks, where the basic material is presented and from where the methods in the programs may be accessed. For control engineering education a matrix environment (Matlab) has been linked with a simulation environment (Model Works). Hypercard eases the access to programs and the parameter transfer between them and provides a possibility for the student to link his or her own work into the course material.

Implementation: the DialogMachine

The DialogMachine is the major product of the pilot project on modelling and simulation mentioned above. It is based on Modula-2 and consists of a set of 12 modules with more than 600 procedures that support programming of interactive "Macintosh-like" software. Standard reactions are preprogrammed, so that only application specific parts must be supplied by the programmer. The concept of abstract data types is widely used and the general scheduler linking keyboard and mouse input to the procedures in the program is also part of the package so that message passing programming can be used. The development time of a typical small simulation or animation program has been shortened to a few days by this procedure. The DialogMachine is used in many places inside and outside of ETH. Version 1.0 is available for the Macintosh and will be available for IBM compatibles in Spring 1989 and for Ataris shortly afterwards. Figures 7 and 8 show screen dumps from "sorting algorithms" for Macintosh and IBM compatibles. We believe that this is one of the first possibilities to generate programs for different families of computers from the same source code. This is important for us because we have to support different lines of personal computers. Every staff member has in principle the freedom of this choice.

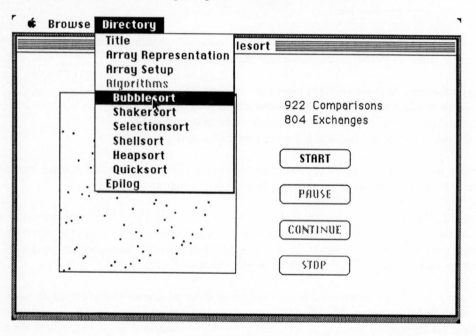

Fig. 7: Sorting algorithms: A program for comparing the performance of different sorting algorithms (Macintosh version)

It took about three man/woman years by senior and junior programmers to implement the DialogMachine in Modula-2 on the Macintosh and one man year of a senior software developer to transfer it to the IBM PC where we use JPI Top Speed Modula-2 and GEM. The following brief description of the major modules provides some insight into the design, which is strongly based on the concepts of abstract data types and message passing programming. As mentioned above, the general scheduler linking mouse and keyboard input to the procedures in the program is part of the environment, providing standard reactions to many events. Only user specific parts must be coded and linked into the system. To do this, the following modules are available:

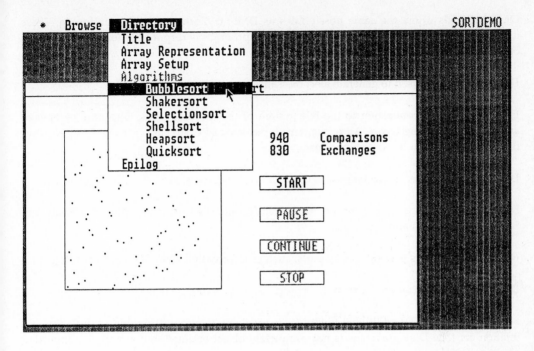

Fig. 8: Sorting algorithms (IBM version)

DMMaster is the main module that controls all actions, especially user input via mouse and keyboard. As far as possible DMMaster reacts directly on events or passes these on to other parts of the DialogMachine. If this is not possible user procedures are called.

DMMenus supports installation and use of menus and commands. The procedures that are activated by the commands can be written completely independently and are then linked into the system.

DMWindows serves for installation and use of windows (with/without scrollbars, close box, zoom box, resizable, moveable etc.). After activation of a window by CreateWindow(..) the DialogMachine takes care of it.

DMWindowIO offers text and graphical output as well as mouse input in windows.Several coordinate systems are supported and texts can be positioned in the graphical output.

DMEntryForms provides possibilities for modal dialogs. Characters, Integers, Cardinals and Reals can be entered with syntax checks. String input is also possible and check boxes, push buttons, radio buttons and scrollbars are provided. Modal dialogs must be terminated with ok or cancel.

DMEditFields offers the same possibilities as DMEntryForms in non-modal mode. These dialogs can be terminated at will, the application program is responsible for the consistency of the data.

DMAlerts may be used to generate alert messages.

DMFiles offers a connection to the File system of the machine used. Files may be opened and closed via dialog boxes. All elementary types such as Characters, Strings, Integers, Cardinals and Reals can be written and read.

DMLanguages supports the languages used for error messages etc.

DMConversions contains routines for the conversion of Cardinals, Integers, Reals and Longreals to Strings and vice versa.

DMSystems exports system specific parts, such as information about the hardware (screen).

DMBase is the interface to hardware, firmware and operating system.

Beside this core many additional modules are available to support graphics, simulation, animation etc. The DialogMachine is not completely object oriented, but a module supporting object oriented programming is also available.

Experience

Part of the software described above has been in use in different departments of ETH for more than two years. Classrooms with 15 to 60 Macintosh computers are available for problem solving sessions for larger classes.

The programs that we develop are usually accompanied by an extensive description. It is our experience that we spend about one third of the total development time for the basic design, another third for the documentation, and only one third for programming. Simple programs can be developed in a few hours. It took about two weeks for the two-term controller and several months for the world model.

The students are pleased by the fact that our programs are easy to use, and spend most of their time on the assigned problem (control, natural science, computer science) and not on questions of how to operate the computer or the program. An introduction of 10 to 15 minutes when the first assignment is given is sufficient for dealing with all questions of the operation. We are convinced that the teaching of complex systems (feedback, nonliearities, complexity) and of algorithms (animation) has been considerably improved since we use computers.

References

Fischlin, A. (1986,1988): The DialogMachine. Projektzentrum IDA ETH Zurich

Fischlin A., Ulrich M. (1988): ModelWorks: an Interactive Modula-2 Simulation Environment. Int. Report 4/1988, IDA-Zentrum, ETH Zürich.

Mansour M., Schaufelberger W. (1989): Software and Laboratory Experiments using Computers in Control Education. IEEE Control Systems Magazine (accepted for publication).

Moler C. (1981): MATLAB Users' Guide. Dept. of Computer Science, Univ. of New Mexico.

Nievergelt, J., Ventura, A., and Hinterberger, H. (1986): Interactive Computer Programs for Education. Philosophy, Techniques, and Design. Addison-Wesley

Norman, D. A., Draper, S.W. (1986): User Centered System Design. Lawrence Erlbaum Ass., London.

Schaufelberger, W. (1988): Teachware for Control. American Control Conference, Atlanta, Georgia.

Schaufelberger, W. (1988): Experiences with group-projects and teachware in control engineering education at ETHZ. ASEE Southeastern Section Conference Proceedings, Portland, Oregon.

Vancso-Polacsek K., Fischlin A. (1988): Automated Construction of Interactive Learning Programs in Modula-2. Comput. Educ., Vol. 12, No. 4, pp. 507-512.

Ventura, A., and Schaufelberger, W. (1988): Benützungsmodelle: Vermittler zwischen Menschen und Maschinen. Bulletin SEV 15, pp. 921-925.

Wirth N. (1985): Modula-2. Springer-Verlag.

Wirth N. et al. (1988): MacMETH, User Manual. Institut für Informatik, ETH Zürich, 100 pp.

THE USES OF THE cT LANGUAGE

Bruce Arne Sherwood
Center for Design of Educational Computing
and Department of Physics
Carnegie Mellon University
Pittsburgh PA 15213

Modern graphics-oriented computing environments are very attractive and friendly to end users but present daunting challenges to programmers. The development of tools for programmers has not kept pace with the tools for users, yet the programming task has become far more complex, due to high expectations for the user interface. The result is that most people are not able to write modern programs. The cT language (formerly called CMU Tutor) fills a major need by providing a powerful tool for even those with limited programming experience to develop graphics-oriented, interactive applications. The cT language has been developed in the Center for Design of Educational Computing (CDEC) at Carnegie Mellon University.

Not only is it surprisingly easy to create modern applications with cT, but such applications have been run *without change* on several brands of professional workstations (IBM RT PC, Sun, and DEC VAXstations) and also on popular microcomputers (Macintosh and PC families). This is nearly without precedent. In the past, any program which had an attractive user interface was tied to one particular computer. Major differences in the handling of graphics, multi-font text, and user interactions such as mouse clicks or menu selections meant that it was necessary to rewrite large portions of each program for every different machine on which it would be run. With cT, programs can be written on one set of hardware and be easily distributed among users having a variety of equipment.

An important aspect of the cT programming environment is the evolutionary development path it has followed. Most new language features are of course additions to the language which do not invalidate existing programs. However, occasionally it has been necessary for further growth to make incompatible changes which would cause existing programs to stop working, were it not for the fact that the cT compiler automatically converts old programs to the new format. A syntax level indicator is kept in the program file to indicate that the appropriate conversions have been done. As a result, despite major growth and change in the language, the oldest programs from 1985 still work. This compatibility from year to year is just as important as the compatibility which cT offers from machine to machine. In contrast, programs written in C on professional workstations at Carnegie Mellon have stopped working periodically due to changes in the software environment.

Summary of cT features

While the cT language includes many of the standard calculational and file-handling capabilities of other languages, it is unusual in providing within the language itself strong graphics capabilities, a rich set of sequencing options, and powerful input analysis routines [1, 2, 3]. Some of these capabilities can be obtained from subroutine libraries accompanying other languages. However, such libraries are usually highly dependent on the particular computer environment, which makes it difficult to move the resulting program to a different computer.

Major features of the cT language include

> interactive graphics in windowed environments
> instant portability across diverse computers
> automatic rescaling of text and graphics to fit the window
> multi-font text
> menus
> mouse and keyset inputs
> analysis of words and sentences
> analysis of numbers and algebraic expressions
> rich sequencing options
> standard calculational capabilities
> numeric and text files

The programming environment has some unique features. The integrated graphics editor generates cT source code, and the resulting statements can be modified either by hand or with the aid of the graphics editor. The source-code editor provides the same mechanisms for making text italic, bold, or centered as one finds in modern menu-driven word processors. In other programming languages it is generally not possible to include italic text directly in the source code. An unusual aspect of the cT programming environment is that one can use the mouse to copy sample routines from the on-line reference manual into the source window and execute them immediately. This provides a powerful resource for learning the language.

Major features of the cT programming environment include

> integrated editing and execution environment
> incremental compilation for fast revision and execution
> on-line reference manual with executable examples
> graphics editor which generates cT graphics statements
> accurate and informative error diagnostics

Educational uses of cT

The InterUniversity Consortium for Educational Computing (ICEC) offered one-week workshops on cT to faculty and staff from the ICEC colleges and universities [4]. The prerequisites were that participants had written at least one program in some language, but generally had no experience with modern windowed environments. In less than a week, most participants wrote significant graphics-oriented programs. Later, Vassar College and California State University at Northridge ran cT workshops themselves.

Examples of educational programs can be found in the ICEC Workshop Guide [4] and in [5, 6]. For an assesssment of the suitability of cT for educational programming, see [7, 8]. General issues affecting the design of educational programs are treated in [9].

Rather "intelligent" programs have been written in cT (for example, see reference 6). These developments suggest that large Lisp machines and large development efforts need not necessarily be required to exploit many of the insights gained from research on artificial intelligence. On the other hand, cT has also been used to build the user interface for a large Lisp program running on a Unix-based workstation, with the two programs communicating through sockets. Similar work is in progress to provide a cT user interface for a Soar program. The importance of cT for this work lies in the fact that Lisp and Soar by themselves offer few capabilities for building good user interfaces.

The cT programming environment provides an excellent tool for interface prototyping. One really can't tell how an interface will work except by seeing it on the screen. Active use, as opposed to static displays, is preferable for such review. Moreover, one should try it out on some users, early and often, with rapid revision based on user experience. The ease of cT programming and the fast turn-around resulting from incremental compilation make possible a very short design cycle.

Designing the interface can be independent of the development of the rest of the program. With a basic interface concept, one that has been shown to work, one can then consider how to implement it in a particular environment of interest. At Carnegie Mellon, for example, several psychology students are currently using cT for prototyping interfaces for their intelligent tutoring systems. Another student, who had previously written in Pascal a simulation program that was used in Engineering and Public Policy classes, used cT to design an improved interface for that program. When it came time to port the original program to a Macintosh, it turned out to be easier to rewrite the whole program in cT than to deal with the differences in the Pascal environments.

Research uses of cT

Some faculty and graduate students have used cT for research computing tasks. Like those writing educational programs, researchers too face a daunting problem when trying to create graphical displays of results on a modern computer. For a discussion of the difficulties of writing modern programs for research purposes, with some assessment of the advantages of cT, see [10]. It is useful to be able to develop and run the same graphics-oriented research program on a workstation in the lab and on a microcomputer at home. The ability to use the same tool for both research and educational programming has encouraged research-minded faculty to develop educational software, in some cases by modification of their own research programs [7].

Development history

Development of cT was begun in June 1985 [11, 12], and it was used on workstations at Carnegie Mellon within a few months. The basic aspects were patterned after the TUTOR and MicroTutor languages developed in the University of Illinois PLATO project. In 1987 it became possible to deliver cT programs on PC and Macintosh microcomputers, but the full development environment was available only on workstations. In July 1988 Carnegie Mellon began distributing the full cT programming environment for the Macintosh (Mac Plus, Mac SE, and Mac II). Again, this version was introduced with the offering of a workshop, this time to precollege teachers and administrators who were able to define relevant applications and produce operational programs in under a week.

Equivalent versions for the PC family and for workstations running the X Window System are planned for first quarter 1989. (Earlier versions for workstations were based on CMU's Andrew window manager, which is no longer generally available.)

In the early development of cT there was an emphasis on the use of high-function Unix-based workstations. This was in keeping with the belief held by many university planners that only such workstations had enough power, graphics capabilities, and operating-system uniformity across different brands of computers to permit truly adequate development of educational applications. The role of microcomputers with respect to cT was, at most, to act as a delivery vehicle for materials created on workstations. However, during the period since 1985 the capabilities of popular microcomputers improved so much as to rival the workstations while providing a much richer selection of interesting applications.

It also became apparent that portability of system software need not depend on the use of Unix but can be largely achieved through writing in the now-ubiquitous C language. C provides a rather high degree of independence from the operating system (with the notable exception of MS-DOS, where memory limits and memory fragmentation require special considerations, even in C). Not only is Unix not necessary to achieve portability, it is also not sufficient, because there is a proliferation of graphics environments within the Unix world, despite attempts to standardize on MIT's X Window System.

C has increasingly provided much-needed independence from the details of the processor and the operating system. However, it has done almost nothing to provide needed independence from the details of the graphics environment. The cT language attempts to tackle this next major level of portability issues, by making it possible for a program to run without change on different processors, different operating systems, and different graphics environments.

An ironic twist to this new level of portability is that we now have faculty writing cT programs at home on a microcomputer, for use by students on Unix workstations in public clusters!

The cT programming environment is currently being distributed by Carnegie Mellon University. For information, write to cT Distribution, CDEC Bldg. B, Carnegie Mellon University, Pittsburgh PA 15213.

Acknowledgements

This work was supported by grants from the Claude Worthington Benedum Foundation, the Carnegie Corporation, the Alfred P. Sloan Foundation, IBM, and Apple Corporation.

References

[1] Sherwood, B. A., and Sherwood, J. N. *The cT Language*. Champaign, Illinois: Stipes Publishing Company, 1988.

[2] Sherwood, J. N. *The cT Reference Manual*. Champaign, Illinois: Stipes Publishing Company, 1988. This is a printed version of the on-line reference manual.

[3] Sherwood, B. A., and Sherwood, J. N. The cT language and its uses: A modern programming tool. Proceedings of the Conference on Computers in Physics Instruction, North Carolina State University (August 1988).

[4] Critchfield, M. *ICEC-Carnegie Summer Workshop Guide*. Carnegie Mellon University internal report (1986). This is a guide for instructors of such workshops.

[5] Trowbridge, D. Quick generation of lecture demonstrations and student exercises. Proceedings of the IBM Academic Computing Information Systems University Conference, Discipline Symposia - Physics, Boston, 2-7 (June 1987).

[6] Trowbridge, D., Larkin, J., & Scheftic, C. Computer-based tutor on graphing equations. In *Proceedings of the National Educational Computer Conference* (NECC '87), 28-33. Eugene, OR: University of Oregon.

[7] Resmer, M. New strategies for the development of educational software. Academic Computing **2**, 22-27 (December-January 1988).

[8] Sherwood, B. A., & Larkin, J. H. New tools for courseware production. The NERComp Journal (in press).

[9] Chabay, R. W., and Sherwood, B. A. A practical guide for the creation of educational software. In *Computer Assisted Instruction and Intelligent Tutoring Systems: Shared Issues and Complementary Approaches*, edited by J. H. Larkin & R. W. Chabay. Hillsdale, New Jersey: Erlbaum, in press.

[10] Lewis, C., & Olson, G. M. Can principles of cognition lower the barriers to programming? In *Empirical Studies of Programmers (Vol. 2)*, edited by Olson, G. M., Soloway, E., & Sheppard, S. Norwood, New Jersey: Ablex 1987.

[11] Sherwood, B. A. An integrated authoring environment. Proceedings of the IBM Academic Information Systems University Advanced Education Projects Conference, Alexandria, Virginia, 29-35 (June 1985).

[12] Hansen, W. J. The Andrew environment for development of educational computing. Computers in Education **12**, 231-239 (1988).

THE CONSTRUCTIVE PROCESS OF KNOWLEDGE ACQUISITION: STUDENT MODELING

Hans Spada, Michael Stumpf and Klaus Opwis
Psychological Institute, University of Freiburg
Niemensstraße 10, D-7800 Freiburg
(e-mail: spada@cogsys.psychologie.uni-freiburg.dbp.de)

Abstract

Despite some optimistic claims of the contrary it is still in the distant future to teach by means of truly self-adapting systems. Nevertheless, one main focus of Cognitive Science lies on this issue of how to construct a system which has the special feature to adjust its behavior to the student/user in a sophisticated way. One answer is student modeling. Findings of Cognitive Psychology and tools of Artificial Intelligence are combined to assess the student's knowledge and the learning process she[1] is subject to, while working with the system. We discuss several approaches towards student modeling namely overlay models, enumerative diagnosis systems, and generative models based on theories of knowledge acquisition.

To address these topics, we have developed the AI-based microworld DiBi (**di**sk **bi**lliard) and FEDS, a **f**lat **e**numerative **d**iagnosis **s**ystem. Both systems are implemented on XEROX 11xx / SIEMENS 58xx machines running InterLISP-D and PRISM.

DiBi is a computerized learning environment for elastic impacts as a subtopic of classical mechanics. The student learns by designing experiments, making predictions about their outcomes and by revising her hypotheses based on a comparison of her predictions with the computer-generated feedback. The constructive process of knowledge acquisition can be understood as experience-based learning.

A form of passive adaptation to the student can be seen as realized in two aspects of DiBi: Having all characteristics of a microworld, the system enables the student to access optimally fitting information in a self-guided way. In addition, DiBi supports quantitative **and** qualitative thinking in several ways.

Active adaptation presupposes some kind of student modeling. By means of FEDS, correct quantitative domain-specific knowledge, but also qualitative knowledge and misconceptions are assessed in form of correct, fragmentary and faulty hypotheses. We are working on an improved diagnosis system which is explicitly based on elements of a theory of knowledge acquisition. As a consequence, we will represent the domain in a way which facilitates knowledge communication between system and student in all phases of the learning process. The long-term objective is to develop a really self-adapting teaching system.

---

[1]

Femine expressions are used as generic terms: No bias is intended.

Introduction: Self-Adapting Systems

In comparison to conventional computerized teaching programs "intelligent" systems are characterized by substantially more **flexible control structures** and more **elaborated techniques for representing and communicating knowledge.** These control structures correspond to one or more of the four main components of an intelligent teaching system: (1) the **domain representation**, (2) the **student component**, (3) the **teaching component** and (4) the **user interface**.

The first component contains the system's knowledge about the domain. It has two main functions: The generation of instructional material (problems, questions, etc.) and the evaluation of the student's domain specific behavior in the tutorial dialogue. The function of the student component is to build a model of the student's preinstructional knowledge and its change in the course of her interaction with the system. The teaching component represents the didactic expertise of the system, especially tutorial strategies. The form of the interaction between the system and the student (graphical, natural language based, etc.) is defined by the user interface.

On a certain level of abstraction, we can think about a tutorial dialogue as an interaction between two learners. The student acquires knowledge about the domain, instructed or coached by the tutor. The tutor learns about the knowledge of the student, using as data the student's reactions. A good tutor systematically adapts her instructional measures to the particular knowledge state of the learner.

From this perspective, an intelligent teaching system has to perform the following tasks while interacting with the student: (a) Based on observations of the student's behavior in the given domain a representation of her knowledge has to be built up. (b) This student model has to be compared to a criterion model, in order to evaluate the state of knowledge at different points of the learning process. And (c), it has to be decided - using the results of the comparison and based on a set of instructional goals and tutorial rules - what should be taught next and how this should be done.

Therefore, a main focus of psychological research in the framework of teaching systems is on the issue of how to assess and model the process of knowledge acquisition. The objective is to develop **self-adapting systems**, i.e. systems that adjust their behavior to the student's preinstructional state of knowledge and to its change during the learning process.

We do not claim that progress in the development of teaching systems solely or primarily depends on improving the student component. But it is a fascinating idea to develop a system that is "able" to really adapt its instructional measures to the state of the knowledge of the individual student.

At least three problem areas call for further research in this context. Valid and much more detailed models of knowledge acquisition have to be developed, considering in particular the constructive characteristics of information search and information processing. The techniques for an automatized assessment of a student's domain specific knowledge and its change over time have to be improved. And the domain representation has to be extended to include not only expert's knowledge but a prescriptive domain-specific theory of learning. The domain representation should allow domain knowledge to be accessed and manipulated easily and should offer a basis for interpreting the student's inputs in a psychologically valid way.

The goal should be to move from an expert-based design to a learner-based paradigm. The performance of a student should not primarily be compared with that of an expert, but with that of an ideal learner, thus taking into account (a) how the knowledge of a novice develops step by step in the direction of an expert's knowledge structure, (b) what knowledge state should be reached considering the preinstructional knowledge of the student and the type and amount of information given in the tutorial dialogue, and (c) what knowledge should be obtainable in the next steps of the dialogue.

To summarize: Two central prerequisites for constructing truly self-adaptive systems are (1) a **prescriptive theory of knowledge acquisition** tailored to the given content domain and (2) a **descriptive dynamic student model** which is based on an automatic assessment of the student's knowledge and its change.

Student Modeling:
From Expert- to Learner-Based Approaches

Often, the domain representation (mostly captured as expert knowledge) is also the starting point in the development of an automatized diagnosis system. As a consequence, the student model is conceptualized by comparing the student's behavior with that of the modeled expert. The student's knowledge is considered to be a subset of the expert's knowledge. Such **difference or overlay models** (Carr & Goldstein, 1977) are often misleading and not very useful, because (a) novices are not empty experts, i.e. not only missing knowledge but also incorrect and, hence, different knowledge has to be considered, and (b) no information is provided to fill the gap between the student's and the expert's knowledge (Reimann, in press b).

In order to overcome some of these problems, **enumerative bug models** - to use a term proposed by Wenger (1987) - have been developed. Aside from correct domain-specific knowledge incorrect knowledge is represented in the diagnosis system. In a narrow sense, a bug is a structural flaw in a procedure that often manifests itself in faulty behavior. In a broader sense, also misconceptions and other types of incorrect knowledge which may account for discrepancies between correct and student behavior may be called bugs. The famous article of Brown and Burton (1978) on 'Diagnostic Models for Procedural Bugs in Basic Mathematical Skills' prepared the ground for the development of many enumerative models, for example by Burton (1982) himself, Sleeman (1982) and Young and O'Shea (1981), to mention only a few. Both British bug models use the production system formalism (Klahr, Langley & Neches, 1987; Opwis, 1988) to represent correct knowledge and bugs, and both show based on this representation language how correct and incorrect elements of knowledge are interrelated.

Enumerative models with a fixed set of correct and incorrect knowledge elements ("bug-library") constitute substantial progress compared with the restrictive nature of diagnosis in the former systems of computer-assisted instruction and with overlay models. By means of this type of diagnosis it is possible to formulate a **computational model** of the student's knowledge, i.e. to reconstruct the behavior of the student based on the diagnostically inferred knowledge elements.

Nevertheless diagnosis systems with fixed libraries face several limitations (Reimann, in press b; Spada & Reimann, 1988; Wenger, 1987). All knowledge elements have to be entered into the diagnosis system, before it can be used for the assessment of the student's knowledge. But inferring bugs from student's data is a laborious and costly task. Furthermore, it is difficult to use this approach in the case of knowledge changes and it is complicated to include an explanation component. Most of the problems can be related to the lack of an explicit theory of knowledge acquisition. Enumerative models are flat. They do not tell how a correct knowledge element or a bug was acquired and how it is embedded in general knowledge.

A truly learner-based approach to student modeling should be based on a model of knowledge and bug acquisition. Steps in this direction were taken, e.g., by Brown and Van Lehn (1980) in their Repair Theory, a **generative bug theory**. The main assumption is that students will invent faulty actions to overcome problems that occur during the execution of a fragmentary (in part forgotten) procedure. Van Lehn (1987) has formulated a generative theory of how correct procedural knowledge in the domain of subtraction is acquired step by step by means of learning from an optimal sequence of worked-out examples.

Another approach to overcome enumerative diagnosis systems is exemplified by the work of Langley, Ohlsson, and Sage (1984). They try to reconstruct the bugs of an individual student by applying machine learning techniques without recurring to a psychological theory of knowledge acquisition. A heuristic search through the space of possible conditions on domain operators is performed, using data on students' performance.

DiBi: A Computerized Learning Environment for Elastic Impacts

In our Research Group on Cognitive Systems we are trying to develop better solutions to two problems. (1) How to assess and model the constructive process of knowledge acquisition of a student in a computerized exploratory learning environment. (2) How to support such a learning process by designing the teaching system such that it will adapt itself to the student's needs.

We have developed DiBi (Stumpf, Opwis & Spada, in press; Stumpf et al., 1988). DiBi is a **computerized microworld** for a physical problem domain, namely elastic impacts as a subtopic of classical mechanics. The DiBi system implements a kind of a **di**sk **bi**lliard. Central and oblique impacts upon disks, disks rebounding off the cushion, and collisions of disks can be explored by the student in a self-guided way. While inter-acting with the microworld, the student learns by designing experiments, making pre-dictions about their outcomes and by revising her hypotheses based on a comparison of the predictions to the computer-generated correct feedback. The experimental set-ting is arranged in such a way that the collected data reflect the student's search for and processing of information. Information selection and hypothesis formation are se-quenced into different steps, thus enabling their seperate assessment. DiBi allows for the simulation of a great range of experiments on the screen, involving multiple disks, forces and velocities. These objects can be arranged in rather unconstrained ways to design experiments belonging to **three basic types of phenomena** (cf. Figure 1):

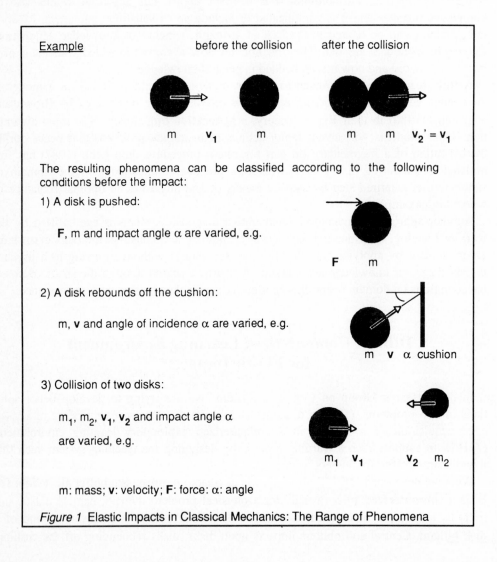

Figure 1 Elastic Impacts in Classical Mechanics: The Range of Phenomena

First, there is the central or oblique impact upon a resting disk. In this case, the mass of the disk, the force and the angle of impact can be varied. Second, a moving disk rebounds off the cushion, where the mass and/or the velocity of the disk and the angle of incidence can be varied. Third, in a central or oblique collision of two disks, the variables are the masses and/or the velocities of the disks as well as the angle of collision.

The quantitative treatment of the different phenomena appearing in DiBi is based on the following presuppositions. We adopt the general laws of particle kinematics in two dimensions. In particular, the impacts are assumed to be completely elastic, friction and rotation are ignored, and we consider the extension of a body only for the impact event. The domain representation is based on the laws of conservation of momentum and energy. The correct **domain-specific quantitative knowledge** is represented in DiBi as a rule-based system, namely as a set of production rules. We used PRISM (Ohlsson & Langley, 1984; Opwis, Stumpf & Spada, 1987) to design the underlying production system interpreter. At first sight, this approach to represent quantitative physical knowledge might look far-fetched. What we obtained was a homogeneous formalism for domain representation **and** for student modeling. It is a basic principle of our conception to use the same formalism to handle both types of knowledge. Thereby, it is much easier to match diagnostically assessed student knowledge with expert knowledge, which should not be restricted to quantitative expertise, of course. We will come back to this point.

The **user interface** of DiBi is highly graphical and makes extensive use of menus and mouse-sensitive graphical objects to support different modes of a "direct manipulation" interface (Hutchins, Hollan & Norman, 1986; cf. also Smith, 1986). Figure 2 shows a dump of the screen during a session with DiBi. The elements of the screen layout visible in this figure are the large window representing the billiard table which contains the disks, a prompt window on top of the table window, a menu at the bottom of the table, a protocol window containing icons which represent the experiments carried out so far, and a menu which displays the current program phase and which may be used by the student to go back to a previous step in the program run. Beside these features, there are many other menus available to the student to cope with the input/output requirements. At the point of time the dump has been taken, the student had selected two of the buttons at the bottom of the screen (marked by inversion), and the system was displaying the situation in the experiment just before the collision together with the student's prediction.

Typically the student's input consists of the following interactions:
- selecting a type of phenomenon (e.g. a central collision of two disks), selecting and positioning disks on the window representing the billiard table, and selecting or constructing forces and velocities (design or selection phase),
- selecting or constructing velocities in the prediction phase, and
- selecting different kinds of feedback, and maybe requesting information about the outcomes of previously designed experiments (feedback phase).

We speak of SPFP sequences, the last "P" referring to the phase in which the stu-

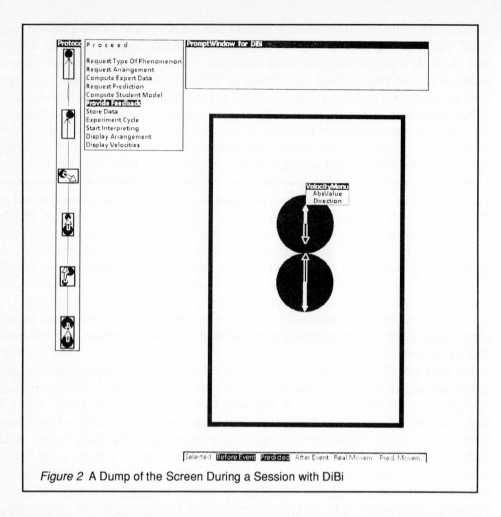

Figure 2 A Dump of the Screen During a Session with DiBi

dent processes the feedback information, compares her predictions with the outcomes and possibly modifies wrong or fragmentary hypotheses.

The feedback concerning an experimental outcome forms the most important part of DiBi's output. Several kinds of static feedback are provided as well as a dynamic one. The static feedbacks include displays of the disks at certain critical events where arrows represent the force or the velocity attached to the disk, as well as a numeric feedback that informs the student about the exact quantitative values of the physically relevant data. The dynamic feedback displays the movement of the disks obeying real-time constraints. Another useful feature of DiBi lies in its ability not only to present the disk movements according to the correct physical laws, but also according to incorrect predictions made by the student. In this way, the student is confronted with her incorrect assumptions in a very direct manner. We will develop a further kind of feedback which will consist of natural language sentences. The student will be provided with explanations concerning the current experiment and the underlying rules which she perhaps may not have taken into account.

DiBi as described above is implemented on Xerox 11xx/Siemens 58xx machines running InterLISP-D and PRISM.

But how is it possible to adapt the system's behavior to the different stages of a learning process? One answer is that DiBi allows for and supports qualitative and quantitative reasoning in several ways. The interaction between the student and the system can take a qualitative and/or quantitative form. This refers to the inputs made by the student, especially with regard to the predictions, and to the different kinds of experimental feedback, which are provided by the system.

A form of **passive adaptation** to the student can also be seen in the following aspect: Embodying all characteristics of a microworld, the system enables the student to access appropriate information in a self-guided way. The basic philosophy of a microworld as a learning environment gives prominence to the assumption that in order to really understand complex relations between multiple concepts, it is considered more important to support a student in learning how to develop and debug her own theories rather than to teach her directly. A potential danger of such a learning environment is that if it is not well-structured, the learner might get confused and come to a deadend. We tried to avoid this problem by structuring the interaction between learner and system by means of the SPFP sequences as discussed above. They subdivide the stream of experimental information and provide a red thread for the process of knowledge acquisition.

Student Modeling:
From FEDS, a Flat Enumerative Diagnosis System, to . . .

Active adaptation of a teaching system to the needs of a student presupposes some form of student modeling. In this part of the paper we describe how we represent the knowledge of a learner and its change over time, we discuss FEDS, the first diagnostic system, which was developed by our group, and we give an outlook on future work reaching beyond FEDS.

From a psychological perspective, the acquisition of expertise by the student taking place during the interaction with DiBi can be understood as a form of **experience-based inductive learning** (cf. Holland, Holyoak, Nisbett & Thagard, 1987). More precisely, we see the process of knowledge acquisition as being **based upon formulating, testing and modifying hypotheses**, the latter of which can be defined as "scope-phenomenon" pairs (cf. Figure 3, especially Examples H1 and H2).

Knowledge of this type and its modification can be characterized as follows: First, by features of concept formation such that each phenomenon is tied to a particular scope, and second, by the development and the application of algorithms that are needed for the prediction of the expected phenomena. In formal terms, the knowledge can be **represented as production rules**. The condition part of the rule specifies the as-

---

- **Hypotheses as "scope-phenomenon" pairs**

  Examples: H1: IF   a resting disk is pushed with some force **F**   ; scope
  THEN the disk will move in the direction of **F** and   ; phenomenon
  its velocity will be the greater, the greater the force **F**.

  H2: IF   a resting disk of mass m is pushed with force **F** ; scope
  and it is a central impact
  THEN the disk will move in the direction of **F** and   ; phenomenon
  its velocity will be **v'** = **F**/m.

- **Formal representation: production rules**

- **Hypotheses may vary according to several dimensions:**

  - Generality of the scope

  - Precision of the prediction of the expected phenomenon (e.g. a qualitative, semi-quantitative, quantitative prediction)

  - Accuracy (correct or false hypothesis)

  - Embeddedness in general knowledge

- **Knowledge acquisition consists of:**

  - generalization/discrimination learning and

  - induction of functional relations (incorporation or deletion of variables, change from a qualitative to a semiquantitative to a quantitative phenomenon prediction, etc.)

  Figure 3 Knowledge Acquisition as Hypothesis Formation

---

sumed scope, and the action part of the rule specifies the expected phenomenon. These hypotheses may include qualitative, semi-quantitative as well as quantitative features, and they may vary according to several dimensions given in Figure 3.

If we take a look at another example of a hypothesis (Example H2 in Figure 3) and compare it with the first one then the roles of the different dimensions can be illustrated in greater detail. The two hypotheses differ from each other in several aspects. Hypothesis 2 allows correct quantitative predictions of the resulting phenomena, whereas Hypothesis 1 allows only semi-quantitative, relational predictions. Furthermore, the scope of Hypothesis 2 considers a greater number of conditions correctly, such as the disk's mass and the angle of impact. Hypothesis 1 is incomplete in this respect and will therefore lead to false predictions in those cases in which these aspects must be taken into account. If appropriate counterexamples are presented, which falsify the hypothesis of the student, her attention might be shifted to the variable "mass of a disk" that has been neglected, so far. As a consequence, she might modify the scope of her hypothesis such that the mass is included. Next, this variable would have to be considered also in the algorithm used to predict the expected phenomena and a semiquantitative rule would have to be replaced by the correct quantitative algorithm. Of course, in general it will take more than one step to come from Hypothesis 1 to Hypothesis 2. Such a kind of inductive learning can be reconstructed as a process, which combines **discrimination learning** (cf. Langley, 1987) **and** the **induction of functional relations** (cf. Falkenhainer & Michalski, 1986).

Having these examples in mind, it is evident that in our case knowledge acquisition entails both a condition and a function component. Modifications occur in a hypothesis' scope (generalization, discrimination) and in the prediction part (incorporation or deletion of variables, change from a qualitative to a semiquantitative to a quantitative phenomenon prediction, change from faulty to correct functional relations). Both variants of knowledge modification can be incorporated in the selected rule-based form of knowledge representation, i.e. the production system formalism (Klahr et al., 1987; Opwis, 1988).

A clear distinction has to be made between predictions and hypotheses. A prediction refers to one experiment. It is the result of applying a hypothesis in the context of a specific trial. A hypothesis refers to all those experiments included in its scope. A prediction might be impossible for an experiment, although the hypothesis is correct, but, e.g. is composed of two semiquantitative assumptions, like: "The greater the force F, the greater the velocity v' " and "The greater the mass m, the smaller the velocity v' ", if in the experiment force and mass are greater compared to a preceding trial with known outcome.

The behavior of a teaching system has to be adapted primarily to the knowledge/hypothesis level of a learner and not to the reaction/prediction level. This leads to the question of how to diagnose this type of knowledge addressed by DiBi.

The first computerized diagnosis system which was developed for DiBi by our group is FEDS, a **f**lat **e**numerative **d**iagnosis **s**ystem. The approach is sketched in Figure 4. FEDS is a rule-based system. It was implemented by Rolf Plötzner by means of PRISM (Ohlsson & Langley, 1984; Opwis et al., 1987). Correct, fragmentary and faulty quantitative and qualitative hypotheses are inferred from the student's predictions of the experimental outcomes. The "hypothesis-library" is formally represented by a set of production rules. For each student those rules are selected which allow the best possible reconstruction of her predictions. In a first algorithm which was implemented this is done via an update of the strength parameters associated with each rule. The development of the hypothesis-library was based (a) on our conceptualization of this type of knowledge, which was outlined above, (b) on empirical investigations using DiBi and paper and pencil tests, and (c) on studies, in which reasoning about physi-

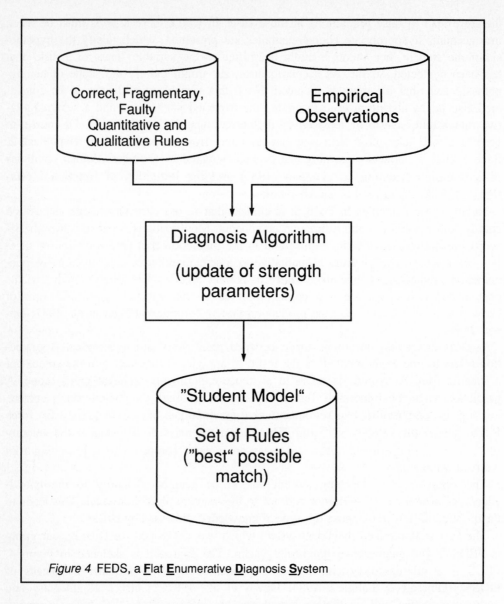

Figure 4 FEDS, a **F**lat **E**numerative **D**iagnosis **S**ystem

cal laws and systems is analyzed (e.g. Bobrow, 1985: DiSessa, 1982; White & Horwitz, 1987).

Not yet implemented, but in consideration, are several tutorial measures based on the results of applying FEDS. The fact, that the same formalism is used to represent domain knowledge and the knowledge of the students facilitates to compare the individual student model with criteria provided by the domain representation. Furthermore, it is possible to visualize the assessed student model in the sense that it can be used to predict the outcome of individual experiments. By presenting the disk movements according to the student's model, the learner can be confronted with her hypotheses in a very direct manner, especially in the case of counterexamples. A counterexample is given, if the prediction derived from the student's hypothesis does not match the correct outcome. Based on FEDS, an automatized generation of counterexamples would be feasible.

Despite the usefulness of FEDS, one encounters the limitations of all flat enumerative diagnosis systems, which do not explicitly correspond with a theory of how knowledge is acquired. Apart of the points mentioned in the second section of this paper it is very difficult to differentiate between incorrect predictions based on wrong hypotheses or missing knowledge and erratic behavior, which is not of diagnostic relevance.

But a domain-specific model of knowledge acquisition would also be necessary to extend the domain representation. Aside from correct quantitative knowledge, it should include semi-quantitative and qualitative knowledge and information on how the different knowledge states are sequenced in the learning process. What are the characteristics such a model should have?

Reimann (in press a), a further member of our Research Group on Cognitive Systems, has developed the HDD (**h**ypothesis **d**riven **d**iscoverer), a system that learns by formulating new rules in the light of experimental data - in this case based on a microworld on geometrical optics. The scope descriptions are learned by discrimination which is triggered by differences between predictions and feedback. The discrimination algorithm used is the one developed by Langley (1987) and reimplemented by Plötzner & Opwis (1987) in our PRISM version. In a first version of HDD the induction of functional relations is done by an algorithm, which takes as input information about pairs of experiments and returns equations, which describe the functional relations between independent and dependent variables. The algorithm realizes a rather "blind" and not very effective search.

With regard to DiBi we are working on the idea to tune the condition induction and the induction of functional relations not only by experimental evidence but also by a transfer of world knowledge to the experimental situation. World knowledge about concepts like weight, effort and distance (an object is pushed) and their interdependencies is understood as influencing the formulation of hypotheses on experimental variables like mass, force and velocity. General mathematical knowledge on the detection of functional relationships comes into play, too. We expect, that it will be possible to reconstruct the generation of correct but also of fragmentary and faulty hypotheses as a function of the correctness and completeness of the corresponding parts of world knowledge a student has and the way she represents the experimental information.

References

Bobrow, D.G. (Ed.) (1985). Qualitative reasoning about physical systems. Cambridge, MA: MIT Press.

Brown, J.S. & Burton, R.R. (1978). Diagnostic models for procedural bugs in basic mathematical skills. Cognitive Science, 2, 155-191.

Brown, J.S. & VanLehn, K. (1980). Repair theory: a generative theory of bugs in procedural skills. Cognitive Science, 4, 379-426.

Burton, R.R. (1982). Diagnosing bugs in a simple procedural skill. In D.H. Sleeman & J.S. Brown (Eds.), Intelligent Tutoring Systems (pp. 157-184). London: Academic Press.

Carr, B. & Goldstein, J.P. (1977). Overlays: a theory of modeling for computer-aided instruction. AI Lab Memo 406 (Logo Memo 40). Cambridge, MA: MIT.

Di Sessa, A. (1982). Unlearning Aristotelian physics: a study of knowledge-based learning. Cognitive Science, 6, 37-75.

Falkenhainer, B.C. & Michalski, R.S. (1986). Integrating quantitative and qualitative discovery. The ABACUS system. Machine Learning, 1, 367-402.

Holland, J., Holyoak, K., Nisbett, R.E. & Thagard, P. (1987). Induction: processes of inference, learning and discovery. Cambridge, MA: MIT Press.

Hutchins, E.L., Hollan, J.D. & Norman, D.A. (1986). Direct manipulation interfaces. In D.A. Norman & S.W. Draper (Eds.), User centered system design (pp. 87-124). Hillsdale, NJ: Lawrence Erlbaum.

Klahr, D., Langley, P. & Neches, R. (Eds.). (1987). Production system models of learning and development. Cambridge, MA: MIT Press.

Langley, P. (1987). A general theory of discrimination learning. In D. Klahr, P. Langley & R. Neches (Eds.), Production system models of learning and development (pp. 99-161). Cambridge, MA: MIT Press.

Langley, P., Ohlson, S. & Sage, S. (1984). Machine learning approach to student modeling (Technical Report CMU-RI-TR-84-7). Pittsburgh, PA: The Robotics Institute, Carnegie-Mellon University.

Ohlsson, S. & Langley, P. (1984). PRISM: Tutorial, manual, and documentation (Technical Report). Pittsburgh, PA: The Robotics Institute, Carnegie-Mellon University.

Opwis, K. (1988). Produktionssysteme. In H. Mandl & H. Spada (Hrsg.), Wissenspsychologie (S. 74-98). München: Urban & Schwarzenberg.

Opwis, K., Stumpf, M. & Spada, H. (1987) PRISM: Eine Einführung in die Theorie und Anwendung von Produktionssystemen (Research Report No. 39). Freiburg: Psychological Institute.

Plötzner, R. & Opwis, K. (1987). Modeling discrimination learning in a production system framework (Research Report No. 40). Freiburg: Psychological Institute.

Reimann, P. (in press a). Modeling discovery learning processes in a microworld for geometrical optics. Proceedings of the European Summer University on Intelligent Tutoring Systems. Le Mans 1988.

Reimann, P. (in press b). Toward general knowledge diagnosis systems for student and user modeling. In H. Mandl, E. DeCorte, N. Bennett & H.F. Friedrich (Eds.) Learning and instruction. European research in an international context. Vol. II & III. Oxford: Pergamon Press.

Sleeman, D.H. (1982). Infering (mal) rules from pupil's protocols. In Proceedings of the European Conference on Artificial Intelligence. Orsay, 160-164.

Smith, R.B. (1986). The Alternate Reality Kit: an animated environment for creating interactive simulations. Proceedings of the IEEE Computer Society Workshop on Visual Languages. Dallas, 1986, 99-106.

Spada, H. & Reimann, P. (1986). Hypothesis formation in knowledge acquisition: Preparing the ground for an intelligent tutoring system. In F. Klix & H. Hagendorf (Eds.), Human memory and cognitive capabilities (pp. 951-961). Amsterdam: North Holland.

Spada, H. & Reimann, P. (1988). Wissensdiagnostik auf kognitionswissenschaftlicher Basis. Zeitschrift für Differentielle und Diagnostische Psychologie, 3, 183-192.

Stumpf, M., Opwis, K. & Spada, H. (in press). Knowledge acquisition in a microworld for elastic impacts: The DiBi system. Proceedings of the European Summer University on Intelligent Tutoring Systems, Le Mans, 1988.

Stumpf, M., Branskat, S., Herderich, C., Newen, A., Opwis, K., Plötzner, R., Schult, T. & Spada, H. (1988). The graphical user interface of DiBi, a microworld for collision phenomena (Research Report No. 44). Freiburg: Psychological Institute.

VanLehn, K. (1987). Learning one subprocedure per lesson. Artificial Intelligence, 31, 1-40.

Wenger, E. (1987). Artificial intelligence and tutoring systems. Los Altos, CA: Kaufmann.

White, B.Y. & Horwitz, P. (1987). Thinker tools: enabling children to understand physical laws (Report No. 6470). Cambridge, MA: BBN Laboratories.

Young, R.M. & O'Shea, T. (1981). Errors in children's subtraction. Cognitive Science, 5, 153-177.

A CONCEPTUAL MODEL OF A COMPUTER-AIDED LEARNING KNOWLEDGE BASE

Krasimir Spirov

Centre of Engineering Pedagogics,
The 'Lenin' Higher Institute of Mechanical and
Electrical Engineering
1156, Sofia
Bulgaria

Mihail Draganov

Programming and Applied Systems Department,
The 'Lenin' Higher Institute of Mechanical and
Electrical Engineering
1156, Sofia
Bulgaria

ABSTRACT

Recent developments in the theory of artificial intelligence and the advent of the expert systems made it possible to actually produce intelligent systems for computer-aided learning (CAL). A major component of such a system is its knowledge base.

The paper presents a model for a knowledge base and an approach to building it.

To solve the task set, a sufficiently abstract hierarchical model has been developed of a knowledge base consisting of notions. By definition the model is recursive and subject-independent.

The transition to a learning-oriented knowledge base is achieved by using a well-known model for a content-information description of the process of learning. The basic element in it is the 'elementary cognitive structure' (ECS), which the authors identify with the 'notion' element of the general conceptual model. On this basis a model has been designed of a learning-oriented knowledge base, comprising ECS.

INTRODUCTION

This study has been made in accordance with the Committee for Science program for the development of the theoretical and practical aspects of mobile CAL software.

Presenting knowledge in a CAL system is a very specific thing to do, as, besides the factual and conceptual data concerning the particular subject, the system must also contain knowledge about the goals of instruction, the mechanisms and techniques of learning, learners' initial and final status, learning strategies and more.

In what way is this knowledge to be structured? Could we avail ourselves of the theoretical knowledge in other fields of study? How, in pedagogical terms, should the data related to the specific subject, be presented? These are questions the answers to which are sought for in the paper.

The currenty used means are traditional. The majority of the existing programs boil down to programming a given scenario, the knowledge, the goals and the learning strategies. To this end special languages are employed (PILOT, COURSEWRITER) or high level ones (BASIC, PASCAL).

This approach makes it difficult to use the same programs for different goals and with different learning strategies.

Therefore, it is the authors' opinion that it would be expedient to separate the knowledge in a given subject from the learning goals and learning strategies. This would make it possible to develop a knowledge base structured exclusively in keeping with the logic of the respective subject area. Such a learning-oriented knowledge base would also solve the problem of courseware mobility both as regards the hardware and the individual schools, or students respectively.

It should be noted that the conceptual model proposed concerns only the manner of presenting knowledge in a certain subject, not knowledge about how to learn.

2. GENERAL OUTLINE

A knowledge base (KB) will be assumed to be a set of notions. If we are to use Bacchus's notation:

    < KB > ::= < N > < KB >, where
    N - is notion

The recursion used in the definition shows the KB not to be limited in breadth, i.e. notions can be added to an already existing KB.
Each notion consists of a contents and associative part:

    < N > ::= < CN , AN >, where
    CN is the contents part of a notion;
    AN is the associative part of a notion.

2.1. CONTENTS STRUCTURE OF THE CONCEPTUAL MODEL

The contents part of a notion is the list of contents parts of its constituent subnotions:

    < CN > ::= < CSN > : < CSN > < CN > , where
    CSN is the contents part of a subnotion.

Here recursion shows the list of constituent subnotions to be open-ended, i.e. the component part of a notion can be ex panded by new subnotions. The term 'subnotion' (SN) is indicative only of the relations of inclusion of a given notion into a notion from a higher hierarchical level. Otherwise, each subnotion is a notion on a certain hierarchical level and is therefore also composed of a contents and an associative part.

If Ni is a notion of the i-th hierarchical level, then:

    < CNi > ::= < CNi+1 > < CNi >

Recursion shows that the number of notions contained in the component part of a notion of a higher hierarchical level can grow. Thus the contents part of a hierarchical system of notions in a given knowledge base can be said to have a tree structure (see Figure 1).

The lowest hierarchical level is different for each branch of the tree. If need be, each notion of the lowest level can be regarded to be composed of subnotions, i.e. hierarchy can be expanded in depth.

<u>Figure 1:</u>

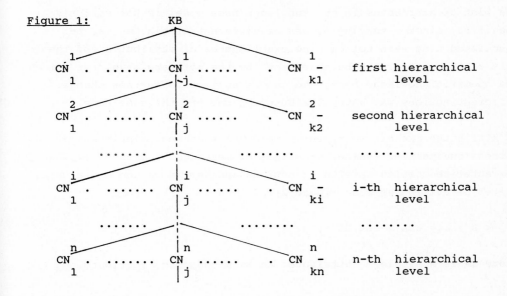

2.2. IDENTIFICATION OF NOTIONS

Each notion is specified by a name (identifier) in the knowledge base, which must be unique. Each notion has both a full and abbreviated name. The abbreviated one is a string of symbols. The full identifier contains the names of all notions of the tree branch leading to the respective notion. Uniqueness of the notion's identification is achieved through its full name. The abbreviated names should be unique in the list of names of notions which are subnotions to one and the same notion.

2.3. ASSOCIATIVE PART OF A NOTION

The associative part of a notion is a list of attributes characterizing various aspects of the notion:

$$< AN > ::= < A > : < AN >,$$

where AN is the associative part of a notion; A is an attribute. The list of attributes in the knowledge base model is not strictly specified, since a varying number of different attributes can be associated with each notion. The exact number of attributes and the form of the list are to be determined by the software developer for the specific knowledge base, and can be subject to further change. Different notions may have attributes of one and the same name.

Attributes are of two types: simple and compound. Simple attributes possess one meaning (value) or a list of meanings. Compound attributes characterize complex aspects of notions and depend on the hierarchical system of attributes (see Figure 2).

$$< A > ::= <SA > : < CA >,$$

where SA is a simple   attribute; CA is a compound   attribute.

$$< CA > ::= < A > : < A > < CA >$$

Figure 2:

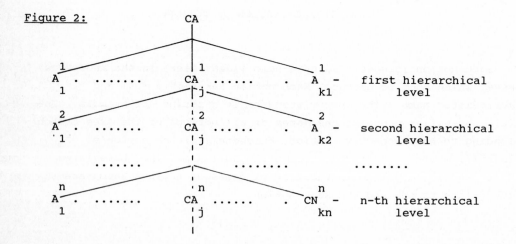

The attributes of a notion can, for instance, define the type of notion, its hierachical level, the parent node of the notion tree, the relationships of that notion to others, etc. Here is a simplified list of attributes:

    AN ::= < type, level, parent, markers >

Each attribute may have properties. The properties characterize various aspects of the attribute just as attributes characterize various aspects of the notion. Let PA be the property of attribute A, and PSA - the list of properties of the A attribute.

    < PSA > ::= < PA > : < PA > < PSA >

Analogically to attributes, their properties can be regarded to be simple or compound, possessing a complex hierarchical system of subproperties. If necessary, the properties may be attributed various definers, etc.

2.4. PRESENTING NOTIONS IN THE KNOWLEDGE BASE

The definitions introduced so far of the contents and associative part of a notion allow a notion to be presented as in Fig.3. Clearly, a complex informational structure can be associated with each notion, characterizing it comprehensively. There are no limitations in principle as to the size and complexity of this informational structure. Thus the knowledge base can be represented in a tree structure. In actual fact, however, an entire system of markers evolves, related to individual notions, attributes and their properties, and these markers enter into multiple relations between the various tree nodes.So the structure of the knowledge base is rather a complex hierarchical network describing the specific subject area. The dotted lines in Figure 3 indicate the directions of recursive expansion of the hierarchical structure.

Figure 3:

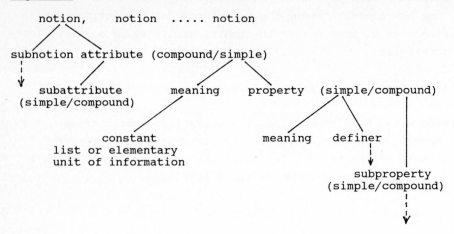

2.5. ADVANTAGES OF THE MODEL PROPOSED

In reality, a KB built on this principle is a complex hierarchical system of notions and attributes of the following advantages:
- extremely complicated structures can be described and presented;
- any information unit is easily accessed;
- the KB is easily updated.

3. A MODEL FOR DESCRIBING THE PROCESS OF LEARNING
IN TERMS OF CONTENT AND INFORMATION

In order to design a model for a CAL knowledge base a sufficiently formalized model of the processes of instruction and learning should be available, presenting the process of instruction as a sequence of operations. There exist a number of psychological theories offering one explanation or another of how man learns, the theory of the stage-by-stage formation of mental action, the cognitive psychology, behaviourism, etc. All of them, however, with the only exception of the programmed learning theory based on behaviourism, are not constructive enough and do not allow a formal description of the process of learning. This is the reason why in introducing CAL, traditional didactics resorts to conceptions which have evolved in practice, in the course of organizing learning, and which do not rest on specific theoretical grounds.

Bearing in mind the destination of the model in question, we are of the opinion that considerable success has been achieved in this area by Djugeli and Vephadze [1], who proposed a content-information-oriented model to describe the process of learning.

The process of learning can be presented as a system composed of a teacher S<T> and a learner S<L>. The functioning of the system in the process of learning is described, in most general terms, by their interaction:

$$S<T> \Longleftrightarrow S<L>$$

The contents structure of the system S<T> and S<L> can be modelled using the Elementary Cognitive Structure (ECS) concept. By definition, it can be defined by constituting two sets: the set of elements and notions and the set of their interrelations. The ESC concept is a systems characteristics of the process of learning, for it can be used to describe simultaneously both the learning material and the processes taking place in the teacher's or learner's mind. Thus, the goal of instruction in a certain subject is to form in the mind of the learner a definite system of ECSs. The initial state of the learner can also be described as a set of definite ECSs he can operate with, and in this stage the role of the teacher boils down to establishing the presence of these ECSs and their interrelations, and to planning and organizing instruction.

Let us assume that M $<m_1, m_2, \ldots, m_l>$ is the set of elements present in the learning material, and R $<r_1, r_2, \ldots r_k>$ - the set of relations in M. From these sets the set of elementary cognitive structures P $(p_1, p_2, \ldots, p_q)$ is formed, each ECS being given as:

$$P_i < M_i R_i >, \quad i = 1, 2, \ldots, q$$

where M_i and R_i are subsets to M and R respectively and should formally satisfy the following constraints:

1. $M_1 \vee M_2 \vee \ldots \vee M_q = M$
2. $M_i \wedge M_j = 0$
3. $R_1 \vee R_2 \vee \ldots \vee R_q = R$
4. $R_i \wedge R_j = 0$

The first constraint means that the conjunction of all notions featuring in ECSs of the respective subject comprise the set total of notions. The second one - that one and the same notion can enter different ECSs. The third and the fourth have the same meaning for the set of relations.

The set of items M_i is termed the notion field of a given ECS, and the R_i set - the possible interrelations. The ordered set P_i of all subsets is called the thesaurus of a given subject and is denoted by Q(P). Then the teacher's work in the course of instruction can be presented as decomposing ECSs according to the logical structure of the section of material taught and presenting them to the respective learner. In other words, the system S(T) acts on Q(P) by means of a decomposition operator Fd and presents all elements of the notion field and all their possible interrelations.

In this context the objective of didactive activity boils down to forming in the mind of the learner the thesaurus of a respective section of the material taught. Let Qn(P) is the share of the thesaurus that is to be acquired by learner S(L).

The system, comprised of < S(T),S(L), Fd, Q(P)and Qn(P) > performing a translation of Qn(P) in S(L), is tantamount to what G. Frank terms "directed learning system" [2]. In such a system learning takes place without a feedback, just through the structure of the respective section of the learning material.

To complete the description of the learning process, it is necessary to account also for the fact that at each step in this process in the S(T) system a respective model of the learner should exist. If these factors are at hand the system can be said to be self-organizing, according to Pask [3].

4. MODEL OF A LEARNING-ORIENTED KNOWLEDGE BASE

What has been said so far justifies us in identifying the item 'notion' in the general structure of the conceptual model with the 'Elementary Cognitive Structure' one of the model describing the process of learning in terms of content and information.

$$N \equiv P$$

Resting on this tenet, the following definitions can be offered:

KNOWLEDGE BASE OF THE SUBJECT - the sum total of elementary cognitive structures depending on learning goals:

$$< KB > ::= < P >:< P > < KB >$$

INFORMATION ITEM (II) - the smallest meaningful item of information in the knowledge base.

Each information item contains one element of the M set of the respective subject and therefore an II cannot be an elementary cognitive structure, according to Pask [3].

Each elementary cognitive structure has a contents and an associative part. The contents part is formed by all IIs included in it. In other words, the contents part of Pi is the subset Mi of the 'M' set of items of the subject. The associative part comprises the relationships between IIs, their type and kind, as well as some other characteristics.

4.1. CONTENTS PART OF AN ECS

Each ECS can contain two kinds of IIs: an information item of the 'Knowledge' kind and an information item of the "Problems to be Solved' kind.

The two kinds of information items differ in the response required on part of the learner. IIs of the "Knowledge' kind expect a response to "Read and Go on", and IIs of the 'Problems to be Solved' kind - a response to 'Read, Solve, Answer and Go on' kind.

The set of information items of the 'Knowledge' kind falls into subsets structured depending on their kind and destination. Thus the following ten subsets can be formed:
- motivational context;
- methodological guidance;
- terms and notions ;
- laws and rules;
- formulas;
- illustrations;
- algorithms and solutions;
- help;
- reference material;
- literature to be consulted.

The division is conventional and could be changed, if occasion demand. What is more important, however, is the idea of presenting the learning material which allows the teacher to structure it depending on instruction goals. Generally, each II can belong to several subsets at a time. Let us consider the following item of information:

Voltage at which breakdown occurs is termed breakdown voltage. Its value depends on the type of semiconductor used, on its resistivity, width of junction, etc. The wider the junction, the greater the voltage.

Clearly, depending on instruction goals, this item could be labelled to be simultaneously a 'notion', 'help', or 'reference material'. Only information items containing methodological guidance, algorithms and solutions and bibliographic data cannot be declared others.

The set of information items of the 'Problems to be Solved' kind can also fall in subsets according to type and kind. An example:
Types of problems:
- questions;
- problems;

- situations to be analyzed;
- design tasks;
- case studies.

Each of these is characterized by its destination, which defines its kind:

- initial level test;
- drill & practice;
- in-course testing;
- final test.

The types of problems form non-intersecting sets, while a problem of one and the same type can pertain to all kinds simultaneously. An example: The information item:

What semiconductors are used for
    semiconductor devices?

1. Pure
2. Non-pure
3. Doped

can belong to the subsets for initial level test, in-course testing and final test simultaneously.

4.2. ASSOCIATIVE PART OF AN ECS

As was already pointed out, the type and kind of the information items, their interrelations as well as some other characteristics of theirs constitute the associative part of an elementary cognitive stucture. In other words, a definite attribute is associated to each item in the contents part of the cognitive structure. This attribute is a compound one and is termed the II's logical description.

The compound attribute of an II - Knowledge kind is composed of two simple attributes - name and type:

CA ::= < NAME >:<TYPE>

The attribute "name" has one single meaning - the absolute address of the II-Knowledge in the knowledge base, whereas the "type" attribute can assume one or several of the ten meanings shown above. As an example we shall discuss the compound attributes of two information items of the Knowledge kind:

$$CA_{17} ::= < II\ 17 >:< FORMULAS >$$
$$CA_{22} ::= < II\ 22 >:< NOTION;HELP;REFERENCE >$$

This would mean the following: the compound attribute of information item number 17 has a name "II17" and type "formulas"; the compound attribute of information item number 22 - name "II22", type - "notion", "help" and "reference".

The compound attribute of II - Problems to be Solved, is far more complicated. It consists of the following simple attributes:

    CA ::= <NAME>:<TYPE>:<KIND>:<DEGREE OF COMPLEXITY>:
           <CORRECT ANSWERS>:<ASSOCIATIVE RELATIONS OF
           CORRECT ANSWERS>:<ASSOCIATIVE LINKS OF WRONG
           ANSWERS WITH II-KNOWLEDGE>:<ESTIMATION OF
           WRONG ANSWERS>:<HELP>:<SOLUTION TIME>.

The simple attribute name of an II - Problems to be Solved is the same as that of I - Knowledge kind. The attributes "type" and "kind" assume: the first - respectively one of the five and the second - one or more of the four meanings pointed above.

"Degree of complexity" is an attribute of three values: "high", "medium" and "low".

The "correct" answer or answers, "trapped or untrapped" wrong answers are simple attributes, characterized by a constant value of numbers, characters, alpha-numeric or other symbols.

The "associative relations" of correct, wrong, and untrapped answers are simple attributes, having as a meaning the names of the II - Knowledge, associated with the respective answer.

The attribute "estimation of wrong answers" is a simple attribute of three values: "insignificant", "significant" and "bad" (mistake).

"Help" is an attribute of the same kind as the answers, for generally this is a learner's answer of a kind.

"Solution time" is an attribute assuming the meaning of a number, indicating the time (in minutes) for solving the respective problem. A value of "0" means unlimited solution time.

Thus, the compound attribute of the question given above would be:

```
CA ::= < II12 >:< QUESTION >:< INITIAL LEVEL TEST;
       IN-COURSE TESTING >:< MINIMUM >:< 2 OR 3 >:
       <II7>:< II8 >:< 1 >:< II9 >:< BAD >:<   <II10;
       II11 >: < BAD >: < 1 >
```

and means: name of the problem to be solved "II12", type-question, kind - initial level test, in-course testing, final test; lowest degree of complexity. Correct answers - second and third. Associative relations of second answer - II7, of third answer - II8. Expected wrong answers - first, associative relations -II9. Estimation of such an answer - bad mistake. All other answers are untrapped, associated with II10 and II11 and their estimation is also 'bad mistake'. No "help" is envisaged. Solution time - one minute.

4.3. IDENTIFICATION OF ELEMENTARY COGNITIVE STRUCTURES

Each ECS has its name in the knowledge base, which, as was pointed out in describing the model, should be unique. The abbreviated name of the ECS is the information about its hierar chical level and its number on that level. The full name of the ECS comprises its contents meaning in the knowledge base. It also features a description of all information items falling within this structure.

An example: A knowledge base contains 20 information items, and II1 : II15 are defined as Knowledge, and II16 : II20 - as Problems to be Solved. The following cognitive structures are defined in it:

ECS1 < II1 : II4 ; II16 : II17 >;
ECS2 < II5 : II15; II18 : II20 >;
ECS3 < ECS1;   ECS2 >;
ECS4 < ECS1; II6; II18; II19 >

These are the full names of the cognitive structures in the knowledge base. Each ECS constitutes a list of the information items contained in it, or a list of the elementary cognitive structures, which is one and the same. The abbreviated names of the cognitive structures in this case are: ECS 1; ECS 2; ECS 3; ECS 4.
Provided these are structures from different hierarchical levels, then they would be denoted as:

$$ECS_1^1 ; \quad ECS_2^1 ; \quad ECS_3^2 ; \quad ECS_4^2 .$$

The superscript indicates the level of hierarchy to which the respective ECS belongs.

4.4. STRUCTURE OF THE LEARNING-ORIENTED KNOWLEDGE BASE

What has been said so far allows us to present a knowledge base as a hierarchy of cognitive structures in the following manner (Fig.4):

The M set of the contents parts of information items will always be on the lowest hierarchical level. The next level will always be occupied by the associative part of the information items. Third level and above will contain the cognitive structures.

The first level is the contents part of the knowledge base, whereas all the rest of the levels constitute its associative part.

As can be seen in Figure 4, the order of hierarchy in this case is reverse to that of the general conceptual model. This reason is that here recursion is possible only upwards with regard to the degree of generalization of knowledge (growing generalization) and outwards with regard to increasing the number of elements and ECSs on a certain hierarchical level. Recursion is not possible from the information items level downwards. This is a peculiarity of a learning-oriented knowledge base, which is not 'pure' knowledge, but knowledge organized in such a manner as to achieve definite educational goals.

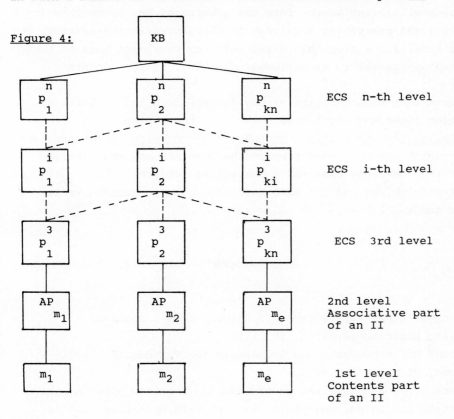

Figure 4:

Thus, depending on the goal, learning may begin at the first hierarchical level with some students, and at the second with others, an so on. Another peculiarity of such a knowledge base is that an ECS of the i-th level could be an element in an ECS of the i+1 or higher level. The reverse does not hold.

The very structure of ECSs that is to be built in the knowledge base could be different, depending on the goals, learning theories and strategies, the students' individual characteristics, etc.

5. SUMMARY

Introducing new technology in schools and its efficient utilization in learning will bring to the fore the problem of the approaches in structuring and presenting knowledge in learning-oriented systems. The proposed model for a computer- aided learning knowledge base is just one of the approaches to be employed, allowing, in the authors' opinion:

1. Invariant presenatation of any subject down to the level of information items and attributes describing their properties.

2. Laying some theoretical groundwork on developing CAL programs.

3. A quick and easy up-dating of the contents and associative parts of the knowledge base for a respective subject.

4. Employing one and the same knowledge base to achieve various learning goals.

6.REFERENCES

1. Djugeli E.P., Vephvadze A.A., "Kibernetika i problemi obuchenia", Metzniereba, 1981, Tbilisi.

2. Frank H., "Kybernetische Grundlagen der Pedagogik", Verlag W. Kohlnammer, Stuttgard, 1971.

3. Pask G., "Obuchenie kak protzes sozdania sistem upravlenia". "Kibernetika i problemy obuchenia" M., Progress Publishers, 1970.

EULE+: An Object-Oriented Authoring and Learner System

W. Stern, G. Schlageter
University of Hagen, Department of Computer Science
Postfach 940, 5800 Hagen, West-Germany

KEYWORDS

Computer Assisted Learning (CAL), Authoring and Learner Systems (ALS), Object-Oriented Systems

ABSTRACT

The deficiencies of current authoring and learner systems lead to the development of a new authoring and learner system. This paper presents the features of this system, which is called EULE+.

The basic concepts of EULE+ is the object-oriented approach. Beyond it many concepts are integrated which are known from other fields such as CAD, HYPERTEXT, OOPS, IR, Simulation and Animation. The main challenge with EULE+ is the integration of all these different concepts to a high level author- and learner system and the consequential usage of object-oriented concepts in the functionalities for the author and learner.

This report is based on a project which is funded by the German "Bundesminister für Bildung und Wissenschaft" (Project No. M0538.00). The authors are responsible for the contents of this publication.

1. INTRODUCTION

Since 1986 the University of Hagen has been engaged in continuing education based on electronic media (personal computer). Electronic courseware has been or is being developed in the field of computer science, especially:

- Introduction to UNIX
- Introduction to C
- Introduction to LISP
- Office Automation
- Introduction to PROLOG
- Introduction to Expert Systems
- SQL
- Object Oriented Programming

(Some of these courses were produced in cooperation with the (HYPER-)COSTOC project at the IIG Graz (Austria), Prof. Maurer) [HUB_88a].

These courses are offered worldwide by the university of Hagen to universities, students and also to companies. The electronic courseware has been accepted very positively, mainly for the following reasons:

- *the contents*

    The courses are authored by experts in their field. Their close connection to research activities results in courses of immediate interest for both universities and companies.
- *the medium PC*

    It is our aim to consequently use the features of the computer in the courses. So the student can learn in a very interesting and motivating way; much more than s/he can do with a conventional book.

It is an obvious fact that CAL, after a phase of depression in the 70ies, becomes more and more important in nearly every area of education (school, universities, *continuing education*). This is also our experience after offering CAL-courseware for more than one year.

But still one great problem exists: the tools. The functionalities of the available tools to build and to learn with courseware are rather rudimentary. Among other things this implies high development costs.

The deficiencies of current authoring and learner systems lead us to the development of a new generation of tools, based on object-oriented concepts. This paper presents the features of this system, which we call EULE⁺ (Eule (German) = owl: symbol of wisdom).

2. Some Pragmatic Aspects on a Suitable Authoring-/Learner System (ALS)

Obviously everyone who offers an ALS maintains that this special ALS is the best one. We have made a special research on 21 ALS (available in Germany and running in a DOS-environment); the result was that none of these systems was really suitable [FAN_88].

But what is a "suitable" ALS?

a) An authoring system is *suitable* when the costs for editing and developing the courseware are very low

(not 1:200 or more as with current tools).

b) A learner system is *suitable* when the learner is so enthusiastic about this learning environment that s/he go on using this environment deliberately

(and is not as frustrated as s/he is by current tools).

So ALS has to be measured against the users of the system: the author and the learner. They have to be satisfied by the system. Of course this is an obvious fact, but you have to consider that some ALS exist on the base of authoring-language (which is more or less a programming language), which is surely not state-of-the-art of computer science.

These statements above are very common but they point on the problems of current CAL tools:

1) *The authoring process is directed by the tool*

An author of courseware spends a lot of time to adapt her/his didactic ideas to the limitations of the used tool (e.g. 40 chars/line, no animation, very primitive answer analysis techniques, etc.).

2) *the editing process is very time intensive*

This aspect derives from the same deficiency of authoring systems: designing a special idea of an author by the means of the used tool often results in a difficult technical analysis of the functionalities of the used tool (e.g. if the author wants a very detailed and complex answer analysis).

3) *the learner is not as free in learning as s/he wants*

Naturally *the typical student* does not exists. Everyone learns on her/his own way. That means that a learning system may not *dictate* the learner but has to offer a flexible and adaptable learning interface. To give an example: the requirement to look into two different parts of the courseware in parallel (e.g. to compare something) fails because it is impossible to open two course-windows parallel on the screen.

It is a very interesting fact that there is a connection between the quality of the tools and the quality of the contents of the courseware: if features of an ALS are to complicated the author (or the courseware designer) will avoid them although it would improve the contents.

What we need is a ALS with the following features:

1) Book World

While designing an authoring and learner system it is most important to bear in mind, that authors and students are used to the conventional learning medium **book**. So the minimum an electronic learning environment has to offer are all the functionalities of a conventional book. This seems to be trivial but surprisingly nearly no commercial authoring system today exists which fulfills this requirement.

To give an example: marking text with a pen is most simple to do in a book, but impossible in almost every commercial electronic courseware.

2) Computer Features

Naturally it is not enough only to redesign a book on a computer. Computer features have to be integrated consequently into an ALS:

- working in parallel (multi-windowing)
- complex but transparent course-structure
- (animated) graphics
- interaction (dialogues)
- electronic laboratory
- communication support (to support cooperative working)

3.   THE EULE-SYSTEM USED SO FAR

The ALS the university of Hagen is using until now is called EULE and is partitioned into the authoring system (AUTOOL), which supports the author of a course (editing, structuring..) and the learner system (EULE-Tutor), which acts as a tutor to the student (presentation,..):

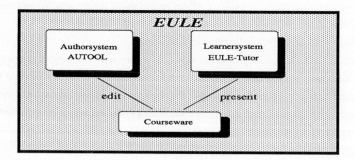

Figure 1: Parts of EULE

The authoring system is AUTOOL, which has its strengths on graphical presentation [GAR_85, GAR_87].

The learner system we have developed in our project presents the courseware to the student with some advanced techniques:

- *Multi Windowing Techniques*

    The student can open several windows to look at different 'course-pages' simultaneously.
- *Navigation support*

    Access via index, but also via course-structure (frame, chapter, course) is supported.
- *Animation*

    Within the course animated graphic is often used to give an intuitive understanding of the concepts. In comparison to more text-oriented courseware the animation feature allows a faster and more motivating learning.
- *Electronic Laboratory*

    Parallel to the presented courseware ('electronic book') it is possible for the learner to experiment with the tools that are the subject of the course (e.g. the PROLOG Interpreter can be used to experiment with some of the concepts presented in the book-part).

The EULE-learner system used so far is conceptually split up into two parts: the electronic book (edited with AUTOOL) and the laboratory (original tool, e.g. language compiler, or simulations).

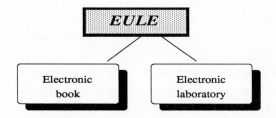

Figure 2: Book and laboratory in EULE

Still both the authoring and the learner system have disadvantages:

AUTOOL and nearly every other commercial *authoring system* are more or less low level text- and/or graphic editors. So the costs for editing a course with such a system are very high (see above). Costs can only be reduced by comfortable authoring-functionalities:

- WYSIWYG-techniques
- large example libraries, from which the author can derive her/his special course (e.g. graphical elements)

On the other side the *learner environment* should be more comfortable; functions are needed as:

- integration of electronic book and laboratory (e.g. Cut-and-Paste)
- sub-intelligent support in question-and-answer dialogues
- flexible navigation functions through the courseware
- support of individualization of the courseware by the learner (notes, highlighting, ..)

All these ideas will be explained in more detail in the following chapter.

4.   EULE⁺

We try to solve the described problems by designing EULE⁺, a sophisticated object-oriented authoring and learner system.

Let us first describe the basic design principles for EULE⁺:

1) *Book World*
   (see chapter 2)

2) *Computer Features*
   (see chapter 2)

3) *Non-intelligent, but object-oriented approach*
   The experience with the 'intelligent' approach to learner systems, the so-called 'intelligent' tutoring systems (ITS) shows, that although the ITS developed so far only work on very small domains, large knowledge-bases had to be built for ITS [YAZ_86, AND_85, DED_86]. So the ITS-approach only allows *domain-dependent* systems, which require high development-costs, too.
   We are thinking about *tools* in the sense that they can be used domain-independent and support a fast development of 'high-level' courseware. The natural approach for such tools is the object-oriented one. This will be explained in detail in the following chapters.

4) *Usage of common concepts*
   We try to make use of the observation that many of the functions we would like to integrate in an EULE⁺-ALS are available in other systems, though scattered on very different ones.
   E.g. the presentation layer of EULE⁺ has many functionalities of a CAD-system; the course-management has to offer many functions already known from office-automation-systems.
   So what we try is to integrate different concepts into EULE⁺.

Similar to the already existing EULE-ALS also EULE⁺ is partitioned into the authoring system (EULE⁺-A) and the learner system (EULE⁺-L):

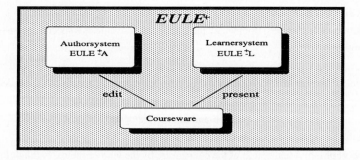

Figure 3: Parts of EULE⁺

Naturally the author of a course has both systems available simultaneously: EULE⁺-A for editing, EULE⁺-L to test the courseware from the learner's view.

4.1   EULE⁺-MODULES AND THEIR FUNCTIONALITIES

Before we describe the functionalities of EULE⁺ let us first show an overview of the different modules:

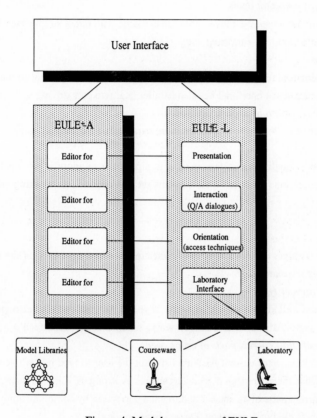

Figure 4: Module structure of EULE⁺

EULE⁺-A offers a set of tools (editors) to edit the items which will be used by the different modules of EULE⁺-L.

From this point of view the functionalities of EULE⁺-L are described first:

EULE⁺-L Functionalities:

Presentation

The presentation layer has to present the content of the courseware to the learner.

1. **Simple presentation features**

   All the presentation possibilities known from other ALS and/or several graphic tools (e.g. MS-WINDOWS DRAW).

   Examples: text, curves, splines, arc, ...

2. **Complex presentation items**

   Complex in that sense, that the presentation items are built out of simple ones, but are as usable as one single item (e.g. mirroring, etc.)

3. **Animation**

   Several animation features are supported. Among others not only serial animation exists (only one item animates at one time) but also parallel (e.g. two cars driving against each other).

4. **Adaptive Presentation - Individualization**

   The learner can select various (presentation) parameters: e.g. animation-speed, color settings, ..

   Also the individualization of the contents is supported: an editor is provided which supports some modification functions on the contents such as annotations, marking, notices, ..

Interaction

The interaction layer analyzes the answer of the learner to questions presented in the course and give appropriate reactions to the learner.

1. **Different answer types**

   Not only the well known textual answers ("Type in the answer!") but also graphical ones are provided (e.g.: "Paint the curve of $f(x)=\sin(x)$ with the mouse on screen").

2. **Detection of (not) correct parts of an answer**

   Answer techniques of current ALS almost want the user to type in a whole new answer to a question when the system has detected an answer as wrong. EULE⁺-L tries to detect the correct and not correct parts of an answer and to get a correction by communicating with the learner (e.g.: "This is ok, but ... is wrong. Do you have an idea?").

3. **Hints**

   Hints (foreseen by the author or derived from the answer by using courseware-links,..) can be given by the system to help the learner to answer a question (e.g.: "Perhaps you should repeat the chapter about xyz, before you can answer this question").

Orientation

By orientation all features are meant which deal with the structure of the course.

1. *Navigation*

   The *book-path* leads the learner through the courseware by offering book-structures (chapter no., page no., next page, last page, etc.).

   Several book-paths can exist, e.g. depending on the learner's level (beginner, specialist, etc.). Naturally the author has to provide these structures.

   Beyond this the learner can create *individual paths*, e.g. to provide the course material to other learners (teacher -> pupils).

2. *Information retrieval (IR) and database query techniques*

   Other structures on the courseware allow several access techniques,
   - via pattern searching/matching
     (e.g. all pages with expression xyz, or
     all graphics which include a special presentation item)
   - via content dependencies
     (e.g. all pages which include suppositions to this special content)
   - via didactic types
     (e.g. all questions of chapter x, or
     all animations of the course).

   Also combinations are very useful:

   e.g. Present all questions which can be answered on the base of the knowledge acquired so far. For this kind of retrieval a *learner-protocol* (not an internal learner-model) is necessary.

Laboratory interface

The laboratory interface connects the underlying laboratory tool to the other layers of EULE⁺-L. Functions are:

1. *Cut-And-Paste*

   Information presented in the course (e.g. a PROLOG database) can be cut from the course-page and transmitted into a laboratory (e.g. a PROLOG interpreter). In the laboratory the learner can directly experiment with such information out of the course.

2. *Control an laboratory exercise*

   The learner has to solve given problems in the laboratory, which are given in the book-part (e.g. to modify a PROLOG-database). This access can be compared with a special Q/A-technique in the course.

   The laboratory-interface installs the exercise into the laboratory (e.g. transmits the PROLOG-database) and tries to analyze whether the learner has solved the exercise when the learner comes back from the laboratory (e.g. by testing whether a developed program runs or not).

Laboratory

Laboratories realize the fields of experimentation for the students. Two types of accessing laboratories can be distinguished:
- *free*: the learner decides to play and experiment on his own.
- *problem-oriented*: the learner has to solve a given problem in the laboratory (see above).

Individualization

Individualization facilities of EULE⁺-L are already pointed out in the modules *presentation* and *orientation*.

For the learner also a *history component* of EULE⁺-L is very useful and acts as an individual learning protocol. This is most important for parts of learning when the learner is in dialogue with the system: question/answer dialogues and laboratory-sessions. E.g. the learner can get the information about his last program-development in the laboratory.

EULE⁺-A Functionalities

As pointed out above, EULE⁺-A offers a set of tools (editors) to the author.

There is one idea which runs like a red thread through EULE⁺-A: the possibility *to reuse* already designed things (out of courseware or libraries) and *to adapt* them very simple and fast to special needs. Courseware development can be much faster by using models or copies. To explain it very clearly: we do not think only about a simple copy of something; the main and innovative idea is the possibility of flexible adaptation.

To give an example:
One model could be VEHICLES. This model includes the information, that there are several WHEELS, how to draw a WHEEL and how to move the vehicle (e.g. "while moving over the screen rotate the WHEELS").

Now the author can use this model to generate a special presentation: e.g. CAR. The only thing s/he has to do: specify the number of wheels and connect the presentation of the car-body. The author has developed the new model CAR.

S/he can simply position the presentation of a car on screen and specify MOVE. Important: the whole movement has not to be edited manually as it has to be in current tools, because the common method "moving a vehicle" can directly be used.

This concept of modelling and adapting can be seen as the object-oriented authoring interface and is consequently integrated into every EULE⁺-A tool.

"Object-oriented" encloses the concepts:
- objects with potentially complex internal structures
- methods which represent the behaviour of the objects
- class hierarchies with inheritance

The main task of the EULE⁺-A tools is to generate und edit EULE⁺-courseware which consists of EULE⁺-objects with a definable behaviour and an assigned graphical representation.

So how can editing of EULE⁺-courseware work:
1) pick up a model (object class) out of a model library
2) generate new models by adapting, composing, editing of existing models
3) instantiate EULE⁺-objects out of models
4) compose EULE⁺-objects to EULE⁺-courseware

This concept is integrated in every EULE⁺-A tool:

1. Presentation editor

- see example above

2. Q/A editor

- model library includes standard types as:
  YES/NO, multiple choice, pairing, puzzle, gaptext, freetext, ..
- possibility to compose new question types such as graphical ones
- build course-dependent Q/A models:
  e.g. the author could generate Q/A models for freetext, which all can handle synonyms for special keywords (e.g. CAI = CBT = CAL = ...).

3. Structure editor

Organization of the courseware network. Hypertext concepts and techniques are used as an object-oriented base for this tool.
- model library includes several course structures
  (e.g.: depending on the count of learning hours, etc.)
- generate individual course structures
  (e.g.: after every chapter a question is placed, ..)

4.2   USER INTERFACE

As already stated above the user interface
- supports a window-surface
- is mouse-driven
- uses WYSIWYG-presentations

All functionalities of EULE⁺-L and EULE⁺-A are offered using this interface (e.g. and not offered by a programmable but object-oriented interface).

To give an idea of working with this user interface:

To get a model out of a library with the presentation editor of EULE⁺-A
- the author clicks a library icon with the mouse
- a window is opened with rough sketches of the available models
- the author clicks a model icon and pulls it into the working area

4.3   INTERNAL REPRESENTATION OF EULE⁺ COURSEWARE

The base for both systems is the EULE⁺ courseware, which is structured as follows:

The courseware can be seen as a "hypertext-like" network of courseware-elements. Courseware elements are called *nodes* which are connected via *links*.

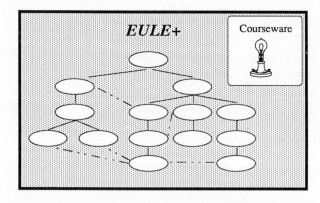

Figure 5: Courseware-structure in EULE⁺

Nodes:

Nodes *represent objectives* of the course. The node itself could be a paragraph, which is conceptually an atomic semantically self-contained learning-unit (e.g. a paragraph could be: "QUICKSORT-algorithm"). But nodes can also be more complex, such as a chapter or the whole course.

The nodes have a description part, a content part and a link part.

Description part:

The node is described in several aspects:
- *structural*
  course, chapter, .., paragraph
  register, index, glossary, ..
- *type of content*
  definition, example, question, laboratory exercise, ..
- *type of presentation*
  textual, graphical, animation, ..

These informations can be accessed by the learner by using the orientation features.

content part

The content of the node contains the concepts which are taught. Technically the content is more or less represented by objects with some graphical presentation. It is important that the contents are *not* a knowledge-bases about a domain.

link part

The link part includes the information about the connection of this node inside the courseware network.
- book paths (e.g. next page, last page,..)
- content dependencies
- individual learning paths

5. SUMMARY

EULE⁺ represents the consequent successor of system EULE. The basic concept of EULE⁺ is the object-oriented approach.

Many concepts are integrated which are known from other fields such as CAD, HYPERTEXT, OOPS, IR, Simulation and Animation. The main challenge with EULE+ is the integration of all these different concepts to a high level author- and learner system and the consequential usage of object-oriented concepts in the functionalities for the author and learner.

EULE+ runs on IBM-PC under DOS and uses MS-WINDOWS (in future also OS2).

ACKNOWLEDGEMENT

The ideas presented in this paper were developed by the members of the EULE-project. We wish to especially acknowledge the contributions of E. Berg, J. Böhme, K. Fankhänel, D. Rosin, Prof. H.-J. Six, Prof. C. Unger.

LITERATURE

[AND_85] J. R. Anderson, B. J. Reiser
        The LISP Tutor
        BYTE, April 1985
[DED_86] C. Dede
        A review and synthesis of recent research in intelligent computer-assisted instruction
        Int. J. Man-Machine Studies (1986) 24
[FAN_88] K. Fankhänel, G. Schlageter, W. Stern
        Lehrsysteme für Personal Computer
        - Autoren- und Tutorsysteme -
        University of Hagen, West Germany 1988
[GAR_85] J. Garrat, F. Huber, H. Huemer
        AUTOOL: Ein BTX-orientiertes Autorensystem
        University of Graz - IIG, Report 206
        Austria 1985
[GAR_87] J. Garrat, F. Huber
        AUTOOL Version 2 Reference Manual
        University of Graz - IIG, Report 237
        Austria 1987

[HUB_88a]   F. Huber, F. Makedon, H. Maurer
     HyperCOSTOC: A Comprehensive Computer-Based Teaching Support System
     University of Graz - IIG Report 258, Oct. 1988
[HUB_88b]   F. Huber
     A proposal for an authoring system avoiding common errors in tutorial lessons
     University of Graz - IIG Report 265, Dez. 1988
[YAZ_86] M. Yazdani
     Intelligent tutoring systems: An overview
     expert systems, 1986, Vol3. No.3

"Interactive COSTOC Tutorials"

M.G. Stone[*]
Department of Mathematics and Statistics
The University of Calgary

Abstract

We describe here a pilot program for the creation of interactive mathematics
tutorials using COSTOC. The design philosophy, and the interactive program
elements, as well as their implementation in HyperCostoc are discussed in detail.
Several lessons have been completed to date, incorporating interactive presentation
material and Self-Test/Review Exercises. Important features of the project are
"problem drivers" and "answer evaluation" routines implemented as PASCAL subroutines
in the execution program. Demonstration of completed Lessons will be the basis for
a presentation of this work at IICAL'89.

1. INTRODUCTION

In a previous pilot project the author created a series of nine tutorial
lessons for a laboratory in Elementary Linear Algebra, using the PLATO authoring
system. Approximately thirty students attended a weekly two-hour lab which
supplemented the usual lectures and tutorials. Experience with this earlier project
suggested that such CAL tutorial lessons could be far more effective if three
additional criteria were met:

1) Lessons should run outside the lab on low end PC-compatibles.
2) Lessons should generate unlimited numbers of drill exercises.
3) Lessons should contain free response questions, which require the student to
   create rather than select an answer.

To this end it was decided to initiate a second pilot project. Internal funding (in
the form of release time) was provided through I.C.A.L. at the University of Calgary
to support the current project. After reviewing a number of available authoring
systems, the COSTOC Authoring System was selected as the environment most likely to

---

[*] ICAL Fellow at the University of Calgary 1988-89. The author gratefully
acknowledges ICAL's support; their help made this work possible.

lend itself to completion of lessons incorporating all of the above features in the required time frame. The Institute IIG in Graz, Austria has generously provided support for development of subroutines related to the more unusual technical aspects of the project. Ten lessons are planned, with a pilot section of 100 students from Math 211 (Elementary Linear Algebra) field testing some of these lessons in the period January - April 1989, at the University of Calgary.

Lessons planned include:

Introduction to Linear Systems	Properties of Determinants
Solving Linear Systems	Applications of Determinants
Matrix Algebra	Vectors in 3-D
Theory of Linear Systems	Lines in 3-D
Evaluating Determinants	Planes in 3-D.

Our decision to create lessons which will run on micros (rather than in a mainframe environment) was in part dictated by resource limitations and student numbers. Full scale use of these lessons at the University of Calgary would require lab facilities for eight or ten sections of one hundred and twenty students apiece, in each of the Fall and Winter terms (about 2200 students annually). Parallel requirements for Calculus (2500 students annually), and for other courses as well generate student numbers for which it has been impossible to provide adequate dedicated laboratory facilities. However, more and more students have, or it appears will have in the near future, access to PC-compatibles ... either at home, through a friend off campus, or at other non-dedicated micro lab facilities on campus. Moreover, the lessons to be developed here were viewed as a study tool, rather than an evaluative one. Thus an effort is being made to develop lessons which students can use in a "self-test -- review" learning cycle, in an environment of their own choosing. It is anticipated that enough laboratory facilities can be made available to accommodate those students who have no other access to a suitable microcomputer.

In the previous project PLATO lessons incorporated random selection of questions from suitable groups of questions in a question file as the components of a quiz. The enormous manpower required to provide such question files is familiar to anyone who has attempted a similar project. It was decided to construct lessons with problems which are produced by algorithms, using random number generation in order to overcome difficulties involved in providing large question banks. The ability to drop down and execute subroutines in a standard programming language is a clear prerequisite for the incorporation of such algorithms into lessons. The PLATO authoring system does not have this capability. The COSTOC authoring system offers an opportunity to incorporate Turbo Pascal subroutines as "calls" in the lesson programme, and thus is suitable for this purpose.

The restricted choice of answer format (multiple choice or variations thereof: limited "matching", "short answer", true/false or numerical answer only) available in PLATO proved to be fundamentally unsatisfactory. If "difficult" questions were constructed (e.g. "For the situation given ... (above) ... which of the following (A,B,C,D,E) are true? Select all correct responses.") student progress was slow, and the frustration level high. For easier "computational" questions, or some "difficult" drill exercises, students were often able to select the correct response ... even though subsequent conventional testing showed they were weak at execution of similar computations. Some of these difficulties with the multiple choice format can be overcome by careful question/answer construction. Nevertheless, our anecdotal evidence (both in Linear Algebra and in a parallel pilot project in Calculus) indicated that the multiple choice answer format conferred a significant learning handicap on students with incomplete understanding, by masking from them their own fundamental deficiencies. For an author of CAL lessons, on the other hand, the syntactic recognition of correct "free" responses supplied by students poses problems not currently within the range of sophistication of programmes which can run on PC's. It was decided to invoke an operational test for the correctness of student responses: by evaluating and comparing the "correct" response and the student response at a number of randomly selected values within an appropriate range for the variable, equivalent answers could be accepted and wrong answers rejected. A preliminary version of a programme to check differentiation of elementary functions (Differenzierungs Trainer) has been created in GRAZ at the IIG Institute, incorporating this idea to recognize correct student responses. The idea is simple, but it appears to work very well. The use of this technique in an interactive mode to check for correct input response in CAL has been proposed by others as well, cf. [5]. It provides a relatively low-cost entry (in terms of programming sophistica-tion) into the use of "free response" format questions (at least in mathematics!) and we regard this as a pedagogically important departure from techniques which "prompt" student response, or which accept only a limited number of "canned" correct responses.

2. BACKGROUND

Some criteria for good mathematical educational software described by H. Flanders in [2] are worth repeating here. We paraphrase his suggestions below:

a) No knowledge of computers should be required to use the software, other than the basics of how to insert a disk, power on, and type in a few letters. No computer programming whatever should be required.

b) The documentation that goes with the disk should be essentially unnecessary for the user. What one has to do at any point should be visibly apparent, and one should never have to stop work to look up a topic in a manual. Therefore the manual should be brief, and essentially a reference work.

c) The software should be truly interactive, with emphasis on the "active". It should neither spoonfeed nor do show-and-tell demonstrations, but should require user input to produce output, require the user to think about what he or she is doing, and enable the user to be correspondingly gratified by the results. The user should always feel he or she is part of the process.

d) The software should be robust: extremely difficult to crash. Input errors should be noted, not punished, with reentry requested.

e) The syntax for input should be as close to the way mathematics is written as possible. For instance .5 Sin 2t, not 0.5*(sin(2*t)).

f) Input of real numbers should allow expressions that evaluate to reals, so the computer does the calculations for you. For instance, Arcsin (.5 Sin 1.7) should be acceptable "constant" input.

The interactive nature of CAL, described above in c) has been the focal point of our own development. The interactive elements of our program design involve both a conscious choice of language (the direct mode of address) in presentation material, and an interactive capability on the part of the program to evaluate and respond to user proposed solutions. Thus it is a requirement not only that the user think about meaningful input, but that the program respond flexibly to a wide range of input. We comment briefly on each of these aspects: language, answer evaluation, and the role of user input before going on to describe the details of our implementation in HyperCostoc.

There is a great temptation, perhaps for mathematicians especially, to write presentation material for software as one would write a textbook. The style is usually in the impersonal third person, with occasional use of the "royal" we in the presentation of ideas. If the software is to be truly an interactive tutorial however, it is our feeling that the lessons should develop more as a dialog. The use of Socratic dialog as a paradigm for mathematical software is explored briefly in [1]. We felt, however, that the language itself should encourage a participatory, even conspiratorial, exchange between the user and the program elements. Thus we have adopted, in one of our pilot courses, a language for the lessons which frequently uses the direct mode of address. Typically this means choosing to replace phrases such as "This system has no solution" with "Notice that there are no solutions to this system..." and "There are three types of operations which leave the solutions invariant." by "You can do the following three things which do not change the solutions." Frequent use of other phrases such as "Let's see what happens when we do this", or "We will next take a look at..." attempt to draw the user into the discussion and engage his or her attention as a <u>participant</u> in a process, <u>rather than</u> a <u>recipient</u> of information dispensed from higher authority.

We have discussed briefly the method used to <u>evaluate</u> student input for the lessons in this project. The "answers" we have in mind here are for the most part mathematical expressions. The problem we hope to overcome is the necessity of constructing a sophisticated parsing mechanism to recognize equally correct answers in different form, e.g.

$$(x - 1)(x + 1), \text{ and } x^2 - 1, \text{ and } x^2 - \sin(\pi/2).$$

Hopefully we may also detect subtle errors, recognizing for example that $x(x - 1/x) \neq x^2 - 1$. An operational approach is used. All answers are treated as functions; functions proposed as answers are evaluated at a number of randomly chosen points in a range appropriate to the individual problem, and compared with the values of the standard answer to determine "correctness". Given the limited keyboard input available, the possibilities for confusion in identifying correct input are not great, and indeed the procedure seems to work very well. For text-based answers, there is a reasonably sophisticated answer evaluation profile available already within COSTOC, wherein one can elect to seek keywords or fatal errors; one can elect to ignore punctuation, capitalization, extra characters etc. The main gain here is to provide a mechanism which recognizes immediately as "correct", answers like $4x^3 - 6x^2 + 2x - 9$ in an infinite variety of presentations, for example $2x(2x^2-3x)+2(x-5)+1$.

The need for meaningful <u>user input</u> to produce output in an interactive program seems clear. There is a balance, however, which must be struck in a lesson which a user will perhaps execute many times. The COSTOC system provides the user with an escape mechanism to consciously bypass the need to really "work through" all parts of the lesson each time it is used. This feature perhaps gives greater freedom to include, periodically, questions which require considerable time to answer, as opposed to those which merely check the user's attention to the material being presented.

The implementation of Interactive Tutorials for Mathematics using this design philosophy is the goal of our project. Lessons in Differentiation and Systems of Linear Equations have been completed. The latter is part of a course in Elementary Linear Algebra currently under development. The ease with which subroutines in a standard programming language (PASCAL) can be incorporated in materials authored in the HyperCostoc System was a major factor in the decision to implement this project in that system. HyperCostoc facilitates the use of interactive design elements such as algorithmic problem generation and operational answer checking through direct calls to subroutines in program execution.

3. HYPERCOSTOC

We will describe briefly here the HyperCostoc environment for those who are
not familiar with it. The system is an outgrowth of COSTOC (Computer Supported
Teaching of Course!) and GLSS (General Lessons Specification System) developed at
the Institute IIg in Graz, Austria. These systems in turn have historical roots in
the evolution of PLATO and the Tutor language developed by CDC.

In the execution mode HyperCostoc Lessons consist of a sequential presentation
of (numbered) Frames. At the conclusion of each presentation Frame, students have
the option to go forward (next), back to the previous (or another specified) Frame,
or invoke a lateral help Frame. Individual Frames may present text or graphics (or
indeed call a special graphics frame), may provide a menu with the opportunity to
branch selectively to other Frames, or may present a question or branch to a
(PASCAL) subroutine. Both text and graphics are presented in PGA or EGA high
resolution color graphics modes. Execution with a hard disk provides good screen
displays with minimum time delay. The presentation is governed by author-specified
branching among the Frames. Each frame itself consists of a sequential presentation
of objects (text, graphics, timed pause, key pause, animation, and repetition
sequences) which allow one to sequentially develop, clear and refresh the image
presented in a single frame. An execution overlay allows an instructor to customize
a lesson by using windowed marginal notes. Students, too, can add their own notes
in a similar windowing system. The same overlay allows the student to use "Alt"
keyboard commands to control a number of the presentation features e.g. alter the
speed of presentation, mark a frame for reference, jump to a numbered or marked
frame, display or hide student/instructor notes etc., providing considerable
flexibility and control to the user.

In the authoring mode, currently, special graphics hardware (Matrox PGA) is
required in order to use a menu-driven Lesson Editor. Menu selection is made
through use of a cursor and screen icons (hence Hyper Costoc?) The graphics editor
is mouse and menu driven. The text editor, however, operates entirely from the
keyboard, with on-screen menu selection for text attributes. Text presentation is
limited to a single font in several sizes. A graphics text mode can used to
overcome some of the shortcomings of the single font, but a choice of fonts or the
ability to load a special font would be a welcome addition. Animation, setting
branching options, and standard question formatting (multiple choice, text recognition) are macro objects which call special menus that simplify the production of
sequences to accomplish these tasks. A description of features of the
COSTOC/HYPERCOSTOC Execution and Authoring system can be found in [3],[4].
Hopefully other presentations at the 1989 IICAL Conference will deal with some of
the details of HyperCostoc.

4. IMPLEMENTATION

We will present, in Dallas at IICAL '89, two prototype lessons consisting of interactive COSTOC tutorials: <u>Differentiation</u>, and <u>Systems of Linear Equations</u>. To illustrate the nature of the project, we focus here on <u>Systems of Linear Equations</u>. We will describe the overall features of this lesson, which is Lesson 1 in a series of ten lessons for a Course: "Elementary Linear Algebra ... an Interactive Tutorial". The Course could be used in conjunction with self-study of any standard text at this level. It has been designed, however, with a view toward use in a tutorial role, either by individual students, or in a Lab setting, in a standard first year university level course. Lesson 1 consists of 53 frames; about half of these are "help" frames. The branching sequence:

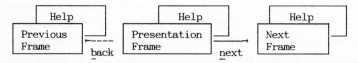

is more or less sequential, with a menu selection after the Title Page which allows the user to select various points in the presentation sequence, or to go directly to the Self-Test at the end of the Lesson. Of course the Alternate keyboard commands allow the user to override the execution mode and access any frame directly at any point in the program.

Individual presentation frames consist of a sequence of from 2 to 98 objects. Three program elements are used to evoke varying degrees of participation on the part of the student in presentation frames.

(i) Dynamic presentation (or animation): Only a <u>low level</u> of interaction is demanded from the user by dynamic presentation; nevertheless it is an important element in constructing a frame. It can be used early on in the development of the frame, and it can be used often, even continually, to command the attention of the viewer; there is definitely a level of viewer involvement that accompanies good dynamic, animated presentation. By the same token, extraneous motion, frivolous use of color etc., can distract the viewer's attention. Our working rule has been to use some dynamic element of presentation only when there is a significant and identifiable advantage to doing so. The graphic capabilities of HyperCostoc are ideally suited to use of dynamic presentation features.

(ii) Keypause followed by text (or animation): Introduction of "key pause" elements in the presentation is the simplest, method of <u>demanding</u> user interaction. It is very successful at one level (no key press, no progress) but has the potential for non-meaningful, reflex, response if not carefully used. This is partly the case because the "key pause" is inevitably used to regulate the timing of the presentation sequence. When a "reflective pause" is required to evoke a level of student participation beyond this reflex response, we have found it useful to combine a key pause with some element of dynamic presentation, such as highlighting text, use of color or animation, or the presentation of a rhetorical question, sandwiched by key pauses. The execution of a Frame in HyperCostoc is essentially a sequential process, regulated in time by timed pause, or key pause interrupts. It would be useful, and would provide an increased level of student interaction, if branching within a Frame, through the creation of buttons, could be introduced. (Perhaps this is something we can look forward to as a future development in HyperCostoc!) The presence of buttons which could be "selected" by a mouse within a frame would permit the use of an "intelligent key pause" or "smart next" which would require the student to pick his way through a frame. It would, moreover, provide the equivalent of a touch-sensitive screen for the construction of questions which ask students to identify qualitative behaviour, e.g. "Where is the curve convex up?", "Where is there an inflection point?".

(iii) Question objects: Question objects, placed at the end of a frame, provide the most highly interactive elements of the presentation material in these lessons. They require a conclusion on the part of the student, provide an opportunity to respond with feedback appropriate to the student response, and permit branching to a suitable frame. We have restricted questions in the presentation material to static questions (the question is the same each time you see the lesson) under the hypothesis that a certain degree of repetition and reinforcement is useful. Some of the questions, however, use a PASCAL subroutine to evaluate student response, and are not standard macros (Formular Answer, Text Matching, or Multiple Choice) available to the author. It appears that skillful use of "question" elements in the presentation mode does more than focus the user's attention periodically; it is the basis for an ongoing internal dialog between program and user. The effect of this type of interaction appears to be critically linked to the appropriateness of level of the question posed - it needs to be neither too hard nor too easy. Moreover, not every presentation frame is suited to the use of this interactive design element. Construction of the presentation material to provide maximum opportunity for the effective use of this device is a design consideration ... such questions are difficult to add afterwards, and the presentation material must be created with this interactive aspect in mind at the outset. One technical device we have employed to enhance the use of question objects as participation elements in a "Frame" is the construction of identical overlays for a succeeding frame. Since question/answer objects result in branching to (the beginning of) some frame, it is impossible to return to the same frame, at any point other than beginning, after a question object. The effect of "continuing" in a single frame, however, can be achieved by reproducing the displayed portion of the present frame as the initial set of objects in a "new" frame.

The major interactive feature of these lessons, however, is the Self-Test. The
Self-Test at the end of the Lesson contains problem "drivers". Through random
number generators these drivers provide different problems each time the test is
taken. Those problems, moreover, require the user to propose an answer, and the
answer-judging criteria accept any mathematically correct response. Problems are
generated, essentially, by working backwards from solutions, to avoid the necessity
to incorporate solution algorithms in the execution routines. Solutions are checked
by operational methods, evaluating and comparing responses with correct solutions at
a set of randomly selected arguments. The procedures are implemented as subroutines
in TURBO PASCAL. Individual lessons can be down loaded to floppy disks, and
executed on PC's with EGA graphics.

5. CONCLUSION

HyperCostoc has been available previously only to authors with a special
graphics environment (Matrox PG-G40A), and hardware availability problems have
delayed our own development of this course. The availability of the authoring
system in an EGA configuration should make it a more attractive authoring alternative. Flanders' criteria for input syntax are not met by the current system; user
input must still conform to the way mathematics is written in Pascal, e.g.
0.5 * (sin(2 * t)) but this does not appear to be a really serious drawback. Apart
from this, virtually all of the criteria advanced by Flanders and cited above are
easily within the grasp of anyone using HyperCostoc. The limitations imposed by the
system are really very few, and it is relatively easy to produce lessons with a
mixture of text, animation, graphics and some of the interactive features we have
discussed, even for an inexperienced author. Some completed lessons will form the
basis of the presentation of this paper for IICAL'89.

BIBLIOGRAPHY

[1]   A. Bork, Learning with Personal Computers, Harper & Row, New York, 1987.
[2]   H. Flanders, Math. Calc. Educ. AMS (summer) Minicourse. Salt Lake City,
        Utah, 1987.
[3]   K.D. Loose, Using Computers to support the Teaching Process.   ICAL
        Bulletin Vol. 3, number 2. (1988) p. 17-22. U. of C.,
        Calgary, Alberta.
[4]   H. Maurer, Presentation Type CAL For Classroom and Lab Use at University
        Level, Proceedings of the ICCAL Conference, Calgary, Alberta (1987)
        p. 27-29.
[5]   Shapiro, D.G., Algorithmic program debugging.   ACM distinguished
        dissertations. MII Press, Cambridge (1983) 210p.

TOURING A HYPER-CAI SYSTEM

R. Stubenrauch

Institutes for Information Processing Graz (IIG)
(Grundlagen der Informationsverarbeitung und Computergestützte neue Medien),
Graz University of Technology and the Austrian Computer Society,
Schießstattgasse 4a, A-8010 Graz, Austria

Abstract

In this paper a concept is presented of how to link instructional material in the context of a hyper-media learning environment, thus creating a hyper-CAI system. Basically, since it is similar to existing non-CAI 'hyper-' systems, it allows to create individual paths for different user-groups and various ways of non-linear linkage of chunks of information. Additionally, it provides a concise interface to the contents of hypermols (as we call the highly independent chunks of lesson material) which are coded in a special new language supporting the tour concept. In particular, conditional branching based on a variety of events is possible.

1   Introduction

Recently, efforts have been made within the CAI world to incorporate hyper-media features into conventional instructional systems. Some of the various reasons for this are:

- There is a need for non-linear navigation through large amounts of instructional material (as an example for a major project see [MM86]). Various ways of touring the database must be provided including cross-lesson touring and referential linkage.

- Hyper-media systems provide valuable resources for CAI which should not be ignored. Thus, it should be possible to seamlessly integrate conventional non-intelligent instructional material and a hypermedia database which consists of large amounts of networked chunks of information, such as text, graphics, pictures etc.

- As the lesson databases grow larger, the need for individualization becomes more urgent and evident. Different user-groups may want to create different lessons from the existing material. Hypermedia functionality can provide such non-linear cross-over kinds of touring.

- Workstations which support window-oriented multi-tasking applications are now available at reasonable prices. Thus, the hardware requirements, such as parallel execution of lessons or of different parts of the same lesson, are fulfilled.

Roughly speaking, in the near future a new generation of CAI systems will come into existence. We have started to call them *hyper-CAI systems*. An example of such a system is the HyperCOSTOC project ([HMM88]) currently under development. Its basic idea is to provide hyper-media functionality within a mainly presentation-type CAI system (which implies among other things that there is little emphasis on artificial intelligence techniques). From the navigational point of view this implies that conventional forms of advanced branching through instructional material (which for example takes into account the student's reactions to some questions) must be combined with encyclopedical types of linkage known from hypermedia systems. To this end, HyperCOSTOC supports both programming-free creation of hypermols, and programming in a dedicated authoring language (see [SM89]) which provides an interface between the contents of individual hypermols and the surrounding information network. Note that inspite of certain references to HyperCOSTOC, the concept of touring outlined on the following pages is a general proposal not limited to a specific system.

2 Non-linear linkage

Various approaches to non-linear linkage have been realized in hypermedia systems so far (for an overview on hypertext systems and applied reference mechanisms see e.g. [Con87]; in [Yan88] you may find a sample session with Brown University's Intermedia; you find more about Intermedia in [Mey86]; see also [HA88]).

Let us first explain some terms used extensively on the following pages. We start with a large database of chunks of information which might be of textual, graphical or procedural kind. No matter of what type these chunks are, we call them *hypermols* (short for hyper-molecules), or simply mols. It is essential that hypermols are independent of each other. For example, pictorial units must not require other units as background in order to be meaningful. Preferably, each hypermol should present just one idea or concept. However, this does not mean that there are no dependencies between the contents of hypermols. On the contrary, hypermols should be organized in an encyclopedic manner, i.e. each one may contain references to related units. We call such connections *referential links*, the most characteristic feature of any hypermedia system.

In hyper-CAI, references can be treated quite analogously as in regular hypermedia systems. Specific *link points* indicate where a referential link is available from a *source hypermol*. Such a link point might appear as a highlighted word or a specific link icon associated with a graphical information, optionally with some attributes. Clicking on such a point causes the system to open a new window which shows the *destination hypermol*. While some hypermedia systems allow references to arbitrary positions within hypermols, we consider it sufficient to restrict reference destinations to whole hypermols (i.e. beginnings of hypermols). In this way the clarity of presentation is increased by encouraging the creation of small and independent units. Note that in contrast to some other systems we suggest referential links to be unidirectional (which does not mean that there is no way to go back to the 'source' mol immediately after following a referential link).

Another type of linkage is covered by implicit *keyword links* which basically correspond to database queries. Unlike referential links which tend to result in a single hypermol, keyword links may yield a large number of hypermols. Thus, the system has to provide a mechanism to restrict them step by step.

3 Tours

What has been lacking so far is a default structure, a suggested way in which we can work through the information material when we follow a certain topic. It should be possible to follow such a route in a simple but meaningful way without exhausting the referential facilities. For example, quick browsing through a lesson should be possible by constantly pressing the same key. The references which are supposed to provide further information are only presented when the user explicitly wishes so.

The simplest kind of such a default organization is the tree structure which in fact is used by many hypertext systems. However, such a strictly hierarchical structure is not sufficient in more sophisticated environments; hyper-CAI systems in particular need substantially more support of guidance. Furthermore, CAI applications require branching which depends on the evaluation of the student's performance, i.e. on the current 'user model'.

The main issue of this paper is to propose a mechanism which covers the above requirements; we call it the concept of *tours*. In a way, tours may be compared to conventional CAI lessons but in a hypermedia context.

When users enter a hyper-CAI system they have to be identified by user-id and password which associates them with a specific user-group. Different user-groups have different access and modification permits which may create quite different views of the information material. A suggestive and somehow hierarchical, but rough classification of users might be the following:

- authors/editors/layouters:
  Only this group of persons is allowed to generate and delete public hypermols as well as to modify them. Deletion and modification must logically be restricted to their 'own' hypermols, i.e. such hypermols they have created themselves. Public mols are available for instructors to build tours across them. Additionally, authors may have all the rights of instructors and students.

- instructors:
  Instructors take existing hypermols and tours and link them in a new way, thus creating new tours. These tours are then available for student classes which are associated with and supervised by the instructor.

- students:
  Students can be members of several classes and work through the tours prepared by the corresponding instructor. In addition, they may create private tours, referential links and annotational hypermols which help to individualize the learning process.

The user's membership in various user-groups and student classes as well as further optional restricting attributes (like date of creation) determine the scope of tours and mols available for the user. This is very important regarding submols. *Submols* are mols which are associated to a mol and are automatically executed together with this mol in a parallel mode, i.e. keypresses are 'sent' to both mols. Each mol may have an arbitrary number of submols. However, a submol is only executed if the user is a member of the corresponding user-group. The main purpose of submols is to provide an annotation facility. Note that care must be taken to ensure correct synchronization (which may be supported by a 'submol editor'). By activating a submol (and by that, its tour) one may look at a set of annotations detached from its 'source'.

One of a hyper-CAI system's characteristics is that completely different lessons may be built from existing material by linking hypermols to different tours. Thus it is necessary to separate the contents of mols from their linkage information. To this end we introduce the notion of *T-nodes* (short for tour-nodes) which are the basic elements of which the tours are built. While each T-node has exactly one associated (main-) hypermol, each hypermol may have an arbitrary number of T-nodes which 'are pointing to it' (which corresponds to the number of tours incorporating it). We might say that the level of tours and T-nodes is the level of control and the hypermol's level concerns the contents. A hypermol is executed only through an associated T-node; i.e., T-nodes have control over the hypermols.

In order to enhance intuitive understanding, we give an example in figure 1. It shows two tours represented by graphs in two planes. The circles represent T-nodes whereas the cubes are supposed to be hypermols. Observe that tours T_1 and T_2 share some mols. Furthermore, note that the black T-node at the right is attached to two mols, a regular one with a solid line (the main mol) and a referenced mol, the referential link symbolized by a dashed line. If users select this reference they may *activate* one of two superimposed T-nodes, provided that they have the required access right. If there is only one T-node to optionally activate, this could be done by just clicking into its according representation window; otherwise, an explicit selection mechanism must be provided. Additionally, it can be specified whether the window of the original, suspended mol should remain on the screen in an inactive manner for optional later re-activation, or whether the window should actually vanish.

It is important to see that regardless how many windows are open on the screen, just one tour and its current T-node is active at any one time. Nevertheless, a hyper-CAI system has to support seamless switches between different tours.

4   T-nodes

Let us now examine in more detail the components T-nodes consist of. They contain two parts: the contents part and the control part. The *contents part* refers to the associated hypermols whereas the *control part* defines adjacent T-nodes. Let us consider the contents part in more detail first. It consists of:

- *Main hypermol*:
  This is the mol which is executed in any case; thus the existence of exactly one main mol is mandatory.

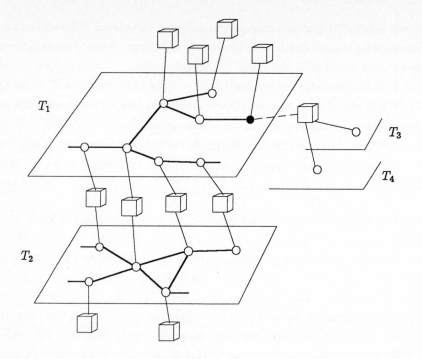

Figure 1: Tours

- *Referenced mols (Refmols)*:
  Refmols are mols which are tied to the main mol via referential links. Such mols are executed in addition to the main mol only when they are explicitly invoked by clicking on the according link icons. Positions and shapes of these icons must be stored together with the link information. An arbitrary number of refmols may be attached to the main mol. Refmols stay inactive unless they are explicitly activated.

We want to use the term *secondary mol* for all mols which are not main mols, including mols which are the result of keyword queries. Observe that this classification of mols is always relative to an actually inspected T-node. I.e. the same mol may at one time be considered a submol and at another moment a main mol (for instance, after activating the tour which is superimposed on it). Incidentially, there is no reason that some mols should not be 'free-lancing', i.e. they might be just refmols for example, but not main mols of any tour of the database. Such a mol can never be activated because there is no T-node which has this very mol as its main mol (i.e. there is no tour to activate). Note that the process of activation is the same for all kinds of secondary mols.

Furthermore, remember that the type of mols and linkage has great impact on the appearance of the material to the user. Refmols, for example, are handled in a way completely different to that of submols. Thus, though one might find it hard to separate the abstract terms, there would be a very clear and suggestive structure in practical use.

Now let us discuss the *control part* which deals with connections to adjacent T-nodes called *branches*. Branches build up the actual tour, the 'backbone' of the network. When the users only follows branches, they may never leave the current tour. A variety of different types control the performance and appearance of branches to the users.

Branches can be considered as an interface between the contents of the main mol and its environment which guarantees that mols may be used within different contexts without changing its contents. We can distinguish between the following *types* of branches:

- *forward*:
  This branch determines the default successor T-node. The existence of exactly one forward branch is mandatory for all T-nodes with the exception of specific 'end nodes' which mark the regular end of a tour. The system provides a system-dependent mechanism for selecting this branch like a specific icon to click on or/and a certain key to press.

- *backward*:
  This optional branch defines the static predecessor of a T-node. If existing, the system handling is similar to that of the forward branch.

- *indices*:
  Indices (or index branches) provide multiple branching similar to indices in books. There might be an arbitrary number of index objects within the main mol, each one paired with an associated set of index branches. Each set of index branches is defined by a corresponding set of T-nodes which will be jumped to when the user either enters a matching text string or clicks on a specific icon which is defined 'inside' the mol.

Index branches and 'sequential branches' (backward and forward) are two of the standard branches which must be supported by the system (as, for example, in TALC [SM89], the language in which the contents of mols is coded in HyperCOSTOC). Basically, they are just for making life easier and to allow a comfortable treatment of the most frequently used types of branching. Nevertheless, in addition to this, there is the very powerful and flexible concept of conditional branching which allows completely free 'programming'. This is also essential for branching determined by the actual performance of the student, thus allowing dynamical branching.

- *conditional branching*:

  Hyper-CAI systems have to provide the definition of specific boolean variables which we call *conditions*. In addition to user defined conditions there are also some pre-declared system conditions, mainly used in answer judging. A T-node 'knows' all conditions defined in its main hypermol; for each condition, the T-node contains a branch which is to be executed when the condition is 'true'. In order to avoid conflicts when multiple conditions are defined, there must be an order for evaluating them. Additionally, for each condition it must be defined whether it should be of *immediate* effect (i.e. the according branch will be executed immediately when the condition is fulfilled) or of *delayed* effect (i.e. the branching takes place only after the last object of the mol has been executed). Conditional branches are considered of higher priority than other types, i.e. they are executed before sequential branches.

Observe that there is a strong relationship between a T-node and its main hypermol. The system must provide comfortable tour editing facilities to ensure that they match. If the definition of conditions within the main mol is modified, the system has to react somehow, in particular by automatically adjusting the T-node's conditional branching part. Furthermore, note that the branching facilities must be disabled when a mol is shown as a secondary mol, e.g. as refmol. Branching is enabled only if the mol is activated as main mol, since only then the correct relationship to the T-node is ensured.

Finally, a branch can be assigned one more attribute: whether it is a returning or a dismissing branch. A *returning branch* implicitly leaves a mark at the T-node from which it is branching away. Later, the user may jump back to this position by invoking a special return function (in order to allow nested returns the system will use a stack). In contrast to this, *dismissing branches* rather behave like a 'goto': once left, there is no automatic way to go back.

Figure 2 illustrates just one T-node within a reasonable dense neighborhood. It shows the T-node in the center with a number of refmols below it and its main mol above it. The main mol has several associated submols. The arrows represent various kinds of branches, indicated by labels like 'b' and 'f' (for backward and forward) or 'correct' and 'incorrect' (for system defined conditions relating to answer judging).

5   Tour sharing and tour priority

It is clear that even for a single T-node such a graphical representation may become quite complex. This raises the question of how to guide the user through a large network of

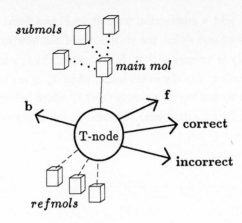

Figure 2: A T-node and its neighborhood

tours and mols without getting lost. Some kind of graphical representation of the network environment is certainly inevitable. One approach is to provide users with maps they may look at with different qualities of 'visual power', e.g. close-ups or overviews. Thus, either a very detailed view of the direct neighborhood is given or a rough outline of a larger area (for example, a whole tour or course) for quick orientation. The network might be made to appear 'thinner' by different methods. Firstly, the submols may be omitted because they are automatically tied to the main mols. Secondly, showing referential mols probably will confuse users rather than support their orientation; hence they can be omitted, too. What remains are the branches making up the actual tours.

Another aspect of reducing the complexity of tours is the following idea. We mentioned in a previous section that the main purpose of tours is to allow instructors to create lessons from existing material, in particular to incorporate parts of other lessons into their own lessons. Figure 3 illustrates structures derived from this practice. In the upper graph two lessons are shown, named T_1 (covering the sequence ABCD) and T_2 (sequence EFGH); in order emphasize the main idea, we simplified the facts, for example by merging mols and T-nodes. The lessons may be distinguished by the different types of lines connecting the units. Now let us suppose an instructor who wants to build a new lesson T_3 quite similar to T_1 but with F and G incorporated between B and C to obtain the sequence ABFGCD.

From the previous section it follows that the instructor has to build a new tour, i.e. a new T-node for each mol. This would result in large amounts of new data to be stored, and in an increased complexity. Considering that in most cases parts of existing tours are combinded into a new one (like in our example) we choose the *tour sharing* strategy: we only generate new T-nodes where there is a branch which did not exist in the original tours. In practical use this would save a lot of overhead. The second graph illustrates the idea: we simply add a connection from B to F and from G back to C, the original tour. Additionally, we must define the start node of our new tour T_3 and introduce a *tour priority*. This priority is to ensure that, for example, the system does not branch from G to C when T_2 is executed. On the other hand, when T_3 is active, the system must branch from B to F because T_3 has higher priority than T_1 which would branch to C. When there is no explict branch for an active tour, T-nodes of lower priority have to be inspected at this position.

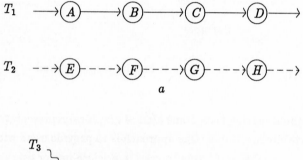

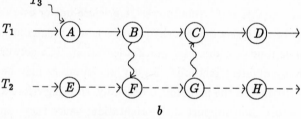

Figure 3: Tour sharing

Conclusion

This paper presents only an outline of my ideas. Within the framework of the HyperCOSTOC project which is at the design stage at the moment, some parts of the tour functionality as described will be implemented. The greatest care has to be taken that the system offers the users a smooth surface because the users are not supposed to be experts in computer science or the use of the particular system. For hyper-CAI as well as for all other 'hyper-' applications one of the most essential criteria is that of touring and orientation.

References

[Con87] Conklin J.:
'Hypertext: An Introduction and Survey', Computer, Sept 1987, pp.17−41

[HA88] Hammond N., Allison L.:
'Travels around a Learning Support Environment: Rambling, Orienteering or Touring?', Proc. of CHI '88, ACM, D. Frye and S.B. Sheppard (Eds.), pp.269−273

[HMM88] Huber F., Maurer H., Makedon F.:
'HyperCOSTOC: A Comprehensive Computer-based Teaching Support System', IIG Report 258, Oct 1988, Graz University of Technology, also to appear in Journal of Micro Computer Applications

[Mey86] Meyrowitz N.:
'Intermedia: The Architecture and Construction of an Object-Oriented Hypermedia system and Applications Framework', Proc. OOPSLA 86, Sept 1986, pp.186−201

[MM86] Makedon F., Maurer H.:
'COSTOC: Computer Supported Teaching Of Computer Science', Proc. IFIP Conf. on Remote Education and Informatics: Teleteaching '86, Budapest, Frank Lovis (Ed.), North Holland, Amsterdam, p. 107−121

[SM89] Stubenrauch R., Maurer H.:
'TALC − The Authoring Language Code', IIG Report, Graz University of Technology; in preparation

[Yan88] Yankelovich N. et al.:
'Intermedia: The Concept and Construction of a Seamless Information Environment', Computer, Jan 1988, pp.81−96

Acknowledgement

Support of part of this research by the Austrian Federal Ministry of Science and Research (Grant Zl. 604.508/2 − 26/86) and the Fonds zur Förderung der wissenschaftlichen Forschung (Grant P6042P) is gratefully acknowledged.

S-TRAINER: An Intelligent Tutor for Mission Assessment

Kathleen M. Swigger
Computer Science Department, University of North Texas
Box 13886, Denton, Texas, 76203

Brigitte Holman
Merit Technology
17770 Preston Road, Dallas, Texas 75252-5736

Intelligent tutoring systems that are capable of diagnosing and explaining complex problem solving strategies require knowledge that is difficult to represent using conventional rule- based representations. The focus of this research has been to integrate frame-based reasoning techniques with constraint satisfaction methods for the purpose of debriefing bomber aircrews. The system was developed on a Symbolics Lisp machine and uses Flavors, an object-oriented programming language, to generate a teaching script by comparing pre-mission training data to actual flight data. The pre-stored mission events serve as script templates which are matched against actual events and the time relation between events. The intelligent training system then generates multiple hypotheses, diagnoses both pilot and crew errors, generates a written evaluation of the mission along with a set of graphics that can be used to supplement the written report. A description of the system and its complex data structure is discussed below.

1   Introduction

This paper describes the research and development of an intelligent tutoring system for the purpose of training bomber aircrews. In recent years, bomber aircrews have been forced to deal with an increasing number of complex situations. Bomber crews encounter sophisticated air defense systems, highly mechanized enemy ground defense weapons, and complicated radar detection systems. At each point in a mission, the bomber crew must react correctly in order to avoid detection as they approach the targets and complete their mission. Thus, in order to train bomber crews to function at appropriate levels of expertise, training systems must be developed that can do in-depth analyses of performance and mission success. The training system must be able to capture complicated time sequences within both local and global contexts. Finally, the training system must be able to evaluate a crew's performance using varying degrees of criteria.

In order to perform these tasks, a training system must have an internal representation that can identify and manage sophisticated time and order relationships. At the representational level, the training system must be able to notice trends and shifts in action and provide clear explanations of its inferencing. This inferencing includes the ability to expect that certain events have occurred based on information about related events within both a local and global context. All this must be done in an environment where information is potentially sparse or misleading.

The Strategic Training Routes Architecture for an Intelligent Effective Reviewer, nicknamed S-TRAINER, is an intelligent training system designed to assist in the debriefing of bomber aircrews. S-TRAINER is made possible by integrating script based event matching [8] and time reasoning with constraint satisfaction [10]. S-TRAINER is designed to generate a teaching script by comparing pre-mission training data to actual flight data. The system detects the ten most significant events, diagnoses errors, and proposes an instructional sequence. Once the instructional sequence has been generated, it is sent to a Graphics Module which produces an automatic, multimedia presentation within one hour of mission completion. The main contributions of this research are script representations of temporal sequences coordinated with constraint satisfaction techniques, the ability to diagnose both individual and crew errors, and the automatic generation of a multimedia presentation. This approach can also be viewed as a first step to plan recognition and plan review.

The next section discusses the rationale for S-TRAINER and the relevant work in the area of plan recognition and generation. Section 3 outlines the logical structures S-TRAINER. Finally, we conclude with a summary of the work and its application to plan recognition.

2 The Rationale and Relevant Work

The rationale for using an intelligent tutoring approach to solve this particular problem was simply that the task was too complex for more conventional approaches. The requirements for the system included an analysis of crew performance, a listing of the ten most significant events and a rationale for selecting these ten events, a mission summary, and a closing statement. In determining S-TRAINER's content, we had to analyze each aircrew member's task and determine its relationship to the total mission. Thus the system had to understand both individual and group problem solving strategies. Each action was analyzed according to its context and temporal position. For example, a bomber crew usually avoids certain actions, if there are no other threats in the area, and if there is time to perform evasive threats in the area, and if there is time to perform evasive maneuvers. If none of these conditions are true, then the bomber crew must prioritize their actions and make global decisions.

The most difficult part in developing S-TRAINER was designing a system that could properly assess a dynamic, reactive environment. Every mission that a bomber aircrew flies is different. In addition, every bomber crew member's reaction to a single event is different. Yet, the training system must be capable of recognizing, categorizing, and critiquing an action within the context of a specific mission. Therefore, we designed an intelligent training system that is capable of assessing 1) the overall performance of the mission, 2) an individual crew member's performance during the mission, 3) the quality of the cooperation between crew members, 4) the engagement skill for specific threats, 5) the interaction skills that occur when a bomber engages multiple threats, and 6) the difficulty levels assigned to specific events within the context of the mission. S-TRAINER emphasizes team performance and an appreciation of shared tasks as well as provides a detailed examination of significant mission events.

S-TRAINER's first design concentrated on a rule-base representation. Rule-based systems [2] are noted for their high degree of modularity because individual rules can behave as independent pieces of knowledge. However, S-TRAINER's rules soon became very complex because the sequences were long and the causal dependencies were not always precisely sequential. The events that took place during the mission had duration, and they overlapped in many different ways. The rules which represented this type of knowledge required long chains of antecedents or long chains of rules to relate the antecedents. Knowledge engineering and debugging S-TRAINER's rules was non-intuitive and quite difficult. In short, the major benefits of using an intelligent system over more conventional software techniques were soon lost.

Further study suggested an alternative knowledge representation of the script representation [8]. S-TRAINER's design was inspired by scripts as applied to natural language processing [8]. However, there are several other types of instructional planners that closely resemble our approach. PROUST [9], for example, uses pre-stored correct and incorrect programming plans to diagnose students' programming errors. Similarly, SPADE-O [5] and ADVISOR [3] represent their problem- solving domains using pre-stored plans. Recently, researchers have introduced the notion of representing teaching knowledge in the form of lesson plans that can be used to drive the rest of the tutor [7; 6]. Indeed, Macmillan and Sleeman [4] hope to construct an authoring system that can adapt to individual student's behavior by modifying its general lesson plan. The power of S-TRAINER lies in its ability to monitor continuously changing situations which contain missing, inaccurate, and/or deceptive data and to analyze multiple adversaries. A more detailed explanation of the data structures follows.

3   The Script-Based Approach

The notion of representing sequences of events as templates or scripts is similar to representing stereotypical information for natural language processing as explored in Shank's research [8]. S-TRAINER is a "goal-detector" which can be used to guide the search of a plan recognizer similar to the plan understander described in [1]

The matching process in S-TRAINER is complex for a number of reasons. Any tactical maneuver unfolds as a sequence of possibly overlapping steps or events that must be fit together like pieces of a puzzle. Because S-TRAINER recognizes events as discrete measurements of continuous occurrences, the start and end times of stored events are rough approximations. Matching must then take place based on guesses as to the ordering and durations of the real events as compared to the hypothesized events. Some events are not recognized at all, while others are re-classified in order to adjust to the planned view. S-TRAINER uses its scripts [10] to categorize knowledge and control execution, while incorporating small direct procedures to drive the reasoning and problem solving behavior. The script structure simplifies both the control and storing of the knowledge.

The small action procedures present an intuitive method of solving small problems.

4 S-TRAINER's Knowledge Structures

The knowledge representation used in S-TRAINER was designed to capture the essence of the project's goal; the goal being to write a program that generates a written evaluation of a bombing mission. Thus, S-TRAINER's knowledge structures represent the authors' idea of a real-world task that closely resembles S- TRAINER's goal. Consequently, the main data structure of the S- TRAINER prototype is called DRAMA and consists of a CAST of physical objects encountered by an aircrew, a TIMELIST of events that transpired, SCENES which are the significant event groupings, and a SUMMARY or synopsis of the mission. Similar to a drama critic, S-TRAINER watches the play unfold and provides a critique of the performance. A detailed discussion of each of the data structures follows.

The CAST consists of a list of PLAYERS, or physical objects that an aircrew encounters during a mission. Each PLAYER object has slot entries for name, location, difficulty level, and aircrew score. Each PLAYER object is associated with a corresponding SCRIPT that describes the appropriate actions that an aircrew can take whenever they engage a specific type of PLAYER. A SCRIPT object contains entries for crew station responses, crew performance scores, and rules or methods that perform the action involved with the PLAYER. As a result, the system can compare actual events to desired actions in order to derive a performance score for the event.

The TIMELIST data structure contains a list of the temporal sequence of events that transpire during a mission. Events relate to either actions that occur inside the aircraft or actions that occur outside the aircraft. A single EVENT object consists of slots for ID, name, type and mode, bomber location, PLAYERS currently engaged, event score, and bomber statistics such as corridor and altitude violations, EW status, and detection status.

SCENE objects store the significant events that are selected by the system for a debriefing. Significant events are defined as time-intervals in which the crew performed either very well or very poorly. Because a single event cannot be briefed out of context, the system first determines which single events are significant, and then compiles a list of events associated temporally and logically with the single events. The related events are then grouped into SCENES. Each SCENE object contains a slot for name, focus or crew skill, student model, a performance score, and a difficulty level.

Summary data is stored in two data structures labelled SKILL-SUMMARY and CREW-SUMMARY. The CREW-SUMMARY contains slots for individual crew station's performance. Most crew members are scored in at least two areas. For example, crew members assigned to flight stations are scored on how well they perform general flight skills and on how well they execute specific actions. Similarly, crew members assigned to the defensive stations are graded on the number of corridor violations they experienced and on how well they operate their equipment. The SKILL-SUMMARY objects contain overall scores for 1) the crew's performance in life threatening engagements, 2) the number of times the crew was able to jam enemy radar, 3) the number of times the crew was detected by radar, 4) the effectiveness of the crew's target execution, and 5) the quality of the crew's internal aircraft checks and monitoring.

A crew score for each PLAYER is stored with the PLAYER summary objects. For example, if the crew encounters an enemy missile, then the system scores the crew's performance with respect to the missile attack as well as determines an overall effectiveness score for evasive maneuvers for all enemy encounters. At the end of the session, these scores are used to determine the most significant events. S-TRAINER scores the aircrew on both individual and group performance.

5   S-TRAINER's Control Architecture

The control structure illustrated in Figure 1 consists of a script inferencing procedure whose main goal is to critique mission performance. In order to do this, S-TRAINER compares the plan to actual events and carefully selects "interesting" events and places them into a proper sequence. S-TRAINER's control structures, therefore, consist of procedures that compare pre- planned data to actual events, diagnose failures and successes, select significant events, and suggest appropriate training sequences. In the end, S-TRAINER produces an instructional plan in the form of a summary report and a list of appropriate graphic displays.

Figure 1 also shows the control flow of S-TRAINER and how it produces the summary report and training script. PREANALYSIS looks at the pre-mission data and initializes the PLAYERS, CAST and TIMELIST data structures. SYNTHESIZER then correlates the pre-mission data with actual mission data and associates different PLAYERS with their corresponding events. Next, OVERLAY determines a performance score for each event and analyzes the interaction between each event. CRITIC then determines which events are significant and organizes this list of events into SCENES. Finally, SCRIPT-GEN computes the amount of time that needs to be allocated to each SCENE, generates a text/graphic training script, and produces a final report. The S-TRAINER procedures are described below.

PREANALSIS is responsible for initializing the CAST and TIMELIST data structures. PREANALSIS uses the information stored in the pre-mission database to create the PLAYER objects that correspond to all known threats and physical objects. PRE-ANALYSIS also uses the pre-mission database to create an initial event list and store it in TIMELIST. All other procedures will consult and/or manipulate these two major data structures.

SYNTHESIZER correlates the pre-mission data with the actual post-flight data. Thus, SYNTHESIZER adds any new additional events to TIMELIST and attaches all PLAYER objects to their corresponding events. SYNTHESIZER also performs inferencing on bomber statistics for the rest of the system. Each event is evaluated with respect to other data in the system to determine which PLAYERS were in range of the bomber at the time of the event, if the bomber was detected by an enemy threat, and if the bomber was outside the flight corridor.

OVERLAY is responsible for evaluating and scoring the bomber aircrew's performance. As previously mentioned, each player's SCRIPT contains methods that simulate the actions between a threat and the aircraft. In this manner, S-TRAINER determines whether an action was performed correctly, incorrectly or not at all. The system records a performance score in the PLAYER object responsible for the action. Performance scores are then computed by multiplying the PLAYER's score times a difficulty measure. This particular formula results in higher scores for more difficult players. Since player scores are then used to compute event scores which, in turn, are used to select significant events, the final significant event list tends to favor events that involve the more difficult threats.

The CRITIC uses OVERLAY's output to select the most significant events and group events into SCENES. The strategy for scene selection is as follows. Target events are examined first. After determining the target events that will be included in the script, the system examines the significant events associated with each crew station and selects a representative sample from these events. The system then examines the summary scores to determine which events indicate deficient skills. Finally, the system examines the events with the highest score values. The selected events are then expanded into SCENES by selecting the most interesting PLAYER in each event and compiling all other events active with this PLAYER.

SCRIPT-GEN produces two outputs, a final training script and a summary report. The training script contains a series of formatted commands that provides information about each display. All the displays are shown on one of two screens. Each of the screens, in turn, can be partitioned into a full, half, or quarter screen display. Thus, S-TRAINER must decide on both the content of the screen and the type of display. In order to accomplish this task, S-TRAINER uses a series of constraints to collect possible displays from each of the PLAYER objects and then decide how to expand or reduce the number of displays to fit the time allotted for each display. After several iterations, the system produces a final script which indicates type, length, location, and begin/end times for each display.

The final training script contains lines of coded text which are translated by the Graphics Module into the real presentation. A printed summary report is also generated at this time. This summary report includes a copy of the training script, the overall student model, and the explanation of why each event was selected for presentation.

6   Conclusions

This paper has briefly outlined a way of looking at the interrelationships between complex problem solving situation. S- TRAINER as an implementation of the script mechanism is able to recognize trends in a mission as well as identify significant events that occur over time. S-TRAINER's scripts incorporate action procedures that simulate the actions of the domain expert. The system then uses this expert knowledge to evaluate both individual and crew performance and present a relevant critique.

A goal for S-TRAINER is to allow an expert trainer to enter expand its current knowledge beyond the toy stage. At the moment S-TRAINER is very limited in both its number and kind of diagnostics.

Finally, S-TRAINER represents only part of the software necessary to generate and recognize details of plausible/implausible plans. Future work includes building on previous research, such as in [7; 4], and identifying more generalizable plan recognition techniques.

References

[1] Azarewicz, J., et. al., Plan recognition for airborne tactical decision-making, *AAAI* (1986), 805-811.

[2] Buchanan, B.G., and Shortliffe, E. H., eds., *Rule-Based Expert Systems*, Addison-Wesley Publishing Co., 1984.

[3] Genesereth, M. An automated consultant for MACSYMA, *IJCAI*, (1977), 789-793.

[4] Macmillan, S.A. and Sleeman, D. H. An architecture for a sel- improving instructional planner for intelligent tutoring systems. *Artificial Intelligence*, 8, (1987) 323-364.

[5] Miller, M.L. A structured planning and debugging environment for elementary programming. *Int. Jrnl. Man-Machine Studies*, 11 (1979), 79-95.

[6] Ohlsson, S. Sense and reference in the design of interactive illustrations for rational numbers. In Lawler, R. and Yazdani, M. (eds.) *AI and Education: Learning Environments and Intelligent Tutoring Systems*, Ablex Publishing, 1987.

[7] Peachey, D.R. and McCalla, G.I. Using planning techniques in intelligent tutoring systems. *Int. Jrnl. Man-Machine Studies*, 24, 77-98.

[8] Schank, R. and Abelson, R. *Scripts, Plans, Goals and Understanding*, Lawrence Erlbaum Associated, Inc., 1977.

[9] Soloway, E.M. and Johnson, W. Remembrance of blunders past: a retrospective on the development of PROUST. *Cog. Soc. Conf.*, (1984), 57-62.

[10] Wilensky, R. *Planning and Understanding: A Computational Approach to Human Reasoning*, Addison-Wesley Publishing Co., 1983.

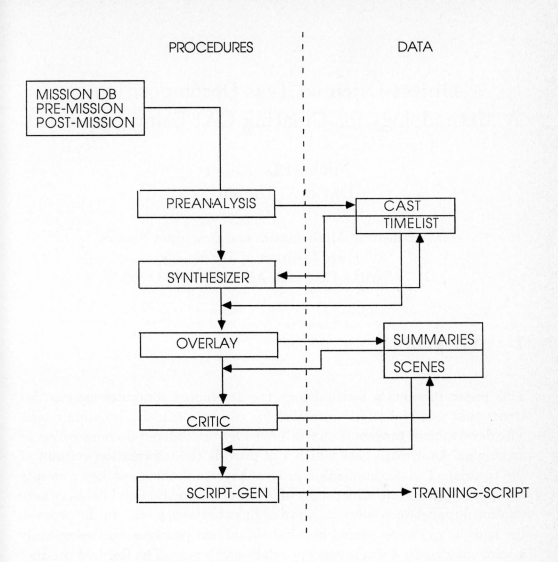

FIGURE 1: CONTROL ARCHITECTURE FOR S-TRAINER

Object-Oriented Text Decomposition: A Methodology for Creating CAI Using Hypertext

Michael L. Talbert
David A. Umphress

Department of Mathematics and Computer Science
Air Force Institute of Technology
Wright-Patterson AFB, OH 45433

1   Abstract

This paper presents a methodology for developing computer-assisted in-structional material (CAI) intended for use in a transfer learning mode. The development process is characterized by the ordered decomposition of an original knowledge base which will provide the information content of the tutorial. The decomposition process keys on fleshing out key concepts and placing them into a hierarchy of levels of abstraction and detail, where relationships between concepts serve as links between levels. In the process, the knowledge base is parsed into individual text passages, each essentially a mini-tutorial on a single concept-relationship pair. The finished product is a formally structured collection of text passages.

Ausubel's cognitive theory of learning serves as the theoretical foundation for the content of the text passages as well as the general hierarchical rela-tionship between one passage and others. Gowin's concept mapping appli-cation of Ausubel's theory provides a basis for a concept-relationship em-phasis. Additionally, the formal direction for the development methodology is borrowed from the principles of software engineering, and the software implementation of the tutorial is done via hypertext.

2   Motivation

In only a decade, computer-based instructional products have grown from computerized programmed text tutorials on personal computers to multimedia, three-dimensional presentations on computer workstations. Sophistication and intelligence have been incorporated with the use of graphics, enhanced human-computer interfaces (e.g., touch- screen, voice-activation), artificial intelligence, and hypermedia. However, the bottom line, the motivating factor for each enhancement, is the desire to use the computer to facilitate learning.

The desire not only to use the computer to educate, but to use it more effectively was a motivating factor in the research which underlies this paper [Talbert 1988]. The goals of the research were threefold:

- Formalize and propose a methodology by which an unstructured or informally structured knowledge base can be mapped into a hierarchically structured, relationship-driven hypertext-based tutorial.

- Using a prototype tutorial structured via the proposed methodology, obtain and analyze both objective and subjective measurements of the structure's learning effect on the users of the tutorial.

- With the formal, built-in structure of a hypertext document, overcome some of the recognized pitfalls and frustrations associated with unchecked, ill-structured, or poorly implemented hypertext.

This paper focuses on the process, results, and significance of achieving the first two goals, with mention of the results of achieving the third goal.

The approach to achieving the stated research goals took the form of a four-phase research effort. With a solid background in software engineering as a starting place, the initial phase was a review of current literature and issues in areas of CAI, knowledge representation, and hypertext. Each of these research areas contributed to a working knowledge base out of which the information decomposition methodology was derived. After detailing the methodology and possible variations on it in the second phase, an actual computer-based tutorial was developed in phase three by following the steps of the methodology. Finally, both the product itself and the educational impact of the product were evaluated, completing the well-rounded research effort.

3 Methodology

The educational aspects of the methodology are founded in the learning theory of Ausubel [Novak 1977] and the concept-mapping applications of Ausubel's theory by Novak and Gowin [Novak and Gowin 1986]. Ausubel's influence is reflected primarily in the hierarchical structure of the network of text passages. Ausubel advocates an "advanced organizer" or "attention step," which provides a high-level focus at the outset of the learning session. From this introductory overview, presumably something which the student can immediately assimilate, more detailed concepts are presented which can be related to the previously understood ideas in the attention step. Each new idea can serve as a new attention step for even more detail. The result is a hierarchy of information.

This general hierarchical structure of knowledge representation is reinforced by Novak and Gowin [Novak and Gowin 1986] through a technique called concept-mapping. In their book, *Learning How to Learn*, they state:

> Because meaningful learning proceeds most easily when new concepts or concept meanings are subsumed under broader, more inclusive concepts, concept maps should be hierarchical; that is, more general, more inclusive concepts should be at the top of the map, with progressively more specific, less inclusive concepts arranged below them [Novak and Gowin 1986, :15].

With a hierarchical document structure as the desired end product, the function of the information decomposition methodology is then to facilitate the transformation from the original information base to the individual text passages. This transformation may be viewed as a mapping from the original information "space" to the final text "space," computer software.

Several modern software engineering methods facilitate the structured decomposition required by such a mapping. Of them, the Object-Oriented Design methodology (OOD) serves well as a pattern for the concept-oriented decomposition advocated in this paper. In particular, the OOD decomposition paradigm provides a mapping from a verbal statement of a real-world problem to a software solution. The "objects" are actors or key players in the software [Booch 1987]. A typical set of high-level objects for a steam compressor might be VALVE_CONTROLLER and TEMPERATURE_MONITOR. These objects might contain operations such as "Open_Valve" and "Close_Valve" and "Sense_temperature" and "Display_Temperature," respectively.

For the readers unfamiliar with OOD and for comparison with the Object-Oriented Text Decomposition methodology to be presented later, the basic steps of are listed below [Booch 1987]:

1. State the problem succinctly in a single sentence

2. Bound the problem at the high level by expanding the problem statement to a single paragraph (5-9 sentences)

3. Identify the objects (nouns) involved in the problem

4. List the attributes (adjectives) of the objects

5. Identify operations (verbs) on the objects

6. Define relations and interfaces between objects

7. Decide on implementations of the objects and operations (software code)

8. Recursively apply the process to the operations as needed.

By applying OOD, the resulting computer software is characterized by modularity, since each object is a separate entity. Additionally, the software modules tend to be highly independent with each module performing a single function. The decomposition method forces a network-like (and often hierarchical) structure on the modules.

The Object-Oriented Text Decomposition (OOTD) methodology presented in this paper closely parallels OOD. Indeed, OOTD can be thought of as simply an extension of software engineering methods to the "engineering" of CAI tutorials. In this case, the text is really the "software" of the computer-based tutorial, exclusive of the underlying hypertext syntax. In other words, the mapping performed by the text decomposition method is from an instructor's base of information (in whatever form that may take) to the hierarchical network of single-theme text passages.

Formally, the steps of OOTD are:

1. State the thesis of the tutorial in a single paragraph.

2. Expand the sentence into a high level paragraph.

3. Identify the key concepts.

4. Identify the relationships between the key concepts and the paragraph theme.

5. Review and revise

6. For each new concept repeat steps 1-5 as needed.

7. Encapsulate related concepts in a single object- module.

8. Implement text links in hypertext.

Expectedly, the methodical progression is essentially the same as for OOD. The highest level concepts are dealt with first, and lower level detail is extracted in subsequent iterations through the process. Similarly, relationships are sought between text objects, particularly relationships which link one level of abstraction to the next lower one. And with regard to levels of abstraction, here as in OOD, there is explicit intent to maintain a constant level of detail during each pass through the process.

More detailed descriptions of the steps in the process are provided below

1. **State the tutorial thesis in a single sentence.** This step is analogous to the first step in the OOD process. The intent is to clarify the theme of the tutorial. This step will establish the highest level of abstraction, the most inclusive concept(s) the tutorial will address.

2. **Expand the sentence into a high level paragraph.** As in the previous step, this step nearly parallels its OOD counterpart. The paragraph should be five to nine sentences long (with exceptions noted below), and should maintain a level of abstraction consistent with that of the single sentence on which it expands. The objective is to introduce applicable terms, principles, etc. which relate to the immediate concept or theme. By the time the paragraph is completed, the scope of the information to follow should be clear to the reader. That is, only progressively finer detail should be encountered throughout the rest of the tutorial.

   In contrast to the OOD method, there is latitude for additional paragraphs, if the tutorial is sufficiently large enough to warrant them. There is an important point to consider which will justify the acceptability of more paragraphs. Since the tutorial structure will be hierarchical, there may be several lower level concepts to explore from the discussion of a single higher level concept. After the reader traverses links to some text several levels of abstraction lower, he must return to higher levels to begin a new path through the document. Consequently, a reader may face the same screenful of text several times as he returns to explore new trails. Thus, the use of more than one paragraph may help the reader feel a sense of progression through the document and closure of the entire document, even as he returns to the same high level many times. In any case, the decision for multiple paragraphs in a single display will be left to the judgement of the tutorial designer on an individual basis. For any paragraph, however, these guidelines apply:

- Write at a constant level of abstraction.

- Provide the reader with the highest level, most inclusive concepts that apply at the current level of abstraction. This allows the reader to view lower level details in relation to these broader concepts.

- Write to call attention to key concepts which will be given lower level, more detailed explanations later in other segments of text. These concepts, the nouns and objects in the text, will become hypertext nodes.

- Write to expound on the relationship between the paragraph theme (a concept-relationship pair) and the higher level paragraph in which it was introduced. Elaboration of the details of relationships is the reason for being for each new text passage.

- Write to make explicit the relationships between the paragraph theme and each lower level concept introduced in the paragraph. Relationships should take the form of object phrases, with the new concept being the object. The objective is to whet the reader's appetite for more detail, while maintaining the current level of abstraction.

3. **Identify the key concepts.** Select only those concepts which are at a level of abstraction consistent with the entire paragraph. These should be the objects in a correctly written paragraph (as per Step 2). Some consideration must be given to the determination of which objects are consistent with the current level of abstraction. It is important to exclude the selection of concepts which, though germane to the topic, are not at the level of abstraction the paragraph represents.

4. **Identify relationships between new concepts and the paragraph theme.** According to the guidelines in the second rule, relationships are articulated as object phrases, i.e., verb or prepositional phrases which take an object. The objects are the concepts identified

in Step 3. Ideally, an entire object phrase will become a hypertext node and a new text object theme. While this step should follow cleanly from well-executed Steps 2 and 3, in some cases adjustments must be made for the sake of clarity and for the final hypertext implementation.

- For implied relationships between the paragraph theme and a new concept, consider rewriting the passage to make the relationships explicit.

- For a series of concepts separated by commas, a relationship will be considered explicit for each concept in the series. For example, consider the sentence "The electronic mail facility delivers mail, error messages, and system notices." The explicit relation "delivers" is attached to "error messages" and "system notices," as well as "mail." The three relationships might each warrant their own detailed paragraphs at a lower level, but the relationship "delivers" must be the linking relationship to each. Consequently, the next level paragraph for each object would key on a "delivers" relationship.

5. **Review and revise.** Review each paragraph to ensure a constant abstraction level is maintained internally. Check for concepts which may best be introduced at a different level of abstraction. Determine which, if not all, concepts and relationships selected in Steps 3 and 4 should be expounded on in more detail. Revise paragraphs as necessary to reflect these decisions.

6. **For each new concept, repeat Steps 1-5 as needed.** Repetition of Step 1 is optional, but is recommended as a good rule for setting the theme of any paragraph [Hodges and Whitten 1982]. Iterate the process until sufficient detail has been revealed; however, there are trade-offs to consider.

Too much detail could force the reader down a path of numerous links. Even within a hierarchy, some form of disorientation due to excessive depth of detail is possible. At this point, the reader may neither understand nor remember the trail of relationships which account for his current position in the tutorial document. In addition, with more than a few such excessively long paths, the reader may become exhausted and frustrated. Consequently, he may no longer desire to browse the document, but instead only to finish, thus mitigating the educational effect of the tutorial.

In contrast, too little detail may not sufficiently satisfy the intellectual appetite of the reader. Of course, the academic objective of the tutorial will ultimately govern the depth of knowledge presented. A depth of two or three new links is a suitable average.

7. **Encapsulate related concepts in a single object.** Recall that in the OOD methodology, the encapsulation of data types and operations specific to a single object provided a modular, abstract representation of a program's structure. One abstract view of an object is as a warehouse of components which can be used within the object itself or by other objects. A similar modular view may be taken of an encapsulated object. Each object contains a text passage which contains zero or more access points (nodes) to additional lower level objects. Objects encapsulated in this way will be referred to as "object-modules."

8. **Implement text links in hypertext.** Once the decomposition is complete, the remaining step is to implement the tutorial using hypertext. Using the constructs of a hypertext "language," (Knowledge Garden's *KnowledgePro*, in this effort) establish links to connect related paragraphs using the node names selected in Steps 3 and 4. In this way, a link connects a concept- relationship pair to the text passage which expounds on it. Additionally, the developer should take advantage of window titles and multiple on-screen windows if the environment provides for them. The window titles can provide additional path markers to aid the reader in orienting himself in the document.

4 Implementation

With the methodology outlined in detail, the next step in the overall process was to actually demonstrate it by decomposing an information base and implement it in hypertext. In the original research effort, the information base used was Jean Sammet's article "Why Ada is Not Just Another Programming Language"[Sammet 1986]. As an example for illustrative purposes only, an abbreviated version of the first-level decomposition is provided here.

The beginning step is the statement of the tutorial thesis in a single sentence. This single sentence introduces the grand picture of the entire tutorial.

> Ada can be distinguished from the majority of other computer languages on many technical and nontechnical merits.

The second step is the expansion of this single sentence into a paragraph, in which all the highest level concepts are presented.

> Ada can be distinguished from the majority of other computer languages on many technical and nontechnical merits. On on-technical grounds, the ordered design and development processes which produced Ada are unlike those of any other programming language. Additionally, Ada has attracted strong interest from users and enthusiasts in the international computing community, outside the Department of Defense. With regard to key unique attributes of its technical elements, Ada offers high-level programming features which contribute to Ada's support for software engineering principles.

The underlined terms represent all the nouns in the paragraph. Of these nouns, the key, highest level concepts were selected from Step 3 as shown below. In Step 4, the relationship between each key concept and the paragraph these (Ada is different) were identified. The resulting relationship-concept pairs are:

CONCEPT	RELATIONSHIP
processes	processes which produced Ada
strong interest	attracted strong interest
programming features	offers high-level ... features
principles	support for ... principles

Included in Step 5 is the evaluation of the concept-relationship pair selections. Of particular concern is the appropriateness of each pair, given the level of abstraction intended not only for this first, highest level paragraph, but also for the next level text passages as well. In Step 6 the next level passages will become separate explanations and elaborations of the concept-relationship pairs which have just been selected. Each explanation, a text passage, will be considered a single-theme object. These new, lower level text passages will be created in the same manner as the original one, following Steps 1–5. Note that this iterative process is the essence of the "decomposition" approach to the methodology.

After interating the decomposition process until a desired level of detail has been achieved (or the original knowledge base has been exhausted), the object-oriented approach to creating the textbase points to the encapsulation of individual objects (Step 7). In this case, since the final textbase structure will be hierarchical, the encapsulation will involve nesting lower level objects inside higher level ones. A pictorial representation of the encapsulated object representations for the top-level object and the four lower level objects is presented in Figures 1-5.

The software representation of the encapsulated text objects must be done using a hypertext environment. With hypertext, direct connections can be made between the concept or concept-relationship phrase in one text passage and the text passage representing the lower level elaboration of the concept-relationship theme. For example, in the illustration used in this paper, the concept "interest" or the phrase "attracted strong interest" will be marked as a hypertext node. When the reader activates a node, the explanatory text passage linked to it will be displayed on the screen. In this new passage, other nodes may be indicated which allow access to still lower level text passages.

Within the pre-established non-linear text structure described above, the reader may browse the tutorial hyperdocument. This involves exploring a chain of concept-relationship pairs, making selections of a new link in the chain from those marked as hypertext nodes at each level. Note that the nodes available at each level are provided by the instructor or tutorial developer during the knowledge base decomposition process. Consequently, as a result of the present methodology, although the reader can choose which link to follow at each level, he cannot dynamically create links.

5   Evaluation

The completed version of the knowledge base decomposition introduced in this paper was presented to a class of graduate-level computer science students in an Ada programming language class as part of an evaluation of the tutorial product. Note that the product was evaluated instead of the methodology itself. Since the impact of the resulting end product of the methodology was of most interest, an "end justifying the means" approach was deemed justifiable as a method of evaluation. As a result, no additional qualifying conditions, assumptions, or proofs of corrects concerning the methodology were explicitly considered.

5.1   Experiment

The experiment itself was in five parts. In the first part, the completed hypertext-based tutorial (developed using the steps described earlier) was compared to the original knowledge base for equivalency of information content. Two instructors of the Ada language completed this evaluation, and their recommendations were incorporated into the final version of the tutorial. The remaining three parts of the evaluation were directly linked as a classroom/laboratory experiment using the class of 20 Ada students as subject.

Second, a pretest was given by the class instructor in lieu of a regularly scheduled in-class feedback quiz. Students were given a list of concepts taken from the original article; the students had not been assigned to read the article prior to the pretest. The test required the students to construct a concept diagram using the list of terms provided. In keeping with the recommendations of Novak and Gowin [Novak and Gowin 1986], the students were instructed to restrict themselves to a hierarchical diagram and to label each link between connected nodes.

The third part of the validation process consisted of control and experiment treatments administered by the course instructor in a regular laboratory following the class in which the pretests were given. Both treatments were computer-based versions of the Ada-related article used as the original knowledge base. The control treatment consisted of several main sections from the article entered directly into a computer file, which could be read only in a strict "page-up — page-down" manner. The sections used were those whose information content was also represented in the hypertext-based tutorial, the experimental treatment. The experimental group was asked to use the hypertext-based tutorial, as designed via the decomposition methodology. Only one group treatment was administered at a time, and each group of students was unaware that its treatment differed from that of the other group.

Fourth, the posttest and two additional measures were given to the students in the following class meeting, four days later. The subjective portion of the posttest was simply a retake of the pretest, so that improvements in individual concept maps could be measured directly, and individual and group gain scores computed. Two additional measures were taken. The students were given an objective posttest quiz, which included questions concerning items of detail expressed in both versions of the treatment. The purpose of this test was to provide an additional basis for comparison of the two approaches to computer-based instructional delivery.

Finally, the experimental group was asked to complete a written attitudinal survey concerning the hypertext-based treatment. Also, both groups later participated in an oral feedback session with the researcher.

5.2 Results

The use of concept diagramming as the primary evaluation tool offered a plausible way to determine if the tutorial design methodology actually influenced the structure students used in assimilating the concepts discussed in reading material. Analysis of pretest concept diagrams revealed that the two groups were equivalent prior to the administration of the treatments. Subjectively, the concept diagrams were generally hierarchical in structure (as required), but lacked a strong sense of perceived levels of abstraction among the concepts in the diagram. Posttest diagrams for both groups revealed improvements in both groups, with the experimental group showing the greatest measurable improvement. Analysis of the average gain scores for each group indicated that the experimental group began to view the concepts in the tutorial reading in a hierarchy of abstraction, more so than did the control group.

The result of the objective quiz were inconclusive. A weakness in the instructions accompanying the administration of the experimental treatment essentially voided any objective measure of the treatment's effect on recall of facts and details. Some comments expressed the post-treatment attitudinal surveys, and reconfirmed in the group interview, revealed that the experimental group students did not fully understand the course-related, information transfer purpose of their laboratory assignment. The students commented that they understood their purpose was to evaluate the hypertext-based method of presentation, and *not* to read for understanding the content of the tutorial. This sentiment was overwhelmingly expressed in the group interview session.

The attitudinal survey revealed a positive response to hypertext-organized information. The students approved of the enhanced topic organization and key topic highlighting which the relationship-driven approach in the tutorial provided. Also, the "select only the nodes you want" opportunity provided by a hypertext structure was noted as beneficial. On the negative side, some students were frustrated by the distraction of the reverse video image of the hypertext nodes, purely a function of the *KnowlegePro* hypertext system used. Additionally, some students would have preferred the written medium over the video display terminal, so quick scanning of the entire document could be possible.

Overall, many of the negative comments were reflections of the students' frustration caused by the software itself. The reverse video, color background, absence of a browsing map, etc., are all restrictions of the environment. Additionally, since several students commented that the hypertext experience was "not the usual way of reading," there is evidence that factors other than the hierarchical approach to text structuring were the key sources of user displeasure.

In the interview session, all ten of the experimental group students stated that they approved of the relation-driven text structuring approach. Also, with more familiarity with the hypertext way of reading, they would have enjoyed the experience more, and gained more benefit from the tutorial. Overall, and of most significance to this paper, the attitudes concerning the portions of the tutorial which can be directly linked to the decomposition methodology were overwhelmingly positive.

6   Summary and Conclusions

This paper has presented a methodical approach to structuring the information content of a hypertext-based CAI tutorial to enhance a reader's assimilation of concepts. The methodology incorporates cognitive theory, knowledge engineering, software engineering, and hypertext. Subjective measures from an experiment used to evaluate the methodology indicated that the tutorial had a positive effect on enhancing its reader's assimilation process.

The methodology facilitates the mapping from a printed source or knowledge base to the textbase of a computer-assisted tutorial. It is solidly founded on the Object-Oriented Design (OOD) paradigm, a proven problem decomposition and software design methodology. In the same way OOD maps from a problem description to a structured network of computer software components, the methodology offered in this work facilitates a decomposition of an information base into a structured network of text components. Particularly, this network of passages represents a hierarchy of abstraction, which learning theorists advocate as an effective presentation of instructional material.

The methodology provides a means for designing formal, relationship-driven structure into a hypertext document. In doing so, it emphasizes the establishment of nodes and inter-text links, solely on the basis of relationships between concepts in the text. Pre-establishing text links in this manner provides benefits to the reader:

- Expressing node names as phrases which reveal a relationship between the current topic and a related topic explicitly draws attention to and reinforces the relationship between the two topics.

- With "up front" information about the text to which a node is linked, the reader is offered additional motivation for exploring the link, i.e., the reader knows beforehand the general theme of the linked text, and will not be surprised by seemingly unrelated information.

- Since the nodes are hierarchically structured and cannot be altered by the user, the potential for the reader to get lost in a web of text links, as is possible in unstructured hypertext, is removed.

- The experimental group members retained the hierarchical, relationship-based structure of the tutorial's key concepts better than the members of the control group. The significance is this: the students who used the structured tutorial began to view the concepts in the reading material as being related through a hierarchy of abstraction.

This result can be attributed to the Ausubelian influence on the structuring the information presented in the tutorial.

References

[Booch 1987]

Booch, G. 1987. *Software Engineering with Ada.* Menlo Park, CA: Benjamin-Cummings.

[Campbell and Stanley 1963]

Campbell, D. and J. Stanley. 1963. *Experimental and Quasi-Experimental Designs for Research.* Chicago: Rand McNally.

[Hodges and Whitten 1982]

Hodges, J. and M. Whitten. 1982. *Harbrace College Handbook* (Ninth edition). New York: Harcourt Brace Jovanovich.

[Novak 1977]

Novak, J. *A Theory of Education.* Ithaca, NY: Cornell University Press.

[Novak and Gowin 1986]

Novak, J., and D. Gowin. 1986. *Learning How to Learn.* Cambridge: Cambride University Press.

[Sammet 1986]

Sammet, J. 1986. Why Ada is not just another programming language. *Communications of the ACM 29*, 8, 722-732.

[Talbert 1988]

Talbert, M. 1988. An object-oriented approach to the development of computer-assisted instructional material using hypertext. Masters Thesis AFIT/MA/GCS/88D-1. Air Force Institute of Technology, WPAFB, OH.

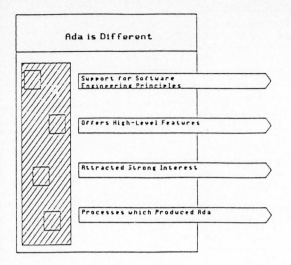

Main Encapsulated Object

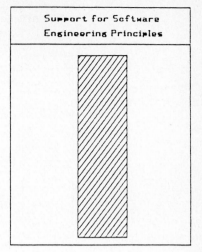

First-Level Object (1)

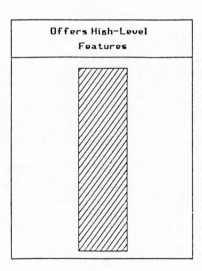

First-Level Object (2)

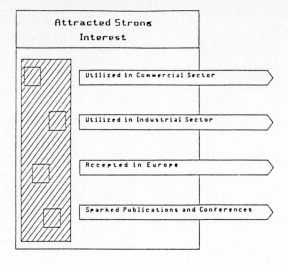

First-Level Object (3)

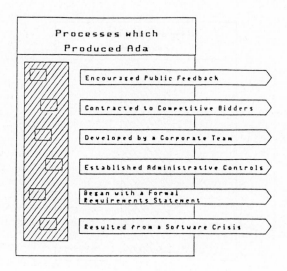

First-Level Object (4)

CAI FOR INTRODUCTORY COMPUTER ORGANIZATION

Ivan Tomek
Jodrey School of Computer Science, Acadia University,
Wolfville, Nova Scotia,
Canada, B0P 1X0

ABSTRACT

We first justify the need for software aids in teaching computer organization. An introductory course on computer organization is then described and personal computer tools developed for it outlined. Several reproductions of screen displays are reproduced.

THE NEED FOR CAI IN TEACHING INTRODUCTORY COMPUTER ORGANIZATION

Introductory courses on computer organization used to consist of basics of digital design, essentials of computer instruction sets and addressing modes, simple examples of machine level programming including an introduction to I/O methods, a brief outline of the design of the control unit, and sometimes principles of interfacing. All this was done at a rather general level.

Increasingly, the coverage is extended to range from the principles of hardware to systems software of a small computer and the course thus becomes a course on the principles of computer systems [Ta84,To89]. It covers topics from logic design through CPU architecture and control design, interfacing, basics of operating systems, and principles of translation of programming languages. An introduction to assembly language programming is included as well. This course and the traditional introduction to programming thus provide an introduction to the use as well as the operation of a computer system.

In addition to a broadened scope, this approach to the course is characterized by greater depth, partly due to the increasing acceptance of hands-on learning, partly because of the increased ease and directness of access to computers brought about by the PC, and partly due to the nature of the modern computer itself. The computer is not any more hidden from the user and enormously complicated in both its hardware and software aspects - it is sitting on the desk in front of the student and its architecture, although sophisticated, can be understood within a reasonable amount of time and effort. Moreover, the student can experiment with it.

Due to these two developments - increased breadth and increased depth of coverage - courses on computer organization are becoming much more ambitious and students need all the help they can get to master the material. The help can come from several sources such as greater access to labs and more tutoring. In the end, however, human resources are limited and must be complemented by machine resources in the form of computer-based tools that demonstrate concepts and techniques, allow experimentation, can correct students mistakes, and, ultimately, provide some tutoring. This is why we consider CAI and its modern variants an essential part of the course.

In the following, we outline the contents of our introductory course on computer organization and then describe the tools that we developed to aid students to master the material. Although our ultimate goal is to integrate these and similar programs into a more sophisticated computer-based teaching environment, this subject is not discussed in this paper.

AN INTRODUCTORY COURSE ON COMPUTER ORGANIZATION

Our two-semester course on computer organization is taught in the first year of a computer science program, in parallel with an introductory programming course using Pascal. Both courses are compulsory for all our computer science students. The contents of the computer organization course are as follows:

Digital systems at gate level

- Decomposition of digital systems into combinational and sequential components.
- Principles of logic.
- Physical implementation of logic with IC technology.
- Analysis and design of combinational functions using SSI components and minimization, MSI and LSI components (multiplexers, ROMs, PLDs, encoders, decoders). Timing, incorrect behavior (hazards).
- Representation of the behavior of sequential circuits, storage components (flip-flops, latches, registers, counters), analysis and synthesis of (mainly synchronous) sequential circuits. Timing, malfunctions (races, cycles).

Codes and operations on them

- Representation of textual and numerical data. Pure binary, two's complement, sign-magnitude, floating-point, and BCD representation and arithmetic - principles, algorithms, and hardware implementation.

Digital systems at register transfer level

- Components of digital systems (ALUs, memories, buses, control units) and their implementation. Hardwired and microprogrammed control units.

Principles of CPU architecture and organization

- Instructions and addressing modes, simple programming examples, hardwired and microprogrammed implementation of control. Timing considerations.

A real CPU

- Detailed examination of the software and hardware aspects of the architecture of the 6800 CPU by Motorola. 6800 programming in assembly language. Outline of the 8088 CPU by Intel.

Principles of peripheral devices

- Hardware and interfacing aspects of keyboards, CRT displays, printers, and disk storage. Basics of communication (RS-232, the modem, etc.), programmable peripheral interface chips (serial and parallel).

Software and hardware aspects of input and output

- Programmed, polled, and interrupt-driven I/O, direct memory access. Decoders and interfaces, programming of interface chips. An elementary computer is explored in detail on the example of the Heathkit tutorial microcomputer [He88] and principles of a more sophisticated computer outlined on the IBM PC.

Principles of small operating systems

- Simple device drivers are explored in detail on the Heathkit microcomputer. The structure, operation, sample system calls, and the file system of a more sophisticated operating system are outlined on the MS-DOS operating system of the IBM PC [Du86]. Practical experience with the use of operating system calls via a simulated operating system for the 6800 CPU.

Principles of translation of programming languages

- Detailed examination of the operation of an assembler. Components and basic algorithms of a recursive descent parser are presented on the example of a very simple high level language without procedures.

The course is accompanied by weekly lab sessions and hardware and software assignments and a hardware project consisting of the design, interfacing, programming, and evaluation of a very elementary "arithmetic coprocessor."

CAI TOOLS FOR AN INTRODUCTORY COURSE ON COMPUTER ORGANIZATION

Examination of the contents of the course reveals that its subject is very well suited to algorithmization and implementation of a variety of illustrative aids on the computer. We will now outline the tools that we have developed or are developing for the individual parts of the course as listed above. Further programs are being explored and their integration into a larger environment contemplated.

A more detailed description of some of the programs with illustration of operation is given in the next section.

Digital systems at gate level:

- Truth tables and product and sum terms. Done.
- Conversion of formulas to truth tables. Done.
- Truth tables and Karnaugh maps. Done.
- Minimization with Karnaugh maps, including don't cares. Done.
- Analysis of sequential circuits with flip-flops and counters. Done.
- Synthesis (design) of circuits with flip-flops and counters. Under development.
- State minimization. Done.

Hardware simulation at gate level based on a hardware description language. Done.
- State machine simulation. Done.
- A series of presentations explaining basic concepts and methods of gate-level digital systems. Done.

Codes and operations on them
- Conversion between various number representations (pure binary, two's complement, BCD, octal, hexadecimal, and so on). Done.
- Arithmetic in various number systems. Done.
- Floating point representation - conversion and arithmetic.

Digital systems at register transfer level
- Register transfer level simulation based on a hardware description language. Done.

Principles of CPU architecture and organization
- Simulation of a TOY CPU at various levels. Under development.

A real CPU
- Assembler for the 6800 CPU. Done.
- Simulator of the 6800 CPU. Done.

Principles of peripheral devices
- None at present.

Software and hardware aspects of input and output
- None at present.

Principles of small operating systems
- Simulated MS-DOS-like operating system for the 6800 CPU. Under development.

Principles of translation of programming languages
- A "visible assembler" for the 6800 CPU. Under development.
- A "visible compiler" for a simple high level language on the 6800 simulator with OS-6800. Under development.

DETAILED DESCRIPTION OF SOME OF THE PROGRAMS

A passive CAI sequence
This is a sequence of computer frames displayed under user's control. The sequence uses IBM's Story Teller program [IBM85]. It allows the student to select a topic and move through the presentation frames back and forth. Subjects covered in the sequence range from basic logic concepts to design of sequential circuits. An "encyclopedia" of parts is also included. Frames use color graphics and "develop" dynamically, providing a certain amount of animation.
Although this program is little more than a computerized page turner, it is surprisingly effective because of its use of color and controlled ability to develop the screen in steps. This makes it possible to show algorithms step after step and display their cumulative effect in the solution of a problem.

Simulation of hardware
Based on a simple hardware description language (HARD) with a rich variety of generic components (gates, flip-flops, latches, counters, multiplexers, and so on) allowing circuits with and without delays and modular design. A sample circuit description and a simulation produced by HARD are shown in Figures 1 and 2.

(All illustrations are slightly edited for reproduction.)

Minimization with Karnaugh maps

The user selects the number of variables, creates the Karnaugh map using a screen editor, and the program displays the solution allowing display of individual steps (identification of prime implicants, essential prime implicants, and finally a minimal coverage of the map). Karnaugh maps with don't cares are also allowed. A sequence of displays produced by this program is shown in Figures 3, 4, 5, and 6.

Analysis of sequential circuits

The student selects a circuit with flip-flops or counters, specifies the number of components, inputs, and outputs, and enters excitation equations. The program converts equations to tables and constructs transition tables in a step by step fashion. A sample sequence of screen displays produced by the program is shown in Figures 7 and 8.

Number representations and arithmetic

After selecting the desired mode (number representation or arithmetic), the user enters operands and the program displays the solution, animating a formal algorithm displayed on the screen and an informal explanation underneath. A typical screen display produced by this program is shown in Figures 9, 10, and 11.

A simulator of the 6800 CPU. This program executes the complete 6800 instruction set and can operate in several modes. In the "visual" mode, it displays all CPU registers, the mnemonic of the current instruction, and a 256-byte segment of memory. In the "non-visual" mode, it executes 6800 instructions and a simulated operating system, allowing the user to access I/O devices. A typical screen display produced by the program running in its "visual" mode is shown in Figure 12.

The 6800 simulator and assembler are used to demonstrate instructions and addressing modes, teach basic programming in assembly language, and principles of operating systems. It is also used in the section on compilers. One advantage of the simulator over a real CPU (which we use in the lab) is that it makes the course "transportable" - the course can be taught even when the hardware is not available. The simulator makes the CPU "transparent," allowing the student to see information not available in regular operation. This is, of course, true for other simulations as well.

A visual compiler. This program compiles programs written in the SIMPLE programming language and displays the operation of the compiler. SIMPLE is a (very simple) high level language developed for the course. It has only I/O and assignment statements, limited arithmetic, and integer variables. More advanced concepts of compilation related to block structure, full arithmetic expressions, and similar topics are avoided and only the fundamental ideas of compilation demonstrated.

The student submits source code and may then select viewing the operation of the the whole compiler or its individual parts - the scanner, the parser, the code generator (generating 6800 code for the simulated operating system and executable on the 6800 simulator described above). A typical screen display produced by this program is shown in Figure 13.

CONCLUSION

All the above programs are written in Turbo Pascal and run on the PC. They do not require graphics or color. We used some of them for several years, others are being introduced this year, and some are still under development. No formal tests of the usefulness of these programs have been made but student reaction has been very favorable.

The author will be happy to consider any offer for cooperation in the perfection of the existing tools, conversion to other computers such as the Macintosh or UNIX, development of new programs, and their integration into a more ambitious teaching environment.

REFERENCES

Duncan, Ray: Advanced MS-DOS, Microsoft Press, 1986.
Heath Company Catalogue, 1988.
IBM Corporation: Story Teller, IBM Corp., 1985.
Tanenbaum, Anrew S.: Structured Computer Organization, Prentice Hall, 1984.
Tomek, Ivan: Introduction to computer organization. Computer Science Press, 1989.

```
CIRCUIT:    ADDER
PARTS:      INPUT:   A,B,Cin
            OUTPUT:  SUM,Cout
            AND:     AND1(2),AND2(2),AND3(2) -  2-input gates
            OR:      OR(3)                    -  3-input gate
            XOR:     XOR(3)
CONNECT:    A    TO: AND1,AND2,XOR
            B    TO: AND1,AND3,XOR
            Cin  TO: AND2,AND3,XOR
            AND1 TO: OR
            AND2 TO: OR
            AND3 TO: OR
            OR   TO: Cout
            XOR  TO: SUM
   END
```

Figure 1. Description of a full adder in HARD.

```
              0         1         2
TIME          01234567890123456789 0123456789

A             ____ ----

B             __ -- __ --

Cin           _ - _ - _ -

SUM           _ - __ - _

Cout          ___ - _ ---
```

Figure 2. Simulation of the full adder from Figure 1.   Simulation
may also be in 0/1 notation.

```
**************************************************
*          TRUTH TABLES AND KARNAUGH MAPS        *
*                                                *
*      0: Quit                                   *
*      1: Truth tables    --> Canonic formulas   *
*      2: Logic formulas  --> Truth tables       *
*      3: Truth table     <-> Karnaugh maps      *
*      4: Karnaugh maps   --> Logic formulas     *
*                                                *
*      Enter choice:                             *
**************************************************
```

Figure 3. Minimization with Karnaugh maps: the initial display.

```
     Prime Implicants         Karnaugh Map
**********************************************************************
                         *
     A'B' AB             *   A\BC 00   01   11   10
                         *       ---------------------
                         *    0 |  1 |  1 |    |    |
                         *       ---------------------
                         *    1 |    |    |  1 |  1 |
                         *       ---------------------
```

Figure 4. Minimization with Karnaugh maps: the display after the
Karnaugh map was created and PIs calculated.

```
          Map cell numbers -> 0  1  2  3  4  5  6  7
(1)  A'B'                    -X--X--|--|--|--|--|--|-
(2)  AB                      -|--|--|--|--|--|--X--X-
```

A'B' - ESSENTIAL -   Prime implicant with 0/ 1/ appearing once

Figure 5. Minimization with Karnaugh maps: calculation of
essential PIs.

```
     Prime Implicants         Karnaugh Map
**********************************************************************
                         *
     A'B' AB             *   A\BC 00   01   11   10
                         *       ---------------------
                         *    0 |  1 |  1 |    |    |
                         *       ---------------------
                         *    1 |    |    |  1 |  1 |
                         *       ---------------------
```

F = A'B' + AB

Figure 6. Minimization with Karnaugh maps: the final display.

```
Select flip-flops or counters (F/C): F
Enter the number of flip-flops (max. 4): 2
Select types of flip-flops (D,T,JK,RS)
  flip-flop 1: d
  flip-flop 2: d
The internal variables will be called Q0, Q1.

Enter the number of inputs (max. 2): 1
The external input will be called a.

Enter equations of flip flops using xor . + ' ( )
  flip-flop 1: a.ql
  flip-flop 2: q0.al

Enter number of outputs (max. 3): 2
The outputs will be called x, y.

Enter output equations:
 x: ql
 y: q0
```

Figure 7. Analysis of sequential circuits: circuit specification.

Results of flip-flop analysis:

1. Excitation equations: 3. Transition table:

```
   D1 = a.ql                          Q1Q0\A   0     1
   D2 = q0.ql                                -----------
                                      00 |  00  |  00  |
2. Output equations:                  01 |  00  |  00  |
                                      11 |  10  |  11  |
   x = ql                             10 |  00  |  01  |
   y = q0                                     -----------
```

Figure 8. Analysis of sequential circuits: solution.

```
***************************************************
*                    NUMBERS                      *
*          CONVERSION AND ARITHMETIC              *
*                                                 *
*                   MAIN MENU                      *
*                                                 *
*            0: Quit                              *
*            1: Conversion                        *
*            2. Arithmetic                        *
*                                                 *
*      Enter choice:                              *
***************************************************
```

Figure 9. The initial menu of the NUMBERS program.

```
***************************************************
*                  ARITHMETIC                     *
*                                                 *
*            0: Quit                              *
*            1: Pure Binary                       *
*            2: BCD                               *
*            3: Two's complement                  *
*            4: Sign-Magnitude                    *
*            5: Floating point                    *
*                                                 *
*      Enter choice:                              *
***************************************************
```

Figure 10. Next step - the ARITHMETIC menu.

```
     Two's complement addition
*****************************************   i: 5
* sum := 0; carry := 0;                 *
* FOR i := 0 TO 15 DO                    *   CARRY          1
* BEGIN                                  *   OPERAND 1 00110100
* sum[i] := (o1[i]+o2[i]+carry) MOD 2;   *   OPERAND 2 11010100
* IF (o1[i]+o2[i]+carry) > 1             *   ------------------
*   THEN carry := 1                      *              10000
*   ELSE carry := 0;                     *
* END;                                   *
* IF (sign_bit_1 = sign_bit_2) AND       *
*    (sign_bit_1 <> sign_bit_sum)        *
*   THEN overflow                        *
*****************************************
            ALGORITHM
```

Add operand 1, operand 2, and carry.

Figure 11. Display showing two's complement addition.

```
MEMORY: 0000..00FF
        0  1  2  3  4  5  6  7  8  9  A  B  C  D  E  F
0000 86 32 8B 25 C6 31 3E 00 00 00 00 00 00 00 00 00    A  = 00
0010 00 00 00 00 00 00 00 00 00 00 00 00 00 00 00 00    B  = 00
0020 00 00 00 00 00 00 00 00 00 00 00 00 00 00 00 00    SP = 0000
0030 00 00 00 00 00 00 00 00 00 00 00 00 00 00 00 00    X  = 0000
0040 00 00 00 00 00 00 00 00 00 00 00 00 00 00 00 00  CC 11111111
0050 00 00 00 00 00 00 00 00 00 00 00 00 00 00 00 00       HINZVC
0060 00 00 00 00 00 00 00 00 00 00 00 00 00 00 00
0070 00 00 00 00 00 00 00 00 00 00 00 00 00 00 00 00  SINGLE STEP
0080 00 00 00 00 00 00 00 00 00 00 00 00 00 00 00 00  A..ASCII
0090 00 00 00 00 00 00 00 00 00 00 00 00 00 00 00 00  E..One step
00A0 00 00 00 00 00 00 00 00 00 00 00 00 00 00 00 00  G..reGister
00B0 00 00 00 00 00 00 00 00 00 00 00 00 00 00 00 00  H..Hex code
00C0 00 00 00 00 00 00 00 00 00 00 00 00 00 00 00 00  I..Instruct
00D0 00 00 00 00 00 00 00 00 00 00 00 00 00 00 00 00  S..Scroll
00E0 00 00 00 00 00 00 00 00 00 00 00 00 00 00 00 00  Q..Quit
00F0 00 00 00 00 00 00 00 00 00 00 00 00 00 00 00 00

PC = 0000
IR = LDAA #32
machine cycles 2
cycles so far  0
```

Figure 12. Simulation of the 6800 CPU - beginning of step-by step execution. Note the display of contents of all registers, machine cycle count per instruction and cumulative, and mnemonic translation of current instruction. The currently active memory cells are highlighted. The program may be loaded from a file (assembler output), or entered into memory in hexadecimal or in mnemonic form. Several other menus are available including commands such as help with 6800 instructions and others.

Displaying operation of SCANNER

SOURCE STATEMENT: READ(x);

OPERATION PERFORMED
  GetWord;
  GetToken;   ...
                 Scan reserved words;
                 ...

SYMBOL TABLE   GENERATED TOKEN: <READ>

Reserved:
  BEGIN
  END
  PROGRAM
  READ
  VAR
  WRITE

Figure 13. Display of one step of the scanner produced by the visual compiler. Similar displays can also be obtained of the operation of the parser, code generator, and the complete compilation process.

Experiencing Programming Language Constructs with TRAPS

Peter Witschital, Günther Stiege, Thomas Kühme
Institut für Betriebssysteme und Rechnerverbund
Technische Universität Braunschweig
Bültenweg 74/75, D-3300 Braunschweig
Federal Republic of Germany

Abstract

TRAPS is an interactive gaming environment. Playing TRAPS, novices in computer programming will gain first experience in using structured programming language constructs and in "putting them together". In doing so, the learners are supported by an intelligent computer coach.

In this paper we describe some major difficulties, which novices have with computer programming and which, we hope, will be overcome playing TRAPS. We mention the influence that natural language has on novice's difficulties with computer programming and outline the roles of concrete models and experience in learning a programming language.

Furthermore, we describe the architecture of the coach, that offers hints based on a student model and an analysis of the student's current move.

1 Introduction

It is well known that people who are concerned with learning a programming language for the first time have various difficulties with it. They consider programming a difficult task and are frightened right at the start by the great deal of detailed information that they have to remember even before they can start writing the first little program [Green 83][Spohrer et al. 85][du Boulay et al. 81]. Despite the fact that computers more and more become part of our every day life, there are many people who suffer from a serious "computophobia", similar to the "mathophobia" described by Papert [Papert 80].

For now four years we have accomplished an introductory programming course for Pascal. The course is offered every semester and, each semester, is taken by about 500 students of all disciplines except computer science. The course is obligatory on students of certain disciplines (e.g. electrical engineering) but optional for others (e.g. social sciences). The voluntary participants not only take part because they are really interested in learning programming, but more often because they believe – and they are right – that they will have to learn a little programming to improve their chances of employment. Therefore the participants of the course are not only those who really want to participate, but equally those who are forced to for some reasons.

With intent to support the students in learning their first programming language and to introduce them to programming in a playful way we have developed the learning game TRAPS (*T*rainer für die *A*nwendung von *P*rogrammstrukturen). TRAPS is an interactive computer game that provides an environment for gaining first experience in using and nesting programming language constructs. The word for word translation of what the name TRAPS stands for is "*T*rainer for the *A*pplication of *P*rogramming *S*tructures", but better would be something like "training environment for using structured programming language constructs". Playing the game, the rules of which we will explain below, the students are supported by an intelligent computer coach that analyses the students' moves and offers hints if it seems necessary. We don't want to replace some existing part of our course by TRAPS, rather we think of it as an additional tool to the conventional programming course [Venezky 83].

2 The game TRAPS

TRAPS is a program written in C and running under COLLAGE, the window management system for SINIX-systems by the SIEMENS company. SINIX is a derivative of UNIX.

One window contains the playing board. The left border of the playing board is the starting area where a little playing man is placed randomly at the beginning of each run of the game. The right border of the playing board is the winning area that has to be reached by the playing man to end each run of the game. The area between starting and winning areas can be seen as a roll so that the playing man leaving the upper border comes in again from the lower border and the other way round. On it's way from the starting area to the winning area the playing man has to take several obstacles. First there is a bogland full of many separate bogs with some firm ground around. Walking through, the playing man has to be careful not to be bogged down. He can jump over a bog or walk around it. Having gone through the bogland, there waits a mountain range with steep cliffs. The playing man can climb up or down the cliffs or can look for a way round them. Having conquered this challenge, only a river separates him from the winning area. Calling it river is understatement. It's more a torrent and can only be crossed using one of three bridges. The bogs, cliffs, and bridges are placed randomly at each new run of the game.

Now, how to move the playing man over the playing board? The player can give him instructions by writing little programs in a Pascal-like pseudo programming language. The program that will control the next move of the playing man is put together in a separate window using a syntax-driven editor. The elements of the pseudo programming language are selected from pull-down menus using a mouse. The pseudo programming language is very simple. It consists of the three structured language constructs *IF-THEN-ELSE, REPEAT-UNTIL,* and *WHILE-DO*. The actions the playing man can take are *step forward, turn right, turn left, jump, climb,* and *idle*. It's possible to ask for the type of the next field in line of sight of the playing man by checking the conditions *bog ahead*, *cliff ahead*, *river ahead*, and *winning area ahead*. The conditions can be combined by the logical operators *not*, *and*, and *or* and additional parentheses. There are no variables included in the language as will be explained later.

The bogs and cliffs are not visible from the beginning. So the player has to check for the content of the next field he wants to move to. Checked obstacles are displayed. At the start the player has got a limited score of one hundred points. Each step of the playing man reduces the score. Normal steps on firm ground cost one point. Jumping and climbing reduce the score by five points. If the playing man fails at an obstacle, ten points are withdrawn from the account. Turning and staying idle is free. First of all, the goal is to reach the winning area. Secondly, the player should aim for a remaining score as high as possible. Trying this means walking round the obstacles, what in turn requires extensive use of nested programming constructs. The limited score prevents the playing man from endless running in case of an eternal loop in the program. Eternal loops not reducing the score are detected before execution, and the player is asked to modify his program.

3   Natural language and computer programming

When people give instructions to other people they normally use their natural language. They assume that the person being instructed already has some previous knowledge that can be based on. Due to this assumption the resulting instruction set is incomplete, but still sufficiently precise for instructing a human being. Unfortunately, constructing a computer program one can not rely on some "base of experience" that the computer will already have. All special cases and exceptions have to be described with equal precision [Onorato/Schvaneveldt 87]. The statement of Green that "nonprogrammers are perfectly able to describe algorithms, but not in the usual programming terms" [Green 83] must be completed by "and not with the precision required for programming computers". Miller did research on natural language programming and found that in computer programming the final actions are deep embedded in massive control structures with regard to handling all exceptions. He called this style "conditionalized action". In natural language, however, the special conditions or circumstances under which an action is to be applied are following the action as qualifications and often are omitted. This style is characterized as "action qualification". Miller's experiments led to the conclusion: "programming language style is simply alien to natural specification" [Miller 81].

Other researchers have stated that programming languages which would "cognitively fit" with the problem-solving skills of naive computer users would lower the barrier erected between those users and computer programming [Soloway et al. 83]. It would be easier for novices to write correct programs if their preferred problem-solving strategy would be supported by the language constructs. Traditional looping constructs, for instance, were not sensitive to the natural concepts of looping used by novices. This all may be right, but nevertheless there still are no such programming languages. Programming by means of natural language interfaces is far away too, so we have to cope with the existing, widespread computer languages.

With TRAPS we tried to narrow the gap between the abstract algorithms often formulated with a programming language and natural language instructions you give, for instance, if you are asked the way.

4 Concrete models and experience

Meaningful learning only takes place if the new material to be learned can be connected with knowledge that already exists in memory. The incoming information that reaches short-term memory is assimilated using appropriate prerequisite knowledge concepts in long-term memory. For learning, i. e. connecting the new material with existing knowledge, the learner must actively use this prerequisite knowledge. Using familiar, concrete models provides the appropriate prerequisite knowledge. High-ability learners are able to build their own concrete models, but low-ability learners are not [Mayer 81].

TRAPS provides the novice programmer with such a concrete model that enables him to connect the new programming knowledge with knowledge that he already has. The playing man of TRAPS has a line of sight and looks in a specific direction. He lives in a "real world" with mountains and a river. So it's easy to identify oneself with the playing man and to "play playing man", as Papert would say [Papert 80]. By the way, TRAPS is also a little LOGO-like with respect to making visible the running of the program by the motion of the playing man. This is very helpful to the understanding of the dynamic aspects of a program [Soloway 86].

Concrete models do have an effect on the encoding of information by novices. They are a resource for avoiding rote representation of knowledge for the benefit of a better understanding. People who have difficulties to apply their knowledge of algebra to a mathematic task given in natural language only have a rote representation of the knowledge needed. Transfer of knowledge to a new task requires deeper understanding. To do successful programming it is not sufficient to know the syntax of a WHILE-loop. Furthermore, you have to understand the substance of a WHILE-loop. The concrete model provided by TRAPS will help to enhance this understanding.

As mentioned above, the active use of prerequisite knowledge is essential for learning. To the evolution from novice to expert experience is indispensable. Experience guides reasoning processes and serves to turn unrelated facts into expert knowledge. New experiences are evaluated and understood in terms of previous ones [Kolodner 83].

TRAPS is providing an environment that is well suited for gaining first experience in programming. Among other things, this is due to the fact that the task given by TRAPS has many different solutions on several levels of complexity. The very beginner can reach the winning area by writing quite linear programs only using simple actions and conditionals and by executing many small moves (i.e. programs) sequentially. Getting further acquainted with programming the player may use single loops without nesting. With increase of expertise solutions may become quite difficult using deeply nested programming constructs. The optimum solution is a program that leads the playing man from the starting area to the winning area in one move spending as few points as possible. Playing TRAPS the player will evolve from novice to expert increasing his programming knowledge by actively using his previous experience and by gaining new experience with support of a concrete model.

The fact that TRAPS is a game will motivate the students and take away their fear of learning programming. Motivated and encouraged students are better prepared for learning.

5 Novice's difficulties

"There is no single component of a Pascal program that is troublesome for the majority of the students" [Soloway et al. 82], but "a few bug types account for a lot of the mistakes made by students learning to program" [Spohrer/Soloway 86]. Novices often have difficulty to determine which programming language constructs to use in a given situation and how to coordinate them into a unified whole. It does not matter, whether these difficulties stem from misconceptions about the language constructs or from buggy plans, because playing with TRAPS will lead to a better understanding of the language constructs as well as improve the player's ability to construct appropriate plans.

A lot of confusions arise from the application of natural language meaning to the programming language keywords [Bonar/Soloway 85]. Details and examples will be described in the following subsections.

5.1 Difficulties using loops

Among the errors concerning the appropriate use of programming constructs the most frequent ones are with the use of looping constructs. In particular, this is due to the fact that the looping constructs offered by common programming languages are not sensitive to the natural looping concepts of novice programmers, as was mentioned earlier. Unfortunately, it's not merely a matter of individual taste which looping construct should be chosen in a given situation. There are, however, definite reasons this decision can be based on. Nevertheless, a correct program can be written using not the most appropriate looping construct, but it will require further effort [Soloway et al. 82]. Unnecessarily, the textbooks moreover contribute to the confusion about the difference between *REPEAT*-loop and *WHILE*-loop: "The (while-) statement is repeatedly executed until the expression becomes false. If its value is false at the beginning, the statement is not executed at all." [Jensen/Wirth 78].

When the students are told, that the body of the *REPEAT-UNTIL*-construct will be executed at least once, whereas the body of the *WHILE-DO*-construct will possibly be executed not at all, they do not really understand the significance of this difference. Without experiencing the difference this knowledge will remain represented in a rote way. TRAPS brings about the necessary experience in a very figurative way. The playing man will be bogged down if he is trying to step forward to the next bog using a *REPEAT*-loop and starting directly in front of a bog. This experience will be very valuable as the student has *seen* what the difference between the two looping constructs is like.

Another common misconception results from transferring the natural language meaning of *while* to the *WHILE*-loop. Novices often believe that the condition under which a loop is executed will be checked continously during the execution of the loop, and that the execution of the loop will be terminated immediately when the condition for the termination is met [Bonar 82] [Covington 84][Bonar/Soloway 85]. TRAPS is well suited to illustrate this misconception to the students.

There are some more errors with loops appearing frequently in connection with variables [Soloway/Ehrlich 84][Soloway et al. 82][Soloway et al. 83][Gannon 78]. As TRAPS not includes variables those errors are not mentioned here.

5.2 Difficulties formulating logical expressions

Using structured programming language constructs the formulation of conditions plays a central role. Difficulties formulating logical expressions again may take their rise from natural language. A novice, who is thinking: "I want to do action A if condition $C1$ is true, *and* I want do the same action A if condition $C2$ is true.", is easily misleaded to formulate "*IF C1 and C2 THEN ...*".

Another frequent error occurs if a *REPEAT*-loop is reformulated as a *WHILE*-loop and the condition is negated neglecting DeMorgan's Rule. As wrong beliefs often are transferred from inappropriate domains like natural language, this misconception may have its origin in the student's knowledge of algebra, where the equation $-(a + b) = (-a) + (-b)$ holds [Spohrer et al. 85] [Spohrer/Soloway 86].

TRAPS is impressively illustrating the consequences of illformed logical expressions and helps the students to become experienced in formulating logical expressions.

5.3 Difficulties to be aware of all exceptions

As was mentioned in chapter 3, people who are not familiar with computer programming normally omit some special cases, when they are describing a particular procedure in natural language. Miller's experiment [Miller 81] showed that non-programmers never use a full *IF-THEN-ELSE*-structure in their descriptions. In human discourse the missing information can be retrieved by some "general base of experience", also called "common sense". As computers (still) have no "common sense", learning computer programming means learning to think of every possible exception that might happen. Indeed, advanced programmers "make greater use of conditional information", "are more likely to look at every possible decision and alternative that could occur along the way" and "are less likely to incorporate their instruction recipient's 'base of experience' into their instruction sets" [Onorato/Schvaneveldt 87].

Playing TRAPS the students will see that it is very important to be aware of all possible exceptions. In TRAPS there is no *IF-THEN*-construct without *ELSE*-case. This will force the student to think about what should be done if the condition is not satisfied. If there is really no alternative action the student has to give explicitly the command to *idle*.

5.4 Difficulties "putting the pieces together"

The most serious difficulties novices have are with "composing and coordinating components of a program" [Soloway 86][Spohrer/Soloway 86].

To understand these difficulties we have to look at the process of program construction. This process has been divided into several subprocesses with various denominations by numerous researchers. Wender et al. propose the discrimination of three phases: the planning phase, the algorithmic phase, and the coding phase [Wender et al. 87]. The theory of Program Development by Stepwise Refinement [Wirth 71] suggests to proceed top-down and breadth-first from the planning phase, via the algorithmic phase to the coding phase. Indeed, this procedure is used by most of the advanced programmers. In opposition to this, "beginners very early leave the planning phase, pass through the algorithmic phase very quickly, and start typing in code", showing a depth-first behaviour "starting at the top level but proceeding at once to the bottom" [Wender et al. 87]. This is because the evolution from novice to expert is done, of course, bottom-up. At first the novice only has mental representations of elementary actions and some syntactic rules. In the next step algorithms are represented but still cannot be handled correctly. Only in the last step the programming language and often-used algorithms are interiorized completely allowing the student to do a complete top-down/breadth-first approach [Hoc 77]. The portion of program development that can be done top-down by novices is based on their general problem solving abilities.

If you want to do stepwise refinement, you have to "break down a problem into subproblems, on the basis of problems that you have already solved and for which you have canned (or almost canned) solutions" as stated by Soloway [Soloway 86]. He continues: "Students must already possess the primitives into which the problem will be decomposed in order to carry out a stepwise-refinement strategy." When a novice does not already have the appropriate primitives or plans respectively he cannot use stepwise refinement straightforward. Therefore, he will use rather a depth-first than a breadth-first strategy.

The task given by TRAPS is very similar to a real-world situation. Therefore, the portion of top-down planning that is absolutely necessary can be achieved with general problem solving knowledge: First travel the bogland, then the mountain range, etc. The next step in a top-down approach would be to refine "travel the bogland". This would mean to write something like: While you have not reached the mountain range do ... The novice, instead, will leave out this loop and will proceed further down to the next subgoal: Go to the first bog. He will, probably, code this subgoal, execute the code and watch for the result. Then he will see how to proceed further.

The advantage of TRAPS is, that there is no need for complete planning at the top level. The novice first may gain experience at the bottom level. Having put the necessary primitives into his tool-box he will be able to plan at a higher level in one of the following runs of the game. At any time he may save pieces of code he has written and load the pieces again later. So he can take a *WHILE*-loop, for instance, and put into it some previously saved components which have proved to be successful.

The task given by TRAPS cooperates with the fact that the thinking of novices is very local and sequential, while experts have a more global view of the problem [Spohrer et al. 85].

Novices have problems in "putting the pieces together", if they have not yet fully understood how the individual pieces work. The difficulties are reduced playing TRAPS, because the player is able to test the components separately before composing them. We hope that the novices will transfer this technique to other tasks: If you have difficulties putting it together, try to break it apart and test the components separately.

5.5   Further difficulties

Of course there are many further difficulties novices have in learning programming that we have not mentioned yet. A wide field of possible errors is opened by variables and data structures. We have not addressed this field with TRAPS but, on the contrary, have concentrated on programming constructs. This was mainly to keep the concept of TRAPS simple. With the results we obtain from our current experiments with TRAPS we will think of possible extensions.

We do not take up syntactical errors with TRAPS. Using the syntax-driven editor the player only can build syntactically correct programs. Strictly speaking, he may indeed make a change that makes his program syntactically wrong, but if he does so the editor immediately comments on the error with a message like: "A condition is not appropriate here!" The player will have to undo the last change in this case. Wender et al. showed that using a syntax-driven editor improves (or at least not impairs) performance related to syntactical knowledge [Wender et al. 87].

6   The coach

Playing TRAPS the student is supported in his knowledge acquisition by an intelligent computer coach that is implemented in C-Prolog [Malinowski 87].

6.1   The representation of knowledge

The knowledge that has to be represented in the knowledge base of TRAPS includes *programming knowledge* as well as *knowledge how to play TRAPS*. Furthermore, we have to include *knowledge of possible misconceptions* to improve the analysis of the student's behavior. For coaching it will be advantageous to include some *knowledge about interconnections* between different knowledge chunks. The coach will be able to generate better explanations if there is some information how the knowledge that is to be explained is related to some knowledge already known by the student.

To embody all these types of knowledge we have chosen a knowledge representation depending on the "genetic graph" proposed by Goldstein [Goldstein 82]. The rules of our knowledge base can be interpreted as nodes of a graph. The edges of the graph are formed by the relations analogy, generalization/specialization, simplification/refinement, and deviation/correction. These relations represent possible paths for the evolution of knowledge and will be used by the coach in generating explanations. As was proposed by Goldstein, we have extended the original genetic graph, that is suited best for representing procedural knowledge, by adding declarative knowledge and planning knowledge. Declarative facts may be linked to rules explaining and justifying their behaviour. Planning knowledge may be represented by declaring an order of efficient application for certain sets of rules.

6.2 The expert component

Diagnosing the student's abilities the coach has to compare the program submitted by the student with an expert solution. The expert component is able to construct an expert program for every possible situation in the game using the rules from the knowledge base. The complexity of the program proposed by the expert component depends on the student's current level of performance given by the student model (see 6.3). Ideally, the expert solution is slightly better than the solution the student is expected to submit.

6.3 The student model

The student model should be good for answering the following questions: *What* does the student already know? *Which* is his preferred learning style.

For modelling the student's knowledge we use some kind of "overlay model". The knowledge of the student is modelled as a subset of the knowledge in the knowledge base. It is not only a subset of the expert's knowledge. Remember that the knowledge base of TRAPS contains more knowledge (e.g. misconceptions) than is needed by an expert for playing TRAPS.

Each rule of the knowledge base is associated with a numerical tag indicating the student's *familiarity* with this rule. The value of the tag is incremented if the student has used the corresponding rule correctly and decremented if the student has not used the rule but should have. If the familiarity of a given rule exceeds a defined threshold this rule *belongs to the student model*. There are mimimum and maximum values for the familiarity.

Similar tags are associated with each type of relation (e.g. analogy) that is used in the graph indicating the *strenght* of this type of relation. If the student uses a rule for the first time that is related to a known rule by a specific relation, it is assumed that he has discovered the new rule with the help of this relation. In this case, the strength of the specific relation type is incremented. The relation with the highest strength value is the relation that is most used by the student in learning.

6.4 The analysis component

The program submitted by the student has to be analysed to find out which rules have been used by the student composing the program. Some (lower-level) rules in the knowledge base contain chunks of program code. The analysis component first tries to identify those chunks of code in the student's program. Then, in a bottom-up fashion, it tries to find some higher-level rules which might the student have used composing his program.

Of course, the analysis component can be fooled by pieces of code that are equivalent but not identical to those expected. Likewise, it does not work very well with very badly structured and incorrect programs (humans have also difficulties in analysing such programs). The quite fair results obtained by the analysis component are due to the very restricted programming language involved and the fact that the students are working on the same problem all the time.

6.5   The teaching component

If the student submits a program for execution, the analysis component is activated first. According to the results of the analysis the student model is updated. Then, the expert component is asked to construct an expert program with regard to the student model. Subsequently, the execution of *both* programs is *simulated*. This dynamic analysis is very important because the coach must not blame the student if his program yields a better result than the expert program. If so, the student will get credit.

Otherwise, the coach looks for a rule which will be opportune for explanation. To find such a rule, the coach constructs the set of rules which have been used by the expert, but have been missed by the student. If this set is not empty, the coach will look for the rule which has the tightest connection with the student model. This rule will be most easily understood by the student because he is able to connect the new information with the knowledge he already has. This means adapting the explanation to the learner's level of knowledge. The tightness of the connection is determined by summarizing the strenghts of the relations between the given rule and the rules belonging to the student model. If no appropriate rule can be found the coach will remain silent.

Having selected a rule for explanation the coach determines the relation with the greatest strength that exists between the rule and the student model. For each type of relation there is a specific type of explanation. Using this type of explanation means adapting to the learner's preferred learning style. The explanations are presented in a separate window with (in most cases) three different levels of detail. On the first level a general explanation is presented, on the second level the goal which should be aimed at in the current situation is given, and on the last level a complete program is proposed. The explanations are assembled from canned text. At each level the student is asked whether he needs more information. After an explanation the student may change his program before executing but also may leave it unchanged to see what will happen.

7   Summary

We have presented an interactive computer game, called TRAPS, that will help novice programmers in learning programming by *guided-discovery learning*. The concept of the game is tailored to help the students learning to avoid some errors frequently made by novices. The students are supported in learning by an intelligent computer coach adapting his explanations to the needs of individual students.

References

[Bonar 82]   Bonar, J. (1982) Natural problem solving strategies and programming language constructs. *Proceedings of the Fourth Annual Conference of the Cognitive Science Society*, 146-148.

[Bonar/Soloway 85] Bonar, J., Soloway, E. (1985) Preprogramming knowledge: A major source of misconceptions in novice programmers. *Hum. Comput. Interaction, 1(2)*, 133-161.

[Covington 84]   Covington, M. A. (1984) A pedagogical disadvantage of repeat and while. *Sigplan Notic., 19(8)*, 85-86.

[du Boulay et al. 81] du Boulay, B., O'Shea, T., Monk, J. (1981) The black box inside the glass box: Presenting computing concepts to novices. *Int. J. Man-Mach. Stud., 14*, 237-250.

[Gannon 78]   Gannon, J. D. (1978) Characteristic errors in programming languages. *Proceedings of the Annual Conference of the ACM, Washington, DC*, 570-575.

[Goldstein 82]   Goldstein, I. P. (1982) The genetic graph: a representation for the evolution of procedural knowledge. In D. Sleeman, J. S. Brown (Eds.), *Intelligent Tutoring Systems*. Academic Press, London. 51-77.

[Green 83]   Green, T. R. G. (1983) Learning big and little programming languages. In A. C. Wilkinson (Ed.), *Classroom Computers and Cognitive Science*. Academic Press, New York. 71-93.

[Hoc 77]   Hoc, J.-M. (1977) Role of mental representation in learning a programming language. *Int. J. Man-Mach. Stud., 9*, 87-105.

[Jensen/Wirth 78] Jensen, K., Wirth, N. (1978) *PASCAL – User Manual and Report*. Second Edition. Springer-Verlag, New York.

[Kolodner 83]   Kolodner, J. L. (1983) Towards an understanding of the role of experience in the evolution from novice to expert. *Int. J. Man-Mach. Stud., 19*, 497-518.

[Kühme et al. 87] Kühme, T., Malinowski, U., Witschital, P. (1987) TRAPS – Ein Trainer für die Anwendung von Programmstrukturen. In R. Gunzenhäuser, H. Mandl (Eds.), *Workshop "Intelligente Lernsysteme", Abstracts*. Deutsches Institut für Fernstudien an der Universität Tübingen.

[Malinowski 87] Malinowksi, U. (1987) *Ein intelligenter Tutor zum Lernspiel TRAPS*. Diploma thesis. Institut für Betriebssysteme und Rechnerverbund, Technische Universität Braunschweig, D-3300 Braunschweig, West Germany.

[Mayer 81]   Mayer, R. E. (1981) The psychology of how novices learn computer programming. *Comput. Surv., 18(1)*, 121-141.

[Miller 81]   Miller, L. A. (1981) Natural language programming: Style, strategies and contrasts. *IBM Syst. J., 20(2)*, 184-215.

[Onorato/Schvaneveldt 87] Onorato, L. A., Schvaneveldt, R. W. (1987) Programmer–Nonprogrammer differences in specifying procedures to people and computers. *The Journal of Systems and Software, 7*, 357-369.

[Papert 80]   Papert, S. (1980) *Mindstorms: Children, Computers, and Powerful Ideas.* Basic Books, New York.

[Soloway 86]   Soloway, E. (1986) Learning to program = learning to construct mechanisms and explanations. *Commun. ACM, 29(9)*, 850-858.

[Soloway/Ehrlich 84]   Soloway, E., Ehrlich, K. (1984) Empirical studies of programming knowledge. *IEEE Trans. Software Eng., 10(5)*, 595-609.

[Soloway et al. 82]   Soloway, E., Ehrlich, K., Bonar, J., Greenspan, J. (1982) What do novices know about programming? In B. Shneiderman, A. Badre (Eds.), *Directions in Human–Computer Interactions.* Ablex Publishing Company. 27-54.

[Soloway et al. 83]   Soloway, E., Bonar, J., Ehrlich, K. (1983) Cognitive strategies and looping constructs: An empirical study. *Commun. ACM, 26(11)*, 853-860.

[Spohrer/Soloway 86] Spohrer, J. C., Soloway, E. (1986) Novice mistakes: Are the folk wisdoms correct? *Commun. ACM, 29(7)*, 624-632.

[Spohrer et al. 85]   Spohrer, J. C., Soloway, E., Pope, E. (1985) A goal/plan analysis of buggy Pascal programs. *Hum. Comput. Interaction, 1(2)*, 163-207.

[Venezky 83]   Venezky, R. L. (1983) Evaluating computer–assisted instruction on its own terms. In A. C. Wilkinson (Ed.), *Classroom Computers and Cognitive Science.* Academic Press, New York. 31-49.

[Wender et al. 87]   Wender, K. F., Weber, G., Waloszek, G. (1987) Psychological considerations for the design of tutorial systems. Paper presented at the *Third International Conference on Artificial Intelligence and Education, Pittsburgh, PA.*

[Wenger 87]   Wenger, E. (1987) *Artificial Intelligence and Tutoring Systems.* Morgan Kaufmann, Los Altos, CA.

[Wirth 71]   Wirth, N. (1971) Program development by stepwise refinement. *Commun. ACM, 14(4)*, 221-227.

THE OTHER SIDE OF THE COIN:
TEACHING ARTIFICIAL LEARNING SYSTEMS

Ian H. Witten and Bruce A. MacDonald
Knowledge Sciences Laboratory, Department of Computer Science
University of Calgary, Calgary, Canada T2N 1N4

Abstract. The burgeoning technology of machine learning is beginning to provide some insight into the nature of learning and the role of teaching in expediting the learning process. A number of systems that learn concepts and procedures from examples have been described in the research literature. In general these require a teacher who not only has an analytical understanding of the problem domain, but also is familiar with some of the internal workings of the learning system itself. This is because the learner is performing a search in concept space which is generally quite intractable, but for the teacher's selection of guiding examples.

A concept learning system's teacher must select a complete, properly ordered set of examples — one that results in a successful search by the system for an appropriate concept description. In some systems the set of examples determines whether the concept can or cannot be learned, while the order of presentation affects execution time alone. In others, both examples and presentation order are jointly responsible for success. Yet others occasionally select critical examples themselves and present them to a teacher for classification. In all cases, however, the teacher provides the primary means whereby search is pruned. Sometimes the teacher must prime the learner with considerable initial knowledge before learning can begin.

Not surprisingly, systems which demand more of the teacher are able to learn more sophisticated concepts. This paper examines the relationship between teaching requirements and learning power for current concept learning systems. We introduce concept learning by machine with emphasis on the role of the human teacher in rendering practical an otherwise intractable concept search. Machine learning has drawn many lessons from human learning and will continue to do so. In turn it can contribute more formal, if simpler, analyses of concept learning from examples.

Teaching *vs* programming

A concept learning system's practical utility obviously depends critically on its teaching requirements. Teaching differs from programming in that a teacher does not have a detailed formal model of the learner. Teachers are always uncertain about exactly how a learner learns. A programmer normally expects to know precisely how his instructions are going to be interpreted. In Dennett's (1981, 1987) terms, a teacher adopts the *intentional stance* while the programmer adopts the *design stance*. In the former case intentions are ascribed to the learner, and its behavior is modeled in terms of those intentions; while in the latter a detailed formal model of the system is available which reflects its behavior *by design*. In the design stance, if by any chance there is a mismatch between the formal model and the system's actual behavior, this indicates a malfunctioning — the design has not been realized correctly at the physical level. In the intentional stance, mismatches do not indicate any fault in the learner but are corrected by the teacher modifying his model.

In principle, a teacher should need to know nothing about the design or physical implementation of the learner, nor about the representation it uses for concepts; although good teachers certainly make and use models at the intentional level. Learning even in the absence of a good teacher is an important skill for human and machine learners, enabling them to acquire knowledge on their own. But as human society has found, unassisted learning can be very difficult and is often impractical.

Teachers do not expect to have to give explicit analytic descriptions to learners in the way that programmers create explicit analytic specifications in their programs. Rather, they use pragmatically established, intention-based techniques, coupled with a carefully selected set of examples, to engender understanding in the learner. Furthermore, domain experts who expect to use concept learning techniques for transferring knowledge to machines are not necessarily skilled teachers. They are unlikely to have a clear analytical understanding of the task domain — otherwise more explicit methods of knowledge transfer will likely prove more appropriate. In general, people find it difficult to translate their own expertise into explicit descriptions. Consequently concept learning systems should be able to work with the kind of examples that a user finds it natural to provide, ordered in a way that seems natural to him.

In practice, the distinction between teaching and programming is not so clearly delineated. The teacher of a computer learning system is often required to construct exemplars which are borderline cases of a concept — either near misses or critical examples — and the boundary in question is not necessarily one which accords with our intuition, but is characterized by the particular way the concept is represented in the machine. This gives teaching some of the model-dependence of programming. Conversely, programming can acquire some of the model-independence of teaching. For example, it has been observed that in logic programming languages, particularly those with non-standard computation rules, a programmer may be completely unable to figure out the execution sequence of his program — and yet know from a declarative perspective that any answer that is computed must be the correct one.

Generalization as search, identification by enumeration

Systems which acquire concepts do so through some sort of searching process. "Generalization as search" was the title of an influential paper (Mitchell, 1982) which equated the process of generalization with searching through a space of structured concept descriptions. Since then other paradigms have appeared, notably the newly-fashionable connectionist architectures which employ relaxation methods such as simulated annealing to embed new concepts in highly-connected networks; but even these are effectively searching for energy minima using hill-climbing. Groping around for solutions seems central to the learning process, and it is hard to see how a program which avoided search could reasonably be described as generalizing or learning.

As an example of the kind of search involved, consider the problem of classifying scenes containing simple objects. (Such problems are typical of the early experiments on concept formation by people, pioneered by Bruner *et al*, 1956.) Figure 1 illustrates a domain in which scenes contain objects with attributes such as size, color, and shape, placed in various positions relative to each other (from Haussler, 1987). It includes a formal description of a scene which has a red circle inside a red square, both being under a green crescent. Also shown is a sample concept, a circle in a particular size range, inside any convex object. The scene contains an instance of the concept. The problem of concept learning is to take many examples of such scenes and induce the description of the sub-structure that they all have in common. This basically involves testing candidate concept descriptions on the example set, and searching through possible descriptions until one is found which fits. The search space of possible concepts is enormous.

Generalization as search is essentially the same idea as identification by enumeration, a basic methodology for inductive inference introduced by Gold (1967) in a seminal contribution†. A number of theoretical results characterize the ability to identify classes of languages from example sentences, through the theory of enumerability (countability) of various infinite sets. Identifying a particular language from a given class by examining sample sentences is the same thing as identifying a description from a given class by examining samples of what is being described. The crux of the matter in practice, of course, is not whether sets can be enumerated but whether the space of possibilities can be cut down sufficiently to make searching productive. This highlights the importance of the example sequence, which largely directs the search.

Although theoretical results about identifiability may seem remote from practical concept learning, and irrelevant to teaching human learners, they do point out that search lies at the root of inductive inference. They may not tell us *how* to search, but they confirm that we will have to do so. Human learners have a powerful ability to generalize from properly selected examples; introspectively this generalisation does not appear as an explicit search of the possibilities, but there is an implicit search carried out at some level.

The "identification by enumeration" paradigm for inductive inference proposes a system that enumerates all possible descriptions in advance. It selects a description and pronounces it to be the target generalization as long as it is consistent with all examples that come along. Once an example is encountered which clashes with the current description, it moves to the next description, checks it against all examples that have been seen so far (for it remembers each example given), and if it passes that test, adopts it as the new target generalization. Suppose that the presentation is such that all possible examples are included. Is such a system bound to come up with the correct generalization eventually?

---

† This arose out of early work in the mid to late 1950s; see Ginsburg (1958), Moore (1956), Gill (1961), Solomonoff (1964). Angluin & Smith (1983) provide an up-to-date survey.

Nominal attribute

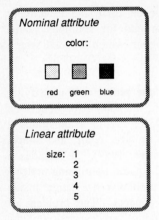

color:

red green blue

Linear attribute

size: 1
       2
       3
       4
       5

Tree-structured attribute

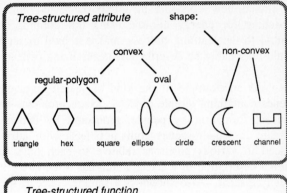

shape:

convex   non-convex

regular-polygon   oval

triangle hex square ellipse circle crescent channel

Tree-structured function

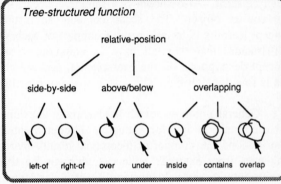

relative-position

side-by-side   above/below   overlapping

left-of right-of over under inside contains overlap

Sample scene

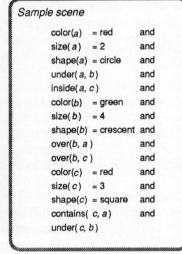

color(*a*)   = red   and
size(*a*) = 2   and
shape(*a*)   = circle   and
under(*a, b*)   and
inside(*a, c*)   and
color(*b*)   = green   and
size(*b*) = 4   and
shape(*b*)   = crescent and
over(*b, a*)   and
over(*b, c*)   and
color(*c*)   = red   and
size(*c*) = 3   and
shape(*c*)   = square   and
contains(*c, a*)   and
under(*c, b*)

Sample concept

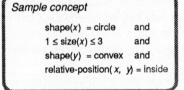

shape(*x*) = circle   and
$1 \leq$ size(*x*) ≤ 3 and
shape(*y*) = convex   and
relative-position(*x, y*) = inside

Figure 1 Example of similarity-based learning
(adapted from Haussler, 1987)

If there are only a finite number of different examples corresponding to any given description, the system will be bound eventually to stumble upon a correct generalization (assuming one exists). However, as Gold (1967) showed, if the class from which generalizations can be selected includes all finite languages and at least one infinite one, the answer is no. He proved this by an intriguing method that develops what has become known as a "frustration" sequence of examples. There exists an infinite sequence of finite languages, such that each is a subset of the next, and all are subsets of the given infinite language. For any learner a presentation sequence can be arranged to "fool" it that the language is one of this sequence, and to fool it an infinite number of times, thereby postponing indefinitely any opportunity for it to identify the infinite language. On the other hand a system which begins by guessing the infinite language will never discover its error if the language is in fact finite, since no examples disconfirm its hypothesis. (An example of this phenomenon is given in the next section.) The possible existence of such worst-case example sequences is a useful tool in the analysis of practical methods, and also highlights the crucial role counter-examples in real teaching situations.

Teaching requirements: theoretical foundations

The paradigm of generalization by enumerating and searching through candidate descriptions highlights the importance of the sequence of examples presented and the role of the "teacher" who selects them. It is obvious that learning can be prevented by showing only a subset of examples. However, even if all examples are presented eventually, the frustration argument shows that a teacher can have the power to inhibit learning by pernicious choice of the example sequence.

There is a basic distinction between presenting positive examples only, presenting both positive and negative examples, and allowing the learning system to choose examples itself and have them classified by an informant. In the first case, we assume that all positive examples are included eventually. In the second, we assume that every member of some universe which contains all possible descriptions is shown eventually; this allows an informant to be simulated by simply waiting until a selected example occurs in the presentation sequence. Gold (1967) showed unequivocally what one expects informally, namely that the second and third methods are more powerful than the first. They permit primitive recursive languages, which include the context sensitive, context free, and regular languages, to be learned eventually, whereas with positive presentations only, as noted above, the inclusion of even one infinite language in the set of potential concepts can destroy learnability.

Figure 2 illustrates some of these ideas with reference to a simple, artificial learning problem. Suppose the concept "integer between 1 and N" (L_N) is to be learned, where N is unknown and may be infinite. Figure 2(a) illustrates the set of possible concepts. Part (b) shows the initial part of sample presentations for each of two target languages, L_{100} and L_∞. Positive presentations contain only positive examples (and eventually every positive example will appear); mixed presentations include all positive and negative examples over some universe (in this case, the integers). Part (c) shows the effect of two different enumeration sequences for the two chosen target languages. With the sequence

(a)

Description	Language
L_∞	{1, 2, 3, ... }
...	...
L_{101}	{1, 2, 3, ... 101}
L_{100}	{1, 2, 3, ... 100}
L_{99}	{1, 2, 3, ... 99}
...	...
L_3	{1, 2, 3}
L_2	{1, 2}
L_1	{1}

(b)

target language	positive presentation	mixed presentation
L_{100}	53,25,2,97,46,... (all ≤ 100)	¬2576, ¬198, 53, ¬1007, 25, ...
L_∞	2576,198,53,1007,25,... (any numbers)	2576,198,53,1007,25,...

(c)

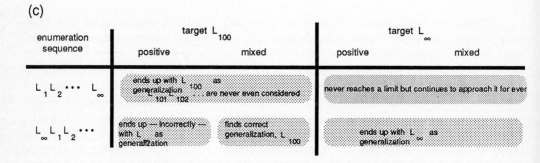

enumeration sequence	target L_{100} positive	target L_{100} mixed	target L_∞ positive	target L_∞ mixed
$L_1 L_2 \cdots L_\infty$	ends up with L_{100} as generalization 101 102	... are never even considered	never reaches a limit but continues to approach it for ever	
$L_\infty L_1 L_2 \cdots$	ends up — incorrectly — with L_∞ as generalization	finds correct generalization, L_{100}	ends up with L_∞ as generalization	

Figure 2 (a) A problem which is identifiable in the limit but only from a mixed presentation

(b) Example presentation sequences

(c) The effect of different enumeration sequences

$L_1, L_2, \cdots, L_\infty$ and target L_{100}, identification by enumeration never even considers L_{101}, L_{102} etc. (Supposing it were to, none could be ruled out if the presentation were positive, but any could be if it were mixed.) With target L_∞, positive and mixed presentations become identical (see part (b)). With the same enumeration sequence the target will clearly never be reached. On the other hand a presentation sequence in which L_∞ occurs early on will quickly identify L_∞. With target L_{100}, identification depends on the kind of presentation. Positive examples will never be able to rule out L_∞, so L_{100} will not be identified correctly. In contrast, a mixed presentation will achieve the desired result. Thus the problem can be solved with an enumeration in which L_∞ occurs early on, if the presentation is mixed.

There is a curious theoretical result which relates to the sequence of examples presented. Gold (1967) showed that descriptions unlearnable from positive and negative examples *can* be learned under a special condition: the presentation sequence must be sufficiently regular. Moreover, positive examples alone suffice! For instance, descriptions from the class of recursively enumerable languages (which includes the primitive recursive ones mentioned above, and more besides) are not normally identifiable even from positive and negative examples, nor indeed using a helpful informant who is prepared to classify arbitrary examples. But a suitable, highly contrived, presentation sequence of positive examples can render such descriptions learnable. In essence the learner can identify the algorithm used to select the examples, thereby identifying the set from which they are drawn. For example, it is much harder to recognize the Fibonacci numbers from the presentation 34, 5, 13, 1, 8, 1, 21, 3, 2, 55 $\cdots$ than from the normal sequence 1, 1, 2, 3, 5, 8, 13, 21, 34, 55, $\cdots$.

Here the importance of the teacher's selected example sequence is clearly reflected at the theoretical level. A good sequence of examples does more than speed the search, it makes learnable the otherwise unlearnable. This regular patterning of examples is a vital skill in teaching humans; experienced learners expect the order of example presentation to be carefully selected to give the maximum assistance to learning.

Teaching requirements: felicity conditions

A skilled teacher will select illuminating examples himself and thereby simplify the learner's task. The benefits of carefully constructed examples were appreciated in the earliest research efforts in concept learning. Winston (1975) showed how "near misses" — constructs which differ in just one crucial respect from examples of a concept being taught — could radically diminish the search required for generalization. Confident that its teacher is selecting examples helpfully, a learning system can assume that any difference between an example being shown and its nascent concept is in fact a critical feature.

The notion of a sympathetic teacher has been formalized in terms of "felicity conditions", constraints imposed on or satisfied by a teacher that make learning better than from random examples (Van Lehn, 1983). One obvious condition is that the teacher should correctly classify examples as positive or negative, and not (intentionally or unintentionally) mislead the student. Another is that if the absence of something is important, the teacher should point it out explicitly. If in the classic example of the concept of "arch" it is necessary that a gap be left between the pillars, the gap should be explicitly labeled in examples. More generally, the teacher should show all work and avoid glossing over intermediate results. Examples should not by coincidence include features that might mislead the learner: one should not illustrate the concept of married *vs* maiden names using a lady whose original family name happens to coincide with her husband's; one should not illustrate the geometric concept of isosceles triangles with ones that happen to be congruent. Finally, the teacher should introduce one essentially new feature per lesson and not try to teach multiple differences at once — a similar condition to Winston's "near miss" approach.

Intermediate results, and other implicit parts of examples, are difficult for a system to learn since they necessarily involve a large search. The system must consider everything that *might* be absent, and the numerous relationships it may have with other parts of the description. Andreae's (1984) "justified generalization" addresses this problem by using the amount of justification associated with a conjecture to determine which of three different levels of search to undertake. When the evidence is sufficiently strong, it will expend considerable resources seeking implicit relationships between parts of a description.

Although it does not increase formal learning power, the possibility of a system constructing its own examples and having them classified by an informant has considerable potential to speed up learning and reduce dependence on the skill of the teacher. This potential can only be realized if the system is able to synthesize "crucial examples" which discriminate effectively between alternative hypotheses consistent with the information seen so far. This ability seems to be one of the chief distinguishing characteristics of people who are good learners. To take the generation of examples one step further, if there is an automatic way of classifying examples as positive or negative, a system can attempt to learn autonomously. This paradigm of "learning by discovery" was exploited most effectively in pioneering work by Lenat (1978; see also Davis & Lenat, 1982, Lenat & Brown, 1984) on automating the theory formation process in mathematics.

The effect of teaching on search

The role of a concept learning system's teacher is to guide its search through an intractably large space of possible descriptions. This section discusses examples of how existing concept learning systems allow the teacher to control search. Particular attention is paid to the extent to which teachers need to be conscious of the system's search space and its internal workings.

Version space. Mitchell's (1982) version-space paradigm is an attempt to construct a learner which processes examples incrementally and yet remains insensitive to their order. This contrasts with the early, and very influential, work of Winston (1975) on learning structural descriptions from examples. While Winston's system was very sensitive to the order in which examples were presented, sometimes failing to learn a concept because of "incorrect" presentation order, Mitchell noticed that by using appropriate data structures and setting up the algorithm in the right way this order-sensitivity could be eliminated.

Essentially, his scheme is a way of representing and manipulating the "version space" of all possible concept descriptions that are compatible with the examples seen so far. Suppose all conceivable generalizations could be listed and stored. When an example is presented, this list could be pruned by removing generalizations that are inconsistent with it. For instance, a positive example may rule out certain generalizations that are too restrictive to encompass it. A negative example may eliminate other generalizations so broad that they *do* encompass it (since it is a negative example, the correct generalization must not). A third possibility is that the example is compatible with all remaining generalizations on the list. A positive example is compatible if all generalizations include it; a negative one if they all exclude it. In either case, nothing can removed from the list on the evidence of that example.

As time goes on, the list of remaining generalizations shrinks. Now the system can classify some examples itself. Given an unknown example, it may be compatible with all remaining generalizations (in which case it must be a positive instance of the concept), incompatible with all remaining generalizations (in which case it must be a negative instance), or compatible with some and incompatible with others. In the last case the system cannot tell whether that example is positive or negative. But if it is told its classification, it can use that fact to eliminate some more generalizations from the list. Ultimately, one hopes, the size of the list will shrink to one generalization, which is the "correct" description of the concept. Then all further unknown examples can be classified as positive or negative. Mitchell showed that the entire version space need not be explicitly stored, but only its upper and lower boundaries in a hierarchy formed by a "more general than" ordering on the concept space.

The reason for constructing and maintaining the version space is to ensure that the final concept learned is independent of the order in which examples are presented. However, while the sequence in which examples are presented does not affect the final result of learning with the version space method, it can very greatly influence the amount of searching required. Indeed, it can be shown that presentation order can have an arbitrarily large effect on the search required. Although this may seem of secondary importance compared with whether the search converges at all, the whole process of concept learning can be viewed as purely a matter of searching large spaces. Consequently the judicious restriction of search is absolutely central, and often makes the difference between successful and failed learning in practice.

In summary, with version space the concepts learned are independent of presentation order, but the amount of search is not. In practice this still places a high premium on the teacher's ability to select a good sequence of examples.

Learning procedures. The version-space machinery, which makes the final concept independent of the order in which examples are presented, cannot be applied inapplicable to domains which are open-ended. For example, Andreae's (1984) NODDY, which learns robot control procedures from sample traces, is sensitive to the order in which examples are presented. On seeing two different executions of the same procedure under different conditions, it attempts to combine the two traces into a single nascent procedure. If they are sufficiently similar it will succeed, and generalize the traces so that they become identical. In the process, however, the individual differences are lost, and in the event that the generalization was premature the system will not be able to create procedures that rely on the small differences, previously thought insignificant, that discriminated the two traces. The obvious solution of retaining all details of individual traces in case they might prove important in the future is fraught with difficulty, not because there is any difficulty with recording the information, but because putting it to good use opens up the search space enormously.

This matches our own intuitions when learning new procedures in a complex domain. It is necessary to generalize in order to simplify enough to see the wood for the trees. But generalizing in the wrong way leads us up blind alleys. Forgotten features of individual examples, previously thought insignificant, now become vital.

A second reason why the procedures learned by NODDY cannot sensibly be represented in a version space is because they involve open-ended functional induction. In order to rationalize two different moves of the robot at the same point of a procedure, an attempt is made to relate the parameters of the motion to other aspects of the current environment. For example, two MOVE orders with quite different numerical parameters may turn out to be the same if the parameters are viewed in terms of the distance and orientation of the goal position from the current one. NODDY bases the functional induction involved on a pre-determined set of operators for the domain, searching combinations of the operators up to a specified depth limit. Such open-ended search does not lend itself readily to the version space technique.

Hierarchical decomposition. One way to search large spaces successfully is to employ hierarchical decomposition of descriptions. Complex concepts are decomposed into constituent parts which are learned separately. Only then are examples of the full concept presented. The system embeds previously-learned constructs into its representation language so that they can be used in subsequent descriptions. Examples of such systems are Shapiro's MIS (Shapiro, 1983), Sammut's MARVIN (Sammut & Banerji, 1983, 1986), and Krawchuk's ALVIN (Krawchuk & Witten, 1988).

In this learning paradigm, the language in which concepts are described is extended to include new concepts as they are taught. This makes learning particularly sensitive to the order of teaching. Since these systems are not tied to a fixed description language, they permit sophisticated concepts to be constructed piece by piece. However, inevitably teaching begins to assume the character of programming. Concepts require debugging, and the effects of undiscovered low-level bugs propagate into higher-level concepts.

The teacher must now select a suitable presentation sequence for concepts, as well as examples within each concept. For instance, in a card-playing domain one might imagine teaching the concept of a *court card* and employing this as a component in the concept of *royal flush*. This is not unnatural providing the teacher can analyze each concept into its constituents (but experts typically find this hard to do). Unfortunately, the teacher must not only teach concepts in the right order, but must refrain from teaching irrelevant concepts

— otherwise the search increases dramatically as all combinations of concepts must be considered. Larger spaces can be searched if the user is asked for more specific information about constituent concepts. For example, MIS requires him to specify explicitly which constituents should be used. Of course, this a step in the direction from teaching to programming.

Automatic generation of critical examples. One way of reducing dependence on the skill of the teacher is for the system to show some initiative by generating its own critical examples and having the teacher classify them. Within the standard generalization-as-search paradigm there are four basic strategies for selecting examples: *randomly*, by *halving*, by *factoring*, and by *conservative selection.*

Choosing examples at random is certainly the simplest, but not usually the most helpful, strategy. Recall that "felicity conditions" were defined above as conditions on example selection that make learning better than it would be with randomly-chosen examples. In order to teach people effectively, one must know something about what they bring to the problem in terms of prior knowledge and experience. Equally, to satisfy felicity conditions one must make assumptions about the operation of the learner. This is a good argument for having the system select examples itself, using something other than random selection.

Suppose a learner contains an explicit representation of the set of descriptions from which the target concept must be chosen, the version space for the concept. An efficient strategy for example selection, in terms of the number of examples required, is to use each one to cut the version space in half. In other words, pick the description whose refutation or verification results in a half-sized version space (Genesereth & Nilsson, 1987). If descriptions are equally likely *a priori*, this strategy will minimize the number of examples required before the concept is identified uniquely. More generally, if the *a priori* distribution is known, one should select examples to maximize the expected information gained by their classification.

One objection to this strategy is the computational burden of identifying examples which maximize expected information. In the worst case, every conceivable example must be evaluated with respect to every possible concept description. A second is that the examples chosen bear no relationship to each other; the sequence seems to the teacher to be disjointed, unmotivated. For example, Shapiro (1983) used the same idea of binary chopping to narrow down the location of bugs in logic programs; it has been observed (eg by Lloyd, 1986) that this strategy poses a series of questions to the user that seem entirely unrelated.

The third approach, factoring, decomposes the version space by independent attributes and applies halving to each sub-space (Subramanian & Feigenbaum, 1986). This is much more efficient than the general halving method, but still suffers from the drawback of disjointedness. Furthermore, to reap full benefit examples must be classified by attribute rather than as an overall yes/no decision. This is often infeasible. Moreover, the method is only possible when the concept to be learned can be factored into independent parts. Many problems cannot be decomposed in this way.

The final approach, conservative selection (Krawchuk & Witten, 1988), uses local, directed search to explore the generalization space. Starting with a positive seed example, it climbs one level of the generalization lattice, selects that concept as its current hypothesis, and generates an instance that tests this hypothesis. In effect this follows the "near miss" strategy of Winston (1975) by selecting a new example which differs in just one way from the seed. However, it is stronger in that the new example is guaranteed to differ by a minimal amount. Depending on the teacher's classification of this example, the system continues to generalize or seeks to specialize the current target concept description. The next step at each state is guided by the teacher's response to the previously-generated example.

Although conservative selection generally requires more examples than halving or factoring (the number grows linearly rather than logarithmically in the number of possible hypotheses), its operation is more perspicuous. It generates a sequence of examples that indicate to the teacher where it is heading. It avoids large inductive leaps by making steady progress at a local level. It does not rely on special properties of the generalization space (as factoring does). Finally, it is computationally feasible, since generating the next hypothesis is a constant-time operation.

Explanation-based learning. Explanation-based learning (EBL) differs from other machine learning paradigms in that it presupposes a general theory which "explains" each example given to it (Mitchell *et al*, 1986; DeJong and Mooney, 1986; Krawchuk & Witten, in press). It provides a way of generalizing a machine-generated explanation of a particular example into a rule which applies not only to the current example but to others as well. The original explanation is normally created by a problem-solver, which relates the given situation to a stated goal using the domain theory that has been provided. EBL takes the output of the problem-solver — in the form of an explanation tree — and processes it to discover an appropriate rule. In effect, EBL provides a mechanism for learning something from the solution to a problem that will expedite the solution to similar problems in the future.

Explanation-based learners do not learn the domain theory; it must be provided to them before they can operate. It follows that since the general rule that they do learn is already implicit in the theory, they learn nothing new. What they do is use examples to guide the operationalization of knowledge already implicitly known, so that it can henceforth be employed more efficiently. The knowledge operationalized pertains to the original example, and probably to many others.

Explanation-based generalization is a two-step process, first creating an explanation that distinguishes the relevant features of the examples from the irrelevant ones; and then analyzing it to determine the minimum constraints that are sufficient for the explanation to apply in general. Because the explanation is created for the given training example, it does not necessarily explain every possible example of the goal concept. The final concept is typically a specialization of the goal concept rather than a direct re-expression of it.

The method of explanation-based learning corresponds to the important role of problem-solving in pedagogy. Posing students apt problems forces them to think through the implications of a theory in a particular context. The act of doing so creates rules which can perhaps be applied to similar problems in the future. We have argued elsewhere (Krawchuk & Witten, in press) against the current trend in machine learning to try and split off the "learning" component and examine it in isolation, separated from the rest of the system. Learning should be put where it belongs, right in the heart of the problem solver. Through practice in problem solving, one comes to have a richer, multi-faceted, view of the domain knowledge which includes short-cut rules for special cases along with the general theory from which all results can be deduced.

Conclusion

This paper reverses the normal roles of machine and human in computer-assisted learning. We introduce concept learning by machine with emphasis on the role of the human teacher in rendering practical an otherwise intractable concept search. In machine learning the importance of the teacher can be clearly reflected in theoretical analyses of example selection and presentation order. Although concept learning systems' abilities do not compare with those of human learners, the teaching requirements reflect interesting similarities, such as felicity conditions and near misses.

Human learning seems quite different from programming, but when the machine is the learner the distinction is not so clear. Still, teachers do not expect to provide explicit analytic descriptions. Examples generally must *guide* the learner, by giving a regular, straightforward sequential development, including near-misses and other counter-examples, pointing out "hidden" aspects and avoiding coincidences. A learner may benefit from selecting its own critical examples for teacher classification, such as randomly, or by halving, factoring or conservative selection. Machine learners have an opportunity to be primed with initial knowledge, enabling some learning from a single example. An important question asks how the initial knowledge is acquired; in humans it too must be learned.

Version space is a powerful but limited technique for maintaining a space of possible concepts. More open-ended methods are required for learning procedures from example problem-solving traces. Hierarchical decomposition of concepts into smaller sub-concepts may facilitate learning. Explanation-based learning can make powerful use of initial knowledge, operationalizing it for more efficient later use.

Machine learning has drawn many lessons from human learning and will continue to do so. In turn it can contribute more formal, if simpler, analyses of concept learning from examples.

References

Andreae, P.M. (1984) "Constraint limited generalization: acquiring procedures from examples" *Proc American Association on Artificial Intelligence,* Austin, TX, August.

Angluin, D. and Smith, C.H. (1983) "Inductive inference: theory and methods" *Computing Surveys, 15* (3) 237-269, September.

Bruner, J.S., Goodnow, J.J., and Austin, G.A. (1956) *A study of thinking.* Wiley, New York.

Davis, R. and Lenat, D.B. (1982) *Knowledge-based systems in artificial intelligence.* McGraw Hill, New York, NY.

DeJong, G. and Mooney, R. (1986) "Explanation-based learning: an alternative view" *Machine Learning, 1* (2) 145-176.

Dennett, D.C. (1981) *Brainstorms.* Harvester Press, Brighton, Sussex.

Dennett, D.C. (1987) *The intentional stance.* MIT Press, Cambridge, MA.

Gill, A. (1961) "State-identification experiments in finite automata" *Information and Control, 4,* 132-154.

Ginsburg, S. (1958) "On the length of the smallest uniform experiment which distinguishes the terminal states of a machine" *J Computing Machinery, 5,* 266-280.

Gold, E.M. (1967) "Language identification in the limit" *Information and Control, 10,* 447-474.

Haussler, D. (1987) "Learning conjunctive concepts in structural domains" *Proc AAAI,* 466-470.

Krawchuk, B.J. and Witten, I.H. (1988) "On asking the right questions" *Proc Fifth International Conference on Machine Learning,* 15-21, Ann Arbor, Michigan, June 12-14.

Krawchuk, B.J. and Witten, I.H. (in press) "Explanation-based learning: its role in problem solving" *Journal of Experimental and Theoretical Artificial Intelligence, 1* (1), Also available as Research Report 88-307-19, Department of Computer Science, University of Calgary, Calgary, AL.

Lenat, D.B. (1978) "The ubiquity of discovery" *Artificial Intelligence, 9,* 257-285.

Lenat, D.B. and Brown, J.S. (1984) "Why AM and EURISKO appear to work" *Artificial Intelligence, 23,* 269-294.

Mitchell, T.M. (1982) "Generalization as search" *Artificial Intelligence, 18,* 203-226.

Mitchell, T.M., Keller, R.M., and Kedar-Cabelli, S.T. (1986) "Explanation-based generalization: a unifying view" *Machine Learning, 1* (1) 47-80.

Moore, E.F. (1956) "Gedanken experiments on sequential machines" in *Automata studies,* edited by C.E.Shannon and J.McCarthy, pp 129-153. Princeton University Press, Princeton, NJ.

Sammut, C. and Banerji, R. (1983) "Hierarchical memories: an aid to concept learning" *Proc International Machine Learning Workshop,* 74-80, Allerton House, Monticello, IL, June 22-24.

Sammut, C. and Banerji, R. (1986) "Learning concepts by asking questions" in *Machine learning Volume 2,* edited by R.S. Michalski, J.G. Carbonell, and T.M. Mitchell, pp 167-191. Morgan Kaufmann Inc, Los Altos, CA.

Shapiro, E.Y. (1983) *Algorithmic program debugging.* MIT Press, Cambridge, MA.

Solomonoff, R.J. (1964) "A formal theory of inductive inference Parts I and II" *Information and Control, 7,* 1-22 and 224-254.

Van Lehn, K. (1983) "Felicity conditions for human skill acquisition: validating an AI-based theory" Research Report CIS-21, Xerox PARC, Palo Alto, CA, November.

Winston, P.H. (1975) "Learning structural descriptions from examples" in *The psychology of computer vision,* edited by P.H.Winston. McGraw Hill, New York, NY.

An Artificial Intelligence Approach to Second Language Teaching

Masoud Yazdani
Department of Computer Science
University of Exeter
ENGLAND

1 Introduction

Many Computer Assisted Language Learning (CALL) systems have been developed within the traditional Data Processing paradigm of Computing. A recent display of such systems is presented by Cameron (1989). These systems are developed in order to help specific, and mostly focused needs of a particular teacher of a particular language. A system may help a learner with French noun gender (Farrington, 1986); another with English adverbs (Fox, 1986) and so on. Although the systems are motivated by practical pedagogical principles they do not have any "knowledge" of these principles.

As Cameron (1989) points out "the aim is not to show how ingenious we are in creating software but to use the computer to help us implement educational aims." This means that as with other forms of computer software the knowledge of the second language teaching is in the head of the programmer and not inside the system.

In contrast, a small group of researchers (Imlah and du Boulay, 1985; Schuster, 1986; Barchan et al, 1986, Pijls et al, 1987; Yazdani and Uren, 1988; Cerri et al 1989) have attempted to address the issue of language learning from the perspective of the Artificial Intelligence (AI) paradigm. As with most other AI workers they feel that any effective form of human computer interaction requires both parties to have "knowledge".

The clearest exposition of the difference between the AI approach and the traditional approaches is presented by Brachman and Levasque (1985):

> "What makes AI Systems knowledge-based is not that
> it takes knowledge to write them, nor just that
> they behave as if they had knowledge, but rather
> that their architectures include explicit
> knowledge-bases: more or less direct symbolic
> encoding of knowledge in the system".

Therefore, the starting point of someone addressing the CALL development from an AI point of view is radically different from someone who is in need of a fix for a specific educational problem. While traditional CALL development is based on storage and application of massive patterns of potential interaction, the AI systems are based on simple but general principles.

2 Background

FROG (Imlah and du Boulay, 1985) aims to trap and comment on grammatical errors in an arbitrary French sentence. In its final form the program was only capable of parsing French declarative sentences only. However, this system showed that a certain level of effectiveness can be offered without the use of anticipated situations.

FROG had a general knowledge of vocabulary and grammar of French. However, when we tried to extend the system to broaden it beyond declarative sentences we found it was not general enough in it's architecture. The main problem we found with this system was that the knowledge and the routines for processing the user's input were so intertwined that the change involved an architectural restructuring.

FGA (Barchan, Woodmansee and Yazdani, 1986) attempted to keep its "knowledge" of French grammar and dictionary separate from the processes needed to deal with the user's input. In addition, we added an explicit taxonomy of the common misconceptions of novice language learners (a "bug catalogue").

While FGA had some success in achieving an architectural generality, it was still not effective enough in an every day teaching situation. In the meantime, similar systems to FGA were developed for German and Italian which shared a good deal of similarity in their structure with FGA.

LINGER (Barchan, 1987) gr w out of a critical appraisal of FGA. If a new system could be developed which copied a good deal of FGA's code why should we not build a language independent grammatical error reporter? The resulting system now known as LINGER 1 has become the basis of a series of interrelated projects in order to explore the potential of applying Artificial Intelligence techniques to language learning. Section 5 provides an overview of these project while section 4 gives the context which motivates the work. Before that we shall provide a brief overview of other AI based language tutoring systems.

3 Related Work

Pijls, Daelemans and Kempen 1987), have developed a prototype of an Author Environment which provides the user with automatic correction and explanation of grammatical errors and spelling errors of Dutch. Based on the same linguistic modules used in the Author Environment, the Nijmegan group has developed and tested knowledge based programs for grammar and spelling teaching and an educational word processor (Vosse, 1988) with spelling and grammar checking for Dutch. These systems go beyond correction of the users error by providing help and advice on grammar and spelling mistakes. The intention is to explain why a word is spelt the way it is instead of just correcting it.

Cerri (1989) has concentrated his efforts with ALICE on how the confusion of the meanings of words leads to mistakes made by novice language learners. Correspondence between words of two languages is seldom one to one and is highly context dependent. ALICE currently deals with subordinate conjunctions in English, French and Italian.

Schuster's (1986) system VP 2 aims to explore how the "correspondences between the grammars of two languages provide an account of grammatical errors made by native speakers of one language attempting to learn a second language."

VP-2 deals with two narrow bandwidth of the language; verb plus prepositional phrase such as

"John ran into the street" and "Into the street ran John"

in addition to verb plus particle such as

"He filled up the bottle" and " He filled the bottle up".

While VP-2 "maintains a model of the student's native language-Spanish. This grammar is assumed to be standard for all Spanish speakers." Also, the system would "fail if input contains unknown words or misspellings or unknown constructions outside the verb phrase"

4 Hypothesis

What happens when someone learns a new language? In order to build a computer system which attempts to be of some help we need to have an answer, however naive, to this question.

Our work has been based on a working hypothesis which is clearly naive and possibly wrong. However, it would be useful to present this hypothesis as it may help the reader understand how our various projects fit together.

The hypothesis is as follows. When someone learns her mother tongue she does not build any explicit (high level) representation of that language. The learning of the language is linked to many other activities. Even if at anytime some "introspective" knowledge of the language is developed, it is not needed in the every day business of communicating with others.

When the person, normally at a later stage in her life starts to learn a second language she starts to become conscious of something called a "language". In learning a new language (L2) the learner attempts to make sense of the this new language in the context of her mother tongue (L1). In so doing she builds a representation of what a language, any language is (L*). She then tries to make sense of both her L1 and the new L2 in the context of this general structure.

If we are to help a learner we need to consider that the learner is involved in a complex task. Not only is she learning specific facts about the structure of the target language (L2) but she is also rediscovering her mother tongue (L1). As she comes across more knowledge of the new language she has to build a more complex L* structure. Accordingly, when she makes a mistake in the target language she not only suffers from confusion between her L1 and L2 but also she may suffer from restrictions or over generalisations of her L*.

This means that while Schuster (1986) is right in taking the mother tongue of the speakers in mind, she is wrong in assuming that all the speakers of one language have the same understanding of their mother tongue or suffer the same identical misconceptions in learning a new language. While a population of learners with the same L1 learning the same L2 share some difficulties, they are also victims of their individual personal backgrounds. For example someone who has learnt another language on the way would experience difficulties or advantages not shared by others.

5 Work in Progress

An AI based system which attempts to facilitate the learning of a second language within the above scenario needs to be both general and specific. General, in so far as it needs to deal with problems that learners would face irrespective of their mother tongue or the target language. Specific in so far as it needs to have knowledge of the specific languages involved and the ways that interference may occur between them.

LINGER 1 in the above sense is neither general nor specific. It does not have knowledge of any particular language nor does it have a general model of users learning process. We could spend many years writing a specification of a grand ideal design and then implement it from scratch.

The one-shot approach (specification to implementation) of conventional software development is not appropriate Artificial Intelligence oriented applications. In our case the discovery of the specification is itself a major problem which can be solved by the use of a throw away prototype such as LINGER 1.

Figure 1 shows how we are growing a number of systems out of our prototype.

$$
\begin{array}{ccccc}
& & \text{SLING}-1 & \longrightarrow & \text{sL}-2 \\
& & \uparrow & & \\
\text{FGA} \longrightarrow & \text{LINGER}-1 & \longrightarrow & \text{eL}-1 & \longrightarrow & \text{eL}+ \\
& \downarrow & & \downarrow & & \downarrow \\
& \text{LINGER}-2 & & \text{eL}-2 & & \text{Le}-\text{Mail}
\end{array}
$$

LINGER 1 was tested with a number of 'toy' knowledge-bases for French, German, Italian, Spanish and English. At one level we need to broaden the coverage of the knowledge of any one of these languages. O'Brien and Yazdani (1988) have been attempting to use LINGER 1 as the basis of an more effective English Error Detector and reporter. In so doing they have devised a new system called eL which gives up the generality of LINGER in dealing with any language in order to gain advantage in efficiency of processing.

On the other hand, Lawler (1989) is planning to keep LINGER 1 as it is and extend the Spanish knowledge bases for his SLING system. It would be interesting to see if in a future phase Lawler's project would attempt to build an engine on the similar lines as eL specific to Spanish (sL).

LINGER 1, el-1 and SLING are all basically error detectors. They need to be incorporated into general environments which motivate the learner to use the system and benefit from it. In this respect the three projects are following different routes. Uren (1989) has been looking at the teaching strategies of practising language teachers has used the French system (almost unchanged, as a subroutine) as the basis of LINGER 2. On the other hand Byron (1989) plans to exploit an object oriented approach and add a wordprocessor-like front-end to eL to help people compose letters (eL-2). Lawler (1989) plans to incorporate his sL into a general exploratory environment using Apple's Hypercard system.

The next stage of our work involves the design of a new system eL+ which uses eL-1 as a prototype. eL+ attempts to use a model of the user's mother tongue Ll in order to diagnose user's errors. In a colaborative project with Pijlis et al's (1987) and Cerri's (1989) projects we plan to develop user models for Italian's and Dutch people learning English.

The environment around eL+ is to be provided by LE-MAIL, an active form of Email, where some tutoring and monitoring. We intend to encourage language learners to communicate with their pen pals electronically. The user composes a message through a special educational wordprocessor. The processor incorporates a spelling checker which explains spelling rules in addition to correcting mistakes. The wordprocessor is also used as the interface through which the grammar analyser checks, offers advice and corrects users grammatical errors.

6 Acknowledgements

The work reported here is sponsored by the British government through its training agency (formerly the MSC) and the Economic and Social Research Council (ESRC). I am grateful to my colleagues Keith Cameron Paul O'Brien, Jo Uren and Don Byron for their continuous support.

6 References

Barchan J., Woodmansee B.J. and Yazdani M. (1986)
   A PROLOG-based Tool for French Grammar Analysis
   Instructional Science Vol. 14   pp 21-48

Barchan, J. (1986)
   "Language Independent Grammatical Error Reporter" (LINGER)
   M. Phil thesis, University of Exeter

Brachman R. J. and H. J. Levesque 1985
   Readings in Knowledge representation
   Morgan Kaufmann

Byron G (1989)
   eL Writer: A Proposal
   Department of Computer Science, University of Exeter

Cameron K (1989)
   Computer Assisted Language Learning: Program Structure and
   Principles, Ablex Publishing Corporation

Cerri S. (1989)
   Acquisition of Linguistic items in the context of Examples
   Instructional Science Vol. 18

Farrington B (1986)
   Computer Assisted Learning or Computer Inhibited Acquisition?
   in Cameron et al(eds.) Computers and Modern Language Studies
   (Ellis Horwood)

Fox J (1986)
   Computer Assisted Reading_ Work in Progress at the University
   of East Anglia in Cameron et al(eds.) Computers and Modern
   Language Studies (Ellis Horwood)

Lawler (1989)
   A LINGER Learning Environment
   School of Education, Purdue University

O'Brien P and Yazdani M (1988)
   eL: A Prototype Tutoring System for English Grammar (Error
   Detector and Corrector) in proceedings of the Third
   International Symposium on Computer And Information Sciences,
   New York, NOVA Science Publishers, Inc

Pijls F, Daelemans W and Kempen G (1987)
   Artificial intelligence tools for grammar and spelling
   instruction, Instructional Science Vol. 16 pp 319-336

Schuster E. (1986)
   'The role of native grammars in Correcting errors in
   second language Learning
   Computational Intelligence Vol. 2

624

Uren J. (1989)
    Teaching Strategies : Languages and LINGER .
    Department of Computer Science, University of Exeter

Yazdani M. and Uren J. (1988)
    'Generalising language-tutoring systems: A French/Spanish
    case study, using LINGER', Instructional Science Vol. 17
    pp 179-188

Computer-Assisted Learning in Dermatology: Two Knowledge-based Approaches

YoungOhc Yoon
Department of Computer Science Engineering
The University of Texas at Arlington

Glen A. Reece
Artificial Intelligence Laboratory for Manufacturing
Automation and Robotics Research Institute
The University of Texas at Arlington

Paul R. Bergstresser, M.D.
Department of Dermatology
The University of Texas Southwestern Medical Center at Dallas

Lynn L. Peterson, Ph.D.
Department of Computer Science Engineering
The University of Texas at Arlington
CSNET: CS_PETERSON@UTA.EDU

INTRODUCTION

Use of an intelligent system to support computer-assisted learning has been envisioned and experimented with for some time in the form of intelligent tutoring systems [e.g., Carbonell (1970); Brown (1975)] and rule-based systems serving as an instructional base [e.g., Shortliffe (1974), Clancey (1979)]. The success of these systems has raised the hope that such instructional tools could be routinely constructed to augment learning in numerous domains.

Workers in computer-assisted learning (CAL) are well aware of the time required for the construction of useful instructional materials. Target domains must therefore be carefully chosen based on a very favorable cost-benefit ratio or a clearly defined need which is difficult to meet with available human instructors. Developers of expert systems are laboring under similar constraints. Tools and techniques exist but the time invested in the development of such systems must promise favorable payback. The use of knowledge-based systems for instructional purposes clearly must be carefully justified in these terms.

This paper describes work being done in a specific instructional setting in which characteristics of the domain appear to permit a knowledge-based approach to CAL which minimizes knowledge-acquisition time and still provides students access to useful knowledge. The task, instruction of medical students in aspects of the diagnostic process for a class of skin diseases, is briefly described. The knowledge-acquisition method is then discussed. Two approaches to the development of a knowledge-based system for use in this instructional setting are then described.

The rule-based expert system, PIEL-2, is first presented. The system is a standard rule-based system utilizing a non-standard approach to the computation of the degree of confidence with which the system supports a particular diagnosis for a given list of symptoms. Then, a connectionist expert system, DESKNET, is presented. DESKNET has been constructed using the back propagation algorithm [Rumelhart, Hinton & Williams (1986)]; its knowledge base has the form of a multi-layered network, and knowledge is distributed over the network so that a pattern of weighted interconnections constitutes an implicit specification of decision criteria. The expert system then uses this knowledge base for diagnosing a patient's disease given a list of symptoms.

Explanation has typically been handled in rule-based systems by means of responding to the questions of "How?" and "Why?". However, additional explanatory techniques are in use in PIEL-2 involving both tabular and graphical presentation. The use of an implicit knowledge base in DESKNET makes more difficult the task of providing explanations of why a particular diagnosis was selected by the system. A method of presentation of explanatory information is suggested for such a connectionist expert system. This paper is primarily oriented toward the enhanced explanation facilities possible in the two types of knowledge-based systems constructed in this project to provide computer-assisted learning facilities in dermatology.

RATIONALE

In a clinical teaching setting during a one-month dermatology rotation, senior medical students working at a large public hospital see patients who present a variety of complaints. The student typically takes a medical history and then examines the patient, working toward the establishment of a diagnosis for the patient's complaint and development of a subsequent treatment plan. The information the student uses in this process is normally obtained from lectures and textbooks, although he/she must consult with a resident physician or faculty attending physician for confirmation of diagnosis and before beginning treatment. It is in this consultation that the experienced physician should guide the student through the elements of making the diagnosis as well as formulating an appropriate differential diagnosis.

Several approaches have been developed for generation of an "expert" computer system for use by medical students for consultation. When used in an instructional setting, such diagnostic systems allow students to focus their attention on those questions which are employed by trained dermatologists in the formulation of a diagnosis. It is believed that students can utilize such systems to assist in learning the relationships among the diagnoses and the parameters employed in making discriminations. It is anticipated that each student will develop a better understanding of how each of the parameters in the diagnostic process interacts with others to form a diagnosis.

Papulosquamous skin disorders represent a broad category of inflammatory skin disease which is unified by the occurrence of inflammation which is directed against structures near the skin surface. This inflammatory phenomenon leads to a combination of two clinical findings, skin thickening and scaling. The class of papulosquamous skin diseases chosen for this study includes ten distinct diagnoses: Psoriasis, Pityriasis Rubra Pilaris, Lichen Planus, Pityriasis Rosea, Tinea Versicolor, Dermatophytosis, Cutaneous T Cell Lymphoma, Secondary Syphilis, Chronic Contact Dermatitis, and Seborrheic Dermatitis. Eighteen discriminating factors (parameters) were believed relevant in formulating a diagnosis for this class of lesions. The domain was chosen for a number of reasons:

(a) Patients may be placed by trainees into the papulosquamous category without great difficulty.
(b) By contrast, trainees have great difficulty in discriminating among the diseases which make up that category.
(c) A relatively large number of clinical observations are required to distinguish among them.
(d) Not only do these clinical observations (discriminating factors) enable one to distinguish among the papulosquamous disorders, but they are also central to making dermatologic diagnoses in general.
(e) Making the correct diagnosis is important, since there exist great differences in methods of treatment.

METHODS

Papulosquamous skin diseases have served as the domain for the development of two knowledge-based systems which are being adapted as aids in learning the diagnostic process for this class of diseases. In the development of these systems, it was recognized that the knowledge acquisition process would be the primary bottleneck in the development of the knowledge base [Waterman (1986)]. In the development of the rule-based system, knowledge was initially gathered from general clinical dermatology texts. It soon became apparent that without extended tutoring sessions with our domain expert, this process would require an inordinate amount of time. A knowledge acquisition process which minimized expert time in the production of an effective system was required. Thus, a non-traditional knowledge acquisition method to minimize the knowledge acquisition effort was attempted. Expert-supplied estimates of frequency of occurrence were acquired for each of the possible diagnoses, based solely on the expert's experience. These estimates were provided on a parameter basis, i.e., a given estimate reflected how a single parameter in the diagnostic process related to a single diagnosis. For example, in the diagnosis of papulosquamous lesions the duration of the presence of lesions on the body is an important parameter whose possible values are *days, weeks, months*, or *years*. Our domain expert provided the estimate that 25 out of 100 patients who have Psoriasis will also have duration recorded as *months*. This estimate reflects only how a single parameter is expected to interact with a single diagnosis. Similar estimates were gathered for all parameters, and for all diagnoses. This estimate-of-frequency data was straightforward to collect and served as the basis for the generation of knowledge bases for both the rule-based and connectionist systems.

A prototypical rule-based system, PIEL-2, was developed to utilize the knowledge base generated from the estimate-of-frequency data [Reece (1988a,b)]. It was developed on a PC-AT 386 machine using the PC-based expert system building tool Personal Consultant Plus in a PC Scheme LISP environment. After numerous trials it became apparent that the certainty model of Shortliffe and Buchanan used in MYCIN [Shortliffe (1975)] and of the type implemented in the expert system shell of PIEL-2 was inappropriate for the papulosquamous domain for the frequency data that was in the knowledge base. Therefore, a non-standard approach was modeled and implemented in Pascal using a modified approach to that of the envoking strengths formulated by Pople in the INTERNIST-1 system

[Pople (1980)]. The approach taken has three distinct modules that comprise the overall certainty or confidence scheme. First is the non-mutually exclusive parameter value calculation module which deals with those paramaters whose possible values are not mutually exclusive and maps them into the integer range of zero to four, called the frequency level, for use in the confidence calculation module. The second module is the classical case pattern matching algorithm module which performs a similar mapping into the range [0-4] of patterns of the lesion locations compared with those locations that are considered classical for a particular diagnosis. The third module is the confidence calculation module. In PIEL-2, each parameter is assigned a priority score that indicates the level of impact it has on the ultimate diagnosis. Excluding the location parameter and those parameters whose values are not mutually exclusive, each parameter also has a frequency level [0-4] determined from the estimate-of-frequency data. The product of the priority score and the frequency level is calculated for each parameter. The summation of all products comprise a measure of the degree of confidence in the diagnosis of a particular disease, as shown in Figure 1.

Student's Diagnosis				Correct Diagnosis		
Frequency Value	Priority	Product	Parameter	Frequency Value	Priority	Product
2	2	4	Duration	3	2	6 ***
0	2	0	Severity	0	2	0
4	2	8	Lymph-Pathy	4	2	8
4	3	12	KOH-Results	4	3	12
0	3	0	Distribution	0	3	0
1	1	1	Num. of Lesions	0	1	0
1	2	2	Shape	1	2	2
2	1	2	Active Border	0	1	0
3	2	6	Color	3	2	6
0	2	0	Amount Scale	3	2	6 ***
0	2	0	Elevation	1	2	2 ***
0	2	0	Pigmentation	1	2	2 ***
0	1	0	Arrangement	1	1	1 ***
4	1	4	Pattern	4	1	4
0	3	0	Pustules	0	3	0
0	2	0	Thick	0	2	0
0	3	0	Herald Patch	0	3	0
1	3	3	Location	1	3	3
		42				52
	certainty factor = 39%				certainty factor = 51%	

FIGURE 1. Frequency table showing the student's diagnosis versus the highest percentage diagnosis. The "*** higher ***" labels are used to highlight which parameters have greater values in the highest percentage diagnosis versus the student's diagnosis in order to show which parameters most likely caused the highest percentage diagnosis to be the most likely diagnosis.

The most likely diagnosis is selected by the system from among the top three competing diagnoses based upon their degrees of confidence. Students consulting the system see the most likely diagnosis and also which other diagnoses demonstrate similar characteristics, as evidenced by the system-calculated degrees of confidence. Hence the student is able to see which diagnoses demonstrate similar characteristics and become familiar with how to differentiate among them in the clinical setting.

Looking again at the problem of generating an effective knowledge base while minimizing expert's time and effort, another problem with a standard rule-based system approach became apparent. Generation of a knowledge base has proven difficult in the development of rule-based expert systems due to the requirement for explicit rules. The knowledge acquisition phase may result in the loss of critical information in casting implicit knowledge into explicit rules. Therefore, the back propagation algorithm is employed to develop a knowledge-based system, called DESKNET (a Dermatology Expert System with Knowledge-based NETwork), due to the ease and appropriateness of the method in dealing with implicit knowledge [Yoon (1988a & b, 1989)].

DESKNET, called a connectionist expert system due to the interconnections of many nodes in its network, has a three-layered network consisting of an input layer, a hidden layer and an output layer. The units on a given layer have excitatory or inhibitory connections to units on the adjacent layers. Input for DESKNET is a list of symptoms organized by the 18 parameters, and output is the set of 10 papulosquamous skin diseases, each with an "activation value". In this network, each possible value of each of the parameters is represented in an input unit, as shown in Figure 2. Training data consists of 200 sets of symptoms, as input, and an expert's diagnosis, as the desired output, with input in the form of 0's and 1's representing the existence or non-existence of each symptom.

Once a set of appropriate initial weights is found, the back propagation learning algorithm is used to compute the weights of a feedforward network. It is a gradient descent algorithm in which weights in the network are repeatedly modified to minimize the overall mean square error between desired and actual output values for all output units and for all patterns. In this algorithm, the input vector, representing symptoms, propagates forward to the hidden units and output units by the product of weights on the interconnections and the

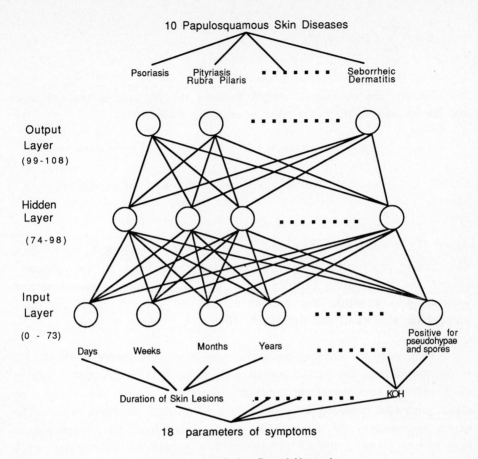

Figure 2. Knowledge Based Network

(Courtesy of Auerbach Publishers. Reprinted with permission from Yoon, 1989)

activation values. A sigmoid function of equation 1 is applied to determine the activation value of a given unit, Aj, at the L th layer.

$$A_j^{(L)} = \frac{1}{1 + Exp\left(-\sum_{i=0}^{n} W_{ji}A_i^{(L-1)} - \theta_j^{(L)}\right)} \qquad (1)$$

where θ_j is a bias of the jth unit, Wij is the connection strength between the i th unit in the Lth layer and the jth unit in the L+1th layer, and Ai is the activation value of the ith unit. The output value from the final layer is compared to the desired one, Dj, and an error computed from equation 2 is propagated back through the network.

$$E = \frac{1}{2} \sum_{j=0}^{n} \left(D_j - A_j \right)^2 \tag{2}$$

Finally, the connection weight between the jth unit in the Lth layer and the ith unit in the L-1st layer is modified according to

$$\Delta W_{ji} = \alpha \, \delta_j^{(L)} A_i^{(L-1)} \qquad \delta_j = (D_j - A_j) \, A_j \, (1 - A_j) \quad \text{for an output unit}$$

$$\delta_j = A_j \, (1 - A_j) \sum_{k=0}^{n} \delta_k W_{kj} \quad \text{for a hidden unit}$$

where α is the learning rate, and A_i is the activation value of the ith unit. The above procedure is applied repeatedly in order to incrementally encode the association between input and output into interconnection weights of a network. For further details and discussions of the back propagation algorithm, see Rumelhart, Hinton & Williams (1986).

Thus, once the learning process is completed, knowledge in DESKNET is distributed over the multi-layered network in such a way that a pattern of weighted interconnections accomplishes for implicit knowledge the effect otherwise achieved by specification of explicit decision rules. The expert system uses this network as a knowledge base for diagnosing a new patient given a list of symptoms. The system is implemented on a VAX 11/780 using the C programming language.

In the inferencing process, the sequence of questions is predetermined and the interface system asks a student to supply the patient symptoms as determined by the history and physical examination. Once the values of input parameters are known, the sigmoid activation function of equation 1 is used to compute the activation values of the hidden layer and, finally, the output layer. A disease is "diagnosed" when represented by a sufficiently high activation value at an output node for a given list of symptoms. During the interface session, all questions must be asked in order to reach a conclusion because the activation values of the output units can change dramatically (even from 0.9 to 0.1, and vice versa), based on one input value. Therefore, partial reasoning appears to be risky in this problem. However, the system accepts *unknown* as the value of a parameter and then eliminates the effects of the parameter on the conclusions. After an initial conclusion is reached, a student can test the effect of a parameter by arbitrarily attributing to it a value of true or false, and observing the result.

A personal computer running an interface to both PIEL-2 and DESKNET will be placed in the examination room to prompt the student in gathering historical, physical, and laboratory test result information needed to establish a diagnosis and to recommend a course of treatment. We are working with these two approaches to determine which yields the best results. The intent of this paper is not to compare the two systems since a valid testing procedure is being devised for that purpose. The intent of the paper is, on the other hand, to elucidate the explanation facility developed for the rule-based system PIEL-2 which goes beyond that of a typical rule-based system and to describe an explanation facility for a connectionist system which has not been done, to our knowledge, for such a system.

RESULTS: Diagnostic Systems

The PIEL-2 prototype is in the second of three phases of development. The first phase tested the performance of the system in determining the most likely diagnoses using hypothetical patients. The second phase will test performance of the system using patient records collected prospectively by a trained professional using a set of parameters (modified slightly from the set used in phase one, as suggested by the results of phase one). Finally, the system will be tested with medical students, using control groups to test the hypothesis that students consulting PIEL-2 do in fact demonstrate a greater understanding of the interactions between parameters in diagnosing this class of skin diseases than students without this tool.

At present, after phase one using test data sets of hypothetical patients, PIEL-2 shows an 85% success rate, defined as including the correct diagnosis among the top three likely diagnoses returned (Table 1). On the same data, the correct diagnosis was indicated by the system as being most likely in 67% of the cases and was among the top two most likely diagnoses in 78% of the cases. Of those diagnoses considered to be the most likely, 41% obtain a degree of confidence of 90% or higher. This success rate is judged as being sufficiently promising to warrant further development, but not adequate to begin to use the system in instruction of students. The second phase, in which actual patient data is being collected, is therefore intended to improve the knowledge on which the system is based.

Table 1.   <u>PIEL-2 : Phase I Results</u>

Most Likely Diagnosis

Correct Diagnosis	First	Second	Third	Forth
1. PS	PS (76)	PRP (74)	SEBD (69)	PR (61)
2. PS	SEBD (93)	PS (91)	LP (85)	TV (80)
3. PS	LP (87)	SEBD (85)	PS (75)	PR (73)
4. PRP	PRP (85)	SEBD (84)	LP (81)	CTCL (81)
5. PRP	PRP (95)	PS (80)	SEBD (70)	TV (67)
6. LP	LP (100)	PR (86)	CONT (84)	SEBD (83)
7. LP	LP (89)	PRP (82)	PS (75)	SEBD (74)
8. PR	PR (90)	SEBD (75)	CONT (74)	TV (68)
9. PR	PR (84)	TV (82)	PS (77)	SEBD (76)
10. PR	PR (88)	TV (86)	SEBD (79)	PS (77)
11. PR	PR (84)	TV (82)	PS (77)	SEBD (74)
12. TV	TV (99)	PS (87)	PR (83)	SEBD (79)
13. TV	TV (100)	PS (67)	PR (66)	SEBD (65)
14. TV	TV (87)	PS (87)	PR (83)	SEBD (79)
15. DRPH	DRPH (90)	SEBD (78)	CONT (69)	PS (64)
16. DRPH	DRPH (75)	SEBD (69)	PS (62)	CONT (60)
17. DRPH	SEBD (90)	CONT (81)	DRPH (78)	PS (76)
18. CTCL	PRP (80)	CTCL (78)	SEBD (65)	PS (65)
19. CTCL	CTCL (81)	LUES (74)	PS (69)	SEBD (62)
20. CTCL	SEBD (76)	PS (74)	CONT (73)	LP (71)
21. LUES	LUES (95)	LP (81)	PR (71)	SEBD (68)
22. LUES	LUES (83)	CONT (73)	PR (69)	SEBD (67)
23. CONT	SEBD (84)	CONT (81)	PR (77)	LP (74)
24. CONT	SEBD (95)	PS (90)	LP (89)	PR (79)
25. SEBD	SEBD (100)	PS (84)	CONT (75)	DRPH (65)
26. SEBD	PS (79)	DRPH (69)	LUES (68)	SEBD (62)
27. SEBD	PS (58)	CTCL (56)	DRPH (54)	SEBD (43)
	67%	78%	85%	93%

PS - Psoriasis, PRP - Pityriasis Rubra Pilaris, SEBD - Seborrehic Dermatitis,
LP - Lichen Planus, CONT - Contact Dermatitis, LUES - Secondary Syphilis,
TV - Tinea Versicolor, DRPH - Dermatophytosis, PR - Pityriasis Rosea,
CTCL - Cutaneous T Cell Lymphoma.

The performance of DESKNET was tested with the same set of hypothetical patient data. A "hit rate" of 75% was achieved, meaning that the diseases "diagnosed" by the system were matched with those determined by the domain expert 75% of the time. 85% of the patient cases included the correct diagnosis among the top two likely diseases. These test cases included several patients who suffered from multiple diseases. For example, the system appropriately diagnosed the skin disease of an AIDS patient as suborrheic dermatitis even though he deviated widely from the classical presentation of seborrheic dermatitis. As in other domains in medicine, large variations may occur in individual cases.

DESKNET will also utilize actual patient data to improve its knowledge base. In both systems, the goal of minimizing expert time while maximizing the effectiveness of the system remains the goal of the knowledge acquisition effort.

RESULTS: Explanation Facilities

It is often difficult to decide the most efficient way to investigate a patient's complaints. On the one hand, the cost and the invasiveness of procedures have to be considered while, on the other, there is the problem of the expected information yield, its specificity, and its reliability [Fox (1983)]. Such foreknowledge can help a doctor optimise the plan of investigation. PIEL-2 and DESKNET were developed to assist students in arriving at the correct diagnosis while still in the clinical environment. To do so, a system must do far more than diagnose correctly. It must be capable of explaining its reasoning and must provide as much insight as possible into its processes.

PIEL-2 has explanation facilities to reduce ambiguities and assist the student in understanding the logic employed to arrive at the diagnostic recommendation. These facilities include hypertext-like capabilities for providing help, and facilities for explaining how information has been determined during a consultation with PIEL-2 and why certain information is necessary to arrive at a diagnostic recommendation. When asked "how", the system displays the value or values assigned to each parameter and the rule or other method that determined the value. The "why" query allows the student to ask why information is required to make a diagnosis by identifying the parameter or parameters that depend upon its value, and in response the system cites the rules currently under evaluation and explains the meaning of each rule.

PIEL-2 also provides the student with "active graphic" screens for easy input. Bar chart plots, of the type seen in Figure 3, are provided to graphically show the differences between the most likely diagnosis as determined by the system and the one chosen by the student.

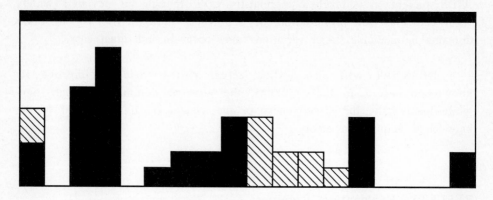

Fig. 3. Bar chart of the eighteen system parameters demonstrating graphically the difference between the student's selected diagnosis (Psoriasis, shown in solid bars) and the system's "most likely" diagnosis (Seborrheic Dermatitis, shown in the hatched bars). The student is intended to see immediately which parameters cause the differing interpretations of the evidence by use of an accompanying legend and figure 1.

A major limitation of connectionist expert systems is that they can not explain decision paths or the underlying knowledge base the way conventional rule-based systems can [Hutchison (1987)]. A rule-based system can be designed to display the rules that it employs to reach its conclusion [Weiss (1984)]. However, conclusions of a connectionist expert sytem like DESKNET are reached by interactions of many units in a synergistic way, and the explanation of its conclusion involves the analysis of many units in the network together. Thus, in order to provide its explanation, DESKNET recomputes activation values assuming parameter information is added in sequence. The system then presents the student with a display showing activation values as a function of cumulative parameter values.

An example of the change in activation values as the value of additional parameters becomes known is presented graphically, as shown in Figure 4. This graph represents all activation values of the output nodes for a patient with seborrheic dermatitis. Note that the activation value for seborrheic dermatitis increased dramatically as location information (parameter 6) was added. Subsequently, this activation value decreased slightly as information on the KOH test (parameter 14), distribution of lesions (parameter 15) and presence of active border (parameter 17) for this patient, atypical for this disease, was added.

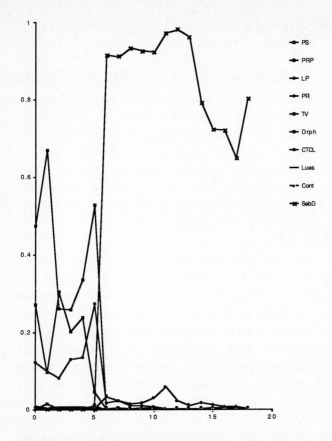

Figure 4:   The graph represents the activation values for a patient as a
function of additional information added in the following
sequence:

parameter 1: amount of scale
parameter 2: perceptability of papules
parameter 3: pattern of lesions
parameter 4: presence of pustules
parameter 5: number of lesions
parameter 6: location
parameter 7: duration
parameter 8: itching level
parameter 9: color
parameter 10: altered pigmentation

parameter 11: presence of thickened
palms
parameter 12: presence of herald patch
parameter 13: lymphadenopathy
parameter 14: result of KOH test
parameter 15: distribution of lesions
parameter 16: shape
parameter 17: presence of an active
border
parameter 18: arrangement of lesions

The activation value for seborrheic   dermatitis is increased by this patient's
values   of   location   of   lesions   (parameter 6), presence of thickened
palms (parameter 11), and arrangement of lesions (parameter 18), and is decreased by this
patient's values   for the KOH test (parameter 14),   distribution of lesions (parameter
15) and   presence of active border (parameter 17).   The reader should be cautioned
that the activation value shown   on the   graph   corresponding   to   parameters added
early should not be interpreted as probability of disease in the absence of much
information.   Specifically,   the   values   corresponding   to   "parameter 0"   has   no
interpretation   in   this   regard.

(Courtesy of Auerbach Publishers.   Reprinted with permission from Yoon, 1989)

CURRENT WORK and CONCLUSION

The rule-based expert system PIEL-2 and the connectionist expert system DESKNET deal with a domain in which effective computer-assisted learning seems possible. The results of the first phase of development with estimate-of-frequency data are promising but phase two has been initiated to improve the success rate by gathering actual data for the knowledge-base. Actual patient data is being collected by a trained professional which is to be incorporated into the rule-based system and will be used to train the knowledge-based network in the case of DESKNET. Preliminary results using data of this sort are promising.

In the meantime, work on the user-interface continues, directed toward providing the most convenient interaction between student and system. Hypertext facilities will be further developed in terms of the actual text of responses, a large task even for the prototype system. Graphic displays of those factors which contribute to a correct diagnosis (Figure 3) are being evaluated with the intent of improving their effectiveness. A neural network approach for pattern matching location values will be examined, and the combining algorithm used for non-mutually-exclusive parameters will be modified.

The neural network design and specifically the back propagation algorithm for the creation of a knowledge base appears to provide a promising method of knowledge base generation for intelligent systems. Effort is now underway to determine ways to enhance the performance of the system and to enlarge its explanation capabilities. The procedure for this further development and the evaluation of its effect on the learning of the diagnostic process are the next steps planned for this portion of the project.

The overall project has as its goals: (1) to categorize clinical information in the outpatient setting, (2) to develop two interactive expert systems for teaching medical students, (3) to combine successful elements of each system into one general system and to employ it as an educational tool when medical students evaluate such patients, and (4) to validate the system's effectiveness by contrasting knowledge of papulosquamous skin diseases and of skin diseases in general between students trained with and without the expert system. A major portion of the effectiveness of this project in meeting its stated goals relates to the strength of its knowledge base, its effectiveness in explaining its conclusions and in elucidating the diagnostic process. Efforts are continuing in this direction.

Acknowledgement

Special thanks to Judy Johns for her assistance in the gathering data from patients.

References

[Brown (1975)] Brown, J. S., Burton, R. R., Bell, A. G., SOPHIE: A sophisticated instructional environment for teaching electronic troubleshooting (an example of AI in CAI). Report no. 2790, Bolt, Baranek and Newman, 1975.

[Carbonell (1970)] Carbonell, J., "AI in CAI: An artificial-intelligence approach to computer-assisted instruction." *IEEE Transactions on Man-Machine Systems*, MMS-11: 190-202, 1970.

[Clancey (1979)] Clancey, W. J., Transfer of rule-based expertise through a tutorial dialogue. Ph.D. Dissertation, Computer Science Department, Stanford University (Also Stanford Report no. STAN-CS-769), 1979.

[Fitzpatrick (1987)] Fitzpatrick, T.B., Bernhard, J.D., "The Structure of Skin Lesions and Fundamentals of Diagnosis," in T.B. Fitzpatrick, et al. (Eds.) *Dermatology in General Medicine*, McGraw-Hill Book Company, New York, 1987, pp 20-49.

[Fox 1983] Fox, J., Alvey, P.,"Computer Assisted Medical Decision Making, " *British Medical Journal*, volume 287, 1983.

[Hutchison, W.R. and Kenneth, R.S.(1987)] Hutchison, W.R., and Kenneth, R.S., "Integration of Distributed and Symbolic Knowledge Representations." In *Proceeding of the First International Conference of Neural Networks*. June 1987, II395-II398.

[Pople 1980] Pople, HE, "Heuristic Methods of Imposing Structure on Ill-Structured Problems : The Structuring of Medical Diagnostics," *Computers in Medicine Applications of Artificial Intelliegnce Techniques Continuing Education Tutorials*, Stanford Univ., 1980.

[Reece (1988a)] Reece, G., Peterson, L., Bergstresser, P., "PIEL-2, a dermatological expert system for instruction in diagnosing papulosquamous lesions," *Proc. Annual Symposium on Artificial Intelligence in Medicine,* Stanford University, March 1988.

[Reece (1988b)] Reece, G., Peterson, L., Bergstresser, P., "Application of a Dermatological Diagnostic Expert System with Dynamic Certainty", Technical Report UTA-CSE-TR88-002, Univ. Texas Arlington, 1988.

[Rumelhart, Hinton & Williams (1986)] Rumelhart, D.E., Hinton, G.E., and Williams, R.J., "Learning Internal Representations by Error Propagation", in D.E. Rumelhart and J.L. McClelland (Eds.) In *Parallel Distributed Processing: Exploration in the Microstructure of Cognition,* pp 318-362, MIT Press, Cambridge, 1986.

[Shortliffe (1974)] Shortliffe, E. H., MYCIN: A rule-based computer program for advising physicians regarding antimicrobial therapy selection. Ph.D. Dissertation, Stanford University, 1974.

[Shortliffe 1975] Shortliffe, EH, Buchanan, BG, "A model of inexact reasoning in medicine." *Math Biosci* 23:351, 1975.

[Waterman (1986)] Waterman, Donald, *A Guide to Expert Systems,* Addison-Wesley, Reading, 1986.

[Weiss (1984)] Weiss, S.M., and Kulikowski, C.A. *A Practical Guide to Designing Expert Systems.* Rowman & Allanheld Publishers, Totowa,1984.

[Yoon (1988a)] Yoon, Y., Peterson, L., Bergstresser, P., "DESKNET: A Dermatology Expert System with Knowledge-based Network." In *Abstracts of the First Annual INNS Meetings,* Boston, MA, September, 1988.

[Yoon (1988b)] Yoon, Y., Peterson, L., Bergstresser, P., "A Dermatology Expert System with Knowledge-based Network." Technical Report UTA-CSE-TR88-001, Univ. Texas at Arlington, 1988.

[Yoon (1989)] Yoon, Y., Brobst, R., Bergstressor, P., & Peterson, L., "A Connectionist Expert System in Dermatology: Construction and Use in Diagnosis with Explanation." Accepted by the *Journal of Neural Network Computing,* 1989.

Author Index